QuickStart

This online teaching and learning environment integrates the *entire digital textbook* with the most effective instructor and student resources to fit every learning style.

With WileyPLUS:

- Students achieve concept mastery in a rich, structured environment that's available 24/7
- Instructors personalize and manage their course more effectively with assessment, assignments, grade tracking, and more

- manage time better
- study smarter
- save money

From multiple study paths, to self-assessment, to a wealth of interactive visual and audio resources, *WileyPLUS* gives you everything you need to personalize the teaching and learning experience.

»Find out how to MAKE IT YOURS»

www.wileyplus.com

ALL THE HELP, RESOURCES, AND PERSONAL SUPPORT YOU AND YOUR STUDENTS NEED!

2-Minute Tutorials and all of the resources you & your students need to get started
www.wileyplus.com/firstday

Student support from an experienced student user Ask your local representative for details!

Collaborate with your colleagues, find a mentor, attend virtual and live events, and view resources
www.WhereFacultyConnect.com

Pre-loaded, ready-to-use assignments and presentations
www.wiley.com/college/quickstart

Technical Support 24/7 FAQs, online chat, and phone support
www.wileyplus.com/support

Your *WileyPLUS* Account Manager Training and implementation support
www.wileyplus.com/accountmanager

MAKE IT YOURS!

INTRODUCTION TO BUSINESS INFORMATION SYSTEMS

SECOND CANADIAN EDITION

JAMES L. NORRIE
Ryerson University

MARK W. HUBER
University of Georgia

CRAIG A. PIERCY
University of Georgia

PATRICK G. McKEOWN
University of Georgia

John Wiley & Sons Canada, Ltd.

DEDICATION

To my students, present and past, who have guided me both in the classroom and while writing this book; to my many colleagues and friends who encouraged me along the way; and most importantly to my family, whose indulgence and tolerance made this book possible. You are all awesome!

Library and Archives Canada Cataloguing in Publication

Introduction to business information systems / Mark W. Huber ... [et al.]. — 2nd Canadian ed.

ISBN 978-0-470-16111-1

1. Information technology--Management--Textbooks.   2. Management information systems—Textbooks.   I. Huber, Mark W.

HD30.2.I58 2010   658.4'038011   C2010-902593-8

Production Credits

Acquisitions Editor	Darren Lalonde
Vice-President & Publisher	Veronica Visentin
Vice-President, Publishing Services	Karen Bryan
Creative Director, Publishing Services	Ian Koo
Marketing Manager	Aida Krneta
Editorial Manager	Karen Staudinger
Developmental Editor	Leanne Rancourt
Media Editor	Channade Fenandoe
Editorial Assistant	Laura Hwee
Cover Image	© Natalia Bratslavsky
Cover And Interior Design	Adrian So
Typesetting	Thomson Digital
Printing and Binding	World Color – Versailles

Printed and bound in the United States
1 2 3 4 5 WC 14 13 12 11 10

John Wiley & Sons Canada, Ltd.
6045 Freemont Blvd.
Mississauga, Ontario L5R 4J3
Visit our website at: www.wiley.ca

ABOUT THE AUTHORS

James L. Norrie, DPM, is an Associate Professor and Associate Dean at the Ted Rogers School of Management at Ryerson University where he teaches in the areas of Introductory IT, Advanced Project Management, Systems Analysis & Design, Business Process, Leadership, and Governance and Ethics. He also undertakes applied research, speaks regularly at industry events, and consults widely in these areas with a particular focus on aligning business and IT strategy to eliminate business risk and improve organization performance. Prior to joining the faculty, he was both an entrepreneur and F-1000 executive with a 20+ year track record of creating, growing, or managing technology-related ventures. He is the author or co-author of two other best-selling titles, numerous articles, and is a frequent media commentator on current issues in technology and society including emerging trends and applications of social media in business.

Mark W. Huber is Lecturer in Management Information Systems in the Terry College of Business, Director of the Terry College and Franklin College of Arts and Science Leadership Excellence and Development Program (L.E.A.D.), and a member of the UGA Teaching Academy. During the past six years he has won nine teaching awards including recognition as Outstanding Faculty at UGA Honors Day, a Terry College Regent's Professor Award Nominee, Outstanding MIS Faculty, a Student Government Outstanding Professor Award, Alpha Kappa Psi (professional business society) Outstanding Management Information Systems Teacher of the Year Award, and three UGA Career Center Student Development Awards. Dr. Huber recently completed a 21-year Air Force career that included the creation and command of a Combat Communications Squadron and the management and development of strategic information systems projects at the Pentagon. His research interests include group support systems and team and group development. He has written numerous papers for various professional and academic journals, and he has co-authored a lab manual published by John Wiley & Sons, Inc. in 2006.

Craig A. Piercy has been teaching large numbers of students in Introduction to Information Systems, Computer Programming, and Web Development classes at the University of Georgia since 2000. Previously, Dr. Piercy taught similar courses at Towson University. As an engineer and later as an academic, Dr. Piercy has long been interested in information technology and how it can be used to solve problems and improve our lives. He was the co-author of *Learning to Program with VB6*, 2nd edition, and he has co-authored a lab manual published by John Wiley & Sons, Inc. in 2006. His primary area of research is in developing algorithms to support decision making. In particular, Dr. Piercy explores decision models that include multiple conflicting objectives. Dr. Piercy has recently been named as the Director for the Masters of Internet Technology program at the University of Georgia.

Patrick G. McKeown is Professor Emeritus of Management Information Systems in the Terry College of Business at the University of Georgia. Until his retirement in 2003, he was the founding head of that department. He was on the faculty at the University of Georgia for 27 years. He has published close to 50 articles in the areas of management science and information systems and has also written more than 30 textbooks in these areas. He is a Fellow of the Text and Academic Authors Association, only one of 15 such honorees out of an organization of over 1,000 textbook authors. In addition, in 2003, he was given the Lifetime Service Award by the UGA MIS Alumni Association and had a student scholarship created in his name by the UGA MIS Department. Dr. McKeown was a Fulbright Scholar in Portugal in 1998 at the Catholic University of Portugal and has taught internationally at universities in France, Finland, South Africa, and New Zealand.

PREFACE

WHY WE WROTE THIS BOOK

During our collective teaching careers, we have developed and taught introductory information systems courses to more than 15,000 business students. For most of our students, this was their first exposure to understanding both business and information systems. From them, we have learned that there is a significant need for an introductory information systems textbook that engages business students across all majors and creates a foundation for their understanding and strategic use of information systems and technology as future business professionals. From our colleagues around the world, we have learned that providing a textbook that leads with the business context, rather than with a technology focus, helps them make introductory IT more interesting.

We hope that as a student or instructor of IT you will agree that this book represents an innovative and creative way of teaching an important subject.

HOW WE WROTE THIS BOOK

Our fundamental philosophy is that within organizations, business professionals use information systems and technologies to enable and enhance the successful achievement of business goals. We believe that the effective integration of IS with knowledge can drive the creation of significant business value. As such, most students, regardless of their major, need to understand information systems and technologies and their importance to the success of business organizations. Numerous features of this book are designed to help students and teachers be successful.

INTEGRATION OF E-COMMERCE

We approach e-commerce as an important component of commerce and not as an aspect of business that stands alone from an organization's efforts to create business value. So, while we discuss e-commerce business models, strategies, and technologies in significant detail in Chapter 5, we integrate this topic into most other chapters where it applies and incorporate relevant examples throughout.

TECH GUIDES

We wanted to provide a way to extend students' learning experiences, as well as enable instructors to tailor the depth of the material to their course goals, without deviating from our goal of focusing on the business context first. To accomplish this goal, we've included five Tech Guides to provide more extensive coverage of hardware and software, networks, SQL and XML, and working in teams. The first Tech Guide, authored by Ron Babin from Ryerson University, is an ICT Career Guide to give students an idea of how to go about pursuing a career in information and communications technology and the benefits of that career path. Instructors can either cover these as links to appropriate chapters or use them to motivate students to go beyond what is required for the class and enjoy a deeper look at base technology and systems architecture. Throughout the book, we include a Tech Guide icon in the margin to alert you to relevant information that can be found in the Tech Guides so both students and instructors will be able to make seamless connections between them.

FEATURES TO ENGAGE STUDENTS

Introduction to Business Information Systems, Second Canadian Edition, is filled with many pedagogical features designed to engage students and enhance the learning process. These features include such things as our chapter opening student ROI, various within-chapter elements, and relevant end-of-chapter material (including an integrative case study).

The next few pages will take you on a tour of some of the special features of this edition. I strongly believe that the approach taken in this text will enhance student engagement and help create a foundation for students' understanding and use of information systems and technology. I hope you'll agree! I'd love to hear from you regarding your experience using this book in the classroom. Please e-mail me with any comments.

James Norrie
jlnorrie@ryerson.ca

FEATURES TO ENGAGE STUDENTS

GET STARTED ON THE RIGHT FOOT!

Student ROI
The *Student ROI* alerts students to the questions they will be able to answer after reading the chapter. In other words, this section helps students see the "return" on their "investment" of time to read and understand the chapter material.

ROI STUDENT RETURN ON INVEST

1. What is an information system?
An information system (IS) is an organized collection of people, information, business processes, and information technology, designed to transform inputs into outputs to achieve a goal

The Voice of Experience
The *Voice of Experience* is a Q&A session with a business professional, focusing on how they use information systems in their jobs. Some of these interviewees are IT professionals, but most are business professionals who have been able to leverage the power of information systems to create business value. These interview boxes are designed to provide motivation for the reader to understand the content covered in the chapter by helping them to see how the chapter material might be useful in their future career.

THE VOICE OF EXPERIENC
Arti Davda, University of British Colu

Arti Davda graduated from the University of British Columbia in 2005 with a Bachelor of Commerce. She then enrolled in

MAKE THE CONNECTION!

Quick Tests
Quick Tests are short quizzes integrated throughout each chapter that provide the student with an opportunity to test their understanding of the material in that section.

Quick Test
1. Fill in the blank. Selling your CD collection on eBay.ca is a form of ___ e-commerce.
2. Which of the following is NOT a known e-commerce business model
   a. infomediary
   b. auction
   c. subscription

What Do You Think?
What Do You Think? boxes are scattered throughout the chapter and are designed to evoke critical thinking related to the topic just discussed. They pose questions to the students to help them think critically about an aspect of the topic and to help them relate it to their own examples or experience. These boxes are further developed in the Instructor's Manual to provide a basis for leading in-class discussions or debates—techniques that we know are important to instructors who wish to engage students in the classroom.

WHAT DO YOU THINK?
In today's networked economy, organizational boundaries zations are blurring the boundary between their suppliers and in their supply chain and create more business value. A recen that suppliers manage the inventory bound for store shelves supplies of a product are low, it is up to the supplier to recog needed to that store. With this in mind, consider the following

Technology Core

One *Technology Core* box can be found within each chapter. These boxes are designed to highlight a technical aspect of the chapter content, showing students how technology facilitates the concept being discussed.

TECHNOLOGY CORE

Many universities across North America worry about their students' ethics when it comes to academic integrity. Recent surveys from a variety of

What's in IT for Me?

At the end of each chapter, three boxes—What's in IT for Me? What's in IT for an Organization? and What's in IT for Society?—provide a discussion of applications of the concepts discussed within the chapter. *What's in IT for Me?* boxes illustrate personal implications of the concepts, such as how ATMs and online banking have allowed for quick and easy transactions, how databases can make you more efficient, and so on. *What's in IT for an Organization?* boxes highlight how organizations have harnessed the power of IT to be more efficient and more competitive. *What's in IT for Society?* boxes demonstrate the far-reaching implications advances in technology and business decisions have on society as a whole. How did technology speed up relief efforts in Haiti after the devastating earthquake in January 2010? What would happen if businesses did not act ethically and practise corporate social responsibility? These and other issues are explored in these boxes.

What's in for me?

Have you Googled yourself lately? What have you found? More and more information can be found about individuals online. Perhaps you were quoted in the school newspaper, had your triathlon results published, or made a charitable contribution noted on a charity's website. Your activity on Facebook, LinkedIn, and Twitter may also come up when searching about you. On one hand, this is good; on another, not so good. With a profile on LinkedIn, for instance, you give employers the ability to find

ASSESS YOUR UNDERSTANDING

Student ROI Summary

The *Student ROI Summary* provides answers to the questions posed in the Student ROI at the beginning of the chapter. As such, it helps the student review what they have learned in the chapter.

Knowledge Speak

The *Knowledge Speak* section is a list of keywords found in the chapter, which the student should understand as a part of the terminology learned in the chapter.

Review Questions

The *Review Questions* contain various types of questions all aimed at having the student assess their understanding of the chapter material. Types of questions include true/false, multiple choice, fill in the blanks, short answer, and essay questions.

Team Activity

The *Team Activity* provides an opportunity for students to work as a team to carry out an activity pertinent to the chapter material.

Software Application Exercises

The *Software Application Exercises* ask students to solve a series of related exercises using word processing, spreadsheet, presentation, database, and Internet software

Case Studies

A *Case Study* at the end of each chapter is a short description of an example where information systems have created value, either for an individual or for a business. Case questions are included with each Case Study. There is also an *Integrative Application Case* at the end of each chapter that follows two students attempting to start up an Internet company. Each Integrative Application Case builds on the material presented in that chapter, showing students how the content ties together. Case questions as well as a student task are included with each integrative application case.

INSTRUCTOR AND STUDENT RESOURCES

ONLINE INSTRUCTOR SUPPORT MATERIALS:
ALL CLASS-TESTED AND IN CURRENT USE BY THE AUTHORS!
www.wiley.com/canada/norrie

As teachers, we understand the value of support materials for classroom activities. In fact, in creating this textbook package, we have tried to create a manageable "course-in-a-box" format. We use an integrated approach to teaching introductory IT/IS courses with a view to enhancing faculty effectiveness and decreasing workload while simultaneously increasing student interest in the discipline and level of engagement in the classroom. To create this course-in-a-box, the textbook is accompanied by a wealth of ancillary materials found on WileyPLUS. Materials are class-tested and in current use by the authors (and other collaborators already using the text!) who are more than happy to help other colleagues implement them in their own classes. Using this book and its support package should provide a department with confidence that students will receive a rigorous and innovative introduction to IS and be better prepared to embark upon their future as business professionals creating business value through IS. To achieve that goal, we provide extensive support materials for both the instructor and the student. Go to *www.wiley.com/canada/norrie* to access the support materials for both students and instructors.

TEACHER'S MANUAL The *Teacher's Manual*, written by James Norrie, Michelle Nanjad, Mark Huber, and Craig Piercy, is based upon their experience teaching the course. Rather than calling it an instructor's manual, it is designed to be a useful *teaching* tool with an overview of key learning themes for each chapter, suggested answers to the *What Do You Think?* boxes, and suggestions for in-class activities and discussions.

TEST BANK The *Test Bank*, which has been carefully reviewed and class-tested, is a comprehensive resource for test questions. For each chapter, it offers numerous multiple-choice and short answer questions to choose from. The questions are labelled based on difficulty—easy, medium, or difficult. The test bank is available for use in Respondus' easy-to-use software. Respondus is a powerful tool for creating and managing exams that can be printed to paper or published directly to eLearning systems such as Blackboard, WebCT, Desire2Learn, eCollege, ANGEL, and others.

POWERPOINT PRESENTATIONS The *PowerPoint Presentations* consist of a series of slides for each chapter of the text that are designed to support the text content, incorporating key points from the text and text illustrations as appropriate.

IMAGE LIBRARY All textbook figures are available for download from the website. These figures can easily be added to PowerPoint presentations.

INSTRUCTOR AND STUDENT RESOURCES

ANIMATIONS Selected figures from the text that involve dynamic activity have been animated using Flash technology. These animated figures can be shown as a part of instructor presentations to demonstrate multistep processes.

WileyPLUS

This online teaching and learning environment integrates the entire digital textbook with the most effective instructor and student resources to fit every learning style.

With WileyPLUS:
- Students achieve concept mastery in a rich, structured environment that is available 24/7.
- Instuctors personalize and manage their course more effectively with assessment, assignments, grade tracking, and more.
- WileyPLUS can complement your current textbook or replace the printed text altogether.

FOR STUDENTS Different learning styles, different levels of proficiency, different levels of preparation—each of your students is unique. WileyPLUS empowers them to take advantage of their individual strengths.

Integrated multimedia resources—including audio and visual exhibits, demonstration problems, and much more—provide multiple study paths to fit each student's learning preferences and encourage more active learning. Resources include:

- Author podcasts
- Video cases
- Microsoft Office 2007 lab manual and projects, prepared by the text authors
- How-to animations for Microsoft Office

WileyPLUS includes many opportunities for self-assessment linked to the relevant portions of the text. Students can take control of their own learning and practise until they master the material. Resources include:

- Automatically graded practice questions
- Pre- and post-lecture quizzes
- Vocabulary flash cards and quizzes
- Animated figures

FOR INSTRUCTORS WileyPLUS empowers you with the tools and resources you need to make your teaching even more effective. You can customize your classroom presentation with a wealth of resources and functionality. You can even add your own materials to your WileyPLUS course. Resources include:

- Media-enriched PowerPoint presentations
- Media resource library
- Optional "hot topics" modules, for example, "Green IS".
- Animated figures

With WileyPLUS you can identify those students who are falling behind and intervene accordingly, without having to wait for them to come to you for help.

WileyPLUS simplifies and automates such tasks as student performance assessment, making assignments, scoring student work, keeping grades, and more.

ACKNOWLEDGMENTS

When we did the first Canadian edition of this book more than three years ago, we had a vision to create a text that would help integrate technology and business in the classroom. The response of the marketplace suggests we succeeded. Of course, a project such as this is never the work of a single group of authors—rather, it is the combined effort of many people. As it was in the first edition, it is equally true in the second. So, we first wish to thank our many students who have challenged us to develop new and innovative ways of teaching the concepts related to information systems and the value-creating role of IS in organizations. Much of what appears in this new text can be directly attributed to what you have told us about your experiences with the first edition. In many instances, you have been a willing audience as we learned what worked, and your pioneering efforts have allowed us to create a product that we feel will significantly benefit the next generation of students who study introductory IT.

Special thanks are due to many people who contributed and worked on this book. To begin with, the original project would not exist had it not been for the vision and support of Darren Lalonde, our Acquisitions Editor. He continues to share our vision and this text is of the highest calibre and quality because of his continued support. Similarly, it was Darren who suggested Leanne Rancourt, our Developmental Editor, and it has been great to have her working by our side, day in and day out, bringing both the first and now the second edition to completion. Our heart-felt thanks go out to the entire Wiley team who has made this book possible: Veronica Visentin, Vice-President and Publisher; Aida Krneta, Marketing Manager; Karen Staudinger, Editorial Manager; Channade Fenandoe, Media Editor; Laura Hwee, Editorial Assistant; and Adrian So, Designer.

And just as there is Leanne and a whole Wiley team behind Darren that makes it easy for him to do great work, I have a team behind me that makes me look good—only, it's a team of one! Michelle Nanjad and I have worked together for many years and still she comes back for more! I enjoy our collaborations immensely and could not do what I do without her research and editorial contributions, knowledge of the subject matter and, of course, her gentle prodding, pulling, pushing, and cajoling to create the best product we can together. You're awesome. I also want to note the contributions of the many authors of the Tech Guides for their contributions as well—many of you are both friends and colleagues and your support means lots to me!

Finally, all of the authors would like to thank our families for the gift of time they gave us to pursue this labour of love. Writing is not always an easy task and it is quite personal, requiring the indulgence of the many to make it possible for the few. To our spouses and children, you know who you are and your love means everything to us!

REVIEWERS

We also want to thank the many individuals who took the time to read and evaluate the draft manuscripts prior to production. Our reviewers generously provided their expertise to help us ensure the book's accuracy, clarity, and focus on the needs of today's information systems instruction. Without their many, many helpful comments, the book would not be what it is today. Thank you for your invaluable contributions.

Ron Babin, *Ryerson University*
Jim Clark, *University of Lethbridge*
Franca Giacomelli, *Humber College*
Robert Hudyma, *Ryerson University*
John Peco, *Ryerson University*
Franklyn Prescod, *Ryerson University*
Rob Sorensen, *Camosun College*
Kim Sunderland, *Humber College*

We would also like to thank the Voice of Experience participants, who took the time to share their expertise and experience with all of us. They are all examples of what can happen when information technology is used to its fullest potential.

Stephen Avanzino, John Wiley & Sons Inc.
Derek Ball, Tynt.com
Tom Beaman, Wmode
Sherrill Burns, Culture Strategy-Fit Inc.
Arti Davda, Google Canada
Ken Killin, Killin Instincts Advisors
John Lennie, Investor in e-commerce and social media–related ventures
Keith Powell, Keith Powell Consulting Inc.
Michael Silagadze, Top Hat Monocle

BRIEF CONTENTS

Chapter 1: IT For Business and Business Professionals 5

Chapter 2: Technology Essentials 35

Chapter 3: Creating Business Value 85

Chapter 4: Enterprise Systems 119

Chapter 5: E-Commerce 165

Chapter 6: Database Management and Business Intelligence 203

Chapter 7: Creating IS Solutions and Managing IS Projects 235

Chapter 8: Web 2.0, Social Media, and Online Trends 275

Chapter 9: Ethics and Professional Practice in IT 305

Tech Guide A: Your ICT Career Guide 337

Tech Guide B: The Details of IT Hardware and Software 355

Tech Guide C: The Details of Networking 397

Tech Guide D: The Details of SQL, Logical Modelling, and XML 423

Tech Guide E: The Technology of Teams 441

CONTENTS

Logon 1

CHAPTER 1

IT For Business and Business Professionals 5

Why IS Matters 6
What Is an Information System? 9
    IS versus IT 11
    The Productivity Zone 12
    The Internet 12
What's in IT for Me? 14
    IT for Your Personal Productivity and Entertainment 14
    IT Is Fundamental for Your Career 16
What's in IT for an Organization? 19
    Business Organizations and the Business Environment 20
    Types of IS Found in Business 22
What's in IT for Society? 24
    The Economy 25

CHAPTER 2

Technology Essentials 35

The Components of IT 37
    Hardware 38
    Software 43
    Connecting Over Networks 46
The Internet 50
    What Makes the Internet Possible? 50
    Accessing the Internet 50
    What's Next for the Internet? 52
The World Wide Web 54
    Basic Components of the World Wide Web 54
    Search Technologies 56
The Technology of E-Commerce 59
    First-Generation E-Commerce Technologies: Establishing a Web Presence 60
    Second-Generation E-Commerce Technologies: Providing Interaction 60
    Third-Generation E-Commerce Technologies: Supporting Transactions 64
    Fourth-Generation E-Commerce Technologies: Transforming Processes 68
Internet Security 70
Meaningful Applications of Technology 73
    Collaboration 73

CHAPTER 3
Creating Business Value   85

Business Organization and Business Processes   87
- Businesses as Open Systems   88
- How Businesses Organize to Create Value   90
- Business Process   93
- Defining Competitive Advantage   95

Applying IT to Create Business Value   96
- Automating to Do Things Faster   96
- Informating to Do Things Better   98
- Transforming to Gain Competitive Advantage   98

Decision Making   99
- Classifying Decisions by Type   100
- Using Information in Decision Making   101
- How to Make More-Informed Decisions   102
- The Decision-Making Process   103

Problem Solving   104
- IADD Model   105

CHAPTER 4
Enterprise Systems   119

The Value Chain   121
- Building an Understanding of the Value Chain   121

Information Systems that Support Business Activities   122
- Functional Information Systems   123
- Workflow Management Systems   124
- Transaction Processing Systems   125
- Management Information and Document Management Systems   127
- Knowledge Management Systems   128
- Decision Support Systems   129
- Supply Chain Management   130
- Enterprise Resource Planning   131
- Enterprise Systems that Support the Value Chain   133
- Software as a Service (SaaS)   140

Strategically Fitting IT to the Organization   142
- Roles of IT Governance and Leadership in Creating Business Value   144

Enterprise Risk Management   146
- Applying the Risk Framework   148
- Risk-Reduction Methods   149
- Control and Controls   151

CHAPTER 5

E-Commerce 165

E-Commerce Defined 167
- Beyond the Basic Definition 168
- E-Commerce and Products: Physical and Digital 169
- E-Commerce Business Models 171

The E-Commerce Advantage 173
- Information Clutter 175
- E-Commerce Competitive Difference 179
- E-Commerce and Business Strategy 181
- M-Commerce 182

Benefits and Limitations of E-Commerce 184

E-Commerce Between Organizations 188
- B2B Transactions and Business Models 188
- Using B2B E-Commerce to Improve Supply Chain Efficiency 190

CHAPTER 6

Database Management and Business Intelligence 203

What Are Data, Information, and Knowledge? 205
- The Data–Information–Knowledge Continuum 205
- Lifelong Knowledge Creation 207
- Knowledge Work Activities 207

Databases: The Primary Data Storage for Organizations 214
- The Data Hierarchy 215
- Relational Data Model 216
- Designing a Relational Database 218
- Storing and Accessing Data, Information, and Knowledge 220

Business Intelligence 223
- Using IT to Support Business Intelligence 224

CHAPTER 7

Creating IS Solutions and Managing IS Projects 235

Critical Pre-Development Questions 237
- What Are We Building and Why? 238
- Is the Project Feasible? 238
- Should We Build or Buy/Lease? 240
- Should We Develop In-House or Outsource? 241

Is Development Teams 242
- The Importance of Stakeholders 242
- A Typical IS Project Team 243

The Stages and Importance of the System Development Life Cycle (SDLC) 244
Standard IS Methodology 247
    Why Do Organizations Need an IS Methodology? 248
    The Traditional IS Methodology: The Waterfall Model 248
    Modern IS Methodologies 250
    IS Modelling 252
IT Tools for IS Development 253
    IS Development Tools 254
Managing an IS Project 256
    Overview of Project Management Tasks 257
    Project Time Management 260
    Risk Management 261
    Program and Portfolio Management 263
    Project Management Software 264

CHAPTER 8
Web 2.0, Social Media, and Online Trends 275

Defining Social Technologies and Utility 278
    Social Utility 279
    Design and Usability 281
    Business Utility 282
    Technology Implications 282
User-Generated Content 285
    Creating Content 285
    Finding Content 286
    User-Generated Content and Brand Risk 286
Creating Business Utility Using Social Media Tools and E-Marketing 288
    Harnessing the Power of Social Media 290
The Social and Business Impacts of Web 2.0 291
    Social Business Models 294
Conclusion 295

CHAPTER 9
Ethics and Professional Practice in IT 305

An Introduction to Ethics and Morality 307
Business Ethics and Conduct 309
    The Business Benefits of Acting Ethically 310
    What Causes Ethical Misconduct in Business? 310
    Remedying Ethical Breaches 311

Corporate and IT Governance 313
    The CIO: Managing IT Governance 314
    Professional Codes of Conduct and Practice 317
    Common Ethical Dilemmas Involving IT 318
The Personal Implications of Ethics and Governance 321
Conclusion 323

Logoff 331

TECH GUIDE A
Your ICT Career Guide 337
Career Trends in ICT 338
    Who Are You? Baby Boomers and the Millennial Generation 338
    The Need for ICT Professionals 339
Career Basics for Resumés and Interviews 341
    What Is a Resumé? 342
    Your Network: It's Who You Know and What You Know 344
    On-Campus Recruiting 345
    Interview Etiquette 346
Starting Your Career in ICT 348
    Show Me the Money 349
Your Career: The Big Picture 349
    Your Career Journey: Going the Distance 351

TECH GUIDE B
The Details of IT Hardware and Software 355
An Overview of Hardware 356
    Evaluating Hardware Devices 356
    The Electronics of Hardware 357
Processing Hardware 360
    The CPU 360
    CPU Performance Characteristics 362
Internal Memory 362
    RAM 363
Input Hardware Devices 364
    Other Input Devices 368
Output Hardware Devices 370
    Display Devices 370
    Printed Output Devices 372

Storage Hardware   373
    Magnetic Disks   373
    Optical Disks   374
    Chip-Based Storage   375
    Storage Performance   375

An Overview of Operating Software   376
    Comparison of Operating Systems   376
    How the Operating System Works   377
    What Does the Operating System Do?   378

An Overview of Application Software   385
    Commercially Developed Application Software   385
    Developing Customized Software   391

TECH GUIDE C
The Details of Networking   397

Network Architecture   398
    Client/Server Architecture   398
    Using Client/Server Systems to Increase Knowledge Work Efficiency   400
    Peer-to-Peer Networks   401

Network Layer Model   402
    Application Software Layer   403
    Network Connection Layer   403
    Data Component Layer   404

Local Area Networks   408
    Wireless LANs   408
    Bluetooth and PANs   409

The Internet: A Network of Networks   410
    How Does the Internet Work?   410
    Using the Internet to Perform Knowledge Work Activities   412

The World Wide Web   416
    Using Browsers to Access the Web   416
    Wireless Connectivity to the Web and Internet   419

TECH GUIDE D
The Details of SQL, Logical Modelling, and XML   423

Using SQL to Query Relational Databases   424
    Relational Database Example   424
    Querying a Single-Table Database   424
    Using SQL to Display Specific Information   425
    Using the LIKE Operator   427
    Inserting or Deleting Records   427

Changing Values with SQL 428
Using Aggregate Functions in SQL 428
Using Logical Modelling to Create a Relational Database 429
Entity-Relationship Diagramming 430
The Relational Data Model 431
Querying Multitable Databases 433
The Join Operation 433
Creating Views 434
Using XML for Data Transfer 435
XML vs. HTML 435
Setting Up an XML Document 435

TECH GUIDE E

The Technology of Teams 441

Why Do Organizations Use Teams? 442
The Business Case for Using Teams 442
Teams vs. Work Groups 443
Types of Teams 445
How People Work in Teams 446
Skills 446
Team Roles 447
The What and How of Teams 449
How Teams Develop 450
Forming 450
Storming 451
Norming 451
Performing 452
Adjourning 452
Hallmarks of Highly Effective Teams 453
Commitment 454
Purpose 455
Communication 456
Involvement 456
Process 456
Trust 457
Bringing It All Together 457
Codes of Conduct 457
Collaborative Technologies 459
Conclusion 459

Photo Credits 463
Index 465

LOGON

Welcome to the start of our journey with you into the era of the IT-enabled business professional. The work world of today is quite different from that of the past. More and more jobs require business professionals who add value to business transactions by transforming data and information into knowledge and wisdom. In support of these activities, organizations acquire current technology and design information systems that help their workers create this value. Almost all employees at any level now use IT-related systems to perform their assigned tasks. We feel strongly that business strategy should drive these technology and system choices. This is often referred to as "alignment." This book will help you align your business choices, your career, and your understanding of the technology required to make this happen.

SO WHAT DO I REALLY NEED TO KNOW?

Depending on the tasks at hand (which will be different if you are a marketing analyst, sales manager, accountant, operations analyst, human resources advisor, or plant manager), you may use different kinds of systems to provide information relevant to your role or function. Regardless of the work you perform, chances are good it will involve a system of some sort. But the degree to which you are interested in the underlying technology of the system, versus the opportunity to improve results you care about, is the essential question.

For example, think about a car that you might like to buy. Are you thinking about a red convertible with leather seats and speed to spare? Or maybe it's an SUV with a sunroof, DVD player, and 21-inch "spinners." The way a car looks and how fast it will go are significant. But the real purpose of a car, or its value, is to get you from place to place safely and reliably.

Let's take this a step further. Think about what happens if you forget to fill the car's tank with gasoline. Like a car, a business will stall without its "gasoline," in this case, information. Drivers use gasoline to make cars go, and business professionals use information to make businesses succeed. This is why we stress business value (transportation) and information (gasoline) first, and then the information technology (big engine) underneath the hood.

Those who are majoring in information technology or information systems (IT/IS) will obviously have a different level of commitment

Just as everyone is looking for something different when shopping for a car, each of you will likely be looking for something different from this text. Whether you want to get engrossed in the details of "what's under the hood," or just acquire the IT knowledge you need to succeed as a business professional in today's fast-paced business world, this book will help you achieve your goals.

to and eventual understanding of the underlying technology being used in the systems—what is actually underneath the hood. However, they also need to make sure they understand the business context, since this is where the systems will be used and where the car will be driven as a means of transportation.

We know that most of you reading this text will not be majoring in IT. And you probably care less about the engine of your car than you do about its features, comfort, and safety. In fact, this course may be your only required course in the subject matter and the level of interest that you have in it will vary, as it should. This is exactly why we wrote this book. We understand your dilemma: you want to understand the practical application of technology, but not necessarily the technology itself.

The authors of this text have all spent many years teaching introductory IT to university and college students around the world. We have come to learn that students vary in their level of interest in and involvement with the subject. Their expectations of the course range from "just get me through it," to "I may want to change my major." Yet there are important opportunities available to you, regardless of how much you initially want to study this subject. Information technology is everywhere; it is an essential component of most everything we do today. We find it in our homes, in our cars, and at the office. It is in our classrooms from preschool to university. We find it in hospitals and in government offices. We use it to shop, socialize, and find out what's happening in the world. It may be hidden or visible; it may be a help or a hindrance, but it is omnipresent. And to succeed in business today, it must be mastered, not ignored.

Yet mastery is so often defined as understanding the definitions and origins of technology. In the Internet age, with its myriad search engines and information-laden sites, this is not the most optimal use of your time as a student. If it is definitions you want, those are easy to get. While we certainly include these in our text (especially in the Tech Guides at the end of the book), we try to provide them in the chapters on a just-in-time basis, to ensure you understand the application of technology in a business context. Only by first understanding the organizational use of the technology are we safe to assume you may be interested in the origins, operation, and acquisition of such technology. This book emphasizes showing you how technology can be applied to create value, and not justifying the value of the technology itself! In short, our goal is to help you acquire knowledge about how to use IT to accomplish personal, organizational, and business partner goals—the really important stuff of business today.

OUR TEXT'S FEATURES

We set out designing this 2nd edition with the feedback of our colleagues and students in terms of what was and what was not working from the first edition. As a result, we have made some changes that we hope will benefit introductory IT students.

To begin with, there is a balance between acquiring knowledge *about technology itself* versus an understanding of *how to apply technology in business settings*. We attempt to make this distinction by focusing our core content chapters (Chapters 1–9) on the knowledge required to build and manage systems, while deferring the supporting knowledge about the technologies themselves to our Tech Guides (A through E) at the end of the book. This design allows both the student and the instructor to participate in decisions about what level of detailed technology knowledge is required for various kinds of students who may be using this text. Therefore, throughout this book you will see this symbol, which directs you to an appropriate Tech Guide for more detailed technical explanations.

In addition, within each chapter we try to identify the usefulness of systems at three distinct levels: for the individual, for the organization, and for society. You will see these clearly highlighted at the end of each core chapter, in the What's in IT for Me? What's in IT for an Organization? and What's in IT for Society? boxes, along with a standard series of features to help you better master and apply the knowledge gained in each chapter.

Team and individual exercises are included in each chapter, along with hands-on applications of the technology that is relevant to each chapter. Again, these are designed to help you and your instructor determine the balance between hands-on and theoretical exercises that will help you learn best.

At the beginning of each chapter, we also include a section called the "Voice of Experience" that highlights people who are putting knowledge about the strategic uses of technology to work in their careers for the benefit of their organizations. They can help you see the value of learning to apply information technology in a variety of professions and different situations.

There is one more essential feature of this text that we would like you to be aware of before we begin our learning journey. An integrative case called *Campuspad.ca* (see below) is included in the nine chapters. This case integrates the knowledge of each chapter with the actual building of an online business. This feature links to WileyPLUS, which you have access to with your purchase of this text.

So our journey begins. You now understand our perspective, our goals in writing this text, and how it might help you get engaged in the value and power of IT in business.

Integrative Application Case: *Campuspad.ca*

Chapters 1–9 throughout the text include part of an integrative application case that will help you apply what you have learned in each chapter to a real-world situation. The hypothetical creation of an online student business closely mirrors the real success story of four former students who began researching a new business concept in their first year of university after taking introductory IT—so it really does happen! As you move through the chapters, more and more information is made available about the case. You will be asked to find out which opportunities and challenges facing this new business can be addressed using information systems and which cannot. You will analyze solutions and sort out problems using information presented in the relevant chapter, both from online sources and your own creativity and knowledge. The objective? To help get this business off the ground and succeed.

Your instructor may do this case in class or assign it as homework, perhaps asking you to work in a team during a lab or on your own. There are no completely right or wrong answers, but there are certainly essential things to think about and apply from each chapter. We hope that this case approach will help build your understanding of the material and the value of information systems.

IT FOR BUSINESS AND BUSINESS PROFESSIONALS

WHAT WE WILL COVER

- Why IS Matters
- What is an Information System?
- What's in IT for Me?
- What's in IT for an Organization?
- What's in IT for Society?

STUDENT RETURN ON INVESTMENT

Through your investment of time in reading and thinking about this chapter, your return—or created value—is gaining knowledge. Use the following questions as a study guide.

1. What is an information system?

2. Why is the study of IT so important to any future business professional?

3. What are the most common types of information systems in businesses?

THE VOICE OF EXPERIENCE
Arti Davda, University of British Columbia

Arti Davda graduated from the University of British Columbia in 2005 with a Bachelor of Commerce. She then enrolled in York University's Schulich School of Business Accelerated MBA program, graduating with honours in 2008. She now works as an account coordinator with Google Canada.

What do you do in your current position? As an account coordinator at Google Canada, my primary focus is working on proposals for prospective clients, outlining how Google products can help achieve their business objectives. For example, I advise clients, both existing and prospective, of advertising opportunities for their businesses on the Google search platform or YouTube. I review the client's objectives—campaign, timing, budget—and present them with various options. Once they've made a decision, I help implement the campaign, set-up accounts, and provide ongoing client support.

What do you consider to be important career skills? I think it's important to be flexible and to easily adapt to change. Working at Google you see that things change quickly—industry and businesses change quickly, and technology is always evolving. Recognize that change is constant, and embrace it; change keeps things exciting! Also, try to take the initiative whenever opportunities present themselves. Volunteer for things outside of your regular role. My role is not a technical one, but it is important that I understand the technology and be able to communicate how it can benefit my clients.

How do you use IT? At Google, technology is ingrained in the company and corporate culture. We use Google Docs, which makes it easier to collaborate, access materials anytime from anywhere, and not have to worry about version control. I use Gmail and its chat feature so I can quickly and easily communicate with people in the office or team members who are on the road. Our conference rooms are set up for audio and video conferencing; we have staff and clients all over the world, and this makes for more timely and cost-efficient meetings. The advertising and sales team members use laptops whether we're in or out of the office, and phones have headsets for ease-of-use. Using the Google Nexus One phone is great, because it allows me to easily check email, voice mail, and so on from anywhere.

Can you describe an example of how you have used IT to improve business operations? We encourage clients to track activity on their website using Google Analytics. It provides them with details about who visits their site, how much time users spend on the site per visit, which pages users access, and user activities such as purchases. This gives our clients a lot of information about how their website is used. I find it rewarding to see clients use this information to make decisions that benefit their business.

Have you got any "on the job" advice for students seeking a career in IT or business? I found that having a mentor is very important. Either before you start your career or when you start your job, find a mentor. This person can help in so many ways. My mentor helped me get where I am today and continues to advise me. Someday you'll be able to return the favour by mentoring someone else.

Arti works for Google in a non-technical sales and marketing role. While in school, she probably never imagined she would work for a technology company—let alone the world's most well-known technology company! In this chapter, we start our exploration of information systems and IT in business and what they might mean to students graduating with business degrees.

WHY IS MATTERS

It should be obvious to you that information systems (IS) are important in your daily life. Without these systems in place, your life would be significantly different. Do you know anyone without a mobile phone? Or anyone who refuses to use an automated bank machine (ABM)? Imagine: in 2004, Research In Motion (RIM) announced the milestone of exceeding two million active BlackBerry users, the majority of whom were members of the corporate and government elite. Today, almost any type of business person uses a BlackBerry, and it also addresses the needs of typical consumers. Perhaps your mother or even your grandmother has one! By

April 2009, RIM reported having 25 million users.[1] If the number of BlackBerry users continues to grow as it has in the past, it is conceivable that there will be over 60 million users by 2012. To put this in perspective, Canada's total population in 2012 is likely to be less than 40 million people. As another example of how quickly new information systems can take hold among users, the commonplace social media websites Facebook and Twitter did not even exist before 2004 and 2006, respectively. Can you imagine your everyday life without these types of systems?

Organizations that ignore the impact of technology and information systems when conducting business will likely risk the business itself. The rate of technology change is greater today than ever before. Consumers have completely adopted the Internet in less than a decade, when previous technology shifts, such as from radio to television, took many decades. Organizations and individuals must keep up with these rapid technology changes or risk becoming obsolete. It has been said that you must "run faster to stay in place." To help understand this magnitude of change, we can look to Moore's Law for insight.

In 1965, Gordon E. Moore, a co-founder of Intel, observed a significant trend in the advancement of technology. This observation, now known as **Moore's Law,** is that computing power (as measured by the maximum number of transistors in an integrated circuit) roughly doubles every 18 months (Figure 1.1). This formulation was printed

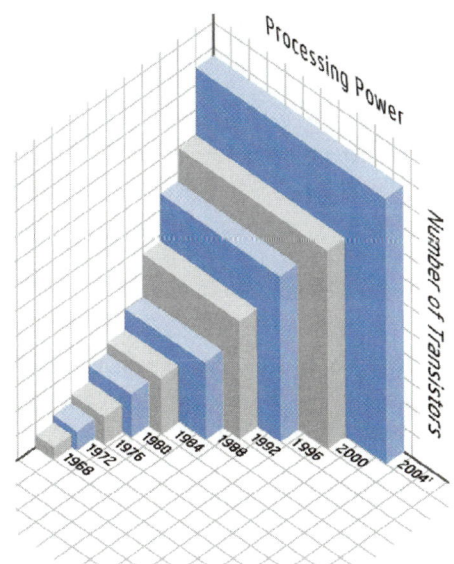

Moore's Law Means More Performance
Processing power, measured in millions of instructions per second (MIPS), has risen because of increased transistor counts.

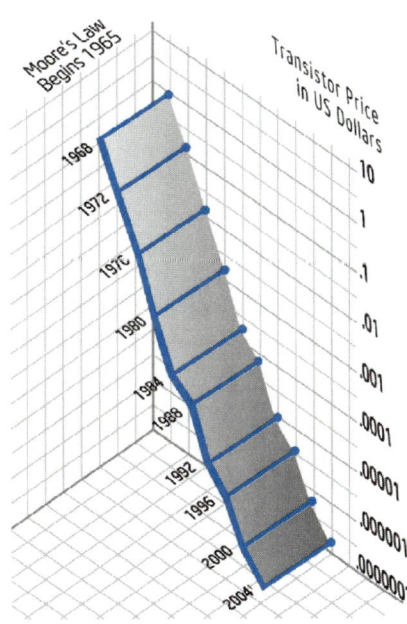

Moore's Law Means Decreasing Costs
Packing more transistors into less space has dramatically reduced their cost and the cost of the products they populate.

1. Estimate only

FIGURE 1.1 Moore's Law illustrates the rate of change in technology capability over time, and the resulting effect on cost.
SOURCE: Intel Corporation.

---
1. http://www.reuters.com/article/pressRelease/idUS215558 + 02-Apr-2009 + MW20090402

in a volume of *Electronics Magazine*[2] and was based on the founding work not of Moore himself, but of VLSI (very large-scale integration) pioneer Carver Mead. However, it was Moore who connected the notion of underlying changes in the pace of technology with consumer access to lower cost and higher performance computing over time.

Moore's Law was initially an observation on only one component of the technology industry (semiconductors). However, the more widely it was quoted and accepted, the more it served as the standard within this huge global industry. As technology engineering and marketing strove to keep up with Moore's Law, a technology revolution was born, eventually leading to the introduction of the personal computer, the forerunning technology to the rapid spread of the World Wide Web. Since every technology company always presumed that one or more of its competitors would soon introduce a newer, faster technology than theirs, the industry became hyper-competitive and one of the most productive and innovative industries in the world.

So what does this mean for business? Well, consider this. If you wanted to express Moore's Law on a different time scale, you could say this technology will improve at an average rate of 1 percent per week. Compounded, this means an increase of 11–15 percent per quarter, depending on the number of days and weeks in any quarter. If you're not in the technology business, but in a business where technology is a part of the business, what must you do to keep up with this ever-present rate of change? Imagine having to either reduce costs or increase sales by that much every single quarter just to "stay in the game." If you worked in a technology industry, you would have to. And in this text you will learn that **information technology (IT)**, as a part of any IS, is a key enabler to all organizations (large and small, private or public sector) and impacts all business disciplines (accounting, marketing, etc.). This makes it pervasive and something that you should be interested in knowing a lot more about, regardless of your ultimate career choice.

As you progress through your career, it will be more important than ever to keep up with changes in technology or risk being left behind. As a professional, you must continually examine everything that you do to ensure that it is optimally efficient and effective, and makes use of the latest technologies required to do your job well, both now and in the future. This is the essence of **knowledge work**, which involves the discovery, analysis, transformation, synthesis, and communication of data, information, and knowledge. In today's work environment, it's impossible to do knowledge work without technology.

This brings up another point: how do you predict the future of technology? Well, you can't. However, you can be sure that the only constant is likely to be change itself. You can anticipate that technologies will evolve and change in the future, and increasing amounts of base computing power, as predicted by Moore, will bring more and more possibilities to you, to the world of work, and to society.

The future often belongs to those whose creativity and innovation are relied on to advance society and change the world. Of course, you could apply this to a technology executive like Bill Gates, or to someone like Helen Keller, whose role in changing the world was less reliant on technology and more reliant on her personal character. And a few of you who are reading this textbook right now will likely change the world of business, of technology, or both. One day, students may be reading your quotes.

---

2. Moore, Gordon E. "Cramming More Components into Integrated Circuits," *Electronics Magazine*, 38(8), April 19, 1965.

One can never consent to creep when one feels an impulse to soar.
—Helen Keller

Success is a lousy teacher. It seduces smart people into thinking they can't lose.
—Bill Gates

So, let's begin your journey to making business history by learning the basics about information systems and how their organization and design impacts business.

WHAT IS AN INFORMATION SYSTEM?

Like most students, you probably surf the Web, shop online, instant-message with your friends on your personal computer, and send text messages on a mobile phone. All of these things demonstrate information systems (IS) in action. So what is an IS?

> An **information system (IS)** is an organized collection of people, information, business processes, and information technology (IT), designed to transform inputs into outputs, in order to achieve a goal.

An information system is much more than just a computer. Sending text messages on your mobile phone, shopping online, or even receiving digital copies of X rays ordered by your doctor are all examples of IS in action.

Are you surprised to learn that an information system is more than a computer? As Figure 1.2 shows, businesses design their information systems to leverage the human ability to achieve business goals through the timely and appropriate application of technology, and the timely delivery of appropriate and useful data, information, and knowledge. That is, information systems enhance work, decision making, problem solving, communicating, and coordinating. Table 1.1 defines the components of an IS model and gives examples for each component.

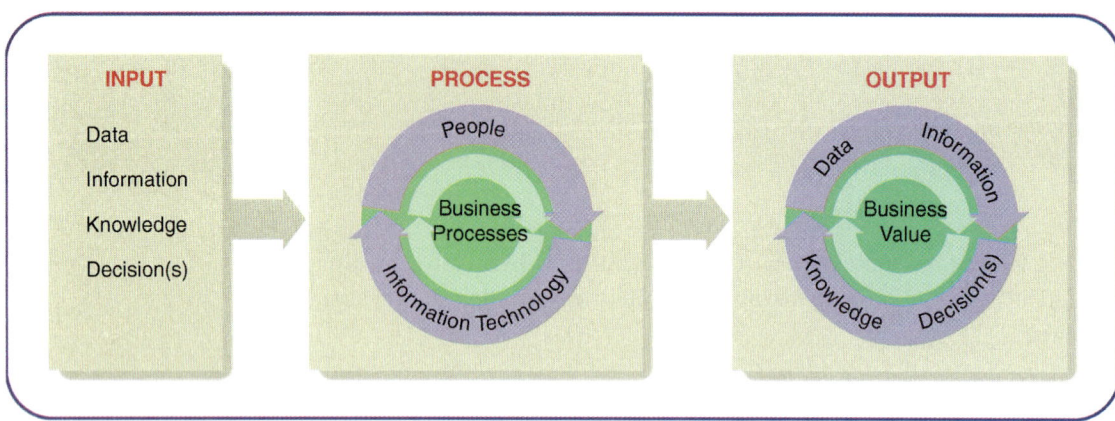

FIGURE 1.2 As this input-process-output (IPO) model shows, a business should design its information system to leverage the human ability to use information technology to its best advantage. By doing this, the output is more than the sum of its parts (data, information, knowledge, decisions)—it is the creation of business value.

Table 1.1 Information System Components

Concept	Definition	Example
Input	Items entered into a system to transform them into outputs.	(1) *Input:* Enter your friends' contact information (email address, Twitter ID, web/blog page, phone number, address, etc.) into your contact list.
Process	A series of one or more steps used by a business to transform inputs into outputs.	(2) *Process:* Save to contact database.
Output	The end result of a process. Information is the result of the transformation (processing) of data. From an organizational perspective, the output of a process is a product or a service.	(3) *Output:* An alphabetical list of friends and their contact information that you can access to make phone calls, send email to, or check on updates from is created. You can use this list to create a group called "spring break trip friends" when planning a trip with your friends for spring break.
Data	Raw, unorganized facts.	(1) *Data:* List of friends who might be interested in a trip on spring break.
Information	Processed/organized/transformed data that are useful.	(2) *Information:* Confirmed list of friends interested in a spring break trip and potential trip locations.
Knowledge	Information plus human experience and judgement.	(3) *Knowledge:* If enough friends can agree on one location, perhaps you can get a group discount on the trip.
Information Technology (IT)	The physical components—typically hardware, software, and connectivity—that make up the IT portion of an IS. Technology is the enabler for processes to perform the steps they were designed to accomplish.	You set up a website for your friends to view the potential spring break location information, with links to tourism boards and travel agencies.

Business Processes	A collection of steps that interact with each other to transform inputs into outputs to achieve a goal.	A function on the website is included for your friends to rank the trip locations in order of preference. Your friends can view which location has the most votes in real-time.
People	People or organizations that have both an interest in and an influence on the creation, implementation, or operation of an IS.	Your friends add comments to the website about what locations they like and why to try to influence the selected location.
Decision	A choice made from one or more alternatives to follow or avoid some course of action.	Based on the number of votes received, you select a spring break trip location.
Business Value	A positive return on the investment of resources created through the effective and efficient integration of an organization's people, information, information technology, and business processes.	You have efficiently coordinated your friends to select a location for spring break and negotiated a group discount. You will now have extra money to spend on the trip! You can continue to use the processes in place to keep your friends updated about the trip and count down the days to spring break.

IS versus IT

It is important to stress the difference between information systems (IS) and information technology (IT). In the example in Table 1.1, would the same results have occurred by simply creating a website? Do you achieve good grades in school simply by having the fastest laptop in your class? Obviously not. While a faster processor can help you do more work more quickly, it is still the quality and insight of that work and your ability to present it well and on time that get you good grades.

IT is simply a collection of tools—hardware, software, and connectivity—that enable individuals or businesses to achieve their goals. Without the context of a clear goal (spring break trip), processes (poll for potential locations, vote), and people (your friends who are interested in a trip), the information technology itself is irrelevant.

Some of you reading this text may end up with careers in IT, but most of you will not. You will be part of the goal, processes, and people components of an IS. It will be to your advantage to have a good understanding of what IT can and cannot do to support you in your career.

WHAT DO YOU THINK?

Consider the components of a typical IS outlined in Table 1.1. Reflect on these questions in terms of the systems you use at school to manage your enrolment, course selection, and payments:

1: What are the benefits to the user of an online information system versus a manual alternative?
2: What are the benefits to the institution of an online system? Are these benefits critical for the institution to achieve in its current environment?
3: Errors occur. In the past, you may have experienced an error in your online enrolment, course selection, or payments. Do you think you would have been better off using a manual system to start with? Did you feel you spent more time trying to fix the error than you would have if you had used a manual system?

FIGURE 1.3 The productivity zone occurs at the intersection of people, processes, and technology. A successful IS system integrates all three of these components to create business value.

The Productivity Zone

As mentioned above, IT is simply an enabler to achieving a goal. IT alone does not guarantee success. Consider this another way. Figure 1.3 shows what we call the productivity zone, which is created at the intersection of people, process, and technology. This is where the design of the information system accounts not just for the optimal technology, but also incorporates elements of human design to accommodate how people will use the system. It also carefully considers the optimal design of the process itself, rather than letting the technology guide those decisions. By applying equal weight to all three of the elements and being able to optimally combine each of these elements, businesses can achieve superior productivity and enhance their competitive advantage. For you, this can mean excellent academic results. For businesses, this can mean increased efficiency and greater profits. For government, this could mean better services delivered at a lower cost. For not-for-profits, this could mean enhanced online donor and event management systems.

Think about this from a personal productivity point of view. Think of a time when you have been incredibly productive. What elements did you combine to achieve this level of productivity? Can you align these elements with those in Figure 1.3? For example, perhaps you were doing a group project with three other students. To get the project done, you assigned clear roles and responsibilities to one another so that you knew who was going to work on what parts of the project (people). You discussed how and when the work was going to get done. You decided how to research the project material and created a schedule for completion (process). To communicate with one another, you exchanged email addresses and began following one another on Twitter. You agreed to use collaboration software (groove, Sharepoint, Blackboard) to share your most recent files and information (technology). By addressing each of these elements—people, process, and technology—you achieved a higher level of productivity and achieved excellent results on your group project, perhaps better than other groups in the class who were not as productive.

The Internet

One information technology that you are undoubtedly very familiar with is the Internet. The **Internet** has become an integral part of personal and business lives for the following reasons: communication, information, and commerce. **Communication** generates business value by making it possible for professionals to share information both between themselves and with business partners. The Internet does this by providing newsgroups, chat rooms, bulletin boards, text messaging using mobile phones, as well as email and instant messaging. You may currently use these Internet communication methods, but as you enter the business world, you may find different Internet tools to use.

Another key to generating business value for any organization and to increasing personal productivity is the ability to both make information available, and to find information in a timely manner. Through the **World Wide Web** (www), the Internet has dramatically reduced the effort required to carry out both activities. For example, the Web makes it easy to publish information in a variety of ways. In fact, the Internet and Web have been called the greatest advances in publishing since the invention of the printing press over 500 years ago. After publishing information on the Web, efficient search engines make it possible to locate it quickly.

However, this ease of creating and distributing information also has the potential for **information overload**, and an absence of quality control means not all web sources are created equal. First of all, as of November 2009, WorldWideWebSize.com reported 21.72 billion indexable pages on the Web. That's an awful lot of information! For your own interest, why not go to that site and see what the number is now? How much has it grown or maybe even shrunk? It might also shock you to know that as of July 2008, Google engineers Jesse Alpert and Nissan Hajaj confirmed over 1 trillion unique URLs in their company's search database.[3] As of May 2009, more than 100 million of those URLs were commercial or business-related sites.[4] The sheer volume of information on the Web is one of the reasons why you need search engines to even begin to locate a place to start when you are looking for something specific. This is also why some people are abandoning the Web as a reliable and useful information source.

Finally, the Internet generates value by being an avenue for the buying and selling of goods, also known as **commerce.** While still just a small proportion of the total commerce in the world, electronic commerce, or e-commerce, is growing dramatically. **E-commerce** is the use of information systems, technology, and computer networks by individuals and organizations to create business value (see Chapter 5 for more on e-commerce). This occurs especially in the information economy, such as travel, insurance, and banking, where often no physical product changes hands.

WHAT DO YOU THINK?

Besides integrating communication, information, and commerce, there's another reason why the Internet has become such an important part of your daily life—entertainment! Think about your own Web usage in this area and then consider the following questions:

1: What are some of the ways you use the Internet for entertainment?
2: Consider the site you prefer most for music or video downloading. What makes it so useful and interesting?
3: Do you spend too much time using the Web for entertainment? Is it the world's number one procrastination tool, or is this time spent valuable?

Quick Test

1. Which of the following is NOT part of an information system?
   a. Internet
   b. Furniture
   c. Mobile phone
   d. Analyst

---

3. "We Knew the Web Was Big," July 25, 2008 entry into the official Google Blog.
4. "Domain Counts," *Name Intelligence,* May 2009.

2. The productivity zone is _____.
   a. the technology implemented at an organization
   b. a measure of the efficiency of an organization's IT infrastructure
   c. the intersection of people, processes, and technology
   d. the time of day where workers are most productive

3. The buying and selling of goods is also known as _____.
   a. revenue
   b. produce
   c. income
   d. commerce

Answers: 1. b; 2. c; 3. d

WHAT'S IN IT FOR ME?

You could interpret this question in two ways: either what's in it for you personally, or what's in IT for you. Both interpretations are important. Most obvious is how IT is involved in your everyday life. It is not only an enabler for you as a student or as someone who is working, but it is also a major source of entertainment and enjoyment. It is safe to say that it would be impossible to be a fully functioning professional today and not use personal productivity tools or have a basic understanding of the Internet, for instance. But more fundamentally, no matter your ultimate career choice, IT knowledge can be a key contributor to your success. You can see examples of this in the Voice of Experience feature at the beginning of each chapter, where both IT and non-IT professionals discuss their engagement with IT systems.

IT for Your Personal Productivity and Entertainment

What does the day of a typical student look like? How many times in a given day do you think you encounter technology?

7:00 a.m. – Awake. Check for messages on BlackBerry. See message from your marketing group that the scheduled meeting will be at the food court. Go back to bed and plan to eat breakfast at the meeting.

9:00 a.m. – Get your breakfast using the money deposited on your student ID card (thanks, Mom!), but can't find your group. SMS a member of your group: 'Where r u?'

10:45 a.m. – Get ready to go to your accounting class. Your professor always posts the class notes at the last minute. Use your PC to access the class website and download the class notes so you can add notes to the slides as you listen to the lecture.

11:00 a.m. – Despite getting some extra sleep this morning, you snooze in your accounting class. Luckily the professor will post a podcast of the lecture later in the day so you can listen to the parts you missed.

1:00 p.m. – Eat lunch and take a break. Sign into Facebook to see what your friends and family are up to. You received a Twitter message earlier that some photos of you at the party last night are posted on Facebook. No wonder you are so tired today. . . .

2:00 p.m. – You are about to get ready to go to your e-commerce class when you receive an email that class is cancelled! You now have extra time to work on your research project. You find a comfy seat at the nearby Starbucks and use WiFi to sign into the school library and do your research online. You use Google and Wikipedia to find other sources of information.

4:00 p.m. – Eek! April will be here before you know it. Better line up a summer job. Post your resume on several job sites and Craigslist (you never know!). Sign up for RSS feeds on a few job sites to get the latest postings delivered immediately.

6:00 p.m. – What's for dinner? Thai would be good, but not the same old place. Use Google to find a good Thai place close to your school. Twitter where you are going for dinner in case someone wants to join you.

7:30 p.m. – You get lost on the way to dinner. Use your GPS to find the way.

8:00 p.m. – Use your BlackBerry to catch up on emails while waiting for friends at the Thai restaurant. You see that an RSS feed from SchoolParty blog indicates there is a party at the campus pub tonight. You mention the party at dinner and your friends agree to check it out with you.

How many times a day do you use technology? Perhaps an easier question to answer is what daily activities do you participate in that *don't* engage technology?

Looking at this simple example, you can see that there are many times in any given day when people use technology to be more efficient and effective, thereby becoming more productive. For example, this student did not need cash to purchase breakfast, as credit was available on his or her ID card. This may have saved a trip to the ATM. Getting an email about a class cancellation saved a trip to the class. Using WiFi at the coffee shop saved a trip to the library. From an entertainment point of view, this person was able to easily connect with friends and family, find dinner companions, and find out about a party they might be interested in. Without enabling technologies, these actions would only have been possible with a lot of effort, or not at all.

IT Is Fundamental for Your Career

You cannot work effectively in any knowledge-intense profession today without superior systems. This means you need to be knowledgeable in the applications of technology in your chosen field, and ensure that you also have well-trained and systems-savvy professionals on board. As an exercise, go to a popular job search site on the Internet, such as www.workopolis.ca. Search for jobs in your chosen career, whether accounting, marketing, finance, or another area. Look at some specific jobs. Can you find any postings that do not mention technology skills (e.g., familiarity with MS Office or other more specific systems)?

The following expands on what you learned in the exercise above, and gives you an idea of how IT will fit into your future career.

I Want to Be an Accountant . . . All basic accounting functions today are done using automated systems, and while they respect the ledger system principles, they have actually replaced the ledgers themselves! This also means that all of the audit trail you need access to, either as an external auditor or as an internal accountant performing business analysis, is contained in various information systems. The ability to understand systems, validate the integrity of the systems operation, and assure management that what is being reported is accurate all require IT knowledge. In fact, most professional bodies that certify accounting professionals now require several courses in IT and IT audit skills to even graduate.

Marketing Is What I Want to Do . . . As any good marketer will tell you, information is power. In this field, it is essential to understand how consumers behave, what influences them, and how to reach them to deliver your message. This is increasingly done online, as you will discover in Chapter 8. An understanding of the power of new media and its impact on society is fundamental for a marketer to figure out how to reach audiences, as traditional media are decreasing in both presence and importance. Furthermore, the information on current customers and their purchasing behaviour is likely all collected by the company's customer relationship management (CRM) or enterprise resource planning (ERP) systems and reported through a data warehouse or data mart. We will explore these systems in detail in later chapters because they are essential to the operation of the modern enterprise and to any aspects of e-government. If you choose to be in marketing, part of your job will include structuring these systems to capture the critical information you will need to analyze customer behaviour and adjust product and service offerings accordingly. It is also likely that you will use Web 2.0 technologies and social networking tools to develop and place indirect marketing messages into cyberspace and to monitor developments around your brand. All of this activity requires IT/IS knowledge.

I'm All about Human Resources... Perhaps you access online job boards when you look for a job. Perhaps you visited an online career fair in SecondLife, or visited the Manpower Island there. Or maybe you investigated an employer rating site to see where the cool places are to work before getting more information about the company from its website. If you work in HR, you better be ready to respond to these new trends because the future generation of workers has moved online. As part of an organization, did you sign up online with an employer for benefits? Or did you report your time into an automated time-tracking system connected to payroll? Or file your taxes online? Modern HR systems are all IT-enabled, and companies increasingly expect professionals in this area to be able to assess the cost-benefit trade-offs of making investments in automation to serve employee and employer needs. IT knowledge is essential to investigating these potential opportunities and making the final business decision about how to proceed. The best HR practitioners understand they need to remain one step ahead of their current and future employees, and therefore need to be linked in to developments in the online world.

Finance Is My Game... Financial analysis, complicated or simple, is always conducted using systems. Like your colleagues in accounting, the trail of information you need to access is usually only available in company or government databases. You will need to interact with the IT professionals in the company to structure these systems to provide not only the knowledge you need, but also to automatically flag important exceptions so management can deal with them before they become a problem. The only way to model complex systems is to use computing power to resolve multivariate equations that would take months to do manually, if they could even be done. As discussed earlier, information is coming online at a steady rate, and finance professionals need to stay on top of fast-moving economic and market news and events—or risk being left behind and letting their employer fall behind too.

The Front-Line Is Where I Belong... Perhaps you are a whiz at working hands-on to get products into the hands of customers in the front-line of business operations. Operations may include roles in manufacturing, transportation, distribution, or service areas of the business. Often these are the most expensive areas of the business to operate, and come under intense scrutiny for efficiency and effectiveness. Complex systems, including customer relationship management (CRM) and enterprise resource planning (ERP), support these areas and provide vital information to other business functions. In your operations role you may need to manage staff to ensure that they use systems appropriately. You may need to analyze the efficiency of operations using data from these systems to find ways of increasing efficiency and reducing costs. Let's look at a few front-line positions more in depth:

- Your front-line role may be in retail, where you need to ensure the products that customers want are in the store at the appropriate times. You rely on automatic inventory replenishing systems driven off immediate point-of-sale data from daily transaction summaries at every store location nationwide.

- Your front-line role may be in hospitality, where it is critical that a VIP customer get the appropriate hotel room upgrade. The room was likely booked online, and the customer will be checked in and checked out using front-of-the-house systems linked to electronic card key access systems in each room.
- Your role may be in health care, ensuring that patient records are accurate and distributed to all required parties. Online systems will maintain the privacy and security of these records and ensure that only authorized medical staff can access them.

Very few professions today do not require the use of technology in some form. Nurses who enter or check patient information are interacting with a complex health care network that needs to be secure and accessible to other appropriate health care providers.

If you are considering any of these types of roles, IT will be an integral part of your job.

I Am Going to Work for Myself . . . Being an entrepreneur can be a very fulfilling vocation, especially if you have a fantastic business idea and the ability to turn that into marketable products or services. Most of these will rely on some elements of technology to create, market, and fulfill the product or service to customers. You will likely rely on a website as a source of promotion so prospective customers around the world can find you easily. At the beginning of your entrepreneurial career, you will often be a company of one. That is, you will be the accountant, marketer, finance department, and operations expert. Once you have some success and can afford some staff, you will be the HR department too. The previous sections in this book described the role that IT will play in your own business. Additionally, you will likely also be the IT department! At the very minimum, you will make technology purchasing decisions like what computer(s) to purchase, who will be your Internet service provider, what mobile and office phone plans you should choose, etc. In the early days, you will likely install all of your computer hardware and software. If there are technical issues, you will likely be your own first level support help desk. Some basic computer skills and IT knowledge will help you to at least understand your requirements and troubleshoot any problems that arise.

The Law Is Where It's at . . . Lawyers today could not cope with the information overload they face without systems. Looking up precedents and codes of law in any jurisdiction around the world in an instant, dealing with colleagues and clients in the firm's offices across the country, or checking on possible conflicts of interest before taking on a new client are all essential IT applications in the legal profession. Collaboration systems have made it easy for multi-team members to create documents, and instantly track and approve changes to improve the speed at which final documents are presented to a client. The volumes of information that must be exchanged between the parties in a typical commercial litigation or merger and acquisition can be done online in the blink of an eye, rather than photocopied, indexed, and bundled into boxes and delivered by truck as was once the case. Furthermore, instead of searching physical documents by reading them, you now search them electronically for the very specific phrase you want, and then the program sorts and presents the results by occurrence including date, time, and document location!

A Career in Consulting Is for Me . . . As a consultant, you will need to quickly understand your clients' businesses and needs. For many businesses, this means IT is the business! You may be asked to evaluate the efficiency and effectiveness of a business and its processes. You may be asked to make business strategy recommendations, or assist in launching a new product. To do any of these activities, you will need to understand the IT the business is using and, perhaps, evaluate new IT that will help your clients reach their goals. If you are an employee of a large consultancy, you will be expected to learn the company's internal systems (including engagement time tracking so your company can bill clients), and knowledge management systems (so that information and tools for engagements can be shared between all members of the firm).

In whatever career you choose, in whatever business environment you find yourself, you need to understand your role in the organization (how what you do creates business value) and your organization's goals and information needs. Further, your success depends on understanding the technology solutions that help meet those goals and needs. Why? Ultimately, the need for and the use of information lies at the heart of every business decision and process.

WHAT'S IN IT FOR AN ORGANIZATION?

Have you ever purchased something online and noticed that the website suggests other products you may be interested in based on what other customers have purchased, or based on what you purchased in the past? This is a key example of organizations using IT to increase sales. Behind the scenes, systems calculate and compile data to understand customer behaviour. A business might learn that a customer who purchased a Dan Brown novel may also be interested in purchasing a John Grisham novel. As the customer, you may not have considered buying a John Grisham novel, but now that it has been suggested, you may check it out.

This kind of intelligent function is exceptionally important for online stores that need to capture as many dollars per visit as possible. Online stores do not have the benefit of eye-catching impulse displays near the checkouts, so they rely on turning as many visitors to their sites into buying customers as they can. These stores also want each transaction to involve as high a dollar volume as possible to maximize profits. In fact, cross-selling or up-selling has been made very simple using technology that matches your current customer profile to your buying behaviour. Either the system itself will prompt you (if the transaction is self-serve), or the salesperson will be prompted to make a personalized offer to you directly (if the transaction is intermediated personally by a sales or service agent).

In addition to increasing revenue per customer or gaining new customers, organizations use IT to increase efficiency and reduce costs. This helps lower their input costs, which can then either be taken back in the form of higher margins on products and services sold, or by enabling them to reduce their selling price to preserve competitive advantage and retain market share or open new markets. And if you are in government or the not-for-profit sector, reduced costs means the ability to deliver more services for the same amount of money, something any taxpayer or donor truly appreciates!

To help you better understand these concepts, in the following section we examine businesses and their environments and compare the IT that contributes to their information systems.

Business Organizations and the Business Environment

To learn about business organizations and the information systems and technology that support them, we need to start with a brief review of the world of business. When we refer to a **business,** we mean any organization with one or more people who:

1. decide on common goals to pursue
2. work together to locate and organize resources
3. create processes to achieve the desired goals

This definition can include businesses in the corporate, government, or not-for-profit sectors. Typically a business's primary goal is to generate economic value (make a profit) over a sustained period of time. For example, when you order coffee at Tim Hortons, this generates value for the company. Or when you sign up for a Rogers Wireless plan, this service creates business value for Rogers by giving you access to voice and data communication via a national wireless network of networks. In other businesses, such as government and not-for-profit, the goal may be to provide clients with a service, or to gain a donation or participation in an event to help support the work of the organization.

In reality, many different factors drive the selection of business goals. One of the most important factors influencing a business is its environment. As Figure 1.4 shows, a company's **business environment** is a complex collection of political, economic, social, and technological factors that organizational leaders must consider when making decisions regarding goals, organizational forms, and the creation of business value. Businesses are now relying on information systems more than ever before to respond to those factors.

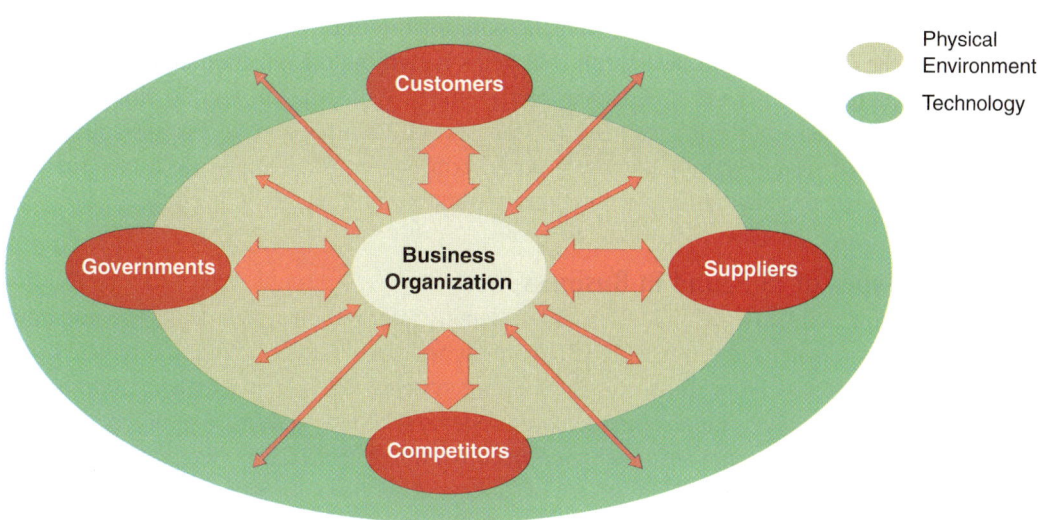

FIGURE 1.4 An organization's business environment is often a complex collection of political, economic, social, and technological factors.

Organizations rely on digital information to gain competitive advantage and to respond quickly to opportunities. As organizations strive to respond quickly, they are changing the way they organize or structure themselves.

Think about an organization from the point of view of a courier carrying documents between the top of the business and the bottom. Perhaps there is or is not a directory to help find the addressee of the package. Or maybe the courier has only the physical address of the big building the company is in and not its specific floor. The taller the organization, the more "stairs" the courier must descend or climb to find and deliver the package to the appropriate party. At each floor, people stop the courier to read the address on the package, see if it's for them, and comment on the weather or whatever. Or maybe the courier needs to stop to clarify if he is getting closer to his final destination. This additional communication may or may not help the courier efficiently and effectively deliver the package to its final destination. The process of discovery can take lots of valuable time before the courier finally delivers the package.

Now imagine that the courier could take an express elevator to deliver the package directly to its intended recipient simply by putting the name into an electronic directory at the front desk of the building. The elevator and directory "flattens" the business into two floors: (1) the floor where the courier gets on; and (2) the floor where the courier stops. Often the pathway the information takes, and how many times and who touches it along the way, will have a significant impact on the design and flow of business information systems. It also affects their efficiency and effectiveness.

So, organizations use advanced information systems, such as *decision support systems (DSS)* and *enterprise resource planning (ERP) systems*, like the courier uses the express elevator—to flatten the organization by eliminating unnecessary stops on floors along the way. Imagine the effect of such de-layering in a business. Now a chief executive officer (CEO) can use a DSS to view and understand corporate data. Such a system could very well eliminate the need for layers of middle managers to filter and interpret the data for the CEO. By eliminating the need for these management layers, the DSS helps flatten the organization and may make it more responsive to its business environment. As a student, you do similar things using IS. You no longer need to visit several libraries and access specialized research resources individually to write term papers. You simply use a tool such as Google or your school's online library portal to find what you need.

Types of IS Found in Business

Now that you have an idea of what a generic information system looks like and how it works, let's take a brief look at some types of IS that you'll find in a typical business today. From *transaction processing systems (TPS), management information systems (MIS),* and *decision support systems (DSS),* to *enterprise resource planning (ERP) systems* and *customer relationship management (CRM) systems,* information systems perform a wide variety of tasks and services. These types of systems use all of the components of IS listed in Table 1.2, and each of these IS is vital to the efficient and effective operation of most modern businesses. As you read about the different types of IS in Table 1.2 you'll see that, regardless of the type of IS, businesses connect people, information, hardware, and software to achieve goals and to create value.

Table 1.2 — The Business Value of IS Types

IS Type	What Does it Do?	How Does it Help to Create Business Value?
TPS (transaction processing system)	Captures and processes transactions to make them available to the organization. A *transaction* is the exchange of something of value the business produces for something in return that the business values (e.g., revenue from product sales).	If a business cannot track its transactions, it will have no way of making decisions about the success or failure of its business processes.
MIS (management information system)	Through processing and reporting features, an MIS provides timely information to decision makers.	Timely reports enable managers to monitor critical processes and avoid costly mistakes.
DSS (decision support system)	Provides analytical and visualization tools to support and enhance decision making and planning.	Enables managers to make data-based decisions and to discover new business opportunities through the use of its tools.
ERP (enterprise resource planning) system	Integrates and standardizes processes, and centralizes and standardizes the storage and management of data.	Reduces costs associated with duplication of processes and effort. Also, can minimize decision-making mistakes due to multiple versions of the same data, information, and knowledge.
CRM (customer relationship management) system	Integrates data collection, transformation, storage, and analysis of customer transaction data, including purchases, service requests, and other forms of customer contact.	Greatly increases the understanding of customers' purchasing and service behaviours and needs. Facilitates the timely and proactive management of customers.

Table 1.3	IS Components of a Transaction Processing System (TPS)
Input	Sales records are gathered at point of sale (POS), when a product's bar code is scanned.
Process	The data are added to a sales database table and removed from an available inventory database table.
Output	The product is sold.
Data	9 780470 840306
Information	1 medium, white, Concordia University T-shirt, $19.95, Sept. 9, 2010, 4:06 p.m.
Knowledge	Customers who purchased white Concordia University T-shirts were also likely to purchase Concordia University beer mugs.
System	As part of the TPS, the POS bar code reader allows for a sale to take place by managing the sale's inventory. The payment module enables the customer to purchase the T-shirt using a credit card.
People	The clerks in the university bookstore have been trained on the system and are able to serve customers efficiently.
IT	The POS hardware (the bar code reader) uses software to read data that are then input into inventory databases, the accounting system, and banks through network connectivity.
Decision	Move the beer mugs closer to the T-shirts to encourage cross-selling of products during the first weeks of September.
Business Value	More beer mugs and T-shirts were sold in the month of September as students and their parents arrived for the start of the school year.

You are probably most familiar with the transaction processing system in Table 1.2. That is, of course, if you have ever purchased anything at a retail store. Table 1.3 illustrates each of the IS components within a transaction processing system (TPS).

The next time you purchase something at a store, think about these various components. Are they visible and obvious to you now? Did you purchase more items than were on your list? This may be the result of an IS in action!

Quick Test

1. True or False. Businesses rely on information systems to help them respond to their environment.

2. Of the following types of IS, which type primarily captures and processes data?
   a. DSS (decision support system)
   b. EIS (enterprise information system)
   c. MIS (management information system)
   d. TPS (transaction processing system)

3. A career in the following will involve some knowledge of IS/IT
   a. finance
   b. law
   c. consulting
   d. all of the above

Answers: 1. True; 2. d; 3. d

WHAT'S IN IT FOR SOCIETY?

As part of information systems around the globe, IT has had a significant impact on society. Not more than 30 years ago, it would have been inconceivable for you to maintain contact with even one friend in another country on a daily basis without incurring prohibitive phone charges. You might have had an international pen pal with whom you exchanged letters on occasion. Without extreme persistence, this often ended within a short period of time. Now you are in contact with friends and family through email and social networking sites such as Facebook as often as you like, and often 24/7! If you subscribe to Twitter, you can be in contact as much as you like, up to 140 characters at a time, and with many people at one time. You can choose to follow some people, and have others follow you.

While air travel created a revolution in international understanding, allowing individuals to easily leave their country and experience another, the Internet provides an inexpensive and easier way to explore the world. With the ability to enter any search term into a search engine, you can learn about any subject in the world. If you are interested in the Hindu festival Diwali, you simply type it in. In the search results you will find Wikipedia entries describing the festival, pictures of devotees enjoying the festival, YouTube videos of festival events, and perhaps blog entries describing individual experiences of Diwali. If you add a location to your Diwali search term, such as Diwali Calgary, you can learn about Diwali celebrations in Calgary.

As you can see, IT has contributed to globalization on a social level. Globalization has also had an impact on the way business is done around the world. **Globalization** means that modern businesses use information technology to expand their market to customers around the globe, to find the lowest-cost suppliers regardless of location, and even to create 24-hour business days by shuttling work across time zones and nations. Much of the current globalization of business and business's worldwide reach is due to the use of the Internet and Internet-related technologies. Another way to look at this globalization is to consider it as flattening. Just as technology has flattened organizations by requiring fewer organizational layers, the world has become flatter. This idea is explored by Thomas Friedman in his book, *The World Is Flat*.[5] He shows that IT has been a key enabler in making the world flatter and smaller. Of the 10 forces identified by Friedman as responsible for flattening the world, only one is not directly related to technology:

1. Collapse of the Berlin Wall – 1989
2. Netscape – an early search engine allowing the general public to search the Internet

---

5. Friedman, Thomas L., *The World is Flat*, 2005. Farrar, Straus and Giroux.

3. Workflow software – using Internet technologies to allow work to be done without human intervention (e.g., the use of PayPal for financial transactions)
4. Open sourcing – allowing online contribution and collaboration
5. Outsourcing – allowing work to be divided between companies or locations, enabling them to be more efficient; the work is then integrated back to the assigning organization; customer contact call centres are often outsourced
6. Offshoring–allowing companies to take their operations to another location, which allows them to produce items better, faster, and cheaper
7. Supply-chaining – using technology to streamline operations and provide products/services to market faster and cheaper
8. Insourcing – allowing companies, small and large, to use outside firms to manage key operations on their behalf, thus allowing them to focus on core business (e.g., a company may insource its warehouse and distribution activities so that it can focus on product design)
9. Informing – the ability to find any type of information online
10. "The steroids" – technology such as mobile phones, iPods, instant messaging, and voice over Internet protocol (VoIP)

As you can see, all of the forces involve technology, with the exception of the fall of the Berlin wall in 1989. The flattening of the world caused by these forces has brought countries and individuals closer together for interpersonal relationships, as well as for business ventures. With the evolution of technology and especially the Internet, business is done 24 hours a day around the world. It is not uncommon to have project team members located in the Canada, the United States, Europe, Japan, and India doing work around the clock. It is also not uncommon to be able to more easily sell or purchase goods and services from other countries. For example, elance.com is a service that connects a variety of professionals looking for contract work with clients that require their services. Using a service like this, a Canadian company can easily hire web designers from Hungary, Turkey, or India for short-term assignments.

The Economy

The information and communications technology (ICT) sector is a major contributor to the economies of the world. In Canada, the ICT sector is divided into several industries, as shown in Figure 1.5. This graph shows the contribution to 2008 GDP made by each of these ICT industries. As a whole, the ICT sector was a source of 4.8 percent of Canada's GDP at a total value of $59.2 billion. Surprisingly, the ICT sector outpaced the Canadian economy. The ICT sector grew 2.7 percent from 2007 to 2008, whereas the Canadian economy grew only 0.6 percent. As seen in Figure 1.6, the ICT sector has had a higher rate of growth than the Canadian economy since at least 2002.

In terms of employment, the ICT sector employed 572,712 people in 2008.[6] Fifty percent of these people were employed in the software and computer services industry of the ICT sector. From 2007 to 2008 employment in the ICT sector grew from 3.30 percent of all Canadian employment to 3.34 percent.

---

6. Canadian ICT sector profile, *Industry Canada*, August 2009.

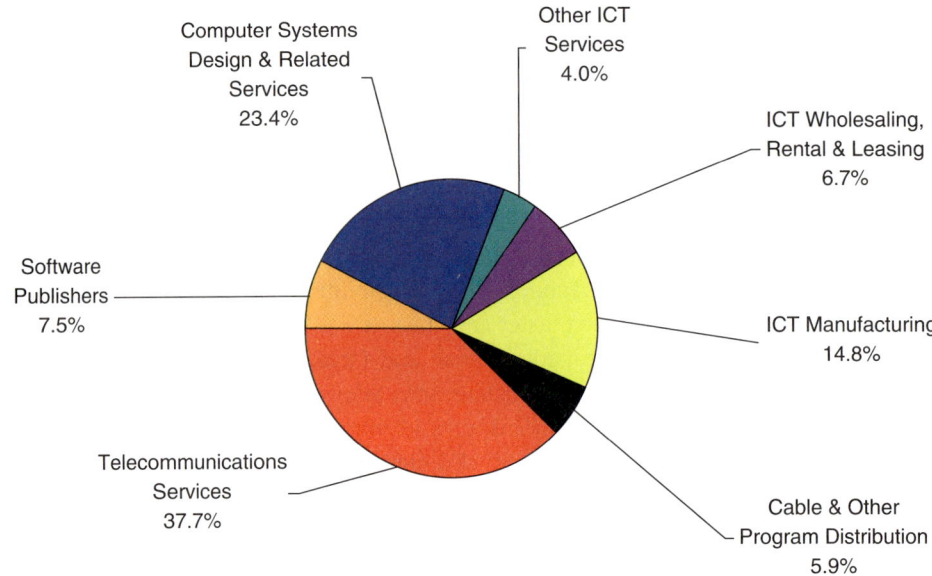

FIGURE 1.5 Distribution of GDP at Basic Prices by ICT Industry, 2008.
SOURCE: Information and Communications Technologies Statistical Overview, Information and Communications Technologies Branch Spectrum, Information Technologies and Telecommunications Sector, Industry Canada, updated April 2009.

What is especially remarkable about ICT GDP and employment growth is that in 2008, all of the economies of the world were slowly sliding into a recession, unlike any other time in history. While the ICT sector is not recession-proof, the sector fared much better than other sectors.

You must not only consider the ICT sector, but also the impact of the outputs of this sector. Technology is critical to the success of businesses within other sectors of the economy. Without the products and services provided by the ICT sector, financial services, resources, energy, manufacturing, health, education, and

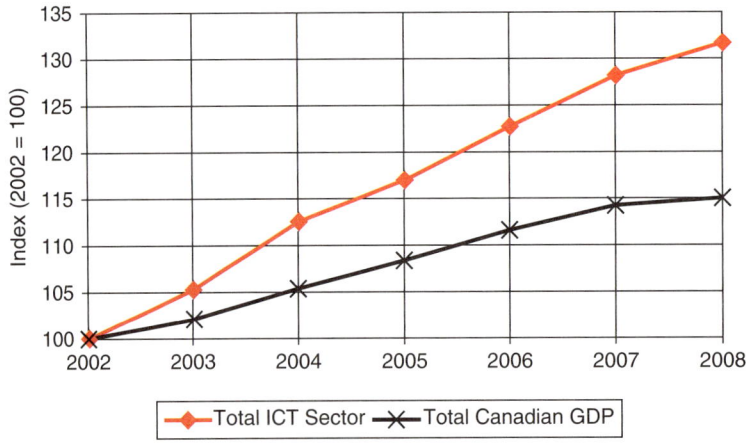

FIGURE 1.6 Indexed Growth in GDP at Basic Prices for the ICT Sector and the Canadian Economy, 2002–2008.
SOURCE: Information and Communications Technologies Statistical Overview, Information and Communications Technologies Branch Spectrum, Information Technologies and Telecommunications Sector, Industry Canada, updated April 2009.

Table 1.4	Key Global Telecom Indicators for the World Telecommunication Service Sector											
	1997	1998	1999	2000	2001	2002	2003	2004	2005	2006	2007	2008
Telecom market revenue (current prices and exchange rates), US$ Billions												
Services	712	767	854	920	968	1,039	1,126	1,329	1,419	...	...	...
Equipment	234	248	269	290	264	275	300	...	...	...	...	...
Total	946	1,015	1,123	1,210	1,232	1,314	1,426	...	...	...	...	...
Other statistics												
Main (fixed) telephone lines (millions)	792	838	904	975	1,034	1,083	1,135	1,204	1,262	1,263	1,278	1,267
Mobile cellular subscribers (millions)	215	318	490	738	961	1,157	1,417	1,763	2,219	2,757	3,305	4,100
International telephone traffic minutes (billions)	81	91	103	114	120	127	141	166	179	183	...	...
Personal computers (millions)	325	375	435	500	555	615	650	775	808	...	...	...
Internet users (millions)	117	183	275	390	489	616	721	867	989	1,168	1,344	1,542

SOURCE: International Telecommunication Union, ICT Statistics, *Key Global Telecom Indicators for the World Telecommunication Service Sector*, http://www.itu.int/ITU-D/ict/statistics/at_glance/KeyTelecom99.html.

entertainment industries would be very different. In fact, growth, innovation, and throughput of these industries would be significantly decreased. Imagine the entertainment industry without the Wii, or eBay without PayPal.

To help put the worldwide ICT industry into an appropriate context for Canadian business students, Table 1.4 shows just a few comparative statistics on a worldwide basis for the period 1997 to 2008, as published by the International Telecommunications Union (ITU.int).

These statistics provide just a glimpse of how large the global ICT industry is, and how much impact it has had as it has grown globally. Notice especially the growth in mobile phone devices (confirming the future of mobile commerce), and also the rapid rate at which both personal computers and associated Internet access has occurred. This is driving the size of the global ICT market—adoption of core technologies at unprecedented rates. And it does not appear to be stopping any time soon.

It is also clear that the trend of technology intensification has a social impact, creating both have and have-not nations, and within any nation a group that has easy access and can afford it and a group that cannot. This is referred to in the literature as the "great digital divide," and is a very real social concern since access to technology is increasingly associated with access to opportunity. Government and social agencies around the world are wrestling with this important issue, as it is clear that investments in technology infrastructure at the national level have an impact on a country's GDP and ability to innovate and prosper in an online world. This is something you need to be aware of and consider as you become a citizen of the world, rather than just a citizen of your own country.

TECHNOLOGY CORE

Throughout this chapter, we have introduced you to the world of information technology and information systems and their role in your daily life, business life, and society at large. At the core of this is what we will generally call technology. None of the things discussed in this chapter and subsequent chapters can occur without it. So how did technology as you know it get started?

For the purpose of this text, we have selected some key events in computing history to highlight.

1951	1954	1957	1960	1962	1969	1971	1972	1975	1981	1983	1984	1985	1989
UNIVAC The first commercially successful computer. Produced by RAND	FORTRAN The first high-level programming language invented	Digital Equipment Corporation (DEC) founded	EDI, Electronic Data Interchange, developed	'SPACE WAR!' The first computer game created	ARPANET The predecessor of the Internet created	INTEL processor introduced	C Programming language created	Microsoft founded	IBM introduces the PC TCP/IP protocol established	DNS (Domain Name System) for the Internet introduced	Apple Macintosh computer launched	Microsoft Windows launched	World Wide Web invented

1991	1992	1994	1995	1996	1998	2003	2004	2005	2006
LINUX, open source software, introduced	Microsoft Office, including Word, Excel, Powerpoint and Mail, launched	Netscape, an early search engine, developed	Java and Javascript introduced; SONY launches Playstation; Microsoft Internet Explorer available; Amazon.com founded; eBay founded	Hotmail released	DEC goes bankrupt and is acquired by Compaq; Google founded	MySpace	Facebook	You Tube	Nintendo Wii; Twitter

RO↑ STUDENT RETURN ON INVESTMENT SUMMARY

1. What is an information system?

An information system (IS) is an organized collection of people, information, business processes, and information technology, designed to transform inputs into outputs to achieve a goal. Information systems combine people, information, and technology to address business needs and to achieve business goals. Table 1.2 on page 22 summarizes the different types of IS and how they help to create business value. It is important to distinguish between IS and IT. IT is simply the collection of technology used in an IS and that enables the other components of an IS.

2. Why is the study of IT so important to any future business professional?

This chapter demonstrates how IT is an enabler in business. In every business discipline, whether finance, marketing, accounting, or another, IT provides essential tools for these business functions. As a future business professional, IT can help make you more efficient and effective. By using IT, you can be more organized and faster. A knowledge of IT is also critical when you are working in an organization. You will be expected to understand the IT in use at the company, both standard and custom systems, as well as evaluate them for improvements. It may be your role to assist the company in developing innovative new products using IT, or to find efficiencies and reduce costs using IT. Regardless of what you will be doing in business, IT will play a part. This chapter explored how IT applies to all business disciplines.

3. What are the most common types of information systems in businesses?

Table 1.2 summarizes some key information systems used in business: TPS, ERP, CRM, MIS, and DSS. Each system supports key business processes, parts of the business's value chain, and ultimately the business strategy. Without these systems, businesses would have a more difficult time operating and significant challenges innovating and growing. Chapter 4 looks at these information systems and others in more detail.

KNOWLEDGE SPEAK

business   20
business environment   20
commerce   13
communication   12
CRM (customer relationship management) system   22
data   10
DSS (decision support system)   22
e-commerce   13
ERP (enterprise resource planning) system   22
globalization   24
information   10
information overload   13
information system (IS)   9
information technology (IT)   8
Internet   12
knowledge   10
knowledge work   8
MIS (management information system)   22
Moore's Law   7
TPS (transaction processing system)   22
World Wide Web   12

REVIEW QUESTIONS

Multiple-choice questions

1. Enterprise resource planning (ERP) systems can reduce:
   I. costs associated with duplication of processes and effort.
   II. decision-making mistakes due to multiple versions of the same data, information, and knowledge.
   III. reliance on data and information as the basis for decision making.
   a. I
   b. II
   c. I and II
   d. I and III
   e. I, II, and III

2. Data are _____.
   a. letters
   b. numbers
   c. symbols
   d. all of the above

3. To arrange the following terms in order from least complex to most complex, which of the following sequences is correct?
   a. knowledge, information, data
   b. knowledge, data, information
   c. information, data, knowledge
   d. data, knowledge, information
   e. data, information, knowledge

4. Which of the following are included in Friedman's 10 forces that flattened the world **and** involve technology?
   a. inshoring, offshoring, insourcing
   b. the collapse of the Berlin wall, "the steroids," open sourcing
   c. Netscape, Nintendo, In-forming
   d. workflow software, supply chaining, insourcing

Fill-in-the-blank questions

5. _____ are raw unorganized facts, numbers, and pictures.

6. For a manager, examples of _____ might include the names of clients, their phone numbers, and their email addresses in an address-book program in a personal digital assistant (e.g., a Palm Pilot™).

7. _____ is created when a person combines experience and judgement with information.

True-false questions

8. Moore observed that computing power roughly doubles every 18 months.
9. As an entrepreneur, you will not need to have any knowledge of information technology or information systems.
10. The only factor of importance in a business's environment is competition.

Matching questions

Choose the BEST answer from column B for each item in column A.

Column A
11. data
12. information
13. knowledge

Column B
a. You listen to the weather report and discover that it predicts a blizzard.
b. Milk.
c. You need to buy milk at your grocery store before it starts snowing, or you may find that the stores have sold all their milk.
d. None of the column B choices are appropriate matches.

Column A
14. process
15. input
16. output

Column B
a. Raw sales data.
b. Organize and format the sales data to create a monthly sales report.
c. A manager's monthly sales report produced by the IS department.
d. None of the column B choices are appropriate matches.

Short-answer questions

17. Apply the model of an IS to an information system of your choosing. Based on the IS you choose, give an example for each of the following components:
    a. input
    b. process
    c. output
18. Explain how the productivity zone works. Give an example of the productivity zone in action.

Discussion/Essay questions

19. Explain the difference between IS and IT. Expand using examples.
20. Using the input-process-output model of an information system presented in the text, create an example that describes how an information system can create business value for an organization.

TEAM ACTIVITY

As you probably have already discovered, teams can be both fun and frustrating. How can you maximize the fun and minimize the frustration? Here's one way that might help.

If your team is willing to use them, good agendas can facilitate productive meetings. Creating an agenda requires your team to think about why it is meeting and what it wants to accomplish. Agendas help teams to break down meetings and project discussions into manageable chunks. They also provide a way to structure discussions from start to finish. If you have access to Microsoft Word, open Help and use the Answer Wizard to find out how to create an agenda. You can find additional sample agendas by searching the Web.

SOFTWARE APPLICATION EXERCISES

These exercises are designed to complement the material covered in each chapter, as well as to help you as a student and as a future business professional.

1. Internet
The Internet provides a number of resources for internship and job seekers, such as Workopolis.com. Use your favourite search engine to locate government (federal, provincial, municipal) sites for information on careers and future job prospects.

2. Presentation
Assume that you have to give a presentation about your background and qualifications to a graduate school admissions committee or a prospective employer. Create a presentation that highlights your strengths and experiences, relates why you chose your major, describes your goals, and then ties it all together to describe why you should be accepted or hired. (This exercise will also help you focus your thinking about possible majors or careers.)

3. Word Processing
Regardless of where you are headed after graduation, you will very likely need two important documents: a cover letter and a resumé. However, many people postpone creating these documents because they don't know where to get started. Further, in the case of the resumé, it is often difficult to highlight and convey the importance of past accomplishments in the space of one page. You can find examples of effective cover letters and resumés by searching the Web. These resources will give you ideas for creating your own resumé. Your school's career centre can also help you create and fine-tune your cover letters and your resumé.

4. Spreadsheet
Are you applying for summer internships? Attending career fairs? Applying for scholarships? Who did you meet? When did you send the thank-you note for that interview? Throw in all your normal school activities, and things can get hectic. However, a well-planned spreadsheet can help you reduce the stress inherent in managing your activities. Visit the course website to view a PowerPoint presentation on creating effective spreadsheets. Then, use this knowledge to create a spreadsheet that will help you track important activities.

5. Database
Here's a chance to see how others create those form letters you receive in the mail. Word processors typically have a MERGE function that will allow you to import or *merge* data from a database (or other source) directly into the document. For this exercise, use database software to create a database of potential employers or graduate schools. Decide what data you need to store (e.g., company name, internship title, school name, graduate program name, and so on). Once you have entered the data into your database, return to your word processor and use its merge function to merge the data into your cover letter (usually called the *merge document*). If you have created your database properly, it's easy to add new companies or schools to your database and print out a cover letter that contains the new data. CAUTION: When using the MERGE function, in a matter of seconds you may create 10 cover letters with the same error. Carefully proofread your cover letter before merging your data into it!

6. Advanced Challenge
Why not create a database that will manage your activities and allow you to provide data for merged documents? If you track activities by date, you can see what has been done in your meetings, as well as what you still need to do. You can use a database to track contacts with companies, the type of contact (phone call, email, thank-you letter, etc.), the employees you contacted, and much more for your internship or job-related activities.

ONLINE RESOURCES

Companion Website
- Take interactive practice quizzes to assess your knowledge and help you study in a dynamic way.
- Review PowerPoint lecture slides.
- Get help and sample solutions to end-of-chapter software application exercises.

Additional Resources Available Only on WileyPLUS
- Take the interactive Quick Test to check your understanding of the chapter material and get immediate feedback on your responses.
- Review and study with downloadable Audio Lecture MP3 files.
- Check your understanding of the key vocabulary in the chapter with Knowledge Speak Interactive Flash Cards.

CASE STUDY: A DAY IN THE LIFE OF A UNIVERSITY STUDENT

Ashley Hyatt attends university, where she is majoring in business administration. The following is a typical day in the life of Ashley.

7:00 a.m. Ashley awakens to new music videos by her favourite artists playing on her computer. These files have been automatically downloaded overnight in compressed format and charged to her credit card. After five minutes, the flat-screen monitor switches from the music videos to a web page displaying news customized to Ashley's interests, including scores from the latest university sporting events.

8:00 a.m.–9:15 a.m. Ashley's first class is Globalization, Regionalism, and Information Technology Systems (commonly known as GRITS), an elective course examining how nations' leaders can use IT to solve global problems. Today the class features speakers from the School of Business Leadership at the University of South Africa, as well as speakers from Botswana and Kenya. The live broadcast is seen by students in Canada, Singapore, Norway, Brazil, and South Africa.

9:15 a.m.–10:30 a.m. After class, Ashley heads off to the combination computer lab–coffee shop where she purchases a bottle of fruit juice and a muffin. As she leaves the food area, she checks the wall-mounted LCD panel to verify that the correct amount was deducted from her account. The mobile device in her backpack communicates automatically with the checkout device. Since her university now uses contact-less smart cards that do not require swiping, all she needs to do is walk through the food area exit. Her mobile device handles all these transactions in addition to other chores. In fact, she can program her mobile device to display selected information on a regular basis; wireless access is continuous throughout the university. For example, for her Finance class, Ashley's team is managing a portfolio of mature Internet stocks, and she has programmed her mobile device to display the portfolio's latest value every 15 minutes. The bottom line of the LCD window shows that the portfolio is down 1.5 percent for the day, based on a number of stock exchanges around the world.

Choosing a seat at a table with an available flat-screen display device, Ashley uses the school's wireless-access capabilities to logon to her network account. Her Web-based to-do list reminds her that she has a quiz to take for her Networked Economy class and a report to finish on Toronto.com for the Strategic Management course. The quiz takes about 20 minutes, and she is relieved to immediately find out that she scored 92 on it. Next, to finish her Toronto.com assignment, Ashley consults an online collection of databases and checks a few websites.

When she finishes the report, she emails it to the professor. Even though the professor is working with an MBA team on a consulting assignment in New Zealand, she knows that he will grade the report within a couple of days and return it with attached audio and text comments. She thinks this mix of classroom lectures and independent learning is good preparation for her business career because she is learning how to learn by herself. She could have done all of this on her mobile device using audio output, but she likes to see the graphics available on the flat-screen display.

10:30 a.m.–11:45 a.m Ashley attends her Networked Economy class and, via the Web, participates in an interesting class discussion that includes the use of voice over the Internet. Whereas some of her fellow students are in her classroom, others are at home or in offices as many as five time zones away. However, all work from the same web page and wear a special headset–microphone combination that allows them to hear and respond to other class members' comments.

1:00 p.m.–2:30 p.m. After lunch, Ashley's Data Management class team members (Ashley, Eduardo from Brazil, and Tore from Norway) meet to review their design for a data model. They participate in an audio conference with a shared screen, so the team members all see the same high-fidelity model of the timetable for the Sao Paulo subway. They take turns changing it until they agree. The Data Management class is simultaneously taught with partner business schools in Brazil and Norway, and students learn how to design and query databases as they hone their skills in working in cross-cultural teams. After completing the project, Ashley catches a bus to the recreation centre to play racquetball. During the bus ride, Ashley listens to a podcast of her Strategic Management professor's latest lecture to confirm her understanding of the class material.

5:00 p.m.–6:00 p.m. Ashley's Strategic Management class team meets at the video booth in a school lab. Jennifer, an alumna working in Vancouver, has agreed to review the team's presentation. As she watches the presentation on her computer in Vancouver, Jennifer's software tags her comments so that the team knows the portions of the presentation that need more work.

6:30 p.m.–7:30 p.m. During dinner, Ashley's sound system stops playing the latest U2 music downloads stored on her computer and announces the receipt of a priority voice mail. Ashley uses the remote to instruct the system to play it for her; it is from the alumna who viewed her team's presentation that afternoon. Impressed by Ashley's role in the presentation, the alumna asks Ashley to cut and paste her section of the presentation and mail it to the company's recruiter. It takes Ashley about five minutes to locate the video on the university server, edit it, and email it to the recruiter.

11:00 p.m. Before going to bed, Ashley adds comments about her day to the blog she is keeping for the GRITS class.

Case Questions

1. How many of the innovations in Ashley's home or school life are available to you? How many are you actually using?
2. This case mentions many acronyms and technical terms. Research and write a short paragraph about each of the following terms:
   a. blog
   b. wireless access
   c. LCD display panel
   d. podcast
3. Do you believe that any of the information systems involved in Ashley's daily life create only limited value for her?

Integrative Application Case: *Campuspad.ca*

Sarah has been a great friend since you met in your student lounge during frosh week. Since you both live in residence, you hang out quite a bit. After IT class today, she approached you to talk about an idea she has for a new business and invited you to help her with it. You were curious—but cautious—as she told you about it.

She recently made the decision to live off-campus next year and was beginning to search for a place. Obviously, her first step was to hop online and search for "off-campus housing" and "student accommodation." During her search, she found a huge number of sites created to help students find economical places to live—although she certainly wouldn't want to live in some of the places she saw online!

The sites she had visited already left her feeling frustrated. Many of them were focused on the United States or were mostly focused on general rental accommodation, and didn't seem to understand her specific search needs. For instance, when she visited roommate-click.com, she found that they did indeed serve Canada, but were only listed on google.com, not google.ca. While homes4students.ca was clearly a Canadian site, it didn't allow her to search for places specifically near her downtown city campus, and she couldn't see the value in searching through the hundreds of listings posted. What to do?

A visit to the student housing office had been very helpful, but so many of the listings she saw had either expired or had been rented by the time she got to them. This wasn't going to be as quick or easy as she had thought. Finals were just around the corner, and this housing search would have to take second priority to studying!

That's when the idea for campuspad.ca was born. In fact, she had already registered the domain name—the first step to launching an online business. As she continued explaining, you became more and more excited. She had some really good ideas and might be on to something...and she wanted your help!

Guiding Case Questions

1. Research organizations, businesses, and sites that exist to serve student renters.
2. List the inputs, outputs, and transactional processes that currently exist in this system.
3. How could the power of the Web and other technologies improve this system?
4. What do you think some of Sarah's ideas for this market are?
5. What ideas do you or your team have to improve on existing sites?

Your Task

Write up your findings in a two-page summary. You will use this in the next phase of the case to continue your investigation of Sarah's business idea.

2

TECHNOLOGY ESSENTIALS

WHAT WE WILL COVER

- The Components of IT
- The Internet
- The World Wide Web
- The Technology of E-Commerce
- Internet Security
- Meaningful Applications of Technology

ROI STUDENT RETURN ON INVESTMENT

Through your investment of time in reading and thinking about this chapter, your return—or created value—is gaining knowledge. Use the following questions as a study guide.

1. What are the fundamentals of information technology that will help increase your productivity as a business professional?

2. How do software and hardware come together to create business capability?

3. What makes the Internet and World Wide Web so valuable?

THE VOICE OF EXPERIENCE
Derek Ball, University of Calgary

With a Bachelor of Commerce specializing in finance, Derek Ball started out in banking. He recognized the ability of technology to create business value, and soon became involved in the start-up of several technology companies. After selling his company, Sonic Mobility, to U.S.-based Avocent in 2004 for over US$8M, Derek is now CEO of Tynt.com, which tracks what is being copied from websites and provides analytics to help drive traffic and identify valuable content.

What do you do in your current position? I am currently the CEO and co-founder of Tynt Multimedia, a company that helps online publishers benefit when their readers copy and paste their content. I coordinate financing, investor relations, and business development, and I ensure that we are delivering a viable product to market.

What do you consider to be important career skills? Understanding the value technology can deliver and whether it can solve a real-world problem. Just after graduation, I was working in Zurich for a bank, doing financial control. The bank bought computers and dumped them on everybody's desk and didn't tell them how to use them. I was willing to learn and I figured out how to use Lotus 123 to automate financial control functions. Despite the fact that I didn't have any formal IT training, the bank ended up giving me the role of applying technology to streamline operations.

What I am doing currently is probably less about education or skill and more about experience. I have enough technical knowledge to know what is possible. I can be realistic about what problems technology can solve. I learned that technology is a tool. It's a means to an end, but not the end itself. It will always be changing, so it's important to be flexible and adaptable.

How do you use IT? Personally, I don't do voice mail. I try to focus all my communications through email as a way of managing my time. I'm also big believer in mobile devices as productivity tools. I have one central point of contact for all my communication: email, contacts, calendar—it's all there with me. I have used the Internet extensively for research and I'm a big fan of software as a service, something that is accessed on a remote server, not installed on an individual hard drive.

Can you describe an example of how you have used IT to improve business operations? In my previous business venture, Sonic Mobility, we used IT to provide a secure connection from a handheld wireless device to a company's backend network. It was an encrypted TCP-IP connection with secure identification. The hand-held would connect with the Sonic Admin server, which would act as a proxy and communicate with the servers that needed to be adjusted through a variety of different protocols, depending on the required action. As an example, our client's IT support staff were about to board a plane to go to a conference when they were contacted about a virus attack. They were able to connect remotely to the network from their BlackBerry devices and use Sonic Admin to stop the virus without returning to the office and missing their trip.

Have you got any on-the-job advice for students seeking a career in IT or business? Your most important resource is the people sitting on your left and right. There's no way that any one person is ever going to understand everything there is to know in any field. Information technology has grown exponentially and will continue to do so. The most important thing you can do is make as many contacts as possible.

Although Derek did not start out in the IT field, he recognized that IT plays a critical role in business success. Early in his career, he had a willingness to learn about new technology and continued to build that learning into successful businesses. This chapter will introduce you to the components and terminology of IT to equip you with a foundation for applying IT in business.

Think about how often you come in contact with information technology (IT) beyond the use of a desktop or laptop computer. For example, a grocery store uses IT to allow you to purchase items more quickly. A bank relies on IT to provide you with ATM access. You probably carry IT with you, such as a mobile phone, PDA, or MP3 player. We could spend all day adding to this list!

Now think about what IT allows you to do. IT allows you to *communicate* with others, such as through mobile phones and instant messaging. IT *enables transactions* between you and the organizations with which you deal, for example, through online purchases. IT helps you to *obtain, organize, analyze,* and *store data* and *information* that you need through online searches and specific software tools. Finally, IT can *provide entertainment* through MP3 players and game consoles. Information technology can help you do all of these things and more, with greater efficiency and value.

Most people are uninterested in opening up IT devices and tinkering with the circuits or boards. They just want to be competent users of technology. However, your use of IT will improve if you know and understand some basic concepts. It's a lot like owning and operating a car: To be a competent driver, you need to know when to get an oil change or that an unusual sound means a trip to the mechanic. And, just like paying for gas at the pump using your credit card, doing many things with your IT devices yourself can save you time.

In this chapter, our goal is to equip you with the IT knowledge that you will need to support your future career. Knowledge of fundamentals, and using available technical tools, will also help you understand new innovations.

THE COMPONENTS OF IT

When you think about it, all IT, including computers, mobile phones, and PDAs, are actually limited to the following capabilities:

- accepting and storing information
- performing mathematical calculations
- applying logic to make decisions
- retrieving, displaying, and sending information
- consistently repeating the above actions many times

The power of IT comes from the fact that it does these things amazingly well. IT devices combine these capabilities in a number of ways to help you work with information more efficiently and effectively. How is this possible?

Information technology consists of three basic categories: hardware, software, and networks. **Hardware** is the electronic and mechanical components that you can see and touch, such as your computer monitor. **Software** is the set of instructions that direct the hardware. While not necessary for all IT devices, **network** technology increases their power by allowing users to share resources, including hardware, software, and information. The three basic categories (hardware, software, and networks) together create a **platform**, as Figure 2.1 shows.

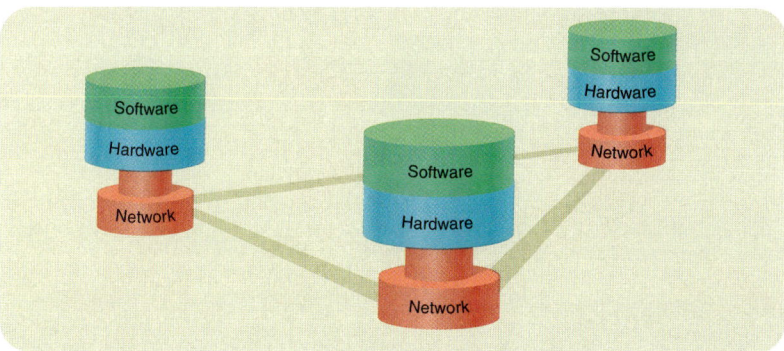

FIGURE 2.1 The IT platform consists of hardware, software, and network technology.

TECHNOLOGY CORE

This chapter discusses the technology that you need to be aware of to be a successful business person. In whatever career you choose, you may need to know more than these basics. When searching for information about technology on the Internet, try these sources:

- *www.mashable.com*: Mashable is a very popular blog that reviews new websites and services, especially in social media.

- *www.cio.com*: This news site for chief information officers provides overview information on technology and related business issues.

- *www.cnet.com*: This technology news site covers all types of technology, including PCs, mobile devices, software, and more.

- *www.gartner.com* and *www.forrester.com*: Gartner and Forrester are technology research firms that often issue press releases on the latest technology and technology usage.

Other sources of information include technology leaders' blogs, such as those of Bill Gates or Steve Jobs, and leading technology companies' websites, such as Cisco or Microsoft.

Hardware

Hardware components represent the physical (hard) parts of a system, as distinguished from the more adjustable (soft) parts, the software. The working parts of IT hardware consist primarily of electronic devices (mostly digital) with some electromechanical parts used with input, output, and storage devices.

When it comes to hardware, IT devices share a common set of system components. In our discussion of these system components, we focus on the personal computer (PC). However, the same architecture and components are common to most modern IT devices.

These general components can be categorized into six basic IT hardware categories (see Figure 2.2), which are discussed in the following subsections.

Processing Hardware Processing hardware directs the execution of instructions and the transformation of data using transistors A *transistor* is an electronic switch that can be either on (represented by 1) or off (represented by 0). A tiny chip made

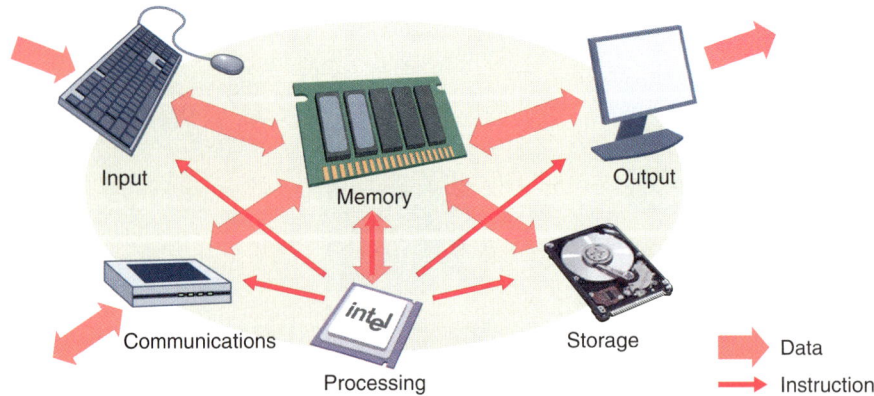

FIGURE 2.2 All IT devices share a common set of six system components.

up of transistors is called a *microprocessor*. This chip contains most of the components that make up the *central processing unit (CPU)*. You notice the speed of the CPU when you are performing a task on your PC. Have you ever done a search or opened a file and had to wait what seemed like an eternity? This speed is called the *clock speed* and is measured in *megahertz (MHz)*, millions of cycles per second, and more recently *gigahertz (GHz)*, billions of cycles per second. Higher clock speeds usually translate into faster performance, which is something to consider when you purchase your next computer.

Just as processing hardware is at the heart of any individual IT device, it is also at the heart of business IS. The main difference here is that rather than making decisions about a single processor, organizations typically need to select combinations of processors with varying processing power. A common categorization scheme for processors used in IS is known as the computer hierarchy.

As Table 2.1 shows, the **computer hierarchy** categorizes processors according to their power. Note that processing power also often corresponds to the computer's physical size. However, comparing computer types on processing power alone can be deceptive. For example, it is possible to combine the processing power of several smaller computers, like personal computers, to exceed that of a small supercomputer. An organization, therefore, has many options to meet its processing needs and will select the most efficient and cost-effective option possible.

Table 2.1   Computer Hierarchy

Computer Type	Relative Processing Power	Purpose	Example
Supercomputer	Largest and fastest	Performs processor intensive computations using parallel processing.	Environment Canada uses supercomputers to analyze data and forecast the weather.[1]
Mainframe	Large	Carries out many of the organizational processing needs using high-speed processing chips and large amounts of memory.	Health Canada uses mainframes to process health care benefit claims not covered under federal and provincial health care plans.[2]
Server farms	Medium/many	Allows multiple servers to handle network processing activities.	Google relies on its server farm to operate efficiently.
Personal computer (PC)	Small to medium	Enables users to carry out processing tasks needed to perform their job; usually networked together.	All of the major Canadian banks provide Internet banking to their personal and business banking clients. Over their websites, the banks allow clients to manage their accounts, order cheques, apply for loans, and download their account activity in accounting software to manage household finances or create business financial statements. *(Continued)*

---
1. Environment Canada, http://www.ec.gc.ca/media_archive/press/2005/050110_n_e.htm. Retrieved March 1, 2010.

2. CGI Case studies, http://www.ams.com/web/en/library/case_studies/application_management/71037.htm. Retrieved March 1, 2010.

Table 2.1	(Continued)		
Computer Type	Relative Processing Power	Purpose	Example
Personal digital assistant (PDA)/ Smartphones	Very small	Provides users with portable computing power; often used to communicate with PC or other users.	Real estate agents across Canada are able to access MLS home listings using their mobile devices (mobile phone, BlackBerry, Internet-enabled PDA) while on the go with their clients.
Embedded processors	Extremely small	Provides low-scale processing and/or identification; embedded in appliances and products.	Procter & Gamble incorporates embedded processors into packaging to monitor expiration dates.

DSPs process signals in real time, perfect for applications that cannot tolerate any delays, such as mobile phones.

In fact, the smallest type, embedded processors, which provide small amounts of processing power, may actually provide the greatest value to businesses. *Embedded processors* are programmable chips built into products to make them "smart." Recent creative uses for embedded processors include digital signal processors (DSPs). DSPs are special microprocessors that include more math-related functions in their instruction set than the typical processor. DSPs can also process signals in real time.

Memory Memory temporarily locates data and instructions before processing. Long-term memory helps you keep track of facts, like the name of the first Canadian prime minister, or processes, like how to brew coffee when you're only half awake. Short-term memory, on the other hand, is only for items that you need to remember for a relatively short time, such as the start time of a movie. After leaving the theatre, you forget that time, or replace it with other things to remember.

Computers have long-term memory (ROM) and short-term memory (RAM) stored on chips. Memory capacity is measured as the number of *bytes* that the ROM and RAM chips store. Capacities of memory devices range from thousands (kilobytes–KB), to millions (megabytes–MB), and on to billions (gigabytes–GB) of bytes. **Read only memory (ROM)** contains instructions and data that only special devices can alter. **Random access memory (RAM)** stores data only until they are no longer needed, or until you shut down the computer. This type of memory is called random access because the CPU can access any item stored in RAM directly (randomly).

Whenever you load software—like Microsoft Word to work on that 10-page term paper that you've been putting off—the CPU retrieves the software instructions and loads them into main memory. As you begin typing the paper, the CPU stores the text that you see on the screen in RAM. As you have no doubt found, if your computer shuts down inadvertently and you have not saved your paper, it will be lost, since the RAM is cleared at shutdown.

Eventually, your computer reaches its RAM capacity. What happens then? It becomes necessary to continuously exchange items stored in RAM with new items from slower storage devices. This can profoundly affect the overall performance of your computer. Consequently, increasing your RAM capacity can be one of the cheapest and most effective ways of extending the life of your computer.

Input Hardware Input hardware provides the interface used for data entry *into* a device. The choice of input device should be tailored to the task to be performed. Have you ever been in a situation when you were using a self check-out counter and the barcode scanner did not read the barcode of an item you were attempting to purchase? Having to enter the 12-digit barcode by hand on a keypad demonstrates that the scanner is a much better way to input barcode data. Input devices you are familiar with include keyboards, pointing devices (such as a Wii, mouse, or touchpad), scanners, and digital cameras.

Controlling a computer with a pointing device, such as a touchpad or mouse, allows more natural movements, thereby requiring less user training.

WHAT DO YOU THINK?

You have no doubt used a Wii. The Wii gaming remote, invented by Nintendo, connects wirelessly to the gaming console and allows the gamer to move the remote to perform activities as if they were in the game itself by sensing motion (e.g., swinging a tennis racket or steering a car).

1: Are there business applications for this technology?
2: Why would this input method be preferable to others in terms of usability? Are these the same reasons why some gamers prefer this method of input over others?
3: What are the drawbacks? Does this technology make you feel more a part of the machinery than you are comfortable with (e.g., Cyborg)?

Output Hardware Output hardware provides the interface used to retrieve information *from* a device. *Output devices* convert IT-processed information into a usable form. When choosing output devices, business professionals are primarily concerned with the quality and speed of the output. Secondary considerations may include ergonomics, portability, compatibility, and environmental considerations. Display devices make up the most common category of output device, such as computer monitors. However, most users also require printers, and many users now rely on other output devices, such as speakers or MP3 players.

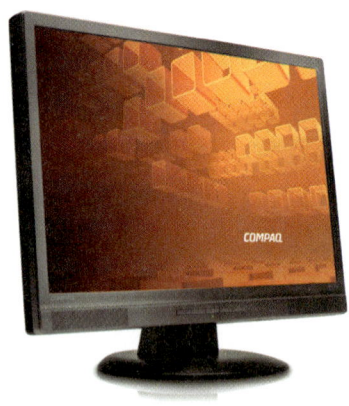

LCD monitors are slim, light, and don't use a lot of power to run.

Modern monitors come in all sizes and resolutions. LCD screens are light, thin, and consume less energy than other types of monitors. Printers and plotters output data to paper. Are you familiar with the terms "paperless society" or "paperless office"? In the 1970s, with the adoption of computer technology in business, some predicted that we would no longer require paper output and would simply view documents on screen, and that society would adapt to decrease paper consumption significantly.[3] What happened in reality was quite the opposite. As it became easier to access documents and information, it became easier to print it! The result, for a period of time, was an increase in paper consumption. Today, we do view a lot more information online rather than printing it, but we have not eliminated the need to print altogether.

Think about your personal printing habits. Are you signed up for on-line billing, for example, as a way to reduce cost for businesses and reduce the use of paper? What types of things do you tend to print rather than view on a screen? Do you think you could go completely paperless? Some of you may be reading this textbook as an eBook. Have you printed it out to read it? Be honest!

Storage Hardware Storage hardware stores data, information, and instructions for the long term. Examples of storage include the computer hard drive, CDs, DVDs, USB flash memory, and external hard drives. How often do you back up your PC? Do you remember to put critical files on an external hard drive or memory key just in case? Have you been in the unfortunate situation of losing your data? To prevent the loss of your data, you can now sign up for an online backup service that will automatically back up the files that you specify on a scheduled basis. If you have bought a Dell computer recently, they may have provided you with a trial of their Dell DataSafe product, which automatically backs up your data and stores it at a secure storage site.

Not only is this a concern for individual business professionals, it is a major concern for businesses. In Chapter 4 we discuss disaster recovery as a way of reducing the risk of data loss. Often businesses keep critical data off-site in case something happens to their internal systems or facilities. This way they can retrieve their data and resume business as quickly as possible.

USB flash memory will store large amounts of data and instructions for the long term.

Communications Hardware Communications hardware connects one IT device to another. Communications hardware, such as the **network interface card (NIC)**, provides the physical connection between a computer and a local network. This ability is vital to many knowledge work activities.

When you are not physically connected to a network, you can use a modem. **Modems,** both wired and wireless, allow you to connect to a remote network over a telecommunications line, such as the telephone or cable TV service. A modem converts (*mo*dulates) the digital signals going out from your computer into an analog signal appropriate for the connection medium used. When receiving a signal, it converts (*dem*odulates) the analog signal back into a digital signal that your computer can recognize.

---

3. "The Office of the Future," *Business Week* (2387), June 30, 1975, pp. 48–70.

Modem speeds, measured in bits per second (bps), significantly affect knowledge work activities. For example, if you frequently research information on the Internet, you will lose valuable time waiting for a telephone modem to download the data. At top transmission speeds of 56 Kbps, telephone modems cannot compete with cable or DSL modems, which offer higher transmission speeds—up to 3 Mbps and higher in many areas.

Finally, recent IT technology has increased knowledge work effectiveness by allowing mobile devices to connect to wireless networks by using wireless NICs.

We have now discussed the main categories of hardware that exist in any IT system (each of these components is discussed in further detail in Tech Guide B). However, each and every IT device, from your MP3 player to your desktop PC, includes a component that you can't touch but that your device cannot work without. In the next section, we discuss this important component: software.

Software

As discussed, IT devices help you with your knowledge work activities and thereby contribute to creating business value. As such, they always involve working with information in some way. You can think about software as information that specifies how a hardware device should work with other data, information, and knowledge.

To begin to understand the relationship between software and hardware, think about cooking from a recipe. Your mother makes an amazing chicken pot pie, and it has been a while since you had a home-cooked meal. She emails you the recipe and you buy the ingredients. You follow the recipe exactly: 2 cups of chicken, 2 carrots sliced, and so on. You also follow the baking instructions: 1 hour at 350 degrees Fahrenheit. Does the chicken pot pie turn out the same as your mom's? Probably not.

By now you're probably wondering: "What in the world does this have to do with computer software?" Recall that a computer performs functions based on instructions; that is, software. The process by which a computer follows instructions is similar to how you learn and follow instructions for the tasks that you do.

For example, even if your mother gives you the exact recipe, she may omit some of the steps that she takes to ensure the perfect chicken pot pie (such as adding a little more salt or pepper to taste). She is able to execute these instructions routinely and without thought. The instructions for this have become instinctual or built-in, like firmware. Similarly, when you turn on a computer, firmware built into ROM chips allows the computer to start and prepare for use (i.e., boot up). Once the computer is ready, the CPU loads more software into RAM, and the computer can get to work.

After your chicken pot pie is cooked, you begin to do more tasks, such as finding dishes and utensils to eat with. Your *personal application software* for setting the table may instruct your body which utensils (fork or spoon) to select. However, it's your *system software* that controls your hands as you place items on the table. Similarly, while you may select the Print command within an application software package, it is the operating system that takes over and carries out the actual print job.

We can divide computer software into three main categories: (1) system software, (2) application software, and (3) middleware.

System Software **System software** includes any software required to control the hardware components and to support the execution of application software. System software includes the operating system and utility software. The **operating system (OS) software** coordinates and handles the details of working with the computer hardware. After the boot program in ROM successfully tests and starts up the hardware, the CPU loads the operating system (OS) software into the computer's memory. The OS software performs two main tasks:

1. managing the hardware and software resources of the computer
2. providing a stable and consistent interface between application programs and the hardware

To manage the hardware, the operating system works like a police officer who directs traffic at a busy intersection. Given its role of directing all computer operations, OS software has the most impact on your experience, efficiency, and productivity when using a computer.

Do you recall the controversy about Windows Vista when it was released worldwide in 2007? In its first year of availability, *PC World* rated it as the biggest tech disappointment of 2007[4] and it was rated by *InfoWorld* as number 2 of the 25 all-time technology flops.[5] Although Vista implemented much needed new security features and a different/improved user interface, it was criticized for the hardware requirements needed to run it and its incompatibility with other software. In an effort to encourage adoption, Microsoft decided to no longer support the previous operating system, Windows XP, and no longer provide it as an operating system to its channel partners, such as Dell. Soon, this left new PC buyers with no choice but to use Vista. Due to public backlash and criticism of Vista, Microsoft retracted and began to allow the use of XP again. They also increased their efforts on the next operating system release, Windows 7. Who knew that an OS could make such a big impact and create such passion in computer users!

Utility software provides additional tools that you can use to maintain and service your system. For example, users often add utilities such as file management software and security programs. A firewall application is an example of utility software that helps guard your computer against unauthorized access when connected to a network.

Application Software **Application software** is a complete, self-contained program or set of programs for performing a specific job. For example, you would use a word processing application software, like Microsoft Word, to write your term paper.

An important group of application software for business professionals is known as **productivity software**. Business professionals frequently use productivity software to more efficiently and effectively work with data, information, and knowledge, as follows:

- *Document preparation software*, for creating documents composed of text, images, and supporting graphics

---

4. Dan Tynan. "The 15 Biggest Tech Disappointments of 2007." *PC World*. (December 16, 2007) http://www.pcworld.com/article/id,140583-page,5-c,techindustrytrends/article.html. Retrieved March 1, 2010.

5. Neil McAllister. "Tech's All-Time Top 25 Flops." *InfoWorld*. (January 21, 2008) http://www.infoworld.com/article/08/01/21/03FE-25-tech-failures_6.html. Retrieved March 1, 2010.

- *Electronic spreadsheet software*, for performing general calculations and analyses, such as financial analysis, budgeting, and forecasting
- *Presentation graphics software*, for preparing professional-quality slides and graphics for business presentations; often requires a business professional to be able to access and manipulate large amounts of data
- *Database management system (DBMS)*, for designing, creating, updating, and querying data
- *Personal information management (PIM)*, for managing personal information, such as to-do lists, schedules, and email

In addition to these uses of application software for individual business professionals, enterprises also employ application software for business units (e.g., finance, marketing, etc.) or for the enterprise as a whole. This software tends to be specialized for a certain business process and may be further customized for the organization itself. An example of this type of enterprise application software is customer relationship management (CRM) software, which helps organizations manage customer data and interactions. Because these types of application software are so important and prevalent in business today, we discuss them in depth in Chapter 4.

Middleware Middleware is software that is more common in enterprises. Its purpose is to link applications that use dissimilar software or hardware platforms and act like a specialized messenger/translator to manage the exchange of information. Figure 2.3 illustrates where a layer of middleware software would fit within an organization's IS to support efficient communication between various business applications and the systems environment.

Middleware is often essential when an organization is implementing new types of software that need to communicate with existing systems. For example, your organization may acquire another company and need to integrate the purchased company's financial systems with your organization's. Middleware may be written to interface with the source system (the acquired company's financial system) and the target system (your company's financial system).

Open Source Software Open source software is software that can be used, modified, improved, and redistributed. Open source software is usually developed by a community of developers that are interested in the subject matter of the software and want to share their work with others. Open-source programs are often free or have very low cost. The combination of low cost, flexibility of use, and decreasing reliance on a single software vendor has made this software a very popular choice for many e-commerce applications. Commonly used open source software in e-commerce include:

- Linux—used as the operating system for the servers (and possibly the clients)
- Apache—a Web server software application
- MySql—a database management system
- Perl, PHP, or Python—a selection of script programming languages
- Ruby on Rails (RoR)—a Web application framework

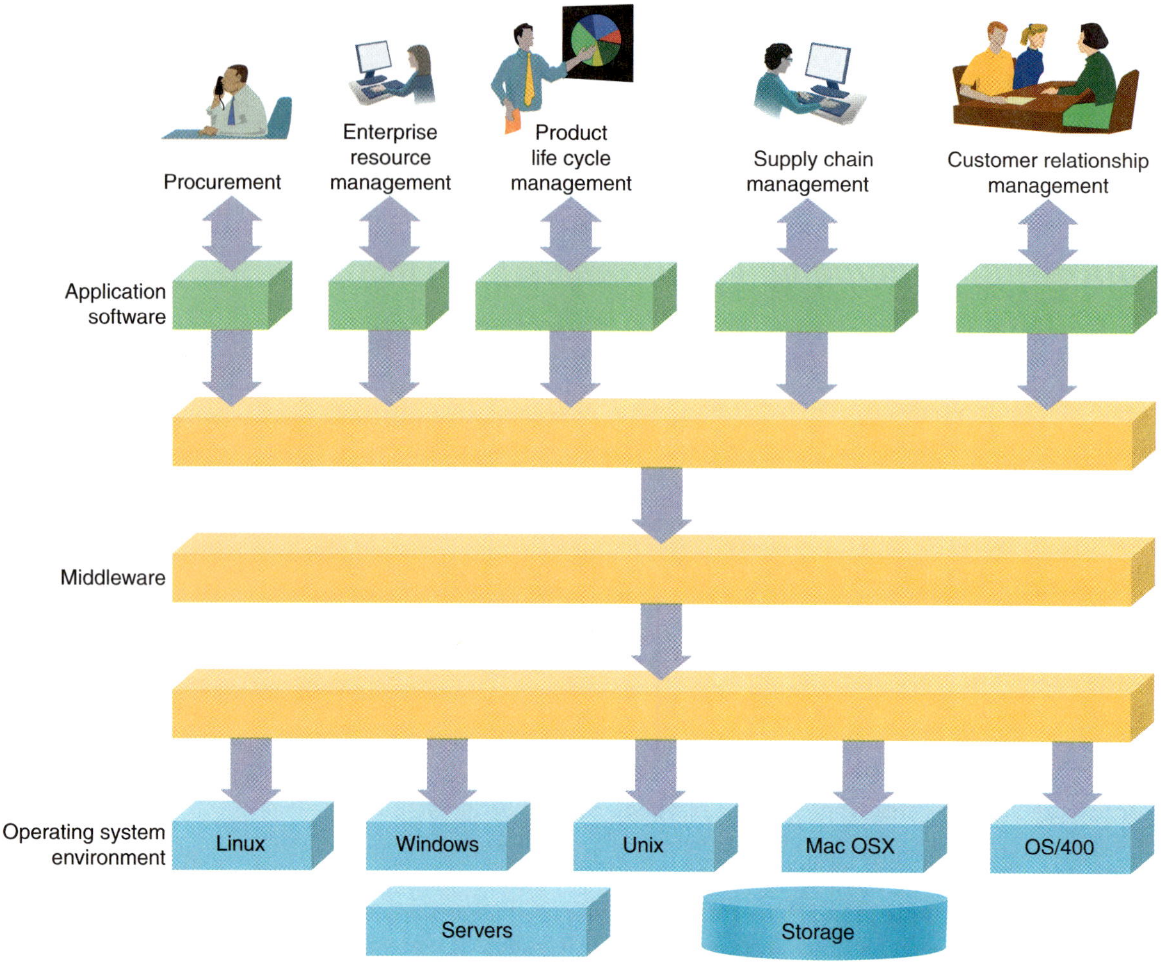

FIGURE 2.3 Middleware, as this figure shows, fits within an organization's IS to support efficient communication between various business applications and the operating system environment.

A report by Standish Group states that adoption of open-source software models has resulted in savings of about $60 billion per year to consumers.[6]

Now that we have discussed hardware and software (both of which are discussed in more detail in Tech Guide B), we can examine how these connect to other organizational resources and how those resources are accessed and shared.

Connecting Over Networks

Look around. Networks are everywhere! Humans are networking maniacs. Social networks link people through family relationships, friendships, acquaintances, and business contacts. Global transportation networks link cities and towns via roads and highways as well as by train, bus, and airline routes. There is also a long history of communication networks, such as the Greek message runners, the Pony Express,

---

6. "Standish Newsroom—Open Source" Press release, April 16, 2008. http://standishgroup.com/newsroom/open_source.php. Retrieved March 6, 2010.

telegraph systems, and the international telephone system. Today, the fastest-growing network is arguably our global computer network, known as the Internet.

A computer network consists of *nodes* that represent computer hardware and the network users, with various types of hardware, software, and *communications media* forming the links between nodes. As such, a computer network requires four primary components:

1. data (the resource) that computers share on the network
2. special hardware
3. software that allows computers to communicate and share the data
4. communication media to link the computers together

Networks of connected computers support the core function of data transfer in an organization. But networks serve another critical function: Computer networks are the main technology supporting communication between managers and employees, between employee and employee, and between the organization and its suppliers and customers. They provide a platform for collaboration, allowing users to share data, information, and knowledge.

In the following sections, we briefly review network hardware and software. For a more in-depth discussion of networks, see Tech Guide C: The Details of Networking.

Network Categories To better understand why so many options exist for network technology, it helps to know the different types of computer networks that exist. The categories we discuss here are important because they represent why different networking components or techniques may be required.

One common method of describing computer networks relies on how much geography the physical size of the network covers. The two extreme sizes are a local area network (LAN) and a wide area network (WAN). Technology requirements are generally more complicated as the physical size of the network gets larger. As Table 2.2 indicates, organizations use all sizes of networks, including PANs, LANs, MANs, WANs, and the Internet, as well as networks based on the Internet protocols.

Table 2.2	Computer Networks		
Network	Size	Purpose	Examples
PAN (private area network) (private)	Covers a very small space that ranges from the size of a human body to a small office	Communication among computer devices in close proximity	A PAN allows your MP3 player to connect to a wireless headset, your PDA to "sync" with your PC, and your car to respond to commands from a Bluetooth-enabled mobile phone.
LAN (local area network) (private)	Within the immediate location or building	Share files, resources, servers, and other hardware among the members of an organization	Common LANs include university computing labs, small office or household networks, and a wireless hotspot. *(Continued)*

Table 2.2	(Continued)		
Network	Size	Purpose	Examples
MAN (metropolitan area network) (private/public)	Ranges in size from a few blocks to an entire metropolitan area	Provides data and voice transmission typically at high speeds (≈100 Mbps)	A university may use a MAN to connect LANs across campus; many city libraries use MANs to support centralized cataloguing and searching of resources.
WAN (wide area network) (private/public)	Over a large geographical area	Share data, information, and resources among units of an organization distant from one another	A WAN connects various university MANs/LANs to share research; a corporate network uses a WAN to link national and international locations.
Internet (public)	Worldwide	Share data and information with all stakeholders in the organization, as well as with the general public	The Internet is the largest public WAN; sometimes known as a *global area network (GAN)*.

Network Hardware Forming a network requires a number of devices for making network connections as well as for managing data transmission over the network. There are three basic categories of network hardware:

1. Hardware to connect a device to a network: Hardware that connects computers or other devices to a network includes modems, cable modems, network interface cards (NICs), and wireless cards. Each of these devices serves to connect your computer or device to a specific network. The device that you use depends mainly on the media that connects to your computer.

    A physical link that forms a network connection is referred to as a *carrier* or *communications medium*. There are several different options including the *plain old telephone system* (*POTS*) network, which is the most common for transmitting electrical signals. Alternatively, there are coaxial and fibre optic cables that can transmit information at faster speeds. What type of connectivity do you have?

    Finally, technologies such as infrared light, radio waves, and microwaves also allow networks to transmit signals through the air. This form of transmission is increasingly important as you seek more mobility with your IT devices. You have likely used Bluetooth technology to speak on your mobile phone using a wireless earpiece, or "beamed" a friend your phone number from your mobile phone to theirs.

2. Specialized hardware for handling network traffic: Devices that help coordinate the data traffic on a network include routers, bridges, repeaters, and hubs. A *bridge* is a device that lets you connect to networks or break a large network into two smaller, more efficient networks. A *router* connects, translates, and then directs data that cross between two networks. A *hub*, also known as a *concentrator*, serves as a central connection point for cables from the devices on the network. A *repeater* is sometimes needed to strengthen or amplify signals that are sent along a long transmission route. Finally, a wireless *access point (AP)* is a special bridge that connects between wireless

devices and a wired network. All of these are important because they contribute to the speed of a network.

3. **Specialized computers that control the network and the delivery of data on the network:** On most networks, specialized computers, called *servers*, manage the various functions of the network. Servers are often assigned a specific task, such as handling email (*email server*), Web traffic (*Web server*), or running programs (*application server*).

A *file server* is a fast computer that requires a large amount of RAM and storage space. Why? Because not only does it store and run the network operating system software, it may also store shared software applications and data files. Further, the file server manages all communication between the devices on the network. (Any computer connected to the file server on a network is called a *client* or a *workstation*.) Because many users may request services from the file server at the same time, you can also see why a computer that can store a lot of data and share it quickly is required. We discuss other types of network servers in Tech Guide C.

Network Software Like PC software, we can divide network software into operating system software and application software. Network operating system software manages network functions and the flow of data traffic over a computer network. Network application software provides the instructions that allow for the creation of data and for this transformation to fit appropriate *protocols* for transmission over a network. A **protocol** is a standard set of rules that allows the communication of data between nodes on a network.

You have no doubt used network application software when you composed an email to a friend and sent it over the Internet. These days, we can include just about every productivity software category as network application software. For example, modern word processing software usually includes features that allow you to email or fax a document directly, or transform and post the document as a web page.

Quick Test

1. All other things being equal, which mix of components allows a computer to simultaneously run multiple programs faster?
   a. 1-GHz processor with 256 MB RAM
   b. 1-GHz processor with 512 MB RAM
   c. 1-MHz processor with 256 MB RAM
   d. 2-MHz processor with 512 MB RAM

2. Imagine that you are in charge of tracking the dues paid by each member of a large student organization. To store these data in an organized form that allows you to easily look up data, which type of application software would you most likely use?
   a. spreadsheet
   b. database management
   c. presentation
   d. word processing

3. Which one of the following is a primary component of a computer network?
   a. communications media
   b. data to share
   c. software
   d. all of the above

Answers: 1. c; 2. b; 3. d

THE INTERNET

Strictly speaking, any computer network that connects several networks together is an internet (short for inter-networking). We simply refer to the single largest and most popular internet in the world as the *Internet*. With the Internet, all of the IT components we have discussed so far—hardware, software, and networking technologies—come together to make what is arguably the most useful technological tool of the last few decades. Almost three-quarters (73 percent), or 19.2 million Canadians aged 16 and older, went online for personal reasons in 2007.[7] In 2010, it is estimated that over 1.7 billion people have access to and are using the Internet.[8]

What Makes the Internet Possible?

The foundation technology that makes the Internet possible is the adoption of standard protocols. The Internet uses the *TCP/IP* suite of *packet switching* protocols. This is a very general, non-proprietary set of communication rules. By adopting these rules and making use of software compatible with the TCP/IP standards, any computer, regardless of the platform, processor, and OS, can connect and communicate over the Internet.

Another aspect of the Internet, important to its near global adoption, is that no single organization or governmental entity owns it. Instead, several international organizations provide committees that discuss and propose Internet standards. These committees include the *Internet Engineering Task Force* (*IETF*), the *Internet Architecture Board* (*IAB*), and the *World Wide Web Consortium* (*W3C*). These and other groups have developed standard protocols, sometimes referred to as the Internet protocol suite. This suite offers many useful protocols, such as *HTTP*, *SMTP*, and *FTP*, which we discuss in detail in Tech Guide C.

Accessing the Internet

At home, users access the Internet through dial-up (over traditional phone lines) or broadband (through cable or ISDN). At work, they often connect directly to the organization's LAN or WAN. The organization in turn provides connection to the Internet if needed. All Internet-access methods require specialized hardware—a modem for dial-up access, a cable modem for cable access, and an NIC or wireless NIC for direct connection to a network.

Most users do not connect directly to the Internet. Instead, they contract with an **Internet service provider (ISP)**. ISPs, like Sympatico, Primus, Shaw, and

---
7. http://www.statcan.gc.ca/daily-quotidien/080612/dq080612b-eng.htm. Retrieved March 6, 2010.

8. http://www.internetworldstats.com/stats.htm. Retrieved March 6, 2010.

Rogers, purchase the expensive equipment needed to connect to the Internet. ISPs then provide connections for customers to use via dial-up or cable.

Internet access also requires software. Software used to make the connection includes OS utilities and special software that the ISP usually provides. To access and process content, Internet users also need application software, such as an email client and a Web browser.

You will not only find Internet access at home or the office, but in public locations like libraries, airports, and coffee shops. Access at these places is increasingly simple and universal with the increase in *Wi-Fi hotspots*. **Wi-Fi** is the popular name for the 802.11 standards for wireless network access. A hotspot refers to any public space within which a wireless device can connect. With Wi-Fi and other forms of wireless access, business professionals can now go mobile and stay connected to the Internet using laptop computers, PDAs, or a number of other wireless devices. You will find wireless access, free and paid, in all major cities in Canada. For a list of free Wi-Fi hotspots in Canada, the United States, and Europe, visit *www.wififreespot.com*.

Beyond Internet Access While the creation of and the ability to access the Internet were revolutionary in themselves, it is now what can be done with the Internet that is remarkable. Later in this chapter we discuss the most popular application of the Internet, the Web. But more and more, researchers are finding ways to use the Internet for other purposes. We will first discuss these other notable Internet applications.

One purpose, now commonplace, is the use of **voice over Internet protocol (VoIP)** to make calls anywhere in the world and bypass traditional switched telephone networks. VoIP uses the Internet's foundation technologies of packet switching and TCP/IP to carry voice instead of data. VoIP does this by converting the analog voice signal to digital, creating packets and sending the packets over the same infrastructure as you do your email or Internet searches. This process is shown at a very high level in Figure 2.4.

There were challenges when VoIP was first introduced. Packets may have been lost or delayed along the network, resulting in conversations sounding choppy.

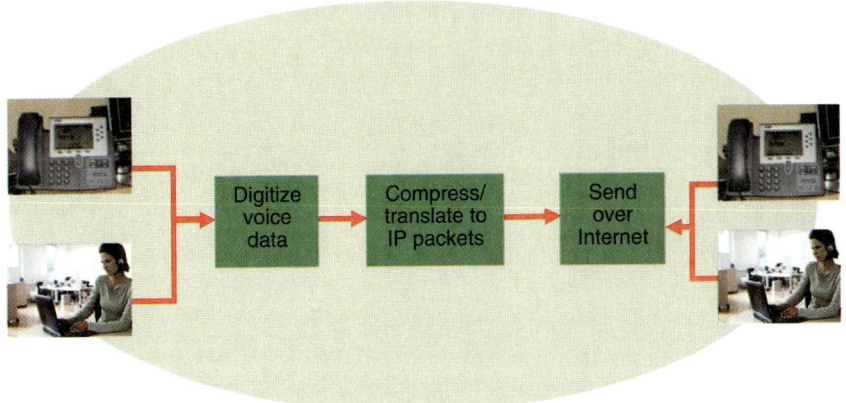

FIGURE 2.4 VoIP takes analog voice calls, digitizes them, and delivers them over the Internet, avoiding the costly PSTN network.

Over the years, however, quality has improved and services such as Skype have become very popular. Skype is especially popular because the calls are free between Skype users. Using the traditional public switched telephone network (PSTN), a call from Toronto to Calgary might cost as much as $3/minute, whereas a Skype VoIP call between those same locations using VoIP-enabled phones or a PC with microphone and speakers is free.

Businesses can also use VoIP to reduce costs, such as reducing the cost of phone calls over the telephone network. More valuable though, is the ability to use VoIP for unified communication. In this context, VoIP can be used for telephone calls, faxing, voice mail, and more over a single network, which can significantly decrease infrastructure costs. Some business professionals, such as a senior executive at Bell or Telus, might not be so enthusiastic about this cost-cutting measure. How would you respond to this competition if you were one of those senior executives?

Another advancement in the use of the Internet is **cloud computing**. The term *cloud* has been used as a synonym for the Internet for many years. Cloud computing simply means computing over the Internet. The Internet has made it easy to remotely access computing resources, separating users from the infrastructure they are working on. That is, users can use any Internet connection to access their resources on virtual computers anywhere in the cloud. There is no need to see or even know the location of the server they are using. There are several benefits to cloud computing:

- Reduced cost because technical infrastructure is not required—Cloud computing is often paid for on a usage, user, or flat fee basis that is significantly cheaper than building and maintaining a technical infrastructure.
- Scalability on demand—The cloud has many resources available to it, including the ability to increase bandwidth and access common application protocol interfaces (APIs) for extending services.
- Accessibility—Cloud computing is accessible from anywhere there is Internet access.

As you can imagine, cloud computing is especially beneficial for small or medium-sized businesses that do not want to invest in technology and the resources to manage it. We discuss cloud computing more in the form of software as a service (SaaS) and application service providers (ASP) in Chapter 4.

What's Next for the Internet?

There is seemingly no limit to what can be done over the Internet. Did you know that the Internet has only been used by the general public for the last 20 years? But look at the advancements made in that short period of time! Below are a couple of projects in the works that will take the Internet to the next level.

- The Next-Generation Internet—This project is working on replacing the basic protocols that make the Internet possible, namely IP (currently version 4), with a next generation protocol called "Internet Protocol Version 6" (IPv6).

IPv4 is already more than 20 years old and is sorely in need of an update for the Internet to continue to grow. IPv6 seeks to repair a number of problems with IPv4.[9] These include increasing the number of available IP addresses, and improvements to routing and network configurations. As of 2008, IPv6 accounted for a minuscule fraction of the used addresses and the traffic in the publicly accessible Internet, which is still dominated by IPv4.[10] The 2008 Summer Olympic Games were a notable event in terms of IPv6 deployment, being the first major world event that had a presence on the IPv6 Internet at *http://ipv6.beijing2008.cn/en* (IP addresses 2001:252:0:1::2008:6 and 2001:252:0:1::2008:8). Further, all network operations of the Games were conducted using IPv6.[11] It is believed that the Olympics provided the largest showcase of IPv6 technology since its inception.[12] You can think of the Next-Generation Internet project as giving the Internet an overhaul.

- Internet2—A consortium of professionals from more than 200 universities and industry and government agencies is developing advanced network applications and technologies to enable the creation of revolutionary Internet applications and ensure the rapid deployment of new technologies and services to the global community.[13] Internet2 applications are already in use. Check at your school to see if some of the Internet sites that you visit are already part of Internet2.

WHAT DO YOU THINK?

There is no doubt that the ability to access the Internet anywhere at any time using wireless technology is changing the way we work and live. Just imagine, there was a time when you could only access the Internet or email by using special terminals in the library! However, some argue that using wireless technology may make us too productive. Consider the following:

1: Have you ever heard the term *Crackberry*? What does this mean to you?
2: Do you think being able to access your email at all times using a wireless device keeps you more or less socially connected?
3: What do you think of the expectation some organizations have that if you are connected wirelessly, you are available 24/7?

For more on this topic, see the article by two professors at Ryerson's School of Information Technology Management: Catherine A. Middleton and Wendy Cukier, "Is Mobile E-mail Functional or Dysfunctional? Two Perspectives on Mobile E-mail Usage," *European Journal of Information Systems,* June 2006, *15*, p. 252.

---

9. "What Is IPv6?," http://www.ipv6.org, 2010.
10. Geoff Huston: An Update on IPv6 Deployment (RIPE 56).
11. The Beijing Organizing Committee for the Games of the XXIX Olympiad (May 30, 2008). "Beijing2008.cn leaps to next-generation Net." Press release. http://en.beijing2008.cn/news/official/preparation/n214384681.shtml.
12. Kaushik Das. "IPv6 and the 2008 Beijing Olympics". *IPv6.com.* http://ipv6.com/articles/general/IPv6-Olympics-2008.htm. Retrieved March 7, 2010.
13. http://www.internet2.edu, 2010.

THE WORLD WIDE WEB

For many, the Internet is synonymous with two of its most popular applications, the *World Wide Web* (*WWW*), including e-commerce, and *electronic mail* (*email*). However, the World Wide Web, often called simply the Web, is not the same as the Internet. Think of the Internet as the technology platform, and the Web as an application that works on that platform.

Some very basic technologies are required to make the Web work:

- client/server networks—the networks over which data travel
- browser—application software that lets users request and view web pages
- HTTP protocol—the standardized rules for exchanging data over the Web
- HTML—the language that guides the display of a requested page

Figure 2.5 shows how these technologies work together. Although there are more complicated technologies on the Web than depicted in this diagram, it provides you with a general overview of the technologies that are still in use today, which are discussed in detail in the following sections (all of these components of the Web are discussed in more detail in Tech Guide C).

Basic Components of the World Wide Web

Client/Server Networks When you open a Web browser on your computer, you start a client application. If you type a **uniform resource locator (URL)**—which specifies a unique address for each page that indicates the location of a document—into your browser or click a hyperlink, the browser sends a request out over the Web that makes its way to the corresponding server. The browser formulates the request under the rules of HTTP (discussed below) so that all computers on the Web, especially the destination server, will know how to handle it.

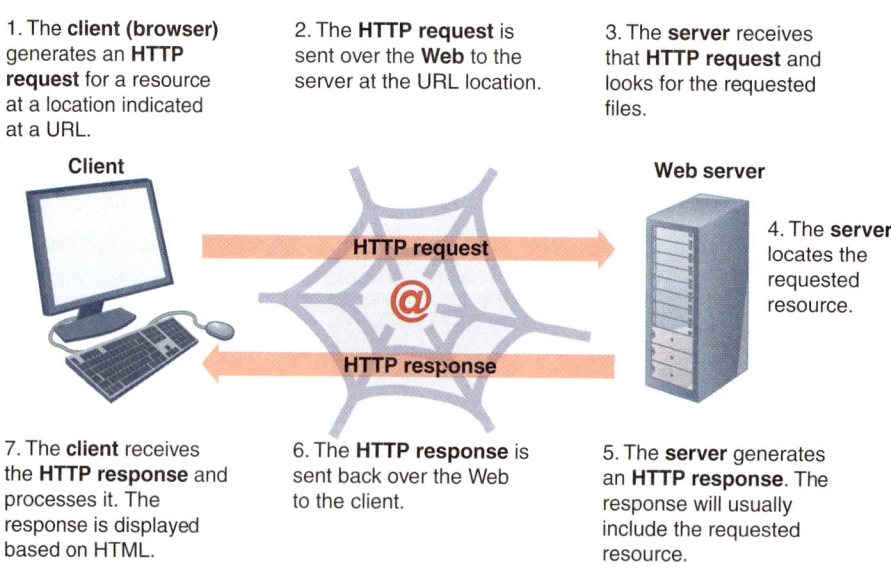

1. The **client (browser)** generates an **HTTP request** for a resource at a location indicated at a URL.

2. The **HTTP request** is sent over the **Web** to the server at the URL location.

3. The **server** receives that **HTTP request** and looks for the requested files.

4. The **server** locates the requested resource.

5. The **server** generates an **HTTP response**. The response will usually include the requested resource.

6. The **HTTP response** is sent back over the Web to the client.

7. The **client** receives the **HTTP response** and processes it. The response is displayed based on HTML.

FIGURE 2.5 The sequence of activities on the Web over a *client/server network*.

When the request reaches its destination, the server generates a response that includes the requested item and conforms to HTTP (note that a *Web server* is a software application that handles Web requests, not necessarily a separate computer). The server then simply loads the text data from storage, adds the appropriate HTTP information, and sends the item back to the client. This sequence of activities provides a **client/server network.**

A static web page file will typically hold a combination of text content and *hypertext markup language* (*HTML*) commands. Other requests may include other static file formats such as images, sound, or video. While sound and video might seem interactive, they are nevertheless static because the file contents do not change.

Web Browsers A **Web browser** is a software application that allows you to easily navigate the Web and to view the content that you find there. At its most basic, a browser will let you request, either by typing a URL or clicking a hyperlink, and display a hypertext-based file. Hypertext organizes content into units that are connected using associations called *links*. Figure 2.6 shows an example of a browser displaying a web page and identifies the typical components of a browser.

HTTP—Hypertext Transfer Protocol A client and a server communicate with each other using messages. To do this, they need a standard set of rules for formatting and transmitting these messages. That is where HTTP comes in. The **hypertext transfer protocol (HTTP)** comprises the set of rules for exchanging messages on the World Wide Web. HTTP governs both the request (*HTTP request*) for a file and the transmission (*HTTP response*) of the requested file.

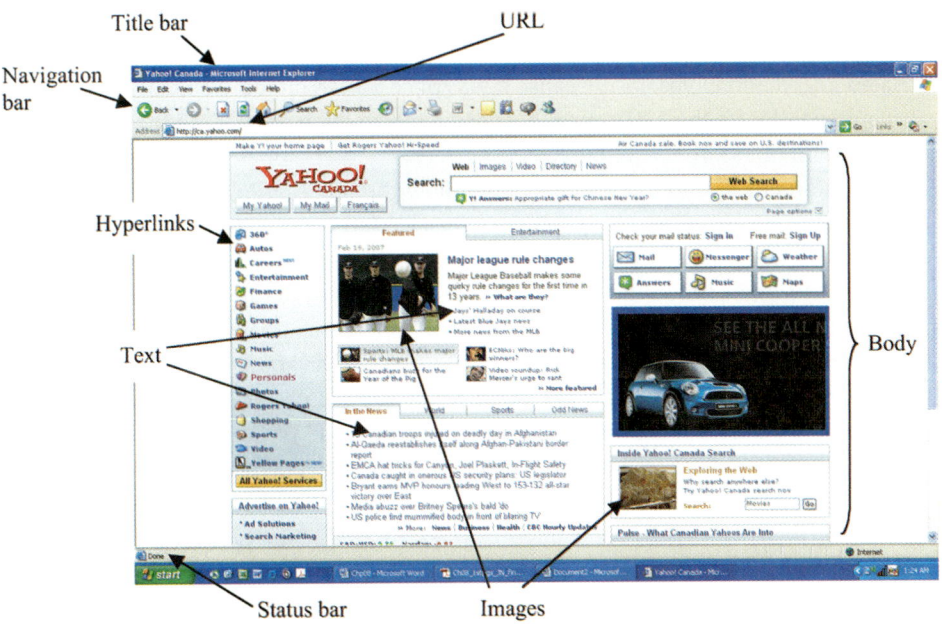

FIGURE 2.6 Most browsers, including Internet Explorer shown here, provide similar components for displaying and viewing a web page.

Tim Berners-Lee, the inventor of the World Wide Web, first implemented HTTP while at CERN, the European Centre for High-Energy Physics in Geneva, in 1990 and 1991. He developed HTTP to live at the application layer of networks. That is, once the application composes the HTTP message (request or response), lower-level protocols such as TCP/IP transmit the message. Berners-Lee originally designed HTTP as a lightweight, speedy method of sharing hypermedia information over a client/server network.

HTML—Hypertext Markup Language **Hypertext markup language (HTML)** is the primary language for creating web pages. It is not a true programming language, as the computer does not generally process HTML instructions. Instead, browser software interprets HTML instructions through the use of *tags*, which are interspersed with content. The tags, surrounded by angle brackets (< and >), mark the placement and appearance of the various components of the page. A web page usually consists of several different types of components, such as page layout instructions, formatted text, hyperlinks, tables, graphics, and form objects. Go to any website, right mouse click and select "view source," and you will be able to see the HTML for that particular web page.

Of course, all of the above happens when users are able to find a website they are looking for. Without search technologies, users would have to know a specific URL to find the website they are looking for. Luckily, sophisticated search technologies are available to help you find what you are looking for, even when you enter the most vague search criteria.

Search Technologies

Have you searched the Web for information lately? If you have, you realize the vast amount of data available. In 2008, Google reported indexing one trillion web pages, and further indicated that more were available.[14] In fact, many claim we are at the point of information overload, where huge volumes of useless, old, or unsubstantiated information lives, just because it was once posted on the Web. As a result, how could you locate the best source of specific information on any product, service, or topic without search technology?

Internet **search engines** generally follow the process shown in Figure 2.7. For most sites, users access an HTML form-based web page that allows them to enter their specific search criteria to a greater or lesser extent. Search criteria generally consist of one or more keywords and possibly other data to limit the search and keep the list of results to a manageable level. The search criteria data are sent to the search engine Web server, which in turn passes it to the application server to search through the sites' databases. In reality, when you search the Web you are actually searching a database that was compiled from previous Web searches.

The main difference between most Internet search engines is how the database of Web locations is created and organized. To search the Web and compile location data in their databases, most Internet search engines use either special software called *Web crawlers,* human submissions, or a combination of the two. Many web pages incorporate special tags, known as *meta tags,* which contain information that

---

14. http://googleblog.blogspot.com/2008/07/we-knew-web-was-big.html. Retrieved March 6, 2010.

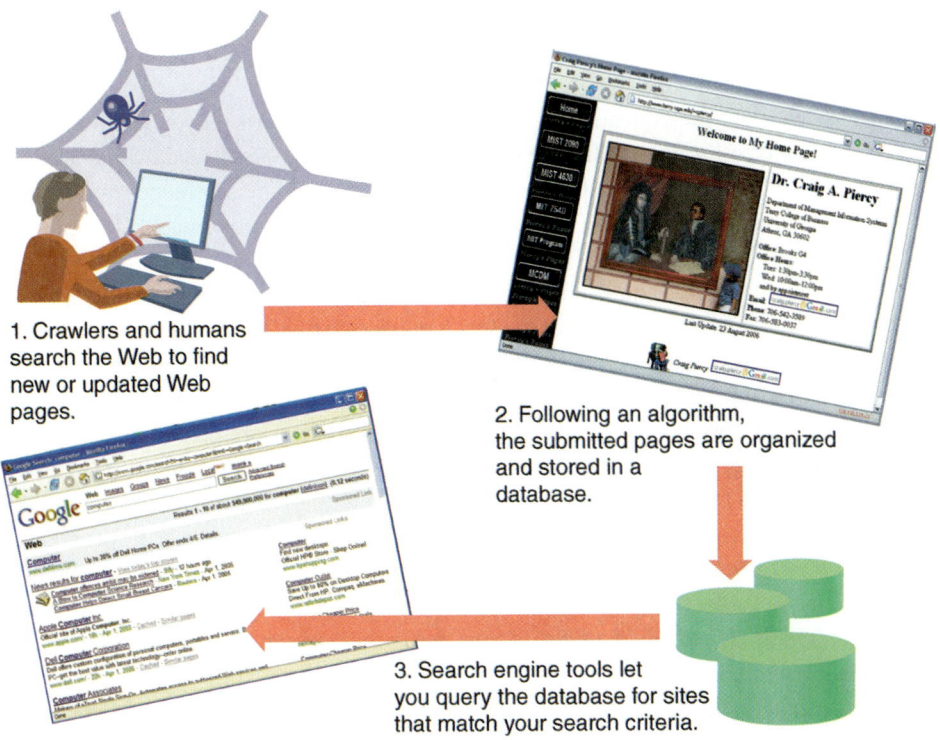

FIGURE 2.7 How search engines work.

describe what a site is about. Crawlers, or spiders, move around from site to site, read these meta tags, and report the data back to their database for storage.

People can also submit sites, which the database also stores. Since people often discriminate between sites better than crawlers, human submissions are often of higher quality or fit a specific profile better than sites found by crawlers. In either case, the actual sites stored in each site's database can vary, depending on what the crawlers and humans find and submit.

Perhaps more important than how the sites are found is the manner in which the database organizes, or *indexes,* the Web data. Each search engine typically uses a different algorithm for indexing the data and applying the search criteria to query the indexed data. For example, a search engine may rank web pages based on the frequency and location of keywords in the page content. Those pages with a higher frequency of relevant keywords may receive a higher ranking. Another method, such as the one made popular by the Google search engine, ranks each page based on the number of other pages that link to the page. A page with a larger number of relevant linked pages is considered to be more important to the Web community, and thus would receive a higher ranking.

When it comes to search engines, there are a lot of questions that can be asked, including:

- What responsibility should search engines have to make sure that the information they are collecting and indexing is accurate and valid?
- What if the information collected is deliberately vague, false, or misleading?

- How can you structure your organization's online presence to ensure that the right information from the right source is displayed to those searching out your business?
- What are the ethical, legal, and related issues that arise if you try to manipulate or otherwise influence search engine "hits" to favour your business?
- To what extent do the business models of search engines influence how, when, and what they display and how they disclose this to you once it is displayed?

Given all of these questions, do you think that using search engines helps you find the information you are looking for? Not necessarily. This is where your experience and skills come into play. If you don't know which search criteria to enter, you may not be able to locate the information you need to succeed. Therefore, learning more about query languages, the construction of Internet search engines, and how that technology works is very useful. You may also consider using a *metasearch engine*, a Web-based tool that allows you to review the search results generated by other search engines. A metasearch engine sends out a search query (formats the word or words that you enter for use by search engines) to other search engines, and then returns the list to you. The metasearch engine uses criteria to select which results it will display. So, if you use a metasearch engine like Mamma.ca (*www.mamma.ca*) or Copernic.com (*www.copernic.com*), your results will be the top listings from other search engines such as MSN (*www.MSN.ca*), LookSmart (*www.looksmart.com*), and Google.

Quick Test

1. Which one of the following represents the set of primary rules for transmitting and receiving data over the Internet using packet switching?
   a. FTP
   b. HTTP
   c. SMTP
   d. TCP/IP

2. Which of the following is a true statement about the Internet?
   a. Dial-up access generally provides faster access to Internet resources than broadband.
   b. Most home users require an ISP to connect to the Internet.
   c. The Internet is owned by the U.S. government.
   d. It is impossible to use a wireless device to connect to the Internet.

3. _____ is the primary language for defining how web pages are displayed in a browser.
   a. HTTP
   b. HTML
   c. Java
   d. VoIP

Answers: 1. b; 2. b; 3. b

THE TECHNOLOGY OF E-COMMERCE

An Internet search often turns into a purchase. If you have ever used credit/debit cards, ATMs, or the World Wide Web, then you've used e-commerce! **Electronic commerce** (or e-commerce for short) is a transaction carried out using computer networks. While the broad definition of e-commerce includes using credit or debit cards, withdrawing money from an ATM, and making purchases over the Web, many people today apply the term e-commerce to making or researching purchases over the Web.

E-commerce is a large reason for the popularity of the Internet. Statistics Canada reports that Canadians placed $12.8 billion worth of orders on the Internet in 2007, up 61 percent from 2005. This increase was driven by a larger volume of orders, which rose from 49.4 million in 2005 to 69.9 million in 2007.[15] The largest online retailer, Amazon.com, reported its best holiday season ever in 2008. The company announced that more than 6.3 million items were ordered on its site worldwide for the peak shopping day of December 15, amounting to 72.9 items ordered per second. On its peak day, it shipped more than 5.6 million units.[16]

The growth in e-commerce results from the ease with which computer users can search for information on a wide variety of products, jump to those products' web pages, and then purchase desired items with a few clicks of the mouse. While items like books, music CDs, DVDs, and computer games are the most popular items, it is now possible to purchase almost anything using e-commerce.

Even if you don't decide to buy an item over the Web, you can find comparative data on products that can help you with your purchase. For example, websites like *www.pricegrabber.ca* and *www.shopbot.ca* provide a wide range of price and quality information on electronics and computers, making you more knowledgeable when you visit an electronics store.

Chapter 5 contains a detailed discussion of the business of e-commerce. Because it may be important in your future career, and because it may be useful to you as an educated e-commerce consumer, we discuss the evolution of e-commerce technologies below.

In its relatively brief history, e-commerce has been through several distinct generations of growth. These generations, shown in Figure 2.8, represent important shifts in the evolution of e-commerce and its enabling technologies. Note that the increasing heights of the bars in Figure 2.8 represent both the growing number of users and increased technology capability. Also, do you see how the time frames listed on the bottom of the figure overlap somewhat? That's because we can

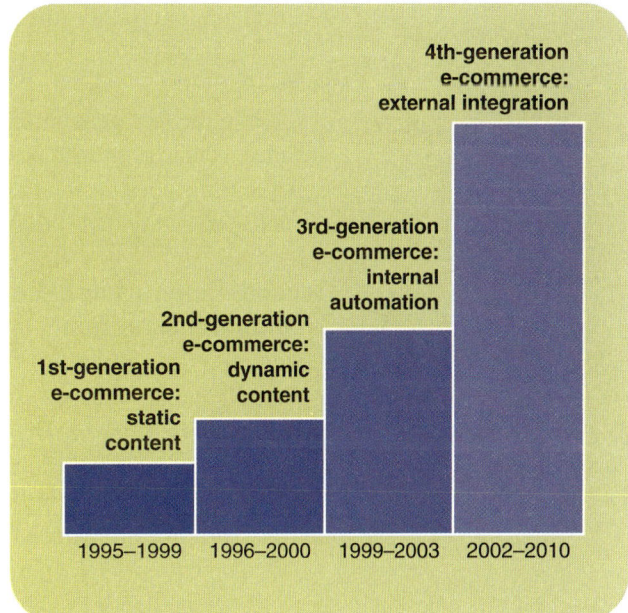

FIGURE 2.8 Generations of e-commerce.

---

15. http://www.statcan.gc.ca/daily-quotidien/081117/dq081117a-eng.htm. Retrieved March 6, 2010.
16. http://www.reuters.com/article/idUSTRE4BP1UJ20081226. Retrieved March 6, 2010.

only approximate the dates when each stage began. Similarly, we can also only estimate the end of each stage; that is, the point at which most Web users adopted the technologies of that generation and began to move on to the next stage.

First-Generation E-Commerce Technologies: Establishing a Web Presence

In the first generation of e-commerce, the available technologies delivered static content through a Web presence. **Static content** refers to fixed information, such as company information, online marketing, and electronic versions of company brochures. A *Web presence* means the business has established its existence on the World Wide Web by creating a set of pages that users can access. Very simple technologies are required to create a website with static content only. These standard web technologies include client server networks, web browsers, HTTP protocol, and HTML, which were all discussed in detail previously in this chapter. Businesses that use only these technologies for their websites are limited to providing static content, but these technologies also represent a low-cost and relatively easy way for new businesses to begin e-commerce transactions.

A term often used to refer to sites with only static content is *brochureware*—a direct reflection of how today's consumers negatively view this low level of sophistication. What is interesting to note, however, is that some companies have downgraded from more sophisticated e-commerce sites. In early 2009, Canadian Tire stopped selling merchandise on its website, indicating that the website did not make enough money to justify its expense. They felt that the site was being used primarily for research purposes prior to a consumer visiting a retail location.[17] Canadian Tire didn't downgrade quite as far as a first generation e-commerce site, since their site contains many interesting features including "do-it-yourself" tutorials and additional product suggestions when a product is selected.

While the first generation of e-commerce technology represented a significant advance in sharing information, it was the ability to exchange dynamic information that allowed e-commerce to really take off. Let's turn next to the second-generation e-commerce technologies that made this possible.

Second-Generation E-Commerce Technologies: Providing Interaction

At some point in the mid-1990s, newer technologies allowed for the delivery of dynamic content, moving us into the second generation of e-commerce. With **dynamic content**, information on a web page can change depending on a number of factors. For example, the time or date, user profile, or browser location might trigger web page changes. In addition, other capabilities became available, such as delivery tracking and personalization of content to match user preferences.

Dynamics and interaction occur based on input data and programming instructions. To create dynamic content, the following needs to occur: obtain input data, pass data to the server, hold data in memory, and execute programming instructions to process the data. Input data can come from several sources:

---

17. http://www.financialpost.com/story.html?id = 1195152.

The Technology of E-Commerce 61

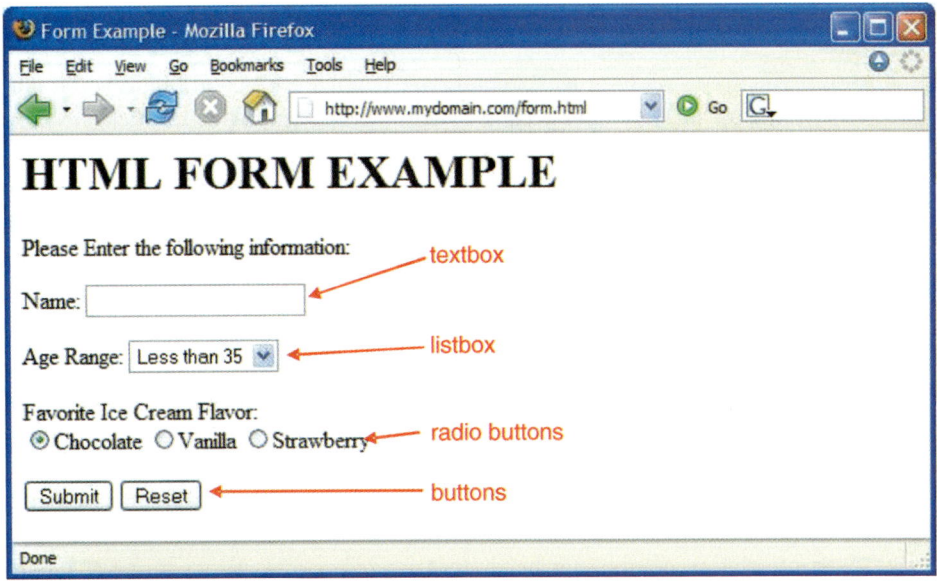

FIGURE 2.9 HTML forms, such as the one shown here, are the primary means by which a business can get the data it needs for online transactions.

- the header in the HTTP request contains data about the client requesting the page
- the server system clock
- client data from a *cookie* along with the request. A **cookie** is a small bit of data, usually created by programs running on the server, stored on the client machine, and passed back and forth in the HTTP request and response. With a cookie, the server can store one or more data items on the client that it may need for subsequent requests.
- user input in an HTML form. You have probably come across a web page that asked you to enter data. The components of a page that allow you to enter input are called HTML *form controls*. Figure 2.9 shows some common form controls. HTML forms are the primary means by which a business can get the data it needs for online transactions. For example, think about the type of information you may have input when ordering items online, such as your name, address, and credit card information. Because this information is critical to successful e-commerce transactions, a business will carefully select the form controls with two major goals in mind. First, the form components must fit the data needs of the transaction. Second, a business selects the form components for ease of use and to minimize the chance of incorrect data entry.

Storing Data on the Client Side With second-generation e-commerce, once data are received, they can be stored. This overcomes the issue that first-generation HTTP protocol is stateless and connectionless, meaning that every request is independent of any other so that a server could not recognize that a previous client was making another request. Now that a cookie can be stored on the client side, data can be retrieved that identifies the client and the application can then respond specifically to that client. Of course, you are used to "signing up" for this type of function already. This action is exactly what happens when you click on a "remember me" box or, if you are using Internet Explorer, you might see a box asking if you'd like Internet Explorer to remember your password. When you agree or click the box, this creates a cookie that is stored on your PC.

By allowing a cookie to store data on the client side, the cookie data can remain until the user returns to the website. When data remain available for a period of time, it is known as *persistent data*. Persistent data allow Web applications to benefit both users and the businesses that run the sites. Because the main use of the cookie is to identify the user, this allows websites to provide *personalization* (an advantage of e-commerce that will be discussed in Chapter 5). Businesses also often use cookies to keep up with data, such as a shopping cart of products that customers want to buy.

A database is an essential component for any interactive e-commerce site. Databases provide another means of maintaining the state of client interaction with the server and storing persistent data on the server side.

For interaction, a computer needs to execute programming instructions. The server, the client, or both may execute instructions. Let's take a look at the primary technologies used for executing program instructions with Web applications.

Making the Client Side Dynamic and Interactive On the client side of a Web application, the browser generally executes instructions by using a scripting language, downloadable code components, or a plug-in. A **scripting language** is a high-level computer language that another program—in this case the browser—interprets when executed. Businesses often use client-side scripting for data validation to ensure that user information is in the correct form before sending it to the server. The most common client-side scripting language is JavaScript. Scripts are primarily used for simple processing tasks such as enabling those annoying pop-up windows you are likely blocking. For more complex tasks, a browser relies on specialized components designed to interact with the user and perform advanced instructions, such as ActiveX, Java applets, and plug-ins:

- *ActiveX* is a set of technologies that Microsoft designed to support the sharing of information among different applications. The ActiveX technology allows you to link data from one document to another. For example, a marketing report created using a word processor might link to a chart in a spreadsheet. Businesses generally use ActiveX controls in their e-commerce applications for more complex actions. Depending on how you have set up your browser, you may have blocked sites that use ActiveX. Some believe that sites using ActiveX are vulnerable to viruses and malware and any users who access those sites may be infected.
- A *java applet* is a small independent Java program that is typically used for online games.
- You undoubtedly have several *plug-ins* installed on your PC right now. Do you use Adobe to view documents? That is a plug-in. What about the Google toolbar or a media player? All plug-ins.

The Technology of E-Commerce | 63

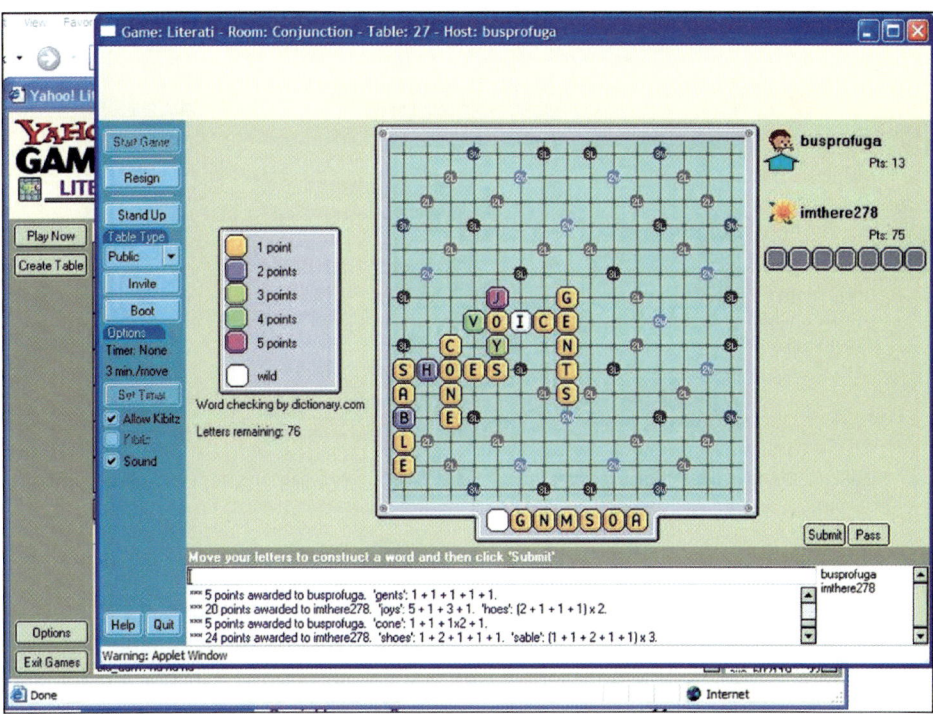

Due to their small size, applets are ideal for applications such as online interactive games.

Most businesses use server-side programming to deliver truly dynamic content. **Server-side programming** is just what it sounds like—programs that run on the server in response to browser requests. Server-side programming is more powerful and can therefore do much more than client-side scripting. It also allows the owners to retain control over their programs so that they can better manage their websites.

Almost every major e-commerce site that you have visited uses server-side programming. When a site requires you to log in, a program on the server checks that you are a registered user. When you type keywords into a search engine, a server-side program queries a database and returns the results to you. When you shop at an e-tailer, server-side programs display the products and handle your transactions.

A short listing of some things that server-side programming can do should convince you why it is important for e-commerce applications. With server-side programming, a business can:

- Deliver content that it customizes for the individual user
- Dynamically modify content for any page
- Access data stored in a server-side database and send it to the client's browser
- Take action on queries and data sent from HTML forms
- Provide access control and security for a website
- Optimally manage the traffic to the site

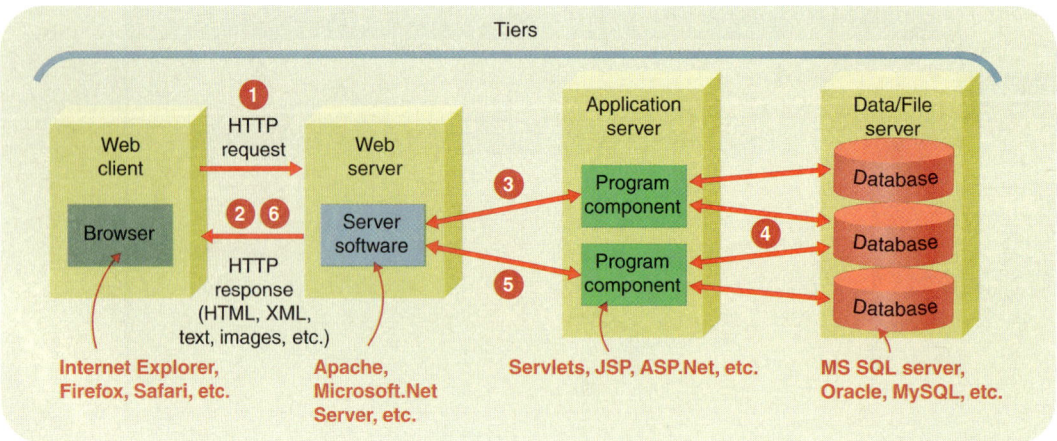

FIGURE 2.10 A four-tier e-commerce infrastructure; depending on its capabilities, any e-commerce application that you build or use might consist of one or more of the Web, application, and data tiers.

When we discuss second-generation e-commerce technologies, we often refer to it being implemented in a tier system. Figure 2.10 and the explanation below it illustrate how a typical transaction would travel through a four-tier e-commerce system.

1. By entering a URL, clicking a button, or any of several other ways, you send an HTTP request to a *Web server*.
2. The Web server receives the requests and determines how to generate a response. If the request is for a static HTML file, the server simply retrieves the file and sends it back as part of the response to the client's browser.
3. If the request requires a dynamic response, the Web server acts as a controller that routes messages and data between the client and the *application server*.
4. When needed, applications contact the *data server* to perform queries on the databases that it controls. The application uses the data to perform its tasks.
5. The results of an executed application will be formulated into a browser-compatible web page that combines the output of the application with the appropriate HTML tags.
6. The Web server includes the dynamically generated page in an HTTP response and then sends the result to the browser.

Third-Generation E-Commerce Technologies: Supporting Transactions

As the power of the World Wide Web became clear to businesses, demand for new technologies grew. Consumers liked using the Web and organizations moved to respond. The third generation of e-commerce saw demand for technologies that would extend to support real-time, online transactions. Companies began to automate both internal and external business processes. Automated transactions enabled advanced capabilities on the Web, such as data mining and the delivery of instant status information through portals (as FedEx or Canada Post now do with full-cycle individual-item tracking systems). Companies sprung up around the globe with new business models that took advantage of enhanced technology and network capabilities, often challenging well-known incumbent firms to catch up and move more quickly into the e-commerce age.

Early in the evolution of e-commerce, businesses recognized that they must contend with several important aspects of commercial transactions for e-commerce to work. That is, prospective customers must have a way to order and pay online and feel secure in doing so.

Order and Payment Systems and E-Commerce System Security An e-commerce site needs to include components for processing orders and accepting payments. The four primary components of a typical e-commerce site are: (1) the shopping and ordering system, (2) the merchant account, (3) the payment gateway, and (4) the security system.

Many e-commerce firms manage the shopping and ordering processes on their own servers or privately leased servers. The main tasks are to track the products that the user selects to purchase during browsing of the site, and then to record the order for those products so that the firm can gather and ship them to the user. A site may use several methods to do this, such as:

- A non-secure HTML order form, with the results sent to the firm's email address
- A secure HTML order form, with the results sent to the firm's email address
- A "shopping cart" system that tracks customer orders using a database
- A shopping cart service provided by a third party

Possibly the best and most popular choices are to use a secure HTML order form or an in-house shopping cart system. The secure HTML order form is simpler to use and is a viable choice if users typically order a small number of items. Firms use shopping carts for more complex sites with lots of shopping options. This makes the users' shopping experience easier by allowing them to continue their browsing after selecting each product and then checking out only once.

Concerning the payment process, firms again have several options. In fact, many sites offer more than one of these options. Businesses can allow payment in more traditional ways, such as billing for payment by cheque or by manually processing credit card information. This is known as *deferred payment*. Smaller sites with limited infrastructure can also use third-party merchant accounts like those provided by PayPal, CCBill, or ClickBank. These sites process payments between the customer and merchant for a transaction fee. While this can be a good solution for those with limited site capabilities, the fee can eat into profits. However, consumers love services like PayPal. Originally born by a group of entrepreneurs who worked together at eBay, and later purchased by them, PayPal essentially created a form of online currency that made a series of smaller consumer transactions possible and convenient by aggregating them through one account that is settled automatically. Especially popular with eBay and other trading site addicts, PayPal has now become an essential part of online commerce.

For large sites, the preferred method for processing payments is to use real-time credit or debit card authorization that they process themselves. This eliminates a "middle man" and improves margins on sales. However, it also makes the sites responsible for all of the issues (security, privacy, etc.) that come with accepting payment information directly into their own systems. This method is compatible with the most popular form of payment by customer, namely a credit card. With real-time processing of credit cards, the merchant handles the payment almost immediately. The merchant then simply needs to ship the goods. This type of payment system, however, requires the merchant to set up a merchant account and to establish a connection to a payment gateway. The same or a similar system is used for debit card payments.

A *merchant account* is basically a bank account that allows merchants to receive the proceeds of credit card purchases. After establishing a merchant account, the acquiring bank agrees to pay the merchant for all valid credit card purchases in exchange for the right to collect the debt owed by the consumer. A **secure gateway provider** is a company that provides a network to process encrypted transactions from a merchant's website. It then passes the transactions on to the issuing banks of the customers' credit cards for approval. Some of the most popular gateway providers include Verisign, Symantec, and *Authorize.net*.

A secure gateway provider will generally offer a payment gateway and a processor. A *payment gateway* links an e-commerce site with the banking network. The processor handles the financial data submitted by the shopping cart application by accepting the data from the shopping cart, properly formatting it, and entering it into the banking network. It is then handled just like any other credit card transaction. Figure 2.11 shows the steps involved in this payment system.

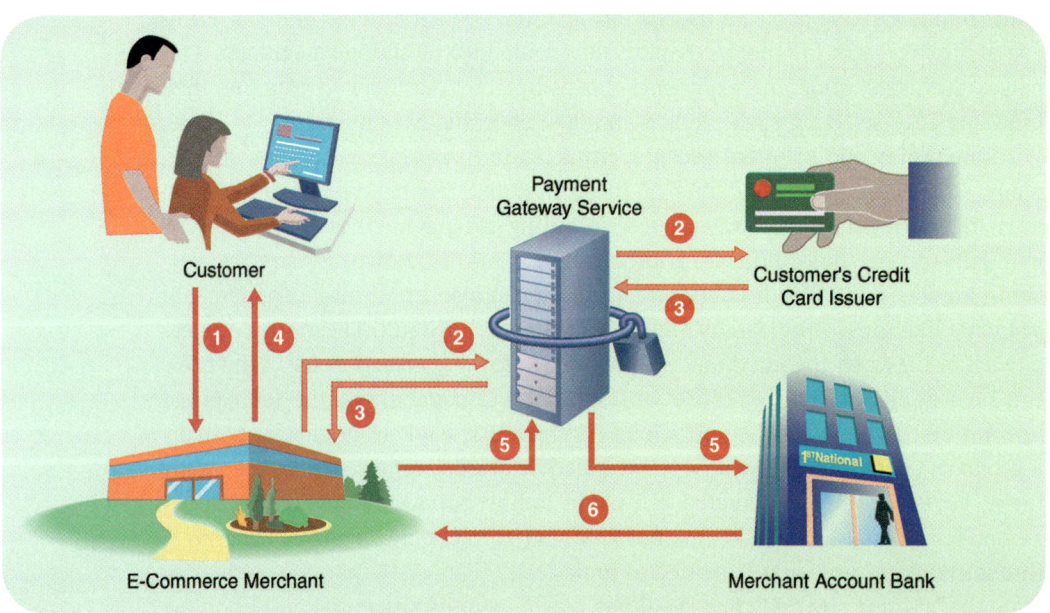

FIGURE 2.11 A payment gateway links an e-commerce site with the banking network.

1. The customer places an order with the merchant through the e-commerce site.
2. The payment gateway provider detects the placement of an order. The provider securely encrypts the transaction data (discussed below) and passes an authorization request to the bank to verify the customer's credit card account and available funds.
3. The gateway provider returns a response, indicating whether or not the transaction is authorized, to the e-commerce merchant. This process typically takes less than three seconds.
4. Upon approval, the e-commerce merchant notifies the user and fulfills the customer's order.
5. The gateway provider sends a settlement request to the merchant account's bank.
6. The merchant account's bank deposits the transaction funds into the e-commerce merchant's account.

The order and payment systems must be secure to protect both the customer and the merchant. In 2007, half of all Canadians reported that they were very concerned about online credit card use. This level of concern dropped to 34 percent among those who had actually made an order (with or without online payment), and it was even lower (30 percent) among the minority who were the "top online consumers."[18] While this seems to be trending down, it is still a concern that must be addressed. Have you ever been on an e-commerce site that did not make you feel comfortable about making a purchase? What made you uncomfortable or suspicious?

Most e-commerce security technologies relate to the **secure socket layer (SSL)** protocol. SSL, developed by Netscape and RSA Data Security Inc., allows a client and a server to communicate in a way that prevents eavesdropping, message forgery, or tampering. A server that encrypts data using the SSL protocol is known as a *secure server*. How do you know if you are connected to a secure server? You just need to look at the URL. The URL of a secure server starts with HTTPS in place of the usual HTTP. You may also see a closed lock icon in the lower corner of your browser. A website can signal that it uses SSL to encrypt data by purchasing an *SSL site certificate*. The site can own the SSL certificate itself, or a hosting service can provide it. When you connect to a secure server, the server will first identify itself to your browser using the SSL certificate. The SSL certificate works to verify the identity of the secure server, much like your driver's licence can be used to identify you (except the SSL certificate is much more difficult to fake). When a customer connects to a secure server, the server and the browser use SSL to provide each other with the information needed to encrypt the data. SSL is currently being replaced by a newer protocol called the *transport layer security (TLS)*. TLS and SSL cannot work together, but a message sent with TLS can be handled by a client that uses SSL.

Microsoft, Netscape, Visa, MasterCard, and others also endorse another security standard called the *secure electronic transaction (SET)* protocol. SET combines several security standards to provide a system that can ensure private and secure transactions.

---
18. http://www.statcan.gc.ca/daily-quotidien/081117/dq081117a-eng.htm. Retrieved March 7, 2010.

Finally, we should also mention the importance of cookies to payment and security technologies. Previously, we discussed how businesses use cookies to track activities on the Web. However, the payment and security systems that we have reviewed in this section may not work without cookies. For instance, these systems often use cookies to authenticate users or to hold data to match users with their shopping cart. In this case, businesses and consumers must consider the trade-off between convenience and security.

Fourth-Generation E-Commerce Technologies: Transforming Processes

We are currently in the midst of the fourth generation of e-commerce, characterized by increasing integration of all enterprise systems with external customers, partners, and suppliers all linked over the World Wide Web. The Web itself is undergoing a transformation, from enabling transactions between humans and Web applications to allowing transactions between two Web applications. In fact, fourth-generation e-commerce technologies are moving to the realm where computers at one business automatically interact with computers at another business. These newer technologies are improving the ability to exchange small amounts of data via the Web and to standardize the support of transactions. We will look at the primary fourth-generation e-commerce technologies of XML and Web services here, which are quickly becoming web standards.

The **eXtensible markup language (XML)** organizes data based on its meaning rather than how it should appear. HTML's goal is to describe how to display data. As such, XML complements HTML, and the two are often used together. XML has become a major component in a set of technologies that are helping to make the Web even more interactive. By combining XML with JavaScript and dynamic HTML and HTTP protocols, a technology called *AJAX* is being used to allow web pages to respond more quickly to user actions. With AJAX, much of the processing related to user actions happens on the client side rather than sending a request to the server and having the user wait for the server's response. Instead, requests for only a small amount of XML formatted data are made when needed and then used to adjust the web page interface. This speeds up overall interaction for the user because an AJAX engine on the client side can handle any action that doesn't require a request from the server, like simple data validation. These cutting-edge uses of JavaScript and XML provide a much richer user experience.

Web services are a standardized way for one computer program to request and run another computer program over the Internet. The two applications may reside on different computers that are connected in some way, for instance by a LAN or more commonly by the Internet. The most popular and most discussed Web services are self-contained business functions that operate over the Internet.

A Web service is a platform-independent software component that can be:

- Described using a standard description language
- Published to a public registry of services
- Discovered using a standard method
- Requested through an application program interface (API)
- Combined with other services and procedures to compose an application

Web services are important because they enable different systems to interact more easily than before, meaning that partners can more efficiently and quickly link and share data. Web services give companies the ability to do more e-commerce business, with more potential business partners, and in more different ways than before at a reasonable cost. There's no doubt that Web services are valuable for e-commerce. First, a Web service is like a spare part, which can be incorporated into any program that has access. Once written and made available, developers can simply request a Web service as needed. This saves time. Second, Web services provide a way for two computers to automatically pass data between each other. This saves more time. These two advantages are so important that many organizations are setting up an infrastructure known as **service-oriented architecture (SOA)** to support full-scale use of Web services.

Web services continue to gain in use and popularity as they create value for companies. For example, Amazon.ca and Google both provide Web services that others can use to access their huge databases. One recent trend is to cobble together Web services from various sources to make an application known as a mashup. A *mashup* is a Web application that seamlessly combines information from more than one source into an integrated experience. Mashups are not only creating new services for existing companies, but also entirely new companies. For example, Jobloft.com, a mashup site created by Ryerson University graduates, combines job postings and Google maps to help job seekers find jobs in their local area.

Quick Test

1. Which of the following is a small data file that can be used to store data on the client's computer?
   a. ActiveX
   b. cookie
   c. crumpet
   d. plug-in

2. Which of the following is a company that provides a network to process encrypted transactions from a merchant's website?
   a. merchant account gateway
   b. payment processor server
   c. secure gateway provider
   d. shopping cart system

3. Which of the following is true regarding XML?
   a. XML tags define the look and feel of a web page as it is displayed in a browser.
   b. XML is platform-independent and can be used by many different applications.
   c. All devices using XML must use primary XML with no new tags defined.
   d. XML is only used for database query data.

Answers: 1. b; 2. c; 3. b

INTERNET SECURITY

This chapter has explored how the creation and phenomenal growth of the Internet has spawned the emergence of e-commerce, a global information society, and an increasingly global IT infrastructure. With this growth comes risk. Risk, in the context of the Internet, means security. Internet security is seen as a serious issue around the world. In 2009, the Internet Crime Complaint Center ranked Canada as fourth in the world for the origin of Internet crime perpetrators and second in the world for the number of complaints about Internet crime.[19] It is important to remember that both individuals and enterprises can be the victims of Internet crime. Table 2.3 describes some of the most common Internet security threats. However, there are many more in addition to these. In fact, in 2005, Sophos—a developer of anti-virus software—received around 50,000 new malware samples every day.[20]

Table 2.3	Common Internet Security Threats
Security Threat	**Description of Threat**
Malware	The use of malicious code as part of a subversive, organized scheme. Such schemes are resulting in massive intrusions into sensitive financial and intellectual property areas. Viruses, worms, and trojans are all types of malware.
Scareware	A type of malware designed to trick victims into purchasing and downloading useless and potentially dangerous software. Ironically, scareware is often disguised as virus protection software and shows a window telling you that your PC is not being protected or is currently infected.
Virus	A program that is able to copy itself and infect a computer. Viruses are designed to spread to as many computers as possible. It usually needs some human action, like opening an email attachment, to occur in order to spread. There are thousands of known viruses on the Web. Most PC users use anti-virus software to prevent viruses.
Worm	Destructive software that can spread by itself, such as MyDoom and its later version, DoomJuice. The MyDoom worm is particularly nasty. Once started on a computer (by clicking an email attachment), it automatically sends out infected emails to everybody in the user's address book, using one or more of the names on the address book as the sender. In addition to overwhelming email servers around the world (at one point, the virus generated as many as one in three emails in circulation), it creates a "back door" to allow a system to be used to further propagate viruses and malware.
Spam (electronic)	Unsolicited and undesired emails. Aside from being annoying, spam may facilitate the installation of malware or phishing.
Phishing	An attempt to gain personal and confidential information (e.g., passwords, credit card information) for fraudulent purposes such as identity theft.
Denial of Service Attack (DoS)	An attempt to make a website unavailable to its users. An attacker will do this by sending a target so many communication requests that the target server eventually goes down and becomes unavailable. No website is safe from DoS attacks. Both Twitter and Facebook have been the victims of DoS attacks.

---

19. http://www.ic3.gov/media/annualreport/2009_IC3Report.pdf. Retrieved March 10, 2010.

20. https://secure.sophos.com/sophos/docs/eng/papers/sophos-security-threat-report-jan-2010-wpna.pdf.

The risk of these threats has increased substantially with the advent of social networking. Social networking provides a breeding ground, if you will, for malware. Those worried about the dangers of social networking sites have a right to be concerned, as many malicious attacks, spammers, and data harvesters take advantage of under-cautious users. Most notably, the notorious Koobface worm family became more diverse and sophisticated in 2009. The sophistication of Koobface is such that it is capable of registering a Facebook account, activating the account by confirming an email sent to a Gmail address, befriending random strangers on the site, joining random Facebook groups, and posting messages on the walls of Facebook friends (often claiming to link to sexy videos laced with malware). Furthermore, it includes code to avoid drawing attention to itself by restricting how many new Facebook friends it makes each day.[21]

Twitter is just as vulnerable. Imagine that a friend of yours has tweeted a link to a cool song, except that the link to the song contains a virus. It is possible that every one of your friend's followers will click on the link and be infected. Some of those friends might even re-tweet it to their friends and so on and so on.

Social networking sites can also contain a lot of information about individuals. For some reason, people feel it is safe to post information that normally they would keep private. For instance, it is not unusual for people to post pictures or update their status on Facebook when they are on vacation. With some investigative abilities, it would not be hard for someone to take the individual's profile information, the knowledge that the person is on vacation, and use other information on the Internet to eventually find the person's address and rob his or her home.

Both individuals and organizations can take the following actions to minimize Internet security threats:

- Install, and keep up to date, both antivirus software and a personal firewall.
- Update your software, such as Windows, to patch security holes or move to less vulnerable systems, such as Linux.
- Do not open email messages or attachments from unknown sources.
- Follow safe computing practices, such as effective password policies.

We often take passwords for granted, however they play an important part in both online and offline security. Is your password your account name or simply the word *password,* or a common name like that of a friend or relative? Do you use the same password for most or all of your accounts? According to research reported by the Computer Crime Research Center, 21 percent of people use their own or their partner's nicknames for their passwords, 15 percent use their birthdays or anniversaries, and another 15 percent use their pets' names. About 14 percent had a family member's name as their password, 7 percent relied on a memorable date, and 2 percent even unimaginatively used the word *password*.[22]

Why do so many people use weak passwords, especially considering passwords are an important part of authentication for many computer systems? *Authentication* is the process of identifying individuals and ensuring they are who they claim to be.

---

21. Sophos Security Threat Report 2010, http://www.sophos.com/sophos/docs/eng/papers/sophos-security-threat-report-jan-2010-wpna.pdf. Retrieved March 10, 2010.

22. http://www.crime-research.org/news/17.08.2001/567/

Coupled with a username, a password is perhaps the most common authentication technique used today. Since most of us have important private information stored on various computer systems, using a weak password is like providing easy access to the key to our safety deposit box.

To ensure that your password is and remains as strong as possible, you should follow these guidelines:

1. Use at least eight characters.
2. Include digits, punctuation, and nonprinting characters.
3. Use both upper- and lowercase characters.
4. Use different passwords on different accounts.
5. Change your password regularly and don't reuse passwords or make minor variations such as incrementing a digit.

Of course, these guidelines are hard to follow. The main reason we don't use strong passwords is that they can be hard to remember, and it is more difficult still to remember more than one. So what can you do? Try this: come up with one or more rules that you can use to derive a strong password from something easy to remember—your own password-making algorithm. For example, (1) start with something easy to remember, such as a favourite song (the *key*) like "Mary Had a Little Lamb." (2) Take these initials: MHALL. (3) Make every other initial lowercase: MhAlL. (4) Insert a punctuation mark between each letter: M*h*A*l*L. (5) Append the initials of the account that you want to access; for the office desktop, the password may become M*h*A*l*Lod. By memorizing just a few items—the song title, the punctuation, the account initials—you can create a fairly strong and memorable password that is different for each account.

Another area of concern with respect to Internet security is in network systems. As a student, you surely enjoy wireless access on your campus or when you are out at the coffee shop and are able to connect to your email and browse the Internet. Wireless networks enabled in various hotspots are very convenient but, if unsecured, can pose a security threat. Although we usually think of hackers breaking into computer systems through the Internet, the growing popularity of wireless networks for organizations and homes has created a new type: wireless hackers.

As an example of what could happen, a security expert noticed his physician using a notebook to set up appointments and wondered about the level of security in this wireless network. Outside, he noticed a chalk mark on the side of the building put there by a hacker indicating an open network was available inside—so-called *warchalking*. Sure enough, when the security expert got to his car, he could access the physician's appointment notes, including the one just created for him! While data about appointments are relatively harmless, diagnoses and prescriptions could also have been on this network, leading to a potential loss of privacy or other problems. If you're using an unprotected wireless network, be aware of the potential for so-called *drive-by hackers* to access your files. A hacker may not bother with your files, but instead use your network to assist in propagating malware or creating denial of service attacks that can be traced back to your network. If you are setting up a wireless network at home, be careful to secure it properly to prevent any of these security issues.

Lastly, in this chapter we discussed the popularity of cloud computing. One of the major advantages of cloud computing is that data are not resident on one PC or one network, but available over the Internet from wherever someone would have Internet access. From a security point of view, this may make it easier for hackers to access the information as they no longer need to worry about an individual's authentication, operating system, or firewall. Instead, they can focus their efforts on the system running the cloud computing application (e.g., Gmail) and gain access to many accounts and a lot of information. In January 2010, Google shocked the Internet community by announcing that it (and more than 30 other companies) had been the victim of a targeted hack attack, seemingly focused against the Gmail accounts of Chinese human rights activists.[23]

MEANINGFUL APPLICATIONS OF TECHNOLOGY

You have now learned the basics of hardware, software, networks, the Internet and its most popular application, e-commerce, and Internet security. This technology is meaningless unless it has a function and creates a benefit. For businesses, this benefit might be the creation of value and competitive advantage. For individuals, it may mean being more efficient and productive. In this section we highlight some applications that might be of interest to you now as a student, or in the future as a business professional.

Collaboration

One of the most important applications of technology is collaboration. Never before have we seen this number of technology tools that allow us to collaborate and communicate with colleagues and friends across the globe. In this section we highlight a few of the technologies that you may be already using, or that you are certain to use as a business professional.

Groupware Software tools known as *groupware* help individuals and teams keep up with their scheduled meetings, monitor projects, share work files, and even conference online. You are likely using some form of groupware now with your professors and classmates. Many universities and colleges use a system called Blackboard that allows professors to post content to all students, send group messages, set up working and discussion groups, and send out and receive assignments. Some businesses use Microsoft Groove. Groove is groupware made specifically for small to medium-sized businesses or ventures to help them manage small project teams. Groove offers support for virtual teams, discussion forums, and information repositories.

Another commonly used collaboration software in business is called Sharepoint. Sharepoint is a very robust system offered by Microsoft that offers many features, including an information repository, a work flow manager, and the ability to manage content, all readily available over a secured Internet connection. Many organizations use Sharepoint to store and share all of their files. Files are easily searched for, retrieved, modified (if allowed), and re-saved for the next employee to view. The workflow aspect of Sharepoint is valuable from a business process perspective. Imagine a document that requires input from various individuals. Sharepoint

---
23. http://www.sophos.com/blogs/gc/g/2010/01/14/google-china-censorship-hacking/.

can manage this interaction through assigning workflow and ensuring that each individual contributes and then makes it available for the next person. This works especially well when approvals are required. Of course, there is an audit trail that shows the progress through the process. Using a system like Sharepoint can really improve operational efficiency. A recent example of Sharepoint in action was at the Vancouver 2010 Winter Olympics. The United States Olympic Committee relied on the test version of Sharepoint 2010 to power the website used to deliver statistics, photos, news, and other information to the many journalists covering the games.[24] Even the U.S. government uses Sharepoint for some applications.[25]

A key feature of collaboration systems is their ability to store documents that can be worked on and shared with several people. You may be using some free tools to do this now with your school colleagues. Google docs provides spreadsheet, word processing, and calendar functions as well as other applications for free. As the documents are created and saved in Google's technical infrastructure, you can share the documents with anyone who has Internet access.

Intranets A less recent method of collaboration for businesses is the use of an intranet. An **intranet** is a set of services for distributing private information throughout the organization using a collection of private computer networks brought together to form an organization-wide, private network (ranging in size from LAN to WAN). At first, most businesses used intranets to reduce publishing and distribution costs for such items as policy and procedure manuals, benefits information, and phone directories. Today, however, the use of intranets has moved beyond the goal of paper reduction to support automated internal transactions, as well as to improve communication, teamwork, and knowledge management.

Using the technologies of the Internet and the World Wide Web, intranets transmit data according to the TCP/IP and HTTP protocols of the Internet, and share the advantages of these protocols. For example, using the Internet as a bridge, an authorized user can access the intranet from any physical location—not necessarily within the organization's physical walls. Further, as with the Internet, employees can also access an intranet using a Macintosh, Windows, or any other PC platform. This is known as *platform independence,* which is usually not the case with traditional LANs and WANs. Finally, intranets can store data using Internet-compatible file formats, such as HTML and XML, thereby allowing users to access the data using a Web browser.

However, an intranet's use of Web technologies, which allow users to access outside resources over the Internet, also make maintaining the privacy of organizational information more crucial. An intranet often incorporates security measures, such as a firewall, and requires users to authenticate themselves with usernames and passwords.

Instant Messaging (IM) Do you think you are collaborating when you use a tool such as Skype? Likely not, but you are. Skype is a very popular tool for not only free long distance calls from computer to computer, but also for instant messaging

---
24. http://news.cnet.com/8301-13860_3-10463102-56.html. Retrieved March 10, 2010.

25. http://blogs.technet.com/sharepointexperts/archive/2010/03/10/the-us-government-bets-on-sharepoint-for-internet-sites-to-track-stimulus-spending.aspx.

(IM). IM is an online communications service that allows users to communicate in real time over the Internet. In 2008, IM had become so popular it led research firm IDC to predict that it would overtake email as the preferred form of business communication by the second half of 2010.[26]

There are two main categories of IM applications: public or enterprise (EIM). Examples of public IM include Skype, MSN Messenger, and Yahoo! Messenger. EIM systems, on the other hand, provide features such as restricted access, and security precautions such as encryption. Developed for corporate use, EIM services include Sun ONE Instant Messaging, IBM Lotus Instant Messaging & Web Conferencing, and Microsoft Office Live Communications Server.

Users of IM in the workplace cite improved teamwork, time savings derived from faster sharing of information, decrease in email and voice mail, and moments of relief from the daily grind. IM can also be used for communicating with customers. For example, the online clothing retailer Lands' End provides Lands' End Live service, which allows customers to get assistance, in real time, with a service representative while they shop online. The representative can even redirect the customer's browser to an appropriate page on the Lands' End site. Lands' End, which has been recognized as a leading e-tailer by various organizations and awards, credits the technology as an integral part of the company's online success.[27]

Risks of using IM include a rise in needless interruptions and distractions, potential security problems, and increased workplace gossip. Have you ever been working on a term paper or studying and just couldn't resist opening your IM tool? Many, however, see that the benefits are starting to outweigh the risks, especially those already accustomed to IM, meaning that IM is becoming more commonplace in many organizations.

Virtual Meetings As a business professional, you may need to conduct a meeting but may not be able to attend it in person. How will you do this? Some excellent web meeting tools are available to facilitate online meetings. This is especially important if you are working with colleagues in many locations. One of these services is called goto meeting. Goto meeting offers web meetings, voice, and chat for invited participants. To have your meeting, you simply set it up in the meeting scheduler and invite your participants. Participants are given a URL, meeting code, and password so they can attend the meeting. Once in the meeting, you can use your computer screen to run a presentation or a product demo, and all meeting participants will be able to see it. If your meeting participants have questions, they can enter these in the chat function.

Other technologies you may be interested in include:

- RSS feeds—Get updates from your favourite websites and blogs by signing up for an RSS feed. When you sign up, you will receive an email alerting you of new content you may be interested in.
- Survey Monkey—Survey Monkey is an online survey tool that allows you to set up simple surveys online for free.

---

26. http://www.computerworlduk.com/technology/networking/messaging/news/index.cfm?newsid=9887.

27. http://www.landsend.com/newsroom/corp_info/customer_service/index.html. Retrieved March 10, 2010.

- Convergence technologies—You may have heard the word convergence before and you may be experiencing it now. Convergence in the context of technology means the merging of technical devices, media, and functions. A current example of convergence is your ability to browse the Internet on your mobile phone. Many more converging technologies are on the horizon.

What's in for me?

Most of you probably own an MP3 player, such as the Apple iPod, to which you can download and listen to your favourite tunes. But, did you know these devices offer more than entertainment value? These personal digital audio/image players and personal computers with digital audio playback capabilities create new opportunities for discovering and learning from experts and others. The primary technology that has allowed for this arguably more productive use of audio devices is known as *podcasting*, a name derived by mingling the words "iPod" and "broadcasting." Podcasting is a method of publishing audio programs via the Internet that allows users of just about any digital audio device to download broadcasts or to subscribe to a feed of new files (usually MP3s).[28]

Podcasting makes all types of audio content portable and available on demand. Listeners can catch up on audio content—news, entertainment, or learning—while completing other tasks like working out at the gym. Like many Internet technologies, podcasting brings "power to the people" by allowing almost anyone to broadcast audio content. However, podcasting has more recently gained interest in the corporate world. Companies can use podcasts to spread the word about their products and services or to complement other media. For example, CBC Radio offers several podcasts that you can subscribe to at *www.cbc.ca/podcasting*.

One of the more well-known IT-related sites is PodcastAlley.com, which lists over 4,000 podcasts related to technology alone. If you need to increase your knowledge of agile or extreme programming, or IT security, or even what Microsoft is up to next, then the Internet and podcasting can provide you with this knowledge.

Finally, podcasting is one of the ways that professors supplement university and college classes. According to the University of Calgary, it was the first university in the country to introduce podcasting on a large scale when it launched four courses in 2006 featuring portable MP3 technology as a teaching tool.[29]

Podcasts will help you become more knowledgeable in the future. For now, you can become more knowledgeable in your classes by downloading audio files about topics in this book from WileyPLUS.

What's in for an organization?

Technology obviously has many benefits for an organization, one of which is putting together virtual teams. A *virtual team*, sometimes called a geographically dispersed team (GDT), is a group of people who work across geographic distance, time, and boundaries between organizations. They stay connected through telecommunications technology. Like any team, however, the members should have complementary skills, focus on a common goal, and hold themselves mutually accountable.

---

28. http://en.wikipedia.org/wiki/Podcasting.

29. http://www.ucalgary.ca/oncampus/online/march-06/ipod.html. Retrieved March 10, 2010.

Meaningful Applications of Technology 77

The number of virtual teams has grown along with improvements in communications, especially with the file-sharing capabilities available over networks like the Internet. Reasons for virtual teams revolve around the differences in the locations and work times of team members. Members may not be physically located at the same place, and it may be impractical or too costly for the team members to travel to meet face-to-face. In addition, the members may work at different times.

Technology to support virtual teams includes hardware, software, and networking. Hardware may include computers, telephones, and videoconferencing apparatus, either connected over private WANs, or more often using public networks like the Internet. The primary software category in use is groupware. Groupware features can include email, meeting facilitation, group scheduling, and project management tools. In a nutshell, a team, plus groupware, plus a communication network, equals a virtual team.

An organization can derive several benefits by using virtual teams:

- People can work from any place and at any time.

- Organizations can recruit the best people regardless of their physical location.

- Travel and sometimes facilities expenses are reduced.

- There is greater flexibility for workers.

However, virtual teams may need to overcome time zone, culture, and organizational responsibility differences to function effectively as a group. Teams and teamwork and the technology used to support teams are discussed in more detail in Tech Guide E.

What's in IT for society?

Technology has the power to mobilize people from around the world. On Tuesday, January 12, 2010, an earthquake with a magnitude of 7.0 on the Richter scale had a devastating impact on Haiti. From the moment the earthquake struck, people turned to technology to find information and organize relief. Below are a few examples of how technology was used in this crisis:

- Almost immediately after the earthquake, tweets and twitpics were posted to Twitter with details of the devastating earthquake. A Twitter group called *#relativesinhaiti* was created and flooded with traffic trying to find out about loved ones. Another Twitter group called *#rescumehaiti* was used to direct rescue efforts where trapped survivors were located. According to Twitter.com, five of the most popular topics posted Thursday, January 14, only two days after the earthquake, were related to Haiti, "Following the earthquake in Haiti, Twitter once again became a platform to disseminate the news and, more important, a way to quickly raise money to support relief efforts," said Mark Evans of social media monitoring and analytics firm Sysomos Inc.[30] Several celebrities posted links to Haiti charities urging their followers to donate.

- Google responded to the devastating earthquake that hit Haiti by working with satellite imagery company GeoEye to quickly make images of the destruction available in Google Earth and Google Maps. The images were taken at approximately 10:27 a.m.

---

30. http://blogs.wsj.com/digits/2010/01/14/twitter-helps-in-haiti-quake-coverage-aid/. Retrieved March 10, 2010.

Eastern time on Wednesday, January 13 and proved to be a helpful tool for aid organizations.

- A website called *Haitian Earthquake Registry* came online Wednesday, January 13 and allowed people to register and look for missing friends and relatives.

- People were able to donate to various charities for Haiti by sending text messages via SMS and donating flat rate amounts.

- The Facebook group called *Earthquake Haiti* had more than 160,000 members,[31] and celebrities quickly added links to Haiti charities on their Facebook pages to increase awareness.

- Journalists, unable to use conventional media broadcast methods, used the Web and Skype to broadcast the first reports of the devastation caused by the earthquake.

It is hard to measure the impact that technology had on the crisis in Haiti, but what is certain is that without it, the situation would have been much worse.

ROI STUDENT RETURN ON INVESTMENT SUMMARY

1. **What are the fundamentals of information technology that will help increase your productivity as a business professional?**

An information technology (IT) device can accept and store information; perform mathematical calculations; apply logic (e.g., compare values of numbers to make decisions); and retrieve, display, and send information. As such, IT allows you, a business professional, to *communicate* your thoughts, ideas, and feelings with others. IT *enables transactions* between you and the organizations with which you deal. IT helps you *obtain data and information* that you can use. IT provides tools you can use to *analyze data and information* to help in your decision making. IT can help you *organize and store data and information* that is important to you. IT can *provide entertainment*. Information technology can help you do all of these things more efficiently and with greater value.

2. **How do software and hardware come together to create business capability?**

A computer network is built with nodes that can represent computer hardware and the network users, with various types of hardware, software, and communications media forming the links. A computer network requires four primary components: (1) data to represent the resources that are shared between computers on the network; (2) special hardware; (3) software to allow computers to communicate and share the data; and (4) communication media to link the computers together. This infrastructure creates capability. The meaningful application of this technology will achieve efficiencies, gain competitive advantage, and create business value.

3. **What makes the Internet and World Wide Web so valuable?**

The Internet is arguably the most useful technological tool of the last few decades. The Internet uses the TCP/IP suite of packet switching protocols, a very general, non-proprietary set of communication rules. By adopting these rules and making use of software compatible with the TCP/IP standards, any computer, regardless of the platform (processor and OS), can connect and communicate over the Internet. Further, another aspect of the Internet important to its near global adoption is that no single organization or governmental entity owns it.

If the Internet is the technology platform, the World Wide Web is an application that works on that platform. The Web is the primary Internet application that supports many types of e-commerce. The Web basically provides a hypertext system that operates over the Internet. Hypertext allows an easy way to publish information on a network. Hypertext documents can include references (hyperlinks) to other information on the network. Using Web browser software, business professionals can view hypertext documents and use the hyperlinks to browse (or surf) other related documents. The Web enables e-commerce, the Web's most popular application. With each evolutionary step, e-commerce changes the way we interact with the Web and provides us with capabilities we previously did not have.

---

31. http://news.bbc.co.uk/2/hi/8461240.stm. Retrieved March 10, 2010.

KNOWLEDGE SPEAK

application software   44
client/server network   55
cloud computing   52
computer hierarchy   39
cookie   61
dynamic content   60
electronic commerce (e-commerce)   59
eXtensible markup language (XML)   68
hardware   37
hypertext markup language (HTML)   56
hypertext transfer protocol (HTTP)   55
Internet service provider (ISP)   50
intranet   74
middleware   45
modem   42
network interface card (NIC)   42
networks   37
open source software   45
operating system (OS) software   44
platform   37

productivity software   44
protocol   49
random access memory (RAM)   40
read only memory (ROM)   40
scripting language   62
search engines   56
secure gateway provider   66
secure socket layer (SSL)   67
server-side programming   63
service-oriented architecture (SOA)   69
software   37
static content   60
system software   43
uniform resource locator (URL)   54
utility software   44
voice over Internet protocol (VoIP)   51
Web browser   55
Web services   68
Wi-Fi   51

REVIEW QUESTIONS

Multiple choice questions

1. What hardware location temporarily stores data and instructions?
   a. hard drive
   b. RAM
   c. ROM
   d. USB flash drive

2. _____ software manages and controls the resources of a computer system.
   a. Application
   b. Operating system
   c. Productivity
   d. Utility

3. Which of the following technologies can be used to make a website dynamic?
   a. a Java applet
   b. an ActiveX control
   c. server-side programming
   d. all of the above
   e. none of the above

4. Which of the following components of a four-tier client/server e-commerce system will display results of a request in a browser?
   a. application server
   b. data/file server
   c. Web client
   d. Web server

Fill-in-the-blank questions

5. The _____ speed of a processor can be measured in megahertz or gigahertz.

6. A major category of productivity software that business professionals primarily use for quantitative analysis is known as a(n) _____.

7. The message that contains the web page sent to a client from a server is part of an HTTP _____.

8. A _____ is a small Java program that can be downloaded and executed within a browser window.

True-false questions

9. A pointing device is generally easier to use than a keyboard when entering text data.

10. The Internet is controlled by several independent, international organizations.

Matching questions

Choose the BEST answer from column B for each item in column A.

Column A
11. communications
12. input
13. output
14. processing
15. storage

Column B
a. Hardware used to save data, information, and instructions long term.
b. Hardware used to connect one IT device to another.
c. Hardware that provides an interface for retrieving information from an IT device.
d. Hardware that provides an interface for entering data into an IT device.
e. Hardware that directs the execution of instructions.

Short-answer questions

16. Briefly explain why more RAM can speed up your computer.

17. Review the network categories and describe LAN and a MAN that you are familiar with. How do you know it is a LAN and a MAN?

18. List the tiers that make up the typical four-tier e-commerce infrastructure. What is the purpose of each tier?

Discussion/Essay questions

19. Describe the four generations of e-commerce. Provide current examples of sites in each generation.

20. Discuss the impact of open source software on the software industry.

TEAM ACTIVITY

Effective teamwork relies on good communication among team members, as well as between the team and its organization. In this activity, you will explore how information technology can help you with each. First, organize yourself into a team of at least five people. At your first meeting, select a team coordinator and an assignment (e.g., a problem that you've noticed on campus or a team assignment for one of your classes). Then send everyone off with the task of thinking about possible solutions to the problem. Over a period of days, the team coordinator should use information technology to communicate with team members to come up with a set of possible solutions to discuss at the second meeting. The coordinator will also use information technology to schedule the second meeting and inform the team members. At the second meeting, in addition to discussing the problem, discuss how the team used IT to perform these tasks. What worked well and what didn't? How could your team use IT more effectively?

SOFTWARE APPLICATION EXERCISES

1. Internet
Information technology is constantly changing, and many new IT devices can seem exciting and cutting-edge. Search the Web and select five new or future information technologies that interest you. Bookmark these sites for use in the Presentation activity that follows.

2. Presentation
Create a presentation to discuss the technologies that you found for the Internet assignment above. For each technology, use two or three slides to provide a brief description and possible uses. Give your presentation a professional look by incorporating an attractive layout, informative graphics, and appropriate slide transitions.

3. Word Processing
Think about an e-commerce site that you would like to create. A very important aspect of an e-commerce site is the user interface. The designers must make sure that they design the site to convey the right message (e.g., that supports the business strategy). Several design factors are important to consider for any website. For example, the content must be appropriate to communicate your message to the user and to hold their attention. In addition, the overall site must be organized so that the user can easily understand how to use it (as well as navigate it). You can use most word processors to create quick web pages. Use a word processor to create mock-ups of how your pages will look on your website (see assignments above).

4. Spreadsheet
Acquiring information technology can be expensive! Personal computers and laptops can range from a few hundred to a few thousand dollars, depending on the capabilities and options selected. Assume you are interested in purchasing a new computer. Create a spreadsheet to help you evaluate the relative costs of several options. For each system, include cells to record the possible options and their prices. Be sure to include extras such as shipping or tax, which may apply to some options but not others. Use formulas to calculate the overall cost for each system. For a challenge, try to use special cells and IF statements to reflect various decisions such as Plasma versus LCD flat-screen monitor, or 512M versus 1024M RAM.

5. Database
Creating an e-commerce site can be a big project. As the project progresses, your team will need to resolve many issues (problems). You can use a database to keep up with the issues in a big project to help ensure that no issues are overlooked.

Create an issues database to track the issues that will inevitably come up in your Web development project. Your database should include at least two tables. One table should include the names and contact information for each person on the development team. The other table should include the data related to each issue. At a minimum, record an issue ID, an issue description, the date when work on the issue began, the date when work on the issue ended, and the issue status. Assume that each issue will be assigned to only one development team member for resolution.

6. Advanced Challenge
A lot of groupware is available in the market. Search the Web and find the five most popular groupware applications. Create a document to compare their functionality, technical requirements, and pricing. Recommend which groupware application your class should use.

ONLINE RESOURCES

Companion Website
- Take interactive practice quizzes to assess your knowledge and help you study in a dynamic way.
- Review PowerPoint lecture slides.
- Get help and sample solutions to end-of-chapter software application exercises.

Additional Resources Available Only on WileyPLUS

- Take the interactive Quick Test to check your understanding of the chapter material and get immediate feedback on your responses.
- Review and study with downloadable Audio Lecture MP3 files.
- Check your understanding of key vocabulary in the chapter with Knowledge Speak Interactive Flash Cards.

CASE STUDY: SELECTING A COMPUTER

In the end-of-chapter case for Chapter 1, you met Ashley Hyatt, a student in business administration at university. In this case, we continue Ashley's story.

After a successful fourth year, during which she interviewed with a number of companies, Ashley accepted a position with one of the large consulting firms. She starts her new job within a few weeks. Because Ashley will telecommute one to two days per week, her company will fund the purchase of a Windows-based, desktop PC system for her home, worth up to $3,000. However, she is unsure of what system will work best for her job.

Ashley realizes that she should begin by considering her job requirements. Because she'll be carrying out extensive financial analyses, she needs a system with a significant amount of processing and hard disk storage. Because she may be doing some serious number crunching in her new job, Ashley should probably go for the maximum processor speed she can afford. Because she will be storing large data files on her hard disk, she should try to purchase a hard drive with as much capacity as possible, but not less than 500 GB. Further, because Ashley will need to transport large files between work and home, she needs a system that reads and writes DVDs.

Finally, Ashley decides that a large (at least 19-inch) flat-panel monitor, which can also display high-definition television signals, will allow her to check breaking news stories while working on her assigned projects.

Case Questions

1. Using a budget of $3,000 and the requirements mentioned by Ashley, make specific suggestions as to what computer system she should purchase, including a brand name, model, and options.
2. You realize Ashley has overlooked printed output. Considering her budget of $3,000, what options would you recommend?
3. Do you think that Ashley's choice of DVD as a portable secondary storage media is a good one? Why or why not?
4. What upgrades would you recommend that Ashley purchase in the future?

Integrative Application Case: *Campuspad.ca*

After your chat with Sarah and agreement to help, you decide that you probably need to know a little bit more about creating and running an online business. To begin with, although you hadn't wanted to admit it to Sarah, you didn't even know how to go about registering a domain name. That was the first thing you researched, and you were surprised at just how easy it was. But of course, the first step is often the easiest and you know there is much more to know about running an online business, especially if it needs full e-commerce capability.

At your last meeting, you and Sarah decided to divide the tasks based on your areas of expertise. Sarah is going to explore marketing, advertising, and regulatory or licensing issues, and you will be putting together a high-level technology plan and getting some estimates of costs. Between the two of you, you will get an idea of how much money it will take to get this business started.

As always, you can only start with what you have, and that is a simple laptop. Using that and your own ingenuity, you have some serious work ahead of you.

Guiding Case Questions

1. Research what is required to register a domain name in Canada and how to do it.
2. List the various IT components required to support a transactional e-commerce site.
3. What additional information might you need before you can make cost estimates?
4. What assumptions would you make about this new business based on what you know?

Your Task

Create two simple documents. The first is a brief description of what is required to register, launch, and host a simple e-commerce site in Canada serving the Canadian market. The second document (best done in Excel or other spreadsheet program) will highlight basic starting assumptions about the IT infrastructure and its associated costs (or cost options) to support the business. Assume that these documents have to be clear and concise enough so that Sarah, someone with very limited IT knowledge and whose major interest is the business, will be able to understand them.

3

CREATING BUSINESS VALUE

WHAT WE WILL COVER

- Business Organization and Business Processes
- Applying IT to Create Business Value
- Decision Making
- Problem Solving

ROI STUDENT RETURN ON INVESTMENT

Through your investment of time in reading and thinking about this chapter, your return—or created value—is gaining knowledge. Use the following questions as a study guide.

1. What is competitive advantage and how do businesses achieve it?

2. How do the structure, quality, and presentation of information influence the nature of the decisions made by business professionals?

3. How can business professionals solve problems to create business value?

THE VOICE OF EXPERIENCE
Tom Beaman, University of Western Ontario

Tom Beaman graduated from the University of Western Ontario in 1996 with a degree in computer science. He is now a senior vice-president with Wmode, a technology company that provides business outsourced services, such as mobile portals and mobile content stores, for operators and mobile virtual network operators.

What do you do in your current position? As senior vice-president of global sales and marketing for Wmode, I sell turn-key outsource solutions to mobile operators. Essentially we run the business for them under their brand. I am involved in the full sales cycle with potential clients, which is typically three stages. In the first stage, I'm not just selling a product or service—I'm selling the Wmode team and what we can do. The client is, in effect, handing over its services to be run by Wmode, and it needs to be confident that we can do what is necessary. I act as consultant and work with the client to determine the actual problem or issue that needs to be solved. The second stage is more about information gathering and digging deeper into requirements. Sometimes this is facilitated by conducting workshops with the client. The third stage is the actual sales stage, during which we create contracts that spell out the details of products and services to be provided to the client. The full cycle can take anywhere from eight to 24 months to complete. By completing the full sales cycle, we figure out what best serves the client and we can customize packages for specific clients.

What do you consider to be important career skills? In this industry, innovation is important. It's no longer acceptable to have just a good product or service to sell to customers. Every business has a good product or they would not be in business. The same is true for you as an individual. You need to have something that differentiates you from the competition.

How do you use IT? IT is everywhere in our company; it's integral to what we do. Mobile access is most important for me, as I'm away from the office so often. We have clients around the world, and I need to be able to access their company information and my own business information wherever I am. I use a laptop and a handheld computer. I use the handheld to check everything from email to reviewing documents, spreadsheets, and the like. We have an analytics package that we sell to customers, but we also use it internally. It allows me to analyze consumer user behaviour. For example, when consumers access a client's site, where do they browse? What don't they use? I can also answer questions like, what is the general consumer behaviour on the mobile Internet?

Can you describe an example of how you have used IT to improve business operations? I use our analytics tool as part of my sales package, and use it internally to help improve operations. It can help me determine how to improve the operations of a service and optimize it. I can look at traffic loads and determine where to change architecture or where to add infrastructure. It works to improve a client's bottom line.

Have you got any "on the job" advice for students seeking a career in IT or business? One important thing I've learned is to always be changing. Early in my career I was a software developer, and I was good at it, but I moved into other areas and increased my skill set. I took on product development and project management. All of that gave me credibility, with staff and clients, when I moved to the business side of operations. You don't have to constantly change companies to do different things, but you should do different jobs during the course of your career. The ability to change and learn new and different skills got me to where I am today.

In this chapter we discuss business strategy, competitive advantage, and the activities businesses undertake to create business value. In Tom's job, he helps mobile operators, such as Rogers, use IT to gain competitive advantage. In the sales process, Tom is actively involved in the problem solving and decision-making process of bringing mobile services to market.

By now you may realize that technology is not an end in and of itself, but rather a means to an end. That is, technology is a collection of tools that enable. From an individual perspective, technology may enable you to be on time for appointments, for example. From a business perspective, technology enables strategy, business processes, problem solving, and decision making.

BUSINESS ORGANIZATION AND BUSINESS PROCESSES

Because of the sheer number of different tasks that need to be coordinated to deliver the end-result product or service, a company needs a **business strategy**. Properly constructed, the strategy becomes a road map for what needs to be done to create business value and competitive advantage. One of the better-known thinkers on strategy, Michael Porter, states that a *strategy* is:

> *a broad-based formula for how a business is going to compete, what its goals should be, and what plans and policies will be needed to carry out those goals.*[1]

He suggests that the intensity of the competitive rivalry in any industry can be attributed to forces that define the industry. If the industry is attractive and there are few barriers to entry, then more competitors will enter the industry, thereby increasing competition. If there are barriers to entry (such as requirements for large amounts of capital or government regulations), then it will be harder for new competitors to gain entry. Similarly, consider the threat of consumers substituting a new product or service for existing ones, and the bargaining power of both suppliers and buyers to determine strategies to create and sustain competitive advantage.

Porter's five forces model, shown in Figure 3.1, illustrates the forces described above. You can find more detailed information on this model and how to apply it to an industry analysis on the WileyPLUS site associated with this text.

In today's world, of course, IT is an essential element of any organization's strategy. IT professionals must ensure that their efforts are aligned to help the business deliver its intended end result. However, before we discuss how businesses use IT productively, you need a good understanding of business fundamentals. Let's begin by considering the analogy of business organizations as open systems.

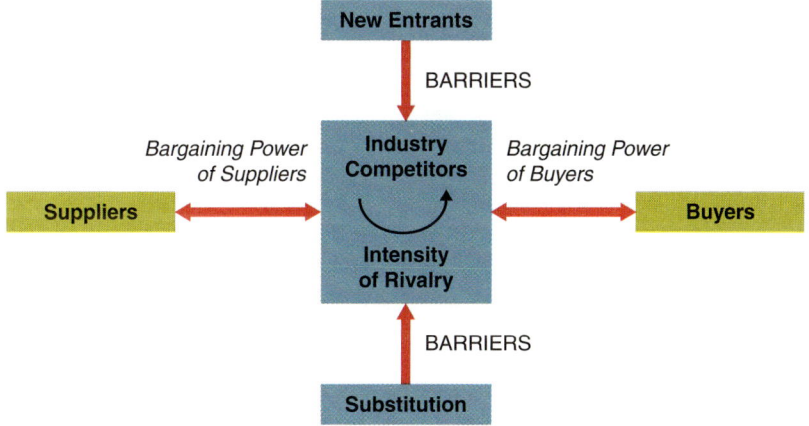

FIGURE 3.1 Porter's five forces model.

---

1. Michael Porter, "What Is Strategy," *Harvard Business Review*, November 1996, pp. 69–84.

Businesses as Open Systems

Looking at an organization as a system helps you see how organizations use various resources, processes, and structures to create business value. In Chapter 1 we used an input-process-output model to define an information system. In this chapter, we expand the model into a general model of an organization, known as an open systems model.

As Figure 3.2 shows, the **open systems model** indicates that a business operates by transforming inputs into outputs and by constantly interacting with its environment. To understand this model better, we will begin by discussing two significant components of the business environment: stakeholders and boundaries.

Stakeholders and Boundaries in the Business Environment Different businesses face different business environments. How businesses adapt to their environment contributes greatly to how their structure develops, and helps determine whether they succeed or fail as a business. What is in this environment that has such a profound effect on organizations? Stakeholders.

A **stakeholder** is a person or entity, for example a government agency or a shareholder, that has an interest in and an influence on how a business will function in order to succeed (or in order not to fail). A stakeholder may be external (in the environment) or internal (within the organizational boundary) relative to the system. Note that *influence* is an important part of the definition of a stakeholder. That influence may be actual or potential, great or small. It all depends on how the organization's decision makers perceive it in relation to a stakeholder's interests.

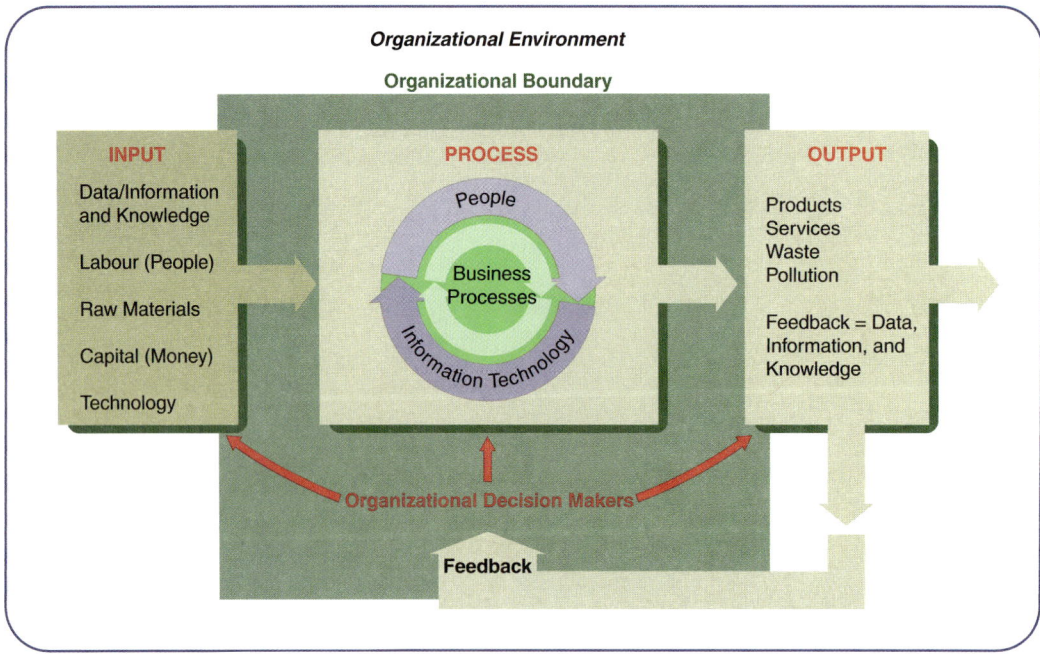

FIGURE 3.2 As this open systems model of an organization shows, a business operates by transforming inputs into outputs and by constantly interacting with its environment.

Business Organization and Business Processes

For example, you may be interested in how a certain company handles online shopping transactions. But if you don't shop at the company's website, you probably have no influence over how the company conducts its e-commerce operations. However, if you are a frequent customer and you email the company describing problems with its website, your suggestions may influence future e-commerce operations. Because you had both an interest and an influence, you are a stakeholder in the organization's environment. Figure 3.3 shows other examples of external and internal stakeholders for a business.

Another important aspect of an open system is the **organizational boundary** (the perimeter of the green rectangle in Figures 3.2 and 3.3). Businesses must remain open to their environment. Why? Primarily, an open boundary allows a business to receive inputs and to produce outputs. Further, a business must be aware of what is going on in its environment so it can take steps to remain competitive by responding to opportunities or threats. In addition, a business needs external information to run its operations or processes on a daily basis. For example, before making business decisions, soft drink manufacturers like Coke or Pepsi need information about purchases of their competitors' products in various regions of the country, the expected cost of high fructose corn syrup (sweetening ingredient), and even the government's recent changes to tax laws.

However, interaction with that environment carries risk, especially when the environment changes constantly. New

Because stakeholders of any company are a varied group, press conferences are an easy way for companies to keep all of their various stakeholders updated on happenings within the company. Companies will often hold a conference to introduce new products, such as Steve Jobs introducing Apple's iPad here.

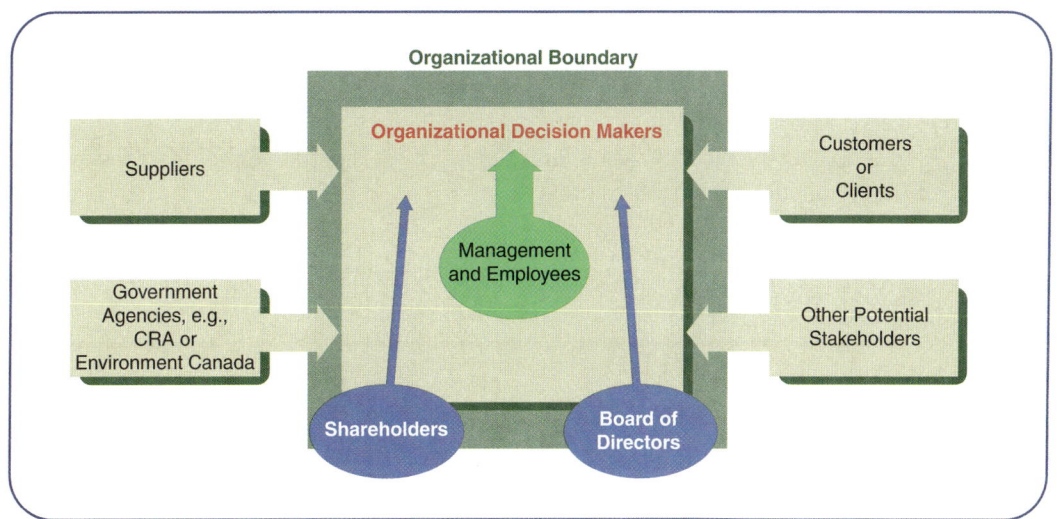

FIGURE 3.3 Organizational stakeholders, whether external or internal, have both an interest in and an influence on how a business will function in order to succeed.

> ### WHAT DO YOU THINK?
>
> In today's networked economy, organizational boundaries are not always clearly defined. Many organizations are blurring the boundary between their suppliers and their organization to gain greater efficiencies in their supply chain and create more business value. A recent evolution by some large retailers requires that suppliers manage the inventory bound for store shelves using sales data provided by the retailer. If supplies of a product are low, it is up to the supplier to recognize this and immediately ship whatever is needed to that store. With this in mind, consider the following questions:
>
> 1: How might retail businesses gain or lose from having suppliers manage their in-store inventory levels directly?
> 2: Are suppliers who don't provide this level of service to retailers at a disadvantage? Do they ultimately have a choice about complying?
> 3: Are there any risks associated with expanding an organization's boundary in the way these retailers have?

technologies (such as the Internet) can become a serious threat to an organization if they are not managed proactively. For example, organizations that use the Internet face threats by criminals that include the use of stolen or fraudulent credit cards and attacks against their online infrastructure. Yet, for all of its security challenges, most businesses and organizations must use the Internet because so many customers and clients do business this way. It is really a double-edged sword: you have to be in the game to stay competitive, but playing the game is risky!

Quick Test

1. Which one of the following is not an input to the organization as an open system?
   a. labour
   b. productivity
   c. information
   d. technology

2. True or False. Stakeholders are part of the environment of the open systems model of an organization.

3. Fill in the blank. A business carries _____ when it interacts with its environment.

Answers: 1. b; 2. True; 3. risk

How Businesses Organize to Create Value[2]
If you want to get something done in an organization, you need to know where to go for the information and how to get to the authority required to accomplish your

---
2. To learn more about these and other organizational topics, consult an introductory management book, such as *Management*, by John R. Schermerhorn, Jr., John Wiley & Sons Canada, Ltd.

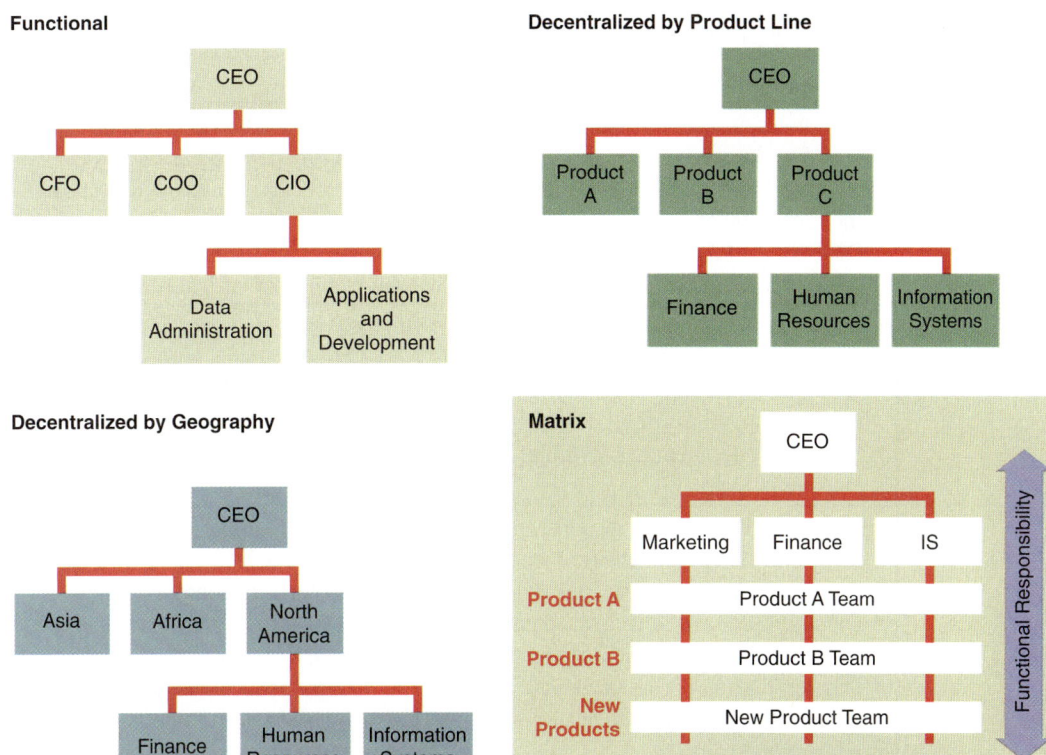

FIGURE 3.4 Functional, decentralized, and matrix organizational structures: modern organizations blend and extend these forms to adapt to a complex and changing global business environment.

SOURCE: Adapted from Weinshall, 1971, from *Understanding Organizations*, Charles Handy, Oxford University Press, 1993, p. 257. Matrix organization diagram added by authors.

task. To some degree, all business organizations possess structures that organize information, responsibility, and authority. When used appropriately, organizational structure helps get the job done. When misused, organizational structure can grow to an unmanageable size and density and can create a bureaucracy that seems to inhibit rather than facilitate productive work.

Figure 3.4 shows four representative types of organization structures. Companies often adapt these structures to their unique business situation or combine them in novel ways that suit their competitive environment, strategy, and preferences.

Consider Figure 3.4 from the viewpoint of a CEO. What do you notice? In **functional** and **decentralized structures,** the lines of authority (who has the right to tell whom to do what) and communication are vertically oriented. However, the **matrix structure** blends the functional and decentralized organizational structures. From top to bottom, the matrix is organized as a functional structure; from left to right, the matrix follows a product-focused (or project or customer-focused) structure that creates teams across business units. Teams are an important part of business, and you would be hard pressed to find a business that does not rely on the work of teams. We discuss the technology of teams in Tech Guide E.

Table 3.1	Advantages and Disadvantages of Functional, Decentralized, and Matrix Organizational Forms	
Organizational Form	Advantages	Disadvantages
Functional	• Economies of scale through efficient use of resources • Significant technical expertise found in the functional areas • Clear chain of authority and communications within a function	• Poor communication and coordination between functional areas • Relatively inflexible or slow to respond to change in the business environment • Employees may focus on functional area goals rather than organizational goals
Decentralized	• Faster response and greater flexibility • Greater communication and coordination between organizational units • Greater development of breadth of managerial skills	• Duplication of resources and efforts across organizational units • Technical knowledge not as in-depth relative to functional organizational form • Less direct control by upper management
Matrix	• Increased flexibility and responsiveness to business needs and environmental changes • Enhanced problem solving, cooperation, communication, and resource sharing • Decision making occurs lower in organization and closer to customer	• Frustration due to dual lines of authority and responsibility • Increased need for coordination between functional areas consumes time and resources • Potential for goal conflict between functional and decentralized components of matrix (e.g., marketing manager vs. product A manager)

SOURCE: Based on R. L. Daft, *Management*, 3rd ed., pp. 300–312; and J. R. Schermerhorn, *Management*, 7th ed., pp. 259–264.

In addition to the benefits of teams, a business might use a matrix structure to take advantage of the strengths, as well as make up for the weaknesses, of functional and decentralized forms. That is, the business would hope to combine the efficiency of a functional structure with the flexibility of a decentralized structure. Table 3.1 lists some advantages and disadvantages of matrix, functional, and decentralized organizational structures. Finally, although functional, decentralized, and matrix structures represent more typical forms, modern organizations blend and extend these forms to adapt to a complex and changing global business environment.

Quick Test

1. Which one of the following is not an organizational form?
   a. matrix
   b. functional
   c. CEO-based
   d. decentralized by geography

2. Which one of the following is an advantage of the functional organizational structure?
   a. decision makers are closer to the customer
   b. economies of scale

c. flexibility
d. greater communication between organizational units

3. True or False. Teams are a key part of the matrix organizational structure.

Answers: 1. c; 2. b; 3. True

Business Process

The preceding sections introduced strategy and the concept of businesses as open systems. They also discussed how businesses organize themselves to create business value. So, there is a goal in mind (strategy), and people are organized in a way to make it happen (organizational structure). What comes next? The business processes to bring the strategy to fruition.

To transform inputs to their main outputs (products and services), organizations need to perform a series of steps known as a **business process.** A business process, as defined by Michael Hammer and James Champy in their influential book *Reengineering the Corporation* is:

> *a collection of activities that takes one or more kinds of input and creates an output that is of value to the customer.*[3]

Modern businesses are full of processes. Some, like manufacturing processes, directly create output—a product like a car or a DVD player—while others may create a service—like a help desk for product support. Before examining business processes, consider what a process is and how we go about studying them.

A process is often shown as input → process → output (refer to Figure 1.2). A process receives input(s), undertakes some action(s), and then produces output(s). Processes are all around us. As you read this book you are in the process of studying, for example. In this case, the input is this book, the process is studying, and the output, hopefully, is knowledge about information systems in business. This is a simple example of a process at a very high level.

There are typically hundreds of processes involved in running a business. These processes link together and interact with one another to achieve the various goals of the business. Business processes can be incredibly complex and layered. The study of business processes is often compared to peeling the layers of an onion. You begin by looking at a high level view of the processes of an organization and continually delve deeper, uncovering more and more detailed processes and sub-processes. A sub-process is one or more tasks that accomplish a significant portion or stage of a process. Figure 3.5 illustrates a simple example of a process and a sub-process.

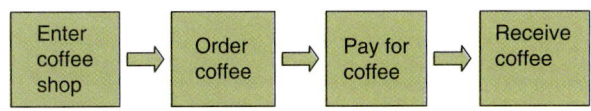

FIGURE 3.5 The process of buying a cup of coffee.

---

3. Michael Hammer and James Champy, *Reengineering the Corporation: A Manifesto for Business Revolution*, Harper Business, 1993.

94 | CREATING BUSINESS VALUE

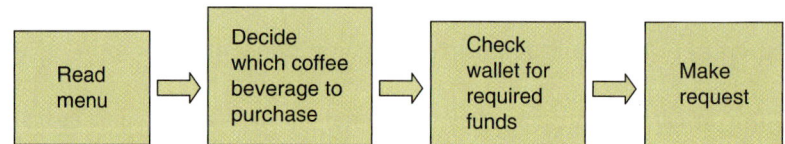

FIGURE 3.6 The sub-process of the process *Order Coffee*.

This string of actions (or sub-processes) constitutes the process of buying a coffee. Does this process look complete and detailed? It might be surprising to learn that you can break this process down further into detailed sub-processes. Figure 3.6 shows the sub-process, *Order Coffee*, in more detail.

As you can see, even the most seemingly simple process can involve several sub-processes and steps.

One method used to analyze and better understand processes is called **IGOE**. Shown in Figure 3.7, this is a method used in process mapping that illustrates the inputs (I), guides (G), outputs (O), and enablers (E) of a process.

Inputs to a process are those resources needed to start a process. (Table 3.2 lists representative types of inputs that are, at a high level, essential to an organization.) *Guides* are rules or policies within which a process must operate. *Outputs* are the results of a process. *Enablers* are a special kind of input or resource that facilitates a process.

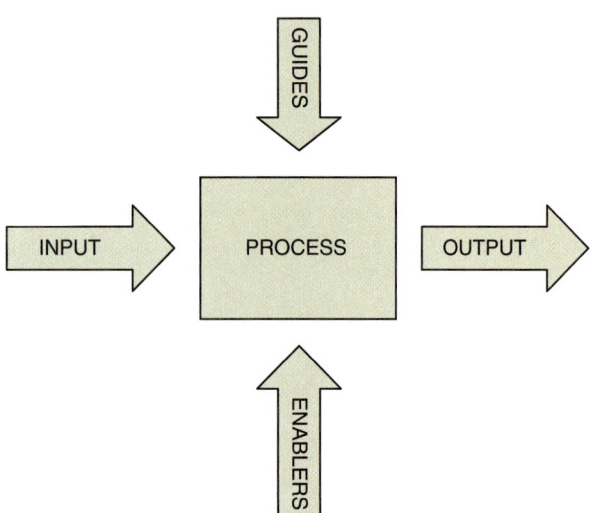

FIGURE 3.7 The IGOE model of analyzing processes.

Table 3.2	Examples of Inputs
Input Type	**Description**
Data, information, and knowledge	Raw facts, summarized data, information derived from research, and expert knowledge relevant to a business's goals (e.g., census data, consumer purchasing data, industry analysis, and a consultant's assessment of a business's IS security capabilities)
Labour	People hired to carry out all or part of the essential business processes or supporting functions (e.g., a production employee hired to make a product or a human resource analyst who manages an employee benefits program)
Raw materials	The "ingredients" from which the company makes its products (e.g., for an automobile manufacturer, a partial listing of raw materials includes steel, plastics, glass, and rubber)
Capital	The money that businesses need to operate (different forms of capital include cash, debt instruments like bonds, and stock—shares of company ownership)
Technology	Available in many forms, and greatly extending beyond PCs and software applications (e.g., robotic welders, computer-controlled assembly lines, mobile phones, and database and Web servers)

If you consider the process of studying, you would find the following:

1. Inputs – you, your book
2. Guides – you want to re-sell your book, so you do not use a highlighter
3. Output – your knowledge about information systems in business
4. Enablers – you download the lecture notes to follow along when reading the book

Now consider a high level business process, *Provide Customer Service*, using an IGOE diagram (Figure 3.8).

In this case, either a customer or customer service personnel initiates the process. The process can only occur during service hours and only when the customer in the interaction proves his or her identity. The process is enabled by the technology used to provide customer service. All of the process elements contribute to the output of the customer's inquiry being answered.

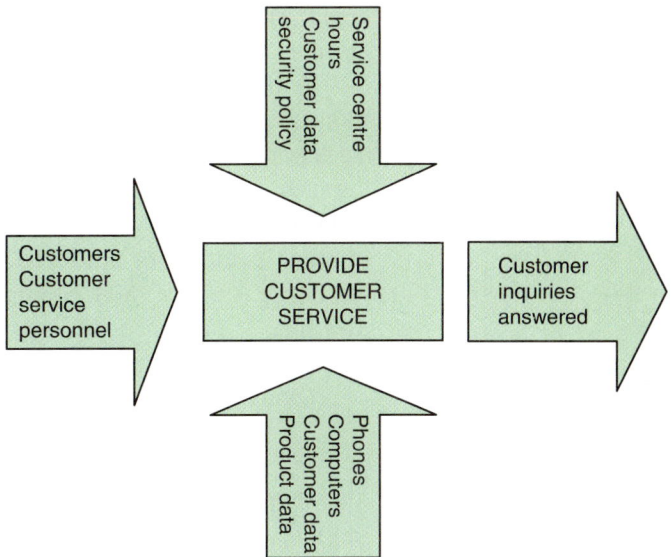

FIGURE 3.8 The business process of providing customer service analyzed using the IGOE model.

Now consider the role that feedback plays in the business process. **Feedback** is a special kind of measurement created by a business process that is then returned to the system ("fed back") to control the system's future inputs, processes, and outputs. Normally, this feedback will include information such as error or failure rates, processing speeds, process costs, and information on approvals and controls required in the process and if they are being respected. Businesses often use this performance feedback to monitor the efficiency and effectiveness of a given process. For example, if a company assembles personal computer systems and has a lot of small parts left over, it should realize it needs to adjust its assembly and/or inventory management process to reduce unused or wasted parts and thus lower manufacturing costs. In fact, the perfect process would theoretically have no waste at all! However, the costs of creating a perfect business process outweigh the benefits in all but a few cases (such as medical services). In the case of extra computer parts, the physical presence of "too many leftovers" is feedback to the system that the process is not working as it should, and the company must decide what to do about this.

Business process reengineering (BPR) is the study of business processes to find ways of making them more efficient. The goals of BPR are usually to reduce costs, increase throughput and speed, and increase quality and service. By undertaking BPR and achieving these goals, a business will likely increase its competitive advantage.

Defining Competitive Advantage

In today's hypercompetitive business environment, all organizations must focus on improving results all the time. This is often referred to as *continuous improvement*, and it is the hallmark of successful enterprises—those that are never satisfied with good enough, but strive to set new standards and benchmarks.

To achieve this, all employees in an organization must be empowered to think and act at the top of their game. They must be encouraged to creatively seek ways to make things better. The notion of *better* is often thought of in terms of reducing the costs of a business process, decreasing the costs of goods sold or the price of raw materials, or improving revenue by increasing prices through branding or improved product quality. And while all of these are important and valid, think of **competitive advantage** as an equation that looks like this:

$$\text{Competitive advantage} = \text{quality of insight} + \text{speed of execution} + \text{cost competitiveness}^4$$

Simply put, unless your efforts at work improve the quality of insight of your organization (into markets, products, consumer needs, pricing, competitor behaviour, or anything else you can think of that matters in business) or improves the speed of execution or cost competitiveness of your organization's response to that insight, then your effort is futile and will not add value.

Similarly, good IT systems are deployed to improve the quality of insight of those making decisions, to improve the speed of execution, to reduce costs, and/or to increase the efficiency of processes. There is no other reason to spend money on a system.

APPLYING IT TO CREATE BUSINESS VALUE

This section focuses on three aspects of strategically applying IT to create business value and competitive advantage: automating, informating, and transforming.

Automating to Do Things Faster

One of the first ways that a business seeks to apply IT is through **automating** (using automation to execute repetitive, routine tasks without human intervention). This frees up employees to concentrate on tasks that have the potential to add high value, or tasks that require judgement or insight to complete. By automating, a business can also complete tasks with more speed, economy, consistency, and possibly accuracy. Automation may provide additional benefits by allowing a business to perform work in different ways than before.

When automating a process, a business first tends to apply technology to do the same things as before, but with greater efficiency and accuracy. Later, as the organization learns from the new technology, it looks to use technology to do new things. Table 3.3 presents several examples of how companies have used IT automation to increase business value.

Bar code scanners are one of the more obvious ways automating can help companies do things faster. The bar code contains all of the information the store needs to keep track of its inventory and sales.

---

4. Adapted from Carol-Ann Hamilton and James Norrie, *The A to Z Guide to Soul-Inspiring Leadership,* Epic Press, 2003, p. 129.

Table 3.3 Using IT Automation to Create Business Value

Industry	Automation	Benefits Derived from Automation
Banking	ATM machines, online banking	• Reduces costs associated with the processing of deposits, withdrawals, and money transfers • Increases flexibility and improves access of services to customers
Grocery/Retail	Bar code inventory systems	• Increases speed and accuracy of product transactions • Improves accuracy (assuming correct entry of products' prices into the system) • Reduces costs and transfers control to customers (e.g., self-service kiosks and check-outs)
Travel	Reservation and scheduling systems	• Allows airline reps and travel agents to process reservations more efficiently and with less cost • Allows transfer of processes to customers (self-serve model) through online services

When applying automation within an organization, management usually thinks in terms of improving a single process. It starts by considering answers to questions such as:

1. What is the main goal, and what are the steps of the process?
2. What data and information are required to carry out the steps? What data are generated in each step? How do data flow between the steps? (Keep in mind that IT works with data and information. The amount of data and information inherent in the process will determine the extent to which IT can automate the process.)
3. How is the process affected by other processes of the organization? When should it occur? What triggers the process to start? How does the output affect other processes?

These questions do not address specific IT hardware or software. Instead, the most critical issues when applying IT automation are related to how the process fits the business organization and its goals.

For example, consider automated teller machines (ATMs), which operate 24/7/365. Prior to ATMs, the bank had to be open and a teller had to be available for a customer to withdraw cash. The bank customer filled out a withdrawal slip to present to the teller to receive cash. The teller accessed the customer's account, determined if there were enough funds for the withdrawal and, if so, updated the account and gave the cash and a receipt to the customer. The use of 24-hour ATMs, however, eliminated this requirement for serving customers. Relative to the old way of serving customers who needed cash, ATMs met a bank's goals of increasing customer service (e.g., cash is "always" available) and saving money (e.g., no teller or branch visit is involved in the transaction so the bank need not be open).

Informating to Do Things Better

Another way companies view the application of IT is known as informating.[5] **Informating** is recognizing that executing processes (e.g., customers accessing their bank accounts to make deposits or withdraw funds) also creates new data and information. An organization may then process the new data to improve its decision making and to change or improve the process itself.

In most cases, companies derive informating and automating benefits from some of the same applications of IT. For example, building on the examples in Table 3.3, installing ATM machines not only reduces costs and increases flexibility, it also tracks the use of services to provide the most popular and profitable services to customers. Likewise, a barcode inventory system improves the ability to track inventory and predict demand for various items. With an informating view, IT can deliver more long-term benefits than from automation alone. In addition, an automation-only view may result in simply speeding up a "bad" process. Informating, however, allows a business to identify flaws in the process and then use its new-found knowledge to do things in entirely new ways.

To gain the benefits of informating when applying IT to a process, a business needs to step back from the details of executing the process and ask three crucial questions:

1. Does the IT store data so that it can also be used for learning and decision making?
2. Is the business process being IT-enabled already optimized for high performance?
3. How could IT enable a better (more efficient or more effective) business process or capability that delivers higher value or additional competitive advantage?

Transforming to Gain Competitive Advantage[6]

The primary goal of most for-profit companies is to achieve a sustainable competitive advantage that results in high profits. In some cases, companies are concerned with competitive necessity: the need to stay in step with competitors and continue to stay in business.

As a result, most businesses have a **transforming** view of IT; that is, they use IT to help them acquire or maintain a competitive advantage over or in line with their competitors. A company possesses a competitive advantage when it sustains higher-than-average profits for its industry. Organizations in the not-for-profit or government sector often have efficiency as their objective, but often see IT in a similar transformative light.

---

5. The concept of informating was first described by Dr. Shoshana Zuboff in 1988 in her book *In the Age of the Smart Machine*.

6. The two types of competitive advantage were first identified by Michael Porter in his book *Competitive Advantage: Creating and Sustaining Superior Performance*, 1985, which is now considered a classic text on organizational strategy. "Transforming" is a term suggested by Professor Richard T. Watson to complement and extend the concepts of automating and informating.

There are two basic ways of obtaining competitive advantage: cost and differentiation. A company gains a cost advantage when it delivers the same benefits to customers as its competitors, but at a lower cost. A company gains a differentiation advantage over its competitors when it delivers superior benefits to customers. By trying to achieve a cost or differentiation advantage, a company can provide better value for its customers and increased profits for itself. It is often difficult to obtain both a cost and differentiation advantage, however, because attempts to achieve greater differentiation usually result in greater costs. This strategy will only work if the differentiation delivers higher market share that results in more revenue.

In a simple resource-based model of competitive advantage, a company gains competitive advantage through the development of distinctive competencies. A company forms its distinctive competencies from a combination of its capabilities and its resources. Distinctive competencies enable innovation, product quality, process efficiency, and customer responsiveness. Applying IT strategically can assist in all these areas. Through automation with IT, a business can use its resources and capabilities more efficiently to achieve a lower cost structure. Through informating with IT, the business can learn new ways to increase or transform its capabilities, and better ways to manage its resources to differentiate its products.

To be successful and continue to be successful, businesses must be armed with data and information about their business, competitors, and the business environment. In Chapter 6 we discuss, in detail, how businesses source, gather, analyze, synthesize, transform, and communicate (all knowledge activities) data and information. Once armed with this knowledge, business leaders must make decisions and solve problems based on this information. These decisions and solutions often lead to changes in the business, which might include automating, informating, and transforming.

DECISION MAKING

To truly create business value, however, a company needs to decide how to best apply the information it has gathered. This section defines a basic decision-making process and the next section will tackle problem solving, both critical business activities.

Before discussing effective decision making, we need to have a common understanding of what a decision is. A **rational decision** is a choice that you make about what actions you will take (or not take) in a given situation after analyzing the consequences of each option. It may involve trade-offs between options, or trying to optimize an outcome given a set of current circumstances and preferences balanced with risk. There may be legal or environmental factors or ethical or moral concerns about certain aspects of the decision.

However, rational decision making normally occurs as part of a larger problem-solving process within a specific context. This creates natural boundaries and limits around the available options. In other words, you usually make a decision, for example, choosing between University A or College B, in the context of solving the problem of what you want to study and why (the problem-solving process). This involves considerations such as distance from home, climate and language

Putting gas in your car so you can drive it is an example of a routine decision; you don't have to think very hard about whether this is a necessary action!

preferences, tuition and living costs, your knowledge of the institution involved, recommendations or rankings by others, quality of program or faculty, accessibility, and perhaps likelihood of being admitted. Once you consider all these factors, the outcome will dictate the first step of choosing where you will go to school (the actual decision). Further, you may also need to consider the ethics of a decision, such as whether or not it is important for you to attend a public or private institution whose selective admission criteria or policies you may not personally agree with, but whose education might be superior. Lastly, the more practice you have making decisions and learning to anticipate their consequences, the better you become at making them!

Some decisions may be routine, whereas some decisions are more difficult, involving ethical considerations (ethics are discussed further in Chapter 9). Think about some of the other decisions that you have made (e.g., what to wear today, what route to take to school, and what career to pursue). These decisions are not equal in consequence or in the need for careful thought and planning.

TECHNOLOGY CORE

Organizations can use IT in several ways to support decision making. For example, businesses use expert systems, a type of knowledge management system. Expert systems originate from the field of artificial intelligence (AI), which attempts to provide computer applications that mimic characteristics of human intelligence. Many other applications use AI technology, from neural networks used for recognizing patterns in stock prices, to genetic algorithms that incorporate theories from genetics into programs that can quickly find an optimal solution to a problem. Expert systems capture and store the knowledge of a human expert so that the organization can permanently store and share it. Special techniques have been developed to capture and codify tacit knowledge (knowledge gained through experience) into an expert system, such as observation and interview techniques. This knowledge includes how an expert performs work and makes decisions. To store the knowledge, special formats capture how the facts relate to the decision rules used by the expert. Expert systems and artificial intelligence will never replace humans, but they can help to advise humans to make better decisions and solve difficult problems.

Classifying Decisions by Type

Your college or university degree program likely requires you to take certain prerequisite courses. When you make your course selections, you know that you must register in these classes. Here, you carry out the required actions associated with a very structured decision. A **structured decision** is one that can be programmed; it is routine or repetitive.[7]

---

7. H. A. Simon, *The New Science of Management Decision*, Harper & Row, New York, 1960 and 1977 (re-release); P. G. Keen and M. S. Scott Morton, *Decision Support Systems: An Organizational Perspective*, Addison-Wesley, Mass., 1978.

However, not all decisions are so clear cut. Sometimes even simple decisions may have increased uncertainty, or doubt about consequences and outcomes, associated with them. This is the case when you register for optional or elective courses. You may decide to take a course based on your interests or when the course is offered. Some of your classmates may have recommended an elective course that is "easy" or entertaining. Other classmates' opinions may have differed. The choice is not so easy. You are now faced with a **semi-structured decision**.

Let's further complicate this example. You graduate from your course of study and are now faced with doing graduate studies or starting your career in the business world, which is a third kind of decision: the **unstructured decision**. This is a novel, complex situation, with no obvious or single correct decision or decision process. Further, your decision will significantly affect the next few years of your life. What do you do?

To help you decide what to do, you may meet with some graduate students, survey some of the courses you would take, and talk to people working in the business area you are considering. You may also consult your family and friends. Money may also be a consideration. You do some research on the Internet and find that having a graduate degree does not significantly affect initial annual salaries. You make your decision: you will enter the work world and not do graduate studies. But there is still a lot of uncertainty as to the correctness of this decision. If you don't do graduate studies now, when will you? Perhaps you will miss studying with an influential professor. However, given the available information, you have made the best decision you can.

Using Information in Decision Making

This is what rational decision making is all about: using information to reduce uncertainty in the outcomes of your decisions. The above example highlights aspects of the three different types of decisions and their relationship to uncertainty. In general, uncertainty complicates the decision-making process and underscores why information systems are so important to businesses. Information systems help businesses reduce uncertainty by providing information to decision makers. Less uncertainty due to more complete information can lead to better decisions, thereby enhancing the creation of business value.

However, business professionals also have a responsibility to recognize that there is no such thing as perfect information to eliminate uncertainty. Therefore, they also have some responsibility to know when they have enough valuable information to go ahead with a decision, and then to push themselves and their organizations to execute those decisions, even when there is some lingering uncertainty.

Another important element of good decision making is what to do when you receive new information. Is it valuable and should it influence your decision? You will be called upon to make these judgements throughout your career as you make important decisions about all kinds of things, both more and less certain, that can affect the organization you work for.

WHAT DO YOU THINK?

People can endlessly analyze information—a never-ending process known as *analysis paralysis*. At some point, analysis should end and lead to some conclusion: a decision or a solution to a problem. To gain competitive advantage, organizations often analyze productivity. **Productivity** is the ability to create business value with the least cost. Examining productivity forces organizations to look at efficiency and effectiveness, defined as follows:

Efficiency: Getting the most output from a given input ("doing the thing right")
Effectiveness: Pursuing the goal or task that is appropriate for the given situation ("doing the right thing")

Therefore, productivity can be thought of as "doing the right thing, right."

Consider the following scenarios to better understand knowledge activities and decision making concerning productivity:

1: Imagine you are a sidewalk vendor of frozen drinks in Saskatoon, Saskatchewan. You get more drinks per amount of ingredients than your competitors; that is, you are highly efficient. But you sell only one frozen drink in January (when the average temperature is −17°C), so your efforts are ineffective.

2: Now imagine you are the owner of a T-shirt-selling business on campus. It is so successful that you always sell out of T-shirts by the end of frosh week. You know you could sell more if you were able to produce more T-shirts by the beginning of September.

For each of these scenarios, what decisions will you make to improve your productivity? What knowledge work activities will you undertake to assist in making these decisions? What role could IT play in improving productivity?

How to Make More-Informed Decisions

As a business professional, recall that your work will often centre on finding and using quality data, information, and knowledge. As a decision maker, the quality of your decision often depends on the quality of the inputs you use to inform your decision.

In every decision that you make in life, you should always carefully consider the characteristics of the information on which you are basing your decision. Obviously, you must have already considered the source when you either accessed or were provided with the information, and you must assume that the source is a good one. However, beyond that are the nuances of the information itself. Is it complete? How accurate or reliable is it likely to be? If it is not, have efforts been made to address the degree to which it is or is not accurate or reliable? And is the information up-to-date and provided in a timely way?

All of these information characteristics, which are summarized in Table 3.4, affect the usefulness of data and information for decision making. As someone living in the most intense knowledge era ever, you need to become a good judge of the quality of information.

Decision Making | 103

Table 3.4	Information Evaluation Criteria
Information Characteristic	**Example**
Complete	Your new project team member's mobile phone is 555–1212. Is this enough information? Maybe, but you may also need an area code.
Accurate	You check your printed course schedule and find out that your Intro to IS class meets at 11 p.m. You suspect the schedule is wrong.
Reliable	You receive an unsolicited email offering you a share in millions of dollars if you will help this person transfer money out of his home country. You realize this is a frequent email scam and is, therefore, unreliable information.
Timely	When deciding what to wear, a forecast of yesterday's weather is recent information, but it could be worthless if today's weather is different than yesterday's. Timely information includes recent information, but also requires that the information arrive close enough to the decision to be useful to the decision maker.

The Decision-Making Process

Figure 3.9 summarizes a typical rational decision-making process. Initially, decision making requires you to engage in knowledge work activities so that you can make an effective choice about some issue or challenge. You have seen that not all decisions are the same with regard to the structure or uncertainty present in the decision-making environment. Normally, as you progress through the process, you will become more certain and the structure of the decision will become clearer. To make the best decision you can, you need to carefully consider the quality of the data, information, and knowledge and put it into proper context. During the analysis stage, you sort, transform, and organize the data to define options. Of course, in this sense, decisions are just like computer programs: garbage in, garbage out! The quality of the final output of this process (the decision) will likely be based on the quality of the inputs (the information and analysis you create).

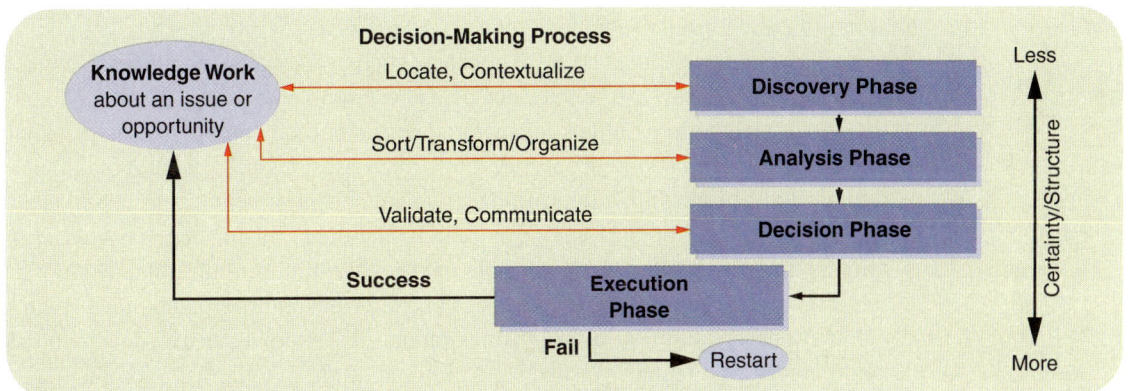

FIGURE 3.9 To make the best decision possible, you should carefully consider the amount of decision certainty and structure, as well as assess the quality of data, information, and knowledge available in the context of the decision to be made.

Once you have narrowed the options to a final decision, you communicate the conclusion so the organization can implement the decision. Obviously, the result will either be a success or a failure. Either of these contributes learning to the process for the next time. You can use this learning to either tackle a new problem or refine your understanding of the current problem, and repeat the process to make a new decision about a new course of action.

Quick Test

1. Fill in the blank. The level of uncertainty faced by a decision maker can be reduced through the discovery and use of _____.

2. True or False. The more you make decisions, the better you will be at anticipating the consequences of making them.

3. The need for data that are from a trusted source determines if the data are _____.
   a. accurate
   b. complete
   c. timely
   d. reliable

Answers: 1. information; 2. True; 3. d

PROBLEM SOLVING

The purpose of decision making is often to solve a problem. In general, a **problem** exists when you find yourself in a situation that fails to meet your goals, needs, or expectations. Further, that current situation often results from a past series of events, or lack of events, that did or did not happen. For example, if you studied and failed to make the desired grade on a test, it's a problem. But it's a different problem if you didn't study at all and failed to make the desired grade on the test. So the first step in problem solving is not only recognizing that a problem exists, but why it exists. You can then take effective and efficient steps to change the situation, to more productively meet your needs and goals.

Fixing some problems is relatively easy, such as using an umbrella to stay dry if it's raining. However, resolving most business problems poses a real challenge. How do business professionals reliably and consistently fix problems? They engage in problem solving. **Problem solving** refers to a series of steps or a process (logical sequence of activities) taken in response to some event or activity.

Consider this example to help you understand the problem-solving process. It is January and time to pay the next installment of your tuition. Unfortunately, the first semester of the year cost a lot more than you expected, and you do not have enough money to cover tuition (problem). You examine the alternatives and decide to ask your parents for a loan. This solves the problem—at least the original problem!

As a business professional, you will often repeat the problem-solving process. Furthermore, each stage of this process may require individual decisions that use the decision-making process discussed above. To make this process as effective as possible, you could use the IADD problem-solving model. The steps in this model provide a tool that you can consistently apply to most problems, either as an individual or within an organization.

IADD[8] Model

The **IADD** model is a more formal expression of the problem-solving process that you probably already use intuitively. The model, as Figure 3.10 shows, consists of four major steps: **i**nvestigate, **a**nalyze, **d**ecide, and **d**o.

- *Investigate:* Determine if there is a problem or an opportunity, and if it is possible to solve the problem or take advantage of the opportunity.
- *Analyze:* Gather data that are relevant to the heart of the problem, or that pertain to the benefits, challenges, and risks associated with a given opportunity.
- *Decide:* Evaluate solutions and make choices regarding how to implement the solution.
- *Do:* Implement the solution and monitor the results.

The following example demonstrates how to use the IADD model. Assume that you have not yet declared an academic major. To solve this problem, apply the IADD model in a question-and-answer format, integrating knowledge work activities as needed.

Investigate In the *investigate* stage, you identify a challenge or problem and gather data to determine if meeting the challenge or resolving the problem is possible. Problems tend to be defined or identified in terms of what went wrong with a process or action, or they may be defined by comparing a desired future state (profitability) to the current situation (expenses exceed revenues).

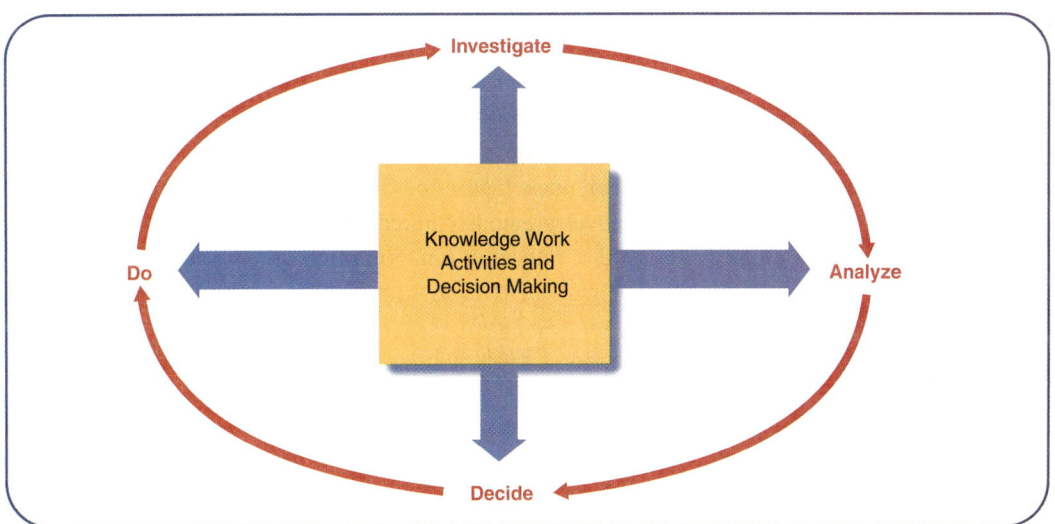

FIGURE 3.10 IADD problem-solving model.

---

8. This model is a synthesis of various problem-solving and decision-making models, especially Simon's *Model of Intelligence, Design, Choice, and Implementation*.

Problems can also be defined as opportunities or challenges. For example, Larry Page and Sergey Brin, frustrated with trying to find information on the Web, thought about how to overcome this problem and help others, too. Who are Page and Brin? They are the co-founders and chief executives of Google.

Now use the example to illustrate how to work through the *investigate* stage. Begin by asking questions: "What's wrong?" "Is there a business or learning opportunity present?" You realize there is a learning *and* business opportunity! You have the opportunity to decide what subject you wish to study and the courses you will most likely take for the next two years or so. You also realize this knowledge will help you in your future business career.

Now that you have identified the opportunity, take action and find information that will help to solve your problem. You might talk to your academic advisor or conduct a search on your school's website using the phrase "choosing a major" or "academic major." Where else can you find data, information, and knowledge about your major? You could talk to your friends who are majoring in the subject, or you could attend a meeting of the student organization related to your intended major. You could also contact a professor who teaches classes in the major.

Analyze In the *analyze* stage, your brain needs to go into "detective" mode, looking for clues and evidence that will let you piece together what happened. Just as crime scene investigators do on television, try to decipher what each piece of data means and how each piece relates to the other pieces. As you continue your analysis, try to describe the problem or challenge, as well as all of the factors that influence the situation. Think of analysis as developing a list of suspects that you interview to help develop a reasonable solution for the crime (problem).

Next, think about how information systems can help with the *analyze* step of problem solving in general. If your problem or opportunity is complex, you will have an abundance of data to organize, classify, store, and so on. Fortunately, databases and database management systems (DBMS) software are excellent tools for organizing and storing data. Further, certain types of DBMS can even harness the power of the relationships that exist in the data (we discuss how in Tech Guide D). Once you have organized and stored the data and relationships, you can use other tools to manipulate the data. For example, you can ask questions of your database through structured query language (SQL) queries, or use special software programs to explore the data to discover previously undiscovered relationships and patterns.

Returning to the issue of choosing a major, although you will want to effectively and efficiently analyze your data, the problem is not so large as to require huge amounts of data or complex information systems. As with other IADD stages, begin to analyze your situation by asking questions, such as: "If I am interested in learning about _____, or if I want to be a(n)_____ in the future, what subject should I major in?" Choosing good questions to focus your analysis is an important part of the problem-solving process. Your questions must fit the decision you need to make.

While you analyze, you may find new data and decide what data are relevant. Finally, you may communicate with others for ideas, assistance, and opinions. The *analyze* stage brings all your knowledge work skills to bear in grasping the problem and moving forward through the model.

At the end of this stage of the model, you will determine alternative solutions or choices. Take the time to think creatively to generate as many viable solutions as possible. Much of the data you have gathered will probably pertain to one or two majors in which you were already interested. However, there may be some surprises as well. Maybe you visited your university or college's career or student centre and took an aptitude test. You can use the results as data to generate alternative majors. Remember, as you generate alternative solutions or choices, you may need to gather more data.

Assume that you came up with three choices: (1) accounting, (2) finance, and (3) management information systems (MIS). To analyze your choices, first determine selection criteria. **Criteria** are the factors that you think are important and relevant to solving the problem. For example, think about your interests or what you like or don't like to study. You might include your estimate of success in the course work required for the majors as criteria. Or perhaps you view your major as a stepping-stone to your future career. If so, your criteria may include future job opportunities, opportunities for travel and advancement, starting salaries, or lifelong earnings potential.

Another approach might help you develop useful and relevant criteria. Of the proposed solutions, think about the positive benefits or characteristics of each. As you list these characteristics, consider which ones you view as more important than the others. This method may help you develop criteria for choosing which solution to develop further.

Which criteria you apply to your decision greatly affects the data that you gathered. For example, if you select future job opportunities as a criterion, but you didn't gather the data, it will be difficult to use this as a meaningful criterion. You will then need to find more data about your proposed solutions to complete your analysis.

Decide At some point in the problem-solving process, you need to stop gathering and analyzing data and generating alternative solutions. Your analysis may offer several good solutions to choose from, maybe even the best solution. However, if you don't choose a solution or you fail to implement it, the problem remains unsolved. In the *decide* stage of the IADD model, you choose the best solution from those available and describe how that solution will solve the problem, meet the challenge, or capitalize on the opportunity.

Is it just that easy? No, not usually. As discussed previously, decision making is often more complex and uncertain. One choice may not be clearly better than the others, or you may need to combine elements from one or more solutions to create a more comprehensive one. Or, if none of the proposed solutions seems workable, you may need to go back and generate more alternatives.

How do business professionals actually decide which solution to pick? It all depends on the criteria they established and the agreed-upon decision process. For your problem, you might enter the possible solutions in the rows of a spreadsheet, and the criteria for choosing in the columns (see Table 3.5). You can then score each possible solution by evaluating it against each criterion according to some scale [e.g., 1 (low) to 5 (high)]. You may also want to add some kind of emphasis or weighting on one or more of the criteria. For example, ask yourself if it is more

Table 3.5 Scoring Alternatives Based on Criteria

Criteria Scale: 1 (low) to 5 (high)	Personal Interest	Estimated Starting Salaries	Forecasted Job Demand	Friends in Major	Total Score
Accounting	4	4 [$41,000.00]	5	3	16
Finance	5	3 [$40,000.00]	4	5	17
Management Information Systems	4	5 [$44,000.00]	5	5	18

important to study what you are interested in or to earn the highest possible starting salary upon graduation. In a sense, before you can rank your solutions, you may have to rank your criteria. Once you determine how to account for the scores you assign, then the solution with the highest point total could be the top candidate for implementation in the *do* stage.

At this stage you change ideas into reality and begin the transition from thinking into doing. By deciding, you determine how you will solve your problem and then translate these thoughts into planned actions. After you select the best solution for you, determine the what, when, where, and how of implementing your choice. Note, however, that although you select a solution in the *decide* stage, you can modify your solution in the future (e.g., you can switch majors if needed).

Do Once you decide on a solution and a way to implement it, conclude the problem-solving process by carrying out the actions necessary to make the solution a success. This *do* step of the IADD model is where you implement tasks and other physical activities according to your solution. At the individual level, you are responsible for doing these activities. You must complete the necessary paperwork and enroll in classes required by your intended major. You must carry out many of these tasks in sequence and by certain dates.

Making a solution work is an especially important part of the problem-solving process. In fact, it can be as much or more of a challenge than the three previous steps. To help with this task, you can use an *action grid*, as shown in Table 3.6.

Table 3.6 Example of an Action Grid

Person Responsible	Action Required	Resources Needed	Due Date	Date Accomplished	Comments
You	Make appointment with advisor	Email or maybe a Web-based form	MM/DD/YYYY	MM/DD/YYYY	Do this before midterm to ensure priority registration for major courses

You can make the action grid even more effective by using information technology. For example, the action grid in Table 3.6 could represent a report that was the output from a database designed to track and manage activities. Or you might use project management software or CASE tools (we discuss these tools in Chapter 7). These sophisticated IS tools can help with your knowledge work activities, decision making, and problem solving.

Communicating your choice of major is important to your success in that field. For example, you may need to meet with faculty and/or advisors to enter into your chosen major, and to work with others to achieve your goal of graduating with a degree. You may also want to let others such as your parents and friends know of your choice. They can provide valuable insight and support as you work toward your goal.

To monitor and modify your solution (if needed), you need to establish metrics. Decision makers use metrics to determine what is measured and how to measure it. For example, you may select your major GPA as a metric. At the end of each semester you can calculate your major GPA. You also need to determine what GPA will indicate satisfactory progress. Or, if you think that a semester is too long to wait for feedback on your progress, you can calculate your major GPA after midterm. Depending on the outcome of your calculations, you may need to alter your studying habits. Basically, metrics should be measurements that help you monitor the implementation and progress of your solution.

As part of the do stage, you should review your solutions. Ask yourself the following questions: (1) What was the solution designed to do? (2) What actually happened or is happening as a result of implementing (doing) the solution? (3) What might explain both the good and bad differences between planned solutions and results? (4) What can I learn from this effort so I can do a better job now and in the future? Based on your answers to these questions, you can modify or scrap your current solution. Simply return to the step(s) in the IADD model that will help you create and implement a more effective solution.

The best organizations use their most precious resource (people) to focus on their most strategic and urgent priorities (their goals). These resources gather data and information, analyze it, and identify problems or opportunities. Problems may include inefficient processes in need of reengineering or faulty outputs that are reducing profits. Opportunities may be innovative product improvements or new market opportunities. Whether problem or opportunity, business leaders must engage in problem solving and decision making to take action. IT plays a part in problem solving and decision making by providing critical information and organizing it to increase the quality of the information. IT may also be part of the solution. For example, IT can automate the less useful and more routine tasks to free up resources to concentrate on the priorities. These activities make organizations successful, and also make them great places to work.

As a business professional, be sure to look for opportunities in organizations that are going to help you use your skills to make decisions and solve problems that help your employer have competitive advantage.

Quick Test

1. Fill in the blank. In order from first to last, the four steps in the IADD problem-solving model are _____.

2. An action grid is a tool that is especially useful in the _____ step of the problem-solving process.
   a. analyze
   b. decide
   c. do
   d. investigate

3. In the *decide* step, _____ are applied to evaluate each alternative's relative value and applicability.
   a. criteria
   b. action grids
   c. metrics
   d. queries

Answers: 1. investigate, analyze, decide, do; 2. c; 3. a

What's in for me?

What if organizations did not automate, informate, or transform? Can you imagine waiting for the bank to be open to withdraw money or having to use a card file in the library to do the research for your term paper? Successful organizations and businesses are constantly looking for ways to improve. Those that do not are unsuccessful and may even cease to exist. Would you choose a bank that did not offer online banking, for example? IT helps organizations understand their business environment and the needs of their customers by providing vital information. With this information, organizations can then solve problems or capitalize on opportunities that help gain or sustain competitive advantage. When this happens, you, as a customer, benefit. You benefit by dealing with an efficient and innovative organization that knows what you want. IT may also be part of what is offered to you as a customer. Somehow Apple recognized the need for the iPod and invented the required technology to enable it. Because of this one innovative product, the entire music industry has been forced to transform to meet customers' needs. We can only guess what the future will hold as you become business professionals and join in the activity of creating business value and competitive advantage.

What's in for an organization?

This chapter covered a lot of ground, from strategy to process to decision making and problem solving. A key member of the executive team who contributes to all of this is the chief information officer (CIO). This person normally reports to the CEO/chair, COO/president, or sometimes the CFO. He or she leads the organization's information and technology efforts, especially as they relate to the creation of business value and competitive advantage. What does it take to become a CIO? Several studies concluded that critical skills for CIOs include strong communication skills, the ability to think strategically, and a thorough understanding of the business processes and operations of the company. With these skills, a CIO champions the use of IT in identifying efficiencies and information that will help sustain or gain competitive advantage. The CIO is also responsible for understanding how new technologies might enable existing business processes and potentially automate, informate, and/or transform.

As you continue through this text, keep in mind that you are gaining the basic foundation for becoming a CIO. Through experience and increased business and technical knowledge, you may one day aspire to fill the CIO position.

What's in IT for society?

Corporate social responsibility (CSR) and the role that business has to play to ensure that we remain a sustainable society are currently hot topics. This implies an increasing scrutiny on businesses about the decisions they make and the rationale for them, including an effort to address the ecological, social, and moral implications of their decisions. This situation is most evident in the recent United States banking crisis and President Obama's accusation of the "fat cat Wall Street bankers not getting it" as they took government bailout money on the one hand, while paying themselves and their executive teams stunningly large bonuses based on improved results. However, the results were only improved (from the verge of bankruptcy in many cases!) by the government injecting capital into the banks. In this case, although the information was perhaps available to make another decision, self-interest likely influenced the decision—it is not clear that IT outcomes would have changed it.

However, in many other business decision-making contexts, improving the quality of the decisions that businesses make can have a profound overall impact on society and its well-being. Bad decisions are often made in the absence of good information. IT can play a significant role in making sure that information required to make informed decisions is easily available. By improving the quality of decisions, we can improve the quality of life generally for everyone. Especially as society holds business more and more accountable for the quality of its decisions, the importance of making data-driven decisions based on high quality information will continue to rise in importance.

ROI STUDENT RETURN ON INVESTMENT SUMMARY

1. **What is competitive advantage and how do businesses achieve it?**

Competitive advantage is the result of creating more business value than competitors. Businesses continually analyze their competitive position to, at minimum, maintain competitive advantage and, hopefully increase advantage. In these endeavours, IT helps businesses to both identify and implement ways to increase business value and competitive advantage. Firstly, IT enables businesses to more efficiently gather, process, and analyze data and information. Through these actions, business professionals can identify areas for improvement or opportunities that will lead to competitive advantage. Secondly, IT may be a crucial part of the business product or service that is offered to market. It certainly may be part of the way the product or service is produced. IT may assist by automating or informating processes to be more efficient and informative, or may transform products to be highly successful in the marketplace.

2. **How do the structure, quality, and presentation of information influence the nature of the decisions made by business professionals?**

A decision is a choice you make about what actions you will take (or not take) in a given situation. Decisions can vary in the amount of structure and uncertainty, from structured and certain decisions (e.g., selecting prerequisite courses) to unstructured decisions that give little guidance about what to do, how to do it, and what the likely outcome will be. The amount of structure and the level of uncertainty can influence how much time knowledge-enabled professionals will spend in different knowledge work activities, and how certain they might be about the outcomes of their decisions. Further, because the gathered data and information form the foundation for the analysis, the quality of data and information directly affects the quality of the decision.

3. **How can business professionals solve problems to create business value?**

The four steps in the IADD model are: (1) investigate, (2) analyze, (3) decide, and (4) do. Business professionals often focus on creating business value for their organization by solving problems and by recognizing and responding to new business opportunities. For example, they do this by gathering new information (*investigate*), considering which information is most important (*analyze*), outlining how to apply this information to the problem or opportunity at hand (*decide*), and then taking the necessary actions to implement and monitor the decided-upon solution or course of action (*do*).

KNOWLEDGE SPEAK

automating   96
business process   93
business process reengineering (BPR)   95
business strategy   87
competitive advantage   96
criteria   107
decentralized structure   91
effectiveness   102
efficiency   102
feedback   95
functional structure   91
IADD model   105
IGOE model   94

informating   98
matrix structure   91
open systems model   88
organizational boundary   89
problem   104
problem solving   104
productivity   102
rational decision   99
semi-structured decision   101
stakeholder   88
structured decision   100
transforming   98
unstructured decision   101

REVIEW QUESTIONS

Multiple-choice questions

1. For a business to begin, it must start with
   a. strategy
   b. processes
   c. organizational structure
   d. all of the above

2. Which information characteristic do you use to determine if an information source can be trusted?
   a. complete
   b. timely
   c. accurate
   d. reliable

3. Which of the following is NOT a type of organizational structure?
   a. autocratic
   b. matrix
   c. decentralized
   d. functional

4. Which is the first step in the problem-solving model highlighted in this chapter?
   a. analyze
   b. decide
   c. do
   d. investigate

Fill-in-the-blank questions

5. _____ is the study of business processes to find ways of making them more efficient.
6. When _____ a process, a business might apply technology to do the same things as before, but more efficiently.
7. Using information in decision making reduces the amount of _____ in the outcome of the decision.

True-false questions

8. The G in IGOE, the process analysis method, stands for gather.
9. An unstructured decision includes little or no inherent uncertainty.
10. The investigate phase of the IADD problem-solving model generates criteria to evaluate options to help ensure the selection of the best solution.

Matching questions
Choose the BEST answer from column B for each item in column A.

Column A
11. input
12. guide
13. output
14. enabler

Column B
a. fermentation tank
b. raw materials, including barley
c. beer
d. heat measurements

Column A
15. structured decision
16. semi-structured decision
17. unstructured decision

Column B
a. How should I invest my money today to ensure a comfortable retirement 40 years from now?
b. What is the correct dosage of a prescription medicine that I should take to get well?
c. Given that I have decided to buy a hybrid car, which one should I buy?
d. None of the above

Short-answer questions

18. Apply the IADD problem-solving model to a problem or opportunity of your choosing. Based on the problem or opportunity that you choose, give an example for each of the following steps of the model:
    a. investigate
    b. analyze
    c. decide
    d. do
19. Decisions can be characterized as structured, semi-structured, or unstructured. Define each type of decision and give a personal example for each type.

Discussion/Essay questions

20. One of your friends is faced with a welcome opportunity: deciding between two internship offers. Apply the IADD problem-solving model to help him or her decide which offer to take.
21. Is decision making the heart of problem solving? Argue for or against this belief. Use examples from your own experiences to support your position.

TEAM ACTIVITY

Assume that your school requires that students all have laptop computers. Administration has asked your class to provide detailed, written recommendations for the best laptop for incoming students. Work in groups of 4–5 students to apply the IADD model to complete this assignment. Be sure to list and discuss your criteria.

SOFTWARE APPLICATION EXERCISES

1. Internet

Many students pursue careers in the private (non-governmental) sector. For a listing of potential jobs, go to your school's homepage and search the website for "Career Centre" or "Job Placement." Use Google.ca or Mamma.ca to perform a similar search. Alternatively, you may want to investigate careers with federal, provincial, or municipal governments. Although the starting salaries for government jobs are often lower than their private-sector equivalents, they have other benefits, such as job security and stability. Look at jobs at the federal level (www.jobs-emplois.gc.ca/) and use your favourite search engine to find your provincial and municipal governmental employment sites.

2. Presentation

Based on your research for the previous Internet assignment, prepare a presentation that highlights the essentials regarding three jobs that you would consider. For one job, discuss what companies you might work for, what you would be doing, and where you might live.

3. Word Processing

A critical business skill is the ability to communicate clearly and to the point. An executive summary (search the Web for an example) provides a brief background of the problem or issue; highlights the key factors, constraints, or opportunities; and may answer the question posed by the executive or decision maker for whom the summary is intended (e.g., recommends actions to take). Prepare an executive summary of the job search process.

4. Spreadsheet

Prepare a budget for the salary that you anticipate you will receive upon graduation (use one of the three jobs that interested you in the previous presentation assignment). Include items like savings, rent, car payment, food, auto insurance and maintenance, utilities, vacation, and entertainment. Assume that you have a choice of cities to call home. Visit www.homefair.com to use the salary calculator to compare salary relative to choice of city.

5. Database

As you continue through your academic and professional careers, start collecting professional contacts. Although software packages are available to manage your contacts, designing and creating your own database may prove more useful. Why? As you think about what data to store, you will recognize certain unique aspects of your relationships with certain professionals (e.g., your professors). You may need database fields to track if a professor wrote you a recommendation, what it was for, when he or she wrote that recommendation, and any follow-up actions (e.g., a thank-you email). Also, you may need to complete and track different types of contacts or documents if you apply for government jobs in addition to private-sector jobs.

6. Advanced Challenge

Imagine that you and three friends are living off-campus, and you are all trying to discover which career is right for each of you. Your roommates do most of their research using a dial-up Internet connection. You are the only roommate paying for high-speed Internet access through the cable company. You all have mobile phones, and each of you has a traditional phone connection through the local phone company. The others, tired of connecting via relatively slow dial-up connections, agree to help pay the bill if they can share your high-speed connection. You are willing to do this, but are unsure how to go about it. You decide to use the IADD model to create a solution. Briefly outline your thoughts and actions for each step of the model, highlighting at least one knowledge activity for each step. Then, fully describe your solution and how you will implement it.

ONLINE RESOURCES

Companion Website
- Take interactive practice quizzes to assess your knowledge and help you study in a dynamic way.
- Review PowerPoint lecture slides.
- Get help and sample solutions to end-of-chapter software application exercises.

Additional Resources Available Only on WileyPLUS

- Take the interactive Quick Test to check your understanding of the chapter material and get immediate feedback on your responses.
- Review and study with downloadable Audio Lecture MP3 files.
- Check your understanding of the key vocabulary in the chapter with Knowledge Speak Interactive Flash Cards.

CASE STUDY: USING IT TO BUY A CAR

After accepting a well-paying position with a consulting firm, Ashley Hyatt realizes that she can now replace the old car she has been driving since her first year of university. She has narrowed her choice down to two coupes—an import and a domestic brand with similar dealer prices. She has also looked at the interest rates that she could obtain for a car loan, but is unsure about which length of the loan to go with: 36, 48, or 60 months. She asks her father for advice.

Her dad begins by helping her understand the basic concept involved in the length of the loan: depreciation. Cars lose value very quickly, especially in the first year. In fact, after as little as 24 months, the residual value of a car can often be less than one-third of its original value. This means that if Ashley has a 60-month loan, even at *zero percent* interest, she will still owe 60 percent of the original loan amount after the first 24 months, but the car will only be worth 55 percent *or less* of the amount that she owes on the loan. This becomes a real problem if Ashley wants to trade or sell the car, or if the car is damaged in an accident.

Ashley realizes that she needs to compare the *residual values* (considering depreciation) to the amount owed on the loan at the same period of time. She knows that she can use a spreadsheet to calculate the amount she would owe on the loan after a given number of months. But she also needs to know the value of her trade-in to use in calculating the net amount of the loan she'll be taking out. She decides to investigate the wide variety of websites dedicated to automobile purchasing, selling, trading-in, financing, and so on.

Using the information from these websites, such as Driving.ca and BankRate.ca, Ashley determines the trade-in value of her car is $3,450. Table 3.7 lists the residual values for the two cars that she is deciding between.

Table 3.7	Retail Price and Residual at End of Yearly Periods	
Year	Domestic Coupe	Imported Coupe
Retail Price	$21,995.00	$21,745.00
2	$9,200.00	$13,300.00
3	$7,375.00	$11,325.00
4	$5,750.00	$9,450.00
5	$4,450.00	$7,850.00

	A	B	C	D	E	F	G	H
1		**Import Coupe**				**Domestic Coupe**		
2	List Price	$ 21,745			List Price	$ 21,995		
3	Trade-in	$ 3,450			Trade-in	$ 3,450		
4	Taxes	$ 1,098			Taxes	$ 1,113		
5	Net Loan	$ 19,393			Net Loan	$ 19,658		
6	Residuals				Residuals			
7	Year 2	$ 13,300			Year 2	$ 9,200		
8	Year 3	$ 11,325			Year 3	$ 7,375		
9	Year 4	$ 9,450			Year 4	$ 5,750		
10	Year 5	$ 7,850			Year 5	$ 4,450		
11								
12	36 Month Loan							
13	Interest Rate	5.25%						
14	Payment	$583.40			Payment	$591.37		
15		Loan Balance	Residuals	Difference		Loan Balance	Residuals	Difference
16	2 years	$ 6,805.67	$ 13,300	$ 6,494		$ 6,898.66	$ 9,200	$ 2,301
17	3 years	$ 0.00	$ 11,325	$11,325		$ 0.00	$ 7,375	$ 7,375
18								
19	48 Month Loan							
20	Interest Rate	5.50%						
21	Payment	$451.01			Payment	$454.93		
22		Loan Balance	Residuals	Difference		Loan Balance	Residuals	Difference
23	2 years	$ 10,227.90	$ 13,300	$ 3,072		$ 10,367.66	$ 9,200	$ (1,168)
24	3 years	$ 5,254.23	$ 11,325	$ 6,071		$ 5,326.02	$ 7,375	$ 2,049
25	4 years	$ 0.00	$ 9,450	$ 9,450		$ 0.00	$ 5,750	$ 5,750
26								
27	60 Month Loan							
28	Interest Rate	5.75%						
29	Payment	$372.67			Payment	$373.22		
30		Loan Balance	Residuals	Difference		Loan Balance	Residuals	Difference
31	2 years	$ 12,295.61	$ 13,300	$ 1,004		$ 12,463.63	$ 9,200	$ (3,264)
32	3 years	$ 8,429.80	$ 11,325	$ 2,895		$ 8,515.24	$ 6,899	$ (1,617)
33	4 years	$ 4,335.76	$ 9,450	$ 5,114		$ 4,374.41	$ 5,750	$ 1,376
34	5 years	$ 0.00	$ 7,850	$ 7,850		$ 0.00	$ 4,450	$ 4,450

FIGURE 3.11 Spreadsheet comparisons of car values.

She found that the interest rates for a 36-, 48-, and 60-month loan are 5.25 percent, 5.50 percent, and 5.75 percent, respectively. Using this information, she calculates monthly payments for each length of loan for the net loan value (MSRP minus trade-in value plus 6 percent taxes) for both cars.

She also determines the loan balance at the end of each year after the first from the amortization tables (in BankRate.ca), and enters this information along with that from Table 3.7 in a spreadsheet. Figure 3.11 shows the resulting spreadsheet.

Case Questions

1. Given the information shown in Figure 3.11, what would be Ashley's best decision if she can't afford more than $600 for a monthly car payment? What about $500? What about $400? Justify your recommendation using quantitative data.
2. If the car dealership offers Ashley a cash rebate of $1,500 or low-interest financing on the original price (assume the low interest rates are 2 percentage points lower than the standard rates), how will this affect her decision?
3. Should Ashley consider a lease instead? Research this lease-versus-buy decision and write a two-page report on your findings. List any online and IT devices that you use in your research.

Integrative Application Case: *Campuspad.ca*

You and Sarah continue to reflect on your business ideas for *campuspad.ca* and remain quite excited. However, you still have lots of unanswered questions.

Having already reviewed the competitors in the student rental space e-world, you are pretty sure you are going to be the first to market a student-centric site design that really meets market needs. But you need to do even more than that to be successful. Although there are very few barriers to starting an e-business, you have to make sure that you continually innovate to stay ahead of future competitors.

You and Sarah decide to each locate your five favourite websites and carefully consider *why* you like them and *what value* they create for you when you use them. You have already discussed the need to pay careful attention to how technology is being used, with the hope of inspiring ways to apply what you like from other sites to your own site design for *campuspad.ca*. You agree to take a week to do this and then meet to sketch out how your homepage might look and define some high-level requirements of the site design. This has you really excited and you want to dive right in. But analysis has to come before decision making, so you go off to do your online research.

Guiding Case Questions

1. Identify your five favourite websites.
2. Analyze why you like them, how they create value for you, and their design features.
3. Do you pay for access to these sites? How do these sites profit from your presence?
4. What kinds of technology do these sites use to support their online business?

Your Task

Use the knowledge you have acquired from this research to make some initial decisions about how your homepage will look when you launch *campuspad.ca*. Using tools of your choice, sketch out how it will look, and add comments about how users will navigate and use the site to meet their needs. Briefly include descriptions of how your intended technology will meet specific user needs to justify your proposed design.

4 ENTERPRISE SYSTEMS

WHAT WE WILL COVER

- The Value Chain
- Information Systems that Support Business Activities
- Strategically Fitting IT to the Organization
- Enterprise Risk Management

ROI STUDENT RETURN ON INVESTMENT

Through your investment of time in reading and thinking about this chapter, your return—or created value—is gaining knowledge. Use the following questions as a study guide.

1. In what ways can organizations apply IT to build business value?
2. How can businesses strategically fit IT to the organization?
3. What is IT's role in managing enterprise risk?

THE VOICE OF EXPERIENCE
Keith Powell, B.Sc., Concordia University, and MBA, McGill University

After 20 years at Nortel Networks, including several across Nortel's value chain and four as chief information officer, Keith Powell established an information technology consulting practice, Keith Powell Consulting Inc. After 10 years as a consultant, Keith calls himself "semi-retired." He spends his business time as a member of five boards, and continues to provide executive coaching services to various entrepreneurs. He spends his personal time on volunteer efforts such as the Vancouver 2010 Winter Olympics, and on travel, golf, skiing, and cycling.

What do you do in your current position? In addition to being semi-retired, I am still involved in executive coaching and development, and I'm a partner in a venture capital company investing in small start-up technology companies. Prior to my retirement, I provided consulting services to large technology companies in the area of IT strategy development. Much of my career has been in value-creating activities such as manufacturing, operations, and customer service, so I have a lot to offer start-ups and executives who are trying to gain competitive advantage throughout their value chain.

I started out at Pratt and Whitney doing supply chain management and then I joined Nortel. Working directly in the supply chain helped me to understand the needs of customers first hand, and showed me how applied IT can create competitive advantage. Because I worked so closely in Nortel's primary activities, I never thought IT was in my career plan. When John Roth, the CEO of Nortel, asked me to take over the IT portfolio for North America, it was a shock to my system.

What do you consider to be important career skills? The ability to bring people, technology, and business thinking together. A lot of my work focused on using business thinking to translate how IT can add value to an organization. But I believe it has to go beyond just adding value. In today's environment, IT should be the strategic lever that organizations use to drive their business. If CEOs cannot understand what technology can do and incorporate it into their strategic thinking, they will fail. There needs to be a focused vision and strategy for information technology in an organization that is tied in with the strategic vision and plan.

Can you describe an example of how you have used IT to improve business operations? I was the chief information officer at Nortel for four years during which I saw Nortel through Y2K. I didn't have the technical background to be the CIO of a company like Nortel. I was lucky enough to have very strong technical people who were able to open their minds to the fact that there was a business that they were servicing. I counted on their expertise in technology, while I was someone who understood and operated in the business and could determine if we were getting a return on our investments in IT. Combining both of these perspectives helped us make the right decisions and have a positive impact on the company.

How do you use IT? I still maintain a home office in both of my homes in Mississauga and Whistler. I do most of my business using high-speed Internet, voice communications, and VoIP. Without the IT capability available today, I would not have been able to perform the roles that I have, certainly not on a global scale. Information technology is a strategic competitive weapon for forward-thinking companies and nations.

Have you got any on-the-job advice for students seeking a career in IT or business? The people side of business is very important: managing others, understanding people and their motivations, and how to work with people to get the best out of them. The relationships you have with people and your network are very important. When you need to find out something, when you need to get help, when you need to make a proposal, you really fall back on that network. Start building a network now and maintain that network throughout your career. It is the most powerful tool you have to help you move forward as an individual and as a business person.

Keith's early career experiences in supply chain management helped him to learn the primary activities of businesses. Later, in his career as a CIO, he used this experience to apply IT to create business value and manage business risk. In this chapter, we explore the value chain and discuss how organizations use IT strategically to create business value and manage risk.

Recall that a business or organization is made up of one or more people and creates products or provides services to earn a profit or satisfy a societal or client need. It does so through core processes it designs and manages that add value. Sounds easy enough, right? Not necessarily. To become successful, businesses must manage many activities. Consider WestJet, a national airline. WestJet provides a service by flying its customers to and from various destinations. To do this productively, WestJet must purchase or lease aircraft; hire pilots, mechanics, flight attendants, and other employees; safely procure, store, and dispense the fuel for its aircraft; and locate and secure capital for current and future operations. And these are just some of the many different resources and processes that WestJet must manage to create business value that customers ultimately pay for by flying WestJet. Putting all of these processes together comprises something called the *value chain*. In this chapter we discuss the value chain and how IT is used to support it.

THE VALUE CHAIN

There are many ways to understand what businesses do to create value. Michael Porter provides one useful way, known as the value chain. In this section, we review all the components of the value chain, and then discuss how businesses use IT, and particularly enterprise systems, to optimize it.

Building an Understanding of the Value Chain

The **value chain** is a connected series of activities, each of which adds value or supports the addition of value to the firm's goods or services.[1]

We begin our exploration of the value chain with the five core components of a typical value chain as shown in Figure 4.1. *Inbound logistics* include the receiving, warehousing, and inventory control of raw materials required to create a product or service. *Operations* are the value-creating and often proprietary activities that transform the raw inputs into the final product. *Outbound logistics* are the activities required to get the finished product to the customer, including packaging, warehousing, and order fulfillment. *Marketing and sales* are all activities associated with getting buyers to purchase the product, including working with distributors, retailers or online channels, marketing, advertising, and pricing. *Service activities* are those that maintain and enhance the product's value, including customer support, repair services, and warranty and recall.

FIGURE 4.1 An organizational value chain is a connected series of processes, each of which adds value, or supports the addition of value, to the firm's goods or services.

---

1. M. E. Porter, "How Competitive Forces Shape Strategy," *Harvard Business Review*, 1979, pp. 137–145.

Obviously, while these five components are more often identified with traditional manufacturing businesses (as shown in Figure 4.1), they can also be associated with IT-enabled businesses such as software companies. These firms use the same five components to hire programmers and other technical specialists, manage the project to create the software product, package and ship the software to the customer, create sales documentation, and provide after-sales technical support.

The value chain components can be further classified into primary and secondary activities. We normally think of *primary activities* as those directly related to the production and distribution of the organization's products and services. These are the activities that create business value for the organization and its customers. Most organizations also require additional *support activities*. Support activities are value chain activities that an organization conducts to support the creation of business value by the primary activities. In his original work, Porter identified four critical support activities:

1. firm infrastructure (which we will call administration)
2. technology development
3. human resource (HR) management
4. procurement

For example, HR management and policy directly affect the people who perform the work that creates business value. HR manages the compensation and benefits that reward employees for their work (e.g., pay, bonuses, and retirement plans). More motivated employees often create more business value. So even though employees might be engaged in operational activities (e.g., programming software or calling on possible customers to buy the software), the HR management efforts support them in their value-creating activities.

When you put this all together, you can see that an organization's value chain is the sum of its primary and support activities, working together to create business value for the organization and its customers. As such, the value chain model is yet another way to view the organization as a system, as discussed in Chapter 1 (inputs → processes → outputs).

The value chain is also a useful tool for defining an organization's core processes and the activities and competencies that it can use to gain a sustained competitive advantage over its competitors. And through the intelligent use of IT, a business can increase its competitive advantage by incrementally changing the value-adding activities themselves, or by making it possible to configure the value chain in a new way.

Now that you have a good idea of what a typical value chain is, we will discuss, at a high level, information systems that support business activities. Later in this chapter we look at specific systems that support each component of the value chain.

INFORMATION SYSTEMS THAT SUPPORT BUSINESS ACTIVITIES

This section explores some general information systems that support the value chain. Within these general types there are hundreds of systems, often specific to an organization. The common information systems include:

Information Systems that Support Business Activities | 123

- functional information systems
- workflow management systems
- transaction processing systems
- management information and document management systems
- knowledge management systems
- decision support systems
- supply chain management
- enterprise resource planning

Please keep in mind that this list does not *begin* to cover all of the various information systems that organizations use to support knowledge work and business processes; however, these are some of the most common types of systems that organizations use.

Functional Information Systems

Traditionally, organizations divided their IS along lines that corresponded to their functional departments, such as operations, accounting, and marketing. Referred to as **functional information systems (FIS)**, they focus on the activities of the functional department to improve its efficiency and effectiveness. For example, an accounting information system focuses on automating and informating accounting activities (see Table 4.1 for more detail).

Table 4.1	Some Common Functional IS
System	Description
Accounting IS	• Typically dedicated to the reporting of a firm's financial health • Relies on input from transaction processing system (TPS) since it must record all transaction data • Provides both internal and external reports of a company's financial status
Marketing IS	• Supports marketing research and decision making in developing and distributing products and services • Includes input from TPS, strategic plans and corporate policies, and external sources • Includes marketing research outputs to support the four Ps of marketing: product development, pricing decisions, promotion, and product placement
Human Resources IS	• Supports activities related to managing the organization's employees • Includes input from TPS, strategic plans and corporate policies, and external sources • Supports human resources planning, recruiting, and hiring • Enables administration of salaries, benefits, and training
Financial IS	• Provides financial information to the organization's financial managers • Includes both internal input items—TPS, financial objectives, and project needs—and external input items—competitor and environmental data • Generates both internal and external audits, supports management of funds
Manufacturing IS	• Supports manufacturing processes and activities • Includes input from TPS, strategic plans and corporate policies, and external sources • Uses outputs primarily for controlling processes: design and engineering, control of inventory, resource planning, and computer-aided manufacturing

FIS remain popular today. However, many companies now find that they need to integrate these systems with the rest of their organization by using middleware (software that links separate systems; see Chapter 2) or turning to large enterprise systems, such as enterprise resource planning (ERP), that are integrated already. Functional information systems continue to be used in specialized areas like medicine (e.g., a patient information system) or for a specific purpose (e.g., CAD/CAM for design). You are probably very familiar with an FIS at your university or college: the registration system.

Workflow Management Systems

A **workflow** represents the steps, organizational resources, input and output data, and tools needed to complete a business process. By focusing on a business process from beginning to end, a **workflow management system (WMS)** (also referred to as *business process management* or *BPM*) supports activities that several departments of the organization may carry out.

A WMS typically provides tools for modelling the steps of the process. The model shows the flow of work, along with the state of components. For example, Figure 4.2 shows an example of workflow for a typical online product order. Information and documentation are needed and generated at each step in the workflow. However, workflow management is not just about how the documents and information flow through the process. A computer program manages the process itself, such as assigning the work, monitoring work progress, and getting the required approvals.

A WMS often leads to several benefits. First, less misplaced or stalled work often occurs, which improves efficiency and quality. Second, managers can focus more time on business decisions rather than on tracking work. Third, because

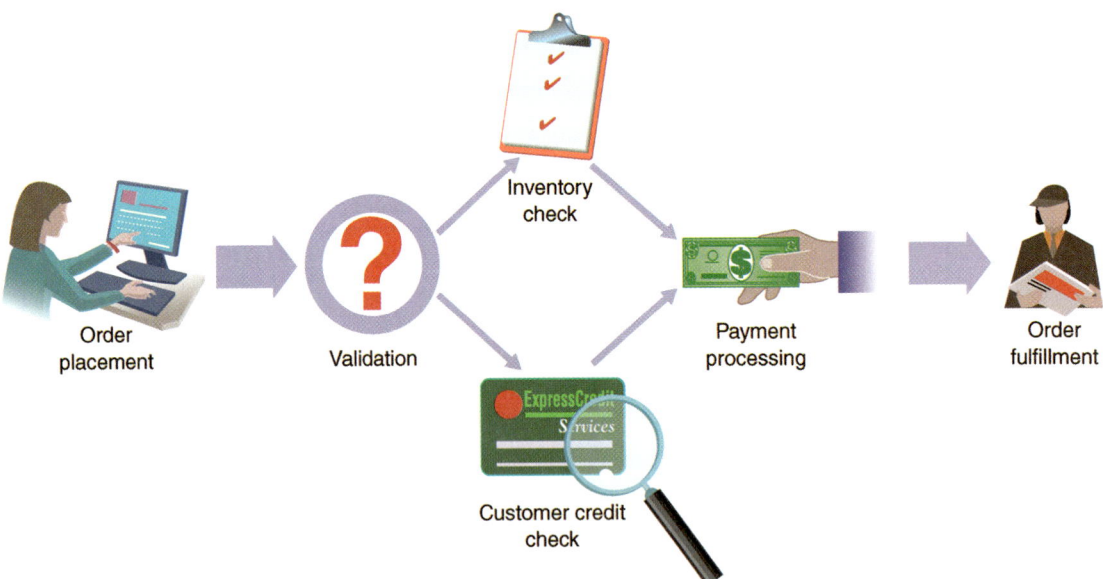

FIGURE 4.2 In a workflow management system (WMS), each step requires and generates information and documentation.

developing a WMS requires formal documentation of all procedures, more analysis and tighter control of the processes often result. This, in turn, leads to better work assignments—the best person for the job—and produces more efficient scheduling.

Workflow systems include tools and features that allow users to work with and manage the processes and the system itself. Administration and modelling tools provide a means for users to create and work with workflow models and definitions. Finally, particular workflow systems will generally not have all of the capabilities needed to support the business rules of the organization. A *business rule* is a statement that defines or constrains some aspect of the business. It is intended to assert business structure or to control or influence the behaviour of the business.[2] For example, a business may decide that it will only accept cash payment. To support business-specific business rules, the system can directly activate plug-in or custom-tailored tools to add capabilities to the system, and the workflow client application manages the interactions between the system and added applications.

Transaction Processing Systems

Business transactions are critical to the core activities of an organization. Without transactions there are no sales, and without sales there is no business! For this reason, we look at transactions and transaction processing systems in depth.

A **transaction** is an exchange of goods or services (value) between two or more parties (businesses, individuals, or a combination of the two) that creates a relationship between the parties. For example, a customer using a bank's ATM to withdraw money is a transaction between the customer and the bank. When you download software you have purchased online, you have completed a transaction.

A customer using an ATM is a transaction between an individual (the customer) and an organization (the bank providing ATM service).

Businesses must record, act on, complete, and report transactions in an accurate and timely manner. This is where transaction processing systems play a critical role. **Transaction processing systems (TPS)** enable transaction activities and capture the key data created by the transaction.

From a technical standpoint, a transaction is a unit of work that has the following characteristics:

- *Atomicity*—A transaction must be unequivocally completed. If an error causes the transaction to fail, then the entire transaction to that point should be undone and the data reset to its previous state (e.g., when a sale is voided or reversed).
- *Consistency*—All unchanging properties of data must be preserved. This means that the data captured by the transaction must fit within the rules of data storage.
- *Isolation*—Each transaction should execute independently of other transactions that may occur at the same time on the system.
- *Durability*—The characteristics of a completed transaction should be permanent.

These characteristics, together known as ACID, allow organizations to create systems that can handle large numbers of simultaneous transactions. Defining

---
2. http://en.wikipedia.org/wiki/Business_rule

transactions that have the ACID properties also helps organizations ensure that the activities of any one transaction all succeed or fail as a group. Why is this important? Think about how a bank relies on its ATM transactions. Say a customer decides to transfer $100 from his savings to his chequing account. This account-transfer transaction has two simple activities: (1) subtract $100 from the savings account, and (2) add $100 to the chequing account. Imagine the problems that would occur if the first activity succeeds but the second one fails. Now think about this problem multiplied by the bank's daily ATM transactions. You can see why a TPS must handle both of these activities together as a single transaction.

Figure 4.3 shows how a TPS brings together the common components of IT—data storage, data processing, data capture, and software. Processing in a TPS must control the flow of both the activities and data involved in the transaction. Depending on the configuration of the system and the network connections, the processing power that handles the transaction can include PCs, servers, and/or mainframes. TPS software applications must incorporate the logic for controlling and enabling the transaction, the business rules of the organization that apply to the transaction, and necessary error-handling logic.

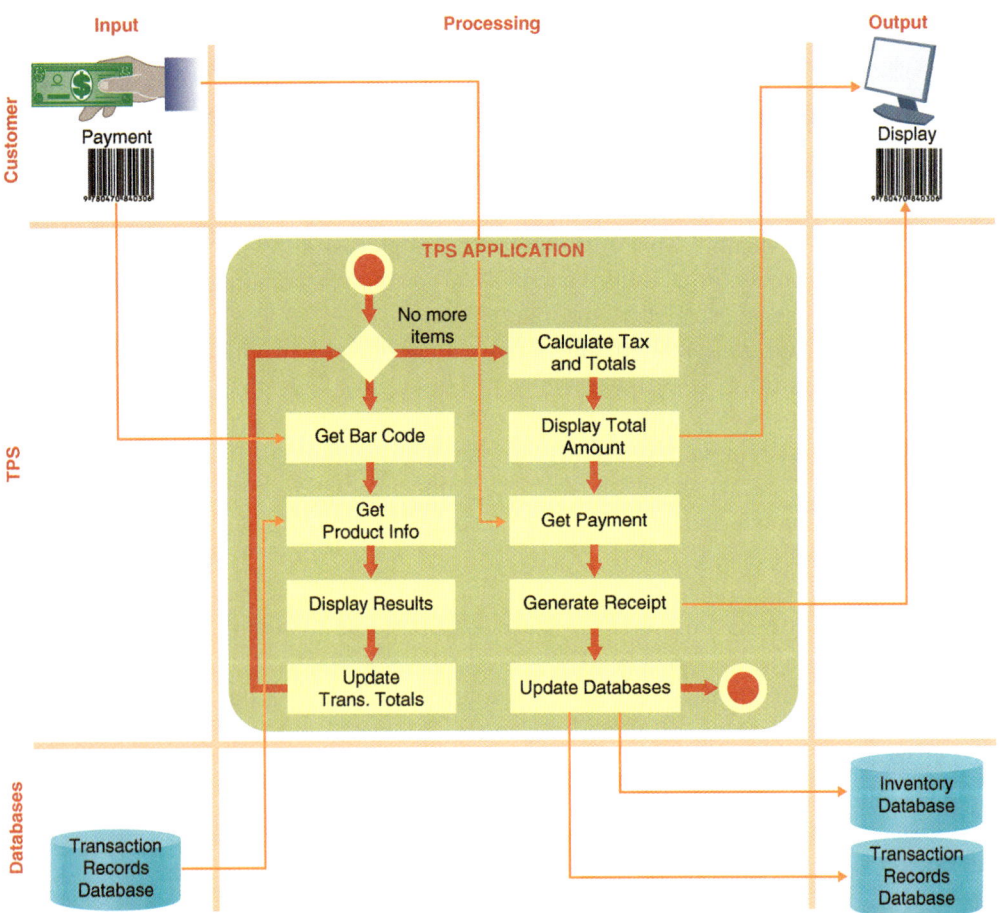

FIGURE 4.3 An automated POS-TPS process brings together the common components of IT—data storage, data processing, data capture, and software—as it creates value for the organization.

Data storage, most often in the form of one or more databases, is very important as a source of input data and as storage for the captured data of a TPS. For example, most retail stores use a point-of-sale (POS) system to capture and store much of the data about their products. A bar code value, assigned as an ID for each product, serves as the primary key for accessing this data, such as the product name and price. Finally, a TPS uses network technologies to connect both its components as well as its system to the organization. The databases that the TPS accesses are usually stored on special database network servers. An important aspect of networks in a TPS is how the company uses the networks to update the central data stores of the organization with the new transaction data.

Management Information and Document Management Systems

In the early days of information systems, businesses typically developed systems known as **management information systems (MIS)** specifically to meet the need of storing processed transaction data as reports for managers. These early systems were often rudimentary and produced large volumes of information because of their limited ability to sort and process data to specific user needs. MIS typically generate three types of reports:

1. *Periodic reports,* such as a company's annual financial statements or monthly sales reports, which are updated and generated after a specific time period has passed.
2. *Exception reports,* to monitor when, and perhaps why, exceptions occur of key values, defined as critical to the operation.
3. *Demand reports,* generated based on user requests. Many systems also include a library of such reports from which a user could choose.

As organizations and systems capability both progressed, many businesses began to create specific systems to serve specific needs. One example is **executive information systems (EIS)** designed to provide summary information about business performance to those making higher-level strategic decisions. This often involved creating "views" of data about business trends that gave rise to graphical displays of information.

Similarly, organizations began to recognize data management needs that revolved around business documents (as distinct from business information). These systems are known as **document management systems (DMS)**. A DMS enters, tracks, routes, and processes the many documents used in an organization, including but not limited to the three types of reports just discussed. A DMS can create the documents electronically or convert them to electronic form using *imaging technology.* Imaging technology includes scanners like those discussed in Chapter 2, as well as special software that can recognize printed characters and convert them to specific data formats to work with application software.

Businesses can use DMS to support workflow systems by managing the storage and routing of documents. They can also use DMS to maintain large archives of forms and documents in a much more efficient and flexible manner than with traditional paper documents.

Knowledge Management Systems

Of the three informational resources—data, information, and knowledge—knowledge is the most difficult to store and share. Why? First, consider that organizations rely on two types of knowledge: explicit knowledge and tacit knowledge. *Explicit knowledge* includes anything that can be written down, stored, and codified (e.g., business plans, patents and trademarks, and market research). On the other hand, *tacit knowledge* includes the know-how that people have through learning and experience, which is difficult to write down and share. Tacit knowledge, while important to an organization, represents a major challenge in that organization's **knowledge management (KM)**; that is, how the company recognizes, generates, manages, and shares knowledge.

To support tacit knowledge, knowledge management systems often rely on collaborative software, which supports teamwork with technologies that enable communication and sharing of data and information. This software category, also known as **groupware**, can be a simple communication tool like email, or it can be more complex, providing shared workspaces to store common files and tools for conferencing and meeting support. Table 4.2 summarizes groupware is divided into three levels of support.

The benefits of knowledge management are often difficult to calculate. Some benefits directly increase revenue or reduce costs, while others do not. To derive the most benefits from knowledge management, clear business goals must drive the process for sharing relevant knowledge throughout the organization. For example, an effective KM program can allow business professionals to streamline the value chain. This in turn will improve customer service and boost revenues as the organization gets products and services out to the market faster. Further, an effective KM program can increase employee morale. Employees often feel greater appreciation when organizations recognize the value and use of their knowledge. They are then often more eager to share their information and ideas, which can foster innovation throughout the organizations.

Table 4.2	Collaborative Software Categories
Communication tools	• Facilitate the sharing of information and data with tools that enable people to send messages, documents, files, and data between each other (e.g., email, text messaging, voice mail, and Web publishing)
Conferencing tools	• Provide a more interactive facility for the sharing of information • At a minimum, can provide real-time text discussions and a common "whiteboard" that each participant can edit • Can also enable voice and/or video using special equipment or computer networks • Some organizations build special facilities for conferencing supported by these tools
Collaborative management tools	• Can help to manage and facilitate the activities of a team (e.g., electronic calendars for scheduling events and automatically notifying participants) • Shared workspaces can be provided to store and share work products that group members may modify • May overlap with project management systems to keep the group aware of a project's status

Decision Support Systems

Decision support systems (DSS) help businesses use communications technologies, knowledge, and models to organize and access data to perform decision-making activities. There are five types of DSS, shown in Table 4.3, each of which has a specific decision-making focus. Although businesses rely on all these types of DSS, model-driven DSS continue to make the most significant contribution to decision making.

Model-driven DSS provide tools that enable analysts to create and work with models, including the following:

- *Financial models*—use financial mathematical models and financial data to support financial decision making
- *Statistical models*—use statistics and probability to describe or forecast possible scenarios
- *Optimization models*—incorporate relatively certain data into a mathematical model of a situation; solving the model helps to find the "best" solution
- *Simulation modelling*—a technique for conducting experiments that test possible outcomes resulting from a quantitative model of a system

Model-driven DSS use data and parameters to help decision makers analyze a situation, but they are not usually data-intensive. Instead, these systems often include smaller databases, with data that may be culled from the larger data stores of the organization. They often incorporate innovative user interfaces that provide analysts with graphical views of their models. Organizations often combine model-driven DSS with other types of DSS to form hybrid systems.

Table 4.3 Types of DSS

Type of DSS	Description	Examples
Communications-driven DSS	Focuses on communications, collaboration, and shared decision making	Conferencing tools; online bulletin boards and chat facilities; email; and meeting support applications
Data-driven DSS	Emphasizes access to and manipulation of internal company data and sometimes external data	Executive information systems (EIS); geographic information systems (GIS); and OLAP-enabled data warehouses
Document-driven DSS	Focuses on retrieval and management of unstructured documents	Document management systems (DMS); search services; and tools for working with oral, written, and video documents
Knowledge-driven DSS	Provides special problem-solving tools that help decision making by suggesting or recommending actions to users	Expert systems (ES); artificial intelligence applications; and data mining tools
Model-driven DSS	Emphasizes access to and manipulation of a model	Financial, statistical, optimization, and simulation models

Quick Test

1. True or False. More value is created by keeping each component of the value chain separate, focusing only on its contribution to business value.

2. A _____ allows the data from a transaction to be processed and passed on immediately to organizational data storage.
   a. decision support system (DSS)
   b. functional information system (FIS)
   c. workflow management system (WMS)
   d. transaction processing system (TPS)

3. _____ are computer systems that support teamwork, communication, and collaboration.
   a. Decision support systems
   b. Groupware
   c. Transaction processing systems
   d. Workflow management systems

Answers: 1. False; 2. d; 3. b

Supply Chain Management

Every business has a supply chain. A **supply chain** is a system of organizations, people, technology, activities, information, and resources involved in moving a product or service from supplier to customer. Supply chain activities transform natural resources, raw materials, and components into a finished product that is delivered to the end customer. In sophisticated supply chain systems, used products may re-enter the supply chain at any point where residual value is recyclable.[3]

An organization's supply chain includes several components of its value chain, as well as links into the value chain of other organizations. Consider the beverage you may drink at the end of exam week. The beverage producer's supply chain includes getting the materials to manufacture the drink. The production of those materials is the end of another organization's supply chain, but the beginning of the beverage producer's. Similarly, the end of the beverage producer's supply chain is the start of the restaurant or bar's supply chain.

To manage the supply chain, businesses engage in **supply chain management (SCM)**. SCM manages materials, information, and finances as they move from supplier to manufacturer to wholesaler to retailer to consumer. A more robust definition is provided by the Council of Supply Chain Management Professionals (CSCMP):

> *Supply chain management encompasses the planning and management of all activities involved in sourcing and procurement, conversion, and all logistics management activities. Importantly, it also includes coordination and collaboration with channel partners, which can be suppliers,*

---
3. Anna Nagurney, *Supply Chain Network Economics: Dynamics of Prices, Flows, and Profits*. Edward Elgar Publishing, 2006.

Information Systems that Support Business Activities | 131

intermediaries, third party service providers, and customers. In essence, supply chain management integrates supply and demand management within and across companies.[4]

Supply chain management systems seek to optimize the supply chain to create business value and competitive advantage. If one organization can produce and distribute its products faster and better than another, it will certainly have the best business results (increased profit and reduced cost).

Typical modules in any supply chain management software system include:

- *Materials management*—the procurement, storage, and use of raw materials to be used in the end product; may connect externally to supplier supply chain systems
- *Inventory management*—finished goods inventory
- *Order management*—orders by customers, distributions, retail outlets
- *Logistics management*—plans for shipping the product and tracking it from origin to destination and related shipping documentation

In addition to the above, supply chain management systems often include various levels of reporting, forecasting tools, and asset management.

Because supply chain management encompasses so much of the value chain, it is often the cornerstone and starting point of enterprise resource planning (ERP) system implementations, which are discussed next.

> **WHAT DO YOU THINK?**
>
> It is easy to see how a supply chain works in a manufacturing or retailing business, but what about a services business such as an accounting firm, a financial planning business, or an IT consultancy? Consider the following questions when thinking about the supply chain for a services business:
>
> 1: What would the supply chain look like for an accounting firm? Would it have the same primary and support activities as a manufacturing business? How might they differ?
> 2: What would the "materials" or other inputs be for an accounting firm?
> 3: How do you think services firms manage knowledge and knowledge-based products to create business value for their clients?

Enterprise Resource Planning

One way to integrate the departments and functions across an organization is to use **enterprise resource planning (ERP)** software. With ERP, a company runs all of its applications from a single database. Each functional unit of a company, such as finance, marketing, and sales, still uses its own supporting enterprise software applications, but ERP links these applications and ensures their compatibility via common data storage. For example, imagine that a customer contacts a company's

---
4. http://cscmp.org/aboutcscmp/definitions.asp. Retrieved February 10, 2010.

salesperson to place an order. Accessing the ERP sales module, the salesperson obtains all the necessary information, such as the customer's contact and billing data, product data, and the product's forecasted availability. The salesperson enters the order data in the ERP sales module, which stores the data in a central database that everyone in the company and other ERP modules can access. This update creates an automatic trigger for all of the other required processes in the value chain related to filling this order. That is, the sales data are updated and the product is taken out of inventory, the financial data are updated to reflect an accounts receivable entry and a customer invoice is generated, the paperwork required for logistics is created (e.g., packing slip), and if the salesperson is working on commission, her commission is updated with the value of the sale she just processed. Further, any of the company's employees can quickly obtain the status of the order at any time by accessing the ERP system. All of these actions are undertaken by the ERP system without any additional human intervention.

Canada Post improved organizational efficiency and effectiveness by deploying an ERP system. This system created value by providing visibility throughout its delivery network (inbound logistics, operations, outbound logistics), enabling new business (sales), and reducing costs through process standardization (administration). Canada Post's ERP demonstrates that the application of IS to its value chain's primary and support activities can support multiple important business processes and can create value for a business.[5]

As this example illustrates, a benefit of an ERP system is to streamline business processes. Companies want to get orders to customers faster and at less cost, and also receive sales revenue quicker. ERP can support all areas of the value chain, both primary and supporting processes, helping to achieve efficiencies not possible with independent systems.

However, the primary disadvantage of ERP is that, like the organizations that they support, the ERP system can become incredibly complex and difficult to manage as it grows. ERP systems need to be customized for the specific business processes and rules that it is supporting. Sometimes this customization is extensive and businesses come to rely on ERP vendors and service providers, such as SAP, Oracle, and IBM, to develop and maintain their ERP installation. These arrangements require close relationships between the client and the service provider. It is important that businesses not become over-dependent on service providers and end up paying expensive fees for support. In these situations, businesses can find themselves losing the cost savings they have achieved through efficiency.

At a high level, ERP systems are called enterprise-wide systems and are used by the entire enterprise through a centralized database and coordinated software modules (applications or sets of applications) that are tightly integrated with one another. Integration between the parts of the value chain represents another very important application of IT: optimizing information flow between and across activities. This allows IT to have an impact throughout the entire value chain.

In the next section we discuss the individual components of the value chain and the enterprise systems that support each component.

---

5. Adapted from http://www.sap.com/solutions/business-suite/scm/pdf/CS_canada_post.pdf. Retrieved February 10, 2010.

Enterprise Systems that Support the Value Chain

Some IT systems are specific to particular parts of the value chain or specific organizational functions. For example, logistics management systems may be specifically designed to support inbound logistics, accounting systems might only serve the needs of that department, and software development tools are generally used by IT in the technology development process. On the other hand, some systems, such as ERP, are used across all parts of the value chain.

The sample systems shown in Figure 4.4 are often known as enterprise systems. **Enterprise systems** are large-scale applications that support business units or functions; they are another way that an organization might apply IT to its value chain. The specific systems listed in this figure are discussed in detail later in this section. By no means does Figure 4.4 provide an exhaustive list of enterprise systems. Further, note that some of the systems listed in the figure may support more than one activity.

To understand the impact of enterprise systems on the value chain, let's examine the activities within each component of the value chain and the enterprise systems that support these activities.

Inbound Logistics The inbound logistics component of the value chain includes activities such as raw material procurement and warehousing. In detail, this involves sourcing and ordering materials from suppliers, keeping track of expected arrival

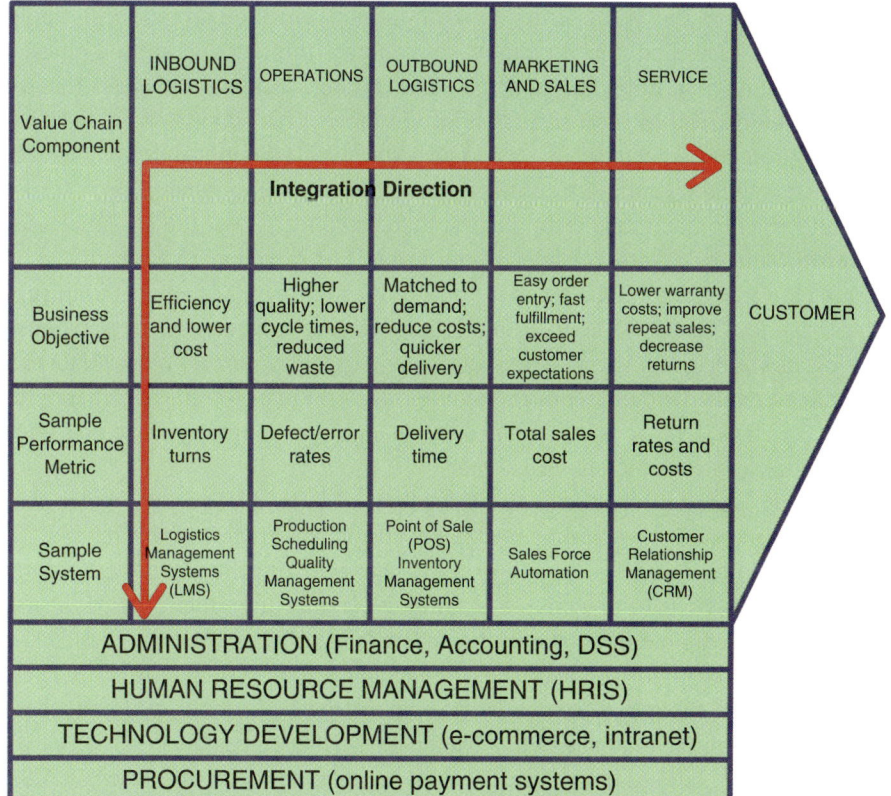

FIGURE 4.4 IT supports the value chain both horizontally and vertically, including some common applications in each component. Performance metrics are associated with the value chain component, business objective, and the sample systems that support the value chain components.

dates of materials, receiving and checking the materials upon arrival, approving the packing slip/bill and authorizing payment, distributing the materials to the correct location, storing the materials, and monitoring supply levels. When the operation is ready for the materials, they must be located and transported to the correct location for use in the operations process.

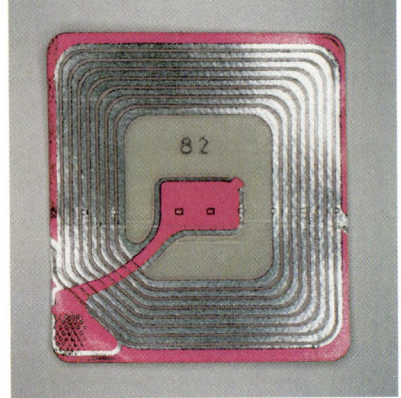

An RFID tag can be invaluable for organizations to keep track of inventory.

One example of a specific technology that is becoming critical to inbound logistics is *radio frequency identification (RFID)*. RFID uses radio waves to automatically identify objects and transmit this information to an IT system. The most common type of RFID stores a serial number on a microchip that is attached to an antenna. The antenna enables the chip to transmit the identification number to a reader. The reader converts the analog radio waves from the RFID tag into digital information. The ID number can then be matched against data stored in a database to obtain information, such as a product's name and price. This kind of technology can greatly assist with tracking inventory, picking orders, and performing inventory counts for audits—just a few examples of its value.

Because RFID tags are small and cheap, they may soon replace bar code technology for many applications. One advantage of RFID over bar codes is that it does not require "line-of-sight" scanning. For a bar code, the scanner uses a laser to read a printed label. To do this, the scanner must have an unobstructed view of the label. Have you ever used a self check-out counter at the grocery store? Did you ever try to scan an item and the bar code just would not be read? Frustrating! Since radio waves can pass through and around objects, a reader can read an RFID tag as long as it is in range. Another benefit is that an RFID tag can be read as soon as a tag is within range. This eliminates the need for a user to present the tag to the reader. Many expect RFID identification to take over because it is quicker and more accurate than other forms of product ID.

But, as with many new technologies, there is concern over the potential uses of RFID. Walmart, a known leader in the use of IS for competitive advantage, is pushing the adoption of RFID by its suppliers. By requiring that products from suppliers have RFID tags, Walmart is able to increase the efficiency of its warehouse and logistics processes. For suppliers, however, especially smaller ones, RFID can be costly to implement and requires them to transform many of their business processes. But since Walmart has mandated the change, these suppliers have no choice but to follow or lose a lucrative customer.

Another issue to consider is that advocates of individual privacy worry that RFID could allow for the real-time tracking of customers. Privacy advocates caution that this could lead to abuses by RFID users who seek to collect data without the consumers' knowledge. For example, a clothing manufacturer might scan a theatre to measure the number of people in the audience wearing a particular brand. The data may then be used to make decisions about product promotions. While this may be innocent enough, the potential for abuse is there.[6] As far as we know, there is not yet an example of abuse of this technology, but it is possible.

RFID or bar code scanning is part of most *logistics management systems (LMS)*. These systems track materials and other assets upon arrival into the warehouse and

---

[6]. David H. Williams, "The strategic implications of Wal-Mart's RFID mandate," *Directions Magazine*, July 29, 2004. http://www.directionsmag.com/article.php?article_id=629&trv=1. Retrieved January 6, 2007.

inventory. LMS are typically highly customized as they need to match the specific organization's business rules and requirements. More general aspects of LMS include transportation management and warehousing.

Operations All of the activities required to create a product or service and make it available to the marketplace are contained in the operations component of the value chain. If you are a manufacturing company, this is where you manufacture the product; if you are a services company, you create and deliver the service. Operations tend to be unique to each organization and tend to have proprietary practices that contribute to competitive advantage. Both supply chain management and enterprise resource planning systems are deployed in the operations of a company to monitor work in progress and the efficiency of the operations processes. Other industry-specific IT is deployed here, such as CAD/CAM (computer aided design/computer aided manufacturing) software that assists in the design and manufacture of products by creating engineering documents and 3D design images. It is quite likely that the clothing that you are wearing was designed using CAD/CAM.

Another common enterprise system used in the operations component of the value chain is production scheduling tools. These automated tools optimize the production machinery and availability of staff to run the machinery. Imagine the operations of Campbell's Soup, for example. It likely uses the same machinery to produce both tomato and mushroom soups. In between making each of these soups, the machinery would need to be cleaned (you don't want mushrooms in your tomato soup!) and new materials delivered to the production area. This takes a specified length of downtime that must be taken into account in production schedules. There might also be scheduled maintenance required on the equipment from time to time. In addition, it is possible that some staff may only work on tomato soup or mushroom soup, and they need to be scheduled accordingly. All of this must be managed so that production meets demand and sales are optimized.

Another critical function in manufacturing businesses is quality management. Quality management systems monitor and control the quality of the products being produced. In our soup example, the quality control system might monitor the temperature at which the soup is cooked. It may specify when and how many taste tests are required. The quality system may also govern any time constraints around canning the soup. If the quality control rules are not followed, defects may occur. Of course, in the case of a food manufacturer or drug manufacturer (think of the recent Listeria outbreak caused by contaminated Maple Leaf Foods' products, for example), the consequences of not following a strict regime of quality control could result in the product causing illness or death. In this case, the company is legally liable and that could result in financial losses, either from reduced sales or law suits.

What about services businesses? Do you remember the last time you stayed in a hotel? Chances are it used a reservations system to manage your booking and assign you a room. Perhaps that system included items like special requests that needed to be booked in advance or specific room requests. These are examples of operations systems that use IT to improve service delivery.

Outbound Logistics Outbound logistics involves the warehousing of finished goods and the distribution of those goods to customers. Customers may be distributors, wholesalers, retailers, or direct customers. As with inbound logistics, logistics management systems and RFID are used in outbound logistics also. *Transportation management systems (TMS)* can be exceptionally important: a lot of time, effort, and cost have been invested in the finished product, and it is important that it ends up in market how and when it is intended to. Imagine Valentine's chocolates arriving in store on February 15!

Enterprise systems supporting the outbound logistics component of the value chain include systems that get products into the hands of consumers. These include transaction processing systems (TPS), which we discussed in detail earlier in this chapter. One extremely popular type of TPS is the point of sale (POS) system. The POS system conducts the transaction between the organization and the customer at the location of the sale. This is often at a check-out counter in the case of a grocery or clothing store, and sometimes even at your table in a restaurant. The shopping cart function of an e-commerce website can also be considered a type of POS. In recent years, a lot of effort has been made to put POS in the hands of customers themselves. Self check-outs, chip technology in credit and debit cards, and mobile commerce are all moves in this direction.

Fulfillment systems are also important outbound logistics systems. These come into play when you order something online or at a retail store, such as furniture. Stock must be checked and released to the order, and the order must picked, packaged, and processed to be delivered to the customer.

As transactions take place and goods transfer to the hands of customers, inventory must be updated. *Inventory management systems (IMS)* constantly monitor the supply of finished goods to ensure that enough supply is on hand to meet demand. Of course, this may involve communicating with operations systems to request that more of certain products be made! IMS help enable the concept of just-in-time (JIT) inventory, which optimizes the manufacturing process (making just enough of something just when it is needed) and ensures that excess inventory does not need to be managed and stored.

Enterprise systems in the area of inventory management have enabled organizations to allow suppliers themselves to manage the inventory on store shelves. Have you ever been in a store and seen a representative from Frito-Lay or Pepsi re-stocking the shelves rather than a store employee? Sales of goods from the POS system are transmitted directly to these suppliers, who then monitor inventory levels and determine when the shelves need re-stocking.

Marketing and Sales Marketing and sales is a critical component in the value chain. The marketing and sales area investigates what customers need and determines the products and services that will meet those needs. Marketing and sales are information-intense activities that rely on enterprise systems to help provide and organize this data. It is essential that companies closely monitor existing sales for trend identification and for input into sales forecasts. Do products need adjusting, or do products need to be discontinued entirely? Much of the data and sales analysis done by marketing and sales is fed back into the other primary activities of the value chain.

You may have heard the term "sales force automation." This term is used for popular enterprise systems that support sales forecasting, contact management, order management, and lead tracking. All of these are critical activities of the sales team. Of late, sales force automation activities have been encompassed in customer relationship management (CRM) systems, which we discuss in the next section.

Service Once a product or service is in the hands of a customer, the service component of the value chain starts. By far the most popular enterprise system supporting this part of the value chain is the **customer relationship management (CRM)** system. CRM systems provide organizations with the tools to service customers better through knowing their past purchases, their purchasing patterns, and even what their future needs may be. Have you ever been shopping online and noticed an area that said something like "Other customers who bought a blue shirt also bought a blue skirt"? This is a CRM system at work, and this action is called *up-selling*. While the CRM system enables servicing a need a customer has about a past purchase, it may also provide information to encourage the customer to make a new purchase. This not only occurs on the Web. A very common installation of CRM systems is in call centres. CRM systems help route customer calls to the most appropriate agent to help them. When the call is answered the agent has all of the customer's information, including past purchase history, and the system may even suggest potential purchases for the agent to offer the customer. CRM systems not only enable companies to be more efficient in servicing customers, they can also increase revenue through up-selling and increased customer satisfaction.

Administration and Finance Systems Administration is an important supporting activity in the value chain, but it is usually seen as being too expensive to perform manually and too costly without directly contributing to the primary activities that generate value in an organization. Because of this, several enterprise systems are aimed at automating and optimizing administrative processes in the hope of reducing costs and ensuring these processes are efficient.

Administrative activities include functions related to finance, accounting, payroll, and legal, as well as activities like knowledge management and decision making, discussed earlier in this chapter. In many businesses, administration may primarily be known as billing or accounting, but it is just as important as actually providing the product or service; without these activities, customers would not be properly invoiced or pay their bills. Think about your mobile phone bill. As you make calls, send texts, and use the Internet on your mobile device, your telecommunications provider is tracking your billable actions. It would be tedious to have to do this manually, so they automate this task and link it directly to your individual mobile phone number and billing account. As a result, they are able to bill you properly at the end of the month—a good thing! This bill is then sent to you and a record of this receivable is added to the company's accounts receivable ledger where it will stay until you make payment.

However, if your provider has good IT systems linked to its value chain, it will also know when you have stepped out of your standard billing package and therefore add a billable event to your bill. Or it may be able to see changes in usage patterns and call you to see if everything is all right or to suggest another kind of plan. If you are not on a pay-as-you-go plan, the provider can also control the volume of calls it allows on credit before calling for additional security or payment terms.

Other administration systems inside an organization handle accounts receivable and payments from customers, generate cheques for accounts payable to others, calculate taxes collected and payable to the government (HST, GST, and PST for instance), and handle the general ledger and account balancing to ensure reliable financial statements are available to management. Other systems (often referred to as treasury management or cash management systems) track cash assets, execute investment and asset management functions, and perform many other similar tasks required to legally operate a company in most places. Often these systems are linked to online banking systems to help a large company reconcile its accounts to its cash balances and to manage its cash flow.

Human Resources If you have ever been an employee of an organization, you have been involved in the human resources component of the value chain. Typically, human resources is responsible for recruiting and hiring staff, and managing staff compensation and training. Even the smallest of companies must manage basic human resources processes like hiring and interact with payroll to ensure that staff members are paid. *Human resource information systems (HRIS)* are enterprise systems that enable this component of the value chain. HRIS systems house information about employees, including contact information, years of service, experience, and training received. All of this information is critical in terms of understanding the costs associated with staffing an organization. HRIS systems should be able to answer critical questions like, What is the monthly expenditure on salaries across the organization? What is the average number of hours per week worked by non-salary staff? What is the company's portion of benefits paid for each employee? Data contained in an HRIS are very important to organizational decision making. Having accurate information that can be accessed quickly is a major benefit of HRIS.

Technology Development The technology development component of the value chain is quite specific to individual organizations. The sole purpose of technology development is to support the value-creating activities of the organization. If the organization is a retail operation, certainly the creation and maintenance of an e-commerce website would be an example of an enterprise system supporting this area of the value chain.

Human resources is an important part of an organization's value chain, since HR directly affects not only who does the work that creates business value, but also how these employees are compensated and rewarded for their efforts.

Most companies now have intranets as a way of supporting value-creating activities. Intranets provide employees with important information about their employer, employee benefits, and administration information such as telephone numbers and locations. Intranets may also act as a knowledge management system, providing information to employees critical to performing their jobs. In addition, organizations may use specific systems or programs to create custom developed enterprise systems to support the business. Development systems, such as integrated development environments (IDE), are discussed in Chapter 7.

Procurement All companies must purchase materials of some kind. As a student you procure books, a laptop, software, pens, paper, etc. to enable you in the business of study. Procurement supports all primary components in the value chain, especially inbound logistics, as the raw materials necessary for the product or service to be produced are acquired in the procurement process. Enterprise systems for procurement are often part of the financial systems of the company. These systems help to manage preferred vendor lists, indicating which vendors supply what items. If suppliers are required to issues bids when a company is purchasing something, procurement systems can assist by tracking and ranking bids. Most often, procurement systems issue purchase orders when it is determined that something needs to be purchased. Depending on the size of the purchase, a procurement system may manage the approval process required for the purchase. Procurement can be a time-consuming and document-intense activity. Because of this, organizations seek to automate many procurement functions using e-commerce and online payment (see Chapter 5).

Of course, any system that a business chooses to install should be linked to its value chain and to a measureable performance metric that helps it manage the impact of that system on its overall success. An appropriate measure (linked to business strategy) can help determine how effective these systems are and, in effect, how effective or efficient the value chain activities become when using them. Some sample performance metrics listed in Figure 4.4 are associated with the value chain component and the sample systems.

As an example, let's say a company invests $2 million in a new quality management system. Once implemented, the company monitors product defect rates and compares them to the rates prior to the quality system implementation. What would you expect to happen? Surprisingly, at first rates may increase. Sometimes the act of monitoring brings previously unknown issues to light. As the underlying issues are resolved, however, defect rates should decrease.

Enterprise systems support every area of the value chain, and an organization may have several. Some of these systems can be bought off-the-shelf; others require a high degree of customization to work with the specific business rules of an organization. Enterprise systems, either bought or built internally, can be very expensive to implement and maintain. Because of this, companies look for more economic ways of fulfilling the need for these systems. Software as a service and application service providers, in some cases, are possible alternatives.

TECHNOLOGY CORE

What makes enterprise software like SCM, ERP, or software as a service (discussed next) possible? In Chapter 2 we discussed network and e-commerce technologies. These are the foundation of enterprise software; without these technologies we could not operate most organizations the way we do today. By using a combination of server-side programming to create the software, payment, and security systems that process and authenticate clients, and Web services for quick delivery of data, enterprise systems are used throughout organizations, with external partners and over the World Wide Web. It is not uncommon for a manager in the U.K. to be monitoring U.S. sales using their integrated ERP system. Again, this is only possible because of both global networks and the associated IT-related technologies that enable e-commerce and web-based systems. Without these advancements in technology, enterprise systems as we know them today would not be possible.

Software as a Service (SaaS)

One way in which companies acquire enterprise systems is by using **software as a service (SaaS)**. That is, they essentially rent software. The availability of SaaS for almost every business application has led many to believe that some organizations will eventually stop buying or building their own software and use this model to ensure they always have up-to-date systems in the areas where automation will help most in their organizations: "I've said it before, I think it's the end of software." This is a quote from Marc Benioff,[7] the flamboyant CEO of *Salesforce.com*. Mr. Benioff's company delivers on-demand customer relationship management (CRM) over the Web. Services at Salesforce.com include sales force automation, customer service and support, and document management, to name just a few.

Salesforce.com is one of the most successful examples of a company that provides on-demand, or **utility computing services**. Instead of the traditional approach of a firm developing its own IS to support its business applications, utility computing provides services hosted on servers, which can be accessed from anywhere. So, software is not really dead, but the concept that a company has to create systems and install the software may be close to extinction. The goal of utility computing is to provide computing resources when and where an organization needs them. Like electricity, clients pay for services only to the extent that they use them. Advantages for clients include:

- Clients no longer have to develop or maintain the applications.
- Applications are available anywhere clients can gain access to the Web.
- Costs are reduced, as clients pay for only what they use and for only as long as they use the service.

These advantages provide powerful motivation for companies to move to an on-demand service provider, but there is a cost. Clients must be willing to

---

7. Alorie Gilbert, "The End of Software," http://news.zdnet.com/2100-3513_22-5281034.html.

relinquish some control over the applications. Further, they must realize that they will probably not be able to gain a competitive advantage by using these applications. Because your organization finds it efficient to use a certain SaaS, it is quite likely competitors will do the same. This implies that these types of services would be best suited for business processes that are common to most organizations, like accounting or human resources.

Does utility computing represent the end of the way we currently think of software? Probably not for all cases, but the $330.5 million revenue and over one million subscribers from about 67,900 companies worldwide that use Salesforce.com seem to provide strong backup for Mr. Benioff's argument.[8]

Do an Internet search on SaaS and you will find a number of different offerings in the market. You may also find SaaS that are offered free of charge. You may already be familiar with Google Docs, as discussed in Chapter 2, which provides word processing, calendar, and spreadsheet software for free. It is very likely you have or know someone who has a Gmail account, Google's free email service. All of these are SaaS offered by Google.

Software as an Outsourced Service Another way software is provided to organizations is through an outsourced service provider known as an **application service provider (ASP)**. An ASP is an online technology company that develops and delivers software tools on the Internet. Payment for the service is often based on fees or subscriptions. If you take a quick look on the Web, you will find many examples of ASPs. For instance, *ASPNews.com* has a directory of more than 2,000 companies that provide ASP services, such as BrightSuite's Web-based groupware, intranet, and team collaboration application. Many of these ASPs are now marketing their wares as SaaS.

Table 4.4 Comparing SaaS and ASP models

	SaaS	ASP
Pricing model	Per use or per user	Monthly, flat fee, or subscription
Ability to customize	Some ability to customize at a price, but major deviations from the core product are discouraged	More ability to customize at a price, as each installation is unique to a customer
Control over the system	None	Some; clients are usually provided administrator tools
Data security and privacy	It may be unknown how data are processed and stored, but data are is likely contained in common databases with other customers of the SaaS	Negotiable; some ASPs will provide a separate database keeping it completely secure and separate from their other customers, at a cost
Security	As the applications are generally available over the Internet, the system is subject to the same vulnerabilities as any Internet application	Option is available to connect to the system over a dedicated connection, which increases security, in addition to accessing over the Internet

8. Reported on the Salesforce.com website on November 17, 2009.

ASPs provide several major advantages that are leading to their increasing popularity. When an organization uses an ASP, an external company builds and operates the system. This means that the organization does not need to acquire its own technical resources or hire staff with technical expertise. Since the ASP is the primary service of the provider, it also bears the burden of keeping it up to date to provide a competitive advantage over other ASPs. Further, as ASPs deliver these services over the Internet, the software is available anytime and anywhere. In addition, any device can use it.

ASPs and SaaS are quite similar offerings, and many ASPs are changing their business model to be more like SaaS. In fact, the terms SaaS and ASP are often used synonymously. Table 4.4 compares SaaS and ASP models.

WHAT DO YOU THINK?

Software as a service is certainly here to stay. Imagine that you are in charge of finding customer relationship management (CRM) software for your small business. Consider the following questions.

1: Are you concerned that your company's customer data are stored outside of your company?
2: What if the software you are renting no longer meets your needs in the future? How will you move from one system to another?
3: Why would a company offer software for free? Should you consider a free CRM system?

Quick Test

1. True or False. Metrics are not necessary when implementing an enterprise system because enterprise systems always improve the efficiency of the value chain.

2. Which of the following is NOT a source of enterprise systems?
   a. ASP
   b. IDE
   c. custom development
   d. SaaS

3. Fill in the blank. Operations and the IT systems that support it tend to be _____ as it is here that proprietary practices are used to gain competitive advantage.

Answers: 1. False; 2. b; 3. unique

STRATEGICALLY FITTING IT TO THE ORGANIZATION

In the previous sections and in Chapter 3, we introduced four views of how a business can derive benefits by applying IT to support the organization and its processes: (1) support of the value chain, (2) automating, (3) informating, and

Table 4.5 Comparing IT Application Views

View	Scope	Benefits	Newspaper Application
Support of value chain	Organization-wide	• Views organization as a system with need for integration of components and activities • Allows a focus on enabling value-adding activities • Helps to fit IT applications and infrastructure to organization	• Use subscription data to forecast demand and to better schedule inbound logistics, production, and outbound activities • Use demographic data for targeted marketing promotions and improved customer service
Automating	Process/transaction	• Allows for cost reduction, efficiency, quality, and consistency	• Use online subscription for newspaper to reduce printing and handling costs of paper-based, mailed subscription forms
Informating	Process/transaction	• Allows for knowledge and learning of core competencies	• Use transaction data to understand subscription process • Collect demographic data during online subscription application and use it to better understand customers
Transforming/competitive advantage	Organization-wide	• Connects automating and informating of processes to organizational strategy	• Develop a unique competency for delivering targeted content to various customer segments as identified by demographic and subscription data

(4) gaining a competitive advantage. These views, summarized in Table 4.5, demonstrate that a business can use IT not only to support current operations, but also to gain long-term or strategic benefits. In addition to listing the scope and benefit of each view, Table 4.5 provides a simple example of applying IT to handle a newspaper subscription transaction.

As you can see from the newspaper example in Table 4.5, the four different views are not mutually exclusive. By using IT to allow new customers to subscribe online, the newspaper company can gain benefits that coincide with all four viewpoints. By focusing on the subscription process itself, it gains greater efficiencies through automation. Through informating, it collects data that may help it further improve the process. The company may use the data it collects when users subscribe to gain a competitive advantage, by using it to support publications targeted at key customers or through some other means. While the process itself may fall within the marketing and sales activity of the value chain model, the company can use the collected data to make decisions about all of its primary activities.

Some would go so far as to believe that companies can gain a unique advantage through an exclusive use or application of IT. This was a widely-held view during the so-called dot-com years of the late 1990s and early 2000s. However, in recent years, some have challenged this view. In his provocative article, "IT Doesn't Matter,"[9] Dr. Nicholas Carr argues that since the core functions of IT—data processing, data storage, and data communications—are available and affordable for anybody, it isn't possible to develop sustained distinctive competencies on IT alone. In other words, if a company can put together an IT system that helps it automate a particular process, then so can its competitors. This is especially true when competitors can simply use the same SaaS. This drives competitive necessity, the need to keep up with competitors to stay in business, rather than competitive advantage. A company can only gain a sustained edge over its competitors by doing things that they can't do.

The IS community continues to debate Dr. Carr's ideas. Dr. Carr maintains that IT is an essential part of the infrastructure of a competitive company, but inconsequential to strategy. Much of the business world agrees with Dr. Carr's view. However, those companies that create and sell IT naturally do not; they note that a sustained competitive advantage has never come from a particular technology itself, but from the intelligent application of IT to support business strategies and leverage distinctive competencies and value chain of an organization.[10] We will not attempt to settle that debate here. Rather, we encourage you to join the debate and continue thinking about the value and potential for competitive advantage offered by IT, and continue to acquire knowledge about how IT can make you a more successful business professional.

Roles of IT Governance and Leadership in Creating Business Value

Recall our earlier discussion of Porter's value chain model, which shows the activities that create business value. Effective IT governance and leadership combine Porter's competitive strategies with the value chain model to help create business value. To see how IT governance and leadership can do this, consider Figure 4.5. The figure includes numbered boxes that correspond to our discussion here.

For example, IT leadership can suggest how a business can integrate technology to reduce or eliminate costs throughout its value chain, until it becomes the lowest-cost producer or retailer (1). From this overall business strategy, IS leadership can develop a specific IT strategy, which enables the business to implement its lowest-cost strategy (2–5). Two possible ways for IT to help reduce costs are to automate a process or to support the **outsourcing** of a process to another location or vendor that can perform the process more efficiently and effectively. This is often

---

9. Nicholas, Carr, "IT Doesn't Matter," *Harvard Business Review*, 81(5), May 2003.

10. E. K. Clemons and M. Row, "Sustaining IT Advantage: The Role of Structural Differences," *Management Information Systems Quarterly*, 15(3), 1991, pp. 275–292; L. M. Hitt and F. Brynjolfsson, "Productivity, Business Profitability, and Consumer Surplus: Three Different Measures of Information Technology Value," *Management Information Systems Quarterly*, 20(2), 1996, pp. 121–112; J. B. Barney, "Firm Resources and Sustained Competitive Advantage," *Journal of Management*, 17(1), 1991, pp. 99–120; and B. Wernerfelt, "A Resource-based View of the Firm," *Strategic Management Journal*, (5), 1984, pp. 171–180.

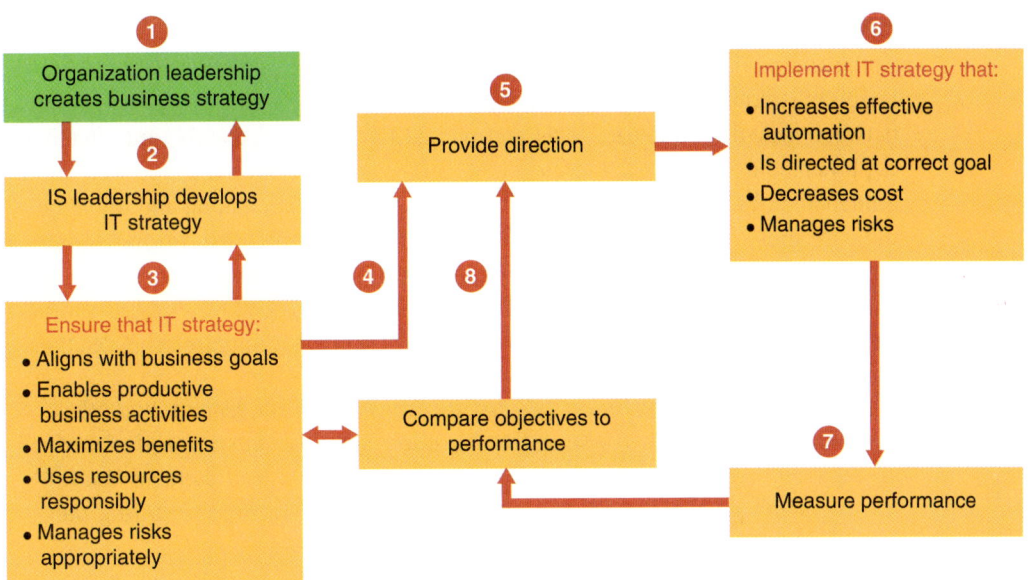

FIGURE 4.5 As this figure shows, effective IT governance and leadership, when combined with Porter's value chain model, can help create business value.
SOURCE: IT Governance Institute®, 2005.

referred to as business process outsourcing (BPO). This could include processes in IT, such as desktop support, help desks, hosting (often called IT outsourcing), or non-core processes in other parts of the business, such as accounting, human resources, or sales. The reduced process cost helps the business offer a lower price for its products or services, thus improving global competitiveness (6). If outsourcing a business process to another country, IT leadership will need to develop a strategy that includes how to support global operations (back to 1). Another way to support the low-cost strategy is to find efficiencies within the value chain. Some businesses do this now by closely integrating business processes and systems with their suppliers to reduce time spent executing value chain activities. Perhaps this means implementing SCM or ERP.

Regardless of whether implementing automation, outsourcing, or optimizing the value chain, the business must measure the performance and total costs of the effort against the unit cost savings for the product or service. This determines if the IT strategy aligns with and meets the needs of the "lowest-cost" business strategy (7–8). If not, the IT leadership must act to bring performance in line with expectations (5). Especially while pursuing a low-cost strategy, a business may not only be trying to create enhanced business value, but simply be trying to stay in business. This suggests some companies may have to constantly improve their use of IT out of sheer competitive necessity.

You will notice in box 6 of Figure 4.5 that IT manages risk. Risk is an essential element of business and no organization, even those in the public or not-for-profit sectors, can eliminate it entirely from their operations. This means that IT has a role to play to both track and manage risk, not only for its own operations but for the whole company in some instances. In the next section we discuss enterprise risk and IT's role in managing risk.

ENTERPRISE RISK MANAGEMENT

All businesses face threats and risks to current and future operations. Value is maximized when management sets strategy and objectives to strike an optimal balance between growth and return goals and related risks, and efficiently and effectively deploys resources in pursuit of the entity's objectives. Obviously, businesses cannot anticipate or plan for all risks and threats. However, when creating and implementing a business strategy, a business must attempt to identify, address, and eliminate elements of risk before they threaten its success. To do this, businesses apply **enterprise risk management (ERM)**. One common definition of ERM is provided by the Committee of Sponsoring Organizations of the Treadway Commission (COSO) as:

> *A process effected by an entity's board of directors, management, and other personnel, applied in strategy setting and across the enterprise, designed to identify potential events that may affect the entity, and manage risk to be within its risk appetite, to provide reasonable assurance regarding the achievement of entity objectives.*[11]

What this means is that everyone involved with planning for and enabling the success of the organization, including any external directors, is responsible for figuring out what can go wrong and how to manage it. This also consists of deciding how much risk they can stand (*risk appetite*) and still achieve their business goals.[12]

To help businesses identify risks and threats, the COSO developed an ERM integrated framework. This framework, shown in Figure 4.6, identifies four overlapping categories of business objectives for focusing on risk assessment and management:

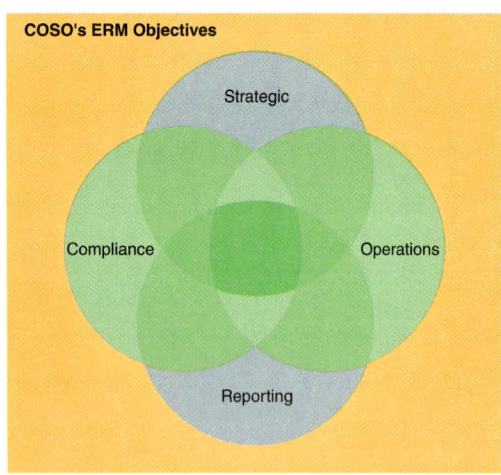

FIGURE 4.6 The COSO ERM framework identifies four overlapping categories of business objectives for focusing on risk assessment and management.

SOURCE: Adapted from the Committee of Sponsoring Organizations of the Treadway Commission (COSO) ERM Integrated Framework Executive Summary, September 2004, p. 3.

- strategic—high-level goals, aligned with and supporting its mission
- operations—effective and efficient use of its resources
- reporting—reliability of reporting
- compliance—compliance with applicable laws and regulations

IT has a role in supporting each of these categories. With respect to *strategy*, IT can provide important data for executive decision making in setting goals and strategies that align with an organization's mission and that mitigate business risk. So far in this text we have seen many ways in which IT supports *operations* by automating, informating, and transforming, and through the implementation of enterprise systems. Through these activities, IT enables the organization to be more effective and efficient. Accurate, timely, and reliable *reporting* is simply not possible without the support of IT. With the appropriate IT systems in place, on-demand

---

11. Committee of Sponsoring Organizations of the Treadway Commission (COSO) ERM Integrated Framework Executive Summary, September 2004, p. 2. COSO (http://www.coso.org) is a "voluntary private sector organization dedicated to improving the quality of financial reporting through business ethics, effective inter-control, and corporate governance." Source: ITGI, "IT Control Objectives for Sarbanes-Oxley," April 2004, p. 27.

12. http://www.coso.org/Publications/ERM/COSO_ERM_ExecutiveSummary.pdf

reporting provides organizations with critical information that they need to manage their business.

Lastly, IT supports compliance. **Compliance** reduces risk through policies and processes that ensure proper financial and accounting procedures. It protects employee and customer data that corporate IS stores, processes, and transmits. Compliance also increases organizational stakeholders' abilities to trust the integrity and accuracy of information reported by corporations. Compliance with laws and regulations ensures that stakeholders and the general public can trust that organizations are performing as stated and are prudently managing risks as they try to achieve their business goals. IT helps organizations with compliance by ensuring that appropriate checks and balances are in place in the systems used by the organization on a daily basis, and that information required for any external audits, accounting or system, is provided.

Why is non-compliance such a risk? Trust is an important cornerstone of global economic and financial systems. Trust is supported through effective continuous compliance practices; non-compliance destroys trust and opens the door to fraud, waste, and mismanagement. For example, after the publication of the financial scandals of Enron and WorldCom, people lost trust in the entire financial market, not just the banks. This mistrust caused markets to decline sharply, resulting in global repercussions for governments, corporations, and individuals. In response, the U.S. Congress intervened in the form of legislation, most notably the Sarbanes-Oxley Act of 2002. Organizations such as the Canadian Public Accountability Board (CPAB) and the Auditing and Assurance Standards Oversight Council (AASOC) have been formed to encourage compliant practices. And because Canadian and U.S. capital markets are co-dependent, the Canadian Securities Administrators (CSA) have adopted multilateral instrument (MI) 52-109, which essentially demands the same level of certification of financial statements for Canadian public firms that the U.S. does. These governance practices are discussed in more detail in Chapter 9.

Why has a piece of legislation that focuses on corporate financial reporting and accounting practices become so important? And why is it relevant to understanding and using information systems in business? Consider technology author Ben Worthen's suggestion: "Imagine, if you will, that Sarbanes-Oxley is a water purity test. What ultimately matters is the quality of the water coming out of the faucet. But no responsible organization would let its water be tested before thoroughly examining and repairing its plumbing, especially when failure means multimillion-dollar fines, a ruined reputation, and possibly jail time for top executives."[13]

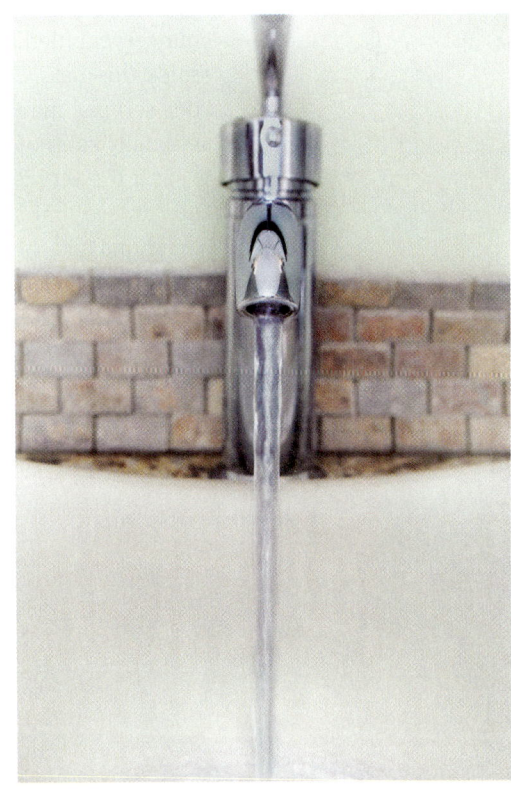

Legislation that focuses on corporate financial reporting has been compared to a water purity test. If the source and all of the plumbing used to deliver the water is clean, then the water itself will be clean. Likewise, if the IT supporting an organization is secure and meets all compliance regulations, then the data from that organization will also be "clean."

---

13. B. Worthen, "Sarbanes-Oxley: The IT Manager's New Risks and Responsibilities," http://www.cio.com/article/31900/Sarbanes_Oxley_The_IT_Manager_s_New_Risks_and_Responsibilities?page=2

If the plumbing (IT) is clean and intact from source to spigot, then as long as the source is clean (IT governance and auditing), so will be the water (data). Because information systems store the majority of a modern business's financial data, these systems must have proper controls in place if the data and the financial reports are to be accurate, reliable, and trustworthy.

Applying the Risk Framework

How do businesses apply the ERM framework to address enterprise risk? They first identify and categorize potential risks. For example, if you are the CEO of a specialty e-tailer (strategy), your customers will buy your goods using the Internet (operations). Accordingly, you need to have secure Web servers (compliance and control) to provide shopping and account management services to your customers (operations), as well as to collect, analyze, and communicate financial, transactional, and other data (reporting and compliance).

Once a risk is identified, the next step is to assess risks and threats using two primary criteria: impact and likelihood. Continuing on with our example, you realize you risk loss of business due to a denial of service (DoS) attack launched against your servers (denial of service is discussed in detail in Chapter 2). How would you assess this risk? You might begin by estimating the dollar-value impact (cost) of your servers' inability to respond to customers' requests. Say your business averages daily sales of $1 million. What if the server problem persists for several days? What if the servers are outsourced to an offshore vendor in a different time zone? You can see that an extended denial of service would severely affect your current operations and the execution of your business strategy.

You next need to determine the likelihood of a DoS attack. How do you estimate this? You can collect data from a reliable source, such as the 2007 e-Crime Watch Survey™.[14] Using the data from the survey, you determine that there is a 49 percent chance your organization could experience a DoS attack. Now you have to decide whether or not this risk is acceptable. Recall that you previously estimated $1 million in lost sales per day if your business experiences a DoS attack. As a result, you decide to implement improved security procedures and invest in IT security infrastructure improvements as necessary.

As in our example, once an organization has addressed its ERM objectives, it needs to focus its greatest effort on managing risk, especially where high-probability risks will have the greatest impact. Figure 4.7 shows the enterprise risk matrix that helps organizations classify risks. The upper-right corner of the ERM matrix shows the area where there are high probability and high impact risks that must be addressed. Businesses should also manage applicable risk (orange area in Figure 4.7) *before* it evolves into high-impact/high-probability risk. Finally, businesses should note the *immediacy* of a risk. Due to the diminished amount of time available to discover and implement

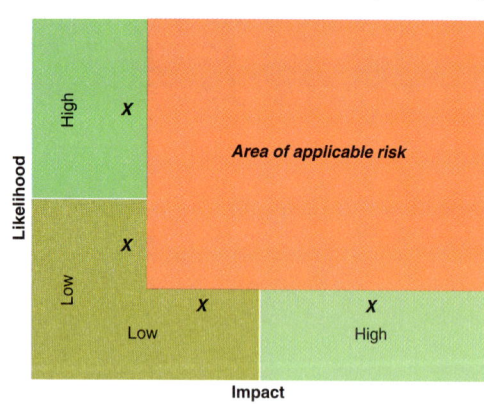

FIGURE 4.7 Organizations use the enterprise risk matrix, where X indicates a potential risk, to ensure that they focus their efforts on addressing high-probability risks that will have the greatest impact (upper-right corner of the ERM matrix).

SOURCE: Applicable risk as defined by the Institute of Chartered Accountants of England and Wales, cited in "How 7799 works," Gamma, http://www.gammassl.co.uk/bs7799/works.html

---

14. "2004 e-Crime Watch Survey," CSO magazine, U.S. Secret Service, CERT® Program, Microsoft Corp, http://www.cert.org/archive/pdf/ecrimesummary07.pdf. Retrieved February 11, 2010.

mitigation policies or processes for immediate risks, businesses need to proactively manage these risks rather than react to them.

Risk-Reduction Methods

Once an organization identifies risk, it must find ways of responding to those risks. Table 4.6 lists some examples of organizational responses to enterprise risk.

IT is a critical enabler in responding to risk. In fact, many risk responses would not be possible without IT. Let's examine how IT plays a supporting role in the risk responses listed in Table 4.6.

Risk Transfer Through the use of IT, organizations can use outsourcing to transfer risk. Earlier in this chapter we discussed outsourcing as a way to make business processes more efficient. Outsourcing can also shift risk outside of an organization to another business that may be better equipped to mitigate risk. For example, several organizations outsource the management of their data centres (facilities housing servers that contain applications and data). Data centre management companies are up to date on the latest technologies and developments in the area of data storage and data facility design. These data centre facilities provide the ideal environment for an organization's hard-working servers and provide staff knowledgeable in monitoring and maintaining this equipment. Because the care of this equipment is the sole focus of these centres, it is likely that the risk of adverse events is reduced. Also, organizations used for outsourcing are often held to strict *service level agreements (SLA)*, which penalize the organization monetarily should the SLA not be met. For example, if an organization's data or applications are not available due to an issue at the data centre, the data centre may be required to reimburse its client for lost revenue, or at least refund any fees paid for the period of the outage.

Interestingly, there is also the opposite of outsourcing, called insourcing. **In-sourcing** refers to the strategic decision made by a business to bring various services or functions back in-house, or keep them in-house, rather than globally source them. Firms concerned with security, quality, and even cost reduction may decide to bring a formerly outsourced IS development, call centre, or other business application back in-house. For example, in 2003, Farmers Insurance Group,

Table 4.6	Types and Examples of Organizational Responses to Risk
Risk Response	**Action**
Risk transfer	Move the risk to someone who is more able to deal with it
Risk deferral	Postpone exposure to the risk until circumstances are more favourable or resources are available to address the risk
Risk reduction	Either reduce the probability of the risk occurring or lessen the impact
Risk acceptance	Realize that some risks are unavoidable and make sure that contingency plans are in place
Risk avoidance	Eliminate the possibility of the risk occurring; however, that may close the doors on some business opportunities as well

an American insurance group with revenues of $11.5 billion and 19,000 employees, in-sourced its IT processes, reassuming operation and control of mainframe IT support, application, and development. According to former Farmers' CIO Cecilia Claudio, Farmers realized an annual savings of $6 million within one year.[15] Of course, in-sourcing reverses risk transfer and the organization must account for the increased risk.

Risk Deferral Sometimes IT is used to defer risks. One example of this strategy in action was during the Y2K crisis. As we approached the year 2000, companies became aware that their existing systems would not be able to handle the year format ending in "00." This created frantic activity to investigate new systems to install to avoid any adverse effects. As many of the systems available at the time were too complicated and difficult to install prior to the year 2000, many companies hired programmers to alter existing programs—sometimes coding line by code line—to defer the risk of adverse activities at the turn of the century. Once the year 2000 arrived, many companies then pursued new systems to ensure long-term stability. ERP systems were among those selected.

Risk Reduction One of the most common ways that IT reduces risk is by enabling disaster recovery. Many organizations have developed disaster recovery, or business continuity, plans. A **disaster recovery plan** allows an organization to resume operations after a major event that interrupts normal business processes. Such events may include data corruption, software bugs, network failures, network attacks, or natural and man-made physical disasters. Even small amounts of downtime could result in lost transactions, diminished productivity, and reduced customer satisfaction. A **business continuity plan** addresses problem prevention, response to crises, resumption of business, recovery of losses, and restoration of systems and processes.

When developing a plan, a company needs to determine its critical functions, the level of disaster, and appropriate procedures for recovery. In a disaster recovery situation, IT focuses on having and making available the important data needed to resume business. Reliable data storage and consistent backup procedures are essential in maintaining data integrity. Imagine if a disaster were to occur and a company lost all of its customer and transaction data. How would it bill customers and receive revenue? Think about your own disaster recovery planning. Would it be acceptable to your professors if you told them you could not turn in your term paper on time due to an unrecoverable hard drive or because your laptop was stolen? Probably not.

Risk Acceptance Not all risks can be transferred, deferred, proactively reduced, or avoided. Organizations must accept some risk; for example, when they go into new ventures or introduce new products. Without risk there is no chance of a greater return. If you have financial investments, you know this to be true. Businesses make changes all the time. We have discussed how businesses pursue competitive advantage through automating, informating, and transforming, as well as implementing strategic enterprise systems. With each of these actions, organizations accept a

---

15. S. Overby, "Bringing I.T. back home," *CIO Magazine*, March 1, 2003.

certain level of risk. Even though the level of risk is acceptable, it is prudent to have a contingency plan in place should something unexpected occur.

In the case of system changes, one contingency plan is to have a roll-back strategy. A **roll-back strategy** essentially involves being able to reverse every action that took place to make the change happen such that everything is returned to its original state with no damage done. Another common contingency plan is to plan a budget contingency should an unexpected expenditure occur on a risky venture.

Here is a very simple example you may have experienced with respect to risk acceptance. You have invited your girlfriend/boyfriend over for dinner and really want to impress him or her. You select a delicious sounding French recipe that you have never made before. You are accepting the risk that it may not turn out exactly like it is pictured on *www.allrecipes.com*, but if it does, your girlfriend/boyfriend will think you're a kitchen superstar! You accept the risk, but buy double the amount of ingredients in case it doesn't turn out the first time and you have to try to make it again (roll-back strategy). You also buy a frozen lasagna, just in case (contingency).

Risk Avoidance Probably the most popular risk response is avoidance. Isn't it human nature to avoid risk at all costs? No one likes to be put in a compromised situation. One way organizations avoid risk is to implement controls, which we discuss in detail in the next section.

Control and Controls

Implementing controls is not only a way of avoiding risk, but it may end up providing a control advantage through IT. We define **control advantage** as the strengthening of internal controls and compliance through the application of IT-based controls to business processes, policies, and procedures. Table 4.7 lists some frameworks that organizations rely on to attain this control advantage.

Table 4.7	Selected Compliance and Control Frameworks and Standards
Frameworks and Standards	**Description and URL**
COSO (Committee of Sponsoring Organizations of the Treadway Commission)	A framework for internal controls, in addition to an Integrated Enterprise Risk Management framework (See *www.coso.org*)
COBIT (Control Objectives for Information and Related Technology)	A framework for effective governance and control of enterprise IT and information (See *www.isaca.org* and *www.ITgovernance.org*)
ISO 17799 and BS7799	ISO 17799 framework from the International Organization for Standardization focuses on information security controls BS7799 is "a specification for an Information Security Management Systems (ISMS). An ISMS is the means by which Senior Management monitors and controls their security, minimizing the residual business risk and ensuring that security continues to fulfill corporate, customer, and legal requirements. It forms part of an organization's internal control system."[16] *(Continued)*

---

16. http://www.computersecuritynow.com/ and http://www.gammassl.co.uk/bs7799/ works.html

Table 4.7	(Continued)
Frameworks and Standards	**Description and URL**
Information Technology Infrastructure Library (ITIL)	A set of best-practices standards for IT and service management. The U.K. Central Computer and Telecommunications Agency (CCTA) created the ITIL in response to the growing dependence on information technology to meet business needs and goals (See www.itil-officialsite.com)
Capability Maturity Model Integration (CMMI)	Guides process improvements across organizations especially associated with software development (See www.sei.cmu.edu/cmmi/index.cfm)
UCCnet, a subsidiary of GS1 U.S.	A standards organization that provides an Internet-based supply chain management (SCM) data registry service for e-commerce companies and companies that have an e-commerce component (See www.gs1us.org)
RosettaNet	An organization set up by leading information technology companies to define and implement a common set of standards for e-business (See www.rosettanet.org)
Institute on Governance (IOG)	A non-profit organization that promotes effective governance, including technology governance (See www.iog.ca)
Communication Security Establishment (CSE)	Canada's national cryptologic agency; provides the Government of Canada with two key services: foreign signals intelligence in support of defence and foreign policy and the protection of electronic information and communication; also provides an IT security program (See www.cse-cst.gc.ca/index-eng.html)
Standards Council of Canada (SCC)	Facilitates the development and use of national and international standards and accreditation services; offers IT security evaluations and accreditation (See www.scc.ca/en/programs/lab/it_secureval.shtml)

SOURCE: Adapted from D. Cougias, "Moving into Compliance Mode: Realizing the Benefits, Cutting the Costs," *Hotel OnlineSpecial Report*, March 2005, http://www.hotel-online.com/News/PR2005_1st/Mar05_MovingIntoCompliance.html

To help you understand how IT can enhance corporate control efforts, we first discuss control and controls in general. We then review the overall process of internal controls, using an example to highlight how IT can enhance the effectiveness and efficiency of controls.

Defining Control and Controls Businesses generally base control around three key concepts:

1. Control is a process that runs throughout the organization.
2. Control influences how people behave at work.
3. Control can only provide reasonable, not absolute, assurance of achieving objectives.[17]

---
17. K. H. S. Pickett, *Internal Control: A Manager's Journey,* New York: John Wiley & Sons, 2001.

Controls are specific actions, including policies and procedures, designed to ensure the achievement of business objectives. *Effective controls* prevent, detect, and correct actions that increase the enterprise's risk of failing to meet business objectives, such as inappropriate financial and accounting practices, fraud, misuse of resources, and ineffective physical and electronic security practices.

COSO defines **internal control** as

a process effected by an entity's board of directors, management and other personnel, designed to provide reasonable assurance regarding the achievement of objectives in the following categories:

- *effectiveness and efficiency of operations*
- *reliability of financial reporting*
- *compliance with applicable laws and regulations*[18]

All these categories should incorporate three broad types of controls: preventive, detective, and corrective. *Preventive controls* are designed to prevent increased exposure to risk by stopping some action or process before it occurs. An example of preventive control is requiring employees to change their corporate network password every 30 days. *Detective controls* reduce risk by discovering when preventive controls have failed and providing notification that action must be taken. For example, if an employee has not changed his or her password in 25 days, then the employee may get a warning email message asking him or her to do so immediately. Lastly, *corrective controls* aim to remedy the situation and try to keep it from recurring. If the employee has not changed his or her password by the 30th day, then he or she could be locked out of the system.

Specific Internal Control Processes Now that you have an understanding of controls, we next discuss seven generic categories of controls, highlighted by K. H. Spencer Pickett in his book *Internal Control: A Manager's Journey*.[19] The seven categories are:

1. segregation of duties
2. authorization
3. security
4. ID codes
5. verification
6. control totals
7. supervisory review

Segregation of duties (Figure 4.8) means that jobs do not span lines of control that would allow mistakes or fraud to go undetected. For example, say you only have one programmer who creates your critical e-commerce applications. A problem can arise if she is also the only person responsible for testing, debugging, and certifying the system. Further, if she leaves the company, who would know if she had created a back door in the e-commerce software, allowing her to hack the

---

18. http://www.coso.org/resources.htm
19. K. H. S. Pickett, *Internal Control: A Manager's Journey*, New York: John Wiley & Sons, 2001.

FIGURE 4.8 Segregation of duties helps to prevent any mistakes or fraud from going undetected.

system and steal sensitive data? Another programmer should review the code and the changes and possibly test, debug, and certify the system.

Authorization controls prevent scope creep and cost overruns in various situations, such as major projects or operations management. Allowing an individual programmer to make minor system changes is efficient. But some changes to the system can be very costly and may commit resources that are already assigned. As a result, another person, such as the project team leader, should sign off (authorize) any significant changes.

If the team leader and programmers are working on an e-commerce application, they will need access to a development database to develop their application. However, for the majority of their application development process, they do not need to access the organization's actual transaction database (production database). Executing untested new code against a production database is a recipe for disaster. To provide *security* for the production database, application developers should therefore log in separately to the development and production databases.

It is also a good idea to track the login IDs and activities of all users, as login IDs are a useful type of *ID code* (as is your student ID number). Tracking login IDs and other ID codes creates an audit trail that organizations can follow to ensure proper controls are in place and working. Organizations can also use them to detect and document attempts at unauthorized use.

Depending on how the application is implemented ("goes live"), *verification* controls can confirm that the application is accomplishing e-commerce functions (e.g., order placement, payment) without error. For example, verification controls can monitor return of merchandise counts to ensure that the new system is sending customers what they ordered.

Control totals can help detect fraudulent actions. Imagine that you return a product. Now say a dishonest employee credits not your account but a fictitious account that he created. If the organization lacks control totals, which compare a customer's paid orders with credits received, it cannot detect this fraud. The item would have been returned and a proper credit in the correct amount given to a customer, just not the right customer.

Finally, supervisors should periodically audit and review processes and transactions. In the case of your e-commerce system, *supervisory review* could consist of ordering an item, calling customer service, returning the item, receiving credit for the item, and documenting the process. The supervisor would share any discrepancies with the responsible person(s), and then make improvements or take corrective actions.

Quick Test

1. Which one of the following is NOT an organizational response to risk?
   a. risk acceptance
   b. risk avoidance
   c. risk behaviour
   d. risk reduction

2. Fill in the blank. _____ reduces risk through policies and processes that ensure proper financial and accounting procedures, as well as protects employee and customer data that corporate IS stores, processes, and transmits.

3. True or False. Corrective controls reduce risk by discovering when preventive controls have failed and providing notification that action must be taken.

Answers: 1. c; 2. Compliance; 3. False

What's in IT for me?

When you are a business professional, you will likely use enterprise systems in your role. This is a good thing. As we have learned in this chapter, enterprise systems make organizations more efficient. They also make individuals more efficient. Imagine a time, not long ago, when accountants had to manually add up revenue numbers receipt by receipt and manually enter them into the appropriate general ledger. Now, with the touch of a button, they can see sales in total, or segmented in any possible way for any possible period, and all transactions are posted electronically directly from the source. The same was true in the marketing field. Marketers had to manually keep track of their product sales to specific accounts. Now it is possible for sales to be made through e-commerce or SCM systems and tracked automatically without any intervention by the salesperson. They simply collect their enterprise system-calculated commissions!

These two examples illustrate how enterprise systems take care of the more mundane or rote functions of a position. These functions are sometimes known as *non-value-added*, meaning that, while necessary, they do not add value to the activity or organization. Using enterprise systems frees up time for individuals within an organization to focus on more knowledge work or *value-added* activities. In the case of the accountant, this might mean having the time to investigate money-saving tax strategies, or in the case of the marketer, being able to focus on new ways to fulfill customers' needs. These activities improve the operations of the organization or increase revenue and are, therefore, value-added. Certainly, from an individual's point of view, these activities are more interesting and ones where business professionals can use their skills to the fullest. Thanks to enterprise systems, when you graduate, you will be able to use your knowledge in your role instead of doing the boring tasks you won't want to do!

What's in for an organization?

We have spent this chapter discussing the benefits of enterprise systems for organizations. One aspect not yet covered is how enterprise systems can benefit not-for-profit organizations. With tight funding and the reliance on donations and grants, not-for-profit organizations can find it challenging to acquire or build systems. With Software as a Service (SaaS), where organizations can pay on a per use basis, not-for-profit organizations are better able to manage software expenditure.

One popular SaaS in the not-for-profit area is called eTapestry. eTapestry offers not-for-profits online fundraising and donor management software. The software tracks donors, prospects, or alumni while managing gifts, pledges, and payments. It is available on the Web and can be accessed by anyone in the organization with login permission. The system is hosted by eTapestry, so in-house technical resources are not required to manage the system. Without a service such as eTapestry, individual not-for-profits may try to manage donor data using spreadsheets or ad-hoc database systems, never being able to analyze or understand their donor data to make the most of donation opportunities. Or worse, by not recognizing the need for a system for this purpose, not-for-profits might invest their hard-earned donor dollars in expensive systems to the detriment of the community or clients they are trying to serve. SaaS is often the perfect solution for the needs of the not-for-profit sector.

What's in for society

Software is big business around the world. In 2009, Gartner Research predicted worldwide enterprise software revenue to be $222.6 billion,[20] indicating relatively flat growth, but growth during a recession nonetheless. Every country in the world has an information and communications technology sector. What does this mean for society? In a word: employment. Of course the research, programming, and marketing of the software create employment, but the sale and purchase of software is just the beginning. Often associated with the sale are consulting and training services. These actions impact employment and maybe even future employment as people acquire new skills by using the purchased software. The software purchased may improve business processes or operations or increase the revenue of the purchasing organization, all potentially leading to more employment. Sometimes the purchased software can lead an organization to obtain a global presence. Perhaps it has purchased web development software that allows it to sell online internationally or work with remote workers around the world. Despite the pressures felt by the software industry from open source software, SaaS, and cloud computing, the software industry is here to stay and the benefits to employment will continue.

---

20. http://www.gartner.com/it/page.jsp?id=923312

ROI STUDENT RETURN ON INVESTMENT SUMMARY

1. In what ways can organizations apply IT to build business value?

Businesses can use IT to automate, informate, and transform organizational processes throughout the value chain to create a competitive advantage. Businesses use IT with a focus on automation to improve the execution of a process—simply doing it faster and more consistently. An IT-informating process recognizes the creation of new data and information about the business each time it executes a process. The business may then process the new data and use it to improve decision making in the organization and to change or improve the process itself. Lastly, transforming organizational processes to gain competitive advantage may involve automating and informating, as well as innovation through application of new technologies like enterprise systems. Using IT may help a business differentiate itself or become the lowest-cost producer—two ways of gaining competitive advantage.

2. How can businesses strategically fit IT to the organization?

Information systems, like the organizations they support, consist of more than IT. When applying IT, a business must consider the interaction of technology with the people who create and use it, the organizational structure and culture, the business processes, and the environment within which the organization resides. In other words, a business must consider the strategic fit of IT within the context of the organization as a system and what it is trying to accomplish. Table 4.5 and Figure 4.5 provide additional insights into IT and its strategic fit with organizations. One specific way that IT supports business strategy is through the implementation of enterprise systems that support individual components of the value chain, like logistics management systems in the inbound logistics component, or across all value chain components in the case of ERP. These systems support business objectives (as set out in the strategy) and are measured by performance measures to ensure that they are creating the expected value.

3. What is IT's role in managing enterprise risk?

IT plays an integral role in both identifying and managing risk. IT helps to identify risk by providing data to management that may help them to recognize a threat. In managing risk, businesses turn to IT to: implement technology and controls supported by technology to minimize or avoid risks; assist with outsourcing to transfer risk; undertake activities to defer risk; and assist with contingency plans to minimize the impact of unavoidable risks. In the case of a disaster, IT is called upon to recover important data and ensure that the business can return to an operational state as soon as possible.

KNOWLEDGE SPEAK

application service provider (ASP)   141
business continuity plan   150
compliance   147
control advantage   151
controls   153
customer relationship management (CRM)   137
decision support systems (DSS)   129
disaster recovery plan   150
document management systems (DMS)   127
enterprise resource planning (ERP)   131
enterprise risk management (ERM)   146
enterprise systems   133
executive information systems (EIS)   127
functional information systems (FIS)   123
groupware   128

in-sourcing   149
internal control   153
knowledge management (KM)   128
management information systems (MIS)   127
outsourcing   144
roll-back strategy   151
software as a service (SaaS)   140
supply chain   130
supply chain management (SCM)   130
transaction   125
transaction processing systems (TPS)   125
utility computing services   140
value chain   121
workflow   124
workflow management system (WMS)   124

REVIEW QUESTIONS

Multiple-choice questions

1. The following is NOT a system that supports the marketing and sales component of the value chain
   a. CRM
   b. production scheduling
   c. salesforce automation
   d. ERP
2. A system that enables transactions and captures key data created by transactions is
   a. a WMS
   b. an ACID
   c. a DSS
   d. a TPS
3. Organizations generally consider control as _____.
   a. a process that runs through the organization
   b. based around people and how they behave at work
   c. providing reasonable, not absolute, assurance that objectives will be achieved
   d. all of the above

Fill-in-the-blank questions

4. The area of _____ includes a set of risks that are predominately high likelihood and high impact.
5. A(n) _____ is designed to provide summary information about business performance to those making higher-level strategic decisions.
6. The risk response where an organization tries to reduce the probability of a risk or minimize its impact is called _____.
7. The value chain model is a useful tool for defining an organization's goals and the activities that it can pursue to gain a sustained _____.

True-false questions

8. The application of IT to an organization can be seen from four different views: (1) automating, (2) informating, (3) competitive advantage, and (4) value chain support.
9. A workflow represents the steps, organizational resources, input and output data, and tools needed to complete a business process.
10. IT is solely responsible in an organization for enterprise risk management.

Matching questions

Choose the BEST answer from column B for each item in column A.

Column A
11. automating
12. informating
13. competitive advantage
14. support of value chain

Column B
a. Amazon.ca's use of patented "one-click" technology
b. Gathering data about search patterns of online purchasers
c. Having customers fill out their own online loan applications
d. Scanning bar codes on incoming materials to determine if they meet purchase orders

Short-answer questions

15. Describe the characteristics of a transaction. What happens if any one of these is not achieved?
16. Think of a business organization with which you are familiar, and list operations that would fall under each primary activity within Porter's value chain model.

Discussion/Essay questions

17. Some businesses create business value by extending the value chain outside of their organization to suppliers and others. From a value chain perspective, argue for or against external company involvement in managing support activities.
18. Considering your answer to the preceding question, how can information technology help transform organizational value chains?
19. Use the ERM framework and enterprise risk matrix to identify and assess risks that you may be facing as a student (e.g., no summer job). Determine a response to each of the risks in your area of applicable risk.

TEAM ACTIVITY

As a team, discuss a business you are familiar with, such as a food outlet in a nearby food court. Discuss the value chain of this business and the potential systems that support it. Create a diagram like the one in Figure 4.4, filling in the specific business objectives, systems, and performance metrics.

SOFTWARE APPLICATION EXERCISES

1. Internet

When you begin searching for a full-time job, you may find several positions require experience with SAP. SAP is the predominant supplier of ERP systems in the world. Go to *www.sap.ca* and learn more about its products. Find some customer testimonials and see how it is used in specific companies.

2. Presentation

Assume that your boss asks you to present one of the information systems that support business in this chapter to the CEO. Your presentation should provide an overview of the system; that is, describe what it is and how the organization could use it. Include both the benefits and risks of using the technology, potential vendors, and one or two examples of how others have used the system. Incorporate graphics as needed. Your presentation should be visually appealing as well as professional.

3. Word Processing

Prepare a disaster recovery and business continuity plan for yourself. Outline each of the critical things that you would need to recover or do to continue to function as a student should you find yourself without your possessions, including your computer.

4. Spreadsheet

Many companies have a lot of money tied up in physical assets such as machinery and IT hardware. To keep up with these physical assets and their value, companies typically maintain an equipment inventory. Often this information is contained in an inventory management system (IMS). Create a spreadsheet to track an equipment inventory for yourself. For each item, record or calculate values related to the physical condition and the financial status of the item as follows:

- **Physical condition:** Provide columns to record an asset or serial number, an item description, a location, a physical condition, the name of the vendor, and the years of service left.
- **Financial status:** Provide columns to record the initial value, a down payment, a date purchased or leased, a loan term in years, a loan rate, a monthly payment, monthly operating costs, total monthly cost, expected value at end of loan term, annual straight-line depreciation, monthly straight-line depreciation, and a current value. You should calculate some of these values as follows:

Monthly payment—if an initial payment is entered and it is not equal to the down payment, use an appropriate function to calculate this value

Total monthly cost—monthly payment + monthly operating cost

Annual straight-line depreciation—use an appropriate function and appropriate parameters to calculate this value; if you are unfamiliar with depreciation, search the Web for more information about it

Monthly straight-line depreciation—annual straight-line depreciation ÷ 12

Current value—use an appropriate formula to subtract the current depreciation amount from the initial value of the item (*hint:* use the now() function in your formula; this one is challenging)

5. Database

Create a database of at least 10 suppliers you use on a regular basis, such as the pizza delivery place. Include the suppliers' names, addresses, phone numbers, email addresses, and other relevant data such as hours of operation. If possible, export this database to your mobile device for easy access. You have now created a database that supports your procurement process.

6. Advanced Challenge

Imagine that you are a sales rep for a consumer goods company. Write a detailed job description for this position including a "day in the life" description. Imagine the types of systems that you need as support in the field as you visit customers. How will you know if inventory is in stock? How will you place orders for your customers? How will you track your sales commission? Develop a set of requirements for the systems you need. With these in hand, search the Internet to find available open source software that could support you.

ONLINE RESOURCES

Companion Website

- Take interactive practice quizzes to assess your knowledge and help you study in a dynamic way.
- Review PowerPoint lecture slides.
- Get help and sample solutions to end-of-chapter software application exercises.

Additional Resources Available Only on WileyPLUS

- Take the interactive Quick Test to check your understanding of the chapter material and get immediate feedback on your responses.
- Review and study with downloadable Audio Lecture MP3 files.
- Check your understanding of the key vocabulary in the chapter with Knowledge Speak Interactive Flash Cards.

CASE STUDY: WALMART

From its humble beginnings in Bentonville, Arkansas, Walmart has grown to be the world's largest corporation in terms of revenue. As measured by the Fortune 500 before the 2006 oil price rise, it surpassed such corporate giants as General Motors and Exxon Mobil, the only two other companies to hold this position. On top of that, *Fortune* named Walmart as the "most admired" company in 2003, the first time the top Fortune 500 company has also had that honour. Reasons for this admiration? Walmart's constant efforts to lower prices for consumers actually influences the U.S. economy by keeping inflation at low levels and forcing productivity up. Famed investor Warren Buffett calculated that Walmart contributes $10 billion a year to the U.S. economy.

Founded in 1962 by Sam Walton, a large part of Walmart's move to the top of the Fortune 500 ranking resulted from its aggressive use of information systems and technology. Unlike many of its competitors, Walmart always considered information technology as a competitive advantage rather than an expense. Walmart was one of the first companies to use POS terminals and bar codes at check-outs.

Other retailers also eventually used this same technology, but Walmart applied it innovatively. For example, rather than hoarding or selling the data that bar codes and POS systems generated, Walmart shared it freely with its suppliers, such as Procter & Gamble, as a way of improving its incoming logistics. The suppliers thus obtained the data necessary to replenish Walmart's products without waiting for the retailer to order them. This process resulted in an average savings of 20 cents per shipping case for both Walmart and the supplier.

In 1991, Walmart took this sharing process one step further. It formalized sharing with an information system named Retail Link, which enabled suppliers to look up sales and prices of their products in any Walmart store. This information helps the supplier plan its production and distribution to Walmart, leading to better and cheaper products. Over 40,000 suppliers now use Retail Link. Walmart is also pushing a Web-based version of EDI as a way to provide suppliers with even more information and data.

Another important part of Walmart's philosophy of sharing information was the introduction in 1995 of collaborative forecasting and replenishment (CFAR). With CFAR, vendors can access Walmart data from their home offices and adjust for causal factors themselves. Walmart does not collaborate with vendors over public exchanges, but instead works with them through Internet connections to its retail link system.

This commitment to the use of IT is most obvious in Walmart's supply chain; that is, the flow of products from its suppliers to its shelves. As one observer put it, "Grocers always invest in new stores. Walmart invests in the supply chain, then in new stores." By using the latest in technology to squeeze inefficiencies out of the supply chain, Walmart keeps its costs down, which enables it to offer lower costs than its competitors. For example, recently Walmart has been a leader in pushing the adoption of radio frequency identification tags (RFIDs) in products coming into its distribution centres. These RFIDs are tiny tags that are aimed at replacing bar codes as a way of identifying products. They have the advantage that they do not require direct contact or line-of-sight scanning to identify the product, and make it possible for retailers to know exactly what is in a pallet coming into the loading dock without having to be near it.

Walmart also uses information technology for competitive advantage in product distribution. For example, Walmart uses its POS data to minimize warehouse inventory. By using the warehouse as a "pass-through" point, where goods come in from the supplier at one side and go out to the store on the other side the same day over miles of conveyor belts, Walmart saves time and money. To improve this process further, Walmart was also an early member of UCCnet, the data synchronization and registry service of the Uniform Code Council that sets the codes used in bar code systems. This avoids problems with pallets with bar codes that fail to match the purchase order listing, which delays processing at the loading dock. If this pallet has a high-demand product on it, the result of the delay could mean lost revenue and unhappy customers.

Case Questions

1. In what ways does IT contribute to the growth of Walmart?
2. How is Walmart using IT to share data and information with suppliers? Why does this lead to lower prices for consumers?
3. What are Walmart's recent IT innovations, and how will they lead to lower costs?

Integrative Application Case: *Campuspad.ca*

You and Sarah are now working as 50/50 partners in the business and are having planning meetings three times a week at the local coffee shop. In fact, if they ever write a *Canadian Business* article on you in the future, the journalist will surely be surprised to know just how much you can write on a napkin!

After compiling the information that Sarah has collected (available for you to review on WileyPLUS) and your work from last week, it's becoming clear that you still don't have sufficient knowledge to proceed—all you have is lots of input and supporting data, but no firm decisions on the path forward yet. You need some advice from someone more experienced who has done this before.

So you decide to approach your IT professor after class today. Turns out he had previously been involved in an Internet start-up and was quite pleased to spend a few minutes sharing what he could to help you launch your own idea. You were grateful and distilled his rather long-winded comments into three simple points to share with Sarah at your next meeting:

1. **Follow the money!** If you can figure out who is paying who for what and how to do it quicker, better, or more cheaply than current business models, then you potentially have a sustainable e-business to pursue. If you can't follow the money then you won't make any . . . unless you're YouTube!
2. **Focus first!** In a start-up, don't try to be all things to all people, and don't try to do it all yourself. Figure out what's at your core, learn to do it better than anybody else, and outsource everything else. Make sure that if you rely on technology for your business it's the best technology you can buy or create because it's easily copied. You've got to stay one step ahead at all times.
3. **Segment your customer!** Where are they and how are you going to reach them? There must be a buyer and a seller in every transaction. Who do you serve and why? If you serve both buyers and sellers, how do you add value to both? What are the ethics of this and can it work? Are there regulatory or conflict issues? How will buyers find you? Can you find them? How much will it cost to reach them and let them know about you? Are you trying to create a new market or move an existing market online? Market makers are market winners!

It now seemed like you and Sarah are destined to become roommates. In fact, you recently located a place not far from campus and *finally* have all the paperwork done—what a hassle! But it was a two-bedroom, one-bath place with a small balcony, and it was just a 15-minute walk or 5-minute bus ride from campus. Sweet! But the worst part was all the money you had to spend—first and last month's rent, damage waivers, key deposits. Oh, and don't forget proof of a tenant's insurance policy to lease here! Then there were references, credit checks, and notary fees to witness the approved standard lease form. Who knew living on your own could be so expensive?

To top it all off, you are now gripped by your new idea and figure that the place is essentially going to become your office as well as your home. That will probably mean a whole bunch of other problems, like the fact that your new lease prohibits you from running a business in your apartment. Oh well, all problems for another day. For now, it's off to meet Sarah for coffee.

Guiding Case Questions

1. Identify all the business processes in your new business and make a diagram of the flows of information, funds, etc. that result.
2. Figure out how you can use enterprise systems to automate these processes.
3. Based on this, decide if the required technology is core to your business or if it can be outsourced or purchased as an SaaS.

Integrative Application Case: *Campuspad.ca*

Your Task

Every new business ultimately needs money to get started. You and Sarah are struggling students—all you have to do is look at your bank accounts to figure that out! So if this business is going to go, it's going to need money . . . and it's not coming from you. To get money, you have to have a simple business plan. Turns out your professor is willing to share an example of what he thinks is an outstanding business plan outline that he gave to a group of students last year (go to WileyPLUS to download a copy). He also says you can find lots of information online about writing good business plans. Although the outline doesn't have any specific information in it, the headings and tables seem like a good place to start when you both look at it. However, it also makes you realize the many things you haven't yet considered. As a result, you both agree that the next step is to fill this in with everything you know (or still have to find out through discovery) for *Campuspad.ca* to become even more real and to eventually get it funded and launched.

5

E-COMMERCE

WHAT WE WILL COVER

- E-Commerce Defined
- The E-Commerce Advantage
- Benefits and Limitations of E-Commerce
- E-Commerce Between Organizations

ROI STUDENT RETURN ON INVESTMENT

Through your investment of time in reading and thinking about this chapter, your return—or created value—is gaining knowledge. Use the following questions as a study guide.

1. What is e-commerce and how is it a part of today's economy?

2. How does e-commerce create value and make a difference to businesses and consumers?

3. How can organizations use e-commerce to enhance the delivery of products and services, manage trade with business partners, and improve their supply chain efficiency?

THE VOICE OF EXPERIENCE
Michael Silagadze, University of Waterloo

Michael Silagadze graduated in 2007 with a BASc from the Department of Electrical and Computer Engineering at the University of Waterloo. He is CEO of the technology start-up company, Top Hat Monocle.

What do you do in your current position? Top Hat Monocle started as a company developing applications for the iPhone, but has recently begun creating a mobile platform for collaborative Internet learning for use in universities and colleges. Our product, *MonocleCAT,* allows students and professors to interact and collaborate using mobile devices and also allows professors to do collaborative authoring. As CEO, my role is that of a generalist. Running a start-up company is different than the same position in an established company; it is not as limited. I'm involved in all aspects of the company.

What do you consider to be important career skills? I don't believe that there is any one specific skill set. My role as CEO requires a broad skill set. The same applies for anyone working in any role at a start-up company. Entrepreneurs require a couple of specific skills. They need to be intelligent, because they deal with many challenges and need to solve problems on a regular basis. They also need to be determined. As a general rule, 95 percent of everything entrepreneurs try—programming, marketing, sales—will fail, and 5 percent will succeed. Also, in IT or with a job involving IT, you have to keep up on current technology developments.

How do you use IT? In a tech start-up, especially one that is Internet based, it's difficult to isolate IT from non-IT. I spend about 95 percent of my day in front of the computer. In business, deciding how you deliver products to your customer is important—the architecture, framework, configuration of services, etc. If you use cloud computing, you reduce your in-house technical needs, especially those for hardware, and you can rent computing hours. Using IT services for our infrastructure allows us to focus on building our product and controlling what runs on our system.

Can you describe an example of how you have used IT to improve business operations? We use Google applications for hosted email, documents, and calendar, rather than using Microsoft Outlook Exchange Server. We also use open-source software. With open-source software there are external communities doing similar work that you can use and then modify for your own needs. Using these services is cheaper and helps improve Top Hat Monocle's bottom-line.

Have you got any on-the-job advice for students seeking a career in IT or business? Many people work along these lines: they're presented with a problem, their manager gives them the solution, and they go do the work. The better way is to do things differently. Take a step back and re-frame the problem: is that really it, or is it a symptom of something else? Once you figure that out, look at it from all possible angles to come up with the best solution. As you gain experience, you'll be more comfortable figuring out the problem and solution rather than letting others do that for you. In IT and business, get as much experience as you can and as broad a range as you can. Students and new graduates are generally in the best position of having time to do this. Take advantage of internships while you're in school. Lastly, choosing a job because it's the safe thing to do isn't worth it. Choose something you enjoy doing.

Perhaps your class is using a tool like MonocleCAT to make your classroom experience more interesting and enjoyable. This application falls into the category of m-commerce, which we discuss in this chapter. We also discuss the business of e-commerce and how companies like Top Hat Monocle fit into the marketplace.

Recall that earlier we defined organizations as creating competitive advantage through a chain of value-producing activities. We also noted that each organization operates in an environment of stakeholders and clients or consumers: those individuals, partners, or suppliers with an interest in and an influence on that particular organization and who ultimately consume the value the organization creates. This implies that *all organizations must have a business model*, regardless of their status—profit-centric or not. Even governments must decide how to efficiently and effectively deliver services, and not-for-profits have to wrestle with how to reach donors. Of course, enterprise systems (discussed in Chapter 4), including ERP and CRM, are elements of the technology designed to help create this value.

Similarly, through the evolution of the World Wide Web and various Internet technologies, these same relationships among customers, partners, and suppliers are rapidly changing. Organizations can now create business relationships and carry out transactions either completely or partially through *electronic commerce*, or *e-commerce*. In this chapter, we discuss the many ways that e-commerce is creating business value for organizations. By the end of this chapter, you will see that for an organization to efficiently and effectively engage in e-commerce, it must tie together business processes, enabling technologies, and its human resources and integrate them into its own unique electronic and digital value chain to enable it to execute its business strategy.

E-COMMERCE DEFINED

For as long as there have been merchants and markets, there has been the desire to improve the efficiency of the retail channel. Advances in technology, product variety, and consumer demand have brought an accompanying change in retailing strategy (as seen in Figure 5.1). The arrival of the telegraph enabled orders to be placed rapidly and shipped by mail. Rail and airline transportation brought new and rapid possibilities for order fulfillment. And the telephone call centre has changed our definition of customer service.

It seems inevitable that the invention of the Internet would create another revolution in commerce, specifically the arrival of *e-commerce* as a way of doing business around the world in an instant without the need for a physical business presence. The Internet also brought along the forces of *build to order* as a way for manufacturers, such as Dell and others, to directly solicit orders from consumers and deliver products directly, rather than relying on a global network of wholesalers and distributors/dealers as a way of bringing products to market.

Some have tried to distinguish between *e-commerce* (transactions that involve buying and selling goods and services through the Internet) with *e-business* (the broader use of Internet technologies to reduce operating costs, such as extending the electronic supply chain to partners and suppliers). We have chosen not to make

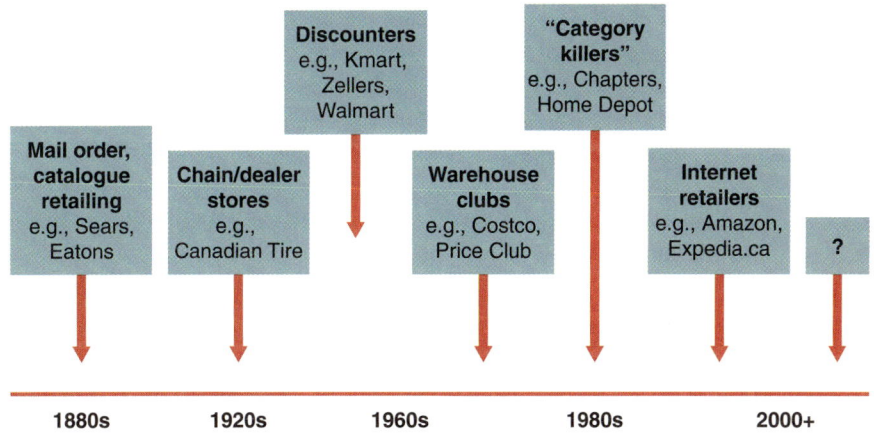

FIGURE 5.1 A brief history of retail innovations.

this distinction. Why? We believe that Internet technologies are still early in their development cycles, and their rapid evolution as a vital part of business operations continues even as you read this. There is still much unexplored potential in these technologies that relate to everything we do as a society, so artificial distinctions will not serve any particular purpose. So, in this text, we group these technologies together and simply call it **e-commerce**.

Beyond the Basic Definition

When you hear the term e-commerce, you may initially think of an online retail company like Amazon.ca. However, the wholesale or business-to-business level is far larger and more important to the global economy than the retail level. In fact, while online retailers measure sales in the billions of dollars, online wholesalers and industrial suppliers measure them in the *trillions* of dollars. But e-commerce is more than just sales. Consider this more formal definition of e-commerce:

> *E-commerce is the use of information systems, technologies, and computer networks by individuals and organizations to carry out transactions in order to create or support the creation of business value.*

This general definition of e-commerce therefore includes all types of computer networks, all types of transactions, and all types of business relationships and models.

To help you better understand the full potential of e-commerce in various settings, we first describe the parties involved on each side of the transaction to identify the type of e-commerce that is occurring. For instance, we refer to a transaction where a consumer buys a product or service from a business as *B2C*. The transaction types are summarized in Table 5.1.

Table 5.1	Types of E-Commerce Transactions and Example Websites	
Transaction	**Description**	**Example Websites**
Business-to-consumer (B2C)	Online equivalent of the retail store as well as other services	www.chapters.indigo.ca, www.barnesandnoble.com, www.telus.ca
Business-to-business (B2B)	Electronic exchanges between companies	http://wwre.globalsources.com/ for the Worldwide Retail Exchange
Business-to-government (B2G)	Online sales to government agencies, as well as electronic payment of taxes	www.doingbusiness.mgs.gov.on.ca/mbs/psb/psb.nsf/index/english?openDocument for businesses wishing to provide goods or services to the government of Ontario
Consumer-to-government (C2G)	Electronic payment of taxes as well as purchase of various types of licences	www.netfile.gc.ca/ to electronically file and pay taxes to the federal government
Consumer-to-consumer (C2C)	Use of online auctions like eBay and similar other sites	www.ebay.com or www.ebay.ca www.craigslist.com or craigslist.ca www.kijiji.com or kijiji.ca

E-Commerce and Products: Physical and Digital

Think about the wide range and types of products that consumers can buy. We can divide such products into two primary categories: *physical* and *digital.* Physical products include anything that requires an actual shipment of the item from a central distribution point to the buyer (whether an end-consumer, wholesaler, or to another company). This also requires an off-line supply chain to handle the sales, order processing, and delivery of these goods, even if they are discovered and purchased online. On the other hand, consumers can receive digital products directly over the Internet or other computer networks (such as downloading an album on iTunes versus going to HMV to buy it). This usually requires the use of a completely IT-enabled supply chain. These differences should be very easy for you understand, given most of you have probably purchased both types of products before!

The main difference between physical and digital products is in the delivery process, as shown in Figure 5.2. Even though a computer network can transmit information about the order, it obviously cannot ship the actual physical goods. So even though a Web presence and online ordering processes and systems may be essential to many e-commerce transactions, the business must still have these *back-office elements* in place to handle order fulfillment. This often requires substantial technology interfaces between the Web and the enterprise's existing computerized business systems (known as *web integration*). Further, any company in the business of accepting orders and shipping goods to customers must also handle returns, the reverse operation of the diagram shown below for a traditional business. This physical process is often as complicated as, if not more complicated than, the actual order fulfillment. Yet, by definition, a returns process may not even be applicable to a pure online business (which may not offer the ability to "return" something once it is successfully downloaded—say iTunes songs or e-books, for instance). This often has to do with the fact that, once downloaded, electronic products or services have immediate value and often cannot be *off-loaded* (deleted or otherwise disabled) with any certainty by the vendor.

Most of you are probably quite familiar with purchasing and downloading digital products. What types of digital products have you bought in the past?

As a result, companies already experienced in physical order fulfillment and returns also tend to be able to more successfully implement e-commerce. Chapters/Indigo, Dell, Lands' End, and many others are good examples of this type of company. Telephone and mail-order companies also have vast experience in handling returns, so returns from Web orders pose no special problems for them. In this situation, e-commerce often simply means extending an organization's existing business model. Or in some cases, it may only mean adding another direct channel for interacting with customers—that is, the Web simply becomes another channel (place) for customers to buy your physical goods.

Now consider digital products. Say that instead of receiving an actual DVD, the company electronically sends you the movie file that you can play back on your

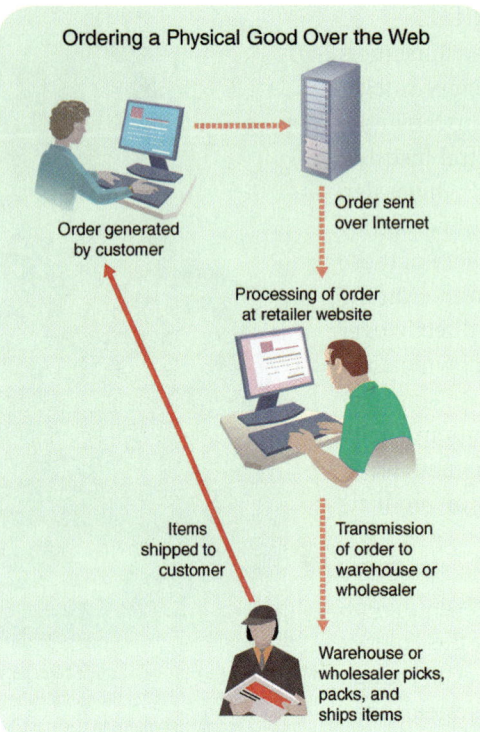 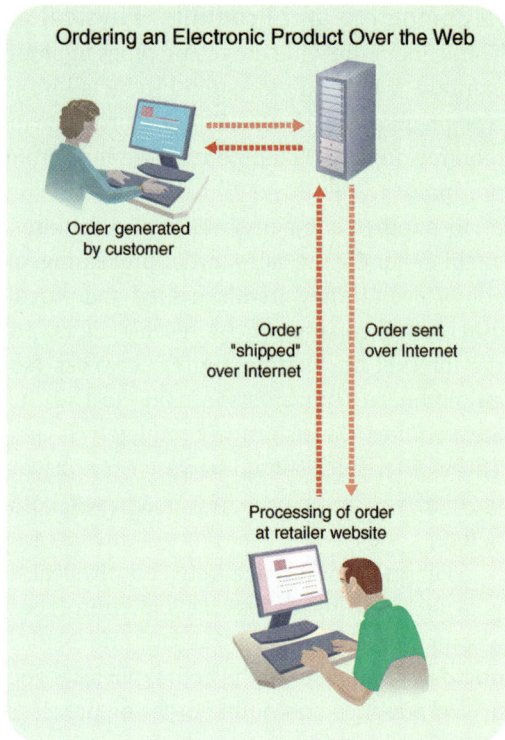

FIGURE 5.2 When buying a physical good over the Web (shown on the left), the company must still pick it from a shelf in a warehouse, pack it for shipment, and physically move it from the warehouse to the customer. The dotted lines indicate electronic communications, and the solid lines refer to physical shipments of products. When purchasing an electronic product (shown on the right), the delivery process is simplified and speeded up as it avoids the need to physically pick, pack, and ship the product. This is often why pure online business models are often more profitable to operate.

computer. In this case, as the right side of Figure 5.2 shows, the company sends you the electronic product directly over the Internet, thereby avoiding any picking, packing, and shipping issues. There are also no return problems. If a problem occurs with the electronic product, the company simply sends a new one for you to download as a replacement, or restores your right to re-download the same content if it is accidentally erased or otherwise compromised.

WHAT DO YOU THINK?

There has been an explosion in online sales in North America in the past few years, and almost everybody has purchased something online at one time or another. In thinking about e-commerce sites you use, consider the following:

1: What features make you choose to do business with an online vendor? What features or aspects make you leery about dealing with one?
2: Are there products or services you would never purchase online? Why?
3: What makes online shopping useful, enjoyable, and fun for you? What types of offers or features encourage you to shop online?

E-Commerce Business Models

The whole story of e-commerce does not involve only questions of how a digital product or service is supplied. In fact, that is often the easiest part of the equation for most e-commerce sites. The harder question is how to develop a business model to ensure you are profitable for the product you produce or offer in an age where consumers often expect everything on the Internet to be free. An **e-commerce business model** combines a specific type of website with a successful revenue model that produces profits for the website owner.

The question of Internet business models is one of the most important strategic questions for most Internet-related businesses, and is tied to the type of site that you plan to operate. This is also an issue you need to address if you are involved in planning for a not-for-profit or government service, and you seek to be profitable or cover your costs as a result of operating online. Of course, if you are an online retailer, the answer is quite simple: sell good products at good prices, delivered on time, that leave you with enough margin (the difference between the selling price and the cost of goods sold) to make a reasonable profit to pay for the website's operation. However, what if you do not actually sell online goods? What if the site you operate is more of a community model based on common interests and shared commitment? How do you monetize that? Or perhaps you are an infomediary, expert site, or news-related site. What other business and revenue models exist that can help you make money online? These models deal with how Internet companies, and traditional companies using the Internet wisely, can make money online. Again, while future innovations are bound to change this list, here are the top ways in which most companies currently make money on the Web:

1. Displaying advertising and being paid for click-throughs from the online community to those advertising products or services (the traffic monetizing or advertising model)
2. Selling goods and services online (typically a transactional, wholesale, or retail merchant model)
3. Earning royalties, access fees, or revenue sharing from selling access to their platform to third party developers (known as the API or applet model)
4. Selling aggregate data about online user behaviour or selling controlled access to users with their permission through targeted offers; sometimes called *infomediaries* (the information or data aggregation model)
5. Getting users to subscribe to your service, usually on a monthly or annual basis (the subscription model)
6. Selling upgrades to a premium subscription service by first offering a free service with more limited capacity or capability (the *freemium* model)
7. Imposing a very slight fee for specific transactions that add value beyond some kind of initial free access, which are added up and billed or deducted from a user account (the micro-payments model)
8. Charging a portion of any transaction that you facilitate for others either as a brokerage or as a re-seller, if you are a traditional middle man (the revenue share or royalty model)

9. Using an auction or co-operative model that is a derivative of a transactional or retail site, but with pricing controlled by the marketplace and the variations in supply and demand (the auction or co-operative model)
10. Selling your company to a strategic buyer! (the build to sell model)

Another way to understand e-commerce is to look at the purpose of the website used to implement the various business models. That is, having a great e-commerce business model will not generate a profit if it is not associated with a website that brings in customers or visitors. As with business models, there are a number of ways to classify websites by purpose, as listed in Table 5.2.

Looking at Table 5.2, note that the same website (Yahoo) is an example of two classifications. That's because most B2C websites try to serve as large an audience as possible, thereby making their sites more valuable to advertisers and serving as a source of information about their Web visitors to other companies. For example, Yahoo started out as a type of search engine, and then became a portal by using its popularity to charge for adding links to other websites.

While none of the business models is particularly complicated, they do not always interact easily. Most online companies choose to focus on only one or two of the models to maximize their focus and their profits. In fact, some of these business models are mutually exclusive and could not even co-exist. Yet there is still room for innovation as we continue to explore how e-commerce and social computing intersect with business in new ways. Perhaps you will become an online pioneer after you graduate by building a company with a new e-commerce business model!

Table 5.2	Websites Classified by Purpose		
Website Type	Purpose	Example	Business Model
Portal	Provides a gateway to many other websites	Yahoo, MSN	advertising, affiliate
Search engine	Finds websites that contain a word or phrase	Google, Yahoo, MSN, Dogpile	advertising, affiliate, infomediary
Browse or search and buy	Sells goods and services	Dell, Chapters.indigo.ca, iTunes, VRBO	merchant, infomediary, manufacturer direct, co-operative
Sales support	Provides information on a product before or after the sale	Microsoft, Dell, McAfee, Telus	community, infomediary
Information service	Provides news, information, and commentary	National Post, TSN, Economist	subscription, community, affiliate
Auction	Facilitates sales between third parties	eBay, Priceline, PayPal	brokerage
Travel	Sells travel tickets and tours	Expedia, Travelocity, Orbitz, itravel2000	merchant, brokerage, co-operative
Special interest or services	Provides information, product sales and support, and contacts between visitors	Microsoft support groups, Google Groups, Lavalife, Craigslist	community, merchant, affiliate, infomediary, advertising

Quick Test

1. Fill in the blank. Selling your CD collection on eBay.ca is a form of _____ e-commerce.

2. Which of the following is NOT a known e-commerce business model?
   a. infomediary
   b. auction
   c. subscription
   d. pay as you go

3. True or False. As long as you have visitors to your e-commerce site, you will have a successful e-commerce business model.

Answers: 1. C2C; 2. d; 3. False

THE E-COMMERCE ADVANTAGE

The use of computer networks, especially the Internet, to carry out transactions between buyers and sellers is creating a significant e-commerce advantage in the worldwide economy. This advantage is often referred to as *frictionless transactions*—the ability of the consumer to move from thought to action (i.e., buying to instantly fulfilling the product) creates new opportunities for businesses to operate at lower costs by easing the burden of the supply chain electronically.

To cite just one interesting example of frictionless transactions, think of Craigslist. How did consumers sell an item in decades past? Likely, if the item had sufficient value, they would advertise it in the newspaper classifieds (now a dying business in many markets). However, that cost money and took significant time: to write the ad, to call the newspaper and book it, to review the proof copy, and then to authorize it to run. And, of course, this also implied waiting another day or so before it actually ran in the printed copy of the newspaper. In turn, the buyer had to respond to the ad itself, normally through a phone call (if the seller dared include a telephone number) or by writing to an assigned post-office box. Such lapsed time and cost meant that this method really only made sense for items of real value—in fact, versus the cost, many consumers would have opted for other kinds of methods to sell the unwanted stuff. For instance, there were flea markets (now almost extinct!), or perhaps a garage sale or lawn sale that would only attract local buyers. Regardless of the method, to actually mount the effort to sell the merchandise took some planning, effort, and cost.

Now think about the Web equivalents—eBay or Craigslist, for instance. In a nanosecond, anyone connected to the Web can post an ad, depending on the site, without cost. Consumers in turn can immediately access an ad from any place in the world and transact business—no more relying on the local neighbours or drive-by types looking for a bargain. There are also interesting business models (auctions, commission-based sites, etc.) that help drive new value into the process of classified advertising, and which have re-invented it. As the cost of posting an ad approaches zero and is so easy to do, sellers do it more often for even lower cost items.

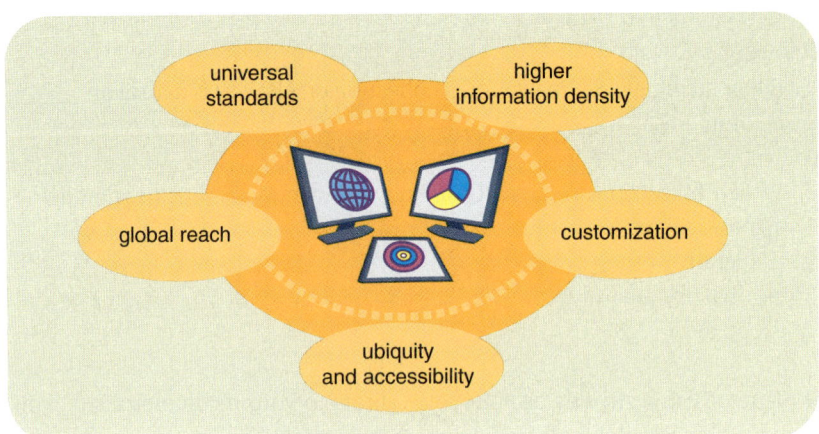

FIGURE 5.3 Impact of e-commerce technologies on business.

This is a great example of the impact of frictionless transactions and the reason why so many newspapers are suffering drops in profit as a result of consumers abandoning an antiquated model for a new, more robust online equivalent.

To understand this better, consider the technology, competitive issues, and strategy associated with e-commerce around the world. When you examine the business use of computer network technologies, especially those associated with the Internet, you find that they offer a number of unique benefits, as Figure 5.3 shows.

People around the world now have Internet access to varying degrees. Some have it only in local Internet cafes; some have a connection directly to their homes or on mobile phones, laptops, BlackBerrys, or other PDAs. This has resulted in the *marketplace* becoming a ubiquitous *marketspace*, with more than 1.5 billion potential customers (people with Internet access) as of June 2009.[1] In Canada, national Internet usage penetration rates are high, with over 82 percent of the population having some form of regular access to the Internet—one of the highest rates in the world.

While still a minority of the world's total population, Internet users are a fast-growing group with significant buying power. That power is often concentrated, because those with Internet access often represent a more economically advantaged economic class overall. Businesses cannot ignore this group when making marketing plans, especially not organizations in North America and Europe, where the Internet is a powerful and growing force for commerce.

The Internet relies on the use of universal technical standards to make it available in the same way, no matter what corner of the world you access it from (see Chapter 2 for more information on the subject of underlying Internet technologies). When combined with open source software applications and development tools, universal standards increase accessibility to the marketplace while also lowering entry costs and encouraging innovation. The innovative uses of the Internet in business have produced truly global competition. Sellers can reach virtually any potential buyer in the world and can easily create a global electronic presence. This

---

1. http://www.Internetworldstats.com/stats.htm, reported as of November 2009.

moves us ever closer to the *perfect market*, described for decades by economists as an ideal situation that theoretically produces the highest consumption at the lowest price for the most goods.

While this global marketplace is great for large retailers like Walmart, it also allows the almost instant creation of niche businesses targeting small markets that would not be dense enough in any single geography to support a small, local retailer. However, when aggregated online, these businesses produce a viable volume of sales to support a global Internet retailer. Smaller businesses like this can compete successfully by targeting specific customers for one-to-one attention. One example of this is the very popular site *www.etsy.com*. Etsy is essentially an online craft fair. Sellers post their handmade items such as knitted slippers, original artwork, or handmade jewellery, and buyers purchase the items through the site's online store. Some products on Etsy are highly customizable and include specific requests from the buyer that might include adding the buyer's name to artwork or selecting custom colours. Without e-commerce, access to these products would be limited to connecting with the artisans directly, likely by word of mouth or seeing them at a craft show. With e-commerce, both buyers and sellers have access to the world's marketplace.

You may not have heard of Etsy and, if some of the sellers on Etsy had websites of their own, you may not have heard of those either. Beyond the need to have a business model that makes you sufficient money that you can afford to offer your service for free, there are the issues of attracting people to your site and marketing to an often overwhelmed consumer. In the following section we discuss information clutter, a growing issue on the Web today.

Information Clutter

The expansion of global e-commerce has also increased buyers' level of **information density**; that is, the quality and quantity of information about products and services of interest to them. For example, websites like *PCMag.com* or *CNet.com* offer product guides, reviews, and prices on many different kinds of technology, from PCs to printers to digital cameras. There are also a wide range of product rating sites that enable consumers to help other consumers, along with online versions of formerly printed buyers' guides like Wine Spectator, Consumers Report, and many others. However, the ability of buyers to obtain almost endless amounts of business information also creates new business challenges. Some businesses have responded by choosing to create business value based on a customization-oriented approach (mass customization or personalization) linked to e-commerce, rather than solely on a low-cost producer strategy.

It is clear that simply having a great website is not enough; you have to make it easy for potential customers to find it. Online merchants use a number of important strategies to accomplish this goal.

Online Advertising The challenge of attracting attention to your site can be partially solved online using the same method as is often used offline—advertising. Google AdWords (see *https://adwords.google.com*) is a way of linking your paid advertising to searches of keywords by consumers. For instance, if you have villas for rent in Hawaii, then you might choose to associate your online ad with searches having to do with vacations, Hawaii, villa rentals, and so on. If you want to be less specific but have a target budget in mind, you can also buy coverage in the form of *cost per click* (CPC) maximums, which work almost like an auction of those competing for placements against popular words and phrases.

Yahoo and other search engines offer similar options and alternatives for online advertising linked to searches, as do certain types of specialized aggregators and placement agencies (e.g., *GoClick.com*). Similarly, banner ad placements (either in bulk or targeted to specific sites) may help you reach your target market online.

Search Engine Optimization All search engines use a technology called *spiders* to crawl the Web and catalogue its content—including your organization's or business's new website. How it then gets labelled and ranked becomes important to its visibility to others online. A variety of techniques are related to making your website both more visible to search engines and more relevant to the way these search engines rank sites to increase the likelihood of appearing higher in the list of any relevant search by consumers. A big part of this is ensuring that your site uses technologies that are easy to search (for example, by avoiding too much use of Flash or embedded video), creating lots of links between your site and others (which increases your rank in many cases), and making good use of meta-tags and content density to appear like a site that offers lots of information and value (a tactic that also creates higher website rankings on search engines). However, like everything on the Web, this space is fast-changing and practices that work today may not continue to work tomorrow, or search engine practices may change as companies develop newer and better ways of providing search results.

Partnering and Traffic Trading You can almost always think of complementary business partners in the offline world that target a similar (or even the same) market as you, but with different products and services, or perhaps different price points and features. An example of this in the offline world is the common dinner and movie pairing. A restaurant near a movie theatre may offer a dinner and movie package for less than the regular cost of one dinner and one movie, thereby encouraging customers to eat dinner at their restaurant prior to the movie. Similarly, in the online world you can partner with other sites and each of you can cross-list the others' website and trade potential traffic that comes to one site. Customers may or may not buy, but they could be interested in something else on your site. In most cases, it's easy to track the origin of traffic and reward the partner site with a commission or fee related to sales it generates for you and vice-versa. This is also a low-cost method of online promotion since it only requires that you identify and contact potential partner sites. Often the parties only pay for results (click throughs, actual sales, etc.) and not any type of set-up or maintenance fee.

Once you have managed to get a potential customer, or *prospect*, to your site, you must find a way to capture his or her interest and, hopefully, encourage a purchase. **Mass customization**, or the ability to create custom products or services on-demand, is one way that Dell has succeeded in the consumer PC business. Through its website, customers can choose from a wide variety of ways to customize a standard Dell PC to match their needs and desires. Other manufacturers have tried this approach as well. For example, you can visit *Bmw.ca* or *Mercedes-Benz.ca* and customize a vehicle that the company will deliver to a dealer in your area.

The E-Commerce Advantage | 177

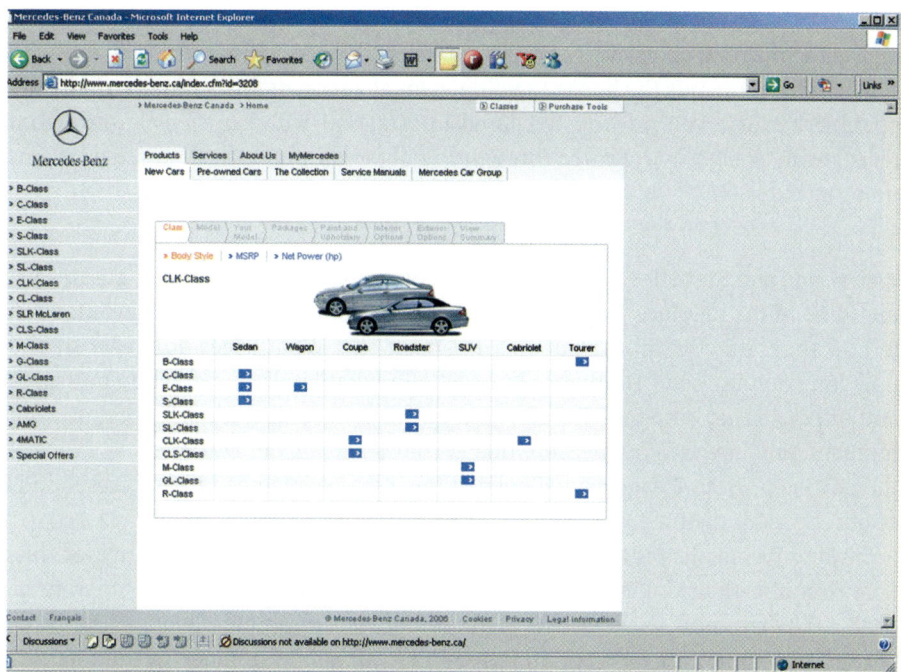

Some businesses use e-commerce to customize their products, such as this website that allows consumers to build their own Mercedes-Benz.

Businesses also use personalization as another way in which e-commerce sites can better reach their customers. **Personalization** is a marketing message that a business customizes for each potential customer's interests, based on his or her searching, browsing, and buying habits. By using personalization, businesses

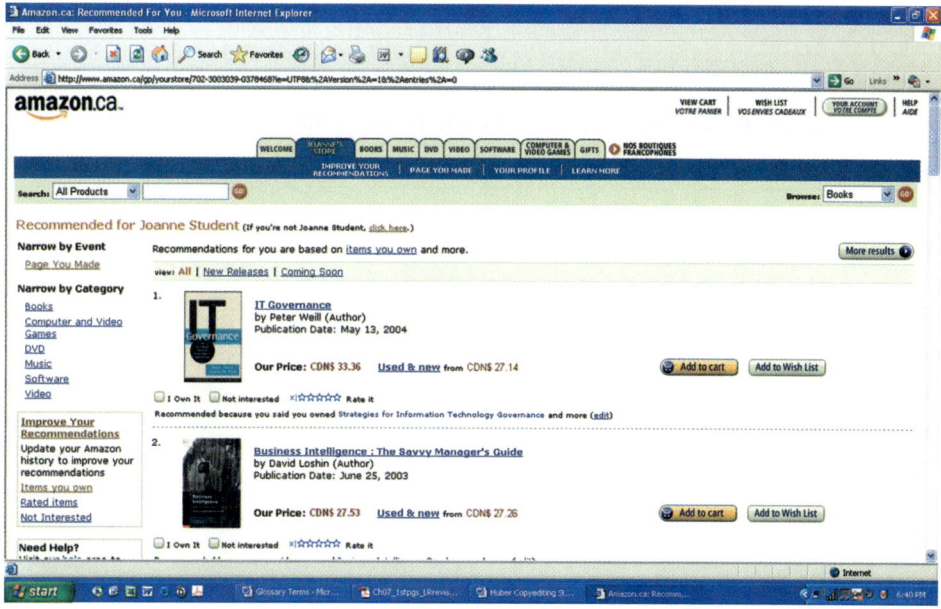

Through personalization, a strategy that Amazon.ca uses effectively, a business customizes its website for each potential customer's interests, based on his or her searching, browsing, and buying habits.

can make marketing messages more effective and efficient. For example if you register with Amazon.ca, you can view a list of book recommendations and why Amazon recommends the books to you. Personalization of this nature is often only possible because you previously shared information with the website through a registration or sign-up form, or through the data you provided to purchase items from the site.

Web Usage and Statistics Once you have your website up and running, besides using some of the methods above to generate new traffic, make sure to pay attention to how the traffic that finds your site uses your site. What pages do they visit and how long do they stay? Do they come back? To what kinds of marketing messages and offers do they respond? Do they join or otherwise indicate some kind of commitment, and how do you measure this in stages and encourage consumers to take the next step? Both IT and non-IT related business people need to ask these kinds of questions all the time.

Many Web statistics reporting software programs are available, many for free. Some require that you install software on your Web server; others operate as SaaS (software as a service). All of these software programs contain the basic required Web metrics for various timeframes, including number of unique visitors, number of page views, where users are coming from (a way to measure the effectiveness of partnerships), which page users exit from on your website, which search engines visitors use to find your website, and more. Figure 5.4 shows the output of one of these programs, indicating the number of unique visitors and page views for several days. Some Web statistics programs offer advanced logging functions, graphing, trend analysis, and integration with other Web programs. For a very comprehensive Web analytics tool, view the Google analytics product tour at *www.google.com/analytics*.

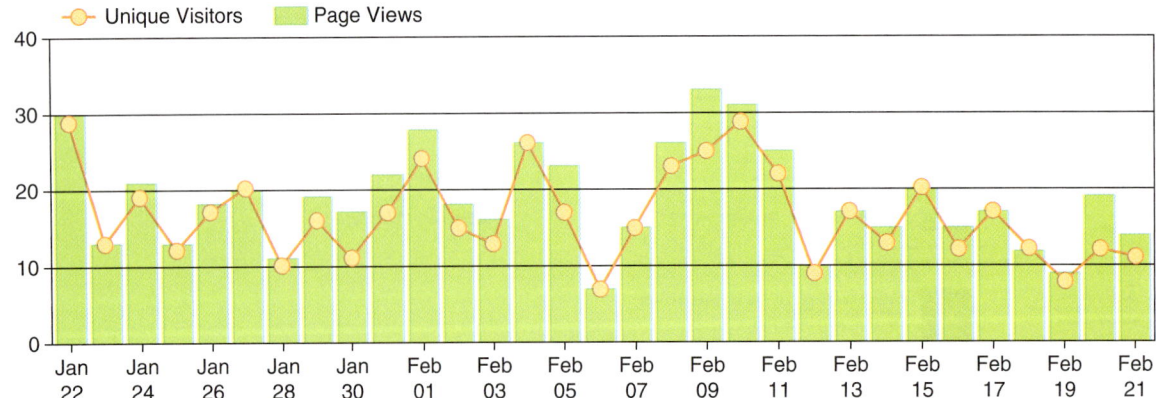

FIGURE 5.4 A simple but important Web statistic is the number of unique visitors to a website. This metric helps to measure if your website is attracting traffic. The sample above, provided by *www.eWebcounter.com*, shows the number of unique visitors and page views by day.

SOURCE: *http://www.ewebcounter.com/summary.jsp?project_id = 54420.* Retrieved February 21, 2010.

E-Commerce Competitive Difference

E-commerce dramatically affects competition between organizations in a number of interesting ways, such as:

- reducing barriers to market entry
- preventing any company from "owning" the market
- enhancing collaboration/alliances
- multiplying market niches
- changing marketplace drivers

To consider each of these impacts, let's use the example of a vacation home rental.

A vacation home is often a sound investment. As the owner, you can use it as well as rent it to others to help cover the costs of the property. Further, because you will probably purchase the vacation home in an area subject to significant increases in property value over time, you can later sell the investment for a large gain.

While investing in a vacation home can be a good idea, it does have problems, especially with traditional commerce. First, you might need to hire a rental agency located in the same area as your property, or advertise in newspapers in those areas where you believe your potential renters might live. However, a rental agency usually charges a significant commission (as much as 50 percent in some cases) and might neglect your property in favour of other rentals that it handles. Advertising in newspapers is expensive and is a hit or miss situation, depending on where potential renters live.

An e-commerce solution to this problem is the use of a **co-operative website**, like *VRBO.com*, *canadavacationrentals.ca*, and *homeaway.com*, where owners of vacation properties co-operate by advertising on the same site. Such websites serve as a meeting place between property owners and renters. For example, the *VRBO.com* (Vacation

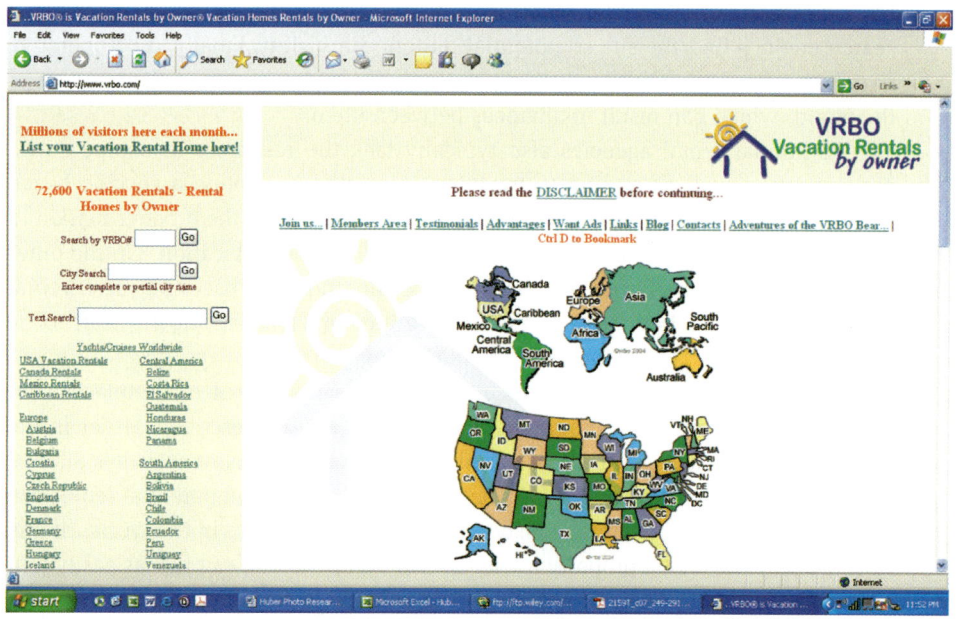

Co-operative websites, such as the one shown here, reflect one significant e-commerce difference in competition by reducing the barrier to entry.

Rentals By Owner) site on the previous page claims to list over 125,000 properties from around the world with 80 million visits to the site each year by renters.[2]

Rental websites, such as those found through search engines like Google, Yahoo, and MSN, also provide an e-commerce solution. Potential renters will find these sites through search engines, advertisements on other websites, or even in traditional travel magazines. These types of websites have quickly become popular with both property owners and renters, for whom the website is basically a meeting place. The actual discussions of availability, price, and rental conditions are handled on a one-to-one basis between the potential renter and the owner. But potential renters can see layouts, complete a virtual tour in some cases, and learn about the property location or community services and so on.

In looking at e-commerce co-operative websites, it should be easy to see how they have dramatically changed the face of the vacation rental market. They have reduced *barriers to entry* by not requiring that a rental agent have an expensive building in a well-travelled location near the vacation area, a list of rental properties to offer potential renters, or a well-known name among past and potential renters. Instead, owners can rely on a much less expensive rental website that will act as a gateway to their individual vacation property website. Even another dominant website does not create any barriers to entry, given the wide open nature of the Internet.

In addition, e-commerce keeps any one rental agency or website from owning the market. The Internet, with the proliferation of search engines, is now the first way that many travellers look for a place to stay on their trips. This bypasses the traditional rental agencies, which often restrict themselves to travellers who happen by their building.

Further, many of the rental websites on the Internet today are co-operative sites that thrive on collaboration—even if the collaborators don't know each other! By co-operating on a popular rental website, property owners virtually ensure that search engines find the site so potential renters can visit it. Finally, a co-operative rental website also enables contacts between property owners in different parts of the world, which can result in alliances between them.

Traditional rental agencies also typically lack the resources to compete in a niche market, such as renting to travellers interested in visiting a specific beach known for its high-quality shells. Such agencies must rent to the broader market to cover the high fixed costs associated with having a physical location. On the other hand, vacation property owners can easily set up and advertise on a niche rental website. **Niche markets** are one area where e-commerce has shown itself to be superior to almost any existing form of marketing.

Finally, time, distance, and price all drive the traditional marketplaces, but e-commerce can easily overcome these limitations (as we described earlier in the Craigslist versus classified newspaper advertising example). Now websites allow a business to stay open on a 24/7/365 basis, and the owner and potential renter can communicate almost instantaneously from virtually anywhere in the world, at any time. This means that a property owner in Canmore, Alberta, can just as easily rent to somebody from Germany as they can to somebody from Edmonton. This was

2. http://www.vrbo.com, as of January 2010.

not really feasible prior to the Web because of time and cost. In terms of price, because the Internet generates so much data, a seller or renter can determine demand patterns based on prior experience or on data from other users. This means that negotiations on price between owner and potential renter can rely on availability and demand, rather than on a one-size-fits-all pricing scheme. And since pricing is a very strategic issue for any business regardless of size, this brings us to our next important topic: the integration of e-commerce into business strategy.

E-Commerce and Business Strategy

Technology advances change business strategy. To better understand this statement, consider *business strategy* in general terms. Henry Mintzberg, a professor at McGill University and a leading thinker on strategy and leadership, suggests that strategy is a plan, pattern, position, and perspective. This is very sound and, when broken down, becomes quite comprehensive in terms of guiding the action of an organization. He argues that strategy emerges and evolves over time in natural response to a constantly emerging competitive landscape and the individual performance level of any competitor in that market space. A change in either a company's performance in relation to the competition or a major change in competition (for instance, the emergence of a disruptive industry force, the emergence of a new competitor, innovations in business models, or the introduction of new government regulations) could necessitate revisiting business strategy. A strategy may start as a perspective (vision, direction) that calls for a certain position, such as being a low-cost provider, and then evolves into a plan that is implemented, and emerges as a pattern that is evident in actions and decisions.[3] Of course, in today's highly tech-dependent world, where the Internet is certainly a major force for innovation and change, no business strategy would likely be complete without addressing the question of how to integrate the Web and e-commerce into the overall business strategy.

E-commerce strategy is a general term for how a business intends to use computer Web-based networks and information systems to compete in its global marketplace. For example, Manheim Auctions is the largest automobile auction company in the world. When the Internet became a reality, Manheim was also one of the first of such companies to explore ways to use it to protect its market share from potential encroachment by competitors. This is a good example of what Mintzberg calls ever-green strategy. This organization chose to strategically apply e-commerce to the wholesale used car market by creating an online purchase system, an online bidding system, and a co-operative system that enables individuals to sell their automobiles. They did this, even at the expense of revenue in their legacy business model, rather than wait for a competitor to do it and change their leadership position. The Internet cannot be ignored. Manheim changed its perspective and looked for ways to use the Internet to further its competitive goals of serving its customers better, demonstrating this co-dependence between strategy formulation and the impact of new technologies as a way of maintaining business performance and competitive position.

Building a meaningful e-commerce strategy requires two different views of an organization's strategy: what it wants to do (conceptual strategy), and how it will

---
3. Henry Mintzberg, *The Rise and Fall of Strategic Planning*, (1994), Basic Books.

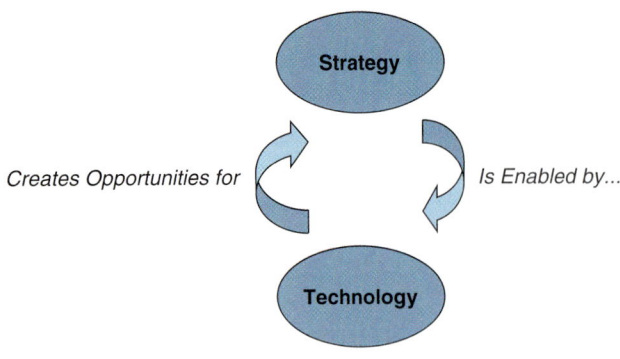

FIGURE 5.5 The intersection of strategy and technology.

do it (technology strategy). Often there will be a gap between the two that must be addressed if you are to successfully execute your strategy. Obviously, the two views are interlinked (see Figure 5.5). For example, having the technological capability to carry out an activity will result in business failure if no market exists. Similarly, relying on a new technology to create competitive advantage has both costs and risks associated with it that will have to be recovered in new sources of profit (see online references to *Pets.com* or the story of Friendster losing its initially leading market position to Myspace and Facebook as great examples of this strategic risk). Just ask the people who lost money in one or more of the dot-com companies in the late 1990s about the business complications of balancing these two challenges!

An important strategy that many companies are using is to connect their online Web strategy to their existing *customer relationship management (CRM)* to create an integrated one-to-one marketing experience for their customers. The Web generates a huge amount of data on customer buying habits and preferences that can be stored and instantly recalled and applied with each new visit (using cookies or other technologies, for instance). With these data, companies can use CRM to tailor the products on their website to the individual buyer, or perhaps create customer-specific offers and campaigns or keep track of specific discount levels or specific inducements or entitlements offered to repeat buyers. For example, your organization could create automatic shipping notifications when orders leave the warehouse so customers know their order is on the way. You can then follow up with automatic online surveys to ensure a highly satisfied customer. This creates a closer match to the customers' real needs, which, in turn, increases the probability they will return to the website for another purchase. However, this can also give rise to privacy concerns, and many of these strategies require customers to give their consent to storing critical information about them (Chapter 9 addresses privacy and other ethical concerns).

The value of overcoming privacy concerns is that the use of CRM can also create switching costs for customers. Going to another seller means that they will have to retrain a new website to understand their preferences. Good service from an existing supplier is a known factor in repeat-purchase decisions, and online vendors should take this seriously.

Other e-commerce strategies that companies use to increase business value to consumers include use of virtual showrooms, increased channel choices, wider component choice, and use of mobile technology. Of course, just as the Web itself was a disruptive technology, the rapid expansion of mobile data networks and phones is another current example of a technology innovation that demands a strategic business response.

M-Commerce

Possibly the largest new channel for many businesses (both online and traditional business models) is the use of mobile devices with wireless networks to access the Internet. This technology, in turn, enables mobile commerce (m-commerce) applications to become a reality, and ensures that consumers can immediately react in the moment to any marketing message (rather than waiting to get home to their computers to access the Internet). **Mobile commerce** is the use of laptops, mobile telephones, and PDAs to connect to the Internet and Web to conduct many of the activities normally associated with e-commerce, but in real time and without regard to where the user may actually be at the moment. Firms now have two-way interaction with customers through these mobile devices and in new ways that can enable entire new applications. For instance, one company is currently exploring the issues of providing consumers with instant-use coupons in grocery stores.

Another great example of mobile commerce is the group buying sites like *Groupon.com* (the U.S. market leader) or *TeamSave.com* (a recent Canadian start-up). If, for example, you are shopping in Loblaws and you have enabled teamsave's application, it will detect small electronic sensors in the aisles of the supermarket to "ping" you with an instant coupon. The sensors can also detect things like you passing rapidly by products (indicating you are likely not interested or possibly only interested if you get pinged) or when you are stationary (perhaps suggesting that you are browsing the shelves of competitive products and that, perhaps, an electronic offer in the moment might cause you to buy one product over another on that shelf). On the other hand, if you like the group buying phenomenon, you can sign up for a limited amount of time for a group buy, redeem your coupon (sent to your mobile device, by the way!), and take home your new treasure—and save money too!

Mobile commerce is continually changing the way people shop. Some stores are equipped with small electronic sensors in the aisle that "ping" your mobile device with an instant coupon as you pass by.

To offer the service to consumers for free, the application charges both the product manufacturers and the grocery stores for the technology and application, as well as occasionally charging a commission or fee (this varies) to the product or service seller. The hopes of the companies involved are obviously to gain the ability to influence sales to consumers by learning more about what offers, purchasing patterns, and available choices interact to cause consumers to buy more or different products through different devices at various times of day.

This is only one example of what will shortly become a flood of m-commerce-type applications available to North American consumers. Again, if you are thinking about an organization's strategy, there is no doubt about the need to address the implications of mobile technology on your existing business model—or else someone else will!

Now that you have a better understanding of e-commerce and the difference it makes, let's look at the business-to-consumer (B2C) and business-to-business (B2B) sectors.

Quick Test

Choose the BEST answer from column B for each item in column A.

Column A	Column B
1. customization	a. competing sellers partnering on a common website
2. frictionless transaction	b. creating products on demand
3. co-operative website	c. providing products/services efficiently and reducing cost and involvement of the provider

---

Answers: 1. b; 2. c; 3. a

BENEFITS AND LIMITATIONS OF E-COMMERCE

Recall our discussion of *business strategy* in Chapter 3, and specifically Michael Porter's five forces model. In general, because having information about and access to larger markets increases the buyer's knowledge of a good deal, Porter's model suggests that e-commerce increases competition. This often results in lower prices and better services for all consumers, online or not. However, there may be disadvantages or limitations for consumers in the form of shipping time and costs, download speeds, security, and payment sizes that create some barriers to the use of this technology for some kinds of transactions or industries. On the flip side, the increased competition, lower prices, and better services that consumers now expect can create problems for inefficient businesses as newer, more tech-savvy competitors enter the industry. Table 5.3 lists some advantages and disadvantages of B2C e-commerce for both consumers and businesses. You are probably familiar with most of these advantages and disadvantages for the consumer.

In looking at Table 5.3, note the number of advantages of B2C e-commerce for businesses. Expansion of the marketplace enables businesses to reach customers far beyond their local area with a minimal capital outlay. Businesses also reduce their cost of dealing with paper-based transactions by carrying out transactions digitally over a computer network.

Customizing individual web pages to the interests of customers also creates greater customer loyalty. Amazon.ca has turned this into a key advantage that keeps customers coming back, since they don't have to train a new website to know their interests. The use of niche marketing helps companies react to changing competition. For instance, many travel agencies have turned to specialized travel niches (for example, those specializing in a specific area such as *www.findcroatia.com*). Finally, more direct communication with customers, even when an intermediary

Table 5.3	Benefits and Limitations of B2C E-Commerce	
	Benefits	**Limitations**
Consumer	• Lower prices • Shopping 24/7 • Greater searchability of products worldwide • Shorter delivery times for digital products • More sharing of information with other consumers • Improved customer service	• Delay in receiving physical products, plus shipping charges • Slow download speeds in areas without high-speed Internet • Security and privacy concerns, especially with the rise of *phishing* (a scam intended to gain private information for fraudulent use) • Inability to touch, feel, smell, try out, or try on products prior to purchasing • Unavailability of micropayments for purchases of small-cost products
Business	• Expansion of marketplace to global proportions • Cheaper electronic transactions • Greater customer loyalty through customized web pages and one-to-one marketing • Expansion of niche marketing opportunities • Direct communications with customers through website, often resulting in better customer service	• Increased competition due to global marketplace • Ease of comparison between competing products drives prices down • Customers want specific choices and will not accept substitutes • Customers control flow of information instead of companies

SOURCE: Some, but not all, of these are from E. Turban et. al., *Electronic Commerce: A Managerial Perspective* (2002), Prentice-Hall: Upper Saddle River, NJ, pp. 26–28.

sells the product, results in better customer service. For example, a large company like Moen (*moen.com*), which markets kitchen and bath products, can provide customers with detailed drawings of its products directly over the Internet, as well as design information prior to the sale.

However, e-commerce carries definite disadvantages for inefficient companies that often mirror the potential advantages. A global marketplace means that companies from around the world can compete for a business's local customers, creating a very intense industry rivalry. More competition driving down prices is like having a Walmart next to every business. If a business is not ready to compete on a price basis, then it must offer some service that its competitor cannot, like more customized products or more individual attention. Finally, with a wide variety of advertising media, companies must know how to attract customers to their websites.

One way to attract customers to websites is to ensure protection of sensitive data, such as credit card information. As a result of consumer concern, many online vendors resort to third-party endorsements of their security practices to help build consumer confidence. An example of this would be overlay brands, such as *www.truste.org*, that an organization qualifies for and then advertises on its site. It is important that online businesses are secure and that they safeguard consumer information.

> ### WHAT DO YOU THINK?
>
> What stalled e-commerce in its early days was consumer distrust of online payment systems, especially if they involved giving out credit card information. Over time, this has become less of an issue as secure computing has gained consumer trust and as various new types of "digital cash" systems have emerged on the Web, such as PayPal. Consider these questions as an Internet user:
>
> 1: Have you ever used an online payment system like PayPal? If so, for what? Did you trust it would work the first time? Why or why not?
> 2: What are the signs of legitimacy that you look for in a website before providing your credit card information for payment?
> 3: Have you ever had a payment problem on the Internet? What were the consequences or solutions to the problem?

Another way companies are attempting to increase consumer comfort levels with e-commerce is through the use of technology provided by credit card companies. Have you ever been on an e-commerce website and been asked to provide your credit card security code as part of the transaction? Figure 5.6 shows the location of the security code on the back side of a Visa and MasterCard. It is assumed that if consumers are able to provide the security code, they have the physical card in their possession, and that the card number is not being used by anyone other than the card holder.

If you have made a large purchase online (e.g., airline tickets, computer) you will have seen a higher level of security offered by credit card companies. During the e-commerce transaction process, an additional screen is presented asking you to enter a special code. This screen is provided by the credit card company, "Verified by Visa" and "MasterCard SecureCode," respectively, and collects a code that is required to authorize purchases that you set up previously. Again, this assumes that only the card holder is doing the purchase online, and that this security code has not been shared with anyone.

FIGURE 5.6 E-commerce sites often ask for credit card security codes during a transaction to provide a higher level of security.

SOURCE: *https://support.swishzone.com/swishstore/csv.htm*. Retrieved February 21, 2010.

TECHNOLOGY CORE

Having an e-commerce business idea would be irrelevant without the technology to enable it. In Chapter 2 we discussed the technology of e-commerce and briefly discussed order and payment systems, including the protocols (SSL) and standards (SET) used for transactions. Here we focus on encryption, the most common method of providing security to e-commerce transactions. Encryption is the process of scrambling a message so that it is meaningful only to the person holding the key to deciphering it. To everyone else, the message is gobbledygook. The reverse process, decryption, converts a seemingly senseless character string into the original message.

There are two primary forms of encryption systems: (1) private key and (2) public key encryption. *Private key* encryption uses the same private key to encrypt and decrypt a message. A key is an algorithm used to encode and decode messages. While private key encryption may sound like the simplest method, there are significant problems with it. For example, how do you securely distribute the key? You can't send the private key with the message, because if the message is intercepted, the key can be used to decipher it. You must find another secure medium for transmitting the key. Do you fax or telephone the key instead? Neither method is completely secure, and each is time-consuming to use whenever the key is changed. In addition, how do you know that the key's receiver will protect its secrecy? Another problem with private key encryption is that you have to create a separate private key for each person or organization with which you will exchange encrypted messages.

In contrast, a *public key* encryption system has two keys: one private and the other public. The public key is freely distributed and used to encrypt messages coming to you. In contrast, the private key remains secret and is only used to decrypt the messages encrypted with your public key. For example, you would distribute your public key to anybody who might need to send you encrypted messages. They would encrypt a message with your public key. Upon receiving the message, you would apply the private key, as shown in Figure 5.7. Your private key, the only key that can decrypt the message, must be kept secret to permit secure message exchange. Public key encryption is widely used in e-commerce to ensure the safety and privacy of transactions.

Did you know that this encryption/decryption process is done each time you provide information on the Web, and especially when transactions are involved? Feeling a bit more secure now?

FIGURE 5.7 The process of public key encryption.

All in all, however, the advantages of e-commerce continue to outweigh any limitations. As a result, businesses are turning to e-commerce business models to find more ways to compete in the global marketplace. Statistics Canada reported that, in 2006, Canadian retailers had online sales of $4.7 billion, with 46 percent of Canadian retail firms having a website.[4] While these B2C numbers are impressive, they pale in comparison to the B2B sales results of $31.4 billion in 2006.[5] Updated figures from Statistics Canada suggest that e-commerce trends continue to rise both

---

[4]. Statistics Canada, http://www.statcan.gc.ca/daily-quotidien/070420/dq070420b-eng.htm. Retrieved November 1, 2009.

[5]. Statistics Canada, http://www.statcan.gc.ca/daily-quotidien/070420/dq070420b-eng.htm and http://www.statcan.gc.ca/daily-quotidien/080424/dq080424a-eng.htm. Retrieved November 1, 2009.

in the private and public sectors, including an increasing propensity for businesses to buy online.[6]

E-COMMERCE BETWEEN ORGANIZATIONS

Even though most of the emphasis in the popular press has been on the B2C form of e-commerce, B2B is by far the larger market in terms of volume of transactions and dollar amounts. One business or organization doing business with another markedly differs from the B2C process. For example, if you decide you need a new computer, you think about what you need in a new PC and then search for computer merchants that sell the product that meets your needs. You most likely make the purchase with a credit card and set it up yourself when it arrives. You then pay the bill from your personal bank account.

On the other hand, if an organization decides it needs new PCs, it's not just ordering one computer at a time, but potentially thousands of PCs. This larger-scale purchase results in a more complex decision-making process, like that discussed in Chapter 3, requiring a great deal of thought and preparation. One or more authorized individuals must consider a number of factors, including the existing organizational technology infrastructure.

B2B Transactions and Business Models

We can broadly divide B2B transactions into two types: (1) spot buying and (2) strategic sourcing. **Spot buying** is much like what you do when you make a stock market transaction; you buy at market prices determined by supply and demand from someone you do not know. Companies often engage in spot buying to purchase goods and services that are commodities; that is, they are usually uniform in quality and differ only somewhat in price. Examples include gasoline, paper, and cleaning supplies. Whenever a company engages in spot buying, it needs to find a public marketplace or *exchange* that sells these desired products and services. Although it can be a physical marketplace, most B2B e-commerce exchange transactions occur through an online intermediary.

On the other hand, **strategic sourcing** involves forming a long-term relationship with another company. The companies set prices through negotiation. Both the buyer and seller are usually well known to each other and wish to continue a trading relationship into the future. A company's large-scale computer purchases probably result from strategic sourcing.

Strategic sourcing often relies on a one-to-one business model, although company-centric and exchange models are also used.[7] In the **one-to-one marketing model**, two companies collaborate to create a trading relationship that is good for both of them. In this form of B2B, both trading partners win from the relationship, as with strategic sourcing transactions. While they are not always of the same relative size, neither company dominates the trading relationship. From an e-commerce point of view, the two companies often seek to use computer networks to facilitate the supply chain from one to the other. (We discuss this model in more detail in a later section.)

---

6. http://www.statcan.gc.ca/daily-quotidien/080424/dq080424a-eng.htm. Retrieved April 7, 2010.

7. E. Turban et. al., *Electronic Commerce: A Managerial Perspective*, (2002), Prentice-Hall: Upper Saddle River, NJ, pp. 220-221.

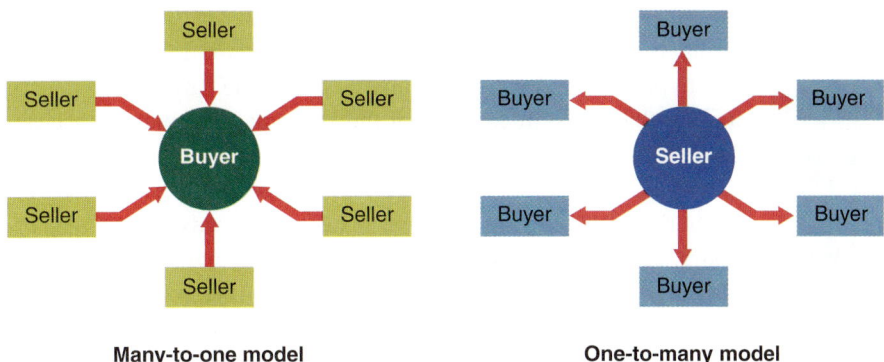

FIGURE 5.8 With the company-centric business model, a company is either a buyer from many companies (many-to-one) or a seller to many other companies (one-to-many).

With the **company-centric business model**, a company is either a seller to many other companies (one-to-many) or a buyer from many companies (many-to-one), as Figure 5.8 shows. In either case, the single company tends to dominate the market. It often completely controls the information systems that support the transactions, including the supply chains between it and its smaller trading partners. In this model, the large buyer or seller wants to use e-commerce to improve its profitability by increasing prices and/or reducing costs of doing business with the many smaller trading partners.

With the one-to-many model, the seller often provides a Web-based private sales channel through a private network, called *electronic data interchange (EDI)*, or through a protected form of the Internet, called an *extranet*, to link trading partners while keeping others out (we discuss both EDI and extranets in more detail later). Such sales can be at a set price or via an auction. For example, *Carbid.ca* uses an extranet to enable car dealers to purchase used cars online, thereby avoiding a costly trip to the physical auction. It has specified prices for cars, as well as online auctions at which dealers can bid on automobiles.

Because the many-to-one model provides a single buyer with products that it needs to carry on business, this is a part of the *procurement process*. When using e-commerce, it is commonly referred to as **e-procurement**. A buyer can conduct this process in a number of ways, including reverse auctions, aggregating catalogues, or group purchasing.

With an e-procurement reverse auction, the buyer posts projects to a secure website to which sellers respond with bids for providing goods and services for that project. In this case, the bidder with the *lowest* bid wins, hence the name *reverse auction*. The aggregating catalogues model assembles together the catalogues from all suppliers on the buyer's server. The buyer then uses them to make all purchases. This tends to centralize the procurement process. Finally, with group purchasing, two or more buyers work together to achieve lower prices from their suppliers. Smaller buyers can do this through websites that aggregate demand and then negotiate prices with suppliers.

In the **exchange model**, many companies use an exchange to buy and sell from each other through spot-buying transactions. The exchange can be a co-operative venture among a number of the companies, owned by an independent organization

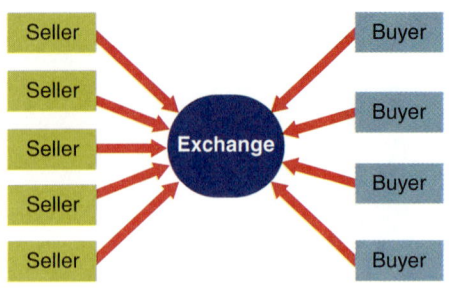

FIGURE 5.9 From an e-commerce point of view, an exchange is typically a website where buyers and sellers post their needs and offerings.

like that run by the National Retail Federation for the benefit of its members. It can also be run by a larger company that has found a way to profit from the transactions. The airplane parts exchange created by Boeing is an example of the last type of exchange (see the Case Study at the end of this chapter).

We can categorize exchanges into two groups: (1) verticals and (2) horizontals. *Vertical exchanges* meet the needs of a single industry, say, retailing. On the other hand, *horizontal exchanges* deal with products and services that all companies need, regardless of the industry (like office supplies). Figure 5.9 shows how buyers and sellers come together in an exchange. From an e-commerce point of view, an exchange is typically a website where buyers and sellers post their needs and offerings. For example, for a fee, the *Workpolis.com* website posts both resumés and job openings.

Using B2B E-Commerce to Improve Supply Chain Efficiency

Recall from our discussion of the *value chain* in Chapter 4 that the inbound and outbound logistics (movement of goods or services from supplier to organization and from organization to customer, respectively) of a company are linked to the logistics of other companies via its supply chain. Also recall from Chapter 4 that a *supply chain* is a system of organizations, people, technology, activities, information, and resources involved in moving a product or service from supplier to customer. More specifically, it is a network of facilities and distribution options that performs the functions of procurement of materials, transformation of these materials into intermediate and finished products, and the distribution of these finished products to customers.[8] Procurement plays a large part in any supply chain, and the use of e-commerce for procurement is an important way for organizations to save money. To understand why, we need to first review the traditional procurement process.

Traditional Procurement Process For procurement to occur between businesses there must be an information flow between the entities in addition to the flow of goods. Traditionally, this paper flow has involved three key elements: (1) the purchase order, (2) the invoice, and (3) the receipt of goods. Figure 5.10 shows the typical steps in the process.

1. The buyer sends a purchase order to a vendor. A *purchase order (PO)* is a document from an organization requesting another organization to supply something in return for payment. It typically provides product specifications and quantities, with this information often coming from the supplier's catalogue.
2. The vendor responds to the PO by sending the goods to the buyer along with a *bill of lading (BOL)*, which describes the contents of the shipment.
3. After receiving the goods and BOL, the buyer sends back a signed copy of the BOL to the vendor and internally files a *receipt of goods*.

---

8. Ram Ganeshan and Terry P. Harrison, "An Introduction to Supply Chain Management," http://lcm.csa.iisc.ernet.in/scm/supply_chain_intro.html.

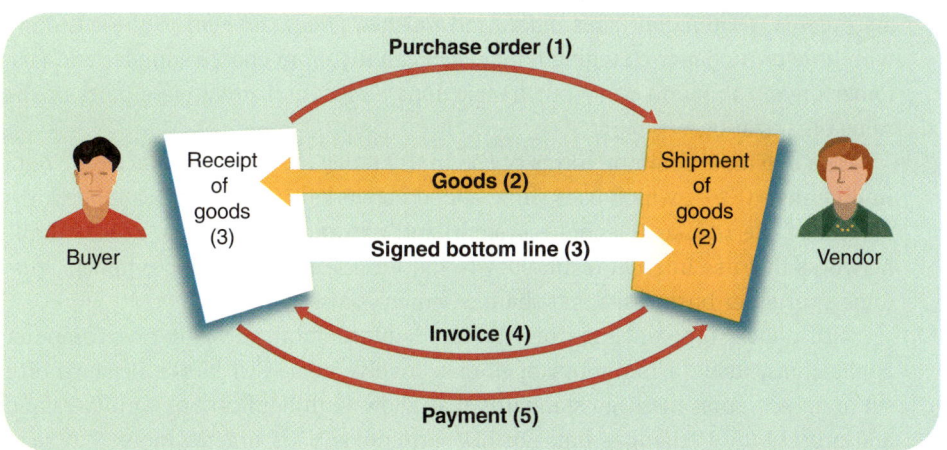

FIGURE 5.10 The traditional procurement method, which requires documents at every step, is often an inefficient process.

4. The vendor sends an invoice to the buyer. An *invoice* is a detailed list of goods shipped from the supplier, along with a list of all costs and discounts. In essence, it is a detailed bill and request for payment.
5. The buyer's accounting department compares the original PO with the receipt of goods and the invoice to ensure they match. After confirming a match, the buyer pays the vendor.

As you can see, the traditional procurement process relies on all paper-based documents. The employees in the accounting department have to pull all of them together and make an item-by-item comparison. Not only is this very tedious and time-consuming, it is also subject to errors and fraud.

Using E-Commerce to Improve the Procurement Process E-commerce, with its digital information, replaces the paper documents in traditional procurement systems. Employees can quickly compare the digital files with far fewer errors and less opportunity for fraud. While companies still compare all three key documents—PO, receipt of goods, and invoice—prior to payment, automating the process is a giant step in the right direction. In fact, some companies have moved ahead by authorizing payment on receipt, thereby eliminating the need for invoicing (Steps 4 and 5 in Figure 5.10).

E-procurement is also evolving into a tighter integration and coordination of the activities of a supplier–buyer relationship through the creation and use of interorganizational systems. An **interorganizational system (IOS)** is "a networked information system used by two or more separate organizations to perform a joint business function."[9] IOS can help to create 24/7 communications between organizations and their suppliers and customers, as well as enable paperless transactions throughout the supply chain. An IOS often involves electronically linking a production company to its suppliers or to its customers in such a way that raw materials

---

[9]. J. I. Cash, Jr., F. W. McFarlan, J. L. McKenney, and L. M. Applegate, *Corporate Information Systems Management: Text and Cases*, 1994, 4th ed. Homewood, IL: Irwin, p. 339.

are ordered, production takes place, and finished goods are sent to the customer with little or no paper changing hands. IOS can therefore enable supplier and customer organizations to carry out transactions almost as if they were parts of the same organization.

The two most common forms of IOS in use today are based on **electronic data interchange (EDI)**, which uses value-added networks (VANs) or private networks instead of the regular telephone system, and **extranets**, which are collaborative networks that use Internet technology to link businesses with their suppliers, customers, or other businesses that share common goals.

EDI allows the exchange of structured information between two computer applications, using a minimum of human involvement. EDI works because of a set of agreed-upon message standards that allow both applications to understand and process the exchanged data. In EDI terminology, the organizations that send or receive documents from each other are called *trading partners*. These partners agree on which specific information to exchange and how to use it.

Although the initial purpose of EDI was to replace the exchange of paper-based documents with more efficient and flexible electronic documents, trading partners have since realized several additional benefits from its use. An EDI system can save unnecessary recapture of data, which leads to faster data transfer, fewer errors, and a more streamlined business process. Firms can also use EDI as a platform for automating existing processes. This can help to reduce costs further, as well as improve the quality and speed of services. Finally, since EDI requires co-operation between trading partners, it can also serve as a catalyst for improving interorganizational processes and improving overall supply chain efficiency.

EDI is older technology that is often overshadowed by the newer cutting-edge technologies such as the World Wide Web and XML. Nevertheless, EDI remains an important part of business. It is still the engine behind a majority of all e-commerce transactions in the world.

An extranet uses Internet technologies to interconnect the intranet of an organization with the intranets of its business partners. Through the extranet, customers, suppliers, consultants, and other trading partners can access selected sites and data available on the internal intranet. Keep in mind that while an extranet extends access to the network outside the boundaries of the organization, usually over the Internet, it is still a private network. Security measures, such as usernames and passwords, usually control access to the extranet. Companies may also use the additional security measures of encryption and firewalls.

As companies realized the advantages of sharing data and information with trading partners, they began to develop extranets as a way to allow these trading partners to access limited areas available on the intranet. An extranet is somewhere in-between a private intranet and the public Internet. There is still a firewall between the intranet and public access, but it is now set to open for selected outsiders. Because EDI requires the use of expensive VANs or private networks, most businesses find it too expensive. However, through the use of an extranet, the Internet enables smaller companies to take advantage of IOS. Another way of connecting with customers or partners is by using a customer portal. A customer portal is available over the Internet and is secured through

Table 5.4	Comparing EDI and Extranet-Enabled B2B E-Commerce		
	EDI	**Extranet**	**Customer Portal**
Security	More secure due to use of private network.	Less secure than EDI due to use of Internet, but can be made safer through use of security measures (e.g., strong passwords, encryption).	About the same level of security as using an extranet. Limits public access by using https:// protocol, but is public facing and is available wherever the Internet is available.
Cost	More costly due to proprietary software and use of VANS.	Less costly because with enhanced features, an organization's extranet can evolve as an extension of its intranet, allowing for the use of existing networks and possible reuse of Internet-enabled applications.	Even less costly than the others as it simply uses a Web front end to access internally available applications.
Flexibility	Less flexible because proprietary software limits use primarily to standard business documents.	More flexible because it is based on the Internet, which permits greater customization and wider access to development tools.	Similar to extranets in that anything that is possible on the Web can be done on a customer portal. Further customization by customer may be possible by changing the look of the Web interface to be specific to each customer when it enters the portal.
Trend	Gradually being replaced by extranet-based applications.	Gaining wider acceptance due to lower costs and increased use of the Internet.	Becoming widely used as it tends to be simple to set up and maintain.

the use of https protocol and customer/partner authentication. Table 5.4 highlights some differences between EDI, extranet-enabled, and customer portal B2B e-commerce.

Does e-procurement work in the real world? Absolutely. For example, Scotland exploited technology to facilitate collaboration and change through use of a common platform, *eProcurement Scotl@nd*. The results so far have been very positive. Since its creation in 2002, governmental entities have placed more than 260,000 orders for goods and services from thousands of suppliers, spending in excess of 271 million Scottish pounds. In fact, this effort has been so successful that *eProcurement Scotl@nd* was a finalist for Scotland's National e-Government Excellence Award.[10] The government of British Columbia has introduced procurement technology called BC Bid®. This software gives businesses that would like to sell to the provincial government the ability to access, create, browse, and compete on public sector opportunities at any time.[11] The federal government and other provincial governments have, at minimum, posted rules and procedures for selling to their governments on their websites to facilitate procurement.

---

10. The eProcurement Scotl@nd home page and other pages on the site. http://www.eprocurementscotland.com/default.asp?page=1

11. http://www.bcbid.gov.bc.ca/open.dll/welcome

Quick Test

1. Which of the following is NOT an e-commerce benefit for businesses?
   a. Expansion of marketplace to global proportions
   b. More expensive electronic transactions
   c. Greater customer loyalty through customized web pages and one-to-one marketing
   d. Expansion of niche marketing opportunities

2. True or False. An extranet is a semi-private network that enables organizations to electronically handle the trading process.

3. Fill in the blank. A(n) _____ is a networked information system used by two or more separate organizations to perform a joint business function.

Answers: 1. B; 2. True; 3. interorganizational system

What's in IT for me?

Have you ever thought of opening your own e-business? Perhaps an e-commerce site? Today, more than ever, opening your own e-business is easy to do as long as you have basic knowledge of how to register a retail business in the province in which you live. Once you have your company name and retail sales tax registrations in hand, you can simply visit *www.ebay.com/stores*, pick your options and—voila—you're literally in business overnight. Much easier than opening a retail store location and, better still, online you can sell to the world!

If eBay stores is not for you, there are several services available online that will help you create an e-business. Check out *www.estore.com* or *www.zen-cart.com*. Both services have a simple, build-it-yourself interface, along with all of the order and payment processing components you need to run your business.

What's in IT for an organization?

Just as you can save yourself money through group buying with *TeamSave.com* or *Groupon.com*, businesses are also starting to participate in consortiums to buy things that all organizations might need. For instance, many industries are similar vertically, with common suppliers, and are therefore setting up group purchasing organizations (GPOs). These entities are created to leverage the buying power of its member businesses. Good examples of this model in the U.S. can be found at *www.higpa.org* (the Health Industry Group Purchasing Association) or the very similar Canadian organization (the St. Joseph's Health System Group Purchasing Organization, at *www.sjhcs-gpo.com*). By joining together and integrating their individual supply chains (process and technology) and using B2B e-commerce, they achieve economies of scale and discounts that they could not achieve individually.

What's in IT for society

Economists have always talked about the creation of a perfect labour market being a panacea for workers—one where workers and employers could find each other and simply interact directly to let market supply and demand set up their employment arrangements. The theory is that this would enable workers to get the best possible price for their skills and abilities and align labour rates to value-added activities created in the business. Today, it's much more common for jobs to be sourced through headhunters, agencies, or others with a vested interest in the outcome of the search, and often with an economic incentive to artificially raise or lower the labour rates being negotiated (depending on their business model).

The Internet gets us one step closer to that perfect market concept by making it possible to create online labour markets. One example of this would be *Elance.com*, a site designed specifically to connect professionals with available projects. This site, for example, enables Turkish programmers to bid for Canadian Web development projects, and Canadian programmers to bid for Turkish Web development projects. Elance's website provides running totals of the number of professionals registered on the site and the earnings these professionals have collected. See *www.elance.com/skills_central* for today's total. As of April 10, 2010, this page listed 107,223 professional with earnings of $260,818,424. Clearly they are doing something right!

ROI STUDENT RETURN ON INVESTMENT SUMMARY

1. **What is e-commerce and how is it a part of today's economy?**

E-commerce is the use of information systems, technologies, and computer networks by individuals and organizations to carry out transactions in order to create or support the creation of business value. Almost all sectors of today's economy rely on it: business (B), consumer (C), and government (G). The primary relationships between these sectors result in C2C, C2G, B2C, B2B, and B2G e-commerce.

2. **How does e-commerce create value and make a difference to businesses and consumers?**

E-commerce makes a difference to businesses and consumers in a number of ways, including technology, competition, and strategy. For example, the use of technology in e-commerce has resulted in information density, which businesses have responded to through mass customization and personalization. In terms of competition, e-commerce (1) reduces barriers to entry for consumers and new businesses; (2) helps keep any one company from owning the market; (3) provides more opportunities for collaboration and alliances among various stakeholders; (4) increases the number of market niches; and (5) affects the traditional marketplace drivers of time, distance, and price.

Finally, e-commerce demands specific strategy, such as CRM, which allows businesses to create a one-to-one marketing experience. E-commerce provides both advantages and limitations to consumers and businesses; see Table 5.3. To emphasize the advantages, most organizations rely on e-commerce models. However, having a great e-commerce business model will not generate a profit if it is not associated with a website that brings in customers, or at least visitors.

3. **How can organizations use e-commerce to enhance the delivery of products and services, manage trade with business partners, and improve their supply chain efficiency?**

B2B transactions are usually of two types: (1) spot buying or (2) strategic sourcing. Companies often engage in spot buying to purchase goods and services that are commodities; that is, they are usually uniform in quality and differ only somewhat in price. On the other hand, strategic sourcing involves forming a long-term relationship with another company. Strategic sourcing often relies on a one-to-one business model, although company-centric and exchange models are also used.

In addition, e-commerce can benefit a company's supply chain. A supply chain is a network of facilities and distribution options that performs the functions of procurement of materials, transformation of these materials into intermediate and finished products, and the distribution of these finished products to customers. Traditional supply chains involve a number of paper-based transactions, but e-commerce-based supply chains involve an interorganizational system (IOS). An IOS can help create 24/7 communications between organizations and their suppliers and customers, as well as enable paperless transactions throughout the supply chain. The two most common forms of IOS in use today are based on electronic data interchange (EDI), which uses value-added networks (VANs) or private networks instead of the regular telephone system, and extranets, which are collaborative networks that use Internet technology to link businesses with their suppliers, customers, or other businesses that share common goals.

KNOWLEDGE SPEAK

business-to-business (B2B) 168
business-to-consumer (B2C) 168
business-to-government (B2G) 168
company-centric business model 189
consumer-to-consumer (C2C) 168
consumer-to-government (C2G) 168
co-operative website 179
e-commerce 168
e-commerce business model 171
e-commerce strategy 181
electronic data interchange (EDI) 192
e-procurement 189

exchange model 189
extranet 192
information density 175
interorganizational system (IOS) 191
mass customization 176
mobile commerce 183
niche markets 180
one-to-one marketing model 188
personalization 177
spot buying 188
strategic sourcing 188

REVIEW QUESTIONS

Multiple-choice questions

1. Which of the following is considered a benefit of B2C e-commerce?
   a. Consumers are uncomfortable about the security of their personal data.
   b. Delivery of the product is delayed and may incur an extra cost.
   c. Distance to markets is shortened.
   d. Micropayment systems are not yet standardized.
2. Which of the following e-commerce impacts would best describe the ease at which new businesses may start an e-commerce site?
   a. reducing barriers to entry
   b. no one owns the market
   c. enhanced collaboration/alliances
   d. market niches multiply
3. Which of the following is an e-commerce site that facilitates how users find web pages of interest?
   a. information service
   b. auction
   c. sales support
   d. search engine
4. With _____, many companies use an online market to exchange products or services.
   a. an exchange
   b. a reverse auction
   c. spot buying
   d. strategic sourcing

Fill-in-the-blank questions

5. _____ is the use of information systems, technologies, and computer networks by individuals and organizations to carry out transactions in order to create or support the creation of business value.

6. A _____ combines a specific type of website with a successful revenue model that produces profits for the website owner.

7. Companies can use the data collected using a _____ system to tailor their products and prices on their website to the individual buyer.

8. A _____ is a network of facilities and distribution options that performs the functions of procurement of materials, transformation of these materials into intermediate and finished products, and the distribution of these finished products to customers.

True-false questions

9. Using a variety of techniques to make a website both more visible to search engines and more relevant to the way they rank sites to increase the likelihood of appearing higher in the list of any relevant search by consumers is called search engine optimization.

10. When you perform a banking transaction at your bank's ATM, you are performing an e-commerce transaction.

11. Due to the popularity of e-commerce, it is more difficult than ever to create business alliances.

12. Websites collect statistics about what pages visitors access and where visitors exit the website.

Matching questions

Choose the BEST answer from column B for each item in column A.

Column A
13. traffic monetizing
14. revenue share
15. infomediary
16. transactional

Column B
a. An e-commerce business model where products are shipped directly from the manufacturer to the consumer.
b. An e-commerce business model where websites are paid a fee when purchases come through them.
c. An e-commerce business model where data on consumers and consumption habits are provided.
d. An e-commerce business model that brings together buyers and sellers for a fee.

Short-answer questions

17. Why is it important for an e-commerce company to have a business model?

18. What are the three main categories of B2B business models?

Discussion/Essay questions

19. List and describe the benefits and limitations of B2C e-commerce.

20. Discuss how e-commerce is changing many aspects of business today.

TEAM ACTIVITY

Find two or three other students in your class who are in, or are interested in, the same major that you are. Think about creating an e-commerce portal/site for your major or your intended major. What information needs to go on the web pages that make up the site? What links are necessary? What about collecting membership dues? Could you also use the site to raise money for the student organization associated with your major? Plan the site on paper first, and then use the activities below to implement it.

SOFTWARE APPLICATION EXERCISES

1. Internet
Research how to build an e-commerce site for your major (see Team Activity assignment above). Look for open source tools that introductory IS students can use (for free) to create and maintain a website. Visit hosting sites to check on hosting plans, and ask your academic department if it is willing to host student sites.

2. Presentation
Create a presentation on how to build and host a major-related e-commerce site (see Internet assignment above). Present your ideas and solutions to your class and/or a professor in your major. Use presentation software to create prototypes of screens that give your audience insight into the look and functionality of your proposed website.

3. Word Processing
Create a promotional brochure to give to the students and faculty in your major. Use this as a basis for a press release to your student newspaper that announces the major-related site (see Internet assignment above) once it is up and working (simulate this if you are not actually implementing the site).

4. Spreadsheet
E-commerce sites cost money, whether you host them at school or offsite. Prepare a budget with projected costs, including an assessment of labour costs (e.g., your hourly rate—research these rates for a realistic cost). Include charts from your financial estimates for the Presentation assignment above. If you decided to deploy this type of website across your entire school (organization), how would the costs increase? Would there be any economies of scale?

5. Database
Research open-source databases, and design and create a database that will support the membership and e-commerce components of your website (see Internet assignment above). You may also use a commercial DBMS like MS Access if this fits better with your school's IT architecture.

6. Advanced Challenge
Think about some of the stakeholders mentioned in the preceding Internet assignment (e.g., fellow students and faculty in your major). Once you have their support, consider what other stakeholders might influence your ability to effectively implement your website. Assume that all stakeholders have approved your e-commerce site. Use an iterative development approach to create the site and test its functionality. Find a suitable hosting site (verify faculty approval to implement) and "go live."

ONLINE RESOURCES

Companion Website
- Take interactive practice quizzes to assess your knowledge and help you study in a dynamic way.
- Review PowerPoint lecture slides.
- Get help and sample solutions to end-of-chapter software application exercises.

Additional Resources Available Only on WileyPLUS

- Take the interactive Quick Test to check your understanding of the chapter material and get immediate feedback on your responses.
- Review and study with downloadable Audio Lecture MP3 files.
- Check your understanding of the key vocabulary in the chapter with Knowledge Speak Interactive Flash Cards.

CASE STUDY: USING B2B E-COMMERCE AT BOEING

Assume that you are the spare parts manager for an airline operating a fleet of Boeing 737s in Asia, and you need to order spare parts in a hurry. At one time, this process would have involved your digging through the Boeing parts manual, finding the correct part numbers, and then calling, faxing, or telexing your order to the company parts warehouse in Seattle. Upon receipt of your order, Boeing would then send you a number of automatic faxes or telexes to acknowledge the order and let you know its status. And this assumes that you have updated your maintenance manual with the continual revisions sent by Boeing—a process that usually took 60 to 90 days.

Sound like a big job? It was! However, today, with Boeing's *MyBoeingFleet.com*, customers and suppliers have a portal to Boeing's Web-enabled, B2B extranet. This site, and the functions it offers, makes the parts-ordering process much less painful for companies operating Boeing aircraft. The password-protected website is open to airplane owners and operators, as well as maintenance, repair, and overhaul shops—basically anybody who needs products or information for their Boeing airplanes. While it is not open to the general public, you can take a guest tour by going to *www.boeing.com/commercial/ aviationservices/myboeingfleet/*.

In mid-2005, there were 30,000 industry professionals from 550 companies who had access to the extranet site, with more than 4,000 logins per day and 4 million hits per month. In addition to ordering parts from *MyBoeingFleet.com*, customers can access engineering diagrams, up-to-date maintenance and flight manuals, service bulletins, and other pertinent information.

The PART Page
A key part of Boeing's global B2B e-commerce effort is the sale of spare parts for the more than 7,000 Boeing aircraft in operation. These parts are handled out of spare-parts centres in eight cities, with the largest such centre being located near the Seattle-Tacoma airport. This centre contains over $1 billion (U.S.) in spare parts stored in a building covering over 6 hectares! In 2004, the centre shipped an average of 3,000 orders each day. These orders contained almost 300,000 different parts and weighed 3 million kg. The centre handled all of these orders using an automated conveyor delivery system more than 3 kilometres long.

To handle this huge spare-parts e-commerce operation, Boeing created a special element for the overall *MyBoeingFleet.com* website. Termed the PART page, this site allows customers to order spare parts on a 24/7 basis and provides tracking information on the orders. Customers can work with the latest information without having to deal with reams of paper updates. This site currently lists more than 6.5 million types of spare parts and handles an average of 130,000 transactions per week. This online supply chain management process is a win–win process for both Boeing and its customers: Boeing dramatically reduces staff required to handle telephone calls, faxes, and telexes, while customers save hundreds of thousands of dollars each year in paper and distribution costs. For example, a customer can now access information equivalent to 80,000 pages of text—a stack of paper 7.5 m high weighing 360 kg!

Spare Parts Economics

Why does Boeing concentrate on the spare-parts business as the keystone of its e-commerce system? There are actually several answers to this question. First, it simply is not possible to sell multimillion dollar airliners over the Web. Second, Boeing makes a great deal of money from its maintenance program. In fact, aircraft maintenance is a much higher-margin business than selling the original aircraft. While Boeing has a 9 percent margin building planes, it has a 20 percent margin servicing them. Finally, even if Boeing stopped building aircraft tomorrow, it would still have a very profitable aircraft maintenance business for many years into the future. Finding ways to more efficiently handle this business, through e-commerce, is just smart.

Case Questions

1. What aspects of the website *MyBoeingFleet.com* qualify it as an extranet?
2. How does this website help enable the Boeing supply chain to assist operators of aircraft built by Boeing?
3. Why is the PART page referred to as the key e-commerce element of the *MyBoeingFleet.com* website? Do you agree with the economic analysis for concentrating on spare parts? Why or why not?

SOURCES: for this case include: James Wallace, "Aerospace Notebook: Boeing's Got Parts—15 Whole Acres of Them," *Seattle Post-Intelligencer*, March 2, 2005. Elizabeth Davis, "Portal Power: E-business at Boeing Gaining Velocity." *http://www.boeing.com/commercial/news/feature/ebiz.html*. Fred Vogelstein, "Flying on the Web in a Turbulent Economy," *Fortune*, April 30, 2001.

Integrative Application Case: *Campuspad.ca*

At your next meeting, Sarah is much less interested in discussing the development problems and much more excited about a call she received from the student union president. It turns out that the student housing office is a source of revenue for the union. If a successful tenant is referred to a landlord by the housing office, the student union receives a listing fee. Although not a huge amount of money, it mostly covers the operating costs, allowing the student union to offer a valuable service to students for free.

The student union president approached Sarah because he had heard you and Sarah might be launching an online business that would compete with the housing office. While not making the statement directly, he said the union had uncovered "unspecified privacy issues" that might force them to recommend students not use your site. On the other hand, he also hinted at wanting to meet to discuss the possibility of the union becoming a strategic partner. Although you and Sarah aren't sure what this meant exactly, you suspect they are interested in how your online business might help them actually improve the service they offer to students. Further, they said that if they could pilot it successfully, then it could be sold to student unions all over Canada.

The union has asked you to think about how you can work together, and wants you to meet with them early next week. Sarah thinks this could evolve into something where they fund the launch of the business in return for some kind of stake in the enterprise, but you're not so sure; you don't feel like they "get it." Again, lots of decisions to make.

Guiding Case Questions

1. What are the risks to an incumbent business with an Internet competitor?
2. How could e-commerce fit into the student union business model?
3. What business model will your new site use?
4. What privacy or other legislation in your jurisdiction might you have overlooked?
5. Could these laws have a negative effect on your future online business?

Your Task

Make up eight to 10 PowerPoint slides that help explain the potential value of the Internet in the student rental market that you will use in your meeting with the student union. Make sure the presentation sells the value of your strategic thinking to ensure that the student union, if it is truly looking for a technology partner, will choose *Campuspad.ca*. Ensure that your presentation addresses the issues of privacy, online security, and secure commerce that you intend to use in the site to make sure it's compliant with local laws, and that it addresses any possible concerns the student union might have about your site's design.

6

DATABASE MANAGEMENT AND BUSINESS INTELLIGENCE

WHAT WE WILL COVER

- What are Data, Information, and Knowledge?
- Databases: The Primary Data Storage for Organizations
- Business Intelligence

STUDENT RETURN ON INVESTMENT

Through your investment of time in reading and thinking about this chapter, your return—or created value—is gaining knowledge. Use the following questions as a study guide.

1. What are the differences between data, information, and knowledge?

2. In what ways can organizations use IT to store and share data, information, and knowledge?

3. How does business intelligence enhance organizational decision making?

VOICE OF EXPERIENCE
Sherrill Burns, Carleton University

After earning degrees in psychology and sociology at Carleton University and graduating from teacher's college, Sherrill Burns built a career in leadership and organizational development in the high-tech industry. She is now a partner in the consultancy firm, Culture Strategy-Fit Inc., which helps organizations leverage culture for breakthrough results.

What do you do in your current position? As an organizational development consultancy, we provide diagnostics, particularly ones looking at organizational culture and change services. We look at the way work gets done in organizations, the way people work together on a day-to-day basis, and the extent to which they collaborate, share information, trust each other, experiment, and innovate.

What do you consider to be important career skills? My first job was as a teacher. The most important skills were planning, organizing, relationship building, and conflict resolution. The skills I use now are surprisingly similar. It is also important that I retain strategic focus while being able to dive into tactical issues. Because I'm now a partner and have assumed the business development side of the business, I've added marketing and alliance building to my skill set. I'm not a "techie" (my partner is the technical guru), but I've learned that you need to leverage technology to gather the data required to identify patterns and dynamics in our clients' organizational cultures. We can then apply this knowledge to help our clients be more productive, deliver their mission and brand promise, and have a competitive edge.

How do you use IT? In the past, we used face-to-face interviews and focus groups to do our organizational assessments. With clients all over the world, this became increasingly costly, difficult, and time-consuming. So we have developed Web-based diagnostics to gather data from our clients. We then use our databases to analyze day-to-day behaviours and the practices that are in use in the organization to uncover culture patterns and to identify causal factors that support and/or inhibit the organization from achieving its strategy. These analyses provide information that helps us uncover the levers that could bring organizations a competitive advantage or help them accelerate their strategy.

Can you describe an example of how you have used IT to improve business operations? Once an assessment is complete, we use Web conferencing to communicate the results to clients. Because we do not often travel to clients, we have reduced the cost of our offering, which makes us more competitive. We also use IT to collaborate with other consulting firms on four continents that are alliance partners with us. We use a collaborative space on our website to share knowledge such as research articles, sample reports, proposals, and methodologies. Having this information available improves efficiency and productivity for us and builds the capability of our alliance partners around the world. We are not constantly responding to requests for information.

Have you got any on-the-job advice for students seeking a career in IT or business? Whether you are working for an organization or client, you have to be willing to experiment to meet business needs. You need to think in three dimensions: first, focus on the work to be done and what you'll contribute; second, look at your workplace's technology enablers, processes, and the base of knowledge you can tap into; and third, examine the way the organization works, its culture, social networks, hubs of wisdom, and experience. You need to realize that you cannot do it all yourself and you will need to lean on capable people and use the resources at your disposal. Consider what you're going to be a master of and what you will leave to others or outsource.

Sherrill has worked in the high-tech industry, but not as a technologist, and now uses technology as an enabler in her own business. By using the Web and databases, her consultancy is able to analyze each client's situation, provide it with the information to break through to new levels of performance, and give it knowledge to create powerful action plans. In this chapter we discuss data, information, and knowledge, the key inputs and outputs of Sherrill's work.

Data and information are as vital to an organization as the water we drink is to us. In addition, both individuals and businesses need these resources delivered in a usable form. Using this analogy, as we did in Chapter 4, we can actually think of IT as the "plumbing" of a business information system (IS).

Let's take our water analogy further. First, we like to get our water when we want it—as soon as we turn on the tap, any time of the day. An organization also likes to get the data and information that it needs when it wants it. Constant access is therefore important. Second, in getting the water, we want a reliable system—the reservoirs, the processing facilities, the pipes that deliver it to our home, and the sewers that drain it away—to provide clean water. Similarly, a business counts on its IS to deliver accurate data and information.

However, it is perhaps more enlightening to think of how data and information differ from the water piped to our homes. With water, we basically need only one standard type—clear and clean. With data and information, an organization's needs are much more varied. It wants data in different forms (e.g., number, text, video, audio) and organized in different ways (e.g., tables, reports, graphs). Just think how complex a plumbing system would have to be to deliver water, coffee, or pop with just a twist of the tap!

In this chapter we discuss the equivalent of "organizational plumbing"—the IT systems designed to support different kinds of knowledge work—gathering and storing data, processing information, and making decisions.

WHAT ARE DATA, INFORMATION, AND KNOWLEDGE?

Let's begin by taking a closer look at what data, information, and knowledge actually are. Much of what you do as a university or college student, and will do in the future as a business professional, relates to data, information, and knowledge. You collect data about various subjects to transform it into information and knowledge. You learn where to look for quality information and how to store it for future use. Sometimes you share information with others. Information and knowledge are not just words on a page; they have tangible value, and knowledge becomes an important asset.

This is also the case in business. The flow of data and information to create knowledge is what creates value in organizations. You can likely think of occasions when the loss of information has had negative results; for instance, a misplaced order from an online supplier. Or a phone number that you didn't have a chance to put into your mobile phone and now can't find. Or how about the registration mishaps where you are sure that you registered for that course that's now full? As a student, learning to apply technology to enable this flow helps you and the organizations you will work for improve their results and avoid just these kinds of situations.

The Data–Information–Knowledge Continuum

Now that you've begun to realize the importance of data, information, and knowledge, let's dig a little deeper into the meanings of each word and their relationship to each other. **Data** are raw unorganized facts, numbers, pictures, and so on. **Information** is data that have been organized and are useful to a person. For example, a hair salon owner might include the names of clients, their phone numbers, and their email addresses in an address book program in a personal digital assistant. **Knowledge** is created when a person combines experience and judgement with information. Applying knowledge is how business people create and add value to organizations.

For example, as an international sales manager, you may know the phone numbers and email addresses of your best clients, but you also know your clients' time zones and normal business hours (information). Suppose you decided to email rather than telephone one client. Why did you do this? Most likely, you based your decision on the *information* you have about the client and your personal judgement regarding past experience with this client. Maybe you've found the client doesn't like to be interrupted by the phone or doesn't have voice mail. Therefore, you made your decision based on the *knowledge* you had about that client.

As a student, you use data, information, and knowledge regularly. Remember your first day of classes in your first semester on campus? You had your schedule and the campus map. How did you find your first class? You probably looked on your schedule and found the building name and/or number (data). Once you knew this, you looked at your campus map (information). Were you on time for class? Maybe you were late because, based on the campus map, you decided to drive and park in a lot near your classroom. Unfortunately, the lot was full, and the only available parking was far away. You had good information (class time and class and parking lot location), so what went wrong?

Because you had never driven to this particular class and tried to park in a nearby lot, you had no experience with the process. Assume that the next time you decided to drive, you left earlier and found a space. Now when faced with the "when-to-leave-for-class decision," you use knowledge, which combines your class time, classroom location, and parking lot location with your "finding-a-space" experience.

You can extend the data-to-knowledge continuum even further to include wisdom (see Figure 6.1). **Wisdom** adds insight and ethics to the experience and professional judgement inherent in knowledge. Wisdom enables business leaders to perceive the underlying meaning and nuances of a business situation and ensures that knowledge from all relevant perspectives, disciplines, and sources is considered in the final decision.

Another important thing to note is that the cost and complexity of the tasks to be accomplished increase as you move up the pyramid from simply accessing data to applying wisdom (see Figure 6.1). Information technology and systems assist primarily with collecting, collating, and analyzing data and information. This is their strongest contribution. While technology is a key enabler, it is still up to humans to take this data and information and turn it into knowledge and wisdom.

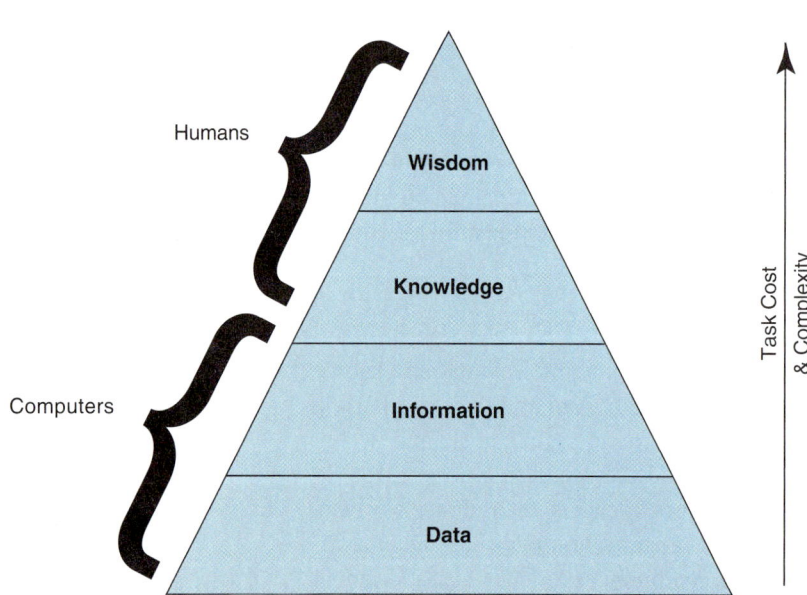

FIGURE 6.1 This knowledge hierarchy shows the relative level of human involvement, cost, and complexity.

Think of it this way: in its simplest form, you have data. These are the raw facts and figures related to the task at hand. By using information technology systems, you can transform this data into information by putting it into context, adding it up or sorting it out, and generally performing mechanical calculations and permutations that would be either boring or subject to error if performed by humans. The system can store and retrieve information quickly and disseminate it throughout the organization. At a higher level, you might also expect these systems to spot and identify basic patterns in the data or point out anomalies. They might generate warnings about potential problems or about processes or values outside of expected or approved levels. However, after this point, the work of the information system is mostly done. It now falls to the business professional to take this information and interpret it in context; that is, turn it into knowledge. You could also add an ethical or legal interpretation to the knowledge to ensure that the appropriate context has been considered before making a decision. Information that is not used to improve the outcome of a business decision is perhaps interesting, but certainly not useful. And you can clearly see the boundary of where information systems can and cannot be helpful.

Lifelong Knowledge Creation

To be a successful business professional, you must always strive to create or acquire new knowledge. Specifically, you need to build on the two types of knowledge that you possess: explicit knowledge and tacit knowledge. **Explicit knowledge** is knowledge that is readily codified, such as the knowledge in this textbook. **Tacit knowledge** is knowledge that you gain through experience, insight, and discovery. These two types of knowledge are complementary halves of a lifelong knowledge creation process.

How does the knowledge-creation process work in the real world? Consider one of your first steps toward becoming a business professional: the business internship or job interview. Interviewers often ask you about their company. They want to assess what explicit knowledge you may have gained about their company by visiting their website or reading the company's annual report. As the interview continues, the interviewer may ask you to describe a situation where you worked as a member of a project team. As you describe your experiences and the lessons you learned from them, you are highlighting your tacit knowledge of working in teams.

You've learned that data are transformed into information, and information can be transformed into knowledge. Then what? If an organization is willing to hire you because you are capable of creating tacit knowledge that contributes to the organization's success, what does the organization do with the knowledge that you've created? In the next section, we discuss the various knowledge work activities that business professionals engage in to create business value for their organizations.

Knowledge Work Activities

Recall from Chapter 1 that *knowledge work* involves the discovery, analysis, transformation, synthesis, and communication of data, information, and knowledge. Examples in the business world include recommending an investment portfolio to clients or interpreting the monthly sales report to plan for the future. However, even

Digital audio devices like MP3 players offer opportunities to incorporate the explicit and tacit knowledge of others into your own knowledge through podcasting, thereby enhancing your own knowledge-creation process.

as a preschooler you were already performing knowledge-based activities. How? Say it was your fourth birthday, and you received a bucket of Lego blocks. Inside the bucket you made a *discovery*—plastic blocks in many colours. So, what did you do? You dumped the blocks on the floor and began to *analyze* the blocks and organize the big pile into smaller piles of colours and shapes. Maybe you first decided to build a car, but then realized, "who needs a car when I can build a really big tower and use all the pieces (*transform*)!" So, you started snapping together blocks, until what began as a collection of pieces came together as a magnificent tower (*synthesis*). You were so pleased with your successful creation that you showed everyone around you what you had built. You also probably told them how you built it. In other words, you *communicated* your Lego-building knowledge to others. To apply this analogy to an organization, the steps you went through are referred to as *work flows* and the outcome of your building efforts as the *work product*.

Figure 6.2 depicts these knowledge work activities and shows how they constantly interact around and through you. You did them when you were young (e.g., playing with Lego), you did them recently (e.g., selecting which university or college to attend), you do them now (e.g., preparing for your current classes), and you will continue to do them throughout your life. Because of their importance, we discuss each activity in more detail in the following sections.

Discovery: Finding Data, Information, or Knowledge Discovery is the finding of data, information, and knowledge relevant to a task, problem, issue, or opportunity (the context). You begin with an idea of what to look for, and then reflect on where information related to the task may exist. You then retrieve relevant data from those various sources and assess its value to the decision at hand. For example, say you work as a marketing assistant for WildOutfitters.com, a hypothetical retail hiking store. Your manager asks you to find the weekly sales data for the store and its main competitors. This request frames your discovery activities. You now need to answer questions such as "Where is the sales data for our store

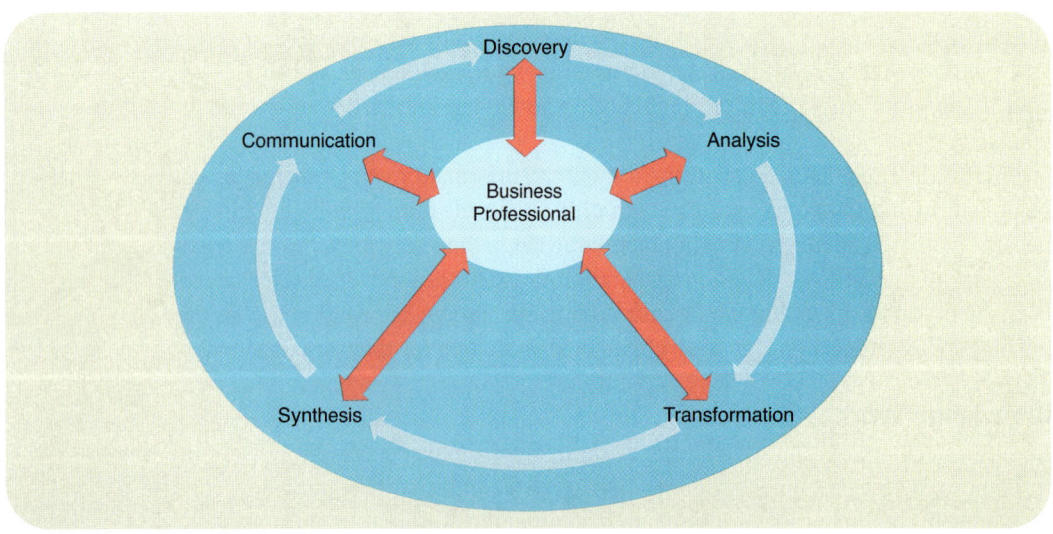

FIGURE 6.2 Knowledge work activities.

located?" and "Who are our competitors?" This type of request is similar to the challenges you face in your search for information to write term papers and create presentations.

You already know how to search the Internet to locate specific data and information. Strong Internet research skills, balanced with an awareness of the limitations of this source of data, can help you create business value for your organization. Reflect on some of the sources you use and trust. What about the sources you reject? Evaluating your search results is an important part of the discovery process. Using sources that you should have rejected will impact the rest of your knowledge work activities, and perhaps lead to incorrect conclusions and poor decision making.

Luckily, discovering information often extends beyond the Internet. In fact, you may have even more powerful job-related information close at hand. The company you work for may have a private version of the Internet known as an intranet. Recall from Chapter 2 that an intranet contains data about the company that only authorized employees can access. If your organization stores information on its intranet about where a similar problem has occurred before and how it was solved, or perhaps tracks the results of decisions made by competitors or partners, it may even help you to discover best practices for solving problems, thereby creating business value for your company.

Learning from your university or college experiences and course requirements will train you for many knowledge work tasks, especially discovering data and information.

Analysis: Investigating and Examining the Available Data, Information, and Knowledge You can think of **analysis** as breaking down the whole into its more discrete parts to better understand how it works. You often perform analysis under other names such as *process mapping* (if you are analyzing a business process), *quality assurance* (if you are analyzing product quality), or *performance testing* (if you are assessing fitness or standards). All of these types of business activities involve some form of root cause analysis to answer the contextual question: "What is happening and why?" Therefore, analysis is a critical knowledge work activity that will help you answer questions and gain understanding through a thoughtful investigation and examination of the available data and information. Once you complete the analysis, put it into the appropriate organizational context, and make a decision or recommendation, you have now created knowledge. If you can extend this to include consideration of any unintended consequences, ethical constraints, or risks so that you safely and quickly put this knowledge to use to create a sustainable competitive advantage, then you have demonstrated wisdom.

To understand better what analysis entails, consider the presentation of the data in Figure 6.3. In analyzing the data, you might ask yourself, "What type of equipment sold the most units?" "What was our total profit?" "How did the sales of each type of equipment contribute to that profit?" Answering these questions helps you to turn this data into information. To better understand the weekly sales and to add business value, you need to continue to analyze the data until you can come to some conclusions. For example, you may come to realize that tents contribute more to profit due to their low cost. For this deeper analysis, you may need more data and advanced analysis techniques. Two information technologies that can help answer

210 | DATABASE MANAGEMENT AND BUSINESS INTELLIGENCE

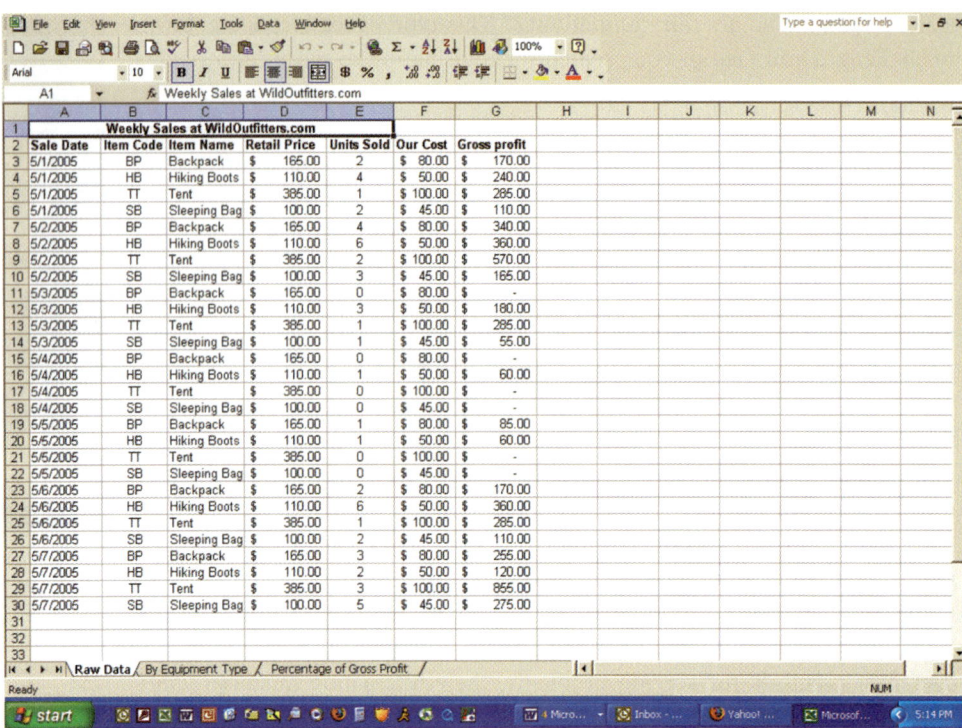

FIGURE 6.3 Sales data for WildOutfitters.com.

questions about underlying patterns and correlations across large amounts of data are data warehouses and data mining, which are discussed later in this chapter.

Transformation: Organizing Discovery Results **Transformation** is knowledge work that requires you to use the results of your analysis to deepen your understanding of the data and information. Why is transformation important? Imagine your university or college course calendar as simply an alphabetic list (e.g., Accounting 350, Acting 102, Art History 210). Each course may contain all the appropriate information, but it is not organized in a useful format. That is, organized this way, you would not know which course is applicable to which degree. When it is organized by course of study (e.g., Business, Fine Arts) or specialty (e.g., Business—Finance) it is *transformed* into information that tells you what courses are required to achieve a particular degree.

Let's revisit your manager's request from the discovery phase, where you need to obtain weekly sales data for WildOutfitters.com and its competitors. Through your intranet and Internet searches, you discover a lot of information. In fact, you find more raw data than you can quickly process. This may be especially true if you work as part of a collaborative project team, where others may discover the data or information and pass it to you to analyze and transform. Fortunately, information technology can help you transform data regardless of who did the discovery and analysis work. For example, spreadsheets and databases are effective tools for organizing and storing information, as Figure 6.4 shows. Note that for this example, you could also use database software. Larger organizations, with many transactions, often use database software for storing and transforming data.

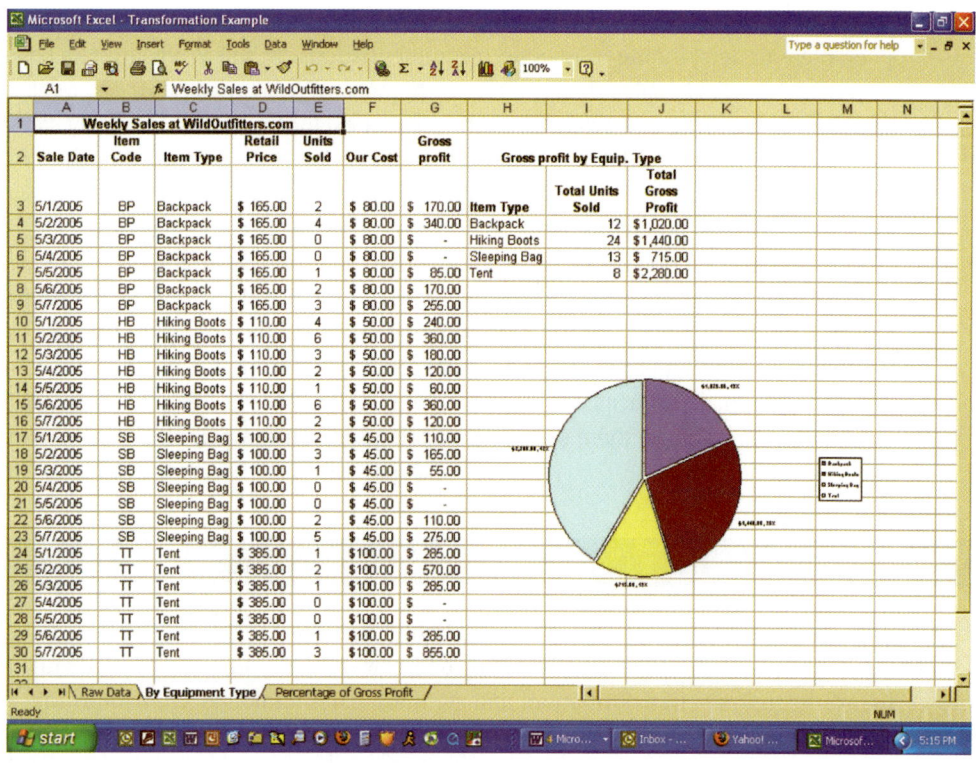

FIGURE 6.4 Further transformation of sales data for WildOutfitters.com.

Figure 6.4 shows additional transformations of the data. Note that you (and your manager) can now easily see that hiking boots sold the most number of units, but tents contributed the greatest percentage to weekly gross profit. By transforming the data into a useful form through the use of a spreadsheet, you begin to make sense of events and issues. You set the stage for the insight and understanding that often result from the next type of knowledge work, synthesis.

Synthesis: The Sum of the Parts **Synthesis** allows you to interpret trends or patterns that seem to explain the past and the present, and may suggest courses of action likely to favourably influence the future. Further, while some of these patterns will stand alone—for example, the WildOutfitters.com sales data for each week of the month—isolated information often paints an incomplete picture. As a result, you will probably need to bring together different pieces of data and information to form a complete picture of your current situation. The essential element of synthesis is in knowing which parts, when combined, will create higher total value than the value of the parts themselves. This is particularly true with the synthesis of information. For instance, national security issues often arise only when one piece of information (otherwise deemed irrelevant or uninteresting) is combined with a similarly unassuming piece of other information to begin to show a pattern of possible terrorist activity. While any one piece of information on its own may seem innocent, when correlated and synthesized into a discernible pattern, there may be a potential terrorist threat to deal with.

Remember, you may need to integrate even more information before gaining a complete understanding or making recommendations. In the WildOutfitters.com example, the weekly sales data may be trending upward, but the last six weeks' data may be trending downward. A synthesis that excludes additional weekly sales data, competitors' sales data, and industry trends may result in an incomplete understanding. For example, if all additional data trend downward except the weekly sales data shown above, this week may be an anomaly (exceptional case). Or, if other weeks show a downward trend and the overall economy is slowing, you may want to investigate what occurred to generate the increased sales. While systems can provide the summary information, only people have the ability to put this information into the proper context and draw conclusions from it.

Once you have an accurate and complete analysis of your results ready, you must then communicate them succinctly to others so you can help the organization make better decisions.

WHAT DO YOU THINK?

You have made your way to university or college by doing knowledge work activities. Of course, you may not have known the names of each of these activities or been aware that you were doing them! Consider the activities of discovery, analysis, transformation, and synthesis, and think about the following questions:

1: What activities did you undertake to come to this university or college? This course?
2: Have you purchased a car? Are you thinking of purchasing a car? Which activities will you use to do this?
3: Are you thinking of getting a part-time job? Again, think about what knowledge work activities you will use to find suitable employment.

Communication: Sharing Analysis with Others As a business professional, you will most likely work for and with others in a business or other type of organization. To help your employer create business value, you must have strong **communication** skills; that is, the ability to share your analyses, ideas, and solutions with others. Even if you work for yourself, you still need to communicate effectively with your customers.

Individuals and organizations can and do use information systems and technologies to help them communicate. Some of the technologies individuals use focus on physically sharing the message, such as email and instant messaging.

Information systems and technology can also allow you to share the meaning behind the message. For example, you can use Microsoft PowerPoint to create a presentation, or other software applications to communicate your knowledge, such as Inspiration (*www.inspiration.com*) and Visio (*http://office.microsoft.com/en-us/visio/FX100487861033.aspx*). These can be collaboratively enabled by using tools such as Groove (*http://office.microsoft.com/en-us/groove/default.aspx*) or GotoMeeting (*www.gotomeeting.com*) to organize and disseminate information throughout a virtual team.

Table 6.1 Examples of Knowledge Work Activities

Knowledge Work Activity	Manager's Request	Helpful IT Tools and Activities
Discovery	Find our company's and our competitors' weekly sales data.	Use data from check-out/point-of-sale (POS) terminals, search tools (e.g., Google), and Web searching.
Analysis	Compare the sales data for the first week of May to similar data from our company for the previous two months.	Import the data into a database or spreadsheet application, and use its features and tools to organize the data. Find the previous months' data and import these as well.
Transformation	Identify any trends in the data by week, month, and day of the week. Indicate how our company's results compare with our competition and with the industry as a whole.	Use the data analysis tools in the spreadsheet application to examine the data from different aspects. Consider what your analysis of the data revealed and combine this with your knowledge of your company's goals to add focus to your analysis. Search the Web for other analyses of your company, industry, and competitors. Integrate this with your interpretation of the sales data.
Synthesis	Given your analysis of our company's relative success or failure, suggest ways to capitalize on our strengths and overcome our weaknesses.	With analysis in mind, obtain feedback about specific company products and services. Arrange a brief Web meeting (e.g., with NetMeeting) of the top sales associates in your company.
Communication	Present your findings and suggestions to management.	Import your spreadsheet data into presentation software. Add the insights gained from your Web meeting.

Summary of Knowledge Work Activities Table 6.1 summarizes and expands on the examples of knowledge work activities we just covered. However, knowledge work activities are only part of the larger picture of a rational decision-making and problem-solving process (see Chapter 3 for more discussion of how decision making and problem solving contribute to creating business value). You'll find that any decision making and problem solving creates the need to engage in the knowledge work activities of discovery, analysis, transformation, synthesis, and communication.

Quick Test

1. If you add human experience and judgement to information, you can create _____.
   a. data
   b. knowledge
   c. resources
   d. facts

2. Either database or spreadsheet software can be very useful as part of the knowledge work activity known as _____.
   a. discovery
   b. analysis
   c. transformation
   d. synthesis

3. In a business organization, the ultimate purpose of knowledge work activities is the creation of _____.
   a. profits
   b. business value
   c. good employer–employee relations
   d. resources

Answers: 1. b; 2. c; 3. b

DATABASES: THE PRIMARY DATA STORAGE FOR ORGANIZATIONS

From our previous discussion on data, information, and knowledge, it is clear that data is important—and often abundant! How do businesses keep track of all this data so that it is readily available and can be found when needed? All business information systems rely on the use and storage of data. The primary technology used to store, manage, and allow efficient access to data is the database.

A *database* consists of interrelated data that are stored in files and organized so that computer programs can quickly and easily access specific pieces of data. For example, a bank stores information about its customers in a database. The bank can then access and update the database as customers make deposits and withdrawals at an ATM. A **database management system (DBMS)** is a collection of software that allows users to create and work with a database. That same bank uses a DBMS to obtain and print a customer's monthly bank statement. Together, a database and a DBMS make up a *database system*. As Figure 6.5 shows, the DBMS controls access to the data stored in the database.

The people who create and manage the database, sometimes known as *database administrators (DBA)*, use the tools in the DBMS to do their

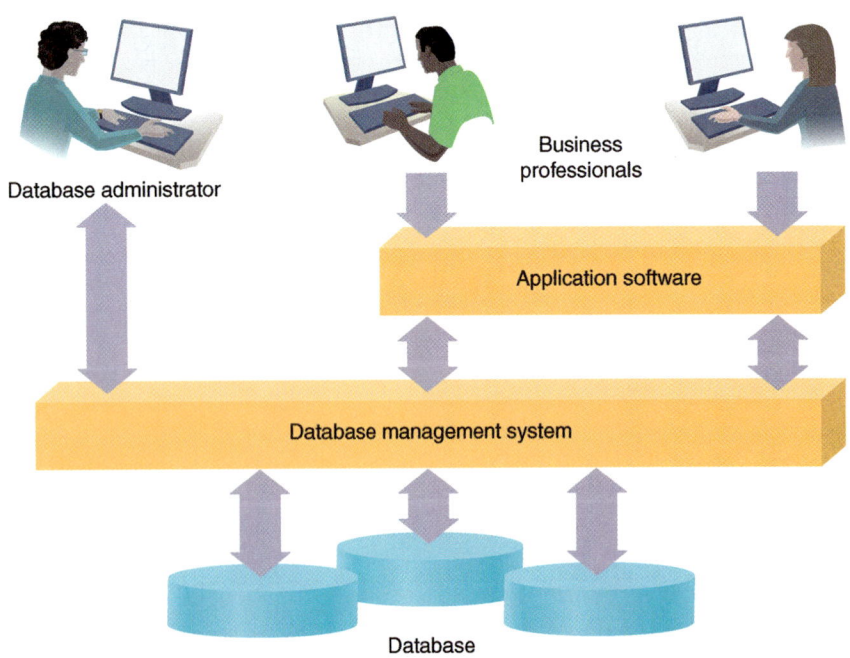

FIGURE 6.5 The DBMS controls access to the data stored in the database.

work. Other business professionals who need to access the database typically do so through other application software that can connect to the DBMS and query the databases that it manages.

In this section, we briefly introduce databases. As a business professional, you will use business applications that depend on databases. Some of the more prevalent databases used today are provided by Oracle, Microsoft, and IBM. You may work closely with other business professionals who are certified as database administrators for Oracle databases and/or Microsoft SQL servers. For more in-depth coverage, including a more thorough discussion of how to design and model a database, see Tech Guide D.

The Data Hierarchy

To organize data in a database, most users rely on the **data hierarchy**. As Figure 6.6 shows, the data hierarchy organizes stored data in increasing levels of complexity. At the lowest level, the data hierarchy stores all data using electronic bits that can be 1 (on) or 0 (off). A specific combination of bits represents each data *character*. The exact number of bits needed for a character depends on the type of data and the encoding scheme. For example, the ASCII encoding scheme will use eight bits (one byte) to store a letter of the alphabet. Unicode will store the same letter using 16 bits (two bytes). A combination of characters representing a data item, such as a name or a price, is known as a *field*.

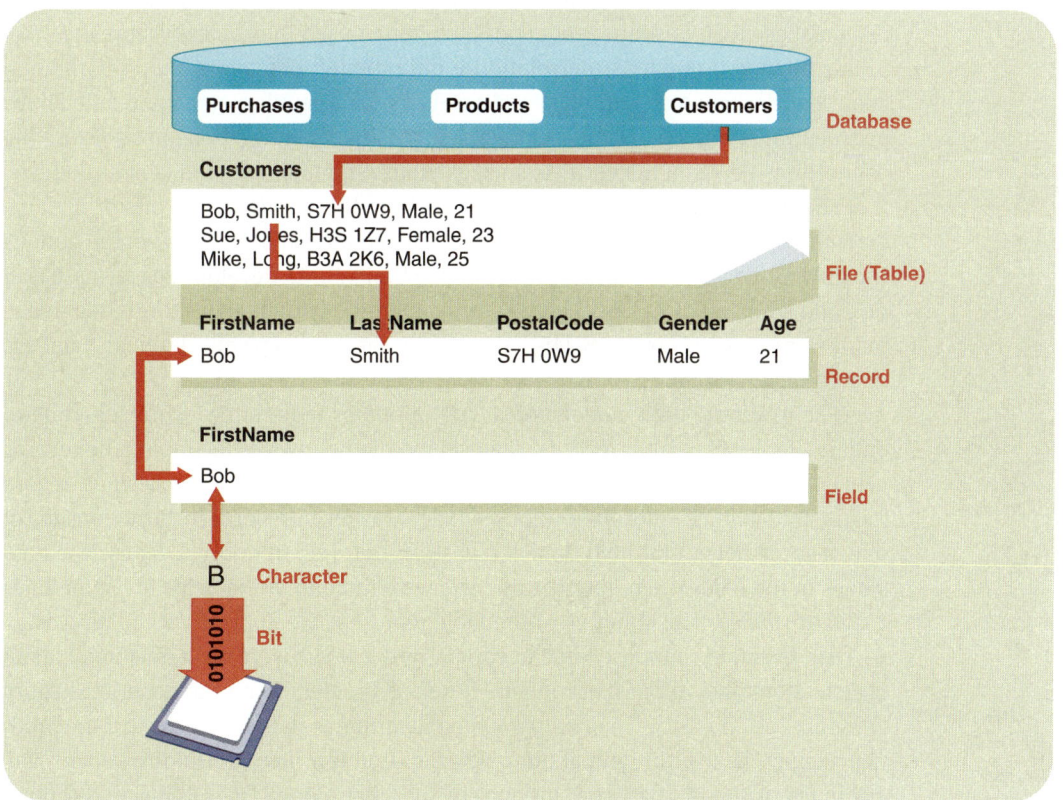

FIGURE 6.6 The data hierarchy organizes stored data in increasing levels of complexity.

The next higher level of the data hierarchy stores collections of fields known as *records*. By using a record that includes fields holding values for FirstName, LastName, Gender, and Age, you find that Bob Smith is a customer who is a 21-year-old male (Figure 6.6). At the next level up, the data hierarchy assembles records into a collection called a *table* or *file*. For instance, at this level you would find a set of records listing the age and gender of all customers, not just Bob Smith. Finally, the top level compiles the organized collection of files into a database.

Using a database system to organize data provides several advantages:

- The organization of the data is independent of any one software application. This allows all applications to access the data in a standard manner.
- The organization of the data reduces data redundancy; a DBMS may need to store only one record of data for a particular product.
- The DBMS can include features for maintaining the quality of the data, handling security, and synchronizing access by simultaneous users.
- The database system allows for capabilities such as improved data access, allowing different views of the data for different users, and report generation.

These advantages improve the accuracy of the data stored (*data integrity*), as well as increase its use.

Relational Data Model

In the early 1970s, Dr. E. F. Codd developed a method for logically organizing data in a database that was independent of the method used to physically store the data. In this method, known as the **relational data model,** databases store information about entities, such as suppliers and products for a retailer, and the relationships between those entities. Databases then use these defined relationships to store the connections between the entities, such as which suppliers provide which products.

The relational data model has since become the standard way of storing large amounts of data. Researchers at various universities and business organizations (notably University of California at Berkeley and IBM) developed systems based on Codd's relational model. These systems are now known as **relational database management systems (RDBMS).** Figure 6.7 shows a typical relational database management system.

The relational data model stores data in one or more tables, corresponding to entities. Tables consist of records, represented by the rows of the table. The records generally hold data about a single instance of an entity. For example, a single record might store contact information for a single supplier. A record, in turn, consists of one or more fields that hold data about an *instance* of an entity. Because the data values in the fields often describe an instance of an entity, the fields are sometimes called *attributes*. The columns of the table represent the fields of all the records.

For example, suppose that a company decides to create a relational database to store data about its products. It begins by identifying the generic category "Product" as an entity. The company then determines that an *instance* of the product category is a set of data about a specific product, such as "hiking boots." The attributes of the hiking boots product include ItemCode (HB), ItemName (hiking boots), RetailPrice ($110.00), and ItemCost ($50.00). Because the company wants

Databases: The Primary Data Storage for Organizations | 217

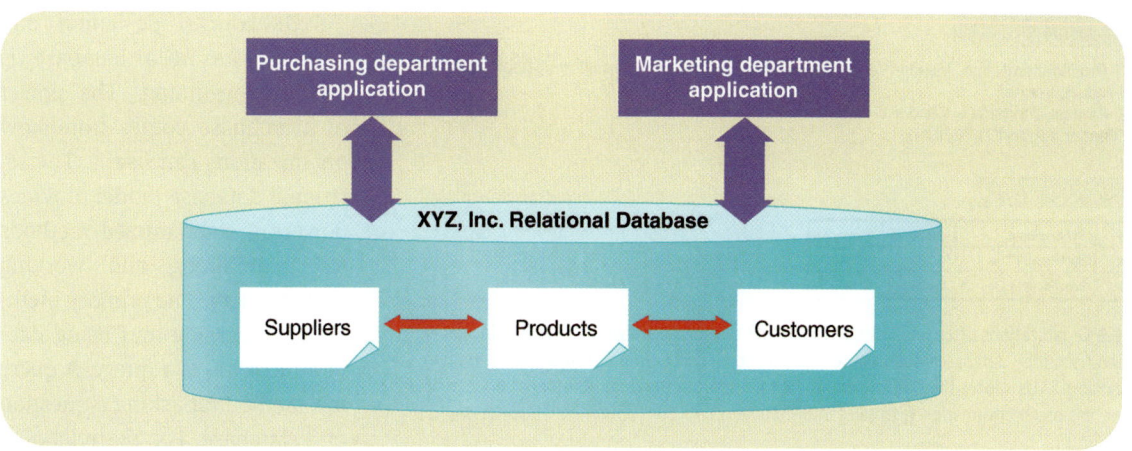

FIGURE 6.7 The relational data model has become the most popular method for organizing and storing large amounts of data.

to store data about the same attributes for all of the products that it sells, its product table will include fields for ItemCode, ItemName, RetailPrice, and ItemCost. (You can imagine that the field names are the column headings for a table.) When the company fills in a row in the table with values for the attributes—HB, hiking boots, etc.—then it has a data record for a product.

As an example of related tables, consider Figure 6.8, which shows a product table and a vendor table. Note that one row of the product table contains our hiking boots example. The product and the vendor tables each store one field that has a unique value for each record, called the *primary key*. In the product table, the primary key is stored in the ItemCode field, while in the vendor table the VendorID stores the primary key.

Note that the product table also contains a VendorID field. To relate the data in one table to data in the other table, the company can simply use the VendorID as a reference. By matching a VendorID stored in the product table with the unique record that it references in the vendor table, the company can pull data about the product and vendor from both tables. In our hiking boots example, you can see that VendorID DOL provides hiking boots, cooksets, and sleeping bags. This code relates to the vendor table that provides all of the details about vendor DOL. When a second table uses the primary key of one table as a reference field in its table, the field is called a *foreign key*.

ItemCode	ItemName	RetailPrice	ItemCost	VendorID
AM	Air Mattress	$100.00	$60.00	SFJ
BP	Backpack	$165.00	$80.00	BRU
CC	Child Carrier	$175.00	$85.00	SFJ
CK	Cookset	$50.00	$32.50	DOL
DP	Day Pack	$105.00	$60.00	WED
GC	Ground Cover	$20.00	$12.50	FEU
HB	Hiking Boots	$110.00	$50.00	DOL
HH	Heater	$75.00	$44.00	BRU
PL	Propane Lantern	$35.00	$20.00	FEU
SB	Sleeping Bag	$100.00	$45.00	DOL
TT	Tent	$385.00	$110.00	WED

Product Table

VendorID	VendorName	Contact	PhoneNumber	Discount
BRU	Backpacks R' U	Nick Estelle	415-555-8328	5.00%
DOL	Doleman Manuf	George Burdell	770-555-4505	6.00%
FEU	Feuters Campin	Chris Patrick	406-555-2103	4.00%
SFJ	SFJ Enterprises	Ashley Hyatt	239-555-0308	5.00%
WED	Waters End	Todd Keegan	715-555-1212	7.00%

Vendor Table

FIGURE 6.8 In this example of related tables, note that the VendorID field (stored as the primary key for the product table and the foreign key for the vendor table) provides the link between the two tables.

Backpack Profit SQL Statement:

SELECT Product.ItemName, Vendor.VendorName, Vendor.Discount, [RetailPrice]-[OurCost] AS Profit
FROM Product, Vendor
WHERE Product.VendorID = Vendor.VendorID
AND (((Vendor.VendorID)="BRU"));

Backpack Profit Query Result:

ItemName	VendorName	Discount	Profit
DayTripper	BackPacks R' Us	5.00%	$85.00
Mountaineer	BackPacks R' Us	5.00%	$31.00

FIGURE 6.9 Organizations often use SQL queries, similar to the one shown here, to obtain specific information from their databases, such as profit calculations. This example shows that of the two items BackPacks R' Us supply, the DayTripper provides more profit per item. Another query can be done to combine this profit information with sales information.

Of course, designing and storing data in a database is just the beginning. The power of a database comes from how organizations can use it. The relational database model provides powerful, standardized methods for maintaining and working with the data. The primary method for accessing and using data in an RDBMS is a query. A *query* is a method for asking a question of a database. For the relational database model, a standard and popular language called Structured Query Language (SQL) (often pronounced "sequel" for short) provides general rules for formulating the queries on relational databases.

For example, Figure 6.9 shows standard SQL queries, which use keywords in capital letters (e.g., "WHERE") and refer to the data by field names and the tables in which they reside (e.g., Product.VendorID). This example also shows that a query can produce values (Profit) that it calculates based on data stored in the database. With one or more SQL queries as a basis, organizations can create forms and reports to simplify data entry and reporting for their employees. A more detailed discussion of SQL is contained in Tech Guide D.

Designing a Relational Database

The following sections discuss the most common methods of designing a relational database.

Data Modelling **Data modelling** is the process of analyzing the data required by the processes of an organization to support it both operationally and strategically. As an example, a business cannot determine what sales tax it needs to remit to the government if it has not gathered this information at the point of sale of its products or services. Therefore, that piece of data must be collected, stored, and able to be reported on when required.

Data models are often the first, high level step in designing a relational database; in this process the required data is defined and any integration with other systems is determined. Typical products of data modelling include a data dictionary, which documents the origin, format, and meaning of the data and other more detailed models such as an entity relationship diagram and a data flow diagram.

Entity-Relationship Diagram and Logical Data Model The **entity-relationship diagram (ERD)** and the **logical data model** are the two most commonly used models for designing the organization of a relational database. The ERD indicates the entities and relationships for the data that the IS will store (see Tech Guide D for a more detailed discussion of ERDs). The logical data model then translates the ERD into a diagram of the tables in the database. Figure 6.10 shows a partial ERD and logical data model for an electronic voting system.

Databases: The Primary Data Storage for Organizations

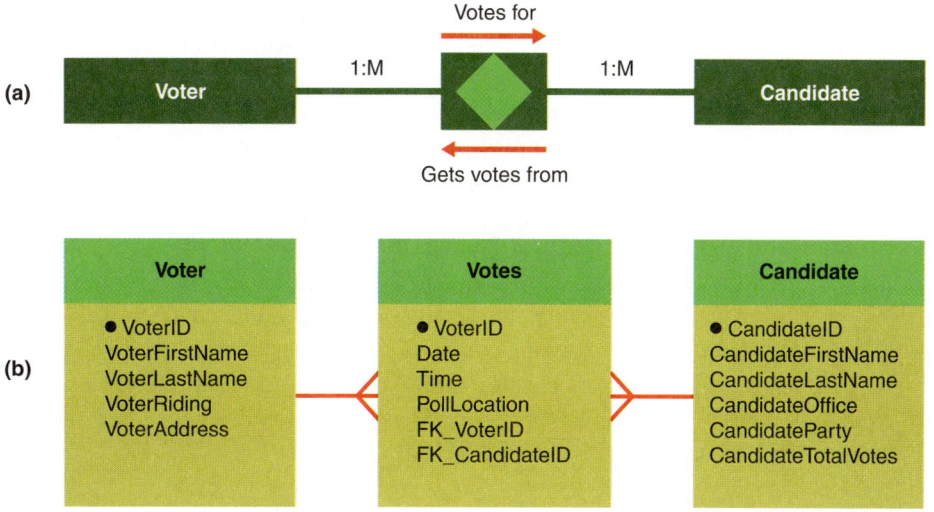

FIGURE 6.10 The two most commonly used models for designing the organization of a relational database are the (a) ERD and (b) logical data model, used here to represent an e-voting system.

Data Flow Diagram As the name implies, a **data flow diagram (DFD)** is a traditional IS model that depicts how data move or flow through a system: (1) the external entities (boxes) that send input or receive output from the system; (2) processes (boxes with rounded corners) that show activities that move or transform data; (3) data stores (open-ended boxes) that usually correspond to tables in the data model; and (4) data flows (arrows) that connect the components.

Figure 6.11 shows a partial DFD for an electronic voting system. In this figure, one external entity, the voter, interacts with the system. Three data stores (tables from the logical data model in Figure 6.10) indicate the need to store various data

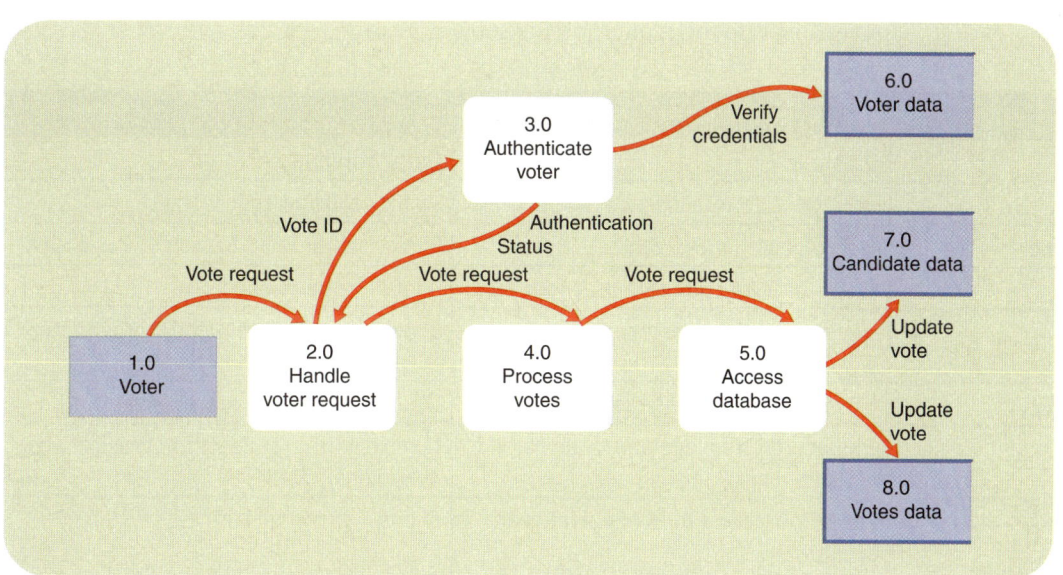

FIGURE 6.11 A DFD depicts how data move through a system; the partial DFD shown here provides more details building on the ERD and logical data model shown in Figure 6.10.

items. The boxes with rounded corners represent four processes, each of which transforms the inputs into outputs. The DFD uniquely identifies all of the components with a number. At this point the model does not specify how to implement the components. For example, to authenticate a voter, the system may rely on an automated process developed by programmers during the construction phase of the SDLC or a manual process (e.g., a polling volunteer).

Storing and Accessing Data, Information, and Knowledge

As it turns out, databases are not the only, nor necessarily the best, form of storage for all business needs. For example, to analyze how a product change might affect sales, a marketing manager may need to access several databases. Or, the manager who needs to examine historical sales data may realize the database does not include this information. In this section, we look at other ways that IT can support the organization, storage, and sharing of data.

Data Warehouses A **data warehouse** is a means of storing and managing data for information access, typically composed of data from one or more transaction databases. It thus consists of *transaction* data, cleaned and restructured to fit the data warehouse model and to support queries, summary reports, and analysis. For example, RBC relies on its data warehouse to incorporate data from its many locations and business units, such as retail banking, investments, and mortgages. RBC uses the data warehouse to provide insight into customer behaviour, manage risks in its lending portfolios, and prevent fraud.[1] Table 6.2 lists several differences between a database and data warehouse technology.

Because data warehouses are very large (in terms of the amount of data stored) compared with the typical database, they work with tools that allow users to more easily deal with these vast amounts of data. For example, a data warehouse may provide information to an area-specific data mart such as a marketing data mart. A **data mart** extracts and reorganizes subject-area-specific data to allow business professionals to focus on a specific subject area.

Table 6.2 A Comparison of Database and Data Warehouse Technology

	Database	Data Warehouse
Supported Activity	Operational (transactions)	Analytical (knowledge work)
Response Time	Fast response time (seconds)	Can be slower (minutes, sometimes hours)
Age of Data	Mostly data for current transactions	A lot of historical data
Scope	May support a limited area within the organization	Should provide view of entire organization
Data Variability	Mostly dynamic, changes often	Mostly static, infrequent changes
Source	Transactions from operational domain; business rules	Combined from multiple sources (including operational databases)
Data Model	Based on business rules of operational application	Aligns with overall business structure

---

1. http://tdwi.org/pages/education/royal-bank-of-canada.aspx. Retrieved April 10, 2010.

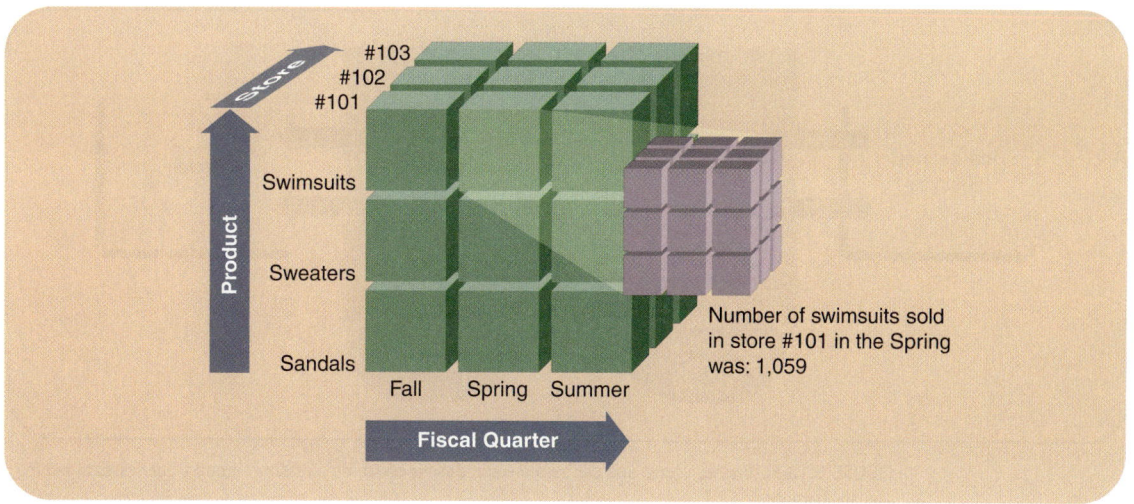

FIGURE 6.12 Data warehouses often provide support for organizing multidimensional data, such as the three dimensions for retail sales shown here, which allows businesses to more easily identify trends.

Data warehouses often provide support for organizing multidimensional data, which are based on two or more characteristics (dimensions), such as time and place. Organizing data in this way allows businesses to more easily identify trends. For example, Figure 6.12 shows data with three dimensions for retail sales. The company can then organize each data item according to three dimensions: store, product, and fiscal quarter. Retrieving data organized in this way is sometimes referred to as *slicing-and-dicing;* that is, the process of cutting off portions of the data until the needed information is obtained.

As Figure 6.13 shows, businesses access and use a data warehouse for four main reasons:

1. *Automatic production of standard reports and queries*—When users need a particular report, they simply view the report that the data warehouse already generated rather than creating one.
2. *Queries against summary or detailed data*—Data warehouse tools include simple query tools like those used with databases. Queries can involve summarized data or be drawn against stores of detailed data.
3. *Data mining in detailed data*—**Data mining** includes a set of techniques for finding trends and patterns in large sets of data. Data mining tools can incorporate advanced technologies such as artificial intelligence. Some provide aids for *data visualization*—organizing and presenting data in ways that allow humans to spot and analyze the patterns better.
4. *Interfacing with other applications and data stores*—A company will often connect a data warehouse to applications that use it as the source of data. A data warehouse may feed data to other data warehouses, data marts, or application programs.

Regardless of how a business uses it, maintaining a data warehouse (or DBMS) can be vital to a company's success. Just think what might happen to a business if it loses all of its data about products, vendors, or customers.

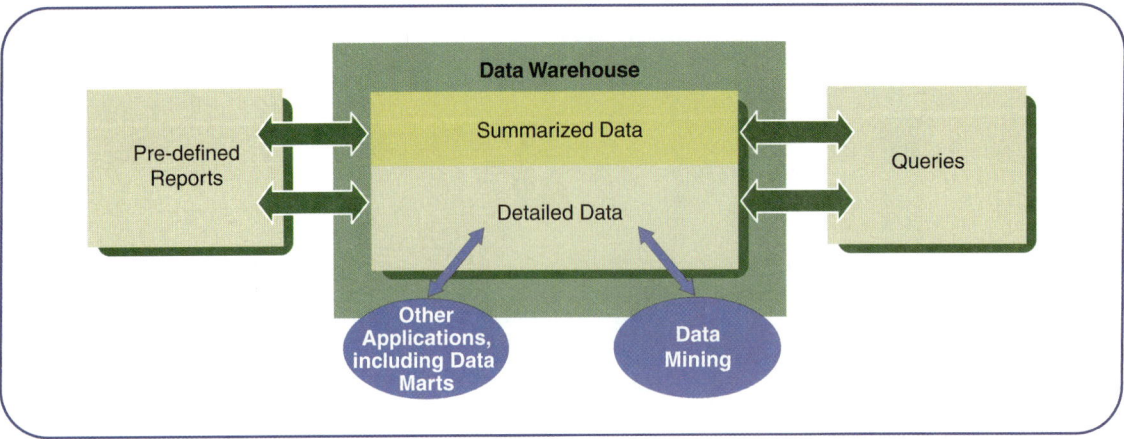

FIGURE 6.13 Businesses access and use a data warehouse for four main reasons: reports, queries, data mining, and applications.

Once captured and stored, businesses process data to create information, which they in turn use for decision making. Although a business can always develop information "on the fly" with queries to a database, this is not always practical. In addition, an organization may periodically need the same information. Therefore, rather than re-creating information from a database, storing that information as-is using a management information system is often more efficient.

Quick Test

1. A _____ is a collection of interrelated data that are stored in files and organized so that computer programs can quickly and easily access specific pieces of data.
   a. database
   b. DBMS
   c. program
   d. none of the above

2. A _____ key is a field that has unique values for each record in a relational table.
   a. primary
   b. foreign
   c. data
   d. relational

3. A _____ combines large amounts of data from many sources, including databases, to provide support for analysis.
   a. data mart
   b. data warehouse
   c. relational database
   d. file system

Answers: 1. a; 2. a; 3. b

BUSINESS INTELLIGENCE

Business intelligence (BI) is a process for gaining competitive advantage through the intelligent use of data and information in decision making. BI is, therefore, a key part of a corporate information strategy. It enables business leaders to make better decisions, which often translate into increased profitability.

TECHNOLOGY CORE

There are a number of business intelligence tools in the marketplace. Some are independent, stand-alone applications that work with any organizational data mart or warehouse. Others come as part of an enterprise resource planning (ERP) system. A company called SAS has been a leading provider of business intelligence tools since 1976 and offers several products that contribute to business intelligence. Their core BI offerings allow companies to integrate and visualize organizational data. They also offer analytics products that help organizations further analyze the data and enable forecasting. SAS and other business intelligence tools provide users with a very simple interface to build their own queries, models, and dashboards. Essential users drag and drop data elements or do drop-down list selections to build their data sets. Once finished the set-up, they may end up with an information dashboard that looks something like the example in Figure 6.14.

On SAS's website, *www.sas.com*, you will find several success stories, including one for Passport Canada. Passport Canada used SAS tools to analyze and predict demand for passport applications. This project came about when Passport Canada was taken by surprise with the increase in passport applications as a result of the United States requiring Canadians to use passports to enter the country. By using predictive models based on combined historical data and external data, Passport Canada can now predict, plan, and act before it experiences increases in passport demand. This has now enabled it to consistently provide passports within 10 business days.[2]

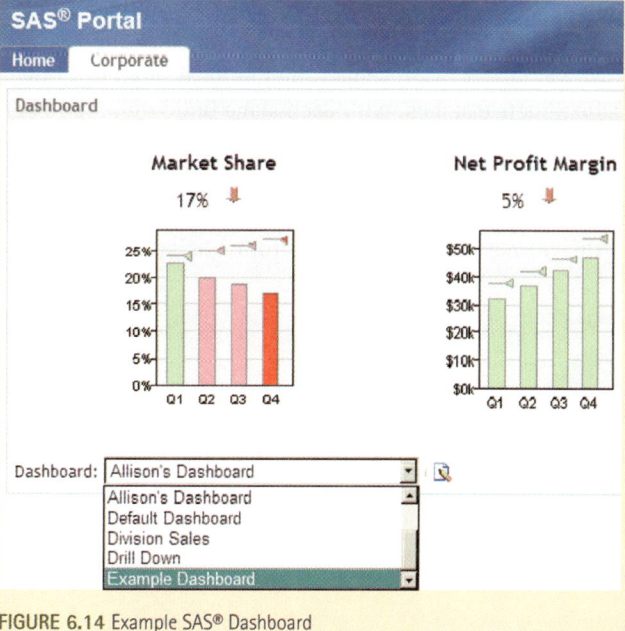

FIGURE 6.14 Example SAS® Dashboard

SOURCE: http://support.sas.com/documentation/cdl/en/bidbrdug/61856/PDF/default/bidbrdug.pdf. Retrieved April 10, 2010.

---

2. http://www.sas.com/success/Passport-Canada.html. Retrieved April 10, 2010.

Table 6.3	The Stages of Business Intelligence
Stage	**Description**
1. Data sourcing (Acquisition)	Mining data and information from text documents, databases, images, media files, and web pages
2. Data analysis (Organization)	Producing useful knowledge from the collected data and information, using tools such as data mining and text/image analysis techniques
3. Situation awareness (Analysis)	Culling out and relating the useful facts and knowledge, while filtering out irrelevant data
4. Risk assessment (Analysis)	Identifying decision options and evaluating them based on expectations of risk and reward
5. Decision support (Decision)	Using interactive software tools to identify and select intelligent decisions and strategies

Using IT to Support Business Intelligence

To enable businesses to reach intelligent decisions, data and information must go through several stages. Table 6.3 lists the stages of business intelligence and how IT assists at every step. In the first stage, organizations get data, often from multiple sources. Then the data obtained generally need further analysis. Analysis may include looking for trends, combining and summarizing data from different sources, or filling in gaps by predicting missing information. Next, to ensure relevant analysis, business professionals must match key items to information needs and filter out irrelevant items. With relevant data in hand, an organization can then evaluate plausible decision or action options. To do this, it may assess risks, compare costs and benefits, and weigh one option against another.

Figure 6.15 presents a hierarchical model of how IT supports these business intelligence stages, with each stage building on and being dependent on the other. For example, it is quite unlikely that an organization would have a data warehouse without operational data, such as transactions, being collected and stored. The transaction processing systems (TPS) at the base of the pyramid represent the primary source of data from business operations. Businesses store and organize the data in databases and, at times, data warehouses. Specialized BI and online analytic processing (OLAP) systems can help analyze, synthesize, and create knowledge. At the top of the figure, management uses the created knowledge to guide its actions and decision making. The BI systems in the third level of the pyramid, decision support systems (DSS), allow rapid and creative knowledge creation by decision makers. Also at this level of the pyramid, you might find knowledge

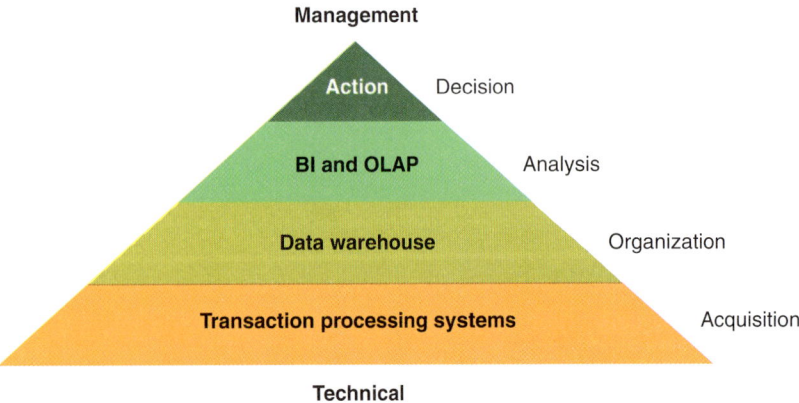

FIGURE 6.15 The business intelligence pyramid.

management (KM) systems. These KM systems facilitate access and distribution of knowledge throughout an organization or a management information system (MIS), which stores management reports. DSS, KM, and MIS are discussed in detail in Chapter 4.

A common way of organizing these systems is using a *balanced scorecard*, *dashboard*, or *measurement matrix* (all terms that are more or less interchangeable). These mechanisms link an organization's strategy to a series of clear measures or indicators that they monitor to determine if they are on-track or not in executing this strategy. This is yet another example of why, regardless of whether the role you play is in IT or within another business function, you must have more than a passing level of knowledge about how to build and use these kinds of systems. They are important for IT to create, but even more important for users in the business to access for a reliable source of data to inform decision making.

Of course, like many other things we have talked about in this text, decision making can occur at a number of levels. At its most fundamental level, **tactical decisions** are made every single hour of every single work day within organizations. They are usually made by the person doing the actual work, based on appropriate guidelines or policies. Systems may or may not be useful or required at this level. For instance, if you are a shipping clerk, you might make choices about which form of shipping to use, which carriers or companies get called, and so on. While these decisions may be informed by information such as what rate was charged for shipping on the invoice, the promised delivery date, or other information contained in a system somewhere, the decisions are not complex or multi-faceted.

At the next level we have **operational decisions**. Continuing with the same example, an organization might do some overall analysis of shipping patterns, perhaps informed by systems that report on these trends by vendor, product type, date ranges, or similar analysis. The organization might determine that it could save money by implementing a preferred vendor program that focuses on volume in return for discounts on rates or improved service commitments to customers. Since this involves a more global perspective across the supply chain and using data from all parts of the shipping department, it is more likely that a manager would look at this issue and make decisions about it rather than an individual shipper. Again, as decision making takes on more impact at a higher organizational level, you see the value of having data and information on overall shipping patterns and trends available to that manager as these decisions are considered.

At the highest level of the organization, executives likely face **strategic decisions** such as whether or not to continue even offering the product in a shippable form. Instead, the organization could move to a self-serve model where the customer interacts directly with the organization's systems, makes product choices and payments, determines how they are to be shipped, and so on. This might involve significant investments in new systems, new ways of marketing the product, changes in internal business processes, and/or staffing levels and functions. This is clearly a decision involving much more than just the shipping department. Here again, systems could be used to model various scenarios, calculate and examine possible impacts on the company's P&L, perform competitive analysis, do detailed customer analysis to pick candidates to invite to a focus group, and so on. At this level, data and information are not only critical, they may come from both internal and external sources, and might include actual data along with modelling, forecasting, or other intelligent extensions of data to improve decision making. Building and using these systems is more complex than tactical or operational systems, and requires a significant understanding not only of IT, but perhaps of statistical analysis, data modelling, and other complex skill sets, in addition to an obvious understanding of database and related kinds of technologies.

Regardless of what systems an organization uses, what is clear is that decisions made in organizations should be based on data and information. Decision support and knowledge management systems are designed to turn basic information into knowledge that can create organizational wisdom. Properly designed systems can improve the quality of decisions made and therefore improve business outcomes—all important goals for IT to contribute to and a major reason why DSS, BI, and related systems and data structures are often a significant focus area for most modern IT functions.

WHAT DO YOU THINK?

Imagine that you are the CEO of a large global retailer. Recently, your CIO approached you to ask about the requirements for a new business intelligence system to replace an aging MIS application. Answer these questions that you are asked during this meeting:

1: What kinds of information about our business would you like to see on a daily, weekly, or monthly basis?
2: How important is it to the kinds of decisions you normally make that this information is accurate and up to date? Does it have to be accurate by the minute, hour, or day, and why?
3: How would you like to have access to this information? Where and why?

Quick Test

1. The process of gaining competitive advantage through the intelligent use of data and information in decision making is called _____.
   a. automating
   b. business intelligence
   c. value chaining
   d. modelling

2. _____ are interactive computer systems that enable the decision and analysis stages of business intelligence.
   a. Decision support systems
   b. Groupware
   c. Transaction processing systems
   d. Workflow management systems

3. True or False. Business intelligence is only used for strategic decision making.

Answers: 1. b; 2. a; 3. False

What's in IT for me?

You may have heard the quote "knowledge is power" by Sir Francis Bacon. Do you think this is true? Certainly accurate and timely data is critical for business success. But it is also true for you as a student and as a business professional in the future. Here is a list of things that can provide you with up-to-the-minute information that might make you more efficient than your colleagues:

- Bookmarks—researching and bookmarking websites provides you with easy access to important information

- Contact databases—maintaining an in-depth contact database on your mobile phone and PC provides you with email and phone numbers at your fingertips

- Organized files in a directory structure—organizing your documents in folders on your PC ensures fast and easy retrieval and makes you more efficient

- RSS feeds—identifying and signing up for RSS feeds keeps you informed about important events and developments

The above are just a few examples of how obtaining and organizing data can help you be more efficient and knowledgeable.

What's in IT for an organization?

It should be obvious to you that data are critical to an organization. One organizational database that you will likely soon come into contact with is the human resources recruiting database. Have you ever applied for a job online? Wonder what happens to your application and resumé when you hit submit? Do you think that an HR analyst reads every submission? HR recruiting databases store submitted applications and resumés and provide search capabilities for HR staff to quickly sort, categorize, and filter candidates. Just imagine how many candidates apply to a company for a position; it would be impossible to manually review each one. One major benefit of these systems is that candidate data can be saved for the long term. Then, when a position opens up again, the HR analyst can simply search the recruiting database for suitable candidates rather than re-posting the position. For this reason, HR databases keep candidate resumés on file for future consideration. On a personal note, because of these systems, it is important for you to ensure that your applications and resumés are a suitable format (HTML, plain text) and have keywords that relate to the position you are applying for. This will help HR analysts find you in their large candidate database.

What's in IT for society

In 2009, the world faced a flu pandemic predicted to be unlike anything experienced in the modern age. The flu strain, H1N1, threatened to become a widespread plague affecting millions of people. Because, by definition, a pandemic is an epidemic over a wide geographical area, it was critical to track and monitor cases from mild to severe, and the number of H1N1-related deaths worldwide. Health organizations and hospitals around the world were equipped with data entry tools to upload their data on the pandemic to various health agencies, including the U.S. Centers for Disease Control and Prevention. This data was then aggregated to the city, region/province/state, and finally country level. With this data, health officials could track the movement of the flu, do statistics to determine if the flu was increasing or declining and in what areas, and measure the impact of vaccination programs.

With this type of data, medical professionals, governments, and individuals could make decisions about how to prevent H1N1 on a global scale.

ROI STUDENT RETURN ON INVESTMENT SUMMARY

1. What are the differences between data, information, and knowledge?

Data is the lifeblood of an organization. It is the raw information that organizations collect to begin to understand their operations and determine whether or not they are achieving their business objectives. Information takes data one step further by organizing it in a way that is useful, meaningful, and more easily accessible. In working with information and applying experience, organizations create knowledge. This knowledge adds value to the business and can create competitive advantage.

2. In what ways can organizations use IT to store and share data, information, and knowledge?

Organizations often store data in a database. The set of rules and concepts that describe entities and their relationships in a database is known as the data model. Relational databases store information about entities and relationships between those entities. Relational databases organize data in tables that consist of records (rows) and fields (columns). Each record provides data about a specific instance of an entity. A field value is a specific data item that is part of the record. Relationships are modelled using special fields known as primary and foreign keys. Each primary key value must be unique in the table, while a foreign key is a field in one table that is used to reference records in another table. Structured Query Language (SQL) provides a standard language that organizations can use to access and manipulate data in a relational database. Databases and data warehouses are the primary systems in use to organize and store large amounts of organizational data. Management information systems (MIS) and document management systems (DMS) are two of several systems geared toward automating business reporting and the dissemination of information. Knowledge management (KM) systems provide tools for working with both tacit and explicit knowledge.

3. How does business intelligence enhance organizational decision making?

Business intelligence (BI) is a process for gaining competitive advantage through the intelligent use of data and information in decision making. The goal of BI is to increase profitability by enabling business leaders to make better decisions. Decision support systems (DSS) provide computer-based tools designed to support business intelligence.

KNOWLEDGE SPEAK

analysis   209
business intelligence (BI)   223
communication   212
data   205
data flow diagram   219
data hierarchy   215
data mart   220
data mining   221

data modelling   218
data warehouse   220
database management system (DBMS)   214
discovery   208
entity-relationship diagram (ERD)   218
explicit knowledge   207
information   205
knowledge   205

logical data model 224
operational decisions 225
relational data model 216
relational database management systems (RDBMS) 216
strategic decisions 225

synthesis 211
tacit knowledge 207
tactical decisions 225
transformation 210
wisdom 206

REVIEW QUESTIONS

Multiple-choice questions

1. Which of the following is not an example of data?
   a. 25 degrees Celsius, 77 degrees Fahrenheit
   b. address book
   c. book, backpack, computer
   d. $345,200, $40, $2,000

2. The knowledge activity where a business professional uses the results of analysis to gain a greater understanding of the data and information is called _____.
   a. analysis
   b. transformation
   c. communication
   d. discovery

3. Which of the following is NOT a characteristic of a data warehouse?
   a. historical data
   b. contains a lot of data
   c. slower than online systems
   d. includes only transactions for the operational domain

4. At what level of decision making would data modelling technologies normally be applied?
   a. strategic
   b. operational
   c. tactical
   d. all of the above

Fill-in-the-blank questions

5. _____ is knowledge that is codified.

6. A(n) _____ is a collection of interrelated data that are stored in files and organized in a way so that computer programs can quickly and easily access specific pieces of data.

7. A(n) _____ key is a field in a relational database table that is used to reference a record in another table and thus represents a relationship between the two tables.

8. A(n) _____ illustrates the relationships of the data in a relational database.

9. Techniques for finding trends and patterns in large data sets are called _____.

10. Identifying decision options and evaluating them based on expectations of risk and reward is the _____ stage of business intelligence.

11. A primary key is a field in a relational database table that must store a unique value for each and every record in the table.

12. Organizational _____ is created when you take base data and information and perform analysis and modelling to turn it into knowledge that can be applied to improve decision-outcomes.

Matching questions

Choose the BEST answer from column B for each item in column A.

Column A
13. synthesis
14. transformation
15. discovery
16. analysis

Column B
a. Find addresses for bars and clubs near campus.
b. Combine all of the data about the bars and clubs including cover charge, hours of operation, location, and ratings.
c. Develop a recommendation of where to go on Saturday night.
d. Review the ratings other students have given the bars and clubs.

Short-answer questions

17. Discuss the advantages of relational database systems.

18. Explain the business intelligence pyramid and why it is a hierarchy.

Discussion/Essay questions

19. Explain the knowledge work activities of discovery, analysis, transformation, synthesis, and communication, using the creation of a term paper as an example.

20. Explain the possible applications of a data warehouse for a manufacturing company and a services company. How would the data differ between these organizations?

TEAM ACTIVITY

As a team, draw the entity relationship and data flow diagrams that you think represent the data contained in your student records. What do you think the major tables are? What are the primary and foreign keys that relate the tables?

SOFTWARE APPLICATION EXERCISES

1. Internet
Do an Internet search and find the website for Cognos, a popular business intelligence tool. Watch one of the demos on the site to get an idea of how business intelligence tools work.

2. Presentation
Create a presentation to explain the importance of data to an organization. Be sure to present all of the uses of business intelligence in an organization.

3. Word Processing
Recommend the purchase of a business intelligence system to your boss. Provide an evaluation of two popular business intelligence tools and recommend which you think is the best one.

4. Spreadsheet
A spreadsheet is basically a rudimentary database. Create a spreadsheet that catalogues the clothes in your closet. Include columns for the major attributes of the clothes (e.g., size, colour, type, short sleeve, brand, etc.). Assign an ID to each article of clothing. Sort and total some of the attributes of the spreadsheet to gain knowledge about your wardrobe.

5. Database
Imagine that you are a business owner and create a database to track your organization's assets. For each asset, include the following: asset ID, description, category, and status; employee to whom the asset is assigned; department to which the asset is assigned; vendor that provided the asset; make and model of the asset; date acquired; purchase price; and date of the next scheduled maintenance. For each employee, store the following data: employee ID; first and last name; title; work phone number; and email address. Store the following for each department: department ID and name. For each vendor, store the following data: name of company; first and last name of company contact; contact's title; and contact's phone number.

6. Advanced Challenge
Think about a relational database that you could create to support your efforts as a student. What would the tables be? How would they relate? What intelligence would this provide you with? Would using a database like this give you a competitive advantage?

ONLINE RESOURCES

Companion Website
- Take interactive practice quizzes to assess your knowledge and help you study in a dynamic way.
- Review PowerPoint lecture slides.
- Get help and sample solutions to end-of-chapter software application exercises.

Additional Resources Available Only on WileyPLUS

- Take the interactive Quick Test to check your understanding of the chapter material and get immediate feedback on your responses.
- Review and study with downloadable Audio Lecture MP3 files.
- Check your understanding of the key vocabulary in the chapter with Knowledge Speak Interactive Flash Cards.

CASE STUDY: DELL INC.

When it comes to purchasing new computers, for many individuals and corporations the top choice has been Dell. What makes this somewhat surprising, considering the salesperson assistance generally required for these purchases, is that Dell sells only directly to its customers, without any retail stores. Dell initially did this by using telephone sales, but has aggressively moved into e-commerce as a way of connecting with its customers. Total 2003 online sales were over $50 million *per day*, resulting from more than 7,000 visits to its website each *minute* of the day.

The Dell website (*www.dell.com*) originally made the direct sales model the heart of its business model, and it was 100 percent reliant on e-commerce as its primary sales method. By providing greater convenience and efficiency to its customers, the site simplifies the process of selecting and purchasing a computer. Dell custom-builds every computer so that customers get exactly what they want and the latest in technology. Dell also improved its support services by making its website work as a front end to its internal databases so that its customers and suppliers can see the same support information it uses internally.

Dell had always sought efficiency in its operations, as evidenced by the fact that its expenses dropped to an almost unheard of 9.9 percent of net revenue in 2003. With this level of efficiency, each Dell employee is generating over $1 million in revenue each year—three times the level of their competitors. This search for efficiency is also demonstrated by its move to the use of radio frequency identification (RFID) chips that it attaches to parts. Using RFID allows Dell to convert online orders into radio signals that instruct automatic parts-picking machines to find the parts needed for each PC. These same radio signals transmit assembly blueprints to workers and track the shipping of the finished product, enabling Dell managers to watch the entire process online. These are examples of using systems at the operational and tactical levels to automate business processes and improve decisions and business outcomes.

Recently, Dell has moved beyond personal computers by offering printers, personal digital assistants (PDAs), and plasma screen televisions. While it does not manufacture all of these products itself, Dell uses its e-commerce engine to sell these products in an innovative way. For example, if you have a Dell printer and it is close to running out of ink, a message will appear on your computer screen. If you agree to order a new ink cartridge, the e-commerce engine will automatically contact the Dell website and arrange to ship an ink cartridge overnight to your home or office. Compare this with the problems of determining which type of ink cartridge you need, finding a retail outlet that carries it, and then scheduling a trip to the store to purchase the cartridge.[3]

Of course, you can now also walk into a computer retailer any place in the world and buy a Dell PC or laptop. This was big news a few years ago when Dell made the decision to participate in the traditional retail channel in addition to continuing to sell its product direct to the consumer. These two business models had not previously co-existed that well. Some of that has to do with the very different systems, processes, and skills required to manage a retail channel versus a distribution business. Given what you have studied in this chapter and the preceding ones, you should be able to discuss what must have been involved in Dell's IT department to make all of this happen in preparation for participating in this new business model.

Case Questions

1. How does Dell use IT to differentiate itself from its primary competitor in terms of its direct sales and distribution of its products? How would this discipline relate to being in the retail channel, or does it?
2. Discuss ways in which Dell is using its online capabilities, business intelligence, and decision-support systems to improve both sales and service.
3. Why do you think that Dell made the strategic decision to begin to sell through traditional retail channels, even while remaining the dominant online supplier of laptops and PCs? What kinds of changes in Dell's systems do you think this would necessitate?

Integrative Application Case: *Campuspad.ca*

You and Sarah have now completed your initial business plan, and things are starting to come together. While you were doing this planning, it became evident that as your business grows, managing data flows will be critical to your success. Listings, members' information, transactional data, accounting data—there is so much to think about!

At the coffee shop today, the question of "device integration" comes up. Last weekend during a party, when discussing your business idea with your potential customers, a student said that what he really wanted was to get beeped or called every time a new listing came up that met his requirements. This made you both realize that you haven't yet thought about how users might need to link to your system if they aren't at their computers. What other technologies do you need to support to make *Campuspad.ca* work for users? What devices will they expect to be able to integrate with your system, and what information and in what forms needs to be available to them on those devices? This initiates a whole new set of analyses and questions, including the following critical ones.

Guiding Case Questions

1. Identify possible devices other than computers that your users might own or carry.
2. How can they be integrated into your site design?
3. What implications does this have for data flows, data integrity, and data security?
4. With your planning progressing this far, have you thought enough about data types and flows to be able to figure out how the back end of your system might work?

---

3. "e.biz 25," *Newsweek*, September 25, 2003, pp. 116–126. Todd Weiss, "Dell Posts Record Revenue of $11.5B for Q4 2004," *Computerworld*, February 12, 2004.

Integrative Application Case: *Campuspad.ca*

Your Task

Pretend that *Campuspad.ca* is going to be up and running within the next 30 days. The programmers are now at the point where they are getting ready to tackle issues around data flows, integrity, and security. The starting point for this is a "data dictionary" that will, at a high level, specify all the information that the system either needs to or intends to collect and store to support its business model. To help you along, the programmers provided a template (provided on WileyPLUS for your use). They asked you to map out all major transactional processes on the site (generic examples might include how new users sign up, how users change/edit/delete their information, how to search listings, how to post a new listing, how to update a listing, how to connect to sellers, etc.). These flow from your initial site design and business plan, of course. Once you have mapped out the process (with inputs, outputs, and associated data flows), you should be able to try filling in the data dictionary template so the programmers can stay on track for the launch of your new business! Do the best you can with the information that you have at your disposal.

7

CREATING IS SOLUTIONS AND MANAGING IS PROJECTS

WHAT WE WILL COVER

- Critical Pre-Development Questions
- IS Development Teams
- The Stages and Importance of the System Development Life Cycle (SDLC)
- Standard IS Methodology
- IT Tools for IS Development
- Managing an IS Project

STUDENT RETURN ON INVESTMENT

Through your investment of time in reading and thinking about this chapter, your return—or created value—is gaining knowledge. Use the following questions as a study guide.

1. What major decisions must organizations address before developing their IS systems?

2. What important activities must organizations consider within each of the seven stages of the system development life cycle?

3. What methods do organizations use to ensure that they obtain the best IS to help meet their strategic goals?

THE VOICE OF EXPERIENCE
Stephen Avanzino, Boston College

Stephen Avanzino graduated from Boston College in 2003 with a BA in political science and a minor in economics. He is a project manager at John Wiley & Sons Inc., the publisher of this book.

What do you do in your current position? As a project manager, I liaise between the business and technology groups within the company. Basically, I work to understand a specific goal, gather business requirements, and help translate them into technical specifications that the IT group can use to design systems and technical solutions. I help define and understand business problems and work with technical resources to devise an effective solution.

What do you consider to be important career skills? Even if you come from a non-technical background, as I did, you can gain knowledge and experience and work in the IT field. With what I've gained, I can talk to people in sales, operations, and so on, understand what they need, and then convey that information to people in IT in a language that they understand. Communication skills are key. You need to be able to communicate well to route information to the appropriate staff and work effectively with others in your team, as well as other parts of the organization.

How do you use IT? I spend most of my days in meetings, either leading them or as a consultant. When I'm not leading the meeting, and as long as it's not disruptive, I can check email with my iPhone. I also use the iPhone outside of the office, as it's easier than using VPN. In today's business world, no one can operate without a level of familiarity and fluency with traditional office applications. We use Microsoft Office—Excel, Outlook, Project, and so on. Collaboration software is increasingly important, and right now we're using SharePoint. We use it for sharing information and documents, tracking issues and bugs for resolution, product testing, and obtaining approval. Although it may appear intimidating, and set-up can be onerous for a project manager, there are significant benefits for everyone. We use Microsoft Project to create and maintain project plans on an ongoing basis. It allows me to quickly report project status and provide accurate, revised delivery dates.

Can you describe an example of how you have used IT to improve business operations? One of the first projects I managed was developing a suite of automated reports on product performance. Staff had to regularly report on sales, shipments, and so on, and a finance analyst had to re-create reports each time from scratch. I partnered with the subject matter experts (SMEs) within the business, and we created a reporting package using a reporting tool called Cognos. Staff could then create reports in five minutes, where it used to take a week!

Have you got any on-the-job advice for students seeking a career in IT or business? Even if you're not a technology major or planning on a career in IT, you can still take advantage of opportunities to familiarize yourself with technology. All business roles today use IT and technology, and will continue to do so well into the future. And while you're in school, polish your written communication skills. Email is essential in business. You need to be able to clearly articulate your thoughts. Everyone saves time and works more efficiently when messages are understood the first time.

As project manager, Stephen is able to work in all areas of Wiley's business and interact with subject matter experts to get projects done that directly support the strategy of the business. In this chapter we discuss the systems development life cycle, project management, and tools that make strategic projects happen.

You may think that creating information systems is easy, but that is not actually the case. We often take the systems that we use every day for granted, rarely giving a second thought to how they were created. Yet all systems start with someone's idea or a group's belief that the system could help the organization achieve its goals. Consider the following examples of successful information systems used in real Canadian companies:[1]

- A collection of three Toronto, Ontario, hospitals—the University Health Network (UHN)—created an information system to streamline the delivery of medication to patients. Prior to the implementation of the Medication

---
1. All examples of recent Canadian Information Productivity Awards (CIPA) winners.

Order Entry and Administration Record System (MOE/MAR), patients did not receive their medication until forms were manually filled in, entered into a records system, and signed off by doctors, nurses, and pharmacists. With the improved ability to deliver medication to patients, UHN has enhanced patient care and increased the efficiency of caregivers. As an additional benefit, physicians, nurses, and pharmacists were brought together to discuss processes and policies, which resulted in needed organizational change.

- The Ontario Ministry of Government Services had a collection of websites that were not meeting the needs of Ontarians. With the implementation of ServiceOntario, a new interactive website, the government reaches the public through the Internet, public kiosks, and access terminals, and provides a variety of services including drivers' licence renewal and business licence application. This implementation substantially improved service by allowing many transactions to occur online at any time, and helped to streamline operations.
- 3L Filters of Cambridge, Ontario, manufactures custom pressure filtration vessels for global clients in the nuclear energy industry. 3L Filters faced the challenge of responding to clients' requests for quotations from its engineering department. As its products are custom made, an engineer would spend a significant amount of time analyzing the client needs and then preparing a quote. In 2005, 3L Filters developed and implemented a Web-based enterprise resource automation application that enables non-technical salespeople to design, price, and present engineering drawings for pressure vessels in just minutes—without engineering assistance. This increased the efficiency of the engineering department and boosted profits.

What do these examples all have in common? These information systems all created business value and helped to provide organizations with a competitive advantage. So, what steps did they take to ensure that these systems matched their needs and were successfully implemented?

In this chapter, we answer these and other important questions that all business professionals in any organization should be asking about their IT systems. Let's first turn our attention to a few critical questions that must be addressed before considering embarking on designing and building a new information system.

CRITICAL PRE-DEVELOPMENT QUESTIONS

To support a complex organization, employees often need complex information systems. And the more complex a system, the more difficult it can be to build, buy, and manage. In addition, not every organizational problem can be solved by building a new system. Often, as we discovered earlier in the text, problems may be related to strategic choices or forces, flawed or inefficient business processes, or an unsuccessful business model. In these kinds of situations, it is unlikely that an information system solution will do anything except hasten failure or speed up the chaos! Before implementing a new system, an organization needs to address four critical questions. We call these "pre-development" questions because they happen *before* an organization decides to start a system design project—referred to as the *concept design and inception stage*. The questions you need to consider, in order, are:

1. What are we planning and why?
2. Is the project feasible?
3. Should we build or buy/lease?
4. If we build, should we do it in-house or outsource it?

Let's look at each of these questions in detail.

What Are We Building and Why?

As already discussed in previous chapters, an organization can plan to improve the performance of its business processes by automating, informating, and transforming (either to seek competitive advantage or out of competitive necessity). It should also look for ways an IS could add value to its new or existing products and services. When an organization recognizes that an IS can help it exploit an opportunity or solve a problem, the process of determining the best IS design for its needs begins. The process starts with the all-important question of what is it building and why. By answering this question early on in some detail, an organization begins to understand its *high level system requirements* and also the *business case* for why it makes sense to build the system. Once it has an understanding of what the IS is going to accomplish and how, it moves to the next important question.

Is the Project Feasible?

A **feasibility study** is a detailed investigation and analysis of a proposed development project that is undertaken to determine whether it is technically and economically possible to successfully build the proposed system. A project is technically feasible if the required technology is available (or can be created—although this is a riskier proposition as we will see below). The study must conclude that the company is technically capable of both acquiring and deploying the required technology for the IS solution it envisions. An organization can determine *technical feasibility* by examining potential solutions and evaluating these solutions based on its capabilities and the capabilities of any technology partners it may choose to work with.

A project is *financially feasible* if the organization can pay for the project, and the project presents a sound investment of the organization's limited resources. To determine financial feasibility, an organization must show that it can afford to build or buy an information system, and that the IS will financially benefit the organization. Organizations often use several common financial measures, such as return on investment (ROI), net present value (NPV), internal rate of return (IRR), and payback period to assess this. Other business texts discuss these in detail and you may already be familiar with these measures from other courses. Keep in mind that IS projects can be very costly to implement, so understanding these financial measures is important to justify their expense. For example, when a company is proposing to implement an ERP system (which can cost hundreds of thousands or even millions of dollars), it will want to use these measures to estimate when it will see the benefits of implementing the system (payback period) or how much benefit it can expect (ROI, NPV, IRR).

The difficulty in calculating the financial measures is in obtaining the exhaustive list of all costs and benefits, and then placing a monetary value on each of them. Some costs and benefits are *tangible*, which means that a value can easily be applied, such as the salary of software developers. Other costs and benefits are *intangible*, meaning they are difficult to measure in monetary terms. Sometimes a company will undertake an IS project for either offensive or defensive strategic purposes that are hard to justify on a purely economic basis.

For example, an intangible benefit of a cosmetics company's website might be the goodwill obtained after customers read about a no-animal testing policy for their products. How would the company measure this goodwill amount? As a result, due to the many intangibles that an organization must often consider in a major IS development project, the financial measures are, at best, good proxies for the project's final costs and benefits. Some of the decision making around IS investments will be based on the judgement and intuition of executives and managers.

Figure 7.1 shows sample calculations for an IS project. You can see that the company is not expecting payback on the investment for either project for three years, and it estimates that the returns on investment (ROI, IRR, and NPV) are greater for Project 2. In this spreadsheet analysis, the Project 1 software has a higher initial cost than Project 2, but a lower ongoing maintenance cost. If all other assumptions are the same, will the organization select Project 2? Not necessarily; financial feasibility and justification are just one piece of the IS development puzzle. Perhaps there is a technical, strategic, or other reason to prefer Project 1. Perhaps the organization is more confident in the maintenance cost estimates provided in

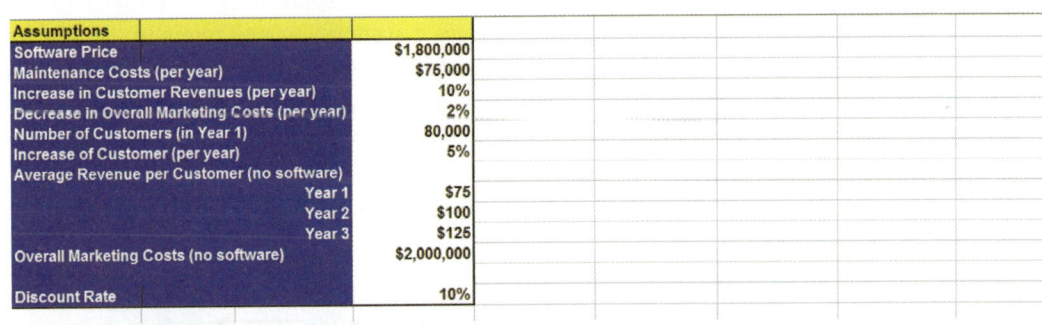

FIGURE 7.1 Decision makers often use a spreadsheet, such as the one shown here, to calculate financial feasibility metrics.

Project 1, or is more comfortable working with the provider of the Project 1 software. Like any major decision, the financial context is only one element of the final business decision.

Should We Build or Buy/Lease?

An organization usually chooses one of three primary options for obtaining an IS: (1) buying, (2) leasing, or (3) building. To select which option is best in any given set of circumstances, the organization needs to examine its requirements and the advantages and disadvantages of each option. Building a new system from scratch often ensures the best matching of an IS with an organization's requirements. It is also the best option for obtaining a sustainable competitive advantage, because the system's capabilities are not easily copied by competitors if they are custom built. However, building a complete IS can be a long and costly process. When time and cost have greater importance than competitive advantage or customization, a firm often pursues buying or leasing.

Obviously, if there is a time-to-market factor in the decision (that is, unless we get to market fast, we are going to lose the opportunity), this may be the most important factor in any decision about buying or building the new system. CIOs today must deliver better systems faster than ever before to support their organization's competitive position, as shown in Figure 7.2.

When buying an existing system, an organization may still need to make adjustments, particularly by compromising its ultimate list of preferred requirements with the actual capabilities of the existing system. However, this option saves time and cost over building a new system. For some systems, like a customer service system, it may be possible to lease a system. Leasing refers to using software as a service (SaaS) or using an application service provider (ASP), discussed at length in Chapter 4. This often involves a pay-as-you-go approach based on transaction volumes or usage, or it can involve renting access to an application on a renewable monthly or yearly basis. In addition to lower development costs and time savings, the major advantage with leasing a system is that the vendor is

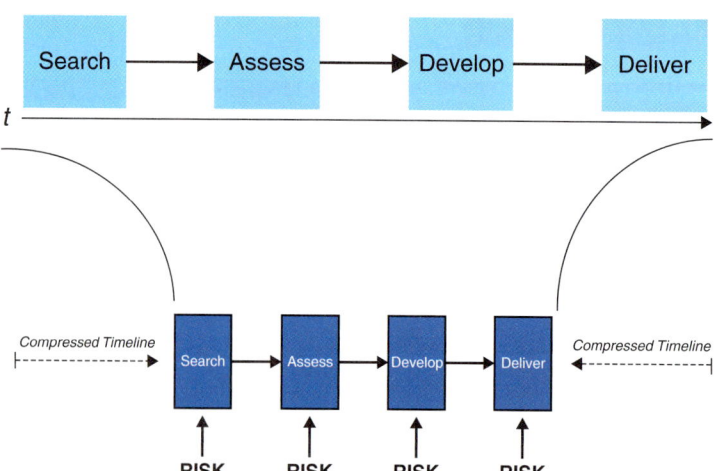

FIGURE 7.2 Globalization has forced organizations to speed up their processes, including system development cycles, to become or remain competitive. However, with increased speed comes increased risk.

Table 7.1	Advantages and Disadvantages of Buying, Leasing, or Building	
Development Choice	**Advantages**	**Disadvantages**
Buying	• Generally faster and less costly than building entire system from scratch	• Little or no competitive advantage; may need to compromise on some features • Dependent on vendor for product updates
Leasing (SaaS or ASP model)	• Lowest cost and fastest to put in place • Vendors are in charge of maintenance and updates • Does not require an in-house IS staff	• No competitive advantage • Little to no control over system features • Dependence on vendor for entire system • Can get locked into an undesirable contract
Building	• Most likely to provide a competitive advantage • Retain complete control over system • Customization of system	• Longest time and highest cost to put in place • Requires IS staff with time and development knowledge

responsible for maintaining and updating it. Table 7.1 provides a more complete listing of the advantages and disadvantages of the three options.

Should We Develop In-House or Outsource?

If an organization chooses to build an entirely new system, the next big question is whether or not to use its own staff (**in-house development**) or hire another company (**outsource**), such as IBM or CGI, to build all or part of it. (When the outsourcing company is located primarily in a foreign country, the practice is known as *offshoring*.)

An organization needs to carefully consider the advantages and disadvantages of outsourcing versus in-house development. As with the build-or-buy question, an organization must examine its present situation and capabilities and choose the option that most closely matches its current needs. Table 7.2 compares these two options. Dimensions to be considered in this decision include any time-to-market imperative (which puts the priority on speed), current financial performance (businesses in crisis or that are under-performing must pay closer attention to costs),

Table 7.2	Advantages and Disadvantages of In-House Development vs. Outsourcing	
IS Development Source	**Advantages**	**Disadvantages**
In-house development	• Firm retains complete control of the project • Process builds internal knowledge through learning and experience	• Generally higher development time and costs • Distraction of in-house IS staff from other duties
Outsourcing	• High level of skill and expertise • Internal staff provides project oversight, which is less time intensive than full development • Generally lower time and costs	• Firm loses some control of project since it is necessary to give outsourcer some decision-making authority • Internal staff has less opportunity to build experience • Requires good contracts and oversight

SOURCE: Adapted from P. G. McKeown, *Information Technology and the Networked Economy*, 2nd ed., 2003, Boston: Course Technology, 328.

and an organization's risk tolerance (which must be greater to take on building a system from scratch versus compromising by buying a system that is not perfect or customized, but meets the most important requirements of the system).

IS DEVELOPMENT TEAMS

The people associated with an IS project usually fall within one or both of two groups: those on the actual project team and those who are stakeholders in the IS. While ultimately the stakeholders must both design and use the system, without a correspondingly excellent IS development team, the system cannot actually be built.

The Importance of Stakeholders

For most IS development projects, identifying the key stakeholders can be a very important task that should be thought about right from the beginning. Why? Because the attitude of a powerful stakeholder toward a project can dramatically affect the project's eventual success or failure. And the various stakeholders who are the subject matter experts (SMEs) can best inform you about various aspects of the system in which you are not an expert. As a result, a **stakeholder analysis** should begin as part of the project feasibility study. The project manager should then continue to use it during the course of the project to reduce the risk of negative stakeholder attitudes.

A stakeholder analysis begins with a list of the stakeholders, including what each has at stake, as well as the degree of impact each stakeholder can have on the project. The analysis must also consider whether the team can expect resources from the stakeholders. Further, the analysis should also attempt to identify each stakeholder's attitude toward the project and any risks. Finally, a project manager should assign team members to different stakeholders, with an anticipated strategy for dealing with each one.

Figure 7.3 shows an example of a stakeholder analysis for a generic IS. Note that this analysis lists potential stakeholders, along with how they will affect and be affected by the project. The analysis also estimates the potential impact on the project's success that each stakeholder can have, along with a strategy for dealing

Stakeholder	Stake in the project	Potential impact on Project	What does the Project expect the Stakeholder to provide?	Perceived attitudes and/or risks	Stakeholder Management Strategy	Responsibility
CEO	Policy and process owner who determines organizational policy and procedures	High	Experienced staff to be involved in user group and user acceptance testing. Commitment to implementing change.	Lack of clarity about preferred approach. Views project team as too technically oriented.	Involvement in Project Steering Board, Regular updating meeting with project leader.	Project Manager
Department Head	Manages admin staff who will operate the new system at local level and secretarial staff who will indirectly input and directly extract data	Medium	Commitment to implementing change.	Lack of interest in project.	Involvement in briefing sessions at quarterly meetings.	Project Sponsor
Admin Staff	Will operate new system	High	Contribute to system and process design and testing.	Concern about increased workload. Worried about what training they will receive.	Involvement in user groups.	Project Team

FIGURE 7.3 A stakeholder analysis lists potential stakeholders, along with how they will affect and be affected by the project.

SOURCE: Stakeholder Analysis Template, JISC InfoNet, *http://www.jiscinfonet.ac.uk/InfoKits/project-management*, 2004.

IS Development Teams | 243

with the stakeholders to ensure they have input into the project and are fully engaged in its eventual success. Finally, the analysis includes the assignment of a team member to oversee and carry out the strategy.

A Typical IS Project Team

The size of both the project team and the associated IS development team will vary with the specific characteristics of the project. These factors can include the scope of the project, the budget, and the available resources. The project team's skill requirements also vary along these lines. However, most IS development projects require teams to possess the following:

- *Project sponsor*—This individual ensures that the project goals correspond to the organization's business objectives and is often a senior executive or someone in a position of authority. Any strategy needs to consider the strengths and weaknesses of both the business and the teams, identify opportunities and threats both internal and external to the organization, understand the financial aspects of the project such as budget and the project's return on investment, and manage risks and planning needs.
- *Project manager*—This role demands knowledge of methods and techniques to ensure delivery of the project on time and on budget, and the ability to communicate project goals and requirements to the project team and to co-ordinate the workflows of everyone on the project team.
- *Account management*—Typically, this group is part of the development team when the project team works as an outsourcer. This team is responsible for the sales and service of the project team. They provide the initial point of contact to the client (the people who need the IS), as well as daily communication with the client.
- *Architecture and design*—The members who work in this group must provide a well-designed user interface. Many user interfaces include multimedia components that require special skills in the areas of art and design.
- *Analysts*—Members in this group may have many titles, but they all provide the methods and processes to translate high level requirements in their

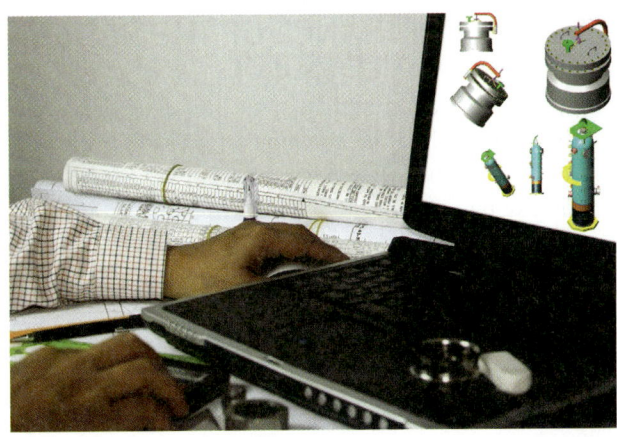

The typical IS project team incorporates many different business professionals with many different skills. Each one needs to contribute his or her expertise to the project for it to succeed.

particular area into lower levels of detail that can be turned into code by programmers. For instance, a *systems analyst* often deals with technical requirements; a *business analyst* more often deals with process and system design; and a *database analyst* handles the data mapping, data dictionary, data structures, etc.

- *Developers*—This group actually creates the system itself by coding and deploying the technical infrastructure of the system and programming it to perform required tasks. This function requires knowledge of both the hardware and software needed by the system to function.
- *Specialists*—This group handles unique aspects of the project and members are often called **SMEs (subject matter experts)**. For instance, a client-facing system may need an artificial intelligence (AI) specialist on the project team to handle specialized interfaces that learn as they go. Likewise, a website for a news organization requires a resource with journalistic or editorial skills on the team to ensure systems meet specific professional requirements of those in the field.
- *Client interface*—A client may be an internal or external customer of the team's organization. In either case, the client has responsibilities toward the successful completion of the project. The client must define system requirements, negotiate contract terms, and maintain oversight of the teams as the project progresses. The client may also need to supply resources to the project team.

The exact mix of jobs required will depend on the nature and scope of the project. The project manager is responsible for assembling a team of talented people who can each fill one or more of these jobs. In fact, the team composition is perhaps the most important aspect of project management. The lack of a good team composition can increase the risks to a project's successful completion. Most successful project teams consist of technical IT people, as well as those with non-technical skills. Non-IT skills range from business skills, such as accounting or business strategy, to creative skills like artistic design and journalism. Thus, no matter what your major, you may have skills that an IS development team needs. You will learn more about teams and team composition in Tech Guide E.

THE STAGES AND IMPORTANCE OF THE SYSTEM DEVELOPMENT LIFE CYCLE (SDLC)

Like many things, an information system goes through a life cycle. The **system development life cycle (SDLC)** is the common term used for the stages and activities of system development. The SDLC is composed of processes that occur from the beginning stages of a system to the end of its useful life when the system is then retired and likely replaced with something new. Or, perhaps the organization may exit a line of business or sell a division, thus eliminating the need for the system altogether. Regardless, you must understand that a system created today, no matter how good, cannot last forever. Therefore organizations are perpetually designing systems.

You must also keep in mind what was said at the very outset of this text: an information system is far more than just technology. Similarly, an information systems project involves more than just technology! Those involved in the systems analysis and design process need to remember there are four distinct pillars that impact an IS project, and all four must be addressed for you to succeed (Figure 7.4): you need the right people with the right skills (your IS development team), they must have the right tools and methods to build the system, and you need to manage the process carefully to ensure success. The failure to pay attention to any one of these pillars can, just as the roof on a house, cause your project to collapse!

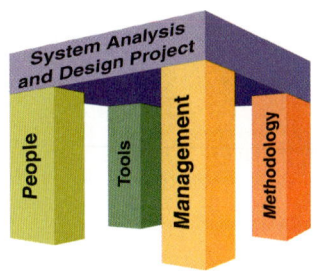

FIGURE 7.4 The four pillars of a system analysis and design project; failures in any one of these areas can cause the whole project to come crashing down.

This also suggests that each stage of the SDLC is associated with a set of activities within both the project team (as we have discussed) and the development team (usually housed in an IT department or outsourced). Therefore, throughout the life cycle, various departments or functions will be doing different things to support the IS as it progresses through the stages of the SDLC.

Diagrams typically show the phases or steps of the traditional SDLC as flowing from one to the next from top to bottom, similar to a waterfall as shown in Figure 7.5. In fact, many systems professionals refer to this as the *waterfall method* for that reason, although we distinguish between the steps of the SDLC and the specific steps the IT development team goes through to build the actual system and the tools and methods they use while doing that (a methodology). At a high level, the SDLC simply starts with an idea. We call this the *concept*, yet early on, the person proposing the idea is unlikely to have details of what the final solution to the problem will be. But the SDLC begins when there is an opportunity that likely involves technology or information systems and flows as follows:

1. *Concept* (also known as pre-inception or idea phase)—This phase involves the environment within the organization that either promotes or inhibits the development of ideas for systems. Obviously, an organization prefers to foster an environment that promotes ideas that can improve its bottom line.

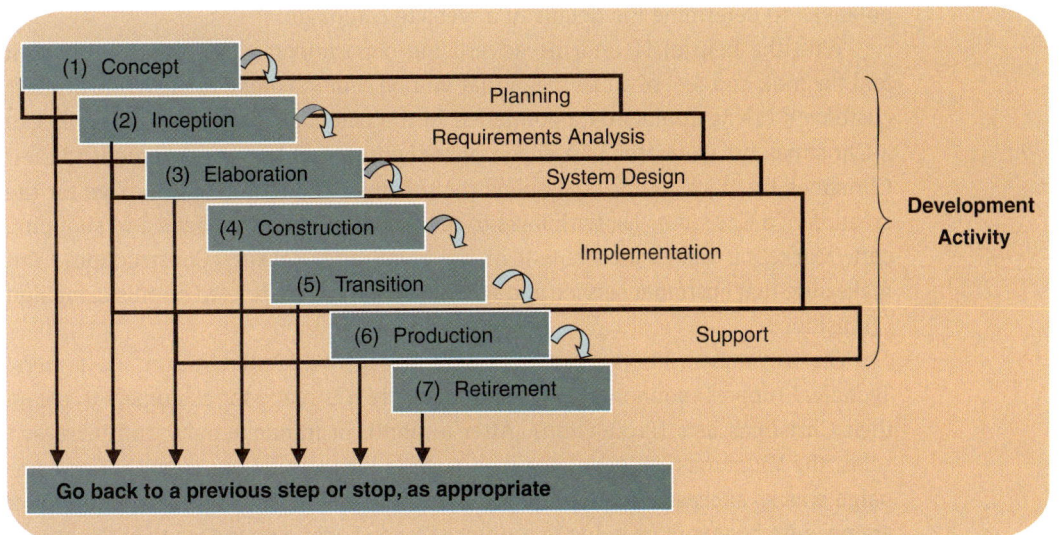

FIGURE 7.5 The *waterfall* presentation of the SDLC steps.

2. *Inception* (also known as the feasibility or planning phase)—This phase begins when an organization has the idea to build an information system. The focus is on understanding the problem to be solved or the opportunity to be addressed and planning the project. Early interactions with stakeholders of the system take place at this time.
3. *Elaboration*—In this phase, the project team finalizes the requirements for the system and the project plan, and designs the system architecture. The team also creates conceptual models of the systems and sub-systems.
4. *Construction*—During this phase, the team builds the initial running system. The team usually implements core functionalities first, and then incorporates additional features.
5. *Transition*—At this time, the team finalizes the system and puts it in place. In addition, the team completes the final training of users and management of users during the transition.
6. *Production*—Once the system is up and running, the organization must continuously monitor, maintain, and evaluate it. The organization must also keep users of the system up to date with the latest modifications and procedures.
7. *Retirement*—At some point, the system may lose its value to the company. This phase often marks the concept of a new system to replace the obsolete one. The old system may retain some usefulness as it is phased out over time by the replacement system.

Let's illustrate the SDLC using an example. As the marketing assistant at WildOutfitters.com, a hypothetical retail hiking-goods store, you suspect that sales are not as high during December as they could be. You come up with an idea to increase website sales for the holiday season (Concept). You analyze sales data for the month of December for the past five years and prove that they are significantly less than sales during the summer. You call a meeting with your manager and your IT department to discuss this information and your idea. They agree that your idea is feasible and should generate a favourable ROI (Inception). You now have the go-ahead to determine the details of a website campaign.

With the help of IT and the advertising department, you design the content and the look and feel of a campaign that will be sent via email to all WildOutfitters customers (using contact data contained in the customer database) with a link to a Christmas list generator that encourages them to add hiking equipment to their Christmas list (Elaboration). IT builds the mailing list and a new web page for the creation of a Christmas list with links to the online product catalogue and shopping cart. Marketing writes the content of the email and website (Construction). You make sure that customer service and technical support are briefed on this campaign (Transition).

On November 30, the email is sent to all WildOutfitters.com customers. Technical support monitors the website to ensure it is ready for customers to create their Christmas lists (Production). After a month of frantic activity and increased sales, the Christmas list generator web page is turned off (Retirement). The campaign was so successful you are promoted to website marketing manager and you are not sure how you are going to top this! You go back to your desk to look at more data and come up with more ideas (Concept again).

> **WHAT DO YOU THINK?**
>
> As you can imagine, answering the pre-development questions and developing an IS involves a significant amount of decision making and problem solving. Review the sections on decision making and problem solving in Chapter 3 to consider the following questions:
>
> 1: What types of information will you gather to determine if the IS under consideration aligns with the strategic goals of the business?
> 2: How would you decide between building or buying a system? What types of information will you gather and how will you evaluate these data to come to a solution?
> 3: During the elaboration phase of the SDLC, many decisions are made about what the system must do. Many times there are a lot of requirements to consider. How would you determine which requirements are more essential than others?

Quick Test

1. A _____ study determines whether a project is technically and economically possible.
   a. hardware
   b. compatibility
   c. feasibility
   d. needs

2. True or False. The system development life cycle of an IS begins when the system is ready to be used by the organization and ends when the organization retires the system.

3. At which phase does an organization finalize an IS and put it in place?
   a. construction
   b. inception
   c. production
   d. transition

Answers: 1. c; 2. False; 3. d

STANDARD IS METHODOLOGY

A **methodology** provides a framework for executing both the project management and technical processes of an IS project throughout the life cycle. Selecting a methodology that matches a project's needs helps to ensure the successful completion of the development project.

There was a time within the IT profession when there was essentially only one accepted methodology, which, initially, evolved from the SLDC. In fact, it was even called the *waterfall methodology* as a result. However, while this methodology works well and is still extensively used in practice, it is also very structured, and as a result is sometimes seen as too slow to respond to the fast-changing business environments of today. Other methodologies have emerged. In this section we briefly discuss and describe the more common approaches to structure IS development and the methods and tools used to implement these methodologies.

Why Do Organizations Need an IS Methodology?

Initially, system developers tended to work in a very ad hoc way, called the **build-and-fix model.** In short, those who knew simply did! In this model, developers sat down briefly with the boss or a customer to find out the requirements, then they wrote programs, created databases, and knit together hardware to create a rudimentary system. After building the system, developers tested and debugged it. As you might imagine, this approach often led to problems. Because developers spent little time analyzing requirements or developing a design, systems developed using the build-and-fix model often did not fully satisfy customer requirements or easily allow new developers to join the project and understand what had already been done. Because of this lack of a common approach or a shared understanding and documentation of the system itself, organizations often depended on the individual developers' knowledge of a system for any future modifications or upgrades that needed to be made. The loss or resignation of a developer often impaired the future evolution of the system as a result.

As a result, IT managers and developers began to think about improving this early process and improving the methods of the development life cycle so that a project team could rely on structure to ensure that everyone, including the developers, was working toward the same project goals. The methodology defines most of the development activities that are part of the plan developed by the project manager, and form a sub-set of the overall activities within the SDLC.

Of course, developers do their work using systems and tools designed to produce software. These development tools are often designed to support a particular methodology. A formal methodology brings several benefits to an IS development project, as Table 7.3 shows. In the sections to follow, we discuss both traditional and modern development methodologies, but many of them offer similar advantages and disadvantages.

The Traditional IS Methodology: The Waterfall Model

The first development model to gain wide acceptance among system developers was based on the **waterfall model**. As discussed earlier, the waterfall model defines a set of phases and a new phase begins only after acceptable completion of the preceding phase. The same is true with the development activities that occur to support the phases of the SDLC, as shown in Figure 7.5. If developers discover mistakes or other problems, they then return, if possible, to a prior phase. As a result, development activities tend to move downstream through the phases in a formal, detailed manner. The idea is that if things are done right in each phase, there will be little or no need to move back upstream to an already completed phase, thereby achieving one of the primary benefits of a structured methodology.

Table 7.3	Importance of Methodology to IS Development
Advantages	**Disadvantages**
• Improvement in fundamentals—methodologies can help team members understand and apply best practices • Avoidance of rework—the process can be oriented toward avoiding repeating tasks in the event of changing requirements • Risk management—because of its structured approach, a methodology systematically helps identify and manage risks • Quality assurance—helps detect errors earlier, when they are easier to correct • Customer orientation—focuses the development team on customers' needs and requirements rather than on building technology for technology's sake • Planning improvement—makes it easy to identify and organize the activities required by the project and helps target resources toward the activities that need them the most at the right time	• Increased bureaucracy—can be overly rigid and bureaucratic • Increased cost—commercial products and services have a substantial cost and often involve training or require hiring in-house experts to support it • Increased structure—because by definition methodologies are designed to avoid ad-hoc development processes, sometimes customers who are developing system requirements may find the process too structured and get frustrated about why IT cannot "simply get it done"; however, without structure the methodology cannot deliver on its benefits

SOURCE: Adapted from Steve McConnell, *Rapid Development*, Microsoft Press, 1996, 14.

The waterfall model is a document-driven and highly structured process. Work during each phase generally produces a document or another type of deliverable. For example, in the inception phase, developers undertake planning activities that result in an initial project plan. During the inception phase, and often at the beginning of the elaboration phase, developers assist users with requirements definition and analysis. That is, they develop the business requirements document for the system to be constructed. At the end of elaboration, a system design document, which often includes logical models (diagrams) that show how the system will satisfy business requirements, is produced. In the construction phase, developers implement the system; they code its components and modules, integrate them, and create user interfaces. As these are completed, the system moves into the transition phase, where the system is tested and implemented into the live production environment. The deliverables of the transition stage include program code, test documents, user documentation, and a completed system. Finally, during the production phases, the developers support the system by keeping detailed records of changes and upgrades. As a result, one of the criticisms of this approach is that it is too focused on output (documents) and not sufficiently on outcomes (the results of the work itself), and sometimes those working with developers on the IS find it too structured and oriented toward an IT perspective rather than the business requirements.

While successfully used for many years and still applied in some organizations, the waterfall model does have other weaknesses. First, the model is usually only effective when users can express their exact needs. Precisely defining the business requirements is crucial for this approach to work. Developers must understand the problem in detail so they can respond with an effective system design. Otherwise, developers may not detect errors or omissions until late in the transition phase when the system becomes available for testing. A closely related problem is that users often cannot adequately express their requirements until they have something to work with and see. This is called a *prototype*. With the waterfall model, there is nothing to show the user until the entire process, through transition, is complete.

In addition, the sequential nature of the waterfall process can delay progress. For example, construction must wait until approval of the system design. In truth, developers can often start some design work in parallel while still finalizing user requirements, and similarly for some elements of generating the actual code. However, a strict reading of the waterfall model prevents earlier starts for tasks or for completing activities in parallel. As a result of all these constraints, developers today rarely use a rigid waterfall model.

Regardless of its limitations, it is still important for you to know about and understand the waterfall model and its associated development activities. It is the most commonly referenced model for describing the development process, allowing developers to share a common language when discussing the development of an IS. This approach also proved the need for consistent documentation and carefully defined system requirements. As such, the waterfall model provided the basis for more modern methodologies, and fundamentally can be credited with adding structure to a formerly ad-hoc approach to development.

Modern IS Methodologies

With more modern methodologies, developers produce a partial running system that they evaluate and then revise and enhance. An **evolutionary model** fits this approach to development. With an evolutionary model, developers first investigate, specify, and implement an important core part of the system with minimal functionality. The team then tests and evaluates this version of the system to plan for the next version. On each iteration of the cycle, the team adds new functionality and features to the system. Figure 7.6 broadly depicts an evolutionary development method.

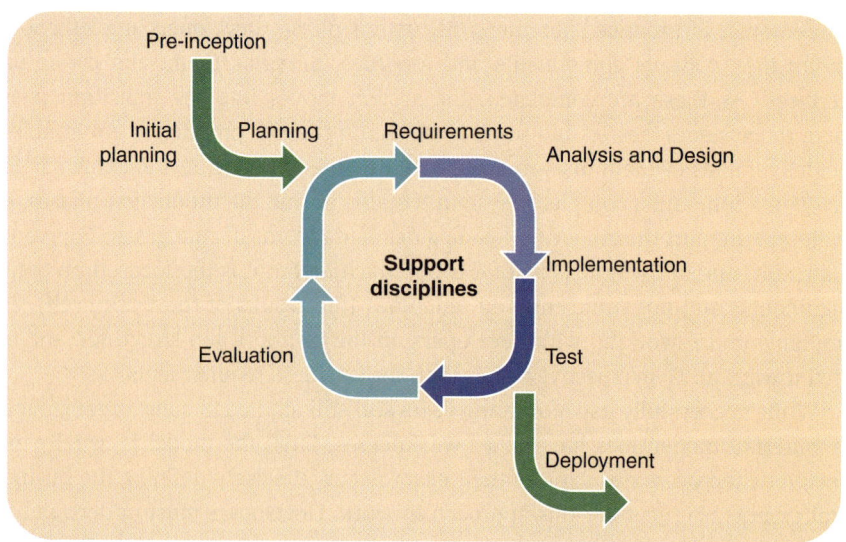

FIGURE 7.6 Using an evolutionary model of IS development, developers produce a partial running system that they evaluate and then revise and enhance.
SOURCE: Adapted from P. Krutchen, "What Is the Rational Unified Process," *The Rational Edge*, Rational Software, January 2001.

As noted earlier, a common approach to the evolutionary model is to use **prototyping.** With prototyping, the project team works with customers to progressively build the system from an initial outline specification using visual mock-ups of screens, diagrams of data relationships, and similar tools that help users see what is going to be built. The final system essentially evolves from that initial prototype. This process can help team members and users better understand the requirements.

However, one problem with an evolutionary model is that developers often neglect to create a well-defined set of documents. This makes it difficult to monitor and control the project, which in turn can cause other problems such as making it difficult to stay on schedule or estimate the true final costs of development, and shifting some of this responsibility onto project managers (something we will discuss shortly). The challenge is that project managers are often experts in their own field and NOT in development, so they become reliant on developers self-reporting progress that may or may not be accurate. If later on it is shown that decisions the developers made were not correct or were inadequate, this will only be obvious significantly later in the development life cycle than would have otherwise occurred with a more rigid or structured approach.

A current trend is to develop systems using an **agile development** methodology. Because an agile process is designed to satisfy continuously changing requirements, the team develops software in short development cycles or increments. Each cycle may include all of the primary phases of the process, as Figure 7.7 shows. Many of these development methodologies also rely on creating mock-ups or templates that show how the system will look once developed; these are then shown to users and compared to the requirements in real-time, often shortening the cycle of getting to a final system design in a similar way as prototyping does.

Evolutionary and agile development methodologies are an attempt to reduce the somewhat constricting formality of the pure waterfall approach. A well-known agile development method is the rational unified process (RUP). This is not only a development method and process, but also comes with software tools of its own to enable the method. RUP is built on six best practices that occur in each development phase: (1) develop iteratively, (2) manage requirements, (3) use component architecture, (4) model visually, (5) verify quality, and (6) control changes.

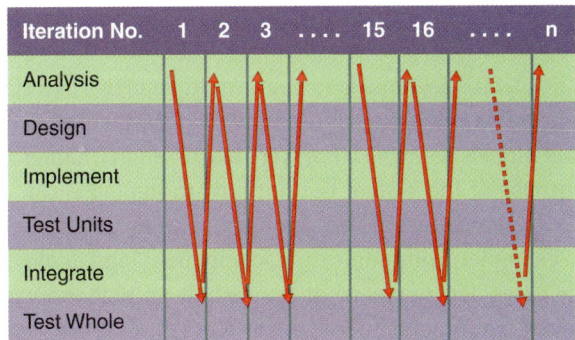

FIGURE 7.7 Because an agile process is designed to satisfy continuously changing requirements, the team develops software in short development cycles or increments.

The choice between any of these development methods can depend on the importance and complexity of the project itself. In general, the greater the complexity and importance of the project to the strategic mission of the company, the more formality is needed in the development process.

WHAT DO YOU THINK?

There is much debate in the IT community about the use of waterfall and evolutionary methodologies for system development. Given what you now know about these methodologies, consider the following:

1: Imagine if you were to do a term paper using *agile* writing. How would this work? What would be the benefits and drawbacks of completing your term paper this way?
2: Do you think that the type of system being developed (e.g., website vs. ERP) should determine the development methodology to be used, or should user preference determine the method?
3: Is it possible to use both methodologies in the development of the same system? How would this work?

IS Modelling

Modelling system requirements is an important part of any IS development methodology. A **model** is a simplified representation of something real, such as a building, weather pattern, or information system that business professionals can manipulate to study the real item in more detail. Models can be of many types, including mathematical equations, computer simulations, and graphs or charts. For IS development, the model usually includes one or more diagrams that developers can use to examine, evaluate, and adjust to understand the system and performance requirements derived from the design of the underlying business process that the system is trying to automate or support. Developers generally create models during the elaboration phase of the SDLC to help them align possible IS solutions to the requirements of each step in the business process.

UML Diagrams **Unified Modelling Language (UML)** has become a very popular modelling tool, as it works particularly well for developing object-oriented systems. The UML consists of several graphical elements that, when combined, form a set of diagrams.

The purpose of UML diagrams is to show multiple views of a system. Together, the set of UML diagrams is known as the *system model*. Like other models, such as ERDs, logical data models, and DFD that were discussed in Chapter 6, a UML model describes the purpose of the system but not how to implement it. The most commonly used UML diagrams include class, object, use case, state, sequence, activity (Figure 7.8 is an example), communication, component, and deployment diagrams. We focus on use cases and sequence diagrams here so that you can see how they help the IS development process.

The UML *use case* diagram notation captures all the possible ways to use a system. It shows which users employ which use cases, as well as the relationships

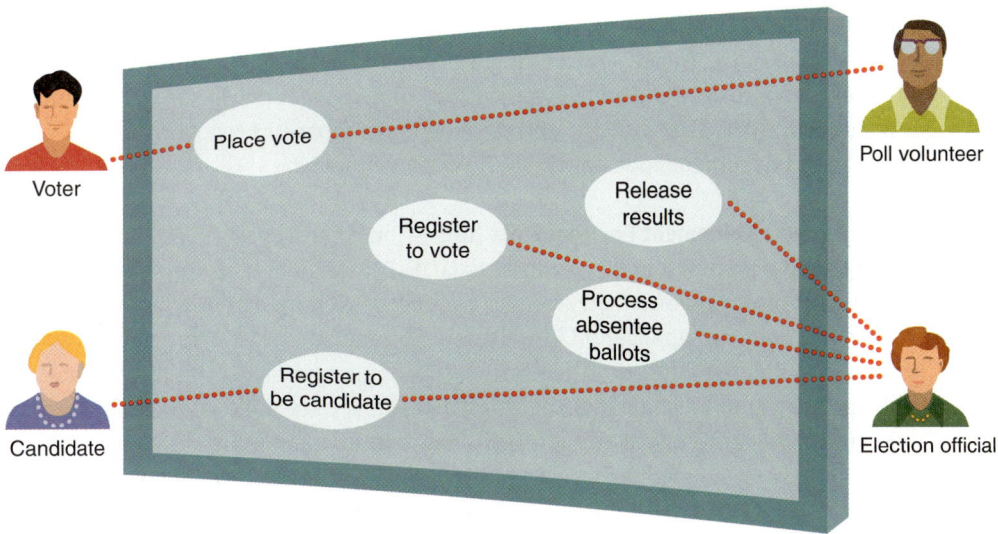

FIGURE 7.8 The UML use case diagram notation captures all the possible ways to use a system, in this case, an e-voting system.

both between the users and between the use cases. A use case describes a system's behaviour from a user's standpoint. Business professionals often create use cases as a tool for determining user requirements. For example, Figure 7.8 shows a use case diagram for an electronic voting system. Here, the use case diagram identifies the possible users of the system and their primary interactions with the system (the ovals). The ovals represent activities that the system needs to support. Business professionals, such as business analysts, can further investigate these activities by using other UML diagrams, such as activity or sequence diagrams. Use case diagrams are usually drawn while gathering user requirements during the inception and elaboration phases of the system development life cycle. These are sometimes accompanied by a *sequence diagram,* which shows the order of various activities and by who, and how they interact with the various system components as they occur in order.

Regardless of the method you use to model requirements, the important point is that they are understood, documented, and shared among the team. This enables the developers to ensure that when the system is programmed, it will actually function as it was intended to, and the data required are available to users.

IT TOOLS FOR IS DEVELOPMENT

What types of IT tools can project teams use in IS development? Well, project teams routinely use personal productivity tools, such as spreadsheet software, to explore financial feasibility or create a budget. They also use word processing software to write reports and documentation, such as the project plan. In fact, most of you have probably used many of these same tools for your group work during your studies, and you know how collaboration software aids group decision making and communications between team members, as discussed in Tech Guide E. Since you should be familiar with these types of tools, we focus next on specific software categories that are geared primarily toward the development of information systems.

IS Development Tools

It is ironic, but software—often the end result of IS development—also supports the execution of IS development tasks! The project team needs software to model the system, write the software, and develop the database. Developers need tools to create and document code, and test and deploy systems.

Integrated Development Environments (IDEs) Today most software programs rely on **integrated development environments (IDEs)**. Instead of using separate software packages, an IDE allows developers to complete several programming tasks within the same software application. The typical IDE includes a text editor to allow the user to write program code, a file system to store programs, a compiler to translate the program into machine language, and debugging tools to find and correct errors. Many IDEs feature visual editors that allow the programmer to develop graphical user interfaces by dragging and dropping components onto a palette. Popular IDEs include Microsoft Visual Studio and Eclipse, an open source IDE.

TECHNOLOGY CORE

The details involved in systems projects can be very difficult to keep track of. A lot of information associated with the SDLC flows from one stage to the next. And then there is the issue of changes! When something changes, many, many people need to be informed and many adjustments made. What if you miss one? Keeping track of the details is essential to the success of systems development projects. Integrated development environments (IDEs) are excellent tools to help in this regard. One of the best-known tools in the market is simply known as Rational.

Rational is a very comprehensive suite of tools that helps systems development project managers and team members keep track of the enormous amount of information required for a system project. Rational starts out by providing an integrated requirements management system that helps to define and manage requirements, especially in the case where requirements change and need to be communicated to team members. Requirements traceability features help determine how requirements are built into the software. Rational, like other IDEs, provides development tools and the ability to develop software collaboratively. Once the software is complete, Rational provides a full quality management system for testing the software prior to implementation. Encompassing all of these activities, Rational offers project management tools to tie it all together. It is funny when you think of it—a project team including programmers worked on a project to create software to develop and manage projects! Now that is hard core!

Modelling Tools and Code Generators Using graphical diagrams in modelling systems is an important activity in information system development. A number of software packages offer a toolbox with common diagramming elements to make building diagrams easier. Perhaps the most significant trend in this category is the move toward code generation.

With **code generation**, a developer can use graphical diagrams to define a system's components and how they are related. Then, with a simple click of a button or by selecting from a menu, a developer generates code that corresponds to the diagram in a language like C++ or Java.

Table 7.4 Authoring Software Categories

Category	Description	Representative Software
Database (DBMS)	Allows developers to build and manage the databases that are a key part of most IS	Oracle Database, InterSystems Caché, MySql, MS Access
Web development	Provides tools for developing web pages and applications. Ranges from simple HTML editors to full-blown IDEs	Macromedia Dreamweaver, IBM Websphere
Animation/video	Provides tools for developing animation and video components	Macromedia Flash and Shockwave
Graphics	Allows users to format and edit visual content	Adobe Photoshop
Audio content	Allows users to format and edit audio content	Adobe Audition

As Table 7.4 lists, a number of specialized tools are also available that focus on the development of specific IS components.

CASE Tools **Computer-aided software engineering (CASE)** is the use of computer-based support in the software development process. CASE tools support the creation and maintenance of the many documents, diagrams, and data that the project team creates over the course of the IS development life cycle and integrates them in a CASE environment accessible to all users. A current trend in CASE environments is to support the analysis and design of business processes, along with the technology to support business processes.

Although project management, development, and CASE tools have dramatically improved the IS development process, there are some risks in using these tools. One common error is to focus on managing the software tools rather than the content of the project itself—which can lead to a quantity over quality outcome where the final product is not going to accomplish the system's objectives, even if it's on time. Another common problem is known as the *silver bullet* syndrome. This occurs when there is an overreliance on the tools for the success of the project, while neglecting the other pillars of a development project. For a successful project, it is important to keep the tools in perspective and view them as support for the primary activities of the project.

Quick Test

1. True or False. Evolutionary development methodologies are considered to be less formal and more agile than the traditional waterfall development method.

2. Through _____, which usually includes one or more diagrams, developers can better understand the system and performance requirements that are

derived from the design of the underlying business process that the system is trying to automate or support.

a. programming
b. prototyping
c. modelling
d. waterfall development

3. Fill in the blank: A(n) _____ allows developers to complete several programming tasks within the same software application, and provides a text editor to allow the user to write program code, a file system to store programs, a compiler to translate the program into machine language, and debugging tools to find and correct errors.

Answers: 1. True; 2. c; 3. IDE

MANAGING AN IS PROJECT

Project management is "the application of knowledge skills, tools, and techniques to project activities to meet project requirements."[2] For IS development, a project manager simultaneously oversees three main project elements: the scope of the project, the resources needed, and the time to complete it, all balanced with a view toward accomplishing the organization's strategy through successful project delivery. The project scope defines what the project should accomplish. Resources can include people, equipment, material, and money. Time estimates consider project activity times and how they depend on each other.

Management of these elements is always a balancing act. A manager often makes decisions to actively set the levels of two elements, and then calculates the third accordingly while always realizing that all three are important and must be accomplished. For example, if the client requires specific software features, these features define the scope and, of course, the ultimate quality of the project. Or the client may prefer to focus on a set time deadline for receiving the final software, often at the expense of incorporating every single last requirement—known as *descoping*. By containing enthusiasm for an endless set of features, the project can often be delivered sooner and additional functionality put into a future release or upgrade. The project manager then calculates the resources, which then result in cost estimates needed to meet the scope and time constraints as demanded by the project sponsor.

As Figure 7.9 illustrates, you can think of the three project management elements as the three sides of a triangle; in some project management circles this is referred to as the *triple constraint*, or *iron triangle*, because of its immutable nature and because it was perceived as nearly impossible to deliver on all three components successfully (on time, on budget, and on scope). And, as you might recall from geometry, once you know the length of two sides, you can calculate the length of the third. However, while Figure 7.9 shows all points on the triangle as equal, it should be clear to you that project scope/quality is often the starting point for arriving at the other two points of the triangle. That's because, among these three

---

2. Project Management Institute. *A Guide to the Project Management Body of Knowledge* (PMBOK® Guide) Fourth Edition, 2008, p. 6.

elements, project scope is often the most important to manage: increases in scope will drive increases in time and/or resources needed. Subsequently, changes or limitations in time and cost can affect the quality delivered by the project.

All that being said, competitive pressures often require the delivery of all three. In fact, we suggest that there is actually a quadruple constraint in most organizations today, where linking project outcomes to strategy is crucial to success. Therefore, the project management triangle, like any other part of the development methodology, must work inside the organization's strategy and mission, as shown by the centre circle in Figure 7.9. By selecting systems projects that enable faster and more certain execution of business strategy, and by executing those projects more successfully, an organization can lock in competitive advantages that make it a force in its industry.

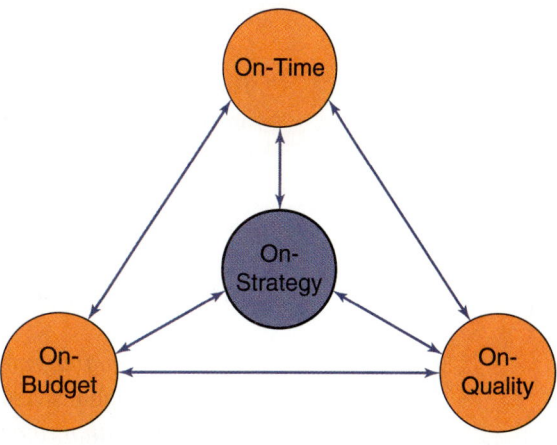

Good People + Good Process + Good Strategy = Extraordinary Results

FIGURE 7.9 The project management triple constraint.

To effectively execute a systems project, each step in the project management process should be linked to a part of the SDLC and have the associated required approvals to proceed to the next step, as shown in Figure 7.10. This requires that project managers of an IS project have at least a comparable knowledge of the steps of the SDLC and the ability to co-ordinate activity between the project team/project sponsor and the development team and assigned IT resources.

Overview of Project Management Tasks

Project management activities may occur as early as the concept phase. However, they normally begin at the point at which the organization has approved a project proposal and selected it to be executed as part of their project portfolio. It is important to note one important difference between the system development life cycle (SDLC) and the project management activities to support a particular project: A project has a beginning and an end, whereas the SDLC is a continuous stream of activities over time. Even though a project finishes when the system is complete and released to production, the SDLC activities continue until the system is retired.

Milestone Approval	Project Selection and Approval	Release to Prototype and Design	Release to Development	Release to Testing	Release to Production	Maintenance Releases
System Development Life Cycle Step	Concept Definition	Concept Development	System Design	System Development	System Development	System Operational
PMI Project Management Life Cycle Step	**Initiating** Planning Executing Controlling Closing	Initiating **Planning** Executing Controlling Closing	Initiating Planning **Executing** Controlling Closing	Initiating Planning **Executing** Controlling Closing	Initiating Planning Executing **Controlling** Closing	Initiating Planning Executing Controlling **Closing**

FIGURE 7.10 The link between project management steps and the SDLC.

While many of the activities in project management occur before the system is constructed, most of the SDLC will not begin for that system until the project is started. The project ends when the system is in production and transitioned to day-to-day operational staff; however, these operational staff monitor and maintain the system until it is retired.

Figure 7.11 shows the nine key components of a project management methodology that support the life cycle of the project. Although the project manager should develop knowledge and skills in all of these areas, the following four core functions lead to specific project objectives:

1. *Time management*—estimating the duration of the project, developing an acceptable schedule, and managing the project to ensure timely completion
2. *Cost management*—preparing a budget and managing the costs of the project to stay within budget
3. *Scope management*—identifying and managing all the tasks required to complete a project
4. *Quality management*—ensuring that the finished project satisfies its defined goals

The facilitating functions support the project activities. Human resources management focuses on making productive use of the team members. Communications management involves the supervision of shared project information. With risk management, the project manager seeks to identify and prioritize potential risks, and develop contingency plans in case a risk occurs. Procurement management involves acquiring the resources needed for the project. Of course, implicit in all of these concepts is that the organization has actually selected projects that are strategic. This is known as **project portfolio management (PPM)**, and is emerging as

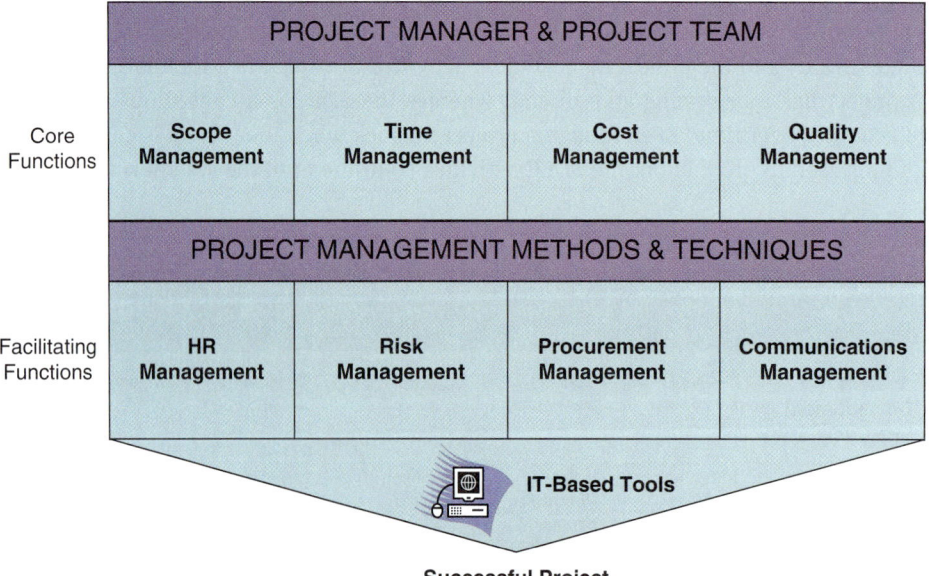

FIGURE 7.11 The nine key components of a project management methodology that create a successful project.

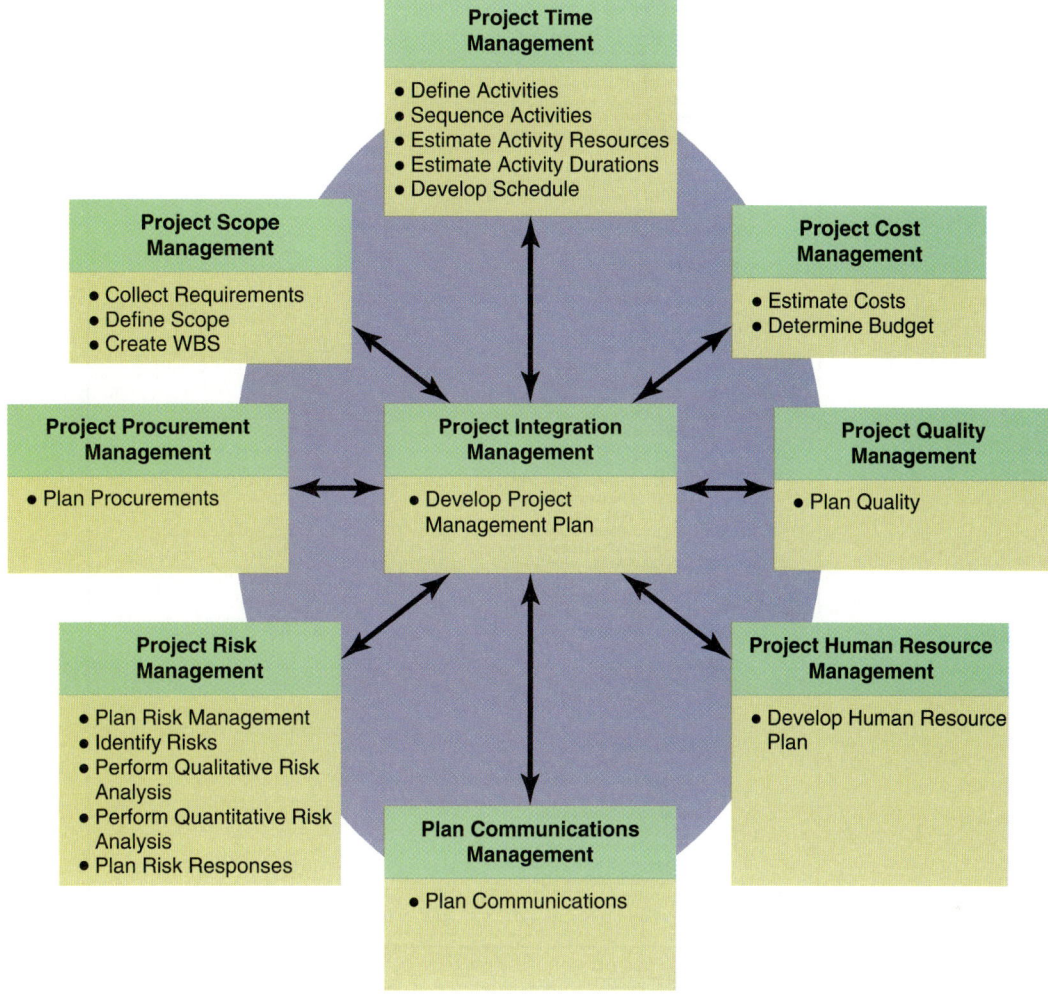

FIGURE 7.12 A project manager must oversee any number of tasks within each of the nine key components of a project management methodology.

SOURCE: Adapted from Project Management Institute, *A Guide to the Project Management Body of Knowledge* (PMBOK® Guide) Fourth Edition, 2008, p. 47.

a critical consideration for companies that are focused on competitive advantage. Therefore, project management should not only be about doing the projects right, but also about doing the right projects!

If you look at Figure 7.12, you can see the number of standard functions and tasks listed under each key component that a project manager must oversee. A project manager ties together all these functions through *project management integration*.

Project management integration includes the development of the project plan, execution of the plan, and the coordination of changes to the plan as they occur. The project manager uses a project plan to coordinate all project documentation and help guide the execution and control of the project. Figure 7.13 provides a sample outline of a software project management plan. Note that creating and managing the project plan is a job in itself!

```
Title Page.........................................................................................
Change History....................................................................................
Preface...........................................................................................
Table of Contents.................................................................................
List of Figures...................................................................................
List of Tables....................................................................................
1. Overview......................................................................................
    1.1     Project summary......................................................................
            1.1.1 Purpose, scope, and objectives................................................
            1.1.2 Assumptions and constraints...................................................
            1.1.3 Project Deliverables..........................................................
            1.1.4 Schedule and budget summary...................................................
    1.2 Evolution of the plan....................................................................
2. References....................................................................................
3. Definitions...................................................................................
4. Project organization..........................................................................
    4.1     External interfaces..................................................................
    4.2     Internal structure...................................................................
    4.3     Roles and responsibilities...........................................................
5. Managerial process plans......................................................................
    5.1 Start-up plan............................................................................
            5.1.1 Estimation plan...............................................................
            5.1.2 Staffing plan.................................................................
            5.1.3 Resource acquisition plan.....................................................
            5.1.4 Project staff training plan...................................................
    5.2 Work plan................................................................................
            5.2.1 Work activities...............................................................
            5.2.2 Schedule allocation...........................................................
            5.2.3 Resource allocation...........................................................
            5.2.4 Budget allocation.............................................................
    5.3 Control plan.............................................................................
            5.3.1 Requirements control plan.....................................................
            5.3.2 Schedule control plan.........................................................
            5.3.3 Budget control plan...........................................................
            5.3.4 Quality control plan..........................................................
            5.3.5 Reporting plan................................................................
            5.3.6 Metrics collection plan.......................................................
    5.4 Risk management plan.....................................................................
    5.5 Closeout plan............................................................................
6. Technical process plan.......................................................................
    6.1 Process model............................................................................
    6.2 Methods, tools, and techniques...........................................................
    6.3 Infrastructure plan......................................................................
    6.4 Product acceptance plan..................................................................
7. Supporting process plans.....................................................................
    7.1 Configuration management plan............................................................
    7.2 Verification and validation plan.........................................................
    7.3 Documentation plan.......................................................................
    7.4 Quality assurance plan...................................................................
    7.5 Reviews and audits.......................................................................
    7.6 Problem resolution plan..................................................................
    7.7 Subcontractor management plan............................................................
    7.8 Process improvement plan.................................................................
8. Additional plans.............................................................................
Annexes..........................................................................................
Index............................................................................................
```

FIGURE 7.13 Sample project management plan.

SOURCE: Reprinted with permission from IEEE Std. 1058–1998, "IEEE Standard for Software Project Management Plans," p. 4, copyright 1998 by IEEE. The IEEE disclaims any responsibility or liability resulting from the placement and use in the described manner.

Project Time Management

After budgeting, the most important function for the project manager is developing and controlling the project schedule. In fact, delays in completing tasks usually go hand-in-hand with increases in costs. However, for many IS projects where gaining a competitive advantage is a goal, creating and maintaining a schedule that produces a quality project as quickly as possible can be more important than costs. For example, think about what might have happened if another company developed its website before *eBay.com*. Could a delay in eBay's development schedule have allowed a competitor to become the first big Internet auction site instead? The main activities of project time management include:[3]

- *Define activities*—identifying the activities required to produce project deliverables

---
3. Project Management Institute. *A Guide to The Project Management Body of Knowledge* (PMBOK® Guide) Fourth Edition, 2008, p. 129.

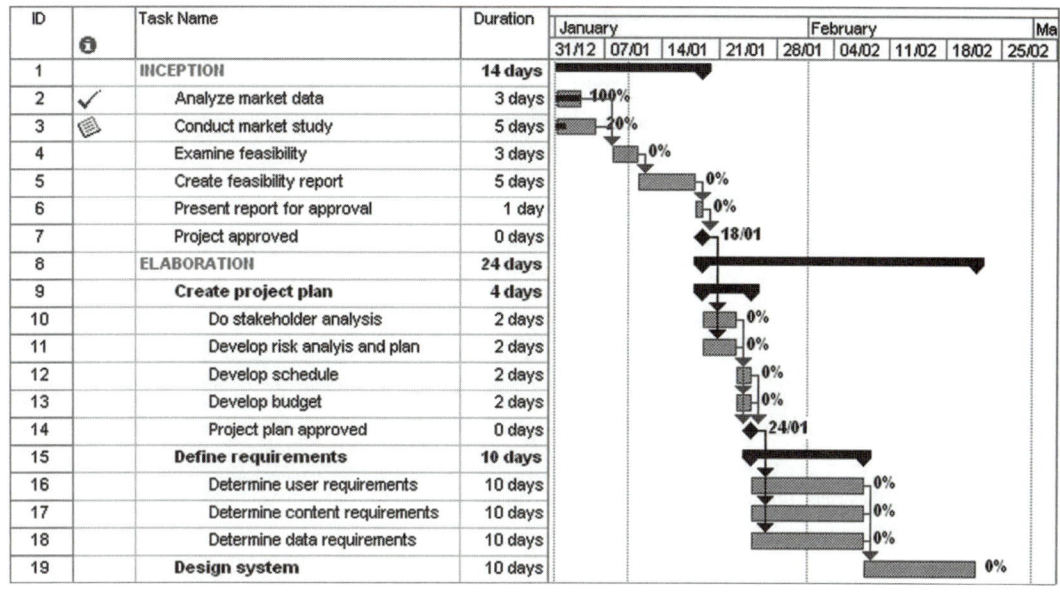

FIGURE 7.14 A Gantt chart provides a standard format for displaying the results of activity definition, sequence and duration estimating, and schedule development; this chart lists the project activities, along with the start and finish dates, in a calendar format.

- *Sequence activities*—identifying and documenting relationships between project activities
- *Estimate activity resources*—estimating the type and quantity of material, people, equipment, or supplies required by each activity
- *Estimate activity durations*—approximating the number of work periods needed to complete individual work activities with estimated resources
- *Develop schedule*—analyzing activity sequences, durations, resource requirements, and schedule constraints to create the project schedule
- *Control schedule*—monitoring the status of the project to update project progress and managing changes to the schedule baseline

To manage all these activities, project managers often use a **Gantt chart**. Gantt charts (see Figure 7.14) provide a standard format for displaying the results of the first four time-management activities. This chart lists the project activities, along with the start and finish dates in a calendar format. On the calendar, horizontal bars that correspond to start and end dates represent activity durations. Patterns or colours on the bars represent various categories of activities. Arrows show when the start time of one or more activities depends on the completion of an earlier activity. While the project is ongoing, the project manager updates the chart to show actual project durations, to serve as a project evaluation and schedule control tool.

Risk Management

Every IS project contains an element of risk. Uncertainties or unexpected events can and do occur. For example, a key project team member might leave unexpectedly, or management might suddenly decide to reduce funding. But most project risks

Table 7.5	Common Areas of Project Risk
Project Risk	Description
Feature creep	As the project progresses, user requirements may increase beyond the team's ability to handle them within the original project scope.
Requirements gold-plating	A project has more requirements than is really needed from inception.
Short-changed quality	If a project is rushed, corners are often cut in areas such as testing, documentation, and design tasks.
Overly optimistic schedule	Setting an overly optimistic schedule can cause abbreviations in critical planning and design tasks, as well as put undue pressure on team members.
Inadequate design	When not enough time is allocated to design, the quality of the design can suffer.
Silver bullet syndrome	Occurs when a project team latches on to a new practice or technology, and expects it to answer all of their problems.
Research-oriented development	This occurs when a design attempts to push the boundaries of what is technically feasible in too many areas.
Weak personnel	Occurs when the skills and knowledge of the team members are not up to the project tasks.
Friction with customers	Can be caused by perceived lack of co-operation on one side or the other or personality conflicts.

SOURCE: Steve McConnell, *Rapid Development*, Microsoft Press, 1996, p. 85.

reflect the fact that much of an IS plan relies on estimates. Since these risks are inherent in the project plan, they can be manageable.

The job of **risk management** is, therefore, to recognize, address, and eliminate sources of risk before they threaten the successful completion of the project. This is the responsibility of all project team members. In general, risk management tasks fall into one of two main categories: (1) risk assessment and (2) risk control.

The first step in risk assessment is to identify potential project risks. A project manager often obtains an initial list of risks by asking several questions: What could possibly go wrong? How likely is this to happen? How will it affect the project? What can I do about it? Since the greatest risks often occur where there is an interface, such as between systems, departments, processes, or organizations, particular attention is paid to these areas. This is where the input of business team members becomes critical: What do you see as being a risky aspect of the project? What can be done to mitigate these risks? Table 7.5 lists some of the most common areas where risks can occur in an IS project.

After obtaining a list of potential risks, the next step is to actually assess these risks; that is, to analyze each of them for likelihood and potential impact to the project. This assessment will come primarily from the experience and knowledge of project stakeholders and others consulted during the risk analysis process. As Figure 7.15 shows, the greatest effort to manage risk will focus on addressing the risks that are most likely to occur (high probability) and those that will have the biggest impact (high impact)

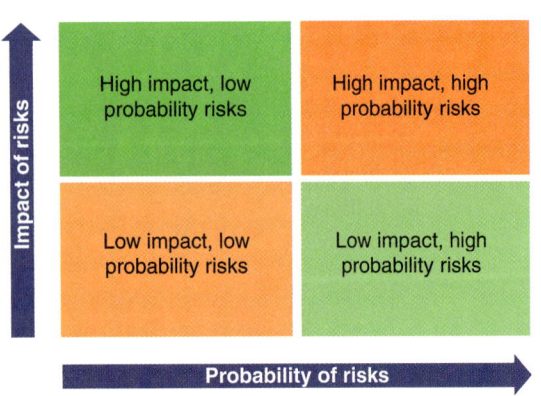

FIGURE 7.15 A project risk matrix helps managers focus on those risks that will have the biggest impact if they occur.

Table 7.6 Risk Response Action

Risk Response	Action
Risk transfer	Move the risk to someone who is more able to deal with it (e.g., a contractor).
Risk deferral	Adjust the plan schedule to move some activities to a later date when the risk might be lessened.
Risk reduction	Either reduce the probability of the risk occurring or lessen the impact; for example, increase staffing resources on the project.
Risk acceptance	Sometimes, you need to accept the risk and then ensure that contingency plans are in place.
Risk avoidance	Eliminate the possibility of the risk occurring; for instance, use alternative resources or technologies.

SOURCE: Steve McConnell, *Rapid Development*, Microsoft Press, 1996, p. 87.

if they do occur. In other words, project managers usually concentrate on those risks that fall in the upper right corner of the matrix.

To manage risk effectively, a project manager directs a team member to allocate each risk to an identified owner. This should be someone within the project team who is responsible for monitoring the situation and ensuring the initiation of any necessary mitigating actions. Table 7.6 lists responses to initial risk assessments.

Managing risk is an ongoing task throughout the project life cycle. The nature of the risks faced by the project team will change as the project progresses. For example, staff recruitment may be a big issue at the inception of a project, while staff retention becomes more of an issue as the project draws near to an end.

As the above discussion illustrates, the scope and complexity of an IS development project is often difficult to manage. To assist project managers and ensure that there are standards in the project management profession, the Project Management Institute (PMI) has developed a guide, the Project Management Body of Knowledge (PMBOK®). Much of the information in this section of the text can also be found in the PMBOK® guide. If project management interests you, we encourage you to visit *www.pmi.org* to learn more about the profession and project management standards. Following standard practices helps project teams do the right things (be effective). Using technology helps project teams be more productive and efficient (do things right).

Program and Portfolio Management

Sometimes it may be useful to either break down a very large project into a series of smaller, interrelated projects, or to group a series of related projects into a single work effort. When this happens, the result is often called a **program** and the activity of managing several projects together is known as **program management**—essentially the same tasks as involved in managing a single project, but across multiple teams. Programs are often created because there are dependencies between projects. Think of a program as similar to graduating with your degree. Inside this program are the individual courses you must take in order to graduate. Think of each of these courses as a project, and some of these courses are pre requisites (dependent). Within each course, specific deliverables and deadlines must be met. Taken together, each course must be accomplished for you to graduate and for the program to end. In systems projects, a program may be created because a project is too large to be organized as one project and the dependencies between large tasks are critical. For example, a project to create a new line of business for an organization would be run as projects within the program, such as creating the technical infrastructure, developing the product for sale, determining customer service practices, etc.

Organizations make choices not only about time, cost, scope, and quality, but even the choice of which projects to undertake in the first place. The selection of projects aligned to an organization's overall strategy that provide the company with a benefit is of utmost importance. This is known as **portfolio management** and is ultimately about selecting and approving projects that will accomplish the organization's strategic objectives. While often considered as part of project management, it is actually a planning process that precedes the project management process by defining which projects will get activated and assigned to a project manager and project team.

In this process, projects are examined to determine which are the most critical and of the highest priority. Once this is determined, resources are allocated across the projects in the portfolio. Of course, new projects begin and projects end or are cancelled all the time. Therefore, the portfolio is always changing. The project portfolio is constantly being analyzed and monitored. It is even possible for projects to change priority over time, and resources may be shifted between projects. Figure 7.16 shows a sample of a very simple project portfolio.

Project Management Software

Project management (PM) software is designed to support and automate project management and decision-making tasks. PM software is usually classified into three levels:

- *Low-level packages*—for entry-level users; include tools for basic scheduling, project control, reporting, filtering, and sorting
- *Mid-level software*—adds to these functions by providing resource-levelling, resource-allocation, cost-control, and flexible-charting capabilities; allows for effective management of large projects, with up to about 2,000 tasks
- *High-level software*—provides advanced functions including scheduling by user-defined rules, programming languages, resource management for multiple projects, and risk management; can identify conflicting demands for the same resources, as well as allow the manager to set priorities among projects that require the same resource

Assigned Priority	Budget	Expected ROI	PROJECTS	Dept	Project Sponsor	Supported Strategic Goal	Project Type	Status	Projected End	PM	Other Allocated Resources (IT and SMEs)
1	$5M	$15M	CRM System implementation	Customer Service	Barb Thomas	Excellence in Execution	Cost Reduction	Execution	Aug 2011	Sam Elliot	Mary Jones, Bob Levy, Sutesh Singh
2	$150K	$3M	VoIP	IT Infrastructure	Ivana Romonov	Stability	Cost Reduction	Initiating	Jan 2011	Linda Chow	Robert Simon, Ted Martin
3	$3M	$10	New product development	Sales and Marketing	Indira Keshavji	Growth	Revenue Generating	Planning	May 2011	Michael Alphonso	Hitesh Bala, Angela Marie

FIGURE 7.16 A simple example of a project portfolio.

Table 7.7 Project Management Software Features

Feature	Description
Task scheduling	Allows the project manager to assign start and end times to a set of tasks that is subject to certain constraints, such as time or resources
Resource planning	Helps determine and control what resources (people, equipment, materials), and in what quantities, are needed to perform the activities of the project
Time tracking	Helps the project manager ensure that the project is meeting the schedule, budget, and quality targets
Estimating	Estimates task-completion times and amount of resources needed for each task
Risk assessment	Helps identify project risks and then develop strategies that either significantly reduce or avoid the risks altogether
Reporting/charts	Includes capabilities for reporting on the project status (e.g., the use of charts)
Collaboration	May include a shared database as well as email, chat, and virtual meeting capabilities
Process/methodology	Provides tools geared toward supporting a particular development method
Hosted or local install	May be locally installed or hosted on the Web by an application service provider (ASP)

Table 7.7 lists common capabilities of PM software.

Most PM software includes graphical tools for scheduling and tracking tasks, such as the Gantt chart shown in Figure 7.14. Another possible tool is the **program evaluation review technique (PERT) chart**. Like the Gantt chart, a project team uses a PERT chart to schedule and manage the tasks within a project. In Figure 7.17, the PERT shows the project as a network of tasks (represented by rectangles) that are linked by arrows. An advantage of the PERT chart is that it clearly shows the sequence and dependencies between tasks. (A dependent task

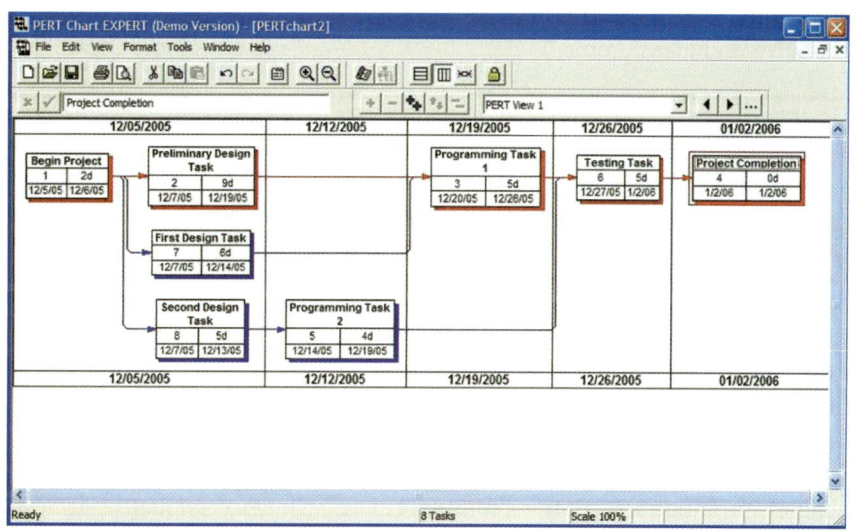

FIGURE 7.17 A PERT chart, such as the one shown here created from PERT Chart EXPERT software, clearly shows the sequence and dependencies between tasks and is used by the project manager to organize and track project deliverables.

cannot be started until another task is completed.) Each task in the diagram is labelled with a task number, the duration of the task, an estimated start date, and an estimated end date.

An important use of the PERT chart is to identify the critical path. The *critical path* is the sequence of tasks that determines the overall completion time of the project. If any of the tasks on the critical path are delayed, then the entire project will be delayed. Tasks not on the critical path may have the luxury of extra time, called *slack*, for completing the work. Note that as the project goes on, the critical path of tasks may change. This can occur if tasks on the critical path are completed early or tasks not on the critical path are delayed beyond their allowable slack time.

Quick Test

1. A _____ chart is used to show sequences of project activities and to identify the critical path.
   a. data-flow
   b. Gantt
   c. PERT
   d. sequence

2. True or False. After setting the project scope and time frame, an organization can then calculate the amount of resources needed to complete a project.

3. The risk that the desired scope of a project will continue to increase as the project progresses is known as _____.
   a. feature (scope) creep
   b. requirements gold-plating
   c. short-changed quality
   d. silver bullet syndrome

Answers: 1. c ; 2. True; 3. a

What's in IT for me?

Project management is a desirable career path for many. It is possible for a project manager to work on projects in many areas of an organization including operations, finance, and human resources, and it is possible for a project manager to manage projects that involve each of these groups in a cross-functional project team. Project management is an important part of an organization's efforts to transform problems into solutions that create business value.

For over 40 years, the Project Management Institute (PMI) has been working to increase the profile and professionalism of project management. Since the 1980s, PMI has been certifying project managers and bestowing the following professional designations:

PMP—Project Management Professional—certifies that an individual has in-depth experience in leading projects

CaPM—Certified Associate in Project Management—certifies that an individual has been a contributor to projects

PgM—Program Management Professional—certifies that an individual has the requisite experience in managing multiple projects as part of a program

PMI also offers certification in risk management (**PMI-RMP**) and scheduling (**PMI-SP**). All PMI certifications are earned by proving experience and writing an exam. If you are interested in project management or becoming a project manager, find out more information at *www.pmi.org*.

What's in IT for an organization?

Project management adds value to organizations. Several studies indicate that project management is beneficial to entire organizations, especially within IT. One study, conducted by Canadians Mark Mullaly, PMP, and Dr. Janice Thomas of Athabasca University, sought to identify the value that organizations receive by managing projects. They studied 65 organizations from around the world and discovered the following key findings:

- Tangible benefits of project management were realized in 47% of the organizations studied. They ranged from cost savings (17%), increased revenues (27%), and decreased write-offs (15%), to customer retention (22%) and increased customer (17%) and market share (7%).

- Intangible benefits of project management included attainment of strategic objectives (63%); more effective use of human resources (63%); improved overall management (61%); improved corporate culture (56%); improved reputation (53%); improved regulatory compliance (24%); improved competitiveness (22%); greater social good (15%); new product/service streams (8%); improved staff retention (8%); and improved quality of life (3%).

- It was found that the fit between the organization's strategy, culture, industry, economic environment, and resources (human and other) and what is implemented to help manage projects seems to determine the level and kind of benefits realized.[4]

For more on this study, see *www.valueofpm.com*.

What's in IT for society?

We don't think that anyone can argue that project management and systems development have not benefited society. We have addressed this many times throughout this text. Two things we commonly access and enjoy that are the result of projects being initiated and executed—systems projects in particular—that followed the systems development life cycle include:

- Text messaging—Text messaging (SMS) was first conceived as a project in the early 1980s. Soon several collaborators came together to develop the technology that allows SMS messages to be sent on GSM cellular networks by simply upgrading the software at each mobile station.

- Microsoft Windows—In the early 1980s, Microsoft began a project in response to growing interest in the marketplace for graphical user interfaces (GUI). At first the product was called Interface Manager, but by the time it went to market it was called Microsoft Windows. Over the years, Microsoft has come to call its strategic projects by a code name with only project team members knowing the details of the "secret" project.

---

4. http://www.financialpost.com/executive/story.html?id=930145&p=2. Retrieved March 30, 2010.

> We could continue and list every piece of technology in place today that started as a project, following the systems development life cycle. Give some thought to technology that provides some benefit to society, and remember that a project team created it.

ROi STUDENT RETURN ON INVESTMENT SUMMARY

1. What major decisions must organizations address before developing their IS systems?

There are four major questions that organizations need to ask when considering obtaining an IS: (1) Do we need an IS? Business professionals in an organization are constantly looking for ways to improve their operations; (2) Is the project feasible? During project inception, an organization needs to determine whether or not the project has a reasonable chance of success; (3) Should we build, buy, or lease the IS?; and (4) Do we build the IS ourselves (in-house), or do we contract with an outside firm (outsource) to build it? Answering each of these questions will require that decisions be made. Sometimes it is difficult to make those choices, and there may not be any "right" answer. See Chapter 3 for a discussion on decision making and problem solving.

2. What important activities must an organization consider within each of the seven stages of the system development life cycle?

The system development life cycle is a series of events viewed over time from the initial concept through to the retirement of an information system. In other words, the system is born, develops, has a useful work life, and then retires. We can divide the life cycle into seven main phases: concept, inception, elaboration, construction, transition, production, and retirement. The retirement of one system often means that an organization is about to transition to another system. Figure 7.5 depicts the SDLC and development activities as a waterfall. As you can see by our very simple example at WildOutfitters.com, there are a lot of activities going on. Every project is unique in terms of the specific types of activities required to bring a system to life, but the SDLC provides a general guideline to the actions required in each of the seven stages.

3. What methods do organizations use to ensure that they obtain the best IS to help meet their strategic goals?

The ultimate goal of any IS methodology is to provide a thoughtful and thorough approach to the process of obtaining information systems. Without a methodology, developers and users usually attempt a make-and-fix or buy-and-fix approach. The waterfall model is a well-known methodology that proceeds from concept through inception, elaboration, and construction, to transition and production. More modern methods involve a more evolutionary approach and use prototyping and agile development to complete IS projects.

KNOWLEDGE SPEAK

agile development   251
build-and-fix model   248
code generation   254
computer-aided software engineering (CASE)   255
evolutionary model   250
feasibility study   238
Gantt chart   261
in-house development   241
integrated development environments (IDEs)   254
methodology   247
model   252
outsource   241
portfolio management   264

program   263
program evaluation review technique (PERT) chart   265
program management   263
project management   256
project management (PM) software   264
project portfolio management (PPM)   258
prototyping   251
risk management   262
stakeholder analysis   242
subject matter experts (SMEs)   244
system development life cycle (SDLC)   244
Unified Modelling Language (UML)   252
waterfall model   248

REVIEW QUESTIONS

Multiple-choice questions

1. In the _____ phase of the IS life cycle, the project team finalizes the requirements for the system and designs the system architecture.
   a. inception
   b. elaboration
   c. construction
   d. transition

2. In the _____ phase of the IS life cycle, the organization recognizes a need for an IS and defines the project.
   a. inception
   b. elaboration
   c. construction
   d. transition

3. Which of the following is NOT a project management task?
   a. activity sequencing
   b. use case creation
   c. resource planning
   d. scope verification

4. Which of the following risk-mitigating tactics means that the project manager will act to eliminate the possibility of a risk occurring?
   a. risk reduction
   b. risk deferral
   c. risk acceptance
   d. risk avoidance

Fill-in-the-blank questions

5. _____ is perhaps the most important aspect of project management.

6. A(n) _____ consists of several graphical elements that, when combined, form a set of diagrams that provide multiple views of a system that highlight the systems purpose.

7. A(n) _____ is a software package that combines several tools used to write software into one package.

True-False questions

8. The IS life cycle enterprise disciplines include configuration and change management, project management, environmental scanning, and operations and support.

9. Program managers actively manage multiple projects as opposed to managing a list of projects.

10. A stakeholder analysis is useful for understanding how well the team members will work together.

11. An important part of a CASE tool is the central repository of project items.

Matching questions

Choose the BEST answer from column B for each item in column A.

Column A
12. buying
13. in-house development
14. leasing
15. outsourcing

Column B
a. Developing an IS by purchasing an already designed system, customizing it, and then installing and maintaining it in-house.
b. Hiring another company to design and build all or part of an IS.
c. Subscribing to IS services from another company, which also maintains and controls the IS.
d. Building an IS using internal staff members to analyze, design, implement, and maintain it.
e. Using computer-based tools to support IS development.

Short-answer questions

16. List and define the stages of an information system life cycle.
17. Modelling is an important part of many business applications in addition to IS development. List some examples of models that you have seen lately.
18. Discuss why an evolutionary development approach is an improvement over the waterfall model.

Discussion/Essay questions

19. What is the ideal system development life cycle? Is this ideal possible to achieve? Why or why not?
20. Should managers rely on purely financial techniques when determining an information system's feasibility? Why or why not?

TEAM ACTIVITY

Form a discussion/study team to discuss the remaining weeks of your classes for the term. Think of the successful completion of the term as a project. Identify the goals and the tasks that you will need to complete, and create a simple project plan that defines and assigns steps required to meet these goals. In your group, brainstorm the risks you might face that can keep you from meeting the goals, and then develop a risk checklist for the remainder of your class term. Consider how using this plan might help you achieve the outcome you want for the term versus not having undertaken any advance planning at all.

SOFTWARE APPLICATION EXERCISES

1. Internet
As you've learned, many methodologies are used to develop information systems. Use a search engine to locate and read about rapid application methodologies. Read the Database assignment below and decide which methodology you would use to develop the database if you were the project manager.

2. Presentation
Assume that you are an IS analyst working for the IS department in a large retail organization. The Database assignment below will be built for use by project managers (not just IS project managers) in your company. Create a stakeholder analysis that shows the interest and influence of organizational stakeholders for the Database project.

3. Word Processing
Based on your stakeholder analysis in the above Presentation assignment, your company should consider the benefits and costs of outsourcing the database development to a third party. Prepare a request for proposal (RFP) that lists the requirements for the projects and any other relevant items. An RFP is a document that an organization provides to vendors to ask them to propose hardware and system software that will meet the requirements of its new system. You can find many sample RFPs on the Web.

4. Spreadsheet
Create a spreadsheet that supports your financial analysis of the Database project. Use the financial feasibility metrics discussed in this chapter: return on investment (ROI), net present value (NPV), internal rate of return (IRR), and payback period. You will find built-in functions for some of these metrics in Excel. Use Excel Help and your own research to determine how to calculate these values. Create two sets of data for each metric: (1) in-house development cost and (2) outsourced cost.

5. Database

Create a database that a manager can use to track projects. The database will need to track information about projects, the employees who work on them, and the activities that they perform.

6. Advanced Challenge

Pull together all parts of your analysis and project management database project work. Create a seamless presentation for management that includes development options, stakeholder analysis, feasibility studies, responses to your RFP, and a prototype of the database. Make the presentation to your professor or to your class.

ONLINE RESOURCES

Companion Website

- Take interactive practice quizzes to assess your knowledge and help you study in a dynamic way.
- Review PowerPoint lecture slides.
- Get help and sample solutions to end-of-chapter software application exercises.

Additional Resources Available Only on WileyPLUS

- Take the interactive Quick Test to check your understanding of the chapter material and get immediate feedback on your responses.
- Review and study with downloadable Audio Lecture MP3 files.
- Check your understanding of the key vocabulary in the chapter with Knowledge Speak Interactive Flash Cards.

CASE STUDY: GOOGLE INC.

"Do you google?" The search engine known simply as Google has become so well-known that some people now use the word *google* as a verb. *Google.com* is the most popular search engine in use today, with over 5 billion web pages indexed and available in less than one-half second. At last count, 53 percent of all searches originated on Google. What spurs this popularity? Basically, Google found a better way to determine which pages match the user's term using an approach called PageRank, which ranks a page in the returned search results based on how many other web pages pointed to it that share similar relevant content. In addition, they refined the natural language search process and its interface to make the search experience for the user easier and (hopefully!) more accurate. This approach usually avoids links to pages that have nothing to do with the user's query. This has made the work of business professionals much easier, including those in IT.

What made Google different from so many search engine start-ups that failed and vanished or merged out of existence? First and foremost, Google added business value by making information much easier to find and much more relevant to the needs of the person doing the searching. Because of this, industry giant Yahoo! picked Google as its search engine, thus giving the company an early source of steady income. Second, Google made money from the very beginning by using innovative advertising on its website. Through a product called AdWords, Google allows anyone to create a simple advertisement for products or services that it displays on related Google search pages.

Third, Google remains open to accepting improvements to its system from its users. Google's open-system approach has resulted in innovative and profitable products being built on top of the Google search engine. Finally, Google constantly looks for new ways to leverage its search engine prowess into other areas, such as indexing images, groups, and products. The company has also added a Web log system called Blogger, as well as a free email system called Gmail, to compete with existing email systems like Hotmail, and which is now integrated with a simple-to-use calendar system. It is now moving into offering applications software in the form of Google Apps.

Learning how to use Google well for business-related searches is an important skill for any student to acquire; that is primarily what this case is about. Using Google to find information about best practices, state-of-the-art tools or resources, and free information on topics you need to know about to be successful are important to your career success. Therefore, you will use Google to help you find relevant and up-to-date information on enterprise systems development and project management related to this chapter.

Case Questions

1. Using Google, develop five different queries related to the same topic (for instance, project management tools or integrated development environments, etc.). State them in different word orders or using different terms. Working backward from analyzing the results you get on the front page, what do you notice?
2. Zero in on three specific sites that offer you free information that you might find useful as a systems development professional. How might you use this information to improve your organization's systems development results?
3. Choose a specific commercially available automated tool that is used either for project management or systems development. Investigate it online and write a simple one-page recommendation to your manager justifying your choice and why the organization you work for should purchase and use this tool by defining how it will help improve your work results.

Integrative Application Case: *Campuspad.ca*

Unfortunately, development has not been going as smoothly as planned (see the issues log and project updates on WileyPLUS). Sarah is getting cranky and it appears as if you are on the verge of a second delay in the proposed launch date for *Campuspad.ca*.

When your uncle (who is in the systems business himself) heard this, he suggested you get in touch with some colleagues who run a software development company with a twist. In return for assuming the risk of development, they *lease* completed systems to you rather than selling you their services. After some initial contact, you met with them earlier in the week. Sarah wasn't available (she had a group project meeting) so you went on your own, but she expected a briefing. After your meeting, they sent you a brief proposal (see WileyPLUS for your copy) and hope they can meet with you again next week.

You aren't quite sure what to do. After investing some money upfront on development (funded by two of your angel investors attracted to your business plan), you don't have much to show for it. This new proposal seems pretty cheap, even if it might cost you more in the long run. And you have personally being toying with the idea of suggesting to Sarah that you invite Adam (a friend from way back…and a *total* technology-guru-geek kinda guy) to become an equal partner and take on the programming and

Integrative Application Case: *Campuspad.ca*

technology stuff, which of course doesn't have any cost. "What to do, what to do?" you think.

Guiding Case Questions

1. How well do you think the current software development firm is doing and why?
2. Do you feel that a lease option is something worth considering? If so, what are the potential risks of that approach?
3. What risks does involving Adam bring?
4. What should your new company do to secure the development resources it needs?

Your Task

You have scheduled a "coffee clutch chat" with Sarah tomorrow and you know all these topics are bound to come up. She is going to expect not only a briefing, but likely will accept your recommendation on how to proceed. What will you do and why? Write your response in the form of a recommendation (no more than two pages), including the rationale to back up the reasons for your proposed solution to the current system development issues.

8

WEB 2.0, SOCIAL MEDIA, AND ONLINE TRENDS

WHAT WE WILL COVER

- Defining Social Technologies and Utility
- User-Generated Content
- Creating Business Utility Using Social Media Tools and E-Marketing
- The Social and Business Impacts of Web 2.0

ROI STUDENT RETURN ON INVESTMENT

Through your investment of time in reading and thinking about this chapter, your return—or created value—is gaining knowledge. Use the following questions as a study guide.

1. What is Web 2.0 and why does it matter to an organization?

2. What features can make a social website more successful?

3. What are the risks and rewards of this technology for society and the organizations and businesses that operate within it?

THE VOICE OF EXPERIENCE
John Lennie, Ryerson University

John Lennie graduated from Ryerson University in 1987 with a Bachelor of Business Management. John previously worked in banking and product management in non-technology roles, but now works with technology companies to help develop technological products. He is a strategic and active investor in e-commerce and social media-related ventures.

What do you do in your current position? I invest in new technology and product development as a strategic—not passive—investor. I work with company management and provide advice on the operations of technology companies. I also help develop sales and service channels for technology-based products. I directly contribute to a company's success by accessing new and expanded markets for its products.

What do you consider to be important career skills? You need to be a realist in business. For example, when planning development time or sales cycles, people with less experience underestimate the time it takes to bring a product to market and the time it takes to close deals in the sales funnel. Being realistic helps to build trust and build a reputation for being trustworthy, which in turn results in market loyalty. When it comes to product development, it is always best to under-promise and over-deliver, if possible.

How do you use IT? IT permeates every aspect of business and I use it to get a full, 360-degree view of customers and prospects. IT is the cornerstone of all of our products, which I use on a daily basis. I've developed our own software platforms for sales, service, etc. There are some technologies that drive engagement, and we've pulled those out and developed products around them. One example of this is the creation of a social media-based project management tool.

Can you describe an example of how you have used IT to improve business operations? These days I don't really get involved in projects at that level. But early in my career I worked on the marketing team that launched Lottario, an Ontario lottery product. We were the first to use computers to create and sell lottery tickets. I understood the IT capability, even though I'm not a programmer. Now I'm trying to help businesses understand the value of social networking tools. Although it might make sense to dissuade staff from using social networking tools while at work, the idea behind them can help businesses. If you can engage employees at work, you'll reduce staff turnover and absenteeism. Social networking tools can improve productivity when used properly. The problem with these tools, though, is that no one knows how to use them effectively. Many companies just try to use all of them in the hope that something will stick. Others ban their use entirely. Neither of these methods is the answer. Skills in social media utility are skills that businesses need to develop.

Have you got any on-the-job advice for students seeking a career in IT or business? Get to know as much as you possibly can, including business processes. That knowledge will enable you to provide more value to the business and inform strategic work. Try to "get into the weeds" of an organization. Find out about sales, operations, finance, etc. The more you learn, the more you know, and the better you'll do.

In this chapter we discuss Web 2.0, social media, and online trends. The companies that John works with are all involved in these areas, creating, implementing, and selling new technologies that are becoming more commonplace every day.

How often have you heard the term "Web 2.0" and wondered what exactly it meant? Or even how someone decided we had suddenly left the world of Web 1.0? And what about Web 1.1 or 1.2? Did you miss those somewhere along the way? Just what is Web 2.0 anyway, and why does it matter? And why are we already talking about the "semantic web," now known as Web 3.0?

Well, you would not be the only one to feel a bit confused. The term means many things, as shown in Figure 8.1. For some, it means technology; for others, it is more about the user experience. Some see it as a revolution, but most simply see it as an evolution.

Web 2.0, Social Media, and Online Trends

Going back into recent history, the term Web 2.0 was first coined by Tim O'Reilly (founder of O'Reilly Media) and used publicly at a trade conference in 2004. By virtue of usage more than anything else, **Web 2.0** has come to represent what most people refer to as the interactive web—that is, moving from a passive site that basically displays information to a site that permits interaction with visitors or users. This interactive site is often supported by significant multimedia capability such as audio and video, combined with some form of **user-generated content (UGC)** such as blogs and conversation threads. The ability for an Internet site to become a two-way communication tool also significantly enhances the ability to promote a sense of online community.

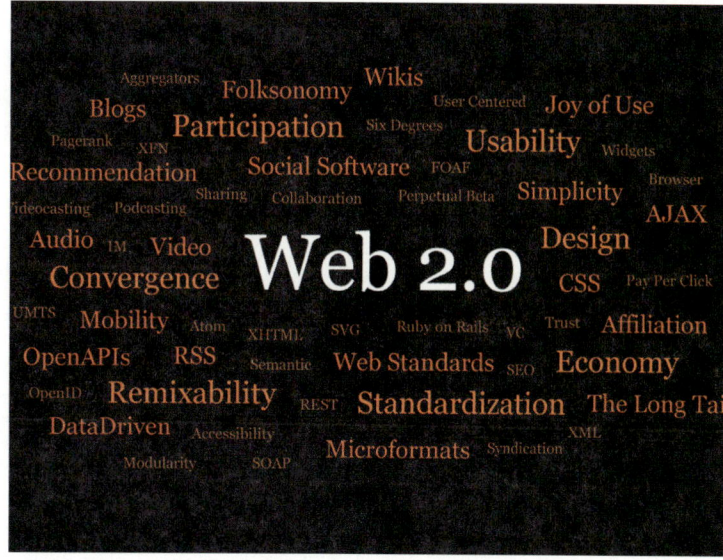

FIGURE 8.1 The term Web 2.0 can mean many different things to different people.

Therefore, the term is often associated with websites that expect higher levels of user engagement and involvement to promote self-expression. The **semantic web** is a next-generation—but not separate—web that makes information sharing and exchange easier by focusing on content, searchability, and interpretability at a technical level. This opens up new possibilities in the future for even more amazing information-sharing applications.

Obviously this trend has significant implications for businesses that use the Web. More particularly, any trend that has a significant social impact will also have a collateral business impact. In this chapter we will explore the intersection of changing social trends on the Web, and their implications for society and businesses alike.

TECHNOLOGY CORE

Without the advances in technology that took us from Web 1.0 to 2.0, many of the social media websites we are so accustomed to today would not exist. The following list highlights a few of these important technologies.

- **Adobe Flash** – Nearly every browser now comes with Adobe Flash. It allows interactivity, animation, and streaming of audio and video. Without Adobe Flash, you would not be able to view your favourite YouTube video or play online games.

- **Javascript** – Simply put, Javascript is the communicator between your computer and the Internet. This program runs locally on your computer and allows you to quickly open windows, menus, and toolbars. It also draws the user's attention to graphical interfaces on mouse-overs, for example. Without Javascript, you would be pressing enter to view a friend's photos on Facebook, and be waiting and waiting and waiting for it to load.

- **API** – In the Web 2.0 world, there is an Application Protocol Interface (API) for everything. Through the use of APIs, developers are able to access established programs and use their functionality. For example, several sites use the Google map API to show the location of bars, restaurants, and even jobs (see *www.jobloft.com*). All those cool iPhone applications would be impossible without iPhone APIs.

These are just a few of the technologies that make social media happen.

DEFINING SOCIAL TECHNOLOGIES AND UTILITY

Technologies that find their centre in the psycho-social fundamentals of human interaction truly constitute social media technologies. For instance, if you think about blogging, the technology is quite simple: a platform gives users the ability to post a story and gives readers the ability to respond with comments in time-stamped threads. There is nothing that is purely "technology" in the traditional sense. Instead, it involves a re-deployment of existing technological capability (threaded conversation) into a specific form that supports a specific function. In other words, these sites are *purpose-built collections of existing capabilities and tools,* in most cases simply bundled together to create a novel technology-enabled online experience paralleling offline socializing.

This linking of *form* to *function* is an important point regarding the social web. Developers are trying to replicate the paradigms of human social interactions and enable them to occur online with technology. For instance, in terms of blogging, it is only a short leap to move from the notion of a speech (blog post) to a conversation (a set of multi-party posts happening in real time). Think also about living in a community, joining a club, or belonging to a particular group, or perhaps even online dating. These notions are originally social in nature, and define how people think about and describe themselves. These activities existed long before technology came along. When you think about the social web, you are really only thinking about doing something that human beings have done forever (converse, connect, gather, join, belong) and translating that into an online context.

Examples of websites that belong to this category include Facebook, MySpace, Orkut, Hi5, LinkedIn, or Twitter, and many others that you may be all too familiar with (see Figure 8.2). Their primary purpose (often stated right in the header of the site!) is to connect you with friends, family, partners, or colleagues. They may help you discover new friends or people of interest, or share your life in the form of pictures, videos, blogs, and updates on your daily activities. They might be oriented mostly toward a specific demographic (e.g., business networks and colleagues in the case of LinkedIn) or aimed more generally at the world (in the case of Facebook). In some cases, different demographics or geographies will adopt one site over another, giving it a social flavour that is different than a similar site elsewhere.

According to Alexa, a global Web information company, the top 10 social sites (excluding search) in Canada in October 2009 were:

1. YouTube.com
2. Blogger.com
3. Twitter.com
4. Facebook.com
5. Flickr.com
6. MySpace.com
7. LinkedIn.com
8. Photobucket.com
9. Blogspot.com
10. Digg.com

FIGURE 8.2 How many of these sites do you visit on a regular basis? Can you find a classmate who has never been to one of these sites?

SOURCE: Alexa, The Web Information Company, "Top Sites in Canada," http://www.alexa.com/topsites/countries/CA. Retrieved October 2009.

Research suggests that the trend crosses all demographic ranges. For instance, a recent poll by TNS showed that the popularity of social networking and blogging is not limited to younger teens and adults:

> *Online teens and young adults are the heaviest users of social networking sites, with 83% of 13–17 year olds and 74% of 18–29 year olds having visited at least one such site. Not surprisingly, older people are less likely to have spent any time on sites such as Facebook and MySpace, but the incidence is still quite high among middle-aged and older online Canadians. Six in 10 people in their 30s have visited at least one social networking site, and 45% of those in their 40s have done so. Among those 50 years and older, one-third claim to have visited such a site.*[1]

In addition, a recent Nielsen Online survey reported that social networking is the fourth most popular online application overall (after search, dating/adult sites, and gambling!) and is now ahead of email. In fact, the 2009 survey indicated that one in every 11 minutes U.S. consumers spend online is now devoted to social computing sites, and that Facebook has the highest average time per visitor among the 75 most popular websites globally. These are startling statistics for such a recent phenomenon.[2]

A website does not have to be a general purpose application to include a social component. A social site may aim to help you share your world through photos and videos (YouTube or Flickr), or to help you find a date in the city in which you live (*meetmeinTO.com*, for example). If you are interested in starting your own blog, consider visiting *blogger.com* or *thoughts.com*. In addition, social media trends follow basic social trends. For example, it is often said that people avoid talking about sex, politics, or religion except in private, safe gatherings. Not surprisingly, you can find blogging sites for politics (*bloggingcanadians.ca* or *bloggingtories.ca*), religion (*religionnewsblog.com*), and, of course, sex (*sexblogs.org* or *erogs.com*, which stands for erotic blogs). Again, many of these sites do not specifically deploy any new technology as such, but they do provide a new technology context for users to do online what they do offline. Form follows function to help create sites enabled by cool technology where people want to participate socially.

Social Utility

In our research at Ryerson University, we have borrowed from other fields (primarily economics) to gain a better understanding of why people are willing to spend so much time online—and what they get out of it. We have coined the term **social utility** to address this. This term suggests that you only spend time on sites that are *useful* to you, and that the time invested on the site somehow contributes to your happiness or social satisfaction, or creates social opportunities for you. Otherwise, you wouldn't do it. In fact, the *only* reason that most people spend any time on Facebook or similar sites is that they provide something of social value in return for spending valuable time creating profiles, updating entries, and so on. Therefore, to

---
1. http://www.newswire.ca/en/releases.archive/June2007/11/c2653.html
2. *Global Faces and Networked Places*, A Nielsen Report on Social Networking's New Global Footprint, March 2009.

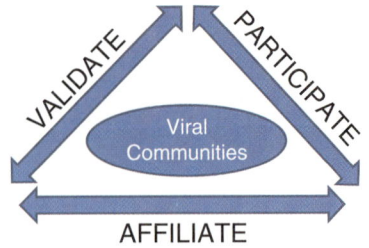

FIGURE 8.3 The Three Pillars of Sociability.

The Three Pillars of Sociability apply to both real life and the online world. The desire to affiliate, participate, and be validated by others is a key factor of the human existence; social networking sites allow users to do this online.

invest time on a site, you need to feel like you get a return or else you will go elsewhere.

One way to better understand this concept is to visualize the **Three Pillars of Sociability**, shown in Figure 8.3. The concepts attached to each pillar are rooted in social psychology, the study of how people congregate and why—often demonstrating almost tribe-like behaviour. Let's consider each of these important concepts in turn to see what they can teach about online social behaviour.

Affiliation The first step, beyond simply being aware of the opportunity to join something, is to ensure that users want to be *affiliated* with your group. The underlying psychological driver of this is the need to belong. This may include wanting to belong to something because it is popular or will make a person popular, or it may be just the opposite and rooted in exclusivity and the fact that only the chosen or a few belong. Regardless of the specific reason why someone wants to belong, you must trigger in your target user the desire to be affiliated with your site. Of course, to create the desire to affiliate, they must know you exist and be able to discover you—this is why you must first figure out where your target user congregates and go to them.

Participation Once they have made the leap to wanting to join your site (that is, to publicly declare their desire to affiliate), you must help users easily understand the rules of *participation*. Every group of humans, no matter how large or small, has both spoken and unspoken rules regarding conduct in the group. Some things might be obvious (for instance, if you join a photo sharing site, you likely want to indulge in photo sharing and understand that others will in turn view your photos), but there might also be other rules (for instance, regarding limitations on the types of photos that can and cannot be shared). These kinds of rules are often printed or implied and are easily mastered by users. However, there are often other, more subtle codes in groups. What if those norms are not obvious to a new user? In a photo sharing context, that might mean it is OK to post photos and invite others to view them, but perhaps it is not all right to follow-up with emails or pokes asking them to comment on them (a common complaint of many sites with an emphasis on sharing).

If it is important for the growth of your online community that users understand rules of behaviour and conduct (both formal and informal), you have to find ways to make participation *socially safe*. Recall your experiences in high school, when every little social gaffe or blunder might have had significant reputational consequences and you worried about doing, saying, and being the right thing. This was not necessarily a socially safe context for many, and it often prevented people from participating fully. And where was the printed rule book that helped you with this? Right, there wasn't one. You learned by doing, as risky as that may have seemed. Similarly, the most successful social networking sites focus on ensuring an **invitational design**, borrowing a psychological term for finding online ways to welcome new people into a group and making it safe for them to learn and master the norms. The best sites encourage play and discovery and make the site design intuitive. This is an essential consideration in the design and marketing of any social networking site. Elements of this may have helped explain why *Friendster.com* was first to market, but ultimately Facebook and MySpace ended up the category winners. Comments at the time suggested that Friendster may not have had the community elements of its design right, and users clearly abandoned it in droves for other sites.

Validation The third pillar of sociability to consider is how to *validate* the user's social experience, thereby constantly reinforcing the social utility of your website. This may not be the same for every user, since each user will have a different level of social comfort, involvement, and confidence. But it does mean finding tangible ways of demonstrating social value—perhaps even involving elements of competition, an age-old concept that human beings have willingly engaged in for centuries. For example, a simple but powerful reason why Facebook may have ultimately beat Friendster in the race to dominate social computing in its early days may have had to do with two critical points:

1. Facebook initially appeared to be a focused and targeted site that had exclusivity (you had to be a registered student in a university or college with an active institutional email ID to join). Friendster was a general purpose site that allowed anyone to join and touted this fact in its marketing. This may have driven down the desire for some to affiliate with it because it was perceived as too easy and too common versus its competition.
2. The *friend* feature in Facebook enabled an instant form of social validation for its participants. In fact, others can easily see how many friends you have and you can find validation by inviting friends to connect with you.

These two facts may have helped create the social desire for people to get in and stay in, contributing to Facebook eventually being forced to broaden its membership base after its initial success.

It is not possible to definitively prove this particular hypothesis about these two sites so late in their respective evolutions and with their now fixed competitive order in the marketplace. However, recent studies of online social behaviour suggest that when a social media platform combines constant social validation of its users (through a variety of techniques that are relevant to its purpose and design), with a slight dose of competition as a way of encouraging users to compete for external forms of validation from other members, it drives up social utility and interest in the site among both users and non-users. This is an interesting and useful finding for those wanting to learn more about what makes a particular social computing website more or less popular with consumers and users, and helps explain why some sites succeed and others fizzle and fail.

Design and Usability

It is becoming clear that design esthetic and usability are critical components to building a successful interactive media site, and that the most powerful of these become almost addictive to users. In fact, as with any social phenomenon, there are going to be users who cannot stay away or keep their desires in proper perspective. This has always been true offline, so it is inevitable that inappropriate uses of social computing will take place as well.

A site has to look good and be attractive to users, while also functioning well and being intuitively obvious to users. If you make it easy to navigate, people will use it; if you don't, they won't. But it is not always easy to create this seamless combination. Close working relationships between developers and designers need to be established to help each discipline maximize its contribution during the site development phase. Companies can no longer afford to code first and then visually integrate good design. The best sites do both concurrently and rapidly, constantly changing and refining the site's technology, flow, and architecture based on users' feedback about what they do and do not like about the site. Successful sites also normally employ a minimalist design perspective that simply says that everything must matter and be just a short click away. This means eliminating the layers, barriers, and complexities of navigating the site by making sure that users can easily find and use a specific function.

Of course, if companies expect users to interact on their sites, they must also design sites that both encourage interaction and make it easy for users to do so. Keep in mind that users are often not very sophisticated in their use of technology. As a consultant in the field once said to a client, "It's not about the technology, stupid!" Rather, it's about what the technology can do for users.

Companies should also be aware of just how possessive users can be about their chosen platforms and interfaces. Recall the number of times that Facebook has encountered controversy for trying to make unpopular changes to its site and how users reacted (for example, see *www.thestandard.com/news/2009/03/19/facebook-protesters-remobilize-protest-design-changes*).

Business Utility

This discussion brings us to a critical question—as students of IT, what can you do to learn how to translate online social utility into business utility that helps drive value for the companies and organizations you serve or intend to create? Essentially, this means exploring how to deploy social media platforms and technologies to create business outcomes (e.g., increased sales, higher customer loyalty, lower transaction costs, etc.) that have real value for an enterprise, but are also acceptable to users. This is harder to accomplish than you might think. Many business models associated with social computing and media are emerging, and the jury is still out on what is and is not working well. We will discuss a few examples of how social media and Web 2.0 technologies can help businesses later in this chapter. However, simply assuming that consumers or clients will share information with you because you want them to is naive—they will only do so when there is utility, when they get something back in return they want (e.g., products and services, information, access to other buyers, etc.).

Technology Implications

When you think about social computing websites from a technology perspective, several obvious issues arise. The first (and likely least obvious) one is the sheer cost

Defining Social Technologies and Utility | 283

of *accumulating and storing* all of this often multimedia intense content. Running a site oriented toward interactive media requires significant bandwidth (to simply serve up all the content on demand) and also massive amounts of storage to keep it all instantly available and properly tagged and indexed. This has a direct operating cost for social media sites, since both bandwidth and storage become more expensive the more volume a site receives. This means that Web 2.0 sites are more expensive to create and run than traditional websites. It also means increasing demand for **compression technologies**, which help reduce the costs of storage and transmission (particularly of image and video-based formats), and developers who know how to code and implement systems that efficiently handle large amounts of information.

The same costs associated with hosting a social website are involved in its use. Over half of more than 220 chief information officers (CIOs) in Canada responded to a 2009 Robert Half organization survey saying that they either already had or were soon planning to limit employee access to what many saw as "irrelevant, non-work related sites" such as Facebook or Twitter.[3] Many experts view this as an unfortunate stance that has several potentially negative consequences. The first is what this tells potential employees about a company's corporate culture (that it lacks trust in its employees). Second, it fails to recognize the way in which work is viewed as an ongoing activity to be woven into a complete 24-hour period, and that multi-tasking is now the norm for most employees.

Many businesses don't like the idea of their workers using social networking sites at work, but others accept that most business professionals today are multi-taskers who might be able to harness the power of social sites for business value.

? WHAT DO YOU THINK?

You are graduating and looking for a job. You recently heard in the news that a company you are considering applying for a job with has banned Facebook and Twitter for its employees at work. Would this affect your opinion of the organization? Would you still apply for a position with the company? Is it fair for employers to restrict access to social sites when they have no problem with you checking your corporate email at home in the evening (and indeed often expect you to)? If you were a business owner, would you allow your employees to access social networking sites at work?

Another concern is what it says about social computing—that it does not belong in the business realm. Yet businesses or organizations will not survive unless they begin to understand the social web. The very employees who "get it" the most and could help an organization do the same will no longer feel attracted to working for organizations that ban social networking sites. An organization cannot deploy technology that employees do not understand. Who is going to help an organization discover what it should be doing about this trend if no one at the company is allowed to participate in it?

---

3. http://www.roberthalftechnology.com/PressRoom?id=2531#

A technological concern also arises from banning social networking sites: many employees will find a way to get around the ban and access the sites anyway. After all, employees can be pretty creative. CIOs around the world are realizing that many employees are becoming technological-savvy, and they can easily deploy proxy servers and other techniques to get around site-specific bans (for instance, check out *hidemyass.com* as just one example of a site targeted at exactly this kind of workplace ban). However, using sites like this can compromise corporate security protocols and open up access to outside intruders. Employees may not be aware of this access, and the average CIO would likely want to discourage it.

Privacy and Security There are also implications for *privacy* and *security* for any social website, both of which are topics covered in Chapter 9 in some detail. These issues have a direct implication for sites where users post and share both public and private information of various types, formats, and levels of risk if they are shared by accident. If you lose your users' trust because of a security breach or because you cannot help them keep their private information protected, you will not succeed at retaining them. Your site will fail to attract new users because of concerns that will likely be widely disseminated on the Web (much to your embarrassment). This is also an area of great *legal risk* since various codes around the world related to privacy protection (such as the Freedom of Information and Privacy Protection Act or FIPPA, and other related codes such as PIPEDA) create obligations that companies and organizations must adhere to by law to operate. While this may not initially seem difficult, imagine you are a global company, or an entrepreneur launching a new site that targets users around the world. Which legal codes do you have to understand and honour? And how would you have to change the design of your technology to accomplish this when the codes are different everywhere and no single solution leaves you globally compliant? These are the kinds of important questions you must ask about this brave new world of social computing. The answers are only starting to emerge as the social web emerges with breathtaking speed as a worldwide force of great social change.

What is already clear is that the answer is not as simple as suggesting that because your site is based in a particular jurisdiction (for instance, Canada), you must only meet the codes of that host country. It would appear from recent precedents that the instant you gain a registered user in another jurisdiction, you may be subject to the privacy and security laws of that country. This was proven recently when the privacy commissioner of Canada engaged in very significant discussions and negotiations with Facebook to ensure its site met Canadian privacy laws. If Facebook does not comply, the commission has the ability to prevent it from operating in Canada or accepting Canadian registrations—a significant business and technical risk for a global firm. This is yet another example of social innovation exceeding the rate of regulatory progress in terms of understanding how the law and local regulations can keep up with what is happening in society at large. The result is a constant challenge for those who develop and implement new technologies like social media websites.

Quick Test

1. True or False. Web 2.0 is clearly a revolution in the web world.

2. Which of the following contribute to the success of a social networking site?
   a. usability
   b. attractiveness
   c. intuitive navigation
   d. all of the above

3. Fill in the blank. People participate on social networking sites only if the site provides _____.

Answers: 1. False; 2. d; 3. social utility

USER-GENERATED CONTENT

Creating Content

An essential ingredient that most experts agree is fundamental to most social media applications is the concept of *user-generated content*. This suggests that in most instances, true social sites focus on providing the *context* in which users generate content themselves, rather than providing the actual content. Participants in social media sites must register, identify themselves, and decide how to present themselves. This may be done by creating and posting a profile (as in the case for LinkedIn and Facebook-type sites) or perhaps by adopting an avatar or fictitious online personality (as in the case of many interactive gaming sites and sites such as *secondlife.com*). Regardless, the primary purpose of a social site is to have participants interact, which means they must actively join and self-identify in some form before they can participate.

Good psychology suggests that before you affiliate with a group, you must *discover* and *trust* its social motives and intentions. For this reason, most successful social media sites permit some form of restricted observation or discovery before requiring registration or identification. If you move to restrict access solely to registered members, you are limiting your growth to those who trust before having reason to do so. Studies suggest these people make fickle members at best, since they move around to the latest, newest sites. Instead, successful sites restrict visitors to watching, observing, or learning about the site, its intentions, and user behaviour by limiting what non-registered users can do. Using this method, before new users can participate fully they must demonstrate a willingness to disclose or create a **participating identity**. They will use this identity to create and post additional content or take the actions required to begin to fully participate in the online community.

Again, this mirrors the offline world: before joining a club, you are often invited by a current member to attend a meeting or learn more about it. If you then decide to join, you become a member, which infers certain privileges but also certain obligations or responsibilities. Similarly, when you join various social sites, you may also face restrictions such as user or member agreements, codes of conduct, or requirements to participate only in certain ways. The community might also be **self-regulating**, where members report conduct they feel is outside the group norms to a moderator who is responsible for drawing the inappropriate behaviour to the attention of the member or removing or restricting the member's privileges. Again, when you consider these functions as technology, you miss the point—these technologies are not actually innovations for technology's sake, but rather are simply *technological interpretations* of normal social conduct. The online and offline worlds mirror each other more in this space than in just about any other found on the World Wide Web.

Finding Content

To make your own content useful to other users, you must label or tag it. **Tagging** involves associating keywords with your content to make it searchable so that other users can locate it and interact with it. In turn, by using collaborative tagging and comparing and coalescing how other users tag the same or similar content, you derive a **folksonomy**, or collective cloud tag, that helps users access information quickly and efficiently.

Again, while the content and how it is tagged and searched will depend on the purpose of the site, the technology of tagging and searching is actually not new and was certainly available in the days of Web 1.0. What is different is how the technology is deployed to permit **viral social interactions**, where something that is funny, unusual, shocking, interesting, or newsworthy almost instantly spreads online from its origins to nearly every corner of the world. If you speak with your classmates or friends, you will likely be able to recall a recent example of something that went viral. What do you think made it go viral? How many people who you know saw it? How did they see it? These are the kinds of questions that marketers are now asking themselves as they try to address how consumer behaviour on the social web is changing, and how it impacts information consumed online.

User-Generated Content and Brand Risk

If you think about business for a second, having something good about your business (perhaps a story of outstanding products or services, for instance) go viral would be wonderful. This might often be a company's stated objective. However, in keeping with the psychological concept of **schadenfreude** (drawing happiness from others' misery or misfortune), negative stories go viral more often than positive ones. For instance, recall the viral video of the bride with her hair on fire as an example that later turned out to be part of a stealth advertising campaign. This kind of example should act as a warning to organizations that might misunderstand the power of the social web and try and harness its benefits without realizing its risks. This also suggests that one essential element of any company's **online social strategy** should be an awareness of the risks of undertaking any kind of online social campaign that might backfire.

Companies need to make sure that they monitor the online messages being posted about their enterprise or organization. Probably one of the best examples of an online campaign gone wrong can be found by searching Google for "Dove Mashup" or "Unilever Disrobed," or going to *shapingyouth.org* and searching the same terms. Unilever is a massive, global consumer products company that owns both the Dove and Axe brands—products aimed at seemingly separate and distinct demographics (older women and younger men, respectively). The world of social media permitted anyone to compare and combine the messages that Unilever was using in two separate campaigns. For Dove, Unilever employed the "talk to your daughters before the beauty industry does" campaign, which stressed the "natural products that bring out the natural beauty in you." For the Axe line, the "spray more get more" campaign had an overtly sexual overtone and was seen by many as being demeaning to women.

Within days of the campaigns being activated in traditional media, there was a user-generated **mashup** of the two campaigns that juxtaposed them side-by-side in a way that Unilever obviously never intended nor thought would happen. This is called a **brandstorm**—a situation where a traditional brand faces an online storm that can quite literally damage the value of its brand overnight. While the intention was not to directly attack Unilever, the online world was imposing *media transparency* by forcing Unilever into the awkward position of justifying its seemingly unauthentic positions. The result, of course, is that the online world was instantly abuzz with negative messages about the two campaigns and the company's intent to deceive its customers, regardless of the company's actual intent. This is what is so damaging about a brandstorm; in many cases, the storm is created not on the basis of fact, but perhaps only by implication, or in some cases from outright fiction. An example of this is the online video showing a Kryptonite bike lock being sprung by a Bic pen cap. It was later proven to be false using time-lapse photography, but it was too late and the damage to the brand was done.

Ironically, the mashups in these instances are often many hundreds of times more popular online and viewed by more surfers than the original product campaign videos or statements by the company defending itself. Even if Unilever had wanted to respond with its side of the story, it would never have been able to purchase the same amount of media coverage that occurred when the original message went viral. This gets to the heart of the matter: indirect messages, whether based on fact or fiction, are increasingly more potent than any equivalent direct message from the company itself, and this can put brands at risk. In fact, there was very little official response from Unilever to the Dove mashup (likely a strategic move to have the tizzy go away over time rather than risk adding to it), yet it remains a nearly perfect example of the importance of social media strategies to companies today.

Quick Test

1. True or False. Tagging your content helps users locate and interact with your content.

2. To join a social media website, you must create:
   a. a mashup
   b. an identity
   c. your own website
   d. a folksonomy of your content

3. Fill in the blank. A situation where a traditional brand is facing an online storm that can damage the value of the brand is known as a _____.

Answers: 1. True; 2. b; 3. brandstorm

CREATING BUSINESS UTILITY USING SOCIAL MEDIA TOOLS AND E-MARKETING

The early advent of desktop computers did not have much initial impact on marketing. Instead, it had an impact on other elements of business, such as accounting, finance, customer service, and fulfillment, for instance. In fact, if you were working in product or service marketing during the 1980s, you were likely dealing only with the need to get aggregate information through electronic data files and databases (e-info). Otherwise, the two disciplines remained fairly separate (see Figure 8.4).

When the World Wide Web started to become more prominent and adoption was rising, mostly through the early and mid-1990s, marketers began to see it as a tool that would enhance their *direct* brand marketing efforts. Most companies and organizations began to create an online presence (see Figure 8.5). **Direct marketing** means just that: messages, offers, or promotions that come directly from the company to the consumer in some form (e.g., advertising, mail, targeted events, or samples). This moved companies into a new phase of computer-enabled marketing

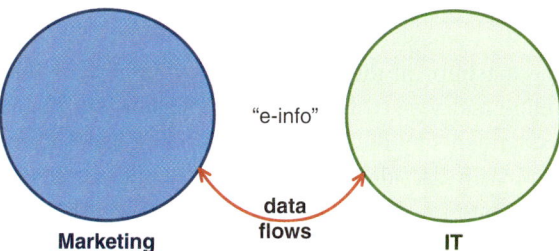

FIGURE 8.4 Phase 1: Early on, marketing's use of IT technology rested solely on gathering and using e-info data.

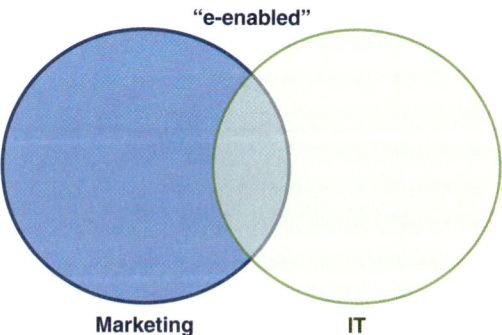

FIGURE 8.5 Phase 2: As the Web began to grow, most companies began to use IT as a way to communicate directly with their customers. However, the communication was still only one way—from company to consumer.

where the two disciplines began to work more closely in tandem. This phase is associated with the creation of mostly passive websites and the slow beginning of basic online marketing techniques such as email lists (and the associated plague of e-spam). Eventually, companies began to refine their efforts to understand online customer behaviour and to track statistics about online buying behaviour to customize offers presented to customers and to refine marketing campaigns. Around this time, most companies began to offer some method of buying products and services online, or at a minimum, introduced store or dealer locator features to make buying easier (see Chapter 5 for more on e-commerce). However, customers were not yet interacting with the company; companies were still only putting traditional marketing materials and information online, and were changing very little about the practice of marketing.

However, the arrival of the social web was about to change all of that. Consumers began to realize the power of interacting online, and began to demand that companies operate with a view to how *they* wanted to access product and service information and buy online when and how they wanted. As a result, the balance of power between marketers and consumers shifted. What *others* were saying or doing with products became more important, and consumers began to seek out **indirect** sources of information (e.g., product and ranking review sites, relying on word of mouth to find new products, etc.). This meant an emerging distrust in some instances for the direct marketing messages coming from companies, and more emphasis being placed on validating what companies were saying about their brands and products.

While not quite creating the notion of "perfect markets through perfect information," as economists suggest is ultimately what happens when buyers have access to complete information, the World Wide Web quickly became an important global source of influence on customers. Consumers were able to share information at such a rapid rate, it was hard for traditional marketing to catch up. To see just one simple example of this, check out *www.tweetedbrands.com*. This site provides information on the most tweeted brands on Twitter in the last 24 hours. It is fascinating to see how this changes over a period of time. Similarly, if you go to Google news, a simple news search engine, and type in any well-known brand name, you will be instantly rewarded with a list of every possible citation of that brand on the Web in the recent past. These kinds of tests will help you see how real the indirect messaging around brands really is online.

Not just marketers have this information—consumers do too. This puts traditional practices such as differential pricing (i.e., the same product sold around the world at different prices that were not purely exchange-rate driven) at risk because consumers became savvy and could shop around globally. Right around mid-2000, just as Tim O'Reilly was introducing the term Web 2.0, the world of marketing was changing so rapidly that marketing and IT became interdependent. E-dominated marketing emerged as a new paradigm as every company, organization, or entity was affected by these trends and had to effectively navigate the risks and rewards of this new online social world to succeed (see Figure 8.6).

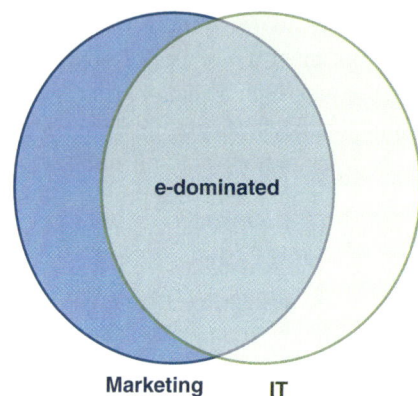

FIGURE 8.6 Phase 3: As the social web began to take over, marketing became e-dominated, where use of the Web is an integral part to marketing's communications with consumers.

Harnessing the Power of Social Media

How should companies strategically use social media technologies in their business? Here are a few examples to explore online to answer that question:

- To facilitate employer/employee engagement (see *www.speechbobble.com*)
- To create brand-related clubs/forums (e.g., Ford Owners Club Facebook Group or others)
- To manage online communities (see *www.charityvillage.com* for a great Canadian example)
- To facilitate online review sites (check out *www.consumersearch.com*)
- To promote geo-purposed sites (find one in your city or try *Toronto.com*, for instance)

Each of these sites has the features that appear to make social-media sense for a business. They have a purpose attached to community, common membership or interests, and they support a specific brand or product and/or a geographical overlay that helps draw local traffic. Of course, this is not to suggest that there is not room for more general-purpose social media sites (often referred to as **platform plays**) that rely on the widespread adoption of their system as a result of a first-mover or technology advantage, making them a superior context for most common social applications. Rather, as a market matures, it tends to fracture into **micro-markets.** These are purpose-built sites (or forums or groups) designed to meet a specific need. It behooves all businesses to consider this trend and to ensure their own social media strategy takes into account how their target market is consuming social media and where. It is almost always better to *go to where they are* rather than trying to *bring them to where you are,* both in terms of the cost and likelihood of success. As a result, one of the more important elements of an online strategy is to find out where your target market is currently "hanging out" online. This is perhaps similar to finding out what they like to do offline, and then advertising or promoting your product or service to them there.

Media transparency—making sure your brand and advertising messages are coherent and consistent—has also become increasingly important in this context.

Any deviation from this practice will absolutely enrage Internet users and likely backfire. Avoid trying to be all things to all people; instead, be who you intend to be for people likely to buy your product or service, and do it well. This often results in organizations moving away from brazen brand marketing (promoting the message endlessly, widely, and without regard to any risk of how it is perceived by other consumers) to a more benign form of marketing involving more emphasis on product placements, targeted sampling, and promoting word-of-mouth awareness through loyal buyers or users.

But if you are going to design, operate, or participate in a loyalty or review site, remember our earlier instructions about self-regulated communities. For instance, early in its online career, Ford North America launched a customer feedback and loyalty site for truck owners. Unfortunately, it seems as if initially they were conducting themselves like a brand-driven company by filtering out negative messages and only leaving positive posts online. They quickly got caught, demonstrating the value of transparency. While it might have scared the company to post negative comments, it would have been better to trust that their loyal, Ford truck-loving customers could take care of themselves online and judge all feedback, good or bad, accordingly. Other sites that operate with clear policies of transparency have demonstrated that unfair comments are quickly corrected within the community; those that are not provide insight into what a company needs to improve or correct, insights that matters to any customer-driven company. This is emerging as a whole new realm of market intelligence for companies. While it may take courage to enable customers to say anything about your product or service online, they are doing it anyway. Why not encourage it to happen where you are aware of it and can count on an active community to participate and correct any unfair comments? This is a new way of thinking about product and service marketing, and it will take some time before online social marketing practices mature and best practices emerge.

THE SOCIAL AND BUSINESS IMPACTS OF WEB 2.0

Another important development for business has been the generational impact of the Web on entertainment choices. For instance, there has been a rapid decline in the consumption of network TV as more and more choices have become available and cable broadcast systems have increased their global penetration, thus ushering in the age of specialty networks.[4] Yet, this alone is not the most fundamental trend. More disturbing to many advertisers is the similar decline in the consumption of newspapers, magazines, radio, and most other forms of mass media. Where are all these listeners, viewers, and readers going? Online, of course. In fact, the amount of time spent online by the average citizen has steadily increased every single year for 15 years as more and more people spend more and more time online. While many thought this trend was mostly related to young computer-savvy people hanging out online, the rates of online usage are rapidly rising across all demographics. Most startling for many advertisers is the recent fact that one of the fastest rising online demographics is retired people! This has driven a corresponding explosion in online advertising spending (see Figure 8.7).

---
4. See http://www.reuters.com/article/technologyNews/idUSTRE5817CE20090902 for a good discussion of the implications for the use of TV and the Internet at the same time by the same user.

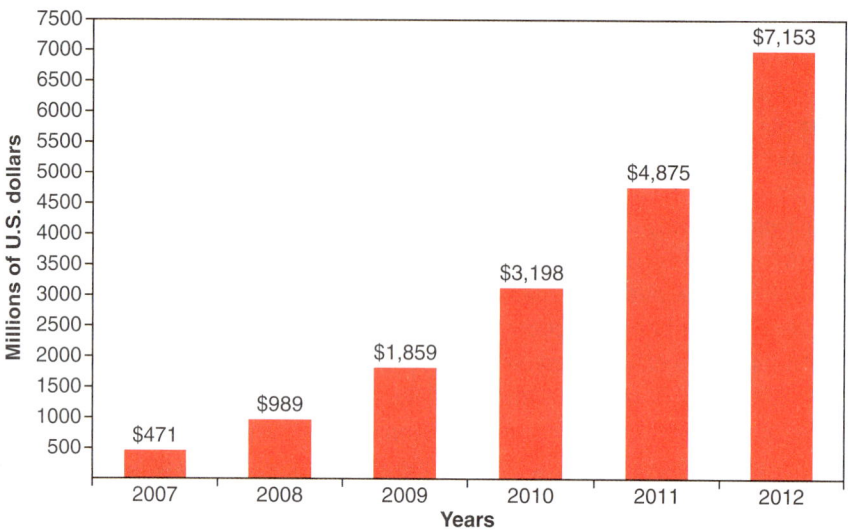

FIGURE 8.7 U.S. online video advertising spending, 2007–2012.
SOURCE: Based on data from eMarketer.com.

As social patterns change and people spend more time online either consuming entertainment (e.g., by watching Internet TV, gaming, or possibly gambling, which now occurs more often online than in licensed casinos) or creating and posting content on sites like YouTube and Flickr, they are not seeing or responding to advertising the way they used to. In fact, the kinds of advertising that will work in a broadcast medium (think the "killer commercial" you used to see during the Super Bowl) are now being replaced by very different efforts that take advantage of the unique technology properties of the Web. For instance, the ability to podcast very specific ads to very specific groups is simply not feasible on conventional TV, but it is on Internet TV.

To understand what this means, look back to the 1950s and the unbelievably quick adoption of the television. Television displaced the earlier and dominant

Today's world is full of multi-taskers. If people are watching TV, especially young people, they are also likely simultaneously online and are fast-forwarding through commercials. The impact of the Web on entertainment choices has had (and continues to have) far-reaching implications for how marketers reach consumers.

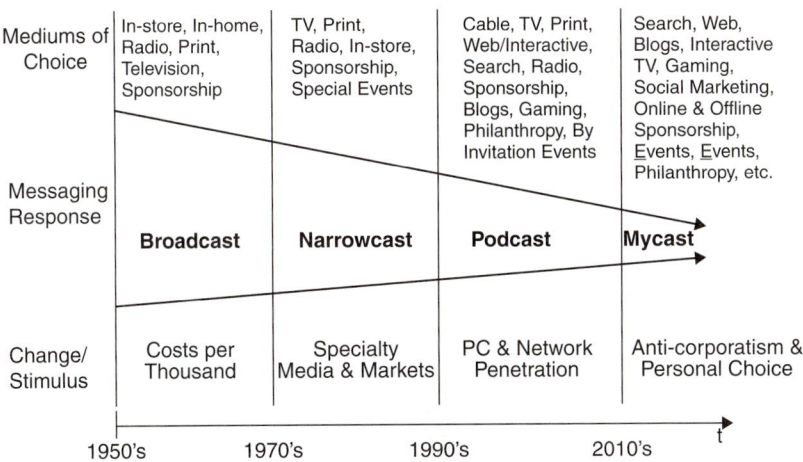

FIGURE 8.8 The way advertisers reach consumers has changed significantly since the advent of the Internet. We have moved from an age of broadcasting to mycasting, and the ability of advertisers to target their audience has narrowed in the process.

technology of radio, particularly as related to having a source of news and current events. While radio was superior in terms of currency over printed newspapers, what is interesting is that newspapers, radio, and TV all co-existed quite nicely until the invention of the Internet. Citizens often consumed all three in a day, reading newspapers in the morning, listening to the radio in the car on the way to work, and then watching television in the evening. As a marketer, this was the heyday of advertising, with lots of ability to bombard the consumer with brand and product-related advertising of all kinds.

However, the Internet changed all that. People have virtually stopped buying and reading newspapers. Why bother when all the news you want is no longer cost effective to print and is only a click away? People are listening to Internet and satellite radio, which are commercial free and subscription based (or even free in some cases!), are watching a decreasing amount of TV, and are more likely to be found online in the evening. In fact, a recent study noted that even when the TV is on in a household, it is likely that a laptop or computer is also running and is being used during the program itself, and most certainly, during commercials. So, as Figure 8.8 shows, there has been a dramatic and continuing decrease in the dominance of broadcast media worldwide and an associated rise in personalized "mycasting" online that seems destined to continue.

WHAT DO YOU THINK?

If you were marketing a product or service to students today, where and how would you market it? What role would the Internet or social media technologies likely play in your strategy?

This presents a significant challenge for companies wanting to advertise, and likely explains the almost 10-fold rise in annual spending in online social advertising that is expected to occur worldwide between 2007 and 2012.

Many companies are realizing the importance of social media in their marketing efforts and are putting more advertising dollars into these sites than more traditional online advertising, such as search and banner ads.

The focus of online advertising is shifting from search and banner ads to social media sites.

Social Business Models

With all this change in marketing and advertising, what are the social business models of the future? How will this trend impact how businesses deal with their customers and build their brands? The answers are still emerging, but there are some early signs that you should pay attention to. The first one is that best practices for social marketing are different. Look for up-to-date sources of what leaders in this space are doing and follow them. Good sources for this information might include sites like *www.mashable.com*, *www.econsultancy.com*, or *www.digitalmarketing.com*. For those of you interested in the not-for-profit space, it too is adopting the social web in interesting ways (see *www.frogloop.com* for the latest and greatest social networking ideas in that space, including a social network return on investment (ROI) calculator!). If you look carefully at any of these sites, you may find that they really do practise what they preach, and they will make it easy for you to find out about them. For instance, on the front page of *Mashable.com* you will see four distinct ways to access information about their latest findings, including Twitter, RSS, daily email subscriptions, or their Facebook group. Of course, as they discover new ways, this list will likely change, as it should for all organizations using social media. To use the social web, you have to be part of the social web!

Companies might also seek the help of a local interactive media marketing agency. This is an emerging field, often linked to traditional marketing agencies. Its sole purpose is to help you maximize your online social presence and brand. But all of this is useless unless there is a way to monetize or assetize your traffic and brand, as discussed earlier in Chapter 5.

What if a company is not an online company, but rather a traditional bricks and mortar company that simply wants to use social networking to its full advantage? What should it be doing in the social web? Here again there is continual innovation and new applications for ways to save money, ways do things more efficiently or effectively, or ways to improve business outcomes with consumers. Here is a short list of some recent things being done in the social web to great advantage, and which begin to help define the business benefits of social computing in new ways:

1. Conducting online focus groups for new product development (faster, easier)
2. Running viral campaigns to launch new products (innovative, cheaper)
3. Holding virtual recruiting and job fairs in Second Life (hipper, more targeted; attracts a different demographic; cheaper than head hunters)
4. Replacing annual online employee engagement or satisfaction surveys with new virtual equivalents that run 7/24 (more cost effective, up-to-date, and interactive)
5. Using social media tools to move from a broadcast to podcast model for training and development and internal communication with employees (on-demand, more flexible, just-in-time)

As shown in the list above, the opportunities to apply social media tools, both internally and externally, are vast for any business regardless of its size, geography, or industry. We are presently in the early stages of adoption. Yet even with the publishing process for this textbook, by the time you read this there will be more and more organizations using these tools online to create, build, and promote their organizations to engaged and involved online consumers. What is clear is that no one can ignore this trend—it is real and it is now.

CONCLUSION

What does all this mean? It means that all businesses and organizations are ultimately affected by any underlying social trend of any magnitude, and that the example of Web 2.0 is no different. As the usage of online social computing in all age groups continues to increase, businesses will have to adapt and figure out what this means for their target markets. It also means that you cannot afford to ignore the technology trends and contents outlined in this chapter, regardless of what role you plan to have in any enterprise, anywhere in the world!

Quick Test

1. True or False. When advertising online, it is more effective to create a place for consumers to come to you rather than finding where consumers already are.

2. Fill in the blank. A more general purpose social media site is known as a _____ because it relies on widespread adoption.

3. Social media is benefiting businesses by
   a. making it easier to respond to negative publicity
   b. using viral campaigns that are more innovative and cheaper for launching new products
   c. increasing favourable mentions on the Web through the creation of brandstorms
   d. allowing for the fracturing of large markets into micro-markets that are easier to manage

Answers: 1. False; 2. platform play; 3. b

What's in IT for me?

Have you Googled yourself lately? What have you found? More and more information can be found about individuals online. Perhaps you were quoted in the school newspaper, had your triathlon results published, or made a charitable contribution noted on a charity's website. Your activity on Facebook, LinkedIn, and Twitter may also come up when searching about you. On one hand, this is good; on another, not so good. With a profile on LinkedIn, for instance, you give employers the ability to find and contact you. This good impression of you may be obliterated, however, by the pictures your friend posted on Facebook of you at Oktoberfest.

It is becoming very important to be aware of your online image and take steps to manage it. Below are some selected tips from Robert Half Technology, a firm specializing in recruiting technical employees, for protecting your professional reputation when using social networking sites:[5]

- Know what's allowed. Make sure you understand and adhere to your company's social networking policy. If you are not permitted to blog or tweet about what you are doing at work, don't. Confidentiality is key.

- Use caution. Be familiar with each site's privacy settings to ensure personal details or photos you post can be viewed only by people you choose.

- Keep it professional. When using social networking sites at work to make connections with others in your field or follow industry news, be professional in the use of your language.

- Stay positive. Avoid complaining about your manager and co-workers. Once you've hit submit or send, you can't always take back your words—there is a chance they could be read by the very people you're criticizing.

- Polish your image. Tweet or blog about a topic related to your profession. You'll build a reputation as a subject matter expert, which could help you advance in your career.

Above all, use common sense. When using social networking, realize that you are broadcasting. The results are much the same as being on TV or radio, but with a more permanent effect.

What's in IT for an organization?

Recently, while conducting research on trends in social computing as related to organizations, we became aware that many innovative organizations respond to new trends by adopting them as a way to promote the organization online. While this is one interesting application of new technology, as researchers we wondered how to apply these kinds of technologies internally within organizations. As a result, a new idea was born. As essentially a collection of social networks (departments, functions, reporting relationships, groups with assigned leaders, a social and power hierarchy, etc.), most companies could benefit enormously from deploying Web 2.0 technologies internally; yet the focus of most organizations has been purely on their use externally. The most innovative CIOs will never forget their internal users, for they are the core of productivity and innovation, something every company should care deeply about. To see more about how this approach might work and what is being done about it, check out *Speechbobble.com*.

---

5. *Robert Half Technology Canada*, http://rht.mediaroom.com/index.php?s = 131&item = 790.

What's in IT for society?

As a social trend, Web 2.0 technologies are game-changing in the world of politics. As just one example, the Obama presidential campaign in the U.S. was able to raise more money than any other campaign in history, and from a larger number of donors, through the use of social media. Rather than relying on targeting large corporate donors or the obviously wealthy, the Obama campaign was a grassroots response to a rising social phenomenon.[6] And, of course, social computing was the enabler of this. Without the ability to reach millions of people, seemingly able to connect with them on their issues and then offering them the chance to donate online, this campaign would never have succeeded. Now that's a social trend in politics worth noting!

ROI STUDENT RETURN ON INVESTMENT SUMMARY

1. What is Web 2.0 and why does it matter to an organization?

The term Web 2.0 represents the interactive web as distinguished from the static, for-information-only web of Web 1.0. Web 2.0 has functionality that allows the creation of communities, input of user-generated content (UGC), and two-way communication. All organizations, businesses, not-for-profits, and governments need to be concerned about Web 2.0 because it is the standard that consumers and stakeholders expect. When you contact organizations, you expect responsiveness and interactivity. In fact, you expect fun! This is why more people are using the Web for information and entertainment than radio, TV, and print.

2. What features can make a social website more successful?

For a social website to be successful, it must have social utility. That is, it must be useful and contribute to your happiness or social satisfaction, or create social opportunities for you. The most successful social websites provide an opportunity for their communities to participate and add content of interest to the whole community. This then attracts more like-minded participants, who add more content. In addition to this, for a social website to be successful, it must be attractive and easy to navigate.

3. What are the risks and rewards of this technology for society and the organizations and businesses that operate within it?

As technology continues to develop, the risks and rewards of using it emerge. Web 2.0 technology has allowed for new online communities to be created that could not have been possible otherwise. You can now connect with a multitude of people online, becoming friends, contacts, or simply participants in a social forum. This has the potential to be a very powerful way to mobilize and inform people. However, along with these interactions, there are privacy and security concerns that need to be addressed. The business models for social media are not yet clear and business benefits are not completely proven. However, businesses are using social media to connect with their consumers in new ways, such as blogging, creating YouTube videos, and using Twitter in the hopes of increasing publicity and profitability. These vehicles can be turned against companies, creating a brandstorm that can be quite damaging. Social media may be a way for businesses to improve business processes. Some businesses are using it for recruiting, online focus groups, and surveys. One thing is certain: organizations must take the risk and use social media and Web 2.0 technologies, or risk being left behind.

---

6. http://webtrends.about.com/od/web20/a/obama-web.htm

KNOWLEDGE SPEAK

brandstorm   287
compression technologies   283
direct marketing   288
folksonomy   286
indirect communication   289
invitational design   280
mashup   287
media transparency   290
micro-markets   290
online social strategy   286
participating identity   285

platform plays   290
Schadenfreude   286
self-regulating community   286
semantic web   277
social utility   279
tagging   286
Three Pillars of Sociability   280
user-generated content (UCG)   277
viral social interactions   286
Web 2.0   277

REVIEW QUESTIONS

Multiple-choice questions

1. Running a social media site requires a lot of _____ to deliver multimedia intense content.
   a. marketing
   b. legal advice
   c. pixels
   d. bandwidth

2. The type of marketing that occurs when marketing and IT are interdependent is known as:
   a. e-info
   b. e-dominated
   c. e-commerce
   d. e-enabled

3. The first step in the Three Pillars of Sociability is _____, which is the step where a user would want to belong to a site.
   a. affiliate
   b. placate
   c. validate
   d. participate

4. Mycasting mediums of choice include:
   a. print, TV, radio
   b. Web, TV, radio
   c. Web, search, social marketing
   d. print, TV, special events

Fill-in-the-blank questions

5. For a user to want to continue to use a social networking site, the site must constantly reinforce its social utility and _____ the user's social experience.

6. Because social media sites must store massive amounts of multimedia content, there is a high demand for _____ and _____ who know how to handle large amounts of information.

7. Due to the amount of user-generated content on social media sites, both the providers and users of these sites need to be concerned about _____ and _____.

8. Some businesses might use _____ as a way to cheaply recruit more targeted and hipper job candidates.

True-false questions

9. In March 2009, it was reported that social networking sites were more popular than email.

10. For a social media site to be successful, it must create and produce a lot of content.

11. If a company experiences a brandstorm, the best course of action is to counter-attack online with competing blogs and videos.

12. It is likely that when a TV is on in a household, so too is a laptop or computer.

Matching questions
Choose the BEST answer from Column B for each item in Column A.

Column A
13. Web 1.0
14. Web 2.0
15. semantic web

Column B
a. You post a cool photo of the sunset on Twitter for your followers to see and re-tweet.
b. You need to sell your mountain bike so you post a classified ad on your school's student association website.
c. After booking a trip online, an automated agent searches for hotels and rental cars that will complement your trip.

Short-answer questions
16. What is media transparency? How is this facilitated in social media?
17. What is a blog? How are blogs used in business?

Discussion/Essay questions
18. Select a social networking site. Map this site to the Three Pillars of Sociability. Explain how the site exhibits the three pillars.
19. Imagine you are a marketer. Which social networking sites would you monitor to stay on top of potential brandstorms? Why these sites? What would give you the indication that something is going viral?

TEAM ACTIVITY

Select a brand as a team. Go to *www.youtube.com* and search for videos about this brand. Review the titles of all of the videos that you found. Watch a few of the videos whose titles appear positive to the brand, and a few that appear to be negative to the brand. Discuss your findings as a group. What do you think is the overall impression of the brand on YouTube?

SOFTWARE APPLICATION EXERCISES

1. Internet
Go to *www.ning.com*. Search through the available networks and see if one is appealing to you. Create a social network based on your course work, a hobby, or as a fan of something if it does not already exist. Invite some friends and/or classmates to participate in your social network.

2. Presentation
Blogging may be a good way for you to earn a little money toward your tuition. Do some research to understand what it takes to set up and maintain a blog. Then do some research to determine how you can make money with your blog. Create a presentation to share this information with the class. Ensure that you cover why your blog will be successful.

3. Word Processing
Choose a local company, perhaps a bar/restaurant that you frequent. Develop an online strategy for it that includes the use of existing social media sites such as Facebook, Twitter, and LinkedIn. Document this

strategy using your word processing software in the form of a consulting recommendation report.

4. Spreadsheet

Go to *www.tweetedbrands.com*. Select one of the brands that appears in the listing and note the number of associated tweets. Using a spreadsheet, list this brand and the number of tweets it receives for one week. Graph the data. Did the number of tweets remain constant, increase, or decrease for your selected brand? What may have contributed to this trend?

5. Database

The website *Alexa.com* is an excellent example of an incredibly valuable database application if you are in business. For any website in the world, it will give you an instant ranking of relative traffic. You can also find out if the traffic to a website is increasing or decreasing, as well as other information. Go to this site and pick your top five websites, including at least one or more social media sites, and compare them on a number of dimensions using the Alexa data. Compare your favourite online news site with CBC, for instance, and see which one has more popular influence.

6. Advanced Challenge

How are you managing your online image? Do you have profiles on LinkedIn, Facebook, MySpace, Flickr, or other social media sites? If so, review all of the content you have put in these sites. Does the content reflect the image that you want to portray? If you are not using any of these sites, research professional social networking sites such as LinkedIn and Plaxo. Determine which one might be best to join as a job-seeking graduate. If you think it is a good idea, set up a profile and start networking.

ONLINE RESOURCES

Companion Website

- Take interactive practice quizzes to assess your knowledge and help you study in a dynamic way.
- Review PowerPoint lecture slides.
- Get help and sample solutions to end-of-chapter software application exercises.

Additional Resources Available Only on WileyPLUS

- Take the interactive Quick Test to check your understanding of the chapter material and get immediate feedback on your responses.
- Review and study with downloadable Audio Lecture MP3 files.
- Check your understanding of the key vocabulary in the chapter with Knowledge Speak Interactive Flash Cards.

CASE STUDY: WEB 2.0 APPLICATIONS AT EASTERN MOUNTAIN SPORTS

Eastern Mountain Sports (EMS; *ems.com*) is a medium-sized specialty retailer (annual sales US$200 million) with over 80 physical stores, a mail order catalogue, and online sales. Operating in a very competitive environment, the company uses leading-edge IT technologies and lately has introduced a complementary set of Web 2.0 tools to increase collaboration, information sharing, and communication among stores and their employees, suppliers, and customers. Let's see how this works.

The Business Intelligence Strategy and System

During the last few years, the company implemented a business intelligence (BI) system that includes business performance management and dashboards. A BI system collects raw data from multiple sources, processes them into a data mart, and conducts analyses that include comparing performance to operational metrics to assess the health of the business.

Figure 8.9 illustrates how the system works. Point-of-sale (POS) information and other relevant data, which are available on an IBM computer, are loaded into Microsoft's SQL Server and then into a data mart. The data are then analyzed with Information Builders' business and analytics tool (BI analytics). The results are presented via a series of dashboards that users can view via their Web browsers; they are invited to make comments via blogs. In this way, users can access a unified, high-level view of key performance indicators (KPI) such as sales, inventory, and margin levels, and drill down to granular details that analyze specific transactions. Communication and collaboration is conducted mainly using blogs, wikis, and other Web 2.0 tools that are described next with the process.

The Web 2.0 Collaboration, Sharing, and Communication System

The company created a multifunction employee workbench called E-Basecamp. It contains all of the information relevant to corporate goals, integrated with productivity tools (e.g., Excel) and role-based content, customized to each individual user. Then, it added a set of Web 2.0 tools (see Figure 8.9). The system facilitates collaboration among internal and external stakeholders. EMS uses 20 operation metrics (e.g., inventory levels and turns). These also include e-tailing where e-commerce managers monitor hour-by-hour Web traffic and conversion rates. The dashboard shows deviations from targets with a colour code. It uses the following Web 2.0 tools:

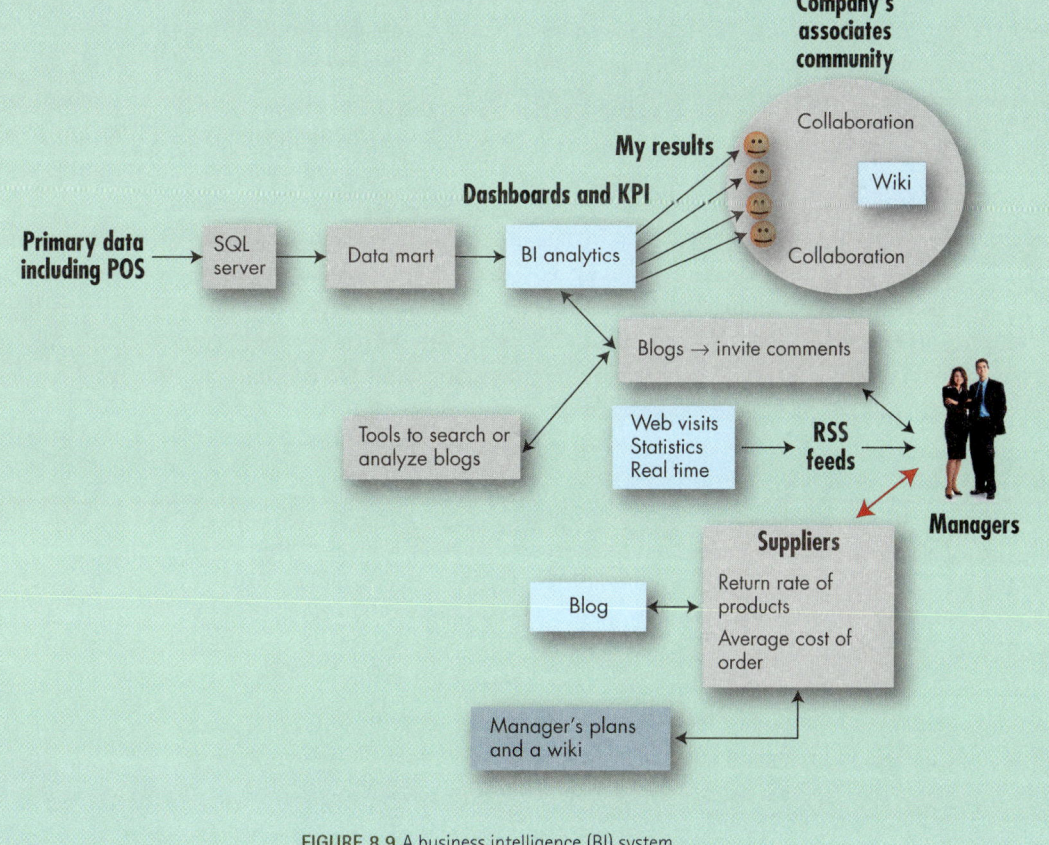

FIGURE 8.9 A business intelligence (BI) system.

- *RSS feeds.* These are embedded into the dashboards to drive more focused inquiries. These feeds are the basis for information sharing and online conversations. For example, by showing which items are selling better than others, users can collectively analyze the transaction characteristics and selling behaviours that produce the high sales. The knowledge acquired then cascades throughout the organization. For instance, one manager observed an upward spike in footwear sales at store X. Investigation revealed that store X employees had perfected a multistep sales technique that included recommending special socks (both online and in stores) designed for specific uses, along with an inner sole. The information was disseminated using the RSS feed. As a result, sales of footwear increased 57 percent in a year.

- *Wikis.* Wikis are used to encourage collaborative interaction throughout the company. Dashboard users are encouraged to post a hypothesis or requests for help, and invite commentary and suggestions, almost like a notepad alongside the dashboard.

- *Blogs.* Blogs were created around specific data or a key metric. The blogs are used to post information and invite comments. Then tools are used to archive, search, and categorize blogs for easy reference. For example, store managers post an inquiry or explanation regarding sale deviations. Keeping comments on blogs lets readers observe patterns they might have overlooked using data analysis alone.

Going to External Business Partners

In the next phase, suppliers are added. For example, suppliers can monitor the return rate of their product on the dashboard and invite store managers to provide explanations and suggestions using wikis or blogs. Assuming proper security of data is installed, suppliers can get almost real-time data about how well their products sell so they can prepare a better production plan.

The objectives are to build a tighter bond with the business partners. For example, by having store managers attach blogs to the suppliers' dashboards, the suppliers view current sale information and post comments to the blogs. Product managers use a wiki to post challenges for the next season, such as a proposed percentage increase in sales, and then ask vendors to suggest innovative ways to achieve these goals. Several of the customers and other business partners subscribe to RSS feeds.

Called *extreme deals* (big discounts for a limited time), blogs are also embedded into the EMS product management lifecycle (PLM) tool. This allows vendors to have virtual conversations with the product development managers.

The major impact of the Web 2.0 collaboration tools is that instead of having conversations occur in the hallway (where you need to be in the right place at the right time), conversations take place on blogs and wikis where all interested parties can participate.

Case Questions

1. Why not just have regular meetings and send emails rather than use blogs, wikis, and RSS feeds?
2. What are the benefits to EMS of combining its BI system and Web 2.0 tools?
3. In what ways is corporate performance bolstered?
4. What kind of community is this? Who are the members?
5. Can the company use any other Web 2.0 technologies? If so, what and how?
6. What information on *ems.com* is typical for what you find in social network sites?

SOURCE: E. Turban and L. Volonino, *Information Technology for Management: Improving Performance in the Digital Economy*, 7th edition. Hoboken, NJ: John Wiley & Sons Inc., pp. 321–322. Reprinted with permission of John Wiley & Sons Inc.

Integrative Application Case: *Campuspad.ca*

There is no doubt that social marketing is becoming one of the most effective ways to promote an online business. In fact, many organizations, both large and small, are moving resources away from traditional online advertising into social marketing. What exactly is social marketing? Think about any effort designed to improve your word-of-mouth, but online. This could include things like having a dedicated Facebook group, or your own YouTube channel, or your island on Second Life, for example. As a small business like *Campuspad.ca*, effective methods might also include having a popular blog (perhaps related to the challenges of renting) or using Twitter to build a community of followers around local rental markets. Or maybe you run an online competition for having your community share the *worst* landlord story they have experienced—imagine how that might go viral! Anything you can do that helps get your market's attention online is valuable to your brand, and that's how social marketing works.

Guiding Case Questions

1. Based on *Alexa.com*'s most current web traffic statistics, which social media platforms are most popular in Canada?
2. What kinds of online social media activity can you think of that might attract the interest of your target market demographic?
3. If you are a renter or landlord, what sites or authoritative online sources are you likely using to get useful information?

Your Task

Based on your research, design a relatively simple online social marketing plan for the *Campuspad.ca* site. Include specifics of any online resources you would suggest building or accessing, what sites or platforms you would use and why, and how any campaigns or social marketing activities would be conducted on these sites.

9

ETHICS AND PROFESSIONAL PRACTICE IN IT

WHAT WE WILL COVER

- An Introduction to Ethics and Morality
- Business Ethics and Conduct
- Corporate and IT Governance
- The Personal Implications of Ethics and Governance

ROI STUDENT RETURN ON INVESTMENT

Through your investment of time in reading and thinking about this chapter, your return—or created value—is gaining knowledge. Use the following questions as a study guide.

1. What is business ethics?

2. Why are corporate and IT governance important?

3. What are some of the common ethical dilemmas involving IT?

THE VOICE OF EXPERIENCE
Ken Killin, Ryerson University

Ken Killin graduated from Ryerson Business Management in 1982, having studied finance, accounting, and entrepreneurial management. He became a Chartered Accountant in 1983 and, after more than two decades as a financial and operational executive in public and private technology companies, is now the president of Killin Instincts Advisors, a consultancy that provides strategic advisory and active management services.

What do you do in your current position? I provide strategic advisory services to C-level (e.g., CFO, CIO, CEO) executives and boards of directors. At different times I've taken on an active management role, including C-level positions and being a member of various boards of directors. In these roles I am often involved in regulatory compliance, governance, and ethical issues concerning IT. I've also helped companies raise capital and execute mergers and acquisitions.

What do you consider to be important career skills? It is essential to understand how technology is used and what is available to you and the businesses you work in. Good management skills are important, whether you're managing a project, a team, or a department. Developing good judgement is also important. Over time, you will learn the right and ethical things to do in various situations.

How do you use IT? Personally, I use mobile devices. For example, my BlackBerry is one device I use that suits my needs. I also use a laptop. Because I am not a technologist, I have a personal technology consultant who helps me with my technology at home and with clients. I need to ensure compliance with customer requirements, regardless of where I am physically. For example, working with a company's email system may sound simple, but even then I need to carefully manage both systems to ensure we meet with information transparency requirements. More specifically, with some clients I use IT relative to finance and operating structures. IT provides financial experts with the materials they need to manage the company and comply with regulatory and audit requirements, while providing operating management with the data and analysis necessary to make better decisions. Finance and IT must provide accurate statements or the business is at risk. IT also needs to provide the proper logistics environment for operations. The value here is data—knowing exact product inventory, shipments, and deliveries, for example. With the relatively new development of enterprise social computing technology, there is a new group of technologies that will allow management to better leverage the human capital within their organizations, as well as client feedback.

Can you describe an example of how you have used IT to improve business operations? While I was chief operating officer (COO) at a large company, they had a patchwork of systems. One system tracked products that were available to customers, another tracked products that had been shipped, another for fill rates, etc. I instituted an SQL-based operating system that tracked inventory, fill rates, and shipments from end-to-end. It was the first true ERP system. The results were increased customer satisfaction and decreased inventory errors. The approach gave birth to a logistics company.

Have you got any on-the-job advice for students seeking a career in IT or business? Take time and get the most out of your academic career as possible. Take advantage of access to various opportunities and be as current as possible with technology. After graduation, find an environment with diverse opportunities that allows you to use the knowledge and skills you gained during your time at school. Seek out the operations people in the company, and discover and understand their needs and challenges. Learn to treat them as customers. As you gain experience, work on your judgement skills. Leverage that with the mistakes you make, by yourself or with your peers, and be open to new experiences. Whenever possible, get involved in the business and offer your expertise to help—be the best you can be. Understand and follow the most ethical and value-added path possible, and remember that your reputation will become your greatest asset.

If you aspire to be a C-level executive, especially the CEO, CFO, or CIO, of an organization, ethics and professional practice will be of concern to you. As Ken's experience illustrates, not only will you need to work in the operations of the company, you will also need to be concerned about governance and regulatory compliance. This chapter first looks at ethics in general, and then discusses issues you may face as a C-level executive.

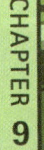

AN INTRODUCTION TO ETHICS AND MORALITY

To conceptually understand ethics, you need to reach briefly into the world of philosophy and answer what initially seems to be an easy question: how do you know what is right and wrong? Think about that for a second—often when this question is first posed to students, they immediately think of examples of what is right or wrong, but they can't always answer why they think something is right or wrong. They just know it is. If this is true for you, and it certainly is for many, then this chapter will focus on how to make your implicit assumptions and knowledge about business ethics into explicit concepts you recognize and can debate, deliberate, and defend. Since studies have shown this is one of the most powerful ways to gain insight into ethics, this is the approach we will take in this chapter.

To begin with, **ethics** is closely linked to morality and a society's widely shared understanding of what is right and wrong. Often a person's moral stance on a particular issue (for instance, sex before marriage) might vary by age, gender, religious affiliation, ethnic or cultural influences, and so on. In turn, your morals are closely linked to your **personal values**—fundamental beliefs that you hold as true about the way the world works and your role in it—which are shaped by those same factors, and also to a large extent by how you were raised as a child. So, there can be no doubt that your ethical position on any decision is informed by your own values, **moral code**, and life experiences. Here's a simple example: Most people learn at an early age that stealing is wrong and you come to accept this as your own personal *moral code*—it is something you know you shouldn't do, and you learn this fast and at an early age (and even those who do it know it's wrong!). You might learn this as the result of religion, or because your parents taught you it is wrong, or because you learned based on the scorn of your peers when you did it to them. No matter how you actually acquired this knowledge, you inherently know that stealing is wrong.

Stealing is also against the law. Society imposes consequences on any member who is caught and proven to have violated certain rules and codes. Therefore, a country's or society's **legal codes** also help define what is right or wrong. In a relatively simple matter like corporate theft, it would be clear to anyone that if you engage in this behaviour, you are acting both immorally and illegally. There is no *dissonance* (that is, simple disagreement between the law and your morals or values), and the right conclusion is to follow both of these tenets and simply not steal. This seems straightforward and easy, right?

Absolutely, but ethics is not actually that easy; very few of the ethical dilemmas you face are so simple that your values and the law make the answer clear. For instance, many deeply divisive issues in society result from instances where morality and the law intersect in interesting ways. For instance, a woman's right to abortion or gay marriage are seen by many as simple issues of human rights and the law. Nobody should be denied a fundamental right because of their gender or sexual orientation is a principle enshrined in Canada's Charter of Rights and Freedoms (see http://laws.justice.gc.ca/eng/charter/Charter_index.html for more on this statute and its place in the Canadian Constitution). On the other hand, some argue that abortion or gay marriage is immoral, and many have a religious perspective on these practices that declare them to be wrong. So what matters more—minority rights or religious freedom? Or can they coexist peaceably with society finding a way to respect both, as has occurred in Canada on many similar issues? These examples demonstrate the complexity of issues where the law and some people's moral or religious codes do not coincide to create an easy answer that everyone will agree to and accept. The result is an **ethical dilemma**.

? WHAT DO YOU THINK?

While it is easy to think of situations like abortion or gay marriage where there is a trade-off between legal and religious or moral perspectives, can you think of a similar situation in a business context where you can identify an ethical dilemma?

When you find yourself facing an ethical dilemma, you need to create your own **hierarchy of values** that help inform your personal decision making so you remain ethical, even when confronting difficult and complex issues. A good example of how this works in a business context is the tobacco industry. While it was not always the case, there is now ample proof that smoking kills. This means that cigarettes, as a product, would never be allowed to be developed and sold today. However, they are a legacy product from a time when people did not recognize the risks as clearly. Since smoking is now a social habit for many (not to mention an addiction!), many would say that smoking should be an individual choice and that society should respect an individual's right to make it. If there was no collective harm, this might be a valid argument. However, in the Canadian context of socialized medicine, smoking imposes long-term costs on everyone. In fact, smoking is the leading contributor to heart and lung disease, some of the most expensive conditions to treat. As a result, an individual's choice to smoke actually does harm everyone in society. This means we must balance an individual's right to choose against the need to protect innocent members of society from harm, thus requiring a trade-off between two opposing rights. Perhaps this implies a need to control smoking, even though it is one that many people view as an issue of choice. The real question for society, especially one with a government-paid health care plan, is should individuals have the right to make that choice?

In addition, many smokers live in family situations where second-hand smoke, a known carcinogen, will be imposed on babies, children, and others who may have no choice or knowledge of those risks. Because society values protecting the vulnerable from the more powerful, there is a plethora of laws against smoking in the workplace, in restaurants, in cars with other occupants, and so on. Many would argue smoking bans are an infringement on "smokers' rights," but there is no such thing. Society does not value an activity that harms others, and cannot condone putting the value of personal choice above harm to innocent victims. The obvious ethical decision is, in the absence of the willingness and ability to completely ban

Did you know that employees were able to smoke at their desks in the early 1980s? Can you imagine?

this product outright, society must at a minimum ensure that smokers who choose to smoke only hurt themselves and not others, and ensure they create no increased long-term health costs that every other taxpayer becomes responsible for paying.

By the way, about the only point where the pro-smoking lobby is on ethically sound ground is the fact that the very same or similar arguments could be made about alcohol, and yet people treat the two substances quite differently. There is also the question of whether or not various levels of governments are engaged in their own ethical dilemma by aggressively taxing or monopolizing vices like liquor, smoking, and gambling, which one might otherwise presume they would want to eliminate or closely control for the good of society, rather than profit from. This point alone should spark significant enquiry about the complexity of ethics and ethical decision making, when even the government appears conflicted between its proper duty versus the lure of unethical profits.

While this introduction has been deliberately brief, we can hopefully conclude that ethics is generally understood to suggest that you need to maintain your personal integrity and act consistently by applying a personal code of conduct about what is right and wrong. This is shaped by trying to act morally, legally, and thoughtfully to make good decisions, even when faced with a dilemma where guidance on the "right answer" may not be all that clear, or may even be contradictory. This means all of your values, morals, experience, knowledge of the law, and understanding of harm and virtue become cornerstones to you acting ethically in business—that is, the ability to apply a very personal lens to how you will behave within your business or organization when faced with an ethical dilemma. But the first step is to actually think about these possible dilemmas in advance and make your own moral and ethical thinking on them explicit, rather than implicit.

BUSINESS ETHICS AND CONDUCT

Corporations or organizations are inanimate. That is, they do not exist in a human form, but rather are animated by the actions of humans who create or belong to them. Yet in many ways they are very similar to people—they are born and die (registration and bankruptcy), they have the right to enter into agreements and own property, and indirectly they vote (although mostly through political donations, advocacy, and influence). This is an important principle of business ethics, because it suggests that society relies on the individual personal ethics of those in business to make the right decisions rather than relying on the business itself to be ethical. Does this seem strange to you? Aren't businesses as a whole bound by rules and regulations?

Yes, but a purely regulatory model will not work. The government can pass laws about general business conduct, and even impose special conditions or processes that create checks and balances on businesses where the stakes are high (for instance, drug approval regimes for pharmaceutical companies, licensing rules for transportation companies, or permit processes for natural resources explorations). However, it is simply not practical to have government be responsible for the ethical conduct of all private businesses or to implement an inspection or compliance regime on anything other than taxes. Why? Because most businesses act ethically, and because most business owners have personal ethics. So, like any quality control process, you have to balance your efforts at finding the outliers—those who are not following the rules or who are at risk of offending.

The Business Benefits of Acting Ethically

There are also a number of tangible business benefits to ensuring that your organization remains vigilant and within the boundaries of ethical behaviour expected in your community. Some of these include:

- Shielding you and your employees from harmful and costly litigation and the associated negative publicity that it draws
- Reducing long-term compliance and audit costs as your organization begins to reliably follow a consistent code of ethics and conduct
- Creating a brand built on integrity and ethical conduct that can increase sales and encourage long-term customer loyalty
- Gaining goodwill in your local community as an ethical and responsible corporate citizen
- Ensuring your organization will be embraced and accepted as it expands to other jurisdictions
- Attracting quality employees and supporting an excellent employee brand

Of course, an ethicist would argue persuasively that you should not need benefits to act ethically, but rather should do so out of moral imperative. While this is to be expected, occasionally you might find this ethical intent in conflict with the profit-maximizing motive of capitalism. This is the primary reason why so many business leaders are now talking publicly about **corporate social responsibility (CSR)**. This school of thought promotes making social agendas and social responsibilities equal to the profit imperative, and balancing economic and social factors in all business decisions. Much of this has come out of recent discussions about the collateral costs of doing business on things like the environment, and how to assess and control the long-term hidden costs of some kinds of industry (for instance, mining and forestry through re-plantation and site rehabilitation, or expecting zero footprint from the transportation industry to help protect the environment). These are referred to as *externalities*, or externalized costs, because the business transfers some of its own responsibilities to society or government by making them responsible for their actions and decisions long after the profits have been earned and spent (for instance, through the costs of site rehabilitation of bankrupt mining or forestry companies). Although still in its early stages, there is increasing acceptance of CSR as a fundamental embedding of ethical behaviour into the fabric of capitalism, and it is expected that this movement will continue to grow in the future.

What Causes Ethical Misconduct in Business?

If there are benefits to acting ethically, what causes ethical misconduct in business? If you work in the private sector, your organization's major purpose is to make profits and maximize shareholder value. Unbridled by any constraint of what is right or wrong, many businesses could make more money by acting illegally or unethically. It is also true that the system of separating management from shareholders might also prompt gaps where actions are undertaken to benefit management more than to benefit shareholders. Inherent conflicts exist because of capitalism and corporate ownership structures, like limited liability. These conflicts are endorsed because they create wealth for society; however they also create a corollary risk that must also be accepted. This means you must then count on the personal ethics of business leaders to balance the pursuit of profits. As evident from recent examples (WorldCom, Enron, and Canada's own Conrad Black), this does not always hold true. Why? And what can we do about this as a society?

Simply put, greed and ego are powerful forces, especially when they are combined. In business, both power and ego satisfaction are offered to those who succeed, and this often comes with society's approval and respect. In this situation, there is the potential for many to confuse the boundaries of right and wrong and act more in self-interest than in the collective interest. However, once you start down this slippery slope, it becomes nearly impossible to admit you were wrong, face the consequences, and right the wrong. Once an initial immoral, illegal, or unethical act is committed, a pattern of cover-ups and systemic deceit or **corruption** occurs to ensure the first occurrence remains hidden. This often requires that employees of the firm in key positions (such as accounting) be co-opted to participate either knowingly or unwittingly in these actions. The conspiracy grows, often unchecked, until there is a spectacular fall from grace. Those conducting themselves in this way often initially benefit (both financially and socially) and can be revered as business leaders. It is only years later, when the truth about their actions emerge, that they feel society's condemnation of their actions and, though not always, face legal consequences as well. For more on this, simply search "Conrad Black" or "Bernard Madoff" in *Wikipedia.com* and you will be amazed by their stories.

Conrad Black is currently serving a six-and-a-half year sentence for fraud-related crimes. While at the helm of Hollinger International, Black and three associates diverted $84 million from investors' pockets. He was convicted after a lengthy and very public trial in 2007.

Quick Test

1. True or False. The law prevents business leaders from acting unethically.

2. Fill in the blank. When the law and an individual's moral code are not in sync, it is a situation known as an _____.

3. It is widely accepted that acting ethically
   a. increases profit
   b. offsets risk
   c. eliminates threats

Answers: 1. False; 2. ethical dilemma; 3. b

Remedying Ethical Breaches

A spate of spectacular bankruptcies in the late 1990s and early 2000s left shareholders shaking with rage because of intentional fraud and deception. When this happens, society tends to swing the pendulum of corporate governance toward regulation.

For example, to restore public and investor confidence in the financial accountability and reporting of publicly traded companies, the U.S. Congress passed the **Sarbanes-Oxley Act** of 2002. Often referred to as Sarbox or SOX, this act is a good example of what can happen when too much regulation is put in place. Although well-intentioned, it is terribly onerous and cumbersome in practice—and whether it actually makes organizations behave more ethically is undetermined. At the heart of its regulatory approach are specific requirements imposed on public companies, such as:

- *Section 302*—Requires CEOs and CFOs to personally certify financial statements and disclosures in periodic reports, as well as the effectiveness of the company's internal controls. In Canada, Ontario's Bill 198 was enacted to allow the Ontario Securities Commission (OSC) to issue rules related to information certification.
- *Section 404*—Requires a separate annual internal controls management report and mandates internal controls that are well-defined, documented, and periodically evaluated by internal (management) and external audits. In Canada, this area is also covered by Ontario's Bill 198.
- *Section 409*—Decreases the time between reporting deadlines into a potentially "real-time" reporting environment, and increases reporting requirements for material changes to business operation that affect financial reporting (e.g., if a main factory burns down, current financial projections are no longer valid).
- *Section 906*—Requires additional CEO/CFO personal certifications of financial reporting and imposes criminal penalties of up to $5 million in fines and up to 20 years in jail for knowingly falsifying certifications.[1]
- *Section 201*—Prohibits a public accounting firm from performing both audit and non-audit services for the same client. Compliance with this section caused several major accounting and IS consultancies like PricewaterhouseCoopers (PwC) to restructure their organization. In 2002, PwC sold its existing global management consulting and technology services practice to IBM, in part to comply with this section of SOX. The Canadian Institute of Chartered Accountants (CICA) has made several amendments to its handbook in line with the rules contained in Section 201.

This type of solution often impacts not just those who may offend, but also those who never would have. It adds a layer of cost and complexity, potentially hinders economic growth in the long-term, and costs everyone something over time. Of particular note is that when it comes to issues of corporate ethics, society often tries to connect organizational outcomes with personal consequences—seen in the requirement of CEOs to *personally certify* their organization's financial statements, thus tying the organization's actions to the leader's responsibility to ensure it acts properly.

Even though this is U.S. legislation, SOX can still apply in Canada if a company has a substantial foreign presence in the United States, and so we should know

---

1. http://www.law.uc.edu/CCL/SOact/sec906.html

something about its scope. For instance, both TD Bank and RBC have significant branch operations in the United States, and their U.S. subsidiaries would have to comply with SOX while other Canadian companies (for instance, Canadian Tire) might not since they operate primarily in Canada. Similarly, there are European codes that might apply if a company operates in Europe. This creates a patchwork of regulations and requirements that apply to large multinational corporations that operate globally.

It is clear that regulating something is an expensive and all-encompassing approach. However, it is also clear that there are times when this approach to regulation, as expensive a mechanism as it is to implement, is the only solution to the ongoing ethical dilemma that business itself refuses to fix. This is a cautionary tale for any future business professional to be aware of.

To move to a more practical level, let's specifically explore the connection between ethics, corporate governance, and IT.

CORPORATE AND IT GOVERNANCE

Corporate governance can be simply defined as the highest level of decision making, involving basic questions of status, strategy, and compliance within an organization. Of course, this suggests a need to include IT in any governance process. Effective governance is a critical enabler for success in the global economy, for securing the enterprise's information resources, and for creating competitive advantage.

Some even contend that good governance is linked to improved financial performance. Noted MIT business scholar Peter Weill estimates that businesses with strong governance create 20 percent more business value than similar firms with less-robust governance.[2] Others say there are companies that follow all the rules of good governance, but still face challenges and suffer from poor performance. There are more factors contributing to performance than simply governance. However, one thing is certain: all companies are re-evaluating their governance in light of high-profile corporate scandals, such as Enron and WorldCom, to bring it in line with emerging global standards and legislated requirements. This is generally improving the overall state of corporate governance globally.[3]

Corporate governance took a front-row seat in everyone's consciousness in 2001 when the Enron scandal broke. Several top-level executives, including founder Kenneth Lay (pictured here) and president Jeffrey Skilling, were indicted and later convicted of several fraud-related charges all connected to the collapse of Enron. Skilling is currently serving a 24-year prison sentence, and Lay died of an apparent heart attack in July 2006, although some speculate it was suicide.

Corporate governance means that the leadership and management of a business are directly accountable to its owners (i.e., shareholders) for *proper operation and financial control* of the organization. This includes deliberate and complete disclosure and reporting of results for a public company. Given the global expansion of businesses and public demand to control what many see as massive corporate excess and global fraud, it is no surprise that stakeholders such as national governments have increased their involvement in ensuring effective governance

---
2. Peter Weill and J. W. Ross, "IT Governance: How Top Performers Manage IT Decision Rights for Superior Performance," Harvard Business School Publishing, Boston, 2004, p. 2.

3. J. McFarland, and E. Church, "Do Better Boards Make Better Companies?," *The Globe and Mail*, October 24, 2006, B1.

and reporting. Government and business leaders around the world are enacting laws (such as Sarbanes-Oxley previously mentioned), writing regulations (such as the 2009 IFRS model financial statements[4]), and establishing policies and guidelines for the control of financial systems (such as new compensation restrictions on banking executives[5]), as well as using existing laws and regulations regarding the security and confidentiality of sensitive data and personal information.

However, most businesses still need to take corporate governance one step further than they have in the past. Since managers and employees are the business professionals who implement and follow governance policies and processes, they need to understand technology and its impacts on both corporate and IT governance. Most modern businesses are heavily invested in and dependent on information systems, technologies, and data. Any requirements, especially around reporting and disclosure, clearly rely on fundamental assurances that what's in an organization's IT systems is reliable, safe, and secure. It certainly would not be prudent to simply assume that because something is "in the system," it must be right! Therefore, for an organization to understand and manage its operations, it must provide governance for all its information-related assets.

IT governance is the "distribution of IT decision-making rights and responsibilities among enterprise stakeholders, and the procedures and mechanisms for making and monitoring strategic decisions regarding IT."[6] This means that IT governance begins as a very high-level process that specifies: (1) how the organization will set goals, objectives, priorities, and policies for IT; (2) how it will integrate IT with business strategies and goals; and (3) which organizational members will make decisions regarding, and be responsible for, the successful completion of these tasks (the "who" of IT governance).[7] This leads to a discussion of the role of IT in an organization and how it must help support proper governance. One of the largest associations of IT professionals in Canada, Canada's Association of Information Technology Professionals, has published a very relevant code of ethics that helps address this responsibility in the context of an IT professional (see *www.cips.ca/ethics*). Of course, if we strive to be better professionals one of our obligations is to continually enhance the role of our profession as it relates to contributing to society and not just remaining self-interested. CIPS, among some other like-minded professional associations globally, has been leading this discussion since the 1980s and is a good starting point for IT students to start exploring these issues even before they begin practising in the field, which brings us to our next discussion about the role of the CIO in promoting good governance practices.

The CIO: Managing IT Governance

Who within a business addresses the IT governance challenges mentioned above? In many businesses, this is the responsibility of the **chief information officer (CIO)** (other titles include VP of IS, director of IS or IT). The CIO must ensure proper and secure use of all the organization's information resources, and particularly the

---

4. See http://www.iasb.org for more details on this global regulatory regime.

5. See http://online.wsj.com/article/SB125324292666522101.html *as an example of this issue.*

6. R. Peterson, "Crafting information technology governance," *Information Systems Management*, http://www.ism-journal.com, Fall 2004.

7. Adapted from IT Governance Institute® website, http://www.itgi.org. Retrieved June 15, 2005.

organization's compliance with privacy laws and regulations in *every jurisdiction* in which it operates. For most organizations today, this has become a complex web of overlapping laws and different standards that takes a significant amount of specialized knowledge to sort out. In fact, IT relies heavily on legal professionals to help sort out these complexities even before systems are designed and implemented. To give you some insight into these complexities, Table 9.1 summarizes just a few of the applicable types of legislation around the world that might apply to various IT operations of a typical organization.

Table 9.1 Selected Governance and Compliance Related Laws and Regulations

Laws and Regulations	Description
Personal Information Protection and Electronic Documents Act (PIPEDA)	The federal government act sets out ground rules for how private sector organizations may collect, use, or disclose personal information in the course of commercial activities. The law gives individuals the right to access and request correction of the personal information these organizations may have collected about them.[8]
Bill 198	This Ontario legislature bill amends to the Securities Act and Commodity Futures Act. Among the amendments are those giving the Ontario Securities Commission (OSC) rule-making authority to require reporting issuers to appoint audit committees and to prescribe requirements relating to the functions and responsibilities of audit committees, including independence requirements. The OSC also has rule-making authority to require reporting issuers to establish and maintain internal controls, disclosure controls, and procedures, and require CEOs and CFOs to provide certifications related to internal controls and disclosure controls and procedures.[9]
EU Data Protection Directive	Each EU member nation is required to pass legislation requiring confidentiality and integrity controls for networks, systems, and data containing personal information for both employees and customers.[10]
Basel II Accord: International Convergence on Capital Measurement and Capital Standards	The regulations from the Bank for International Settlements are designed to encourage banks to adopt and follow rigorous risk assessment, management, and controls practices.[11]
Sarbanes-Oxley Act	The U.S. act holds a company's officers personally responsible for providing accurate public financial information to investors. Emphasis is on internal controls.[12]
Multilateral Instrument 52-109	Since March 2005, CEOs and CFOs (or persons performing similar functions) of reporting issuers are required to personally certify in each interim and annual filing that: 1. He or she has reviewed the filing; 2. Based on his or her knowledge, the filings do not contain any untrue statement of a material fact or omit to state a material fact required to be stated or that is necessary to make a statement not misleading in light of the circumstances under which it was made; *(Continued)*

---

8. Ibid.
9. Ontario Securities Commission Notice of Proposed Amendments to the Securities Act and Commodities Futures Act, http://www.osc.gov.on.ca/en/SecuritiesLaw_ar_20021115_bill-198.jsp. Retrieved January 15, 2010.
10. http://www.cdt.org/privacy/guide/protect
11. http://www.bis.org/publ/bcbsca.htm
12. http://thecaq.aicpa.org/Resources/Sarbanes+Oxley/ SOX Act; http://www.law.uc.edu/CCL/SOact/soact.pdf

Table 9.1	(Continued)
Laws and Regulations	Description
	3. Based on his or her knowledge, the financial statements together with the other financial information included in the filings fairly present in all material respects the financial condition, results of operations, and cash flows of the issuer;
	4. He or she and the other certifying officers are responsible for establishing and maintaining disclosure controls and procedures and internal control over financial reporting, and they have designed disclosure controls and procedures and internal control over financial reporting (or caused them to be designed under their supervision); and
	5. He or she has caused the issuer to disclose changes in internal control over financial reporting with material affect or reasonably likely material effect on internal control.
	In each annual certification, the certifying officers must also disclose under item 4 that they have evaluated the effectiveness of disclosure controls and procedures and caused their issuers to disclose their conclusions regarding their evaluation.[13]
Privacy Act	This federal government act imposes obligations on some 150 federal government departments and agencies to respect privacy rights by limiting the collection, use, and disclosure of personal information. The Privacy Act gives individuals the right to access and request correction of personal information about themselves held by these federal government organizations.[14]
Provincial Privacy Legislation	Every province and territory in Canada has privacy legislation governing the collection, use, and disclosure of personal information held by government agencies. British Columbia, Alberta, and Quebec are the only provinces with laws recognized as substantially similar to PIPEDA. Others, such as Ontario, have their own legislative framework (FIPPA). These laws regulate the collection, use, and disclosure of personal information by businesses and other organizations, and provide individuals with a general right of access to, and correction of, their personal information. In addition, Alberta, Saskatchewan, Manitoba, and Ontario have passed legislation to deal specifically with the collection, use, and disclosure of personal health information by health care providers and other health care organizations (HIPPA in Ontario, for example).[15]

However, since not all organizations have a formally designated CIO, the role of ensuring that IT governance is properly in place is actually the responsibility of the senior executive team and the board of directors. Ultimately, it is up to them to decide who will be responsible for IT governance within their organization. The most basic point here is simply to ensure that IT governance is not an afterthought, but rather a forethought.

Quick Test

1. True or False. All business professionals who use organizational technologies should understand how technology can affect corporate and IT governance.

---

13. http://www.kpmg.ca/unitymail/accountability/en/issues/elert2006-007.html
14. Office of the Privacy Commissioner of Canada, Privacy Legislation in Canada Fact Sheet, http://www.priv.gc.ca/fs-fi/02_05_d_15_e.cfm, Retrieved January 15, 2010.
15. Ibid.

2. True or False. IT governance includes the distribution of IT decision-making rights and responsibilities among enterprise stakeholders.

3. The _____ usually leads the organization's information and technology efforts, especially as it relates to the creation of business value.
   a. CEO
   b. CFO
   c. CIO
   d. COO

Answers: 1. True; 2. False; 3. c

Professional Codes of Conduct and Practice

Industry associations, professional bodies, and industry think-tanks for many professions—IT included—often develop, publish, and promote **codes of conduct**. These codes are relevant to any profession and help guide the professionals within the field in terms of what is and is not acceptable and ethical behaviour. Many professions have very strict codes of conduct (medicine, law, accounting, and engineering, for example), where the consequence of not following them normally results in expulsion and the payment of compensation for malpractice. In many of these professions, a clear duty of care is in place between the patient or client and the professional, and often the relationship is fee-based. In addition to the CIPS example cited earlier in this chapter, other IT-related professions have looser guidelines or lesser means of imposing sanctions and are considered as more voluntary rather than punitive codes of conduct. Specific examples of these in IT include:

- Project Management Institute (PMI) *www.pmi.org/PDF/AP_PMICodeofEthics.pdf*
- Association for Computing Machinery (ACM) *www.acm.org/about/code-of-ethics*
- Association of Information Technology Professionals (AITP) *www.aitp.org/organization/about/ethics/ethics.jsp*
- Computer Society of the IEEE (IEEE-CS) *www.ieee.org/portal/pages/iportals/aboutus/ethics/code.html*

WHAT DO YOU THINK?

There is a school of thought that argues that IT is not a profession in the strict sense of the word. There is no mandatory licensing, no commonly agreed upon body of knowledge and standards of practice, and no self-regulating peer review process for complaints and lapses in standards as there are in many other professions.

However, others argue that many in IT are certainly engaged in *professional practice*. This means that they purport to have expert knowledge in a specific field, on which others must rely, and for which they are paid.

What do you think? Is IT a profession or simply a job? On what basis would you compare and contrast IT to other professions to make this assessment? What could be done to improve IT professionalism in your opinion?

Many large private companies in Canada also have internal codes of conduct that relate to employee conduct and maintaining high ethical standards. The Royal Bank of Canada (RBC) is a good example. RBC's Code of Conduct includes the following principles:

- upholding the law
- confidentiality
- fairness
- corporate responsibility
- honouring our trust in you
- objectivity
- integrity
- individual responsibility

The full Royal Bank Code of Conduct can be found at *www.rbc.com/governance/pdf/RBCCodeOfConduct.pdf*.

These kinds of codes are often in place in organizations with high risk profiles (such as financial services, natural resources, hospitals, community services, etc.), where the risk of unethical behaviour has high financial or human costs.

If the organization or business you belong to has one of these codes, it may be important to review it before you accept employment. If the organization does not have one, perhaps that too should be a question you address during the interviewing and hiring process. Regardless, arm yourself with knowledge about these kinds of issues, the various kinds of codes of conduct that exist, and how different organizations approach and respond to ethical dilemmas. Knowledge is power, and the ability to think about these issues before you face your first real test in business will help you respond better when you do.

Common Ethical Dilemmas Involving IT

Some areas of IT have patterns of potentially unethical behaviour common to an industry rather than specific to any business operating in that industry. These are worth highlighting, as they are things you should be aware of as a future business professional on your way into the business world. These practices need particular scrutiny, and hopefully the brief discussion here will give you pause for thought the next time you think about them or encounter them in the real world.

Copyright and Piracy One of the biggest plagues of the software industry is piracy. It should be clear to any professional that copying any protected software, which the license clearly does not permit, is an unethical practice. It hurts the costs of software in the marketplace (because vendors factor in these costs and pass them along to consumers and businesses alike), does not encourage innovation (why bother if people are simply going to steal your stuff anyway?), and diminishes opportunities for IT professionals (because of less profit to invest in new product development). See the Business Software Alliance website (*bsa.org*) for more detailed studies of this problem.

Similarly, we all sometimes fall into the trap of simply "cutting and pasting" something without referencing it or sourcing it properly. This is another aspect of copyright infringement that is made easier by having access to the Web. It is a significant corporate problem that you have to be aware of, as a CIO or as an employee.[16]

TECHNOLOGY CORE

Many universities across North America worry about their students' ethics when it comes to academic integrity. Recent surveys from a variety of sources show that anywhere from 22 percent to over 50 percent of undergraduate students cheat (to a lesser or larger extent) at some point when earning their degrees. Technology now plays a part in this significant ethical debate. Services like *turnitin.com* use database and matching search technologies that enable professors to quickly detect possible plagiarism from a multitude of sources. Of course, as an American company with onshore servers, they operate under the jurisdiction of the U.S. Patriot Act. This law requires that if something submitted to an electronic network is seen as "threatening to the interests of the United States of America" it be reported and investigated. Many believe that even a simple essay that might ask questions about, for instance, the U.S. role in Afghanistan could be subject to reporting if written in a hostile way. Extreme results of this unintended outcome could include being placed on the "no-fly" list or being listed as a suspected terrorist. This rather draconian legislation bothers many Canadian university students and professors, resulting in arguments against using this service because of the potential risk to Canadians who have their work submitted to a U.S.-based service. Requests to operate local servers (which would presumably be exempt from this type of U.S. regulation) have not been acted on by the company for a variety of reasons, likely including cost and complexity. This is just one example of how the deployment of global systems, even in something as innocuous as cheating detection systems, can become embroiled in ethical, legal, or moral dilemmas and debates.

Patent Violations Although violations rarely happen deliberately, there are still many cases where companies are sued for patent violations. While some of this may be the result of ignorance (in and of itself a potential violation of ethics, since it is easy enough to search for pre-existing patents), much of this is intentional. If you use someone else's work, you should pay for it and almost every developed nation has its own patent codes, arrangements, and royalty requirements. In the case of patents, that normally means acknowledging the use of and paying royalties on any invention you use as prescribed under various patent regimes in place around the world. To use someone else's invention without paying is not only unethical, it is theft of intellectual property.

Reverse Engineering This topic attracts a lot of attention among academics and practitioners alike, and there is substantial debate about its validity as a professional practice. Essentially, reverse engineering is used most often to find out how another manufacturer created a product (software or hardware), and then attempting to learn from this to either make a better one or find a way to replicate it in a different way to avoid infringing on copyright or paying royalties on a patent. If this

---

16. See TYNT.com for an interesting example of a software solution designed to help address this issue within organizations.

process is used as an educational tool (which was its original intention), there are no ethical dilemmas. However, for any other purpose designed to evade respecting other people's originality and intellectual property rights, there is considerable ethical debate about the integrity of this practice.

Spam and Privacy Codes Consumers and businesses hate spam email. However, organizations continue to use it as a marketing tactic, and criminal organizations use it in phishing schemes (e.g., the emails that indicate you are a lottery winner or have been chosen by a foreign national to enter into a business partnership with them). They are all fakes! For up-to-date information on this continuing web scourge, see *www.antiphishing.org*. The ethical dilemma is not the practice of sending promotional email itself; it is seeking permission to do so rather than collecting or buying email addresses where individuals have not provided their consent. This common practice requires IT professionals to implement the systems. However, it is not clear that the profession has taken a stand against unwanted spam email. Similarly, it seems incumbent upon any organization that does happen to have the privilege of obtaining private email addresses to keep them so and not to re-sell them to others without prior permission.

Security Breaches News stories[17] often describe breaches in protocol, usually in IT, or how intrusions or security breaches resulted in the loss or disclosure of valuable personal information. In most countries, including Canada, there are specific requirements to report these privacy breaches and take immediate action to deal with any negative impact of the disclosure. However, there are exclusions for minor breaches, and the system is also voluntary. Without disclosure, there may be no need to act, and there will likely be no media impact. Would you report it? Of course you should, and ethical practice demands that you do. However, it is clear from the frequency with which consumers are affected by identity theft and not informed about it that not every organization adheres to this regimen. This behaviour is unethical; a privacy breach is a serious matter and must be taken seriously. The law is the law—as inconvenient as it may be—and it should be followed.

Competitive Intelligence Competitive intelligence is a common practice in business, including in the IT industry. Competitors want insight into what others in the industry are doing so they can respond to the market and maintain market share. Gaining such insights from customers or partners, or from observation and deduction are all fine, but beyond that there are a whole host of practices that clearly skirt the boundaries of ethical practice. For instance, having someone pose as a potential customer to get pricing information, hiring away a competitor's employees with the sole purpose of obtaining competitive information, hiring a head hunter to seemingly solicit interest for a non-existing job so employees will disclose confidential plans, or hiring investigators to snoop and obtain private information are all clear examples of unethical practices that have been seen or documented in the IT and

---

17. http://www.canada.com/news/Canadian+Tire+cancels+MasterCards+following+breach/1232174/story.html is a good Canadian example and http://www.pcworld.com/article/158003/massive_theft_of_credit_card_numbers_reported.html is an excellent American one.

other industries. Obviously, being a vigorous competitor is one thing; being a crook or a cheat is another.

Hiring Practices, Equity, and Equal Opportunity A vibrant IT sector often helps drive a country's economy through innovation and wealth-creation. As you can see in Tech Guide A, IT careers are solid choices with attractive compensation and long-term security. This often means that demand for talented professionals with the right skills outstrips supply, attracting immigration of qualified professionals to fill that demand. However, there is some evidence that these visa workers are frequently mistreated, not paid fairly, or exploited because they have a limited ability to change employers without affecting their immigration status. They also have to work for a number of years to qualify for citizenship. So, although we need these professionals, we may not always treat them fairly.

The same could be said for those who come to Canada to study in advanced technical programs, often because there are not similar programs in their country of origin. Although they are trained in these programs, they often report having a less than equal access to opportunity. This is a problem within the IT profession; practices that are not completely merit-based are unethical and should be questioned and rectified. All IT professionals should be concerned about this issue.

Green IT The environment is obviously a major global concern of every citizen of every country. And, like any industry, IT is a contributor to environmental damage. IT professionals are becoming aware of what they can do to help protect the environment. Some of the major steps all IT professionals should take are to promote recycling and reduce consumption to create a more sustainable global IT industry.[18]

IT is a contributor to environmental damage. Good IT governance includes finding ways to reduce both the amount of waste associated with computers and other electronics and the negative environmental impact this type of garbage has.

THE PERSONAL IMPLICATIONS OF ETHICS AND GOVERNANCE

At this point, many of you may be asking yourselves what this all means to you. Consider that question using a little bit of visualizing. Suppose you were an employee for either Hollinger International or Bernard Madoff Securities Investment Ltd. Suppose further that you became aware of the frauds that were being perpetuated or somehow were asked, directly or indirectly, to participate in elements of those frauds. To be more specific, suppose you were the IT manager of one of those firms and were asked to do something that seems suspicious on the surface, but that can certainly be done technically. You assess that the action, while not strictly illegal, would not expose you to personal liability, but could clearly result in the company being able to do something that it should not do, and it is unclear to you whether or not the company will do it. The potential for the company to act unethically is directly created by the changes to the system you are being asked to make. Do you do it or not? Do you report it, and if so, to whom? You talk to your boss and it seems

---

18. See *GreenIT.net* as an example of an entire consulting firm dedicated to this emerging trend. Their site has some very interesting and up-to-date information on Green IT trends and practices.

clear that she is fine with the requested changes and may or may not be a part of the potentially illegal activity you suspect. Do you investigate further and ask questions, even though you realize this may have career consequences and may even get you fired? Or do you simply quit?

Every single one of these questions is valid, and responses to each one have their pros and cons. In this case, while what you are being asked to do in its narrowest sense is legal and proper, you know that ultimately, in combination with other information that you hold about the company and its ownership, it is likely improper to do it because it could facilitate a fraud. Because you have chosen to become a professional working in an organization, you are now in an ethical dilemma with potential moral, legal, and personal consequences.

Many in the IT profession would suggest that, providing you have proper documentation of the fact that you were asked to do this and you have no *direct proof* that it is illegal or unethical, you are immune from any consequences and should do as you are told. Of course, you can immediately see the flaw in this line of reasoning if you consider the many times in history when similar situations have occurred and huge numbers of conspirators have claimed immunity based on the principle of lawful direction. This suggests that, when told to do something in an employment, military, or government context that is considered lawful, you must comply with those directions regardless of the outcome.

While there may be kernels of truth and even ethical conduct in doing what you are told, there must also be limits to this type of thinking if society is to remain humane and just. At some point, the most obvious thing to do in a situation like this is to resign and avoid the dilemma all together. But this often comes at a high personal cost, and requires that your moral and ethical code values your personal integrity more than it does your career or monetary gains.

Of course, there is the possibility that you could decide to try and keep your job and deal with the issue internally. This suggests finding an appropriate **internal conduit** for the information and suspicions you have, and dealing with someone beyond reproach and whose integrity you respect. In some institutions, this may be some kind of independent third party such as an **ombudsperson** or **integrity commissioner**. However, private enterprises do not normally have these types of positions, so you may have to selectively use your peers or supervisors for this purpose instead. One positive outcome of even being willing to discuss your concerns about a potential ethical dilemma is that it allows you to test your assumptions and often exposes aspects of the ethical dilemma that you may or may not have been aware of or reflected on. Being able to talk to someone rather than operating in isolation on matters like this lessens the stress and increases the probability of resolving them properly and fully. Silence or tolerance is a form of **complicit or implicit consent**, which means, despite your inklings to the contrary, you did nothing. The law presumes that you consented to act accordingly, either with or without intent, and are therefore complicit. You can be held criminally responsible for these actions if they are illegal, and civilly responsible for damages if it is proved you acted unethically or unprofessionally.

Of course, any solution involving disclosure takes you dangerously close to the issue of **whistle-blowing** which is, in and of itself, fraught with ethical dilemmas of its own. However, the question of whether or not you should report your suspicions to relevant authorities or the media (an **external conduit**) often seems to depend on the extent to which you can back up any claims you make with supporting evidence to ensure you have a credible claim before proceeding. Generally you do not want to undertake something like this unless you are sufficiently sure about your course of action and its potential consequences for both you and the organization you represent. The first step may therefore be to seek the counsel of a professional (such as a lawyer) who can help you understand the risks of your actions and consider how to mitigate them properly and legally before you act. Legal professionals are bound by law not to disclose whatever you tell them, and to act only in your best interests.

CONCLUSION

Ethical thinking is both simple and complex. It relies on each person having values, morals, and a knowledge of the law. You must ensure that you are prepared to confront ethical dilemmas when they arise and make decisions that are defensible and transparent about what is right and wrong. You must not hide or shirk that responsibility if you want to protect your personal character and reputation. Integrity is an explicit requirement of being a solid professional. This is as true for an IT professional as it is for anyone else. In fact, in some areas of explicit risk, it is absolutely up to the IT profession to ensure that the industry acts ethically. The desire to act ethically as a person is what society relies on to ensure that organizations also conduct themselves ethically. Without that, little stands in the way of the unbridled pursuit of profits, increasing the risk of harm to everyone.

What's in IT for you?

A lot of press has been generated about Facebook and the recent changes it made to its website privacy settings. Some of this was in response to significant pressure from the Canadian government (Facebook's current number-two country for market share) and a ruling from the Canadian Privacy Commission, which threatened to shut them down if they did not comply and provide enhanced consumer choices around privacy settings (see *www.priv.gc.ca/* for more information on this trend-setting ruling). In the end, while they did make changes, most users seem quite oblivious to the problem and the risks of things like online identify theft, protection of personal information, and access to IM, mobile phone, or telephone numbers—which can be turned into a reverse 411 lookup to find out where you live, instantly connecting your physical location to your online identity. These kinds of problems, some of which have real consequences, do not seem to register with most of us. We seem more intent on ease of use and easy access than we are on protection of privacy. In fact, some suggest that we now live in a post-private world where governments are increasingly imposing security and privacy regimes that most citizens do not actually care about or comply with. This raises the interesting question of exactly who gets to sit in judgement of Facebook's privacy options—its users or governments? Similarly, what happens in those same debates between employees and employers? Do you feel differently about your right to privacy when your employer wants to make everything you do on your company laptop or pager company information? For another interesting legal precedent in this regard, check out the recent U.S. Supreme Court ruling on IT-related privacy of employee information at *www.washingtonpost.com/wp-dyn/content/article/2009/12/14/AR2009121403689.html*.

What's in IT for an organization?

Why should organizations act ethically when there may be more to gain by not acting ethically? As touched on briefly in this chapter, there may be advantages to acting ethically, especially in the eyes of an organization's customers and partners. The *Report on Business* magazine noted in 2005 that "many business leaders now believe that doing good for others means doing good for shareholders as well." Corporate social responsibility activities that integrate broader societal concerns into business strategy and performance are evidence of good management. In addition to building trust with the community and giving firms an edge in attracting good customers and employees, acting responsibly toward workers and others in society can be in the long-term interest of firms and their shareholders.[19] Michael Sabia, a well-known Canadian business leader, and Michael Porter, a professor at the Harvard Business School, have also commented favourably about the benefits of businesses acting responsibly and ethically.[20] Can you think of a company that you are loyal to that demonstrates good ethics and aligns with your values? Perhaps you support an organization because it is involved in a charity that you support, or promotes environmental sustainability. It is difficult to directly relate whether there is a positive impact on profit of companies acting ethically, but there certainly is a negative impact when unethical actions are disclosed.

What's in IT for society?

Put simply, society needs businesses to act ethically to ensure the safety and security of everyone. Most companies have personal data about their customers that needs to be kept safe, and many of the products you buy could affect your health if the companies that produce them do not make the proper effort to ensure their products are safe. Take food, for example. When you buy food in a grocery store, you assume that it is safe for consumption. Consider what would have happened had Maple Leaf Foods *not* acted ethically when some of their packaged meat products were found to be tainted with Listeria that caused numerous people to become severely ill and, in some cases, die. Instead of trying to cover up the problem, Maple Leaf's CEO, Michael McCain, issued a massive recall, closed the plant, and apologized to consumers during a televised press conference. Maple Leaf also made extensive use of social media, using the Web to provide resources and get their message out. The company handled the deadly outbreak with full disclosure, quick action, and a sense of duty to protect consumers over its own profit motives.[21] This is what consumers should rightfully be able to expect from all organizations.

ROI STUDENT RETURN ON INVESTMENT SUMMARY

1. What is business ethics and why does it matter to business professionals?

Business ethics address ethical and moral issues in the business world. Individuals within businesses are relied upon to conduct themselves in an ethical manner. As a result, businesses then act ethically. Businesses are also bound by law to act ethically, however it is very difficult to know and enforce when a business might be acting unethically. Because businesses are generally led

---

19. *Report on Business* magazine's corporate social responsibility ranking, March 2005
20. http://www.ic.gc.ca/eic/site/csr-rse.nsf/eng/rs00128.html
21. See http://www.theguardian.pe.ca/index.cfm?sid=206223&sc=101 as an example of the coverage of this particular incident.

by those with morals and values, businesses act in a similar fashion. Ethics are important to business professionals because there are benefits to acting ethically. By acting ethically, a business may gain goodwill and, in turn, this goodwill may result in increased customer loyalty and profit. Acting ethically may also allow a company to more easily do business and gain trust. Several companies are showcasing their corporate social responsibility and making company values and ethics public.

2. Why are corporate and IT governance important?

Corporate and IT governance are processes for allocating the decision-making rights and responsibilities for corporate and IT decision making, respectively. They are the link between the business strategy and the IT strategy. As such, they lay the foundation for the implementation of strategy. Governance also includes risk assessment and control.

3. What are some of the common ethical dilemmas in involving IT?

Some of the more common ethical dilemmas involving IT include copyright and piracy, security breaches, and spam and privacy codes. Individuals and businesses make ethical choices in these areas all of the time. For example, did you purchase that song you are listening to on your iPod or "borrow it" from a friend? Sometimes businesses are provided with information that they are only supposed to use in a certain way, or for one time only. As part of their marketing efforts, however, they may decide to send unsolicited emails (spam). What is the harm? Are there times when you trusted your personal information to a company and it was leaked or stolen and used for other purposes? Sometimes it is hard to determine where unwanted phone calls come from. Often it is up to the CIO of a company to use ethics in IT decision making.

KNOWLEDGE SPEAK

Bill 198   315
chief information officer (CIO)   314
codes of conduct   317
complicit or implicit consent   322
corporate governance   313
corporate social responsibility (CSR)   310
corruption   311
ethical dilemma   308
ethics   307
external conduit   323
hierarchy of values   308

integrity commissioner   322
internal conduit   322
IT governance   314
legal codes   307
moral code   307
ombudsperson   322
Personal Information Protection and Electronic Documents Act (PIPEDA)   315
personal values   307
Sarbanes-Oxley Act   312
whistle-blowing   322

REVIEW QUESTIONS

Multiple-choice questions

1. The primary focus of IT governance is on _____.
   a. decision rights associated with IT
   b. information processing
   c. network vulnerabilities
   d. technology acquisition and modernization

2. Contributors to your understanding of what is right and what is wrong are:
   a. personal values
   b. moral code
   c. legal code
   d. all of the above

3. The Canadian legislation governing personal information disclosure by federal government organizations is _____.
   a. Sarbanes-Oxley
   b. PIPEDA
   c. HIPAA
   d. Privacy Act

4. Qualified professionals of any profession need not adhere to _____.
   a. standards of practice
   b. peer review
   c. Bill 198
   d. licensing requirements

Fill-in-the-blank questions

5. Peter Weill suggests that businesses with strong governance create _____ percent more business value than firms with less governance.
6. _____ was a response to bankruptcies, fraud, and deception in business in the 1990s and early 2000s.
7. In an organization, it is often the _____ that ensures the organization is in compliance with privacy laws.
8. If your credit card information was stolen for the records of an online vendor, you are a victim of _____.

True-false questions

9. CEOs must personally certify their organizations' financial statements.
10. If you are asked to do something seemingly unethical, by law you must resign.
11. Hiring your competitor's employees to gain access to confidential information is unethical.
12. All private companies are required to have a code of conduct.

Matching questions

Choose the BEST answer from column B for each item in column A.

Column A
13. copyright and piracy
14. patent violation
15. reverse engineering

Column B
a. Buying a dress, taking it apart, making a pattern from the pieces, and then using the pattern to cut and sew new dresses.
b. Making similar rubber sandals using the same materials and process as other manufacturers.
c. Using your friend's copy of Windows 7.0 to upgrade your PC.

Short-answer questions

16. What is Sarbanes-Oxley? Briefly describe its intended purpose relative to publicly traded U.S. businesses. How has Canada responded to Sarbanes-Oxley?
17. What is PIPEDA? What does this act protect you from?

Discussion/Essay questions

18. Discuss personal ethics, morality, and values. Describe a situation where there is an ethical dilemma.
19. Do you think corporate governance requirements have gone too far or not far enough? As a CEO, how would you feel about personally certifying a corporation's financial statements?
20. What do you think of the business benefits of corporate social responsibility (CSR)? Discuss an example of a company that is benefiting from being socially responsible.

TEAM ACTIVITY

As a team, discuss the Royal Bank of Canada's code of conduct as seen on page XX. Discuss and develop a code of conduct for a company that you would like to work for.

SOFTWARE APPLICATION EXERCISES

1. Internet
Go to the website for the Privacy Commissioner of Canada (*www.priv.gc.ca/index_e.cfm*) and learn how to lodge a privacy complaint. Review some recent findings by the commissioner under PIPEDA.

2. Presentation
Imagine you are the CIO of a company. Prepare a presentation for the executive team on your plan to prevent security breaches. Highlight each issue and its business process or technology solution.

3. Word Processing
Using word processing software, create a word association diagram with words that have meaning to you on the topics of values, morals, and ethics (see Chapter 8, page 277 for an example).

4. Spreadsheet
Use a spreadsheet to chart the stock prices of Maple Leaf Foods on the Toronto Stock Exchange (TSX: MFI) from just before the beginning of the tainted food crisis in August 2008 until August 2009. Review news reports and make conclusions about how the crisis and its disclosure affected the stock.

5. Advanced Challenge
Imagine you will be starting your own business upon graduation. You will rent a small office space for yourself and one partner. Your goal is to have an office that is as green as possible. (1) Describe how your IT will be green. What suppliers will you use? How will you power your IT? Research the cost of your green IT and create a budget for the first year of your business. (2) Create policies and processes to support your green IT initiative.

ONLINE RESOURCES

Companion Website
- Take interactive practice quizzes to assess your knowledge and help you study in a dynamic way.
- Review PowerPoint lecture slides.
- Get help and sample solutions to end-of-chapter software application exercises.

Additional Resources Available Only on WileyPLUS
- Take the interactive Quick Test to check your understanding of the chapter material and get immediate feedback on your responses.
- Review and study with downloadable Audio Lecture MP3 files.
- Check your understanding of the key vocabulary in the chapter with Knowledge Speak Interactive Flash Cards.

CASE STUDY: INTELLECTUAL PROPERTY RIGHTS (OR WHY I SHOULDN'T DOWNLOAD THAT MP3 WITHOUT PAYING FOR IT)

Have you ever downloaded music, videos, or books over the Internet? Do you think you did something unethical? To understand why the *unauthorized* downloading of music files or other forms of copyrighted material may be unethical, it is important to be aware of a concept known as *intellectual property*.

Intellectual property is any creation of the mind, including inventions, literary and artistic works, and symbols, names, images, and designs used in commerce. Canadian laws governing copyrights or patents protect most intellectual properties, making unauthorized copies of such property illegal.

However, the problem is that there are not yet many good ways to enforce these laws. Illegal copying and distribution, brought about by digitization and high-speed networks, is easy. Further, the technological means of copyright enforcement that do exist, called *digital rights management (DRM)*, often seem to violate another important aspect of copyright law known as *fair dealing*. The fair dealing concept of Canadian copyright law allows the use of copyrighted material for purpose of private study or research, or for criticism, review, or news reporting.[22] Material that uses DRM technology often does not allow *any* copies of the work to be made, including copies that would be allowed under fair dealing provisions.

Another challenge is to determine whether or not unauthorized use of copyrighted material has a negative impact on the owner of the material. For the case of music downloads, the jury is still out. Graham Henderson, who heads the Canadian Recording Industry Association, says downloading is damaging the industry, the economy, and the careers of artists: "Downloading, file-swapping, peer-to-peer networks—these are all euphemisms for piracy, pure and simple. It is devastating to the Canadian music industry." Henderson says the recording industry has seen music sales drop almost $500 million in just a few years. That's about a quarter of a million records a month.[23]

On the other hand, a research paper from Dr. Felix Oberholzer of Harvard University and Dr. Koleman Strumpf of the University of North Carolina indicates that there has been little to no effect on the music industry from music file sharing. In fact, the paper concludes that music file sharing has had a positive effect on the industry.[24] A Forrester Research report backs up this claim, advocating that the music industry embrace music file sharing to improve sales.[25] Dr. Michael Geist of the University of Ottawa believes it is not peer-to-peer music file sharing that is negatively affecting the industry as a whole, but rather the Canadian Private Copying Collective—which collects tariffs on downloads—is threatening to kill the nascent online music industry.[26]

Despite the uncertainty surrounding music files, as a business professional, how do you feel about the unauthorized use of intellectual property? Think about how you will earn your living as a business professional—by creating business value through knowledge work activities, decision making, and problem solving. These activities are often highly creative and result in an information or knowledge product that has business value. If someone were to use the knowledge you create, they might be able to "steal" some or all of the business value that resulted from your knowledge work. Your organization might suffer financially. This in turn could adversely impact your salary, pension benefits, profits, royalties, and the value of your company to shareholders. Over time, this could reduce investments in the creative arts and make it less possible for someone to earn a living as an artist. What would this do to society over the long term? So when you download that MP3, you may want to think about how this practice could affect you some day.

---

22. Canadian Intellectual Property Office (CIPO), http://strategis.ic.gc.ca/sc_mrksv/cipo/cp/copy_gd_protecte. Retrieved July 19, 2006.
23. "Musicians call for an update on copyright law," http://www.ctv.ca/servlet/Articlenews/story/CTVNews/110133117830_15?hub = Canada. Retrieved July 19, 2006.
24. Oberholzer, Felix and Koleman Strumpf (2004), "The Effect of File Sharing on Record Sales, An Empirical Analysis," Unpublished paper (Harvard Business School and Department of Economics, University of North Carolina, Chapel Hill), http://www.unc.edu/~cigar/papers/FileSharing_March2004.pdf.
25. Bernoff, J. "Downloads Save the Music Business," August 2002, http://www.forrester.com.
26. Geist, Michael, "Tariffs the real threat to music downloading," *Toronto Star*, http://www.thestar.com/NASApp/cs/ContentServer?page = name thestar/Layout/Article_Type1&cArticle&cid = 1113774609428&call_pageid = 968350072197&col = 969048863851. Retrieved August 25, 2006.

Case Questions

1. Think about the issues outlined above and develop the outline of an online ad campaign that might help others your age think about the impact of illegal file sharing. How could you most effectively communicate a complex issue and its societal impact to overcome individual temptation?
2. Imagine you are an independent artist. How would you protect yourself from illegal copying and why do you think your solution would work?

Integrative Application Case: *Campuspad.ca*

It's almost live! *Campuspad.ca* is ready to go and will soon be launched across North America. You expect transaction volume in Canada (with the help of your student union partnership) to be higher than in the United States, but you are confident growth will happen in the United States over time.

The journey has been interesting. You, Sarah, and Adam (who is now called your CIO) have all learned a lot. The prospects for the future are significant enough that you have all stopped your post-graduate job search and plan to work on the business full time. Soon *Campuspad.ca* will be the largest online student accommodation referral system in the world! Your search engine and social marketing strategy have paid off, and funds spent on marketing have clearly started to drive new sign-ups on the site from both landlords and prospective tenants.

This has also started to generate buzz about your business and there is some initial investor interest. However, in one of those recent investor meetings, someone asked you a question about your privacy policies and compliance efforts. While you know you are responsible for building a secure site and protecting privacy, you are less sure about what a privacy policy is or what it should be. You decide on the spot that this is something you need to deal with.

Guiding Case Questions

1. What legislation applies in Canada and the United States for online privacy and data protection?
2. Since you operate in both countries, what are the differences in what you are required to do to legally operate in both countries in compliance with this legislation?
3. Can you find online examples of other companies' privacy policies you could use as a sample when building your own privacy policy?

Your Task

After doing your research based on the guiding questions, write either a global privacy policy for *Campuspad.ca* OR one for your United States customers and one for your Canadian customers, as you see fit.

LOGOFF

We hope that you have enjoyed this journey, learning to combine your business skills with IT/IS knowledge in ways that create value for the organizations that you will be a part of in the future. We also hope that the practical approach we took helped make the subject matter accessible and useful to you.

Good system design must focus on seamless, connected systems that enable the processes your organization uses to do its work be more efficient and effective. Those systems are best designed with the input of those closest to that work: business professionals like you. You will ultimately use those systems to increase your own productivity and create business impact.

We are now at the end of our journey. You should be equipped with an understanding of the role technology plays in organizations, from enhancing your own productivity to enabling global e-commerce. But are you still wondering why technology matters so much?

One current example of that might be media convergence, something almost every sector of the economy is impacted by. If you are a consumer of any type of media, you are affected. If you produce or sell content or are involved in broadcasting or online media, you are affected. If you are a cable TV or telephone network operator, you are affected. If you are involved in government regulation or cultural policy, you are affected. And if you are an advertiser or promoter, or are responsible for your organization's brand, trends in this important area affect you. That's just about everyone in some way! This is perhaps one of the reasons why you took this course—because the impact of IT affects us in so many ways.

A topical press release that we have reproduced below proves this point. Consider this interesting example of how a media company needed technology business partners to help it address a significant gap in capability required to produce and air a hit TV show in Canada. With the knowledge you now possess as a result of your studies, this case study should make you realize how technologically literate you have become. And perhaps your interest in the content of this press release is just a little bit higher because you can understand the business issues raised and conquered, and some of the required underlying technology. You will also truly understand the point that is being made—that technology is pervasive and persuasive, and its use in business can create an undeniable competitive advantage.

Let's look at the actual press release from Bell Canada.

UNPRECEDENTED TEAMWORK AND TECHNOLOGICAL INNOVATION CONTRIBUTE TO *CANADIAN IDOL* SUCCESS[1]

Canadian Idol mania took the country by storm during the summer of 2003 and accounted for establishing an astonishing telecom industry record. The popular television show became Canada's most-watched English-language Canadian series since the advent of electronic measurement in 1989. Almost 6.5 million viewers

---

1. Reprinted with permission of CTVglobemedia. Please note that Bell Globemedia changed its name on January 1, 2007, to CTVglobemedia.

watched the two-hour finale to see Kingston's Ryan Malcolm become the first *Canadian Idol*. But there would have been no *Canadian Idol* without exciting new technology and unprecedented teamwork among cellular and wireline carriers coast-to-coast, led by Bell Canada.

The incredibly popular *Canadian Idol* TV series generated the highest call volume in Canadian history in the two hours following its finale on September 15. An impressive 3.3 million phone and text message votes from viewers were logged during the two-hour window.

This record was made possible through technological innovations, proactive communication, and cooperation from regional and national telecommunication organizations, led by Bell Canada. The solution Bell designed for *Canadian Idol* merged three essential elements—a robust toll-free network, interactive voice response (IVR) technology, and text messaging. All of this, in addition to the near-live call detail reporting, helped to make *Canadian Idol* such a huge success.

Pioneering a Canadian Industry First

In October 2002, CTV announced that it had partnered with FremantleMedia, one of the largest international producers of entertainment programs in the world, to produce and air a Canadian version of the "Idols" series. The television series had become a huge international hit following the success of *American Idol* in the United States and *Pop Idol* in the U.K. (*American Idol* is still an incredibly popular show that continues to run in the United States.)

Similar to those programs, *Canadian Idol* would feature undiscovered Canadian singing talent vying for the title of Canadian Idol. The show's interactive format allowed viewers to vote for their favourite performers each week via toll-free phone numbers or text messaging to determine who advanced to the next round.

Based on the popularity of the *Idol* shows around the world, CTV anticipated that it would need to partner with a communications service provider that could manage this voting process nationwide. CTV's requirements for *Canadian Idol* were simple: ensure all Canadians had equitable access to vote for their favourite performer and make sure that all votes were counted.

A number of factors contributed to the complexity of this challenge:

- It was not possible to replicate the communications processes used by other *Idol* shows and no similar projects had ever been undertaken in Canada. CTV needed to partner with a company that could design and manage a voting platform for *Canadian Idol,* charting unknown territory. The communications provider would be pioneering a process that could potentially be replicated for commercial applications, such as telephone voting or polling.
- Different telecommunications providers operate in different Canadian regions. These service providers would have to work closely together to ensure seamless communication and network integration.
- Based on the success of other *Idol* shows, CTV anticipated that the show could generate the highest volume of calls over a two-hour time span in Canadian history (which it did). This heightened call volume had caused problems in other countries, where *Idol* shows had placed a significant strain

on local phone networks. Call and messaging volumes were expected to reach peak levels in the communities where the *Idol* contestants resided. This necessitated the close monitoring of network performance and back-up plans in these regions.
- A flexible and intuitive IVR system needed to be rolled out nationwide to automate and process viewer calls and votes.
- Eleven sequential toll-free numbers—one allocated to each finalist—were required by *Canadian Idol* to simplify and streamline viewer voting.

CTV Looks to Bell for Support

After reviewing all requirements, CTV—Canada's largest private broadcaster and a Bell Globemedia company—decided to turn to Bell Canada, the country's leader in communications. Over the next few months, CTV worked closely with Bell to develop and implement a plan to deliver a seamless and reliable platform for *Canadian Idol* voting.

Bell's expertise in wired and wireless voice and data communications for residential and business markets was a strong selling feature for CTV. In addition, Bell Canada was uniquely positioned to manage and integrate the complex communications components of the *Idol* voting strategy. CTV knew that Bell had the scalability and technological expertise it needed to maintain network integrity and meet the demanding requirements of high volume voice and text-based voting.

The timeline was tight and the specifications were daunting. Bell began working on the project in January 2003. The company was faced with a hard deadline of June 11, the air date of *Canadian Idol's* premiere.

A National Network Built on Cooperation and Innovation

"We recognized that *Canadian Idol* could only succeed if our communications requirements were managed on a national basis," said Sam Dynes, director of production at CTV. "With its extensive footprint and partnerships with 80 percent of Canadian telecommunication service providers, we were confident that Bell could manage our project on the scale we required."

Bell's team of network professionals worked closely with specialists at the wireline and cellular divisions of companies such as Aliant, Microcell (Fido), MTS, NorthernTel, Rogers AT&T, SaskTel, Télébec, and TELUS to help ensure the risk to telephone networks would be minimized. This close relationship between CTV, Bell, and the major Canadian telecommunication service providers resulted in an integrated platform that enabled an easy, reliable, and consistent voting process for viewers coast-to-coast.

Communications conference bridges were established throughout the country. Led by Bell, these calls brought together network management personnel from each of the major telecommunication service providers to ensure that calls were being processed quickly and accurately. This task was a challenge because of the variety of IVR systems and networks across providers. Cooperation between regional providers was essential to the success of *Canadian Idol* due to the strong regional nature of voting.

Live communications bridges used during the show enabled telecommunication providers to contact each other as they monitored voice and data traffic and take the proper action should a network issue arise. Essential public-facing service organizations, such as 911, Operator Services, and 611, were also included in discussions so that contingency plans could be implemented instantly if networks suddenly became overtaxed with calls.

Adapting the Solution to Fit Evolving Needs

Delivering a reliable and integrated network nationwide through industry partnerships was the essential first step in the *Canadian Idol* project.

Bell Canada also applied its networking expertise to ensure the integrity of the network week-to-week, as call volumes increased. A near-live streaming of call detail reporting was introduced to provide instant information regarding voting activity across the country. Using this system built specifically for *Canadian Idol*, Bell could identify and monitor potential high volume calling areas and respond quickly to peaks by applying the appropriate routing measures. This system also provided CTV with an additional audit to ensure voting accuracy.

As *Canadian Idol* entered the final few weeks and the number of contestants diminished, high call volumes were expected to be concentrated in the regions where the remaining *Canadian Idol* contestants lived. Innovative actions, such as segregating the toll-free lines, routing 911 on dedicated lines to lower volume areas, and using the cell network to divert calls from high volume areas, were some contingency plans that were applied with great success.

As *Canadian Idol* finalists were selected, each was assigned a dedicated toll-free number to ensure voting accuracy and simplicity. Locating eleven sequential toll-free numbers was a difficult task since toll-free numbers are not typically assigned sequentially. After searching national toll-free databases, Bell was able to identify an available block of toll-free numbers and reserve these numbers for *Canadian Idol* voting.

Planning and Preparation Delivers Results

"The strong partnership between Bell and CTV, along with hundreds of hours devoted to anticipating and planning the right strategies to cover off every aspect of project and network management, were key to the success of the show," commented Ms. Dynes.

For instance, to manage network volume, Bell created key messages for CTV to publicize prior to the broadcast through regional media, as well as live during the show, advising viewers on how to maximize the likelihood of their votes going through. This included instructions such as wait for dial tone; use a cell phone for toll-free or text messaging; and avoid calling during peak periods. CTV also used other vehicles such as its Web site, discussion board, and Bell operators to communicate its key messages about voting. These actions not only supported the high performance of Bell's network, but also benefited regional service providers by redistributing cell phone calls and text message votes processed to available networks.

Bell's commitment to the project extended from its team of network professionals to the president of operations for Bell Canada. Each week, this group worked with CTV to monitor the performance of the national network. It acted quickly and decisively when contingency plans needed to be put in place to maintain essential telecommunications links.

Challenging the Idea of What's Possible

From a network perspective, the success of *Canadian Idol* was largely due to three important factors: technological innovations that enabled Bell to manage the largest call volume in Canadian history; cooperation between the major Canadian telecommunication providers that resulted in a seamless, high performance national network; and proactive communication to encourage viewers to use a variety of voting methods and tactics to log votes.

"We are excited to have collaborated with CTV to deliver a scalable, national network capable of handling over three million calls in two hours," said David Southwell, President, Network Operations at Bell Canada. "The success of *Canadian Idol* is a powerful example of how we work with customers to apply technological innovation and creative thinking to their business problems, challenging the idea of what's possible."

You may have watched *Canadian Idol* or even voted for your favourite singer using text messaging. You now have insight into what it takes to make this type of business product, in this case a TV show, a reality. Did you recognize some of the technology factors: bandwidth, voting database, audit capabilities? Did you see that this endeavour was managed as a project involving a highly diverse team of business professionals, including wireless telecommunications competitors and vice-presidents? Do you understand how this program created revenue and business value for all of the partners involved? CTV gained ratings and was able to sell premium advertising, and all of the wireless providers gained revenue from increased network usage. This is just one example of applying your new knowledge!

Now consider the many phenomena that are a part of our culture that didn't exist only a few short years ago: blogging, Google, MySpace, Facebook, YouTube, etc. The entire concept of social computing (such as online connections, profiling, and chatting) is only a decade old, and yet it has changed the way an entire generation interacts with each other. And who can even imagine what the next "big thing" is? Any of these innovations in isolation would be an interesting enough study about how technology affects society; but all of them together and over such a short period of time is a form of revolution rather than evolution!

FINAL THOUGHTS

One of the most powerful concepts that we keep returning to in our professional and academic lives is the power of properly combining and balancing people, processes, and technology to achieve productivity in organizations. It might help you to think of this concept in terms of this diagram from Chapter 1.

We hope this book has helped you realize the power of this simple concept. Many of those profiled in our Voice of Experience sections spoke about the need to remain on top of technology to master its use in business. We hope they have convinced you of its importance as you progress in your career. If your knowledge of technology now includes how to make yourself and others more productive, and how to ensure business processes run more smoothly in your organizations, then we have accomplished what we set out to do. Good luck!

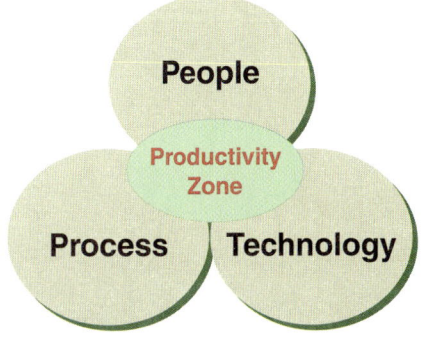

TECH GUIDE A

YOUR ICT CAREER GUIDE

WHAT WE WILL COVER

- Career Trends in ICT
- Career Basics for Resumés and Interviews
- Starting Your Career in ICT
- Your Career: The Big Picture

STUDENT RETURN ON INVESTMENT

Through your investment of time in reading and thinking about this Tech Guide, your return—or created value—is gaining knowledge. Use the following questions as a study guide.

1. What should I expect in my ICT career?
2. Are ICT skills currently in demand?
3. How do I prepare for an ICT career?
4. How do I find a job?
5. What should I expect when I start working in ICT?
6. How will my ICT career change in the future and how should I prepare?

A special thanks to Professor Ron Babin of Ryerson University for authoring this Tech Guide.

Welcome to the rest of your life! As you read this guide, hopefully you will contemplate, plan, and then take action on your career in **information and communication technologies (ICT)**. This is a short guide, but yours will be a long career.

This guide is written for those in the early stages of an ICT career. Right now you're completing your post-secondary studies, but soon you'll be in your first job and wondering how to move on and up. You need to understand where your ICT career can lead and how you can get there.

Your career is *your* career; parents, teachers, friends, and others should not and cannot take responsibility your career. That's why you are reading this guide—it's for you, and for your career. You will make many investments in your lifetime, but what you decide to do for a living will be one of the most important decisions.

Career management is a relatively new concept. For centuries people rarely had the opportunity to choose what they did for a living; they were born into a life that was predestined. In previous centuries, if your father was a farmer, you became a farmer. Your career may have been defined as a wife and mother, raising children and supporting the family. In some societies this career model may still hold true: you don't choose your career, you are born into it. Fortunately for those living in Canada in the current millennium, you can choose what you want to do, and where and how you want to work. Remember, your career is your own.

This career guide starts with a discussion of career trends, examining the ebb and flow in the supply and demand for ICT workers around the world. We then discuss career basics, essentials everyone should know and practise. In the next section we explore what you should expect as you begin your first job in your ICT career. In the final section we paint the big career picture that many of you will live with for several decades.

CAREER TRENDS IN ICT
Who Are You? Baby Boomers and the Millennial Generation

Most of the world was engulfed in a war that was fought between 1939 and 1945. After the war, troops came home and began families in earnest, resulting in what we know as the Baby Boom. This surge in births happened in Canada from about the mid-1940s to the mid-1960s. The **baby boomers**, or simply *boomers*, altered the landscape of society, first straining the education system with their vast numbers, and then fuelling economic growth as they began families, bought houses and cars, and much more.

Fast-forward to the current century. Boomers are now in their 50s and 60s. They are retiring from their careers of 30 to 40 years, leaving a huge gap in the workforce—especially those with ICT skills and knowledge. This gap is a wonderful opportunity for the next generation beginning their ICT careers.

The children of the boomers who were born in the 1980s and 1990s are sometimes referred to as the **millennial generation** because they came of age and joined the workforce in the new millennium, 2000 and beyond. This generation, also known as Generation Y (Gen Y), or the NetGeneration, is as different from their boomer parents as that generation was from the one that fought World War II. Gen Y has grown up with always-on, always-available Internet, personal computers, mobile phones, and many technological innovations that were unimaginable a few years ago. Who could have predicted iTunes, Facebook, and Twitter?

What does this mean for you and your career? A lot! First, those who choose an ICT career will find many opportunities as boomers retire from the workforce. A 2008 study in Canada predicted that over 100,000 jobs will be available by 2012 due to retirements and the ongoing growth of ICT jobs.[1] Second, with an understanding of technology that began at about age four, Gen Y workers bring creative ideas and expectations to the ICT workforce that can result in innovative new products and services. Organizations recognize this creativity and compete to hire Gen Y ICT people. If you decide on an ICT career, you are fortunate to be at the right place at the right time. You have work to do in preparing and managing your ICT career, but there are certainly many career opportunities for you into the foreseeable future.

The Need for ICT Professionals

The first decade of the 21st century was a rough ride. It began with the technology stock meltdown as overpriced technology stocks were devalued and Internet start-ups disappeared. However, many survived and have gone on to become some of today's largest global companies. We now have a hyper-connected world where it is cheaper to call or email halfway around the world than it is to buy a cup of coffee!

A major trend that became evident after society became disillusioned with unfulfilled promises of technology, is the decline in ICT student enrolment at colleges and universities throughout North America, Europe, and Australia. Some programs saw a 40 percent to 50 percent decline in new enrolments beginning in 2003-04.[2] Most programs of study require about four years for an undergraduate degree, so by 2008 we began to see a smaller number of ICT graduates entering the workforce. Gen Y has avoided the ICT career, just as the ICT boomers are getting ready to retire. This has created a wonderful opportunity for those who choose ICT as a career. Chief information officers (CIOs) continue to report overwhelmingly that ICT professionals are hard to find, hire, and keep.

And yet, ICT is vitally important to the economy, and will continue to be for the future economy. Here are some facts:[3]

- The ICT industry plus ICT professionals in other industries comprise nearly 1.1 million workers. More people work in IT than in agriculture, forestry, fishing, mining, oil and gas, utilities, and the transportation industry (including auto manufacturing) combined.
- Of that number, over 600,000 are ICT professionals.
- Canada's ICT industries alone contribute $140 billion to the country's GDP.
- From 2002 to 2007, the ICT sector grew by an average of 5.1 percent annually, compared with only 2.7 percent for the overall Canadian economy.

CIOs continue to look globally for ICT talent. Outsourcing—subcontracting a service or business function to an external service provider—has become a standard

---

1. The Conference Board of Canada, "Securing Our Future: Components of a Comprehensive IT Workforce Development Strategy," January 2008, http://www.ccict.ca/pdfs/Reports_briefs/Securing%20our%20Future%20-%20Final%20report%20-%20January%2022%202008.pdf. Retrieved April 22, 2010.

2. See Ron Babin, Kenneth A. Grant, and Lea Sawal, "Identifying Influences in High School Student ICT Career Choice," In *The Proceedings of IS Education Conference*, 2008, http://proc.isecon.org/2008/2323/index.html. Retrieved April 22, 2010.

3. http://www.ccict.ca/challenge.html. Retrieved April 18, 2010.

business practice to acquire strong talent pools and low cost providers. CIOs and their organizations routinely consider outsourcing because of the lack of local ICT talent and the economic advantages of hiring high quality, low cost talent in distant locations. The impact of fewer ICT graduates, a retiring ICT workforce, and the ability to communicate anywhere at a very low cost has created a "flat world," where programmers in Hyderabad now compete with the software developers in Halifax. Global sourcing of ICT will continue to grow as new regions such as China, Brazil, and Russia begin to compete with India. However, we continue to hear about outsourcing that fails because of poor management or lack of communication. In spite of this, there will be ongoing global competition for entry-level positions, and the pay will be low.

The set of ICT skills required in the coming decades, in your career horizon, will be markedly different from the previous generation. The skills will be less oriented toward programming and computer operations, which can be delivered from anywhere on the global Internet. Skills such as project management, requirements analysis, and systems research and design will be in high demand in Europe and North America. The key skill will be the ability to integrate ICT capabilities to deliver value to business organizations. Outsourcing will alter the ICT skills in demand, and may actually increase the need for higher value ICT skills.

In Canada, industry leaders have taken action to address the growing need for ICT skills. The **Canadian Coalition for Tomorrow's ICT Skills (CCICT)** represents over 20 of the largest ICT employers in Canada. The following describes the ICT skills challenge as described by CCICT:[4]

> *The challenge is this: Employers across Canada cannot find the ICT professionals that they need—even in the midst of the recession. . . . In every region of the country, employers can't find enough qualified business-IT professionals. . . . Deep specialized IT-skilled technologists are critical to innovation and productivity in every industry as we reinvent the economy for the post-recession 21st century.*

David Ticoll, executive director of the CCICT, believes that ICT jobs will continue to proliferate in our society.

David Ticoll, executive director of the CCICT, has described the new ICT career environment as **Jobs 2.0**.[5] He says, "ICT skills will continue to proliferate and seep into ever more dimensions of business and consumer life, and competition will force Canadian firms to close the ICT investment gap." Ticoll says the career profile will change and will focus on innovation, with new jobs such as business-IT leader/advisor, and business IT specialist. The Coalition launched an education initiative in 2009

---

4. http://www.ccict.ca.

5. David Ticoll, "ICTS Jobs 2.0: How Canada Can Win in the 21st Century Global Marketplace for Information and Communications Technologies and Services (ICTS)," *Developing Tomorrow's Workforce Today*, Information and Communications Technology Council, March 2007.

to encourage high school students to consider ICT careers, with an ICT degree that several Canadian universities will call the Business Technology Management (BTM) program.

Recent data from Robert Half Technologies regarding ICT jobs in Canada[6] reinforces the message of a limited supply of ICT graduates. Here's an extract from the 2009 Hiring Outlook for Information Technology in Canada:

> IT unemployment remains low relative to many other occupations, driven by the increasing complexity and proliferation of new technology and the need for professionals to support Web 2.0 initiatives to enhance creativity, collaboration and functionality on the Web. . . . A smaller pool of highly skilled candidates for technology positions, coupled with fewer college graduates with IT-related degrees, is making it difficult for employers to hire and retain individuals within many specialties.[7]

Clearly, employers are constantly looking for employable graduates with fresh technology skills. If you are graduating with an ICT degree or diploma, you have the right stuff; you now need to market yourself.

Quick Test

1. True or False. Baby boomers are not having any significant impact on ICT today.

2. The ICT industry is growing by an average annual rate of 5.1 percent, which is
   a. slower than the overall Canadian economy
   b. faster than the overall Canadian economy
   c. the same as the overall Canadian economy

3. Fill in the blank. CCICT describes the ICT _____ as the fact that employers across Canada cannot find the ICT professionals they need.

Answers: 1. False; 2. b; 3. challenge

CAREER BASICS FOR RESUMÉS AND INTERVIEWS

As a student reading this, you may be thinking "I'm too young to start planning my career!" or, "How can I begin an ICT career when I have no experience?"

Rest assured, it is never too early to begin planning your career. Most people start working when they finish their undergraduate degree. Some go on to additional education, but often after some work experience. As a professional in ICT, you should develop skills and acquire experience throughout your life, because ICT is constantly changing. Think of Moore's Law, which was discussed in Chapter 1. Gordon Moore,

---

6. From http://www.roberthalftechnology.com/HiringInCanada. Retrieved December 1, 2009.

7. Robert Half Technology, 2009 Robert Half Salary Guides Identify Job Market Bright Spots, news release, October 23, 2008. http://rht.mediaroom.com/index.php?s=131&item=137

who co-founded Intel, suggested that the number of transistors we can fit on a chip will double about every two years. This law is generally accepted within the high-tech industry to illustrate that computers get drastically better each year.

This section will help you learn how to structure information about yourself, and how to present that information (you) to prospective employers.

What Is a Resumé?

In its simplest form, your **resumé** is a short summary of you. Think of the resumé as a one- or two-page summary of the skills and experience that you have acquired, and how those skills and experiences will be valuable to your next employer or client.

We won't go into the mechanics of how to write a resumé in this Tech Guide. There are several good online sources available to you, a sample of which is provided in Table A.1. Additionally, your university or college career centre will help you prepare your resumé and can suggest several models or examples to get you started. Your resumé is important, but even more important is the process and planning required to prepare your resumé.

Your resumé is the cornerstone of your career. Potential employers will ask for a copy of your resumé, and you should have different versions to use in different situations. You should prepare or update your resumé whenever you search for a job. You might also prepare a resumé when you are planning for future jobs or career paths. A resumé is never static; as long as you continue to learn and develop your skills, your resumé needs to be updated.

Your resumé should have four sections. The first is simple—your name and contact details. Another section lists your education, including formal degrees and diplomas as well as ongoing professional development. The third section describes your experience in a logical fashion that paints a picture of a progressively developed ICT professional career. The final section describes your accomplishments, contributions, and involvement in your community.

Your Education Education is the foundation of your resumé. You will be hired for the skills you acquired in part as a result of your education. An employer will ask "What can you do for me?" and your resumé answers that question. Education is the easiest part of the resumé to prepare. Usually you complete your foundation education early in your career, obtaining a degree or diploma in your 20s. As an ICT professional, you should constantly upgrade your skills with continuing education.

Table A.1	Resumé Writing Help
Website	**Services Provided**
www.e-resume.net	A wealth of information on resumés under the "Your Resumé" tab
http://career-advice.monster.ca	Resumé and cover letter writing tips Samples of resumés
http://hotjobs.yahoo.com/resume	Numerous articles on resumé basics and cover letters Tips on how to format your resumé
www.bestsampleresume.com	Sample resumés from various professions Tips for writing a resumé

This involves completing additional certificates, attending professional conferences and seminars, teaching, writing articles, and/or giving presentations. These all provide tangible evidence to an employer of your commitment to your skills, and these all contribute to your knowledge and your ability to work in ICT.

Your Experience Experience, especially as you progress in your ICT career, will open career doors for you after you establish your education foundation. We all get older. Some of us build our career experience by progressing from junior roles to levels of more responsibility that require more skill and knowledge, resulting in higher salaries. This progression is often referred to as moving up the **career ladder**. Generally you earn more money as you progress in your career. However, some people do not build their experience; they either rest in one level too long (plateau), or they bounce about with disconnected experiences that are not focused (e.g., a bartender, a call centre clerk, a Web designer, a chef, etc.). A goal for your resumé, and your career, is to develop a set of experiences that fit together, build on each other, are focused, and have a common ICT theme. This starts with your initial career experiences in school, then continues after graduation and throughout your career.

Your resumé should describe how you acquired and developed your ICT skills, through your experience. In its simplest form, your resumé contains a list of the jobs you've had since you left school. But it should describe much more than that: it should convey what you have learned, how you developed your skills and knowledge, and how you can apply those skills to help any potential employer or client. Your list of work experience must be factual, with accurate dates, titles, and employer/client information. When describing your work and responsibilities, present the information as a narrative. Describe your accomplishments, including how you improved the work environment or solved a problem. Outline how a role or job helped you to grow, and describe how the experience is relevant to your overall career.

A well-described set of experiences that are linked together in a rational ICT theme along with your education will make your resumé shine. Next, let's look at how you should present your broader self.

Being a Well-Rounded Person Employers tell us repeatedly that they want smart people with good experience. Further, they say that they prefer to hire well-rounded people rather than hiring the very brightest. In the ICT profession we sometimes find that the very brightest may have limited social skills. So your resumé must also describe how you are more than just a smart, experienced person.

But what is a *well-rounded person*? It is someone who participates in, gets involved with, and contributes to the community. What is your community? It's where you live, go to school, have friends, and play. For example, your college or university is a community. Your sports team is a community. Perhaps you are an artist or a musician, or you enjoy hiking or skiing. Participating in these activities may make you part of a community. Being well-rounded comes from participating in something more than going to school or work, and from getting involved in your community. Your resumé should show that you have interests and skills beyond your education and career. These make you more likely to have developed interpersonal skills—the ability to work well with others—that will help in the work community that you join.

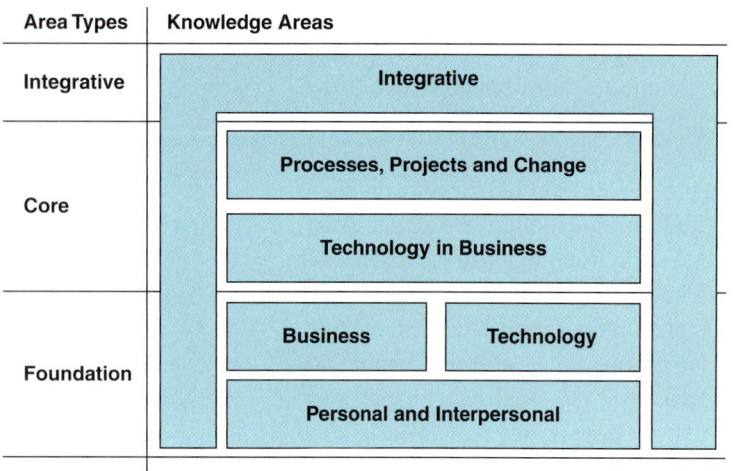

FIGURE A.1 Business Technology Management (BTM) learning outcomes and competency standards.
SOURCE: Canadian Coalition for Tomorrow's ICT Skills, *http://www.ccict.ca/btm.html*.

The Skills You Need In Canada, employers created CCICT with the goal of encouraging young people to consider careers in ICT. The companies, such as Bell Canada, RIM, and BMO Financial Group, recognized that a looming shortage of qualified ICT professionals will be a key challenge for their business in Canada and North America. CCICT defined a set of skills that they expect to find in graduates of ICT programs. Figure A.1 outlines the expected outcomes for ICT programs at educational institutions across Canada.

The **foundation skills** begin with personal and interpersonal skills. Employers look for communication skills, time management skills, personal motivation, an ability to deal with personal set-backs and challenges, and an ability to learn and develop. The second and third foundation skills are the ability to understand business concepts and related business technologies. The **core skill** requirements consist of the ability to apply technology in a business environment and the ability to manage business processes, projects, and change. The **integrative skill** set is the ability to combine all these skills together and provide an appropriate business/technology solution that is relevant and realistic for a given business situation.

Your Network: It's Who You Know and What You Know

Have you heard about **networking** and how people get job opportunities from friends? It's true: it's not just *what* you know (skills and experience), it's also *who* you know. Connecting with friends and allies is the best way to learn of career opportunities and to introduce yourself to prospective employers and clients. The majority of job openings are never advertised, but are filled through word-of-mouth from friends and acquaintances. There are many ways to network; we describe two.

Join a Professional Network The ICT profession has many professional groups that welcome student participants. Professional organizations allow you to learn and develop your skills and provide a natural forum for meeting people and networking. Some organizations to consider include:

- Association for Information Systems (AIS)
- Association of Information Technology Professionals (AITP)
- Certified Management Consultants (CMC)
- IT Association of Canada (ITAC)
- Society for Information Management (SIM)
- Canadian Information Processing Society (CIPS)
- Women in Technology (WIT)

Conduct Information Interviews A common technique for learning more about a company, and potential job opportunities, is the **information interview**. Through a company directory or professional organization you can find out the names or positions of senior ICT staff. Ask to meet with them (perhaps offer to buy a cup of coffee) and discuss careers and career paths. Everyone in a senior position was once where you are now, just starting out in the business. Following are some questions that you might consider asking in your information interview:

- Tell me how you came to be an employee (manager, executive) at this organization.
- What do you enjoy most about your career?
- What advice would you give to a young person starting an ICT career in terms of . . .
  - education?
  - interpersonal skills?
  - industry experience?
  - travel and relocation?
  - work–life balance?
- What personal qualifications or characteristics does your organization look for in candidates?
- Are there others in this field that you would suggest I speak with? Would you introduce me to them?

Keep in mind that this is not a job interview, but you should have a current version of your resumé with you in case you are asked for one. Many jobs are found through word-of-mouth and informal personal networks. Often an opportunity is found by simply being in the right place at the right time.

On-Campus Recruiting

Major companies, such as Accenture, Canadian Tire, Bell, Microsoft, and others, regularly visit university and college campuses to recruit new ICT graduates. They know that the best and brightest will have multiple job opportunities, and each company encourages the graduates to accept *their* job offer.

The cycle begins in the fall, focusing on students in their final year. Usually human resources (HR) staff will introduce their company with an information session. It's a good idea to attend as many sessions as possible to find out as much as you can to properly compare potential employers. The online job application process takes place from October to December (check for cut-off dates). HR staff sort through hundreds of applications and then invite a short list of applicants in for an initial interview. In some cases, the employer may come to campus to conduct interviews. Second round interviews take place in November or December, and job offers are sent out in December or January (or later) for employment starting after graduation.

As you can see, this cycle takes almost a full year from the initial information session to the new employee beginning a job. These large organizations put a lot of energy and time into recruiting ICT students, again recognizing the limited talent pool and the large number of job openings. But what if you don't want to work for a large company?

Finding Your Niche Many organizations need ICT professionals. Some of the large traditional ICT employers use the well-oiled hiring process described above. But ICT is ubiquitous, allowing you more freedom to choose the industry and type of ICT job that you want. For example, health care will see increasing demand for skilled ICT workers. ICT opportunities are on the rise in managing utilities companies, especially as related to environmental issues. The entertainment industry, with online video and interactive games, will continue to grow and offer ICT employment opportunities. The not-for-profit sector offers the chance to use ICT skills in social development or community causes. One example is NetHope, which provides global ICT services to non-governmental organizations (NGOs) around the world with aid projects in developing nations:[8]

> NetHope began as an informal collaboration and now operates as a non-profit corporation governed by its member NGOs. Our members have well-established ICT (information and communications technology) departments that use technology strategically to support their programs.

And all levels of government have increasing opportunities for ICT graduates, since the bulk of their services rely heavily on information.

The key is to find the organization that fits with your personality, your goals, and your aspirations. For example, banks can offer a secure and financially rewarding career, or you may prefer the adrenaline rush of a start-up Internet company with venture capital investors. You may prefer the creative innovation of software development, or perhaps you prefer high-contact ICT sales and marketing roles. A career evaluation may help you focus on the type of company or in what area of ICT you want to work. Table A.2 lists a few websites that can help you better understand your preferences.

Interview Etiquette

If your resumé is a short advertisement or FAQ about you, the interview is a test-drive. If you are successful with networking, with on-campus recruiting, or with simply directly applying for a job with your preferred organization, then someone

Table A.2	Evaluating Your Career Direction and Preferences
Website	Services Provided
www.nextsteps.org/career/index.html	A career planning website that allows you to find out who you are and what you're best suited to do. The site also provides other information on job searching and career maintenance.
www.careerjoy.com	A career counselling service that helps you figure out what job is best for you. There is also a free career test you can take.
www.servicecanada.gc.ca/eng/home.shtml	Service Canada offers a wealth of information on finding a job (choose "Finding a Job" under Life Events in the left navigation bar), including a job bank.

[8]. http://www.nethope.org

at that organization will want to meet you. This section provides some tips on job interview etiquette.

First things first: know the organization. Before you send in your resumé, before you call anyone, and certainly before you meet anyone at the organization where you may someday be employed, you must learn everything you can about that organization. Why? Because the information is almost always available on the Internet, and whoever you meet will expect you to have read about their organization. You make a good impression when you can ask about recent events at the organization. At some point during the interview you will likely be asked a question such as, "What do you find most interesting about our organization and why do you want to work with us instead of our competitor?" You need to be able to respond with something better than "I need a paycheque" or "You have a nice building." Tell the interviewer good things about the company that you read on the website.

Dress and prepare for success; first impressions are key. Your eye contact, handshake, and how you're dressed—everything that interviewers see, hear, and sense—create an impression of you as a prospective hire. One report states that 58 percent of hiring managers take less than 15 minutes to decide whether to hire the candidate, and half of the decision to hire is based on "chemistry." So, leave nothing to chance. Prepare for success by preparing your wardrobe, your presentation, even your handshake and greeting. This is an audition and you are the star.

After the interview, regardless of how it went, thank the interviewer for his or her time with a simple email or a thank you card sent by old-fashioned postal delivery. You may not get the job this time, but leaving a good impression always helps. There may be additional hiring needs in the near future, or perhaps the top candidate will decline the job offer. You want the prospective employer to remember you for the next opportunity.

If you are successful, you will likely go through several interviews. The first interview may be with someone in HR. Then you may meet the person you could work for, and probably several people in your possible work group. It is quite normal to have at least three interviews before you receive an employment offer. These may seem repetitive to you, answering the same questions many times, but the employer wants a comprehensive view of you. Employers are prepared to invest a lot of time and energy selecting the right person, and you should invest the time and energy in demonstrating that you are the right person. Finally, the interview process is your opportunity to learn about the company you may join. Now is the time to ask questions about their expectations regarding work, pay, training, and so on. You should be comfortable that when and if you receive an employment offer, you understand the organization and the people you will work with.

QUICK TEST

1. Design your resumé to _____.
    a. provide enough information to encourage the reader to interview you
    b. demonstrate the depth of your technical knowledge and skills
    c. demonstrate your artistic presentation capabilities

2. Before an interview, you should research the organization that you would like to work for _____.
   a. to confirm they are looking to hire new employees
   b. to learn about the nature of the organization and the work
   c. to demonstrate an interest in your potential employer
   d. All of the above

3. Interpersonal skills include _____.
   a. business acumen, financial understanding, and time management
   b. the ability to work with other team members
   c. communication, time management, and personal motivation

Answers: 1. a; 2. d; 3. b

STARTING YOUR CAREER IN ICT

Your first job is often the toughest. You are likely joining the workforce on a full-time basis for the first time in your life. Many of you will have been in school more or less full-time for 16 years or more, or about 75 percent of your life. Starting your career is a new experience.

A four-month summer break is no longer the norm. As the junior person, you will have a minimal vacation break (two or three weeks). Everything will be new and different. The people you work with will have different lifestyles and priorities, while you may still be living in student mode. You will earn a full-time paycheque, but your expenses will be high as you begin to pay full employment taxes and you start making big purchases (e.g., car, furniture, travel) that you could not afford when you were a student. For some, you will now start repaying student loans.

An ICT career can be demanding; there is much to learn and then re-learn since ICT constantly changes. In addition, we all face the work–life challenge: getting up for work on Monday, commuting, dealing with deadlines, and so on. Your first few career years will be an opportunity to develop your reputation and personal brand. You want people to know you and respect you in a positive way. The actions you take as the "newbie" will set the tone for your reputation. For example, you should

- be known for integrity, reliability, and quality
- volunteer for new work, showing that you are willing to contribute
- respectfully suggest innovative and fresh ideas
- communicate clearly and professionally with your colleagues
- help others get accustomed to the new work environment

Establishing your reputation early in your career will help you in the long run. ICT is a profession that continues to grow rapidly and change constantly. People you work with now will remember you and your early reputation as you move forward in this rapidly changing profession. You want to be remembered as a professional.

Show Me the Money

ICT careers pay well. Industry Canada reported that ICT employees earned, on average, $61,971 in 2008, or 47 percent more than the economy-wide average of $42,143. Workers in the software and computer services sector earn the highest average, at $68,126. Industry Canada also reported that ICT employment continues to grow at 2.8 percent per year, with low unemployment.[9] According to IT World Canada, the average IT manager in Canada makes more than $80,000 a year.[10]

A survey of students graduating from Ryerson University's Information Technology Management program found that starting salaries ranged from $35,000 to $55,000 per year. Students with more experience (e.g., co-op students) attained starting salaries of over $60,000.[11] These are salaries for students in Toronto, and similar ranges might also apply in Vancouver and Montreal. For smaller cities, such as Halifax, Winnipeg, or Edmonton, starting salary ranges may be lower.

At the upper end, chief information officers (CIOs) earn well over $100,000. The CIO Association of Canada (CIOCAN) reported that its members had an average base salary of $155,000. Interestingly, among the 18 percent of respondents who were women, the average base salary was $156,000. When bonuses were factored in, women still came out ahead, at $189,000 on average compared to $186,000 for men. At the very high end, Canadian CIOs in mining and financial services tended to have the highest salaries, at $285,000 and $247,000, respectively.[12]

YOUR CAREER: THE BIG PICTURE

One certainty in ICT is continual change. Moore's Law ensures that ICT affordability and power will continue to increase, and that we will see ongoing innovation of products and services using ICT. The knowledge that you gain in your post-secondary education will need to be replenished multiple times throughout your career, which means that you will need to continually learn as the ICT industry changes.

A significant current shift is the move to a stronger integration of ICT and business. Many of the technology components that were once standalone, fragmented, and unreliable are being completely integrated with business processes and are highly reliable. The common notebook computer is now the personal computer of choice, while only 15 years ago it was costly and not very reliable. Enterprise systems have integrated most business processes both within and beyond an organization.

David Ticoll describes these jobs as focused on innovation and on the application of technology, and less on building or operating the technology. ICT professionals "'package' business knowledge, communications skills, leadership, project management, interpersonal effectiveness . . . essentially client and general management capabilities with an ICTS flavour."[13] He refers to an "Industry-IT Specialist . . . [with] subject-specific business knowledge, combined with applicable ICTS skills,

---

9. Canadian ICT Sector Profile, Information and Communications Technologies Branch, Industry Canada, August 2009.
10. http://www.itworld.com. Retrieved April 22, 2010.
11. Personal communication with Ken Grant, Director of the Ted Rogers School of IT Management, Ryerson University.
12. CIO Association of Canada, "Women CIOs Out-earn Men," news release, July 14, 2009.
13. David Ticoll, "ICTS Jobs 2.0: How Canada Can Win in the 21st Century Global Marketplace for Information and Communications Technologies and Services (ICTS)," *Developing Tomorrow's Workforce Today*, Information and Communications Technology Council, March 2007.

in a domain where a Canada-based IT/business process services centre of excellence,"[14] such as financial services, electrical utilities, and insurance. For Ticoll, ICT skills are most relevant when applied to a business or organizational context.

Table A.3 presents a list of ICT occupation profiles created by the **Information and Communications Technology Council (ICTC)**, which is funded in part by the Government of Canada's Sector Council Program. According to the ICTC website, the program "works to enable partnerships that address skills and human resource issues by establishing, developing, and supporting national partnerships and the capacity of partners to address both pressing and emerging skills and human resource issues."[15]

On their website, ICTC describes the jobs as they are practised in industry today. This does not guarantee that all of the ICT jobs will continue to be viable into the future. Many years ago, people trained for careers as key-punch and computer operators, jobs that are obsolete today. ICT jobs change and some will become obsolete over your career timeframe, so you need to be flexible and change too. One of the most interesting aspects of an ICT career is constant change, usually brought about by quickly evolving technology. However, you need to constantly change as well, adapting and developing your skills, capabilities, and career to stay current with the technology.

Table A.3	ICTC Career Clusters and Work Streams
Career Cluster	**Work Stream**
Software products	Analysis Design
	Analysis Programming
	Application Software
	Business Analysis and Service Level Management
	Programming
	Software Design and Delivery (Engineering)
	Technical ICT Architecture
	Web Design
	Web Development
Infrastructure	Data Administration
	Database Administration
	Capacity and Performance
	Help Desk
	Network Planning and Support
	Operations
	Problem Management
	Security
	Systems Programming
	User Technical Support

---

14. Ibid.

15. http://www.ictc-ctic.ca/en/content.aspx?id=404. Retrieved April 18, 2010.

Management	ICT Management
	Intellectual Property Management
	Production Management
	Project Management
	Supply Chain Management
	ICT Consultancy
Hardware Products	Design Engineering
	Hardware Scientist
	Manufacturing Engineering
	Product Line Management
	Technical Marketing
Testing/Quality Control	Audit
	Validation
	Quality Assurance
	Quality Professional
Documentation and Training	Education/Training Management
	Technical Writing

SOURCE: ICT Competency Profiles: A Framework for Developing Tomorrow's ICT Workforce, ©2009 Information and Communications Technology Council Inc.

The core competencies that apply to all work streams are analytical thinking, information management, and relationship building. Other competencies that apply to several streams are decision making, leadership, writing skills, and project management. For full details, visit the ICTC website at *www.ictc-ctic.ca*.

Your Career Journey: Going the Distance

A long career in ICT can take many paths. Some of you will spend your entire career in one industry, such as banking, retail, or government. Some may spend your entire career in one organization, although this has become increasingly rare. Some of you will become entrepreneurs, perhaps starting one or more ICT companies (remember when Google was just another start-up?).

Although your earning potential in ICT is good to great, you must continue to invest in your ICT skills. Consultant David Maister describes a business professional as a company, with an income statement and a balance sheet.[16] Your income statement measures your annual earnings, usually your paycheque. A balance sheet has assets and liabilities. Your assets consist of ICT knowledge, skills, and experience. Unfortunately, these assets depreciate over time, and must be replenished over the lifetime of your career. All companies must reinvest to remain competitive, and so should you.

The ICT career has many professional paths. If you enjoy project management, you should consider the Project Management Professional (PMP) designation from the Project Management Institute (PMI). If your skills are more toward business or systems analysis, you should join the International Institute of Business Analysts and attain the Certified Business Analyst Professional (CBAP) designation.

---

16. See http://davidmaister.com.

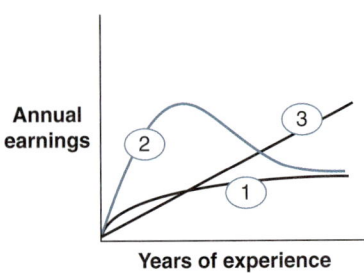

FIGURE A.2 Career salary paths.

Begin with the end in mind. As you start your ICT career you can expect interesting, fulfilling, and rewarding work over many decades. Continually invest in your technical and managerial skills and you will be well rewarded.

If technology attracts you, consider attaining certification in popular technologies such as Cisco Systems communications, Microsoft operating systems, or SAP enterprise resource planning software. You may find that your employer will pay for your certification, either partially or fully, since this will enhance your skills and ability on the job.

As you progress in the ICT field you will likely take on more leadership and managerial roles. Look for opportunities to demonstrate your ability and interests in this area, and invest in yourself. Most colleges and universities offer continuing and executive education courses in management and leadership, as do professional associations. Again, see if your employer will help to pay for this ongoing education.

A key decision that you will face is the need to decide between a technical path or a managerial path. Figure A.2 depicts three salary paths over a career. The first path plateaus after a few years, so that in the second half of the career, the annual earning increases are small. These people have become specialists in a particular area, and repeat that specialty throughout their career. The second path has an early spike, earning a high annual income, but then decreases to a more reasonable level. This profile is often found in specialty technologies that have a high demand for a short period of time, as was the case with many e-business skills before the dot-com crash. The third path is more balanced, with a steady rise throughout the career. This usually reflects continual growth and development, often with a growing portion of managerial responsibilities. This path leads to senior ICT roles, perhaps as CIO. Remember, top CIOs earn well over $200,000 annually.

QUICK TEST

1. True or False. ICT professionals are well-compensated.

2. ICTC stands for _____.
   a. International Council for Technology Currency
   b. Information and Communications Technology Council
   c. Information, Communications, and Technologies of Canada
   d. Information and Communications Technology Corporation

3. Fill in the blank. Analytical skills, information management, and relationship building are some of the _____ that apply to all ICT work streams.

Answers: 1. True; 2. b; 3. core competencies

ROI STUDENT RETURN ON INVESTMENT SUMMARY

1. What should I expect in my ICT career?
Change will be a constant in your ICT career because technology is always evolving. New applications are being created through innovative use of information technology. Some ICT skills are becoming commodities that can be delivered from anywhere in the world. A programmer from Hyderabad competes with someone from Halifax, at a lower cost. In your ICT career you should expect to blend technology and business concepts to provide more than a technology solution.

2. Are ICT skills currently in demand?

As the current ICT workforce retires in the coming years there will be ample opportunities for new graduates to enter the ICT workforce. Because of low college enrolments in ICT programs there will be a shortage of skilled ICT professionals, resulting in a healthy demand for ICT professionals for many years into the future. ICT employment continues to grow at 2 percent to 3 percent and ICT compensation is above industry average.

3. How do I prepare for an ICT career?

Your education is the best starting point, with a degree or certificate from a recognized post-secondary institution such as a college or a university. Be prepared to constantly learn new technologies and concepts. Develop your interpersonal capabilities beyond technology. Get involved in your community.

4. How do I find a job?

Begin while you are at school. Write your resumé and then add to it with work experience, academic achievements, and community involvement. Attend and participate in on-campus career sessions with firms that are hiring. Work through your network of contacts to find opportunities to meet senior ICT professionals for information interviews. Monitor and apply to Internet career postings.

5. What should I expect when I start working in ICT?

The career transition from school to the permanent workforce is challenging. Begin your career by building a reputation for being trustworthy, punctual, creative, and a team player. Develop your career with consistent steps that build on each other, like steps on a ladder. Build your network of contacts by participating in industry events.

6. How will my ICT career change in the future and how should I prepare?

ICT changes rapidly and you should expect to continually learn new concepts to prepare for future ICT opportunities. More work will move offshore, but more work will be created onshore in the application of technologies to business. Join a professional organization and participate in industry events to continually learn about new technologies and concepts.

KNOWLEDGE SPEAK

baby boomer   338
Canadian Coalition for Tomorrow's ICT Skills (CCICT)   340
career ladder   343
core skills   344
foundation skills   344
information and communication technologies (ICT)   338
Information and Communications Technology Council (ICTC)   350
information interview   345
integrative skills   344
Jobs 2.0   340
millennial generation   338
networking   344
resumé   342

TECH GUIDE B

THE DETAILS OF IT HARDWARE AND SOFTWARE

WHAT WE WILL COVER

- An Overview of Hardware
- Processing Hardware
- Internal Memory
- Input Hardware Devices
- Output Hardware Devices
- Storage Hardware
- An Overview of Operating Software
- An Overview of Application Software

STUDENT RETURN ON INVESTMENT

Through your investment of time in reading and thinking about this Tech Guide. your return—or created value—is gaining knowledge. Use the following questions as a study guide.

1. What elements affect the processing capability of hardware?

2. What types of input, output, and storage hardware should business professionals keep current with?

3. Why is the operating system so important to the use of all types of computers?

4. How do business professionals obtain and use application software?

Hardware is the physical component of information technology (IT). The working parts of IT hardware consist primarily of electronic devices (mostly digital) with some electro-mechanical parts used with input, output, and storage devices. *Software* provides the instructions that IT hardware needs. The two major categories of software are operating system software and application software. Except in special situations, both software types run at the same time, each serving a different purpose.

In this Tech Guide, we provide a more detailed look into commonly available hardware, operating systems, and application software. Much of our discussion will focus on the personal computer (PC), as its architecture includes components common to all information devices and it is the system you are most familiar with. Our objective is to provide you with enough knowledge of the technology to allow you to make savvy decisions.

AN OVERVIEW OF HARDWARE

Entire books are written about certain types of hardware. Here we introduce key concepts concerning hardware and discuss commonly used hardware to give you a basic knowledge of this area of IT.

Evaluating Hardware Devices

If you've ever been to an office supply store such as Staples or Office Depot, or an electronics store like Future Shop or Best Buy, you'll know that selecting the right IT devices can be an overwhelming decision. How do you know which ones will serve you best now and in the future? These decisions often include evaluating the following factors:

- *Cost*—You want the device to be within your budget and to provide the most value for each dollar you spend.
- *Compatibility*—Hardware devices work together to form a system. Each device needs to work correctly with the other devices.
- *Data and Information Needs*—You choose devices based on a desired task. You need your IT devices to work with data and/or information in a specific way.
- *Accuracy*—You rely on your devices to handle data and instructions without errors.
- *Speed*—You would like to work with your data and instructions as quickly and efficiently as possible.
- *Portability*—Because you may want to work with information as you travel, you need to easily move the devices as well.
- *Form Factor*—The size, shape, and physical arrangement of IT hardware can affect how and where you use a device.

Some, or all, of these factors influence your selection and use of hardware devices, whether the device concerns processing, memory, input, output, communication, or storage. In this Tech Guide, we will look at various types of hardware devices.

However, before considering many of the types of hardware devices on the market, we first examine the electronics behind them.

The Electronics of Hardware

The primary electronic component of IT hardware is the transistor. A **transistor** is a very small device made out of semiconductor material that acts as a switch to control electronic signals. Millions of transistors, each too small to be seen by the unaided eye, are combined to make the computer's microprocessor and memory chips. Both types of chips are quite small themselves.

Microprocessor chips carry out many different processing operations within a computer, including handling input and output as well as the actual conversion of data into information. Over time, the number of transistors on a microprocessor chip has expanded, resulting in increasingly powerful computers. For example, Intel's popular Core i5 microprocessor chip contains 774 million transistors. Intel chips power the vast majority of all PCs in the world today, including those built by Apple Computer. Microprocessor chips are also built into virtually all electronic devices.

Memory chips also use transistors to store data within the computer. As with microprocessor chips, the amount of internal memory stored on chips has also risen dramatically as more transistors are built into the memory chips.

How Transistors Work Think of a transistor as an electronic switch that can be in one of two states: off or on. You can represent the two states of a transistor using **binary** mathematics, which uses ones (on) and zeros (off). Thus, transistors store and transmit all data in a computer as combinations of 1s and 0s. Data that transistors store as a sequence of discrete symbols from a finite set, like the set {0,1}, are referred to as **digital data**. When you consider technologies like digital cameras or MP3 players, you can bet that the data processed in these devices are represented as binary numbers. Let's take a closer look at binary data.

Binary Data In binary, the basic unit, a **bit**, corresponds to a power of two, or as they say in mathematics, binary is *base 2*. For example, you can use binary to describe the *base 10* decimal number 234 as follows:

$$11101010_2 = 1_{10}*2^7 + 1_{10}*2^6 + 1_{10}*2^5 + 0_{10}*2^4 + 1_{10}*2^3$$
$$+ 0_{10}*2^2 + 1_{10}*2^1 + 0_{10}*2^0$$
$$= 128_{10} + 64_{10} + 32_{10} + 8_{10} + 2_{10} = 234_{10}$$

Similarly, you can convert other binary values to decimal values; and vice versa, you can convert decimal numbers to equivalent binary values simply by taking the decimal number and repeatedly dividing it by two. In each case, the remainder of the division will be 0 or 1. The composite of all such remainders is then the binary equivalent of the decimal number. Let's use the number 234_{10} again. If you take all of the remainders and put them in reverse order from the divisions, you have the corresponding binary number 11101010_2.[1] See Table B.1.

---

1. For an explanation of why this works, see http://en.wikipedia.org/wiki/Binary_numeral_system.

Table B.1	Finding the Binary Equivalent to Decimal Number	
Beginning Number	After Division	Remainder
234	117	0
117	58	1
58	29	0
29	14	1
14	7	0
7	3	1
3	1	1
1	0	1

You may be questioning the usefulness of binary data if they only concern data such as decimal numbers. But many other types of data can also be stored as binary, like the letters and punctuation characters on your keyboard, as well as graphics, music, and videos. How do hardware devices use binary codes to store different types of information? Through character encoding.

Character Encoding Binary codes represent letters and numbers through character encoding. **Character encoding** permits a specific combination of bits to represent each character. Can anyone design his or her own character-encoding scheme? Yes, but that would make it virtually impossible for all types of hardware and software to work together. When software works with a hardware device or when two hardware devices work together, they are said to be compatible. Therefore, independent national or international committees write most schemes, including ASCII, Unicode, and EBCDIC, to ensure IT compatibility.

Standard ASCII The oldest encoding system used on mainframe computers is the *Extended Binary Coded Decimal Interchange Code (EBCDIC)*, which is an eight-bit coding system. For personal computers, the first encoding system was the **Standard ASCII (American Standard Code for Information Interchange)**. Standard ASCII uses seven bits to represent the following: the unaccented letters of the English language, a–z and A–Z; basic punctuation; numbers; space; and some control codes, such as the Enter key. Using binary-to-decimal conversion, the maximum number of characters that standard ASCII can code is $01111111_{binary} + 1_{decimal}$ (for 00000000_{binary}) $= 127_{decimal} + 1_{decimal} = 128_{decimal}$ characters. This limits standard ASCII mostly to English characters and punctuation. However, virtually all computers recognize an extended form of ASCII that uses eight bits to provide 256 characters, thereby adding accented characters from common foreign languages. However, this limit of 256 characters has become a problem with the increasing global use of computers.

Unicode To deal with the increased globalization of business and use of PCs, most IT devices now rely on a more recent standard called **Unicode**, which extends ASCII

Table B.2	Comparison of Coding Schemes—Binary Representations		
Character	EBCDIC	ASCII	Unicode
A	1100 0001	0100 0001	0000 0000 0100 0001
Esc	0010 0111	0001 1011	0000 0000 0001 1011
%	0110 1100	0010 0101	0000 0000 0010 0101
2	1111 0010	0011 0010	0000 0000 0011 0010
π	Not available	Not available	0000 0011 1100 0000
$\frac{2}{3}$	Not available	Not available	0010 0001 0101 0011

by providing a 16-bit character set. Unicode adds eight characters to the extended ASCII eight-bit character assignments to include the characters of the major modern written languages. As with standard and extended ASCII, Unicode is available on virtually all recently manufactured PCs.

Today, virtually all computers can work with all three types of encoding systems. Table B.2 lists some examples of character codes under each of these standards.

Machine Instructions We've seen how a computer can represent numeric and character data, but what about instructions? Hardware devices, such as a computer or PDA, execute instructions as a sequence of binary strings known as **machine instructions**. The sequence used to represent a specific instruction is assigned in a similar manner as that used to assign binary sequences to character data (e.g., the ASCII code). For example, Figure B.1 shows the machine language instructions for a Pentium chip, seen as a series of instructions to sum the digits 1 to 100.

However, there is one significant difference for machine instructions: no default standard exists for how to encode instructions. Instead, this is left up to the manufacturers of microprocessors, which can therefore result in incompatibility between software and hardware. For example, a machine language instruction for an Intel chip will differ from the same instruction on the chips used in larger computers.

The importance of binary mathematics goes beyond the coding of data. You can express most important measures of performance and capacity in computers based on powers of 2. Table B.3 lists some important binary values that you will often encounter when determining hardware capabilities. For example, a **byte** is typically used to represent a character in ASCII, *megabytes* are used to measure the amount of memory in a computer, and *gigabytes* are used to measure the storage on a hard disk.

Instruction	Explanation
10111000 00000000 00000000	Set Total Value to 0
10111001 00000000 01100100	Set Current Value to 100
00000001 11001000	Add Current Value to Total Value
01001001	Subtract 1 from Current Value
01110101 11111011	If Current value is not 0, repeat

FIGURE B.1 The machine language instructions for a Pentium chip.

Table B.3	Important Powers of 2	
Power of 2	Decimal Value	Description
2^3	8	Number of bits in a byte
2^8	256	The number of characters that a byte can code
2^{10}	1024	1 kilobyte (KB)
2^{20}	1,048,576	1 megabyte (MB)
2^{30}	1,073,741,824	1 gigabyte (GB)

Now that you have a basic understanding of the electronics involved in hardware devices, let's look at how they affect processing hardware capabilities.

PROCESSING HARDWARE

At the core of all computing operations is the microprocessor. It contains the majority of the components that make up the **CPU** or **central processing unit**. The CPU works together with memory to control the execution of all instructions and the processing of all data. The CPU is located on the system's **motherboard**, the main circuit board in an electronic device. The motherboard contains the microprocessor as well as other chips and circuits. The motherboard and CPU chip are found in the **system unit**, the box that we often think of as the computer when we look at it.

A computer motherboard is the main circuit board in an electronic device.

Often, the speed and performance of the CPU are the key considerations in determining the processing capability of IT devices. Because it's so vital to IT hardware, let's look at the CPU in more detail.

The CPU

The CPU consists of several components, shown in Figure B.2:

FIGURE B.2 The CPU components, connected by the data bus.

- *Control Unit (CU)*—Performs the following four basic functions: fetch, decode, execute, and store. One time through each of these tasks in a sequence is called a *cycle*.
- *Arithmetic Logic Unit (ALU)*—Executes mathematical and logic calculations. Logic calculations make comparisons between values.
- *Floating Point Unit (FPU)*—Executes mathematical and logic calculations on non-integer values (values that may have a fractional portion after the decimal point).
- *Decode Unit*—Fetches machine language instructions from the instruction cache and translates them into binary code that the ALU processes.
- *Cache Memory*—Provides a staging area for instructions and the data. Because cache memory is faster than RAM, the processor can keep working without waiting on data.
- *Prefetch Unit*—Provides a small amount of memory that stores incoming instructions in a queue while awaiting execution, thereby reducing CPU waiting time.

- *Registers*—Small sections of memory that store data while the microprocessor needs it. A register address is expressed with a small number of bits, making it much faster to access than normal memory.
- *Clock*—A crystal that sits on the motherboard and vibrates regularly, many times per second. The clock speed refers to the number of cycles a CPU performs in the span of a tick of the computer's internal clock.
- *Bus*—A set of wires that transports data from one location to another. A CPU can have internal buses and address buses. Figure B.2 shows the bus as yellow lines.
- *Instruction Set*—A collection of machine language instructions that governs how the processor interprets and executes various tasks that it performs.

Figure B.3 shows how these components work together to execute instructions. Data and/or instructions are input into memory (initially RAM and then into data or instruction cache, or the prefetch unit). After fetching instructions, the control unit then directs the other components based on the instructions. For example, the control unit may direct data either to the ALU or FPU for processing. Memory stores the processed data, which are then available for further processing or output. These four functions—fetch, decode, execute, and store—provide the basic framework for this process.

The Instruction Set Each microprocessor has a permanently stored set of machine language instructions called the **instruction set**. The instruction set governs how the CPU interprets and executes the tasks that it performs to run computer software. There are two main types of instruction sets: *complex instruction set computer (CISC)* instructions and *reduced instruction set computer (RISC)* instructions. Usually, processors that use an RISC instruction set are faster than those using CISC, because an RISC processor needs to understand and execute fewer commands. RISC processors tend to be used in small electronic devices such as mobile phones or MP3 players. Modern chips like the Intel Core i5 combine the speed of the RISC approach with the power of CISC to provide increased speed.

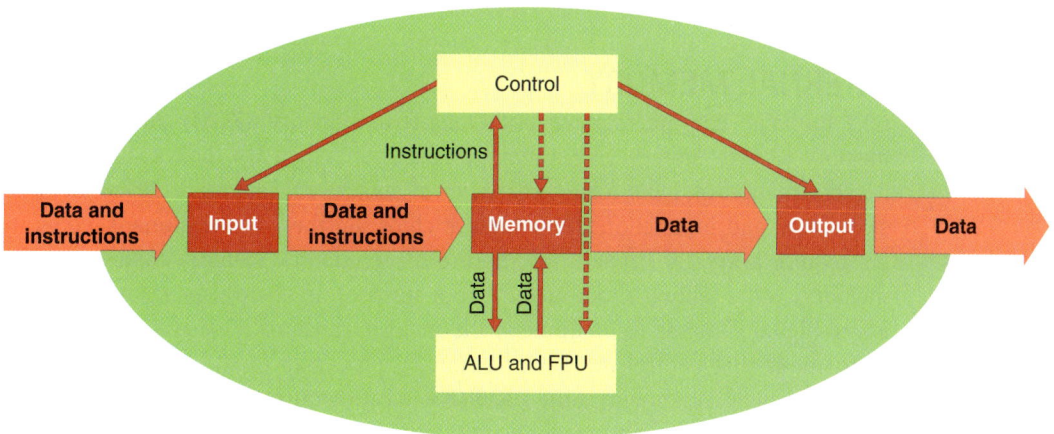

FIGURE B.3 How the CPU components work together to execute instructions.

Bandwidth The size of a CPU's buses determines its **bandwidth**, which is the number of bits the CPU can process in a single instruction. Recall that a **bus** is a set of wires over which data travel from one location to another. In a computer, the main bus is the *data* or *system bus*, which sends and receives data to and from the CPU to other components. However, the *internal buses* control the bandwidth. Internal buses carry data between the components that reside within the chip and *address buses*, which then connect them to main memory.

Bus capacity is expressed as the number of bits of data that can travel over the bus simultaneously. Higher bus capacities usually mean faster processing of instructions and data. For example, assume that a PC has a CPU with a 64-bit internal bus and uses a 32-bit system bus. The CPU internal bus would be about twice as fast as the system bus.

Clock Speed The clock speed is probably the most common measure of CPU performance. Clock speeds are measured in *megahertz (MHz)*, millions of cycles per second, or *gigahertz (GHz)*, billions of cycles per second. In general, higher clock speeds translate to faster system performance. However, other considerations, such as internal memory and video speed, can also affect overall speed. As a result, clock speeds can be a little misleading. Different internal structure and instruction sets can cause two different models of processors with similar clock speeds to perform at different levels.

CPU Performance Characteristics

Microprocessors are typically differentiated by their instruction set, their clock speed, and their bandwidth. As noted above, the clock speed is the most commonly used performance characteristic. All other things being equal, the faster the clock speed, the faster the capability of the CPU chip to process instructions. Many devices contain not only one CPU, but at least two. Dual core processor systems contain two complete processors, often on the same circuit board. The advantage of this configuration is the increased ability to multitask, which allows your computer to do more than one thing at a time.

In addition to the CPU or microprocessor chip, all computers need internal memory to operate.

INTERNAL MEMORY

Like humans, computers have both long-term memory (ROM) and short-term memory (RAM). However, the analogy falls short when we look at the physical implementation and the relative capacity of computer memory. That is, memory stores data and instructions on computer chips. Further, unlike humans, computers require a greater capacity of short-term, temporary memory than long-term memory (we're talking about memory, not storage). In IT devices, from MP3 players to digital cameras to computers, the main purpose of ROM is simply to hold instructions that control the device's start-up processes (booting up). This small set of instructions, known as the **BIOS (basic input/output system)**, activates the hardware components and loads the operating system.

Because ROM's instructions and data cannot be altered and ROM is usually not part of the decision when selecting IT, we focus our attention on RAM.

RAM

The largest number of chips in your computer used for memory is in the form of *random access memory (RAM)*, so named because the CPU can access any item stored in RAM directly (randomly). Personal computers usually have two types of RAM: dynamic RAM (DRAM) and static RAM (SRAM). RAM can also be found in other components of your computer system, such as the printer and video and sound cards. This type of RAM is often referred to as peripheral RAM.

Main memory usually refers to the DRAM in your computer. Like the CPU, **dynamic RAM (DRAM)** has improved over the years to provide faster access and greater capacity. It turns out that one of the easiest and least expensive ways to upgrade an older system is to increase the amount of main memory (DRAM).

Static RAM (SRAM) is so called because it does not need to be constantly refreshed to maintain the data that it stores. This makes it faster and less volatile than DRAM, but it also makes it much more expensive. Due to its high cost, SRAM is typically used for smaller sections of memory known as *cache*. Cache memory typically contains the most recently accessed pieces of main memory.

RAM can also be found in other components of your computer system, such as the printer and video and sound cards. This type of RAM is often referred to as **peripheral RAM**. Peripheral RAM serves as a buffer area between the main system and a peripheral device. For example, the DRAM that exists in most printers is known as the *printer buffer*. This buffer temporarily holds the data until the item is printed. Without a printer buffer, the data processed by the CPU can begin to back up, since the CPU can send the data to the printer faster than the printer can print.

Video cards use another type of RAM, known as **video RAM (VRAM)**. The main difference between VRAM and DRAM is that two devices can access VRAM at the same time. This allows the card to simultaneously receive data from the CPU and transmit data to the monitor.

RAM Performance Two factors affect RAM performance: (1) capacity and (2) address bus bandwidth. Let's consider each factor, starting with memory capacity.

When you open other applications, such as a program to chat with your friends online while you write a report with a word processor and listen to some tunes, the main memory stores the software and data for these applications. Eventually, you reach your main memory's capacity. When you open your favourite game program (and who hasn't done this when they should be working), there is no room in main memory for its instructions. In this case, the CPU either leaves some of the game's instructions on secondary storage until needed, or it bumps instructions and data from other software out to secondary storage until needed again. Remember that accessing secondary storage is much slower than accessing main memory. As a result, your system may also noticeably slow down.

Thus, the memory capacity in a computer can profoundly affect the overall performance of the computer. Memory capacity is measured in terms of the number of bytes that it may store. Capacities of most types of memory are in the range of thousands (kilobytes, KB), millions (megabytes, MB), and in some cases billions (gigabytes, GB) of bytes. The memory in your computer is primarily a hands-off component. In most cases, once you make your initial purchase, you will not need to configure or troubleshoot the memory. What you mostly need to know is that the more main memory available to your system, the better. For example, Microsoft recommends that you have a *minimum* of 128 MB of RAM memory to install and use Windows XP, 512 MB for Windows Vista, and 1GB for Windows 7. For two systems, with all other things equal, the one with the most RAM will be able to process more work.

While capacity is the most important consideration when measuring the performance of memory, there is another limiting factor on memory capacity: the bandwidth of the *address buses* that connect the CPU and other devices to main memory. An address is a number that a computer uses to specify the location of a particular piece of data within memory. The size of the address bus determines the maximum number of memory locations. Early address buses had an eight-bit bandwidth, which limited the amount of addressable memory to 2^8—256 locations. As it turns out, the address bus size is not much of a problem in today's computers. For example, in 2006, Pentium microprocessors used an address bus with a bandwidth of 64 bits. This means that the CPU could access up to 2^{64}—18,446,744,073,709,551,615 (18.45 extrabytes!) eight-bit locations of internal memory. Space and cost limitations with the average personal computer currently make a comparable amount of RAM impractical. But a 64-bit address bus can handle that much if needed.

Quick Test

Fill in the blanks for the following statements.

1. The four functions of the CPU that provide the basic processing framework are the fetch, decode, _____, and store functions.

2. True or False. ROM instructions and data cannot be altered.

3. Because RAM is permanent memory, it is unnecessary to frequently save your work.

Answers: 1. execute; 2. True; 3. False

INPUT HARDWARE DEVICES

Any hardware device must have methods for inputting data. The primary input methods include the keyboard, pointing devices such as the mouse, scanning devices such as bar code readers, and the Internet or other network connection. We consider all of these in Table B.4 *except* the Internet/network connection, which we discuss separately in Tech Guide C.

Table B.4 Input Devices

Device	Description	
Keyboard	A keyboard is generally recognized as the primary and most common input device for computers. When you press a key on a keyboard, a microprocessor in the keyboard determines the location of the button. It then sends the appropriate character in binary encoded digits to the computer. The primary value of a keyboard as an input device rests with its ability and versatility to input text data. Tactile response (how it feels) and ergonomics are considerations when purchasing a keyboard or laptop.	
Pointing Devices		
Mouse	A mouse is the most common pointing device. A *mechanical mouse* uses moving parts, such as a ball and rollers. An *optical mouse* does not require moving parts. An optical mouse, having no moving parts to detect motion, uses the light from an LED (light-emitting diode) reflected off a surface to measure the mouse movement. A *laser mouse* uses wireless technology and an infrared laser instead of LED, and can be more sensitive than other types.	
Touchpad	A commonly used pointing device on laptop computers, touchpads provide a small, flat surface that you slide your finger over using the same movements as you would a mouse. "Clicking" is accomplished by finger tapping, either directly on the pad or on nearby buttons.	
Joystick	A joystick is a pointing device often used to control games. It consists of a hand-held stick that pivots on one end and transmits its angle to a computer. A joystick usually has one or more buttons for entering instructions.	
Touch screen	A touch screen is a pointing device that allows the user to interact with a computer by touching the display screen. Using a combination of sensing technology and software, the computer interprets the location where the display is touched to perform the required operation. A touch screen is often used in public kiosks where a mouse would be a problem.	

(*Continued*)

Table B.4 *(Continued)*

Device	Description
Trackball	A trackball is basically a pointing device that resembles an upside-down mouse. It consists of a ball that rests in a socket containing sensors to detect the ball's rotation. Users roll the ball with their hand to move a cursor. It is used to replace a mouse in situations where physical movement is a problem, for example, when users have a physical disability.
Pen input	A pointing pen looks like a ballpoint pen, but it uses an electronic head instead of ink. Also called a *stylus*, you can use a pen with a digitizing tablet or touch screen. A stylus is often used with PDAs, which also incorporate a form of handwriting recognition that allows you to write directly on the screen.
Light pen	A light pen is a pointing device that uses a light-sensitive detector on a display screen. It allows you to move the pointer and select objects on the display screen by directly pointing it at the objects. A light pen works in a similar way as a mouse, except that you point directly at the objects on the screen.
Wearable device	There are a number of pointing devices that a user can wear. For example, users can wear a data glove on their hand. The computer interprets hand movements to move the cursor. Buttons may be added on the sides of the fingers to provide command input. These are often used with virtual reality games. A Wii is a recent example of a wearable device.
Digitizing tablet	A digitizing tablet is a pointing device that consists of an electronic tablet and a cursor that lets you draw and sketch into a computer. A *cursor* is like a mouse, but it has a window with crosshairs and as many as 16 buttons. The *tablet* contains electronics that enable it to detect movement of the cursor and translate the movements into signals to the computer. It is often used by graphic artists, engineers, and cartographers to convert drawings to digital form.

Input Hardware Devices

Scanning devices		
Bar Code Reader	A bar code reader is a device that reads a printed horizontal strip of vertical bars. The bar widths and spaces between the bars vary in a standard way to represent a group of decimal digits. Most grocery stores use bar codes to encode product codes. Upon reading a bar code, the software then matches the resulting product code with the database records to retrieve such details as the product price, description, and inventory level. Companies number and code all consumer products to a worldwide standard called the Universal Product Code (UPC). A *laser scanner* is a type of bar code reader that projects an oscillating beam that appears as a red scan and senses when an object is placed in front of it. In comparison, a *wand*, or *pen-type scanner*, requires physical contact with a bar code.	
Biometric Scanner	Biometric scanners are devices that scan fingerprints or the patterns that exist in the retina of the eye. They can be used to uniquely identify a person and allow access to a facility, computer, or ATM bank account.	
Document Scanner	A document scanner is a peripheral device on which you scan a printed document. The scanner then uses reflected light to obtain the image, digitize it, and transmit it to the computer. *Flatbed scanners*, where you place the object to be scanned on a glass area, are often built in to other devices such as facsimile and copy machines. In addition to flatbed scanners, there are *hand-held scanners*, where the scanning device is dragged across the page; *sheetfed scanners*, which have a slot where a page is inserted and a motor draws the page across the scanner; and *drum scanners*, which use very sensitive sensors to read the document as it whirls around inside a cylinder.	

(Continued)

Table B.4	(Continued)	
Device	Description	
Magnetic Strip Reader	A magnetic strip reader is a device that reads the data stored on a small magnetic strip as the strip is swiped through the device. These strips are commonly found on the back of credit and library cards. This device could also be considered a form of secondary storage.	
MICR (magnetic ink character recognition)	A MICR system uses a special magnetized ink that can be read by a special scanner. It is primarily used in the banking industry to print information on cheques for efficient processing.	
OCR (optical character recognition)	Usually implemented as software, OCR converts scanned print documents directly to electronic text.	
OMR (optical mark reader)	OMR uses a special scanning device to read carefully placed pencil marks on specially designed forms, such as those used in standardized tests.	
Smart Card Reader	Smart cards are plastic cards that have an integrated circuit embedded inside on which to store information. They are used for credit and debit cards, phone cards, and ID cards, for example. Smart cards can hold over 8 KB of data.	

Other Input Devices

With the increasingly popular use of multimedia information, audio/video input has become a major category. *Audio input* is primarily obtained through the use of a microphone. Applications range from simply storing audio comments within presentations or analysis files, to dictation of text input using specialized voice recognition software. For music, *musical instrument digital interface (MIDI)* devices allow note and effect information, like pitch and loudness, to be captured from a device and stored in a special format on a computer. MIDI devices include music keyboards, controllers, and other electronic music devices.

Video input is captured using a digital video camera, a WebCam, video and DVD players, or from broadcast and cable emissions. A *WebCam* is a video camera that delivers its output for viewing over the Internet. Typically, a WebCam is a slow-scan video camera that captures images about every half-second. This slow rate of capture accounts for the choppiness of the picture relative to full-motion video cameras. This is improving with advances in technology, however. Input from cable and broadcast television antennas can allow the computer and its monitor to serve as a television.

Often, both audio and video input require equipping the computer with special cards. A microphone is connected to a port in the audio card, while a video card processes video input. These cards process the input into a form that the computer can use and store, and usually include their own processor and memory.

Finally, sensory input is another important category of input device. A *sensor* is an electronic device that measures a physical quantity like temperature or pressure, and then converts it into an electronic signal. There are two types of sensors—analog and digital. *Analog sensors* generally produce a voltage proportional to the measurement. The CPU then converts the signal to a digital form. A *digital sensor* captures the measurement digitally, which is then sent directly to the computer for processing. A multitude of applications rely on sensors, such as proximity sensors used in smoke alarms, temperature sensors that control office heating and air conditioning, and pressure sensors used in automatic garage doors.

Considering the extensive list of input devices, how do you select the appropriate input device to use? Ergonomically speaking, the workspace setup can be an important consideration in selecting a device. For example, if space is tight or a flat surface is unavailable, trackballs or touchpads present better choices than a mouse. Users should consider whether or not a device places undue stress on their arm, hand, or fingers, and if the buttons' location makes them easy to reach and use. Biometric scanners must be easily accessible, comfortable, and safe. Hand-held devices should fit neatly into the user's hand, and laser scanners should not be unsafe to the user's eyes.

Environmental conditions can be another important factor when choosing a device. Dust or moisture can make a standard mouse and trackball function erratically or require frequent cleaning or repair. A touchpad or optical mouse is sealed and contains few moving parts, which helps make it more suitable for harsh conditions. Because most scanners depend on the reflection of light off of a medium, surrounding light levels can affect them or the presence of particles in the air can impair their performance.

Performance is also a consideration. Compared with the keyboard, pointing devices are simple to use. Pointing is a natural human movement. Coupled with a good graphical user interface (GUI), controlling a computer with a pointing device can be intuitive and require little training. Pointing devices are most often used to point to items on the GUI, so they are typically more useful for entering commands than for entering data content. For example, you may click on a scroll bar and move it to page through a document on your screen, while you would most likely use a keyboard to enter text.

A way to measure performance is to determine the accuracy of the device being used. You can gauge the accuracy of a device by its resolution and tracking. **Resolution** refers to how precisely the device can pinpoint a location on a screen or the clarity and level of detail of an image rendered. **Tracking** refers to how close the screen cursor follows the movement of the device. For example, an optical mouse usually tracks better than a mechanical mouse, but can provide less resolution. If you are deciding on an input device for bar codes, for example, both resolution and tracking will be important.

Speed is another way to measure performance. All of us have personally experienced the speed of a bar code reader versus keyboard input in the grocery line. These are just some of the things to consider when selecting input devices. Think about your own technology. Do you prefer to text on a BlackBerry or use the touch screen of an iPhone? Do you prefer to use the PageUp and PageDown keys on your keyboard or your mouse to scroll through a document?

OUTPUT HARDWARE DEVICES

Output devices deliver the result of processing operations to the user. Output devices include display and printed output devices, storage devices, the Internet or other network connection, and a wide variety of other electronic devices. We will consider all but the Internet or other network connection here. Internet and other network connections are examined in Tech Guide C.

Display Devices

Because most of us prefer images, display devices continue to be, by far, the most common category of output device. When coupled with speakers, display devices deliver just about every data format to the user, ranging from plain text documents to movies with sound (of course, the sound itself is output by a speaker). Display devices are also a significant component for input. Using a display, mouse, and GUI-based operating system allows the user to interact with the computer by manipulating a pointer on the screen over graphic objects.

The display system is made up of two primary parts: the graphics card and the monitor, as shown in Figure B.4.

The Technology Behind LCD Monitors Display devices vary in shape, size, and underlying technology. Most monitors in use today are LCD monitors. At the heart of an LCD monitor is a piece of liquid crystal material placed between a pair of transparent electrodes. This combination of materials takes advantage of four facts from physics:

1. Light can be polarized.
2. Liquid crystals can transmit and change polarized light.
3. Electric current can change the structure of liquid crystals.
4. Transparent materials can conduct electricity.

A liquid crystal can change the phase of the light that passes through it. Moreover, applying a proper voltage controls the phase change. An LCD display consists of an array of cells (pixels) that can be controlled individually to create the image.

An LCD may be colour or monochrome. For colour LCDs, each pixel consists of three subpixels, one for each of the colours red, blue, and green. By carefully controlling the

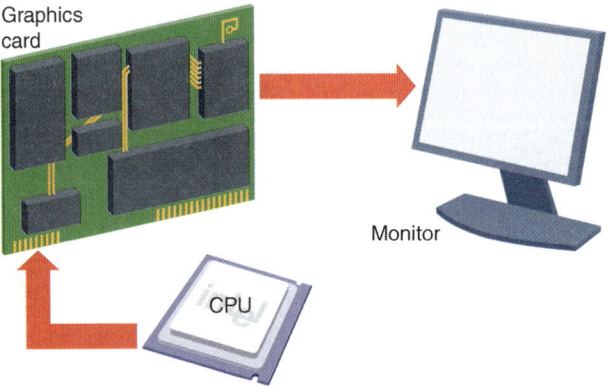

FIGURE B.4 This simple display system is capable of delivering just about every data format to the user, ranging from plain text documents to movies with sound.

applied voltage, the intensity of each subpixel can range over 256 shades. Combining the subpixels produces a possible palette of 16.8 million colours. LCDs may also be either backlit or reflective. Liquid crystals do not emit light; they can only change the phase of light as it passes through. Small, inexpensive LCDs are often reflective, which means to display anything they need to reflect light from external light sources. However, most LCDs are backlit. Backlit displays have built-in fluorescent tubes above, beside, and sometimes behind the LCD. Combined with a white diffusion panel behind the LCD, this redirects and scatters light evenly through the display.

Display Device Performance Display device performance depends on the resolution; that is, the maximum number of pixels that the screen can show, typically measured by dot pitch. The *dot pitch* of a display is the distance between a pixel and the closest pixel of the same colour. For computer monitors, dot pitch is usually less than 0.30 mm. For a display screen of given physical width and height, a higher dot pitch results in a lower resolution.

For LCDs, the voltage to each pixel is refreshed many times a second. How often this occurs is called the *refresh rate,* measured in hertz (Hz). The monitor's horizontal scan rate and the vertical resolution limit the refresh rate, since a higher resolution means more vertical lines to scan. Higher refresh rates mean less flickering, thereby reducing eyestrain. Anything above 60–72 Hz is fine for most users.

The physical dimensions of the screen can also be an important consideration. For LCD displays, screen size is measured on the diagonal in inches. For example, a 20-inch monitor will measure approximately 20 inches from a lower corner to the opposite upper corner of the display. In addition, LCD monitors are generally rated in degrees for their visible *viewing angle* for both horizontal and vertical. A problem with LCD screens is that the colour in the image can only be accurately represented when viewed straight on. The farther away from a perpendicular viewing angle, the more the colour will tend to wash out. A higher viewing angle is usually preferred over a lower angle, unless you want to reduce the attempts of others to look over your shoulder.

Touch Screens: The Future of Display Devices An interesting and increasingly useful twist on display technology is the touch screen monitor. A **touch screen monitor** is a computer display screen that is sensitive to human touch or a special pen. Kiosks (such as ATMs and self-service checkout lanes), PDAs, and newer tablet PCs frequently use touch screens. Using a touch screen, the user can interact with the computer by touching images or words on the screen. Because of this interactivity, touch screens are both input and output devices. PDAs and tablet PCs can also include special software that allows the user to write using a special pen directly on the screen in "digital ink."

There are currently four types of touch screen technology in use. A *resistive* touch screen panel uses a specially coated resistive layer. Touching this layer sends an electrical charge to the controller for processing. *Surface wave* technology uses ultrasonic waves that pass over the touch screen panel. Changes in the ultrasonic waves that result from touching the panel are registered and sent for processing. A *capacitive* touch screen panel is coated with a material that stores electrical charges. Touching this panel draws a small amount of charge to the point of contact. Circuits located at each corner of the panel measure the charge and send the information to the controller for processing. Finally, newer tablet PCs use an *electromagnetic digitizer* that accepts

FIGURE B.5 LCD touch-sensitive displays respond to human touch or a special pen.

input only from a special pen containing an electromagnetic coil. Using the pen can prevent inadvertent movements of the cursor that can sometimes occur with other touch technologies. Figure B.5 shows a touch-sensitive display used for tablet PCs.

Printed Output Devices

The increasing use of PDAs and tablet PCs should reduce our dependency on paper. Think about the ease and lower cost of storing, editing, transmitting, and copying electronic information as opposed to paper documents. Yet we often need printed information. As Table B.5 indicates, a variety of printing devices provide a range of quality and options in outputting both text and graphics.

Table B.5	Output Devices for Print	
Type	Description	
Inkjet	A popular type of printer for home use that prints by spraying dots from an ink cartridge. Capable of high-quality graphics and text printing at speeds over 80 characters per second.	
Laser	A popular type of printer for business and home use that prints by applying dots from a toner cartridge. Capable of very high-quality graphics and text printing at speeds as high as eight pages per minute.	
Multifunction device	A device that combines several types of input and output. Typically, a multifunction device will include a printer, fax, flatbed scanner, and copy machine—all in one device.	
Plotter	Prints very high quality graphics, although at slow speed, by manipulating a pen over a page. Unlike a regular printer, a plotter draws continuous lines. Plotters are typically used for architect blueprints, full-size engineering drawings, or very large printed items.	
Thermal	Uses heat to transfer an impression onto paper either by adhering a wax-based ink from a ribbon or by burning dots onto coated paper. Used in early fax machines and still used for printing receipts like those at pay-at-the-pump gas stations.	

Printed Output Device Performance Printer performance centres on colour, resolution, speed, and memory. Colour is important for most users. In addition to needing colour pages for presentations or maps, colour printers can print near-photo quality, reducing the need to pay for digital photo developing. However, colour printers are more expensive to operate because they require two or more different colour ink or toner cartridges.

Printer resolution is measured similarly to the resolution of display devices. The sharpness of text and images on paper is usually measured in dots per inch (dpi). Higher dpi means higher quality printing. Many inexpensive printers provide sufficient resolution at 600 dpi.

The more print jobs, the more important the speed of the printer. Printer speed is measured as the page rate in pages per minute (ppm). More expensive printers can print faster at about 20–30 ppm, while typical inexpensive printers print only about 8–10 ppm. Note that colour and extensive graphics can reduce these rates.

Most printers come with a small amount of memory called a *buffer*. With a large enough print buffer, the computer can download an entire job for printing and then process other items without having to wait for completion of the print job. As you might expect, higher capacity print buffers perform more efficiently.

STORAGE HARDWARE

Because of the limited amount of internal storage and the volatility of RAM, some form of storage external to RAM is necessary to permanently store data and programs. This **secondary storage** usually comes as magnetic storage media, optical disks, or chip-based flash memory. With all of these, stored information is accessed by internal memory when the control unit decides that this information is needed. Because the secondary storage unit must locate the information, read it, and then transfer it to internal memory, secondary storage is a much slower form of memory than internal memory. However, this slow transfer of information is balanced by the virtually unlimited storage capacity. Table B.6 lists the main types of storage used with personal computers.

Magnetic Disks

Some secondary disk storage uses a *magnetic disk* to store information as a form of **direct-access storage** in which information may be accessed in any order, regardless of the order in which the information was stored. A magnetic disk is composed of metal or plastic covered with an iron oxide whose magnetic direction can be arranged to represent symbols. This magnetic arrangement is carried out on a *disk drive,* which spins the disk while reading and writing information onto it using a *read/write head.* Depending on the type of disk, the read/write head rides either directly on or immediately above the disk.

Almost all computer systems include a hard disk. *Hard disks* serve as the main storage device for programs and data. They have greater capacities and allow for faster access than most other storage technologies. Hard disks can store anywhere from 10 MB to 200 GB or more on the latest drives. A single hard disk usually consists of a stack of several platters. Each platter contains two read/write heads, one for each side. Each read/write head is attached to a single access arm so that they

Table B.6		Storage Devices	
Storage Technology	Type	Description	Capacity Range (as of 2010)
CD-ROM, R, RW	Optical	Capable of storing large amounts of data Some types can be recorded upon (R) or rewritten (RW)	Up to 1 GB; most common is 650 MB
DVD DVD-R DVD-RW DVD-HD DVD-Blu-ray	Optical	A faster, higher capacity type of optical disk than CD-ROM Some types can be recorded upon (R) or rewritten (RW)	4.7 GB–17 GB
Hard disk drive	Magnetic	Very fast and with very high capacity Generally used for permanent but stationary storage of programs and data	Can be more than 750 GB
High capacity diskettes	Magnetic	Higher capacity diskettes such as Zip and Super disk Provide higher capacity while retaining the portability of a diskette	120 MB–750 MB
Tape	Magnetic	Magnetically coated strip of plastic used to store data	Up to 1TB
USB flash drives	Chip-based	Use a special type of ROM chip and plug into a USB port	up to 32 GB and rising

cannot move independently. Each platter has the same number of tracks, and a track location that cuts across all platters is called a cylinder. Each track is divided into sectors, the smallest unit accessible on the disk. Each sector has the same capacity, 512 bytes. When storing data to a disk, the data are divided into portions that can fit within a sector. The operating system and the drive list where data are stored by noting their track and sector numbers.

Hard disk drives are known for their access speed. High-speed disks have an access time of 9 milliseconds or less. Hard disks are generally considered to be stationary, but there are also removable hard disks.

Optical Disks

Unlike diskettes and hard disks, which use electromagnetism to encode data, optical disk systems use a laser to read and write data. The two main categories of optical disk are *compact disk (CD)* and *digital versatile disk (DVD)*. Optical disks have very large storage capacity, but they are not as fast as hard disks. A compact disk is a small, portable plastic medium that includes a reflective surface in its makeup. To record bits of data, the surface of the disk is altered to affect how light is reflected when applying a laser. CDs are commonly used to store large files that need to be portable such as software, music, and video files. The original CDs were read-only memory (CD-ROM) that only the distributor wrote on, and that the user could only read. Now *CD-recordable (CD-R)* and *CD-read/write (CD-RW)* have become widely available, with most computers now coming with a CD drive that writes to CDs as well as reading them.

DVD is an optical technology that is rapidly replacing CD technology. One side of a DVD has a capacity of 4.7 GB, enough to hold an entire feature-length movie. With two layers on each of its sides, a DVD can hold up to 17 GB of data on a disk that is basically the same size as a CD. Because standards for recordable or rewritable DVDs (DVD-R or DVD-RW) have yet to be agreed on, several possible formats exist. More and more computers now come with a DVD drive that will write as well as read disks. Emerging types of DVD storage are high definition (HD) and Blu-ray, both driven by media producers and the need to store more high quality images such as movies.

Chip-Based Storage

Flash memory is a special type of chip-based memory that can be written to as well as read into internal memory. This form of storage has quickly become a very popular way of transporting data between computers. These devices are known as *USB flash drives* and plug into the universal serial bus (USB), an external bus standard that supports transfer rates of 12 Mbps (megabits per second). All personal computer systems sold today contain USB ports, so flash drives are becoming widespread as a portable form of memory.

USB flash drives have advantages over many other storage media, such as higher capacity, smaller dimensions, high reliability, and noiselessness.

Storage Performance

Most personal computer systems include several types of storage devices, such as a hard disk, CD-RW drive, and DVD drive, as well as multiple USB ports that allow the attachment of additional units including the flash memory modules. With all of these available, you should choose the format that is appropriate for the data you wish to store and the method you choose to use. Keep in mind that capacity, portability, and the ability to write to the media are important factors. Also, think about using networks for storage. Storage services exist on the Internet, which allow you to store your data at very little cost. Network storage could provide the ultimate in portability, as most computers have access to the Internet.

Quick Test

1. True or False. A scanning device works with GUI to provide data and instructions to the computer using physical movements.

2. For a display device, the _____ is the distance between a pixel and the closest pixel of the same colour.

3. True or False. Until recently, the most popular form of portable storage has been flash memory, but it is rapidly losing favour among computer users.

Answers: 1. False; 2. dot pitch; 3. False

AN OVERVIEW OF OPERATING SOFTWARE

We introduced the concept of *software* in Chapter 2 as the set of instructions that direct the hardware. This is very much true when it comes to operating system software. Without it your hardware would be useless. Also true is that without application software, your operating system-enabled hardware would be much less interesting!

The **operating system (OS)** serves as the computer's "traffic cop," "office manager," and "chauffeur." As traffic cop, the OS manages all of the message traffic that flows from the user, to the application software, to the computer, and back again to the user. It is an office manager because it handles the allocation of resources and the assignment of tasks to various software programs. Finally, it is a chauffeur because the operating system enables users to get to their destination—that is, carry out needed tasks with application software—without worrying about the hardware interfaces.

For example, the OS monitors the keyboard and mouse to determine when users provide input to the computer. It also manages the video screen and printer to provide output from the computer. The operating system controls the operation of secondary storage to transfer data back and forth between secondary storage and main memory. Finally, the operating system controls the execution of application programs.

For desktop PCs and laptops, the most common operating systems include Microsoft's Windows family, the UNIX family (including Linux), and Macintosh operating systems (Mac OS X). In the next sections we look at operating systems in more detail, including how they work and what tasks they perform. We also compare these operating systems with those for mainframes, networks, and mobile devices such as smartphones.

Comparison of Operating Systems

The operating system functions apply to all computers, regardless of size. However, there are important differences between the operating systems for mainframes, networks, personal computers, and hand-held devices. The primary differences among the four operating systems are the number of users and the complexity of the peripheral devices that they manage. Mainframes and network operating systems manage multi-user systems, while most personal computer and hand-held device operating systems deal with only a single user.

Further, dealing with multiple users requires mainframe and network operating systems to have sophisticated security systems. For personal computers and hand-held devices, most users maintain a minimal security system, depending on their location and use. However, security is becoming more of an issue with hand-held devices due to additional wireless capabilities and storage of important data.

Mainframes must manage a large number of storage, input, and output devices. A network operating system must manage numerous hard drives, backup devices, and printers. On the other hand, a personal computer system usually has at most three or four storage devices: keyboard and mouse, printer, monitor, and set of speakers. Hand-held devices usually do not have peripheral devices. Because of these differences, mainframe operating systems are extremely large programs that require a staff of systems programmers to maintain them. Network operating

An Overview of Operating Software

Table B.7	Comparison of Operating Systems			
Feature	Mainframe	Network	Personal Computer	Mobile Device
Number of simultaneous users	Multiple	Multiple	One	One
Security	Sophisticated	Sophisticated	Minimal/user-enabled	Minimal/user-enabled
Peripherals	Complex	Numerous	Few	Few
Number of tasks	Many	Many	Many	Few
Support	Systems programmers	Networked-certified personnel	User	Provider
Example	OS390	Novell NOS	Windows XP	Windows Mobile

systems may also be quite large, requiring support from individuals with special training and certification on the particular network operating system. On the other hand, operating systems for personal computers and hand-held devices are usually simple and need only periodic maintenance.

All four types of operating systems are multitasking systems, enabling the computer to work on more than one job or program concurrently. Table B.7 compares the mainframe, network, personal computer, and hand-held device operating systems in terms of number of users, security, number of peripherals, number of tasks performed, and support that each requires.

How the Operating System Works

The operating system is the foundation upon which all other software works. As such, the operating system is crucial to the operation of the computer. Yet, it is the computer's least visible form of software. The only direct outputs from an operating system, to either the screen or the printer, are login requests (when the system asks for your user ID and password), error messages, and configuration choices (the settings you can choose for your system).

All operating systems consist of two parts: the kernel and the command interpreter. The **kernel** is the essential part of the operating system that internal memory must always include. It handles requests from either application programs or hardware (often printers or input devices) and then determines the processing order of the requests. Regardless of how fast something seems to happen from a user's perspective, most computers can accomplish only one task at a time (in actuality, this depends on the number of processors—one task per processor at a time). The kernel also handles demands for internal memory from competing applications by parcelling out the limited amount of internal memory as needed.

The **command interpreter** (often referred to as the *shell* in UNIX operating systems) accepts commands from users and translates them into language that the kernel can understand. Users typically communicate with the command interpreter through a **graphical user interface (GUI)**, like that used in Windows or Macintosh operating systems. The GUI acts as a shell to interact with the command interpreter. For UNIX systems, the GUI converts the user's mouse clicks into the appropriate text commands that the operating system understands. The primary exception to

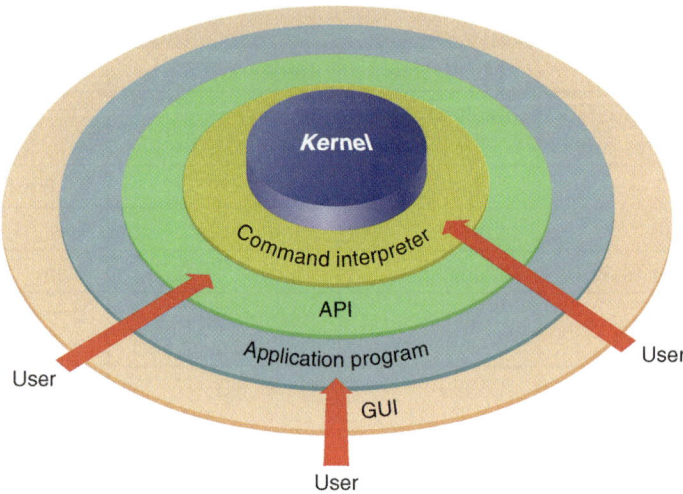

FIGURE B.6 Layers of an operating system.

this is the OS390 operating system used on most IBM mainframes and application servers. That OS command interpreter requires entering text commands that use a special syntax.

In addition to accepting commands from users through text commands or a GUI, the operating system also accepts commands from application programs through its **application program interface (API)**. The API is a specific process that allows the application program to make requests to the operating system or another application. For example, when you click the File|Print command or the Print icon on a Windows program, an API accepts this command and sends it to the operating system. The OS then communicates with the printer hardware to generate the desired output. Figure B.6 shows how the kernel, command interpreter, and API work together. Note that the user either communicates with the operating system kernel through an application program and API or through the command interpreter.

What Does the Operating System Do?

For any computer, regardless of whether it is a mainframe or other large server, a stand-alone or networked PC, or a stationary or hand-held device, the operating system is a collection of software programs that manages the following tasks:

- starting the computer
- managing hardware
- controlling access to the computer
- providing an interface for the user
- ensuring efficient use of the CPU
- providing services to application software

Starting the Computer Users must start, or *boot*, all computers. This start-up procedure relies on the use of the read-only memory (ROM) chip, which permanently stores the booting instructions. Because of its size and the number of hardware elements

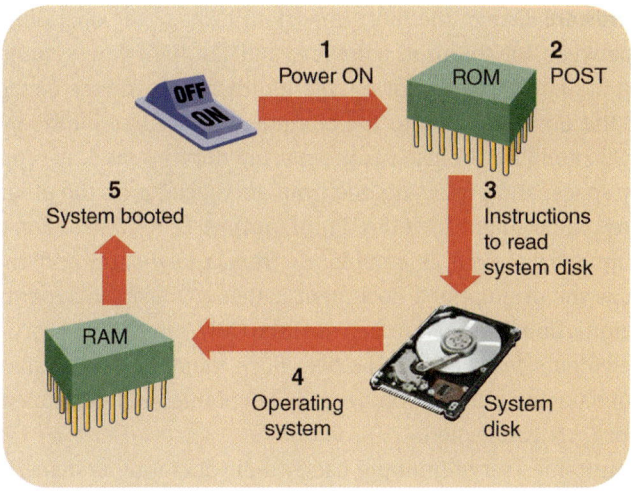

FIGURE B.7 The boot (start-up) process of a computer.

attached to it, booting a mainframe, termed the *initial program load (IPL)*, often takes many steps and some amount of time. On the other hand, to start a personal computer with a hard disk, users simply turn on the computer. The time it takes to start a personal computer depends more on how many application programs will initially be started, rather than how long it takes the OS to boot up. The ROM chip and hard drive then take care of the following booting steps, as Figure B.7 shows.

1. Turning on the computer's main power sends a flow of electricity to ROM.
2. The flow of electricity to ROM causes the BIOS (basic input/output system) to provide instructions to the CPU to perform a *power-on self-test (POST)*, which checks the various components of the computer, including memory, to ensure that they are working correctly.
3. After the POST, ROM/BIOS tells the CPU to find the system disk (usually the hard disk) and read operating system programs from secondary storage.
4. The CPU loads operating system files into internal memory (RAM).
5. The CPU implements instructions in the operating system files and then displays the OS interface.

The hard disk stores the operating system (Microsoft says that your system needs 1.5 GByte of available hard disk space to run Windows XP Professional,[2] 15 GByte for Windows Vista,[3] and 16 GByte for Windows 7[4]) and your PC is instructed, via the BIOS, how to start up the operating system. The BIOS is specific to your PC and prepares it so that other software can load and execute. In the case of booting your computer, you can access the BIOS to change the boot instructions if you want to start your computer from a floppy disk, or more likely, from a CD. Why would you want to do this? This is a common cure for a system failure or when your PC has a virus.

---

2. http://www.microsoft.com/windowsxp/sysreqs/pro.mspx. Retrieved April 13, 2010.

3. http://www.microsoft.com/windows/windows-vista/get/system-requirements.aspx. Retrieved April 13, 2010.

4. http://windows.microsoft.com/systemrequirements. Retrieved April 13, 2010.

Managing Hardware One of the most important tasks of the operating system is to act as a go-between for the user, software, and the hardware system. To do this, the operating system must control a large number of hardware elements. It must also manage the flow of data into the computer, as well as information out of it. Finally, the OS monitors the use of internal memory by tracking application and user memory space, and protecting one from encroaching on the other.

Hardware management includes **input/output (I/O) tasks**. For example, the OS accepts input data, such as commands from a keyboard, and coordinates its output, such as the printing of a document. Other I/O tasks include the transfer of data, instructions, and information between the CPU, internal memory, and secondary storage elements (e.g., CD-ROM drive, flash memory). I/O tasks also include the transfer of data and information over the telephone modem, cable modem, DSL connection, or LAN connection.

Since mainframes serve multiple users, their operating systems must manage numerous hardware elements, including disk drives, tape drives, printers, communications equipment, and user workstations. Further, a mainframe OS must accomplish all this while minimizing delays for users and ensuring their access to the needed hardware elements. On the other hand, with only one user, the hardware control problem for a personal computer is much less complicated. However, it does involve many of the same elements as the mainframe system, plus such items as the mouse for GUI, speakers for audio output, and DVD players.

Finally, in addition to the devices a stand-alone PC operating system must control, a network operating system controls the communications between the local PCs on the network and other network resources, such as various printers and a tape backup for the file server. (We discuss networks in greater detail in Tech Guide C.)

Controlling Access Once the computer is up and running, unless it is a stand-alone PC, the OS must control access to it. For mainframe computers or networked PCs, the operating system must provide security to users' data, information, and programs against unwarranted intrusion. The most recent operating systems require users to enter a password to access the computer, limiting their access to specific areas.

Efficient Use of CPU In any computer system, the CPU always works much faster than the I/O operations. As a result, a key task of the operating system is to ensure that the slow I/O does not hold up the CPU. This is especially important for a mainframe, so that the processing for one user does not delay other users' I/O. Even on a personal computer, it would be inefficient for the CPU to wait on one task—for example, printing a job—before continuing its work.

To keep the I/O from interfering with processing, the OS directs the CPU to run programs concurrently. That is, the CPU processes part of one program, then part of another, then part of a third, and so on until the CPU has worked on all of them. The OS places the jobs in a queue (waiting line) to be executed according to their level of priority. It gives each job an extremely small amount of CPU time, called a time-slice, during which the CPU executes a portion of the job. Thus, the OS allows CPU *multitasking*, which mainframes have done for many years. Personal computers now also widely use multitasking, due to the increase in CPU speed and amount of internal memory. Because a mainframe has multiple users as well as multiple tasks, it usually also has a secondary processor to handle I/O, while the CPU handles the multiple tasks and users. Network operating systems usually handle the problem of efficiently using the server's CPU by shifting a significant portion of the processing burden from the central file server CPU to CPUs of the local PCs.

Multitasking is often confused with *parallel processing*, but they are quite different. With multitasking, the CPU only handles a part of one task at a time. With parallel processing, the multiple CPUs in the same computer handle either multiple different jobs or multiple parts of the same job at the same time.

Think of the difference between multitasking and parallel processing as playing catch with yourself with five different balls. If you multitask, you pick up one ball, toss it, catch it, put it down, pick up the next ball, and repeat the toss-and-catch process. If you parallel process, you are juggling: tossing and catching all five balls at once. We all know that juggling is harder than catching one ball at a time. Similarly, this is why multitasking is much more widespread than true parallel processing. Incidentally, newer microprocessors are being made as *dual-core* or *multi-core processors*; this is like having two or more processors on one chip. Having more than one processor enables PCs to parallel process, to some extent, and begins to address the need to multitask. Intel has introduced its Corei7 processor with multi-core technology to power demanding digital content creation, immersive games, and entertainment.[5]

Providing Services to Application Software While the operating system tasks just discussed are important to the operation of all computers, the main objective of an operating system is to provide services to application software. After all, the primary reason that most business professionals use a computer is to run application software to create business value. Operating systems provide a number of services to application software, including the following:

- running the application software and ensuring the availability of needed resources
- determining the processing order of concurrently running programs
- coordinating file/disk management
- providing memory management

Running Application Software The operating system must make it possible for the user to run application software. It does this by interpreting the instructions from the other software to the CPU and providing resources in the form of hardware devices when needed by the other software program. For example, when the user instructs a word processing program to print a document, the application software issues a command to the operating system, which handles the printing job. Network operating systems are not usually involved in running application software. Instead, the operating system on each individual PC handles this role. It is important to note that only certain applications run on certain operating systems. For example, you cannot run MS Office applications on the Linux operating system without special APIs. Even with the APIs, the full functionality of the application may not be available. Therefore, your choice of operating system may determine the application software you can use.

---
5. http://www.intel.com/pressroom/archive/releases/2008/20081117comp_sm.htm. Retrieved April 13, 2010.

Determining the Processing Order Modern computers are multitasking machines running multiple programs concurrently. For example, you may create a document, work with a spreadsheet, query a database, and print a series of presentation slides, all *seemingly* at the same time. In most cases, one job runs in the foreground, with other jobs processed in the background. The Windows operating systems show programs running concurrently as buttons on the task bar, usually displayed at the bottom of the screen. Figure B.8 shows an example of this process for Windows XP, where the foreground application is Microsoft Word. Background programs include Excel, Microsoft Project, Internet Explorer, Adobe Acrobat, and iTunes.

The operating system must decide which task takes priority, not just between foreground and background jobs, but also between the various background jobs. Setting priorities depends on various criteria, some of which the user may set, others which the operating system defines.

Coordinating File/Disk Management The operating system must manage files on secondary storage (usually some form of hard disk) in such a way to make them available when needed, while also protecting them from unwarranted use or loss. A variety of file types are necessary to use application software, including data files, program files, and utility files. For example, program files execute application software, data files include specific information already entered by the user, and utility files provide assistance, such as spell-check ability.

For example, say you want to create a letter. To run a word processor in the Windows operating system, you click the appropriate icon. The operating system must know the location of the word processor program files, as well as the location of a variety of utility files, known as *dynamic link library (dll)* files. After you specify the location, the OS must also know where to save the result of your work

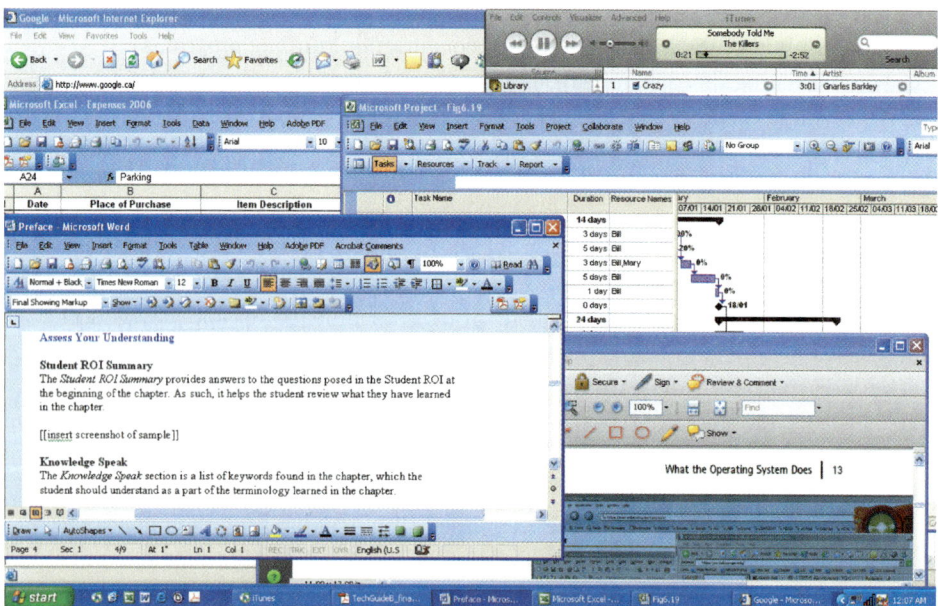

FIGURE B.8 Example of multiple programs running concurrently in Windows.

(or where to find a previously saved document). On the other hand, if you click on a data file, the OS must detect the corresponding application software to launch. The file management element of the Windows operating system handles all of these operations. The same is true of the Mac OS X and Linux operating systems. It is important to note that files such as dlls are often not stored in the application folder on a PC; in the case of Windows, they are saved in the Windows folder. When you want to delete an application, you should always uninstall it, not delete the application folder directly; uninstalling ensures all of the application is removed from memory.

Mainframe and PC network systems have multiple users storing their files on centrally located disk and tape drives, so their operating system must track where files are stored and who may receive access to them. For this reason, security is an important element of a mainframe operating system. For networks, the operating system must also monitor software on the file server to restrict access to only those who have rights to use it.

On personal computers, the operating systems must accomplish the same file management tasks as mainframes and network servers, but usually for only one user. While security is slightly less important, file management continues to be crucial. Also, files on a personal computer hard disk are usually not stored as one contiguous unit. As a result, the operating system must be able to reassemble the parts of a file from many separate locations on the disk. The OS handles this via a table of the various file parts and their locations on the disk, called the *file allocation table (FAT)*. Because files are not contiguous, file fragmentation can occur. When this occurs, fragments of files are not stored efficiently, making it hard for your PC to recombine them and reducing system performance. To solve this problem, you can run a defragmentation utility on your PC. After you have *defragged*, you will usually notice an improvement in the speed of your PC.

The OS also provides file management tools to help users organize files for easy access and retrieval. Virtually all operating systems now use a *hierarchical* (tree) structure that divides a long list of files into several shorter lists, called folders. For example, assume that a company stores personnel files on disk for the employees in its 12 branches around the world. Each branch has between three and six departments. If the company has at least 10 employees in each department, the computer would store at least 360 (12 × 3 × 10) files. With a single folder on the hard disk, finding a particular employee's file might take time. However, as Figure B.9 illustrates, using the Windows Explorer utility to create a hierarchical structure to organize files resolves this issue.

Providing Memory Management Unlike the nearly unlimited secondary storage, internal memory continues to be a scarce resource and must be managed in several ways. First, because multiple programs often run concurrently, the operating system must ensure that these programs don't conflict when using memory or that there is even enough memory to run them. The operating system also tries to partition the various applications in such a way that an error in one does not cause the entire system to fail or lock up (commonly referred to as *crashing*).

Second, even with the large amounts of memory in modern computers, they still need more. One technique, which began with mainframe computers in the

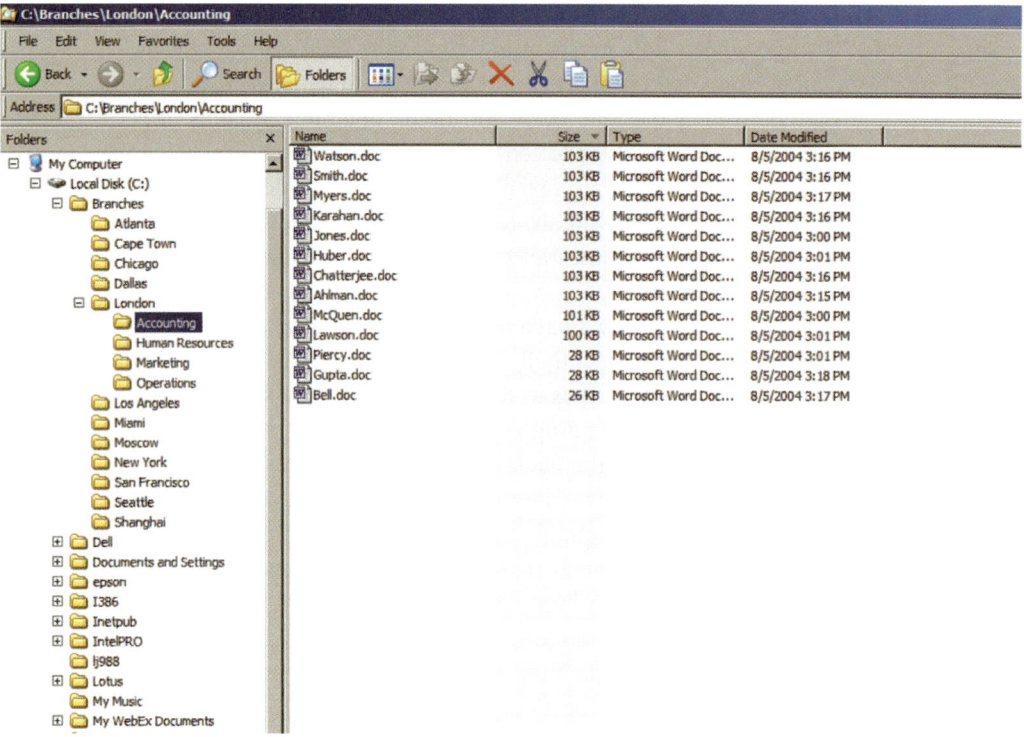

FIGURE B.9 The Windows hierarchical-based file structure.

mid-1970s, provides the appearance of additional memory: virtual memory. **Virtual memory** divides the internal memory into pages, or sections, that match equal-sized sections of memory on disk. The process then exchanges, or swaps, internal memory with the disk or virtual memory when needed. As long as the processing needs only data or instructions that are currently in internal memory, it proceeds as usual. However, when the needed information is on disk, virtual memory swaps a page into main memory. The CPU tries to "think" ahead, to determine which pages from virtual memory will be needed next. As a result, the apparent memory exceeds the actual internal memory without great loss of processing speed. Virtual memory greatly enhances the ability of mainframes to run multiple jobs at high speeds. Personal computers also use virtual memory to expand their apparent memory capacity.

Has your PC ever been so slow that you could have grabbed a coffee before it finished saving your Word document? This could indicate that your PC is not managing memory well. Sometimes this occurs simply because you have too many applications open and your RAM is overloaded. Other times it could be because you have a memory leak or your hard drive needs to be defragged. In the case of a memory leak, you can use the task manager in Windows to identify applications and processes that are using a lot of memory and end them. Because RAM is constantly accessed to randomly write, read, and store to memory, it can get fragmented. You can use your PC's defragmentation utility to correct this. Of course, a reboot, which ends all processes, can also be effective in the short term.

Quick Test

1. Which of the following computer systems is designed to allow for multiple simultaneous users?
   a. mainframe and networks
   b. personal computers and hand-held devices
   c. all types of computers

2. True or False. The ROM chip is most important in the boot operating system function.

3. _____ uses disk storage to give the appearance of additional internal memory.

Answers: 1. a; 2. boot; 3. Virtual memory

AN OVERVIEW OF APPLICATION SOFTWARE

You should now have a better understanding of how operating system software allows you to use hardware devices effectively. However, by far the largest amount of software available to the computer user is in the area of application software. Business professionals typically use either commercially developed (also known as *commercial off-the-shelf [COTS] software*) or custom-developed application software.

Commercially Developed Application Software

Commercially developed application software is used for a wide variety of tasks and is often mass-marketed. The most widely used commercially developed software categories used by business professionals include the following:

- word processing programs to create documents
- spreadsheets and accounting software to carry out financial and other quantitative analyses
- database programs to manage lists and tables of data
- presentation programs to create electronic slide shows
- Web browsers and other Internet-related software
- specialized software for specific industry needs

Many of these applications are often sold together in a bundle known as a **software application suite**, such as Microsoft Office. The major benefit of a software suite is that each application in the suite has similar functions (e.g., Copy/Paste) and these functions can be executed across applications (e.g., copy a table in MS Excel and paste in MS Word). In the next sections, we briefly discuss six common types of software.

Word Processing Software Word processing software, part of a larger category known as *document preparation software,* allows you to easily compose, edit, save, and print various types of documents. Because word processing software almost directly replaces handwritten documents, most business professionals often learn it first (other than games). Among other advantages, word processing software allows efficient creation and editing of text documents. *Desktop publishing software*

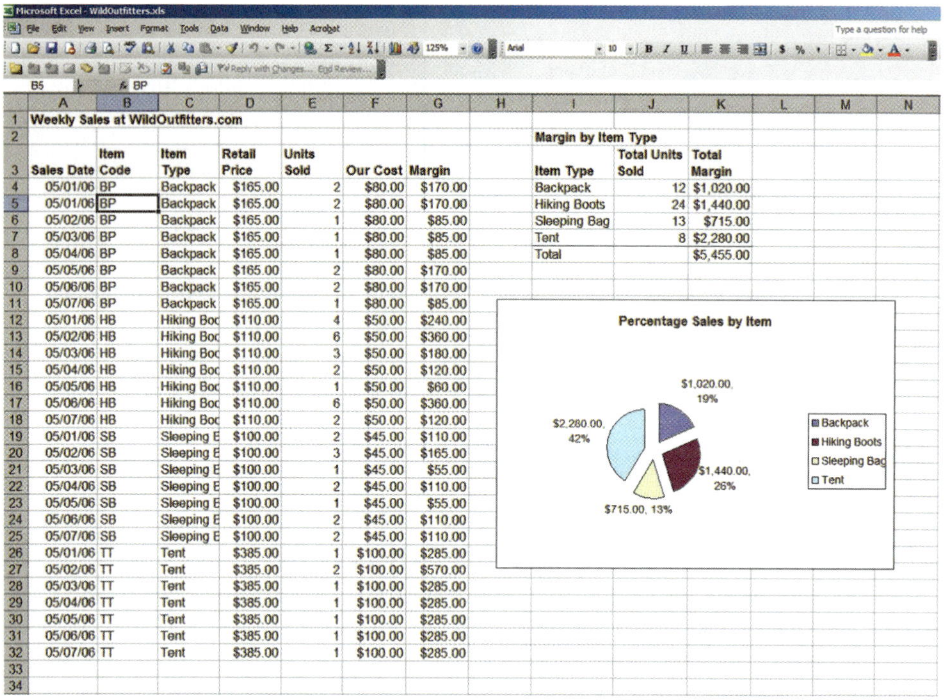

Sales Date	Item Code	Item Type	Retail Price	Units Sold	Our Cost	Margin
Weekly Sales at WildOutfitters.com						
05/01/06	BP	Backpack	$165.00	2	$80.00	$170.00
05/01/06	BP	Backpack	$165.00	2	$80.00	$170.00
05/02/06	BP	Backpack	$165.00	1	$80.00	$85.00
05/03/06	BP	Backpack	$165.00	1	$80.00	$85.00
05/04/06	BP	Backpack	$165.00	1	$80.00	$85.00
05/05/06	BP	Backpack	$165.00	2	$80.00	$170.00
05/06/06	BP	Backpack	$165.00	2	$80.00	$170.00
05/07/06	BP	Backpack	$165.00	1	$80.00	$85.00
05/01/06	HB	Hiking Boc	$110.00	4	$50.00	$240.00
05/02/06	HB	Hiking Boc	$110.00	6	$50.00	$360.00
05/03/06	HB	Hiking Boc	$110.00	3	$50.00	$180.00
05/04/06	HB	Hiking Boc	$110.00	2	$50.00	$120.00
05/05/06	HB	Hiking Boc	$110.00	1	$50.00	$60.00
05/06/06	HB	Hiking Boc	$110.00	6	$50.00	$360.00
05/07/06	HB	Hiking Boc	$110.00	2	$50.00	$120.00
05/01/06	SB	Sleeping E	$100.00	2	$45.00	$110.00
05/02/06	SB	Sleeping E	$100.00	3	$45.00	$165.00
05/03/06	SB	Sleeping E	$100.00	1	$45.00	$55.00
05/04/06	SB	Sleeping E	$100.00	2	$45.00	$110.00
05/05/06	SB	Sleeping E	$100.00	1	$45.00	$55.00
05/06/06	SB	Sleeping E	$100.00	2	$45.00	$110.00
05/07/06	SB	Sleeping E	$100.00	2	$45.00	$110.00
05/01/06	TT	Tent	$385.00	1	$100.00	$285.00
05/02/06	TT	Tent	$385.00	2	$100.00	$570.00
05/03/06	TT	Tent	$385.00	1	$100.00	$285.00
05/04/06	TT	Tent	$385.00	1	$100.00	$285.00
05/05/06	TT	Tent	$385.00	1	$100.00	$285.00
05/06/06	TT	Tent	$385.00	1	$100.00	$285.00
05/07/06	TT	Tent	$385.00	1	$100.00	$285.00

Margin by Item Type

Item Type	Total Units Sold	Total Margin
Backpack	12	$1,020.00
Hiking Boots	24	$1,440.00
Sleeping Bag	13	$715.00
Tent	8	$2,280.00
Total		$5,455.00

FIGURE B.10 Spreadsheets are an effective tool for tracking and analyzing product sales.

takes word processing one step further. It combines word processing, graphics, and special page definition software to create documents that rival those available from professional typesetting companies.

Spreadsheets If you consider word processing as a replacement for handwritten documents, the spreadsheet is an even more powerful replacement for the calculator. Business professionals use this tool for almost any type of financial or quantitative analysis. To understand why, let's consider it in some depth. To start, a *spreadsheet* is an electronic table of rows and columns, with the intersection of a row and a column called a *cell*. The column letter and row number identifies each cell. For example, in Figure B.10, the highlighted cell, cell B5, is located in column B and row 5.

Business professionals enter column values, labels, and formulas into cells to create business models. The formulas typically use the addresses of other cells to create relationships between them. For example, Column G in Figure B.10 automatically calculates the margin for a given item, equal to the selling price (column D), times the number sold (column E), minus store cost (column F), times the number sold (column E). For backpacks (G4), the margin formula in G4 is: = D4*E4 − (F4*E4). Note the use of the asterisk (*) for the multiplication operation in this formula. Note also that the spreadsheet performs mathematical operations in the same order that you do: multiplication first, then subtraction. The spreadsheet software uses the "mathematical horsepower" of your computer to efficiently determine the correct solution.

Spreadsheet software accomplishes other tasks to help business professionals. In the preceding example, the sales manager used the *Sort* tool in this spreadsheet software to automatically list the items according to item type. He or she also added a section to allow the spreadsheet to automatically calculate the total margin for each product type. Finally, the manager used the software to automatically generate a chart showing percentage sales by product type.

Another useful aspect of a spreadsheet is that, when a value changes in a cell that is involved in a formula cell, the value in the formula cell may change also, depending on the relationship. For example, say WildOutfitters (from Figure B.10) sells three backpacks instead of two and updates the value in the spreadsheet. The spreadsheet then automatically changes both the margin for backpacks and the margin for the seven-day period to reflect the increased number of backpacks sold. This capability enables business professionals to perform *what-if analyses* by changing the values in cells and quickly seeing the results.

For example, assume the WildOutfitters marketing department suggests running an advertising campaign for the four products shown in Figure B.10 (that is, hiking boots, backpacks, sleeping bags, and tents). The marketing department believes this campaign will generate a 15 percent increase in unit sales for the four products. However, the cost of this campaign will result in a 10 percent increase in the cost to the company for each of the four items, which, due to competitive pressures, *cannot* be passed along to customers in the form of higher prices. The question is: Given these assumptions, should the campaign be run? On the face of it, it seems like a no-brainer. A 15 percent increase in unit sales should more than outweigh effects of a 10 percent increase in costs. Modifying the spreadsheet by inputting this revised information should back up this assumption.

Figure B.11, the revised spreadsheet, shows the new costs, the new units sold, and the margin figures (columns M through P). Note that the new total margin is $5,850.50, as compared with the existing total margin of $5,455. So, while there is a higher total margin using the assumptions for the advertising campaign given

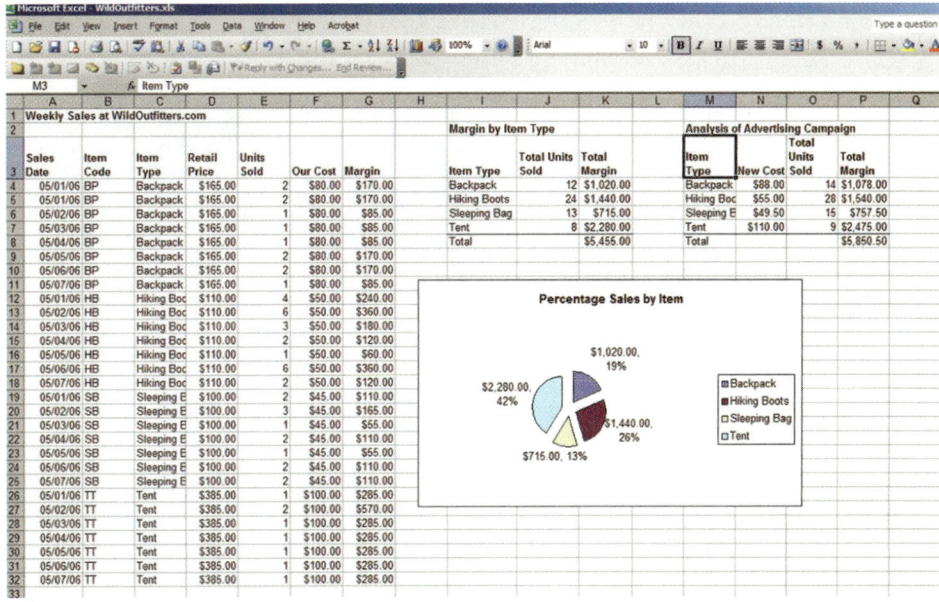

FIGURE B.11 Using existing spreadsheet information, such as that shown in Figure B.10, business professionals can perform a series of what-if analyses.

by the marketing department, the increase is far less than expected, with less than a 1 percent increase in total margin. Based on this what-if analysis, the company should study this issue further before initiating the advertising campaign.

Performing analyses requires the business professional to explore many different possibilities to determine the meaning of the raw data after the data have been transformed. As a business professional, you can expect that your early positions will require that you analyze a question or proposal, like the advertising proposal discussed in the preceding example.

Database Software Another popular way to transform data into a usable form is to organize them by entering the data into *database management software.* (We cover database management systems in greater detail in Chapter 6 and Tech Guide D.) Although the data are often input in a tabular form similar to that of a spreadsheet, the purpose differs. Spreadsheets assist in quantitative analysis, whereas a database locates information that matches some criteria. That is, it can be difficult to alter a database table to calculate margin as easily as you can change a spreadsheet, but you can use it to easily search for all sales of a particular item, say, the backpack.

Using a database often results in less redundancy than using a spreadsheet. Why? The data in a database can be spread over a series of *related* tables. While Figure B.10 shows the name, item code, price, and store cost for every transaction, using related tables in a database, as Figure B.12 shows, reduces this redundant information. Note how Figure B.12 shows the data on hiking item sales as they

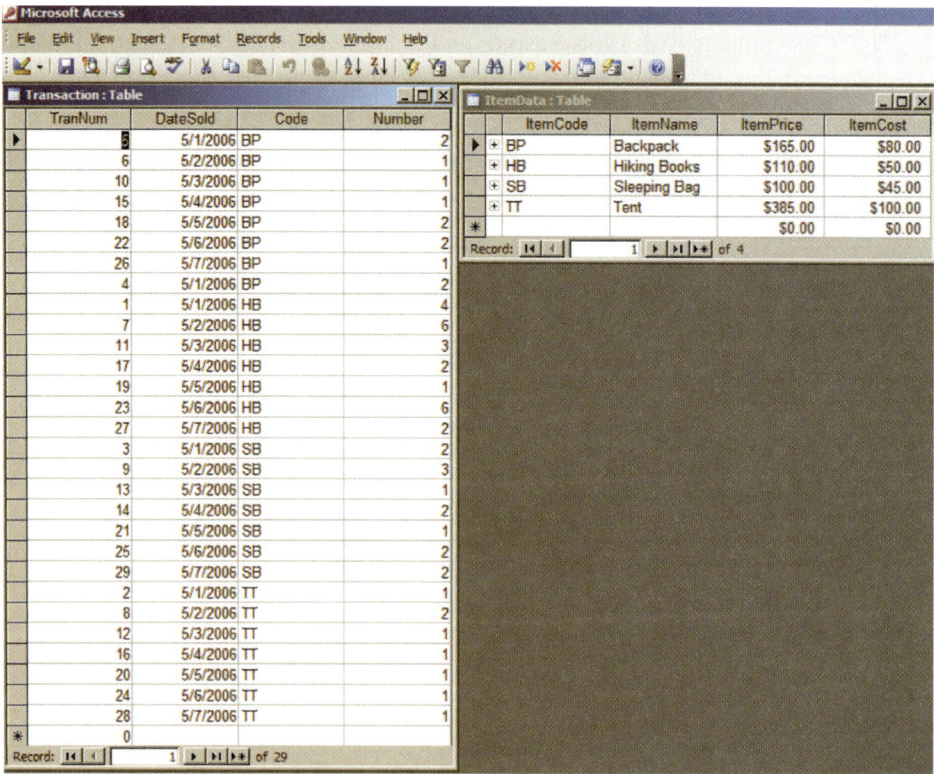

FIGURE B.12 Databases often result in less redundancy than spreadsheets.

BackpacksSold : Select Query

ItemName	ItemPrice	ItemCost	DateSold	Number	Gross Profit
Backpack	$165.00	$80.00	5/1/2006	2	$170.00
Backpack	$165.00	$80.00	5/2/2006	1	$85.00
Backpack	$165.00	$80.00	5/3/2006	1	$85.00
Backpack	$165.00	$80.00	5/4/2006	1	$85.00
Backpack	$165.00	$80.00	5/5/2006	2	$170.00
Backpack	$165.00	$80.00	5/6/2006	2	$170.00
Backpack	$165.00	$80.00	5/7/2006	1	$85.00
Backpack	$165.00	$80.00	5/1/2006	2	$170.00

Record: 1 of 8

FIGURE B.13 A query can provide specific information as well as perform calculations.

would appear in two related tables—a Transaction table and an ItemData table—for a popular database management system, Microsoft Access.

Further, databases allow users to locate information quickly, through queries. A *query* is a specially structured request to a database to locate a desired set of records. In our example, say you want to locate information on backpacks. You would therefore enter a query to find and display—or in database terminology, *return*—all records with the BP item code. You can indicate specific information as part of the query, such as the item name, price, and cost, the date of the transaction, the number sold, and even the calculated gross profit. Figure B.13 shows the result of this type of query.

Presentation Software *Presentation software* allows business professionals to use text in many sizes and fonts, graphics, photos, and even audio and video files to inform an audience. Because of its ease of use, presentation software has become extremely popular for making business, academic, and instructional presentations. For example, Figure B.14 shows a slide from a presentation on teamwork. Presentation software can be used both to support a person giving a speech, and to present information on its own. For example, a product marketing manager may use presentation software to create a slide show that can display automatically at an information kiosk or at a conference booth.

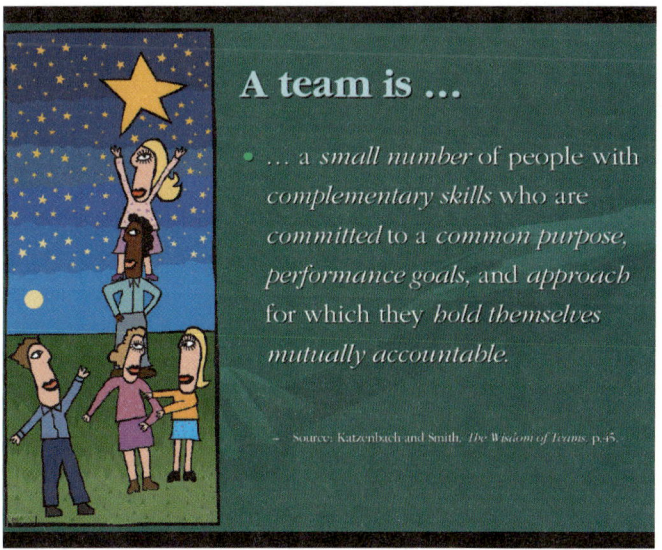

FIGURE B.14 Presentation software allows business professionals to create slides to inform an audience.

Web Browser and Internet-Related Software Since its widespread introduction in 1994, the Web browser has rapidly become one of the most popular (if not *the most* popular) type of software currently in use. The main reason for the popularity of the Web browser is its access to billions of pages of information available on the World Wide Web.

Browsers rely on point-and-click methodology to carry out desired operations. If you know the address of a web page, you simply

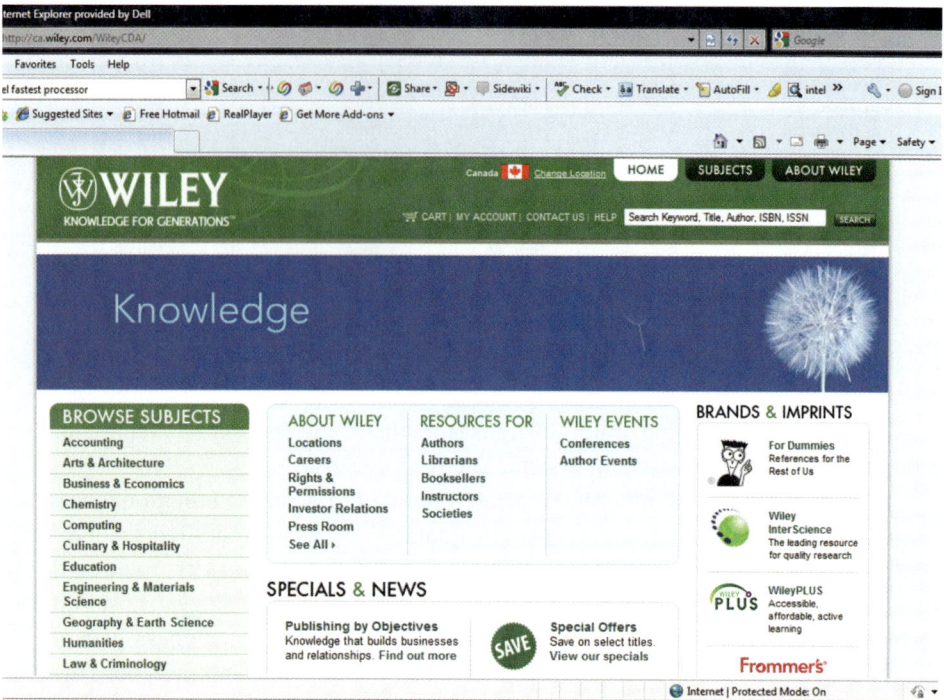

FIGURE B.15 It is possible to jump to other related pages to obtain additional information by clicking on hyperlinks.

enter it in the address box and press the Enter key to retrieve it. Once you have a web page on the screen, you can jump to other related pages by clicking on content that is either underlined or otherwise highlighted in some way, called a **hyperlink**. Of all the types of software that we discuss here, the Web browser is almost certainly the one that you have already used. Figure B.15 shows an example of a web page in a browser for the publisher of this book.

Beyond simply accessing web pages, browsers have become the "jack of all trades" for Internet operations. Web browsers enable searches for web pages based on a word or term; communications with others through email, instant messaging, groups, and chat rooms; and downloading of files of all types, including audio and video files. The power and versatility of the Web result in its almost universal use by business professionals.

Using search engines from a Web browser enables you to search the Web and all of its billions of pages, as well as search discussion groups and even chat sessions. Many public and governmental agencies put their data on the Web in a form that can be searched and downloaded for use in problem solving. For example, in the WildOutfitters example shown earlier, a marketing analyst in the company could use a search engine to compare the company's prices and features with those of all possible competitors.

In addition, many organizations enable their employees to search for internal data and information using search engines on their intranet using a browser. In many cases, employees can send out questions to other employees using email to determine if a problem has already been solved within the organization. This makes it possible for an employee to access the accumulated organizational memory to answer questions and solve problems.

Specialized Software In many cases, business professionals rely on other developed software to handle specific situations. For example, while spreadsheets are the most general form of financial software, most organizations use other financial packages. These include accounting packages, real estate calculators, online stock and bond trading software, and retirement-planning software.

You can see how most knowledge work activities rely on commercially available application software. However, specific tasks require specially created software. Let's look next at developing customized software.

Developing Customized Software

Companies usually buy commercially developed software, like word processing programs or spreadsheets, for routine business tasks. However, to achieve a competitive advantage, a company must often custom develop software to meet its particular needs. As one analyst notes, "software needed to be competitively different is generally not available from off-the-shelf packages" and "building . . . systems for unique [competitive] capability is often the single most important activity for an . . . organization."[6] As a result, there will always be a demand for programmers.

Computer programs are based on algorithms. An **algorithm** is a detailed sequence of actions that, when followed, will accomplish some task. For example, when making the bed, you may follow the steps in this algorithm:

1. Strip the covers and sheets from the bed.
2. Smooth out the fitted sheet.
3. Tuck the sheet under the mattress at the foot of the bed and spread to cover the mattress.
4. Tuck in the comforter and spread it over the top of the sheet.
5. Fluff the pillows and place them in their proper locations.
6. Crease comforter under the pillows and fold it over the top to cover the pillows.
7. Drop a quarter onto the bed to see if it bounces!

Defining an algorithm is just the first step in developing software. The next step is making a computer follow the algorithm; this is known as *programming*. A *computer programmer* takes the algorithm and translates it into instructions written in a programming language that the computer can understand. The set of instructions that follow the algorithm, written using the *programming language*, is known as a **program**.

Programming languages, like the machine language of the CPU, is a set of binary codes. With the first computers, programmers actually had to input binary instructions to their machines. As you can imagine, this was a difficult and error-prone process. Since the 1950s, there has been a trend toward abstracting the machine language instructions into a language that is more natural to human programmers. Unfortunately, the strict rules required for communicating instructions to the CPU

---
6. James Martin, *Cybercorp: The New Business Revolution*, New York: AMACOM Books, 1996, p. 104.

Table B.8	Commonly Used Computer Languages
Language	Common Use
C (including C++ and C#)	Writing a wide variety of applications for PCs or network servers
Java	Writing software for all types of computers; also, for writing browser and server-side Web software
PHP	Writing Web-based applications
SQL (Structured Query Language)	Writing queries to relational database management systems
VB.NET (Visual Basic .NET)	Writing software for PCs; also, for writing browser and server-side Web software

confine programming languages to a formality that today is still far from natural and often difficult to master.

Programs are written in a number of computer languages. Table B.8 lists some of the more commonly used languages and their uses.[7] Each computer language, like a human language, has its own vocabulary and grammatical rules. However, most share a similar logical approach to communication with the computer.

Of special interest is the **Java** language, originally developed to run on networks. Programmers now use it in many different ways, particularly in e-commerce applications. It actually runs differently than many other programming languages, in that it is platform independent. This means it can work on many different kinds of computers.

Java's main competitor is Microsoft's .Net platform of languages, including VB.NET, C++.NET, and C# (pronounced "C-sharp") .NET. As an example of a .NET language, consider Figures B.16 and B.17, which show an application in VB.NET for a video store. The figures show both the interface for this application and some of the corresponding programming instructions (code) necessary to implement the logic behind it.

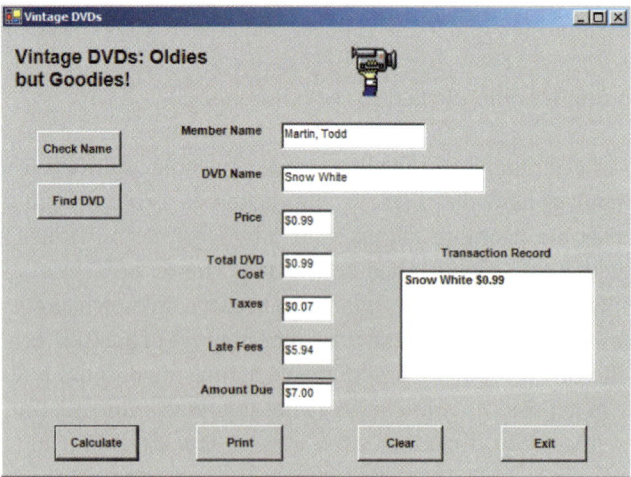

FIGURE B.16 A customized transaction form created using VB.NET.

---

7. Popularity is based on job openings for each computer language on the Craigslist website, as quoted in http://www.dedasys.com/articles/language_popularity.html.

An Overview of Application Software | 393

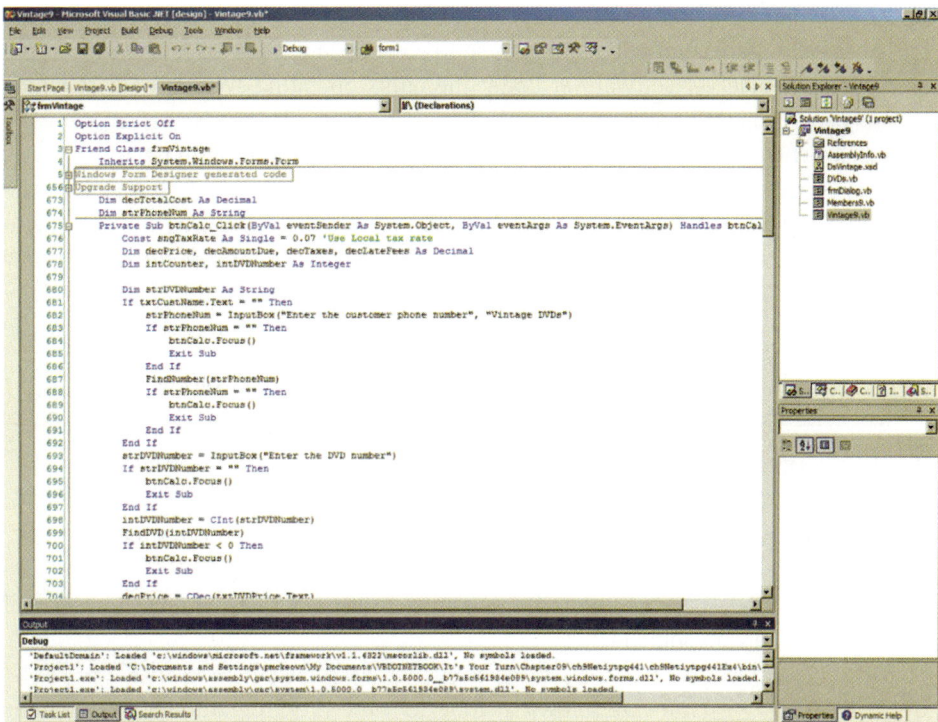

FIGURE B.17 Part of the VB.NET code written to produce the customized transaction form shown in Figure B.16.

Open-Source Software One ongoing argument in the world of software is the use and development of open-source vs. proprietary software. **Open-source software** refers to programs for which the authors allow anyone to view the *source code*—the programming instructions—and make changes. Many open-source software applications are freely available for downloading over the Internet. The only requirement is that any programmer who makes changes to the open-source code must also make those changes freely available to others. Examples of open-source software and languages are the Apache Web server software, the Linux operating system, MySQL database software, the Firefox Web browser, and the PHP Web development language. Open-source software is supported by a community of users who actively participate in newsgroups and websites, like *www.phpfreaks.com*.

On the other hand, **proprietary software** requires a purchased licence and typically restricts access to the source code to the company employees. Examples of proprietary software are the Microsoft Windows operating system and IBM's DB2 database software. Proprietary software is supported by the company that sells it through technical support centres and websites.

The trade-offs between open-source and proprietary software include cost and support. Open-source software is typically free, but often provides no centralized support centres. Proprietary software has a cost associated with it, but has a centralized support system.

There are cases where the software or language is free, but it requires the use of proprietary software to run. For example, it is possible to develop a website using a Microsoft language like ASP.NET using any text editor free of charge, but the website must run on the proprietary Microsoft Internet Information System Web server.

An exception is Java, a proprietary language licensed by Sun Microsystems. Java is typically associated with the open-source movement because it will run on the Apache Web server software or under the Linux operating system, both of which are also open-source software.

As with hardware, software is changing rapidly to meet the needs of users. This is true for both application and operating system software. Further, the continuing contest between proprietary and open-source software will be one to watch. It may greatly influence both the software you use in the future and how much it will cost. If you use a mobile device or smartphone, this is an especially fluid area for software as companies vie to provide you with more ways to use your mobile device.

Quick Test

1. True or False. Spreadsheet software is not as good as database software for storing data records because it often includes redundant information.

2. A(n) _____ is a detailed sequence of actions that, when followed, will accomplish some task.

3. _____ software allows anyone to view the programming instructions and make changes.

Answers: 1. True; 2. algorithm; 3. Open-source

ROI STUDENT RETURN ON INVESTMENT SUMMARY

1. What elements affect the processing capability of hardware?

The microprocessor contains the majority of the components that make up the central processing unit (CPU). The CPU works together with memory to control the execution of all instructions and the processing of all data. The CPU is located on the system's motherboard, the main circuit board in an electronic device. In a PC, the motherboard contains the bus, the microprocessor, and other chips and circuits. The CPU contains a number of components including the ALU, FPU, decode unit, cache memory, prefetch unit, registers, clock, one or more buses, and the instruction set, which enable it to carry out the required processing. Microprocessors are typically differentiated by their instruction set, their clock speed, and their bandwidth, which is the number of bits that the CPU can process in a single instruction. The CPU clock speed is the most commonly used performance characteristic.

2. What types of input, output, and storage hardware should business professionals keep current with?

The primary types of input hardware are the keyboard; pointing devices such as the mouse; scanning devices such as bar code readers; and the Internet or other network connection. The keyboard is generally recognized as the primary and most common input device for computers. Pointing devices, which work along with a GUI, allow the user to provide data and instructions to the computer using physical movements such as *point* and *click*. Scanning devices read data and information stored on some form of non-connected media.

Output devices deliver the result of processing operations to the user. Output devices include display and printed output devices, storage devices, the Internet or other network connection, and a wide variety of other electronic devices. Display devices continue to be the most common category of output device. Display devices are also a significant component for input. Most display devices today use liquid crystal display (LCD) technology, which uses a piece of liquid crystal material placed between a pair of transparent electrodes. Display performance is a function of its dot pitch, refresh rate, and physical size. A variety of printing devices allow a range of quality and options in outputting both text and graphics. The most popular technologies for printers are inkjet, laser, and thermal.

Because of the limited amount of internal storage and the volatility of RAM, some form of external storage is necessary to permanently store data and programs. This secondary storage comes as magnetic storage media, optical disks, and chip-based flash memory. Stored information is accessed by internal memory when the control unit decides that this information is needed. Because the secondary storage unit must locate the information, read it, and then transfer it to internal memory, secondary storage is a slower form of memory than internal memory. However, this disadvantage is balanced by virtually unlimited storage capacity.

3. Why is the operating system so important to the use of all types of computers?

The operating system manages all of the message traffic that flows from the user to the application software to the computer and back again. It also handles the allocation of resources and the assignment of tasks to various software programs, and it carries out needed tasks with application software without worrying about the hardware interfaces. However, there are important differences between the operating systems for mainframes, networks, personal computers, and hand-held devices, depending on the numbers of users and the complexity of the peripheral devices that they manage.

All operating systems consist of two parts: the kernel and the command interpreter. The kernel is the essential part of the operating system that handles requests from application programs or from hardware and determines the processing order of the requests. The kernel may also handle demands for internal memory from competing applications by parcelling out the limited amount of internal memory as needed. The command interpreter accepts commands from users and translates them into language that the kernel can understand.

4. How do business professionals obtain and use application software?

Business professionals rely on both commercially developed and custom-developed application software. The most commonly used commercially developed application software categories include word processing, spreadsheet, database, presentation, Web browsers and other Internet-related software, and specialized software.

Business professionals rely on custom-developed software, composed of multiple computer programs, to meet specific organizational needs. To develop each of these programs, an algorithm must first be defined. The next step is writing the program in a computer language that can be understood by the computer. Computer languages that have been used for programming include SQL, C and C++, Java, PHP, and VB.NET. Of these, VB.NET is an example of a proprietary language from Microsoft, and PHP is an example of an open-source language that is not owned by any one company or organization. Java is a computer language that is proprietary but is often associated with open-source development.

KNOWLEDGE SPEAK

algorithm   391
application program interface (API)   378
bandwidth   362
basic input/output system (BIOS)   362
binary   357
bit   357
bus   362
byte   359
central processing unit (CPU)   360
character encoding   358
command interpreter   377
digital data   357
direct-access storage   373

dynamic RAM (DRAM)   363
graphical user interface (GUI)   377
hyperlink   390
input/output (I/O) tasks   380
instruction set   361
Java   392
kernel   377
machine instructions   359
memory chips   357
microprocessor chips   357
motherboard   360
open-source software   393
operating system (OS)   376

peripheral RAM   363
program   391
proprietary software   393
resolution   369
secondary storage   373
software application suite   385
Standard ASCII (American Standard
    Code for Information Interchange)   358

static RAM (SRAM)   363
system unit   360
touch screen monitor   371
tracking   369
transistor   357
Unicode   358
video RAM (VRAM)   363
virtual memory   384

TECH GUIDE C

 ## THE DETAILS OF NETWORKING

WHAT WE WILL COVER

- Network Architecture
- Network Layer Model
- Local Area Networks
- The Internet: A Network of Networks
- The World Wide Web

 ### STUDENT RETURN ON INVESTMENT

Through your investment of time in reading and thinking about this Tech Guide, your return—or created value—is gaining knowledge. Use the following questions as a study guide.

1. What is client/server architecture, and how does it work?

2. How does the network layer model describe a wide area network?

3. How are local area networks configured?

4. How does the Internet work?

5. What makes the World Wide Web valuable to business professionals?

A special thanks to Robert Hudyma, Franklyn Prescod, and Frances Prychidny for their careful review and feedback on this Tech Guide.

In Chapter 2, we briefly introduced the concept of computer networks and how they can benefit you as a business professional. We described the basic types of networks, network connections, and protocols, as well as network hardware and software. Finally, we discussed the Internet and World Wide Web. In this Tech Guide, we provide more details about these important topics.

We start with the topic of network architecture and its most common type, client/server networks. After that, we review the network software, protocols, and data component using a network layering model. Next we discuss local area networks in more detail, because they are the network that you will work with in your university or college environment. Finally, we take a closer look at the Internet and World Wide Web.

NETWORK ARCHITECTURE

Much like a building, **network architecture** refers to the design of a computer system or network. The term usually covers the overall combination of the hardware and software that makes up the network infrastructure. An *open architecture* is one where anyone can know the design, thus allowing anyone to develop software and hardware to work with it. A *closed architecture* network has a proprietary design, making it difficult for outsiders to design programs that work with the network. Most of today's computer systems are open to allow for easy growth.

In this section, we discuss the most common architecture for computer networks, the client/server network.

Client/Server Architecture

In the *client/server architecture*, each computer on the network is running either server software or client software, or both types of software simultaneously. *Server software* provides data or resources to other computers in the network. Computers running server software are typically referred to as **servers**, with each server typically focusing on a specific task. For example, a *file server* stores and delivers shared files. A *print server* manages one or more shared network printers. Other servers manage databases (*database server*), email (*email server*), and access to the World Wide Web (*Web server*).

Clients are network computers running client software that request services from the servers. The clients depend on servers for network resources like software, files, devices, processing power, and access to the Internet. Figure C.1 shows a client who is requesting database records from a server.

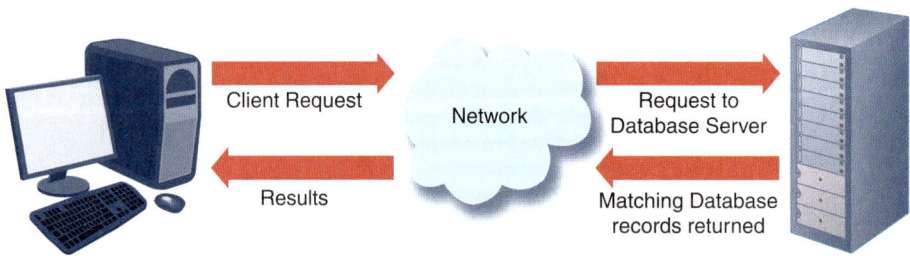

FIGURE C.1 Client/server architecture.

Note that while we use *client* and *server* to refer to hardware devices, it is actually the client software and server software running on the hardware that enable client/server processing to occur. In fact, it is possible to run several different types of client or server software on the same machine. For example, you probably have both Web browser and email client software simultaneously running on your computer.

How is the client/server architecture valuable to business professionals? Recall that in centralized computing, data are stored and processed on a central machine that is remote from the user, while PCs store and process data locally to the user. However, business professionals frequently need both the power of a central computer and the ease of use of a PC. Thus, the client/server architecture combines the best of central computers and PCs. This combination of local and remote data storage and processing leads to four basic computing architectures, shown in Figure C.2. Note that the client/server system overlaps both local and remote storage and processing.

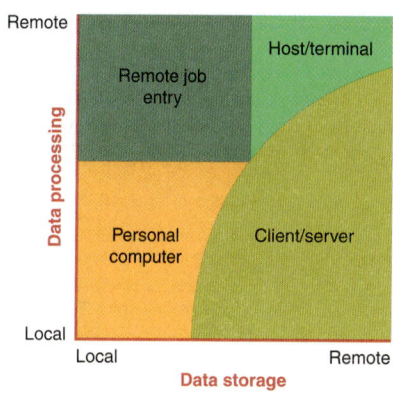

FIGURE C.2 Four basic computing architectures.
SOURCE: R. T. Watson, *Organizational Memory,* 4th ed. (New York: John Wiley, 2004), p. 354.

The simplest form of client/server computing involves a file server, which controls access to the network, manages communications between PCs, and makes data and program files available to the individual PCs. The computing load, however, is still distributed among the individual PCs. This can actually pose a significant problem for many businesses. If a large number of clients attempt to access the server, the client/server performance declines. Therefore, to increase processing efficiency, many client/server networks involve a three-tiered architecture.

Three-Tiered Architecture In many cases, there is actually a series of clients and servers working to provide the data or application software that an end-user client requests. The most common form of series is the **three-tiered client/server architecture**, which uses a client, an application server, and a database server. In this client/server environment, a user working at a GUI-based client PC or workstation requests data or processing from an application server, which decides what data to supply. The application server then sends a query to the database server to retrieve those data. The database server processes the query and returns the matching data to the application server, which processes the data into the form required by the user. Figure C.3 illustrates this process.

One of the strengths of three-tiered client/server computing, therefore, is the capability to string together a series of servers to respond to a client's request while maintaining a single, central database. This allows an organization to maintain data in only one place, which avoids the difficulties of partitioning stored data. In the next section we discuss more advantages of client/server architecture.

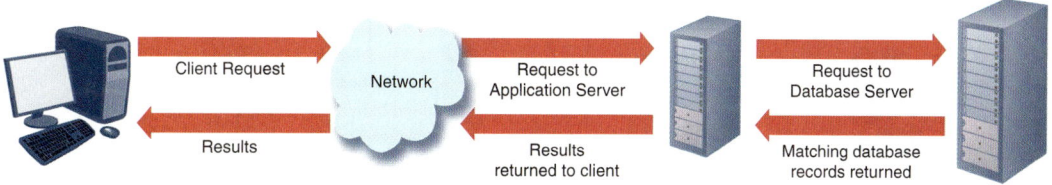

FIGURE C.3 Three-tiered client/server architecture.

Table C.1	Common Types of Servers
Server Type	Purpose
Application	Handles high-speed processing.
Database	Handles queries to a large database and returns matching records.
Fax	Sends and receives faxes for entire organization.
File	Provides both software and data files to users.
Mail	Sends and receives email for entire organization.
Web	Handles requests for web pages.

Using Client/Server Systems to Increase Knowledge Work Efficiency

The client/server environment has a variety of purposes. Table C.1 shows the most commonly used servers, along with their purpose in a client/server network. For example, Web server software handles requests for web pages, whereas email server software sends and receives email. In fact, many organizations now use the application server to replace centralized computers for handling large-scale processing tasks. For example, IBM refers to its large computers as *enterprise servers* to emphasize their use in client/server computing as application servers. Figure C.4 shows a typical client/server network that includes file, fax, mail, database, application, and Web servers and a variety of clients.

Similar to the other types of computing, client/server computing has advantages and disadvantages, as listed in Table C.2. The primary advantage of client/server computing lies in its ability to share processing and data storage responsibilities among multiple machines and to use specialized servers to meet specific needs. The primary disadvantage is the complexity inherent in sharing responsibilities among multiple machines. Overall, however, the trend is toward wider use of client/server computing because of its increased flexibility.

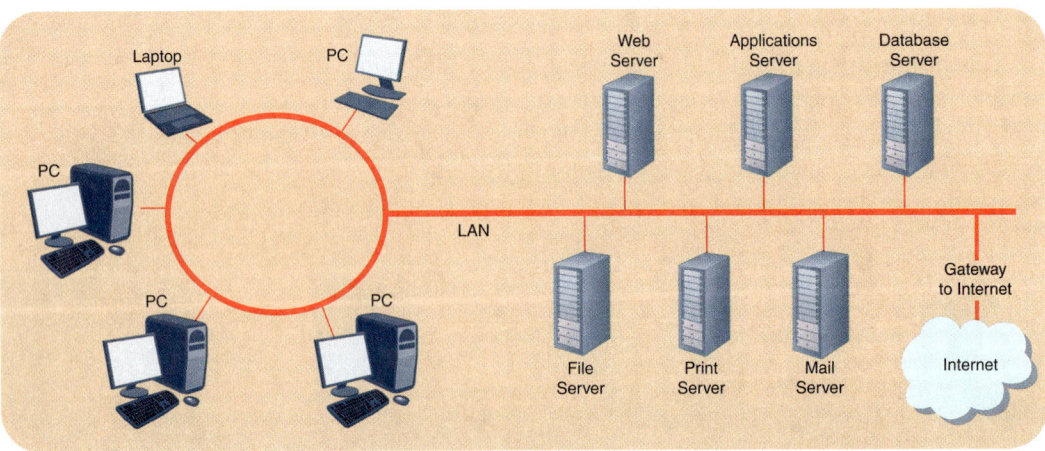

FIGURE C.4 Servers on a typical client/server network.

Network Architecture

Table C.2	Advantages and Disadvantages of Client/Server Systems
Advantages	**Disadvantages**
The computing burden is shared among servers and clients.	There is a more complex programming relationship between clients and servers.
Specialized servers handle one particular type of task.	System upgrades require upgrading of all clients and servers, regardless of location.
The system can be upgraded in small steps.	There are more complex computer and network security issues due to increased numbers of users and client machines with access to networked resources, including data.
The loss of one client does not stop other clients from accessing the server.	

Peer-to-Peer Networks

As mentioned earlier, it is possible for computers on a network to run both server and client software at the same time. This enables organizations to set up a **peer-to-peer network**, where each computer in the network is on the same level as other computers and each computer is equally responsible for overseeing the functions of the network. Depending on the network connection, two computers in a peer-to-peer network may communicate directly with one another, or they may communicate through intermediate peer computers. In a pure peer-to-peer network, the two computers that are communicating with each other share the responsibility for carrying out the communication. There are no central computers or servers to manage the correct functioning of the network. Figure C.5 shows how peer-to-peer networks differ from client/server ones.

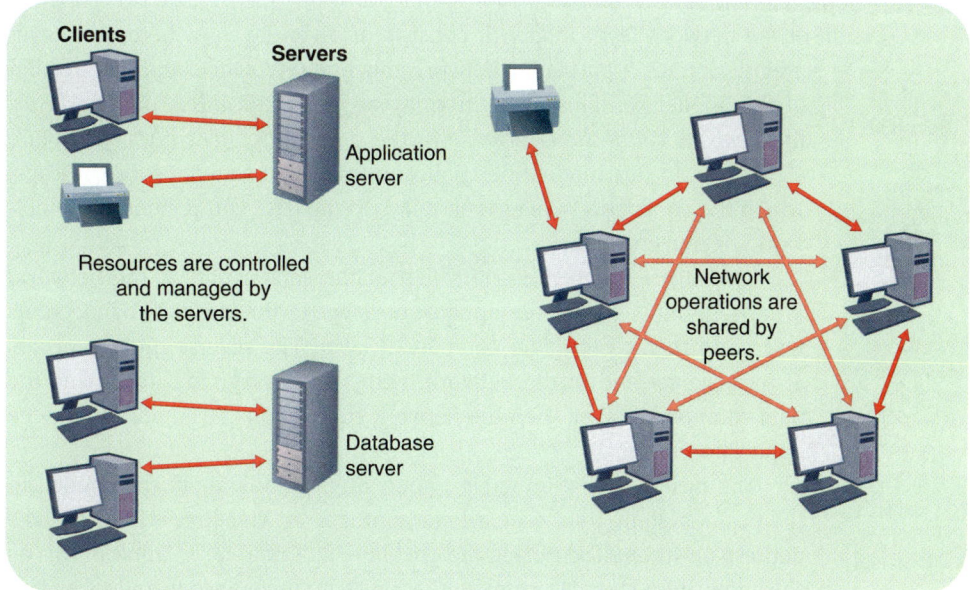

FIGURE C.5 Comparing client/server networks (left) with peer-to-peer networks (right).

Prior to 1999, most business professionals primarily used peer-to-peer networks on small LANs. In June 1999, however, Napster, a famous service for sharing files, began operation. Napster demonstrated how to share files using a virtual peer-to-peer network over the Internet. Today, many companies use peer-to-peer networks for the legitimate purposes of sharing data, information, and services.

Quick Test

1. The most common form of networking architecture is the _____ architecture.

2. A _____ architecture network has a proprietary design, making it difficult for outsiders to develop programs to use with the network.

3. In a _____ network, the computers are running both client and server software with no centralized server.

Answers: 1. client/server; 2. closed; 3. peer-to-peer.

NETWORK LAYER MODEL

Now that you understand network architecture and how its design benefits business professionals, how does the network actually operate? Recall that networks include a data component, as well as network connections, which deliver messages between computers in a network. In addition, networks rely on a wide variety of application software to actually generate the message. A **network layer model** will help you understand how these three elements work together. In this model, each layer handles part of the communications between computers.

The International Organization for Standardization (ISO) created the original version of the network layer model. It consists of seven layers, where each layer of the standard defines a particular network functionality. Our simplified version of this model contains only three layers: the *application software layer*, the *network connections layer*, and the *data component layer,* as Figure C.6 shows. In this model, the application software generates the message, which the connections layer then relays to the data component of the network for transmission.

Looking at Figure C.6, note that at the sender end of the network, a message moves from the application layer to the network connections layer, and then to the data component layer. The reverse process occurs at the receiver end of the network, with the message first traversing the data component layer, then the network connections layer, and finally the application layer.

The postal system provides a good way to think about this model. In the postal system, you write a letter, put it in an envelope with a friend's address on it, and then place the envelope in a mail box. Think of this as the application layer. A postal worker picks up the envelope and takes it to the post office (the network connections layer), which decides how to send

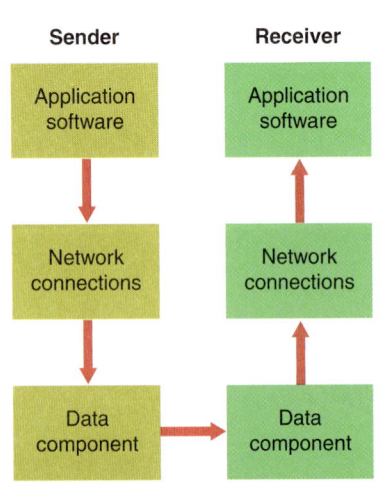

FIGURE C.6 A simplified version of the network layer model.

it to your friend (the data component layer). At the other end, your friend reverses this process to reply to your letter.

Application Software Layer

The application layer includes well-known software applications such as Web browsers and email. This software formats user data by adding information to make it conform to a specific standard or *protocol*, the specific set of rules for communicating. Protocols for the application layer of the Internet include *simple mail transfer protocol (SMTP)* for email, *hypertext transfer protocol (HTTP)* for web pages, and *electronic data interchange (EDI)* for large-scale exchange of data between organizations. The resulting message to the receiver thus combines the message generated by the application software and the protocol.

Application software may also encrypt the data (place the data in a secure, unreadable form) to protect it from unauthorized readers. For example, suppose a customer goes to an e-commerce website and fills out and submits a form to order a product. In this case, the application is a Web browser, the message is the contents of the form, and the protocol is HTTP. In addition, the message is encrypted. Figure C.7 shows the components of the application software layer for any message. For a product order, the message would include the message protocol (HTTP) and encrypted message and encrypted order data. Note that the contents of the message need to be decrypted on the receiving side as well.

FIGURE C.7 The components of the application software layer for a message.

Network Connection Layer

In the network connection layer, the application software layer formats the message according to the network protocol. For example, the protocol for the Internet is the **transmission control protocol/Internet protocol (TCP/IP)**, as shown in Figure C.8.

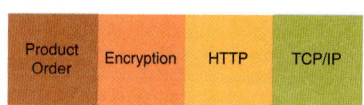

FIGURE C.8 The components of the connection layer for a message.

With the TCP/IP Internet protocol, the network connection layer conducts a series of operations to prepare the message for sending across the Internet to a destination computer. It must first convert the address of the server at the destination from a text form (e.g., somecomputer.somewhere.org) to an *IP address*. The address is converted by using a conversion table stored either on the user's computer or on a computer with which the local computer can communicate. For example, say you want to send an email message to World Vision Canada, whose address is info@worldvision.ca. The domain name server (a client/server application) converts this to the IP address 205.189.149.31.

Next, the network connection divides the message into smaller digital units called **packets**, or *datagrams* in TCP/IP terminology, each of which contains a specific number of bytes. At this step, each packet receives a sequence number and a destination address. Figure C.9 shows this process of converting binary digits to packets and adding the IP address to them.

Because network computers send large amounts of data quickly and then do not send any data for a while, networks rely on a technology called packet switching. **Packet switching**

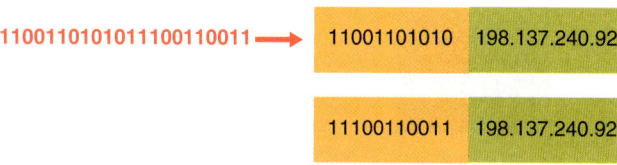

FIGURE C.9 Converting binary data into packets.

routes individual packets through the network based on their destination addresses. It thus allows the sharing of the same data path among many computers in the network. Further, if a switching device on the network is inoperable, the packet finds another way to reach its destination. Packet switching is the key enabling technology that makes it possible to build large-scale, survivable networks like the Internet.

When sending a group of data packets—like product orders or email messages—to a computer with an IP address, software on the sending computer sends the packets to the nearest device that can switch network traffic for retransmission to other switching devices on the network. A common switching device is a *router*, which is a type of computer with the sole purpose of accepting packets and determining the best way to send them to the destination computer. That is, the router specializes in determining the best path for the packet and sending it there.

The original packetized message is reconstructed using the sequence order that is attached to each packet. As a result, packets may follow different paths through the network, as well as arrive in a different order. As they arrive, the destination computer acknowledges received packets. If the sending computer does not get an acknowledgement that a packet has arrived within a certain timeframe, it automatically resends the unacknowledged packets. This ensures the receipt of all packets.

Have you ever tried to make a phone call using voice over IP (VoIP)? Was it a little choppy and out of sequence at times? This occurs because a phone call using VoIP relies on packet switching. Voice is broken into packets (just like data), routed by routers and switches, and re-assembled at the destination. At times this results in poorer quality than calls placed using regular phone lines. Of course, providers of VoIP in Canada are finding ways of improving quality and offering their services at competitive prices.

Data Component Layer

You can share any data that can be converted to electronic signals over a computer network. The sending of data from one computer to another over a channel using electronic signals is known as *data transmission*. Data transmission is concerned with ensuring that the data are sent and received correctly and efficiently.

Data and information transmitted over networks travel over various media, including twisted pair wire, coaxial cable, fibre-optic cable, and microwave and satellite transmission. *Twisted pair*, which consists of twisted pairs of copper wires, is similar to the wiring used in much of the existing telephone system. Networks widely rely on it, both within and between locations.

Coaxial cable, which transmits cable television signals into your home, is also widely used in networks. Although television transmissions used to consist of only one-way signals, television cable across Canada has been converted to a type of cable capable of handling two-way signals. This two-way cable enables the connection of home computers to ISPs.

Fibre-optic cable is the newest medium and consists of glass fibre strands that can transmit a large number of signals at extremely high speeds. However, individual computers are not set up to connect directly to fibre-optic cable, so it is often necessary to use twisted pair cable for the last few feet to the computer. Figure C.10 compares copper wire with fibre-optic cables for transmitting the same volume of information.

FIGURE C.10 Coaxial cable compared with glass fibre.

Table C.3	Comparison of Media		
Media	Cost	Error Rates	Speed
Twisted pair	Low	Low	Low-high
Coaxial cable	Moderate	Low	Low-high
Fibre optics	High	Very low	High-very high
Radio	Low	Moderate	Low
Infrared	Low	Moderate	Low
Microwave	Moderate	Low-moderate	Moderate
Satellite	Moderate	Low-moderate	Moderate

SOURCE: Jerry Fitzgerald and Alan Dennis, *Business Data Communications and Networking*, 8th ed., New York: John Wiley, 2005, p. 85.

Microwaves are high-frequency radio transmissions that can be sent between two Earth stations or between Earth stations and communications satellites. This method is commonly used to transmit television signals. Direct broadcast *satellite transmission* uses microwaves for one-way downloads of data to homes and offices. It provides a way of carrying out transmission of data to a user, especially where traditional telephone lines do not exist or are difficult to install.

A variety of wireless technologies are also becoming popular as a way to provide mobile users with connections regardless of where they may be. The most popular wireless method of sending data relies on radio transmissions. Infrared light used to be a popular method, but is falling into disuse because it requires a line of sight. On the other hand, radio transmissions can pass through walls. However, security is a problem due to the radio waves going in all directions. (We discuss wireless networks in more detail in a later section.) Table C.3 compares the communication media used in the data component layer.

In addition to the media that transmit data, other aspects of the data component layer include the signal type and the data rate.

Signal Type The **signal type** is how data are sent over the network. A signal can be digital or analog. Digital transmission sends bits at different levels. A computer can therefore transmit over a digital communications link without changing the data (other than encoding it to make it suitable to the physical media). On the other hand, analog signals transmit bits as wave patterns, which requires modifying data before transmitting them. Because most telephone and cable systems are analog, to transmit data, *modems* convert digital signals from the computer into analog signals for transmission over the communications link.

Telephone and cable modems convert between analog and digital forms of data using different methods. At the sender's end of a telephone modem, the modem modulates the digital computer data or information into an analog form that can travel over standard telephone lines. At the other end, a modem demodulates the analog signal back into a digital form that the receiver's computer can understand. Cable modems modulate and demodulate the cable signal into a stream of data. In addition, cable modems incorporate a variety of other functions to allow the PC to be linked to a network.

Table C.4	Analog vs. Digital Data Transmission	
	Analog	**Digital**
Advantages	• Reflect natural phenomena; sound, light, and electricity are all analog • Low-cost, existing infrastructure for analog transmission	• Less susceptible to noise, resulting in a lower error rate • Allows transmission of multiple signals over one line at the same time (called *multiplexing*) • Faster rate of transmission • Less-complex and lower-cost circuits
Disadvantages	• More susceptible to noise, distortion, and interference	• Analog phenomena require conversion to digital signals

Both analog and digital data transmission are frequently used. Table C.4 lists some advantages and disadvantages of each form of transmission. The choice of signal usually rests on which of the two is more efficient for the given application.

Data Rate and Bandwidth Issues The **data rate** is measured in bits per second (bps). For example, a telephone modem allows for a maximum data rate of 56 kbps. Even when using a 56-kbps modem, the actual data rate can vary depending on the quality of the telephone line. As a result, most business professionals increasingly use other methods of transferring data, including digital subscriber lines, television (TV) cable, and the various T-carrier circuits. A *digital subscriber line (DSL)* transmits computer data in a digital form along the same telephone line that analog voice communications uses. The *T-carrier circuits* are dedicated digital lines that a telecommunications company leases to users to carry data between specific points. Table C.5 lists the maximum data rates for various methods of transmitting data.

Transmission speed (often referred to as latency or propagation delay) relates to how fast a single message can be transmitted between two nodes. *Transmission capacity* relates to how many bits can be transmitted per second. While speed and capacity are not the same thing, they are highly related.

Table C.5	Maximum Data Rates	
Transmission Method	**Maximum Data Rate**	**Comments**
Standard telephone service	56 Kbps	Available everywhere
Digital subscriber line (DSL)	6 Mbps in; 640 Kbps out	Becoming more available; does not slow down as more people sign up
Cable	As high as 55 Mbps but averages between 200 Kbps and 2 Mbps	Cable must support two-way communication; available in many locations but slows down as more people use it in a specific location
T-carrier circuits (T-1 to T-4)	1.544 Mbps–274 Mbps	Leased lines used for commercial telecommunication

SOURCE: Jerry Fitzgerald and Alan Dennis, *Business Data Communications and Networking*, 8th ed., New York: John Wiley, 2005.

The term *bandwidth*, often used in relationship to data rate, measures how fast data flow on a transmission path. With the increasing demand from users for the capability to view high-quality photos, graphics, and full-motion video on their computers, the competition to provide higher bandwidth access is becoming keen among telecommunications providers.

The two extremes of bandwidth are baseband (which carries only a single digital signal) and broadband (which transmits in a variety of different analog signals). However, broadband is really what makes Web-based services viable and attractive. To place orders on an e-commerce site, the data component layer must include the customer's modem and telephone line, or cable modem and cable. When the message reaches the customer's *Internet service provider* (*ISP*), the ISP's modem and hardware connections then handle the data. Without a high-speed connection, popular applications like MySpace and Gmail would not work well. Certainly without broadband it is impossible to take advantage of software downloads and new services such as VoIP.

Bandwidth is a consideration in any e-commerce venture. Not only do the technical aspects of the website have to take bandwidth into account, the bandwidth of the target customers also needs to be considered. It would be all well and good to have a fantastic video demonstrating your products on a website, but if a target customer does not have DSL or higher, they will not be able to view the video.

Until recently, Canada was a world leader in broadband adoption. Even though adoption rates are at a plateau, we continue to lead the United States in percentage terms.[1] Research on Canadian broadband usage and its social and economic impact is being conducted to answer questions such as: Does Canada's adoption of broadband enhance economic activities? Does it promote societal well-being or does it create a social divide between those who have high-speed access and those who do not?[2] It is certain that consumers will continue to move from baseband to broadband to access the increasing number of Web services offered by businesses and other organizations.

Now that you have a better understanding of how networks operate, let's look next at how business professionals use them.

Quick Test

Match the network layer with the appropriate hardware or software.

1. application software layer   a. TCP/IP
2. network connection layer   b. fibre optics
3. data component layer   c. email software

Answers: 1. c; 2. a; 3. b

---

1. Organisation for Economic Co-operation and Development, "OECD Broadband Statistics, December 2005," http://www.oecd.org/document/39/0,2340, en_2825_495656_36459431_1_1_1_1,00.htm, retrieved July 31, 2006.

2. C.A. Middleton and C. Sorensen, "How Connected Are Canadians? Inequities in Canadian House-holds' Internet Access," *Canadian Journal of Communication*, 30(4), 2005, pp. 463–483.

LOCAL AREA NETWORKS

Most organizations now use **local area networks (LANs)** to share information and resources among employees. Sharing information enables users to work with, and send, the same data or information files. Sharing resources involves the users' ability to share software and hardware.

Sharing software avoids the need for an organization to purchase a copy of a software package for every computer in the organization. Instead, the organization purchases *software licences* for their employees, which allow multiple people to simultaneously use a software package. Sharing hardware allows the use of printers, disk storage, scanners, and so on through the network, rather than purchasing these devices for each user. Making hardware available through a LAN, especially highly specialized types of hardware, can significantly reduce an organization's costs.

The vast majority of LANs use the **Ethernet protocol** to connect computers and move information between computers on the network. With the Ethernet protocol, a computer on the network transmits a message that contains the address of the destination computer. Because all computers are free to transmit at any time, collision-detecting software must be in place. After detecting a collision, the software directs each computer to stop transmitting and wait a random length of time before re-transmitting its message. This system works well and is the basis for most LANs in operation today.

A client on a LAN can not only share information and software with other PCs on the same LAN, but also can communicate through gateways and bridges with other types of computers and with other LANs. A *gateway* is a combination of hardware and software that connects two dissimilar computer networks. The gateway allows LAN users to access a mainframe network without leaving their PC. Similarly, a gateway between a LAN and a WAN enables LAN users to send email over the WAN. In contrast, a *bridge* connects two different networks. For example, if a bridge connects two LANs, computers on each LAN can access the other network's file server without making any physical changes to the data.

Wireless LANs

As its name implies, **wireless LANs (WLANs)** replace the usual LAN cabling between computers with wireless transmissions. They are becoming increasingly popular as mobile users need to connect to their local network and often from there to the Internet. WLANs eliminate the need for cable in remote areas, provide an inexpensive alternative to shared printing, and connect two networks separated by some obstacle, such as a highway or wall, through which cable cannot run.

Business professionals use WLANs to increase the efficiency of many activities in the workplace, including the following:

- Pricing, labelling, handling orders, and taking inventory from anywhere in a store, and then communicating that information directly to the back-office computer
- Connecting a wireless device to a bar code scanner to scan items in a warehouse and thereby produce a list of items and their locations

- Requesting medical tests, checking the results, and then entering the information into a patient's electronic record from the patient's room
- Checking email on laptops and handhelds from anywhere without having to be connected by wiring

Wireless networking hardware uses radio frequencies to transmit information between individual computers, each of which has a wireless network adapter. The individual computers do not communicate directly with each other. Instead, they communicate with a wireless network hub or router. The hub or router bridges the wireless network to a traditional Ethernet and provides a shared Internet connection. Figure C.11 shows how a wireless LAN connects a number of laptops to a hub, which, in turn, connects to the organizational LAN.

The current popular standard for wireless networking supports a data rate of 50 Mbps (or more), with a typical range through open air of about 200–1,000 m. *Wi-Fi (wireless fidelity)* typically uses the IEEE 802.11g standard for short-range radio transmissions. However, the 802.11n standard may surpass it, since 802.11n allows for faster data rates of up to 70 Mbps.

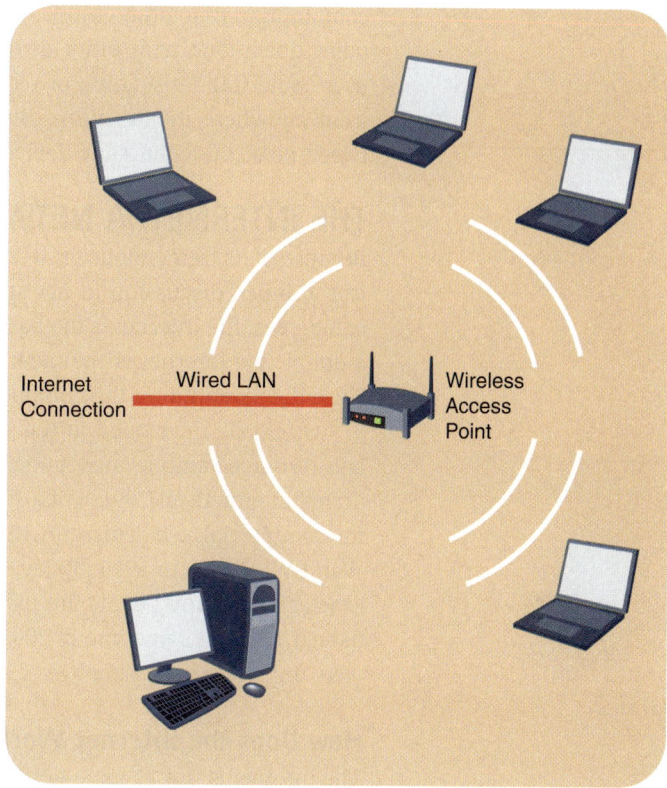

FIGURE C.11 Connection of laptops and PCs to the Internet through wireless LAN.

Any company or individual that uses a wireless LAN should be concerned about security. Access to a wireless LAN must be restricted by using passwords or allowing only certain computer IP addresses, or both. WLANs are even vulnerable internally between a laptop and the router; some form of encryption should be used to ensure that packets are not hacked.

Bluetooth and PANs

One of the newest wireless technologies, developed by a consortium of companies including Nokia, Ericsson, and Motorola, is Bluetooth. Named after the tenth-century king who merged Denmark and Norway, **Bluetooth** is a form of **personal area network (PAN)**. PAN technology enables wireless devices, such as mobile telephones, computers, and PDAs, to communicate over a short distance—less than 10 m. By embedding a low-cost transceiver chip in each device, it allows total synchronization of wireless devices without the user having to initiate any operation. The chips communicate over a radio frequency at up to 2 Mbps.

As envisioned by its developers, a business professional would use a single device adhering to the Bluetooth protocol as a mobile telephone away from the office and as a portable telephone in the office. In addition, the device would work as a PDA and quickly synchronize information with a desktop computer (also containing a Bluetooth chip), or act as a remote control to initiate any number of other operations with other devices (with the appropriate chip). For example, a user could initiate sending or receiving a fax, or printing or copying a document, from anywhere in the office. Bluetooth thus enables pervasive connectivity between personal technology devices without the use of cabling.

THE INTERNET: A NETWORK OF NETWORKS

Because of its tremendous growth over the last decade or so, the Internet is the subject of much discussion in newspapers, books, magazines, and movies. For many companies, the Internet is the basis for the widespread use of e-commerce. Without a doubt, the Internet is the most significant technology innovation to come along since the invention of the computer itself (over 60 years ago).

Originally developed in the 1960s and 1970s as a way of sharing information and resources among universities and research institutions, the Internet began its dramatic growth in 1991 when the United States government opened the Internet for commercial use. This growth further accelerated with the introduction of the World Wide Web in 1994. Today, the Internet is growing so fast that no one can say exactly how many people are using it. We do know that the number of users surpassed 1 billion sometime in 2005, and by the end of 2009 over 1.75 billion people were online, representing over 25 percent of the world's population.[3]

How Does the Internet Work?

The Internet is not a single network, but rather a network of networks. In fact, the name Internet is a shortened version of the term *internetworking* because it allows users to work among multiple networks. To connect to the Internet, as Figure C.12 shows, your computer will usually first connect to a LAN through a network interface card (NIC) or to an ISP through a modem and telephone line. The LAN, mainframe, or ISP, in turn, connects to a regional network, which then links into the backbone of the Internet.

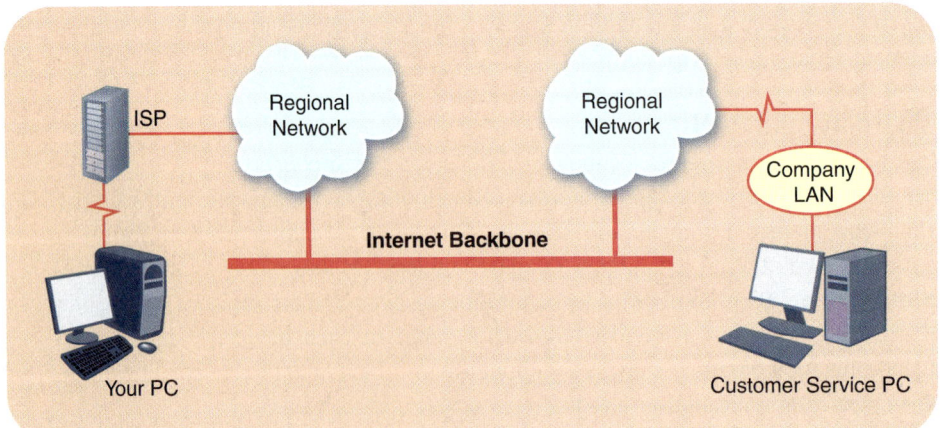

FIGURE C.12 Connecting a computer to the Internet through an ISP.

---

3. Internet World Stats, "Internet Usage Statistics," http://www.internetworldstats.com/stats.htm.

A **network interface card (NIC)** provides the physical connection between a computer and a local network. Most NICs come built into the computer with a jack into which a network cable can be plugged. Wireless NICs convert signals to radio waves that conform to standard wireless protocols and can be sent through the air. Wireless client devices can communicate directly with each other or over the network through a wireless *access point (AP)*.

Within each network, there is at least one host computer that connects to the Internet, with full two-way access to other computers on the Internet and with a unique Internet address. In many cases, all computers in the network are host computers because all have Internet addresses, even if for only a short time, as with a dial-up system.

Each host computer that connects to the Internet uses the TCP/IP protocol for assigning addresses, and packet switching for forwarding information. By having all networks follow the same TCP/IP protocol, users on any network can exchange information with users on other networks, with little or no knowledge of their physical location or configuration.

TCP/IP rules also govern email and other Internet addresses. An email address consists of two parts: (1) the user name and (2) the server address. The user name is assigned to a person or organization that is connected to a server. The "at" symbol (@) separates the user name from the server address. The server address, also known as the *domain name,* consists of groups of letters separated by periods. Moving from right to left, this address goes from the most general (country name or organization type) to the most specific (computer name). The rightmost part of the address is known as the *top-level domain*. Note that these Internet addresses are easy-to-remember versions of the numeric IP addresses that actually identify computers on the Internet.

For example, Figure C.13 shows the email address of the sales department for a fictitious company (WildOutfitters). In this example, the user name is *sales*, the server name is *wildoutfitters.com,* and the top-level domain is *com*. Because the WildOutfitters example is the general email server, it has just the company name (*WildOutfitters.com*) as the server address. Other servers at WildOutfitters may have additional names to distinguish them from this server, say, *returns.wildoutfitters.com* for the email server for the returns department, or *www.wildoutfitters.com* for the Web server.

FIGURE C.13 Components of an email address.

The Internet Corporation for Assigned Names and Numbers (ICANN), a not-for-profit company set up over 10 years ago specifically to administer the domain name system, creates top-level domains for use around the world. Table C.6 lists several top-level domains and the types of organizations that might use them.

How do you know if an email or Web address is for a person or organization located outside Canada? For servers located in another country, a two-letter suffix may be used at the end of the server name as the top-level domain. For example, the server name for the University of Minho in Portugal is minho.pt. Further, businesses often use a second-level domain name of "co" prior to the top-level domain corresponding to their country. For example, the South African Tanda Tula game preserve's domain name is *tandatula.co.za* (where "za" is the top-level domain for South Africa). Many Canadian organizations prefer to distinguish themselves as Canadian by using the popular ".ca" top-level domain (e.g., *www.cbc.ca*).

Table C.6 Top-Level Domain Names

Type of Organization	Designation	Example
Canadian-based	.ca	www.chapters.indigo.ca (Chapters and Indigo bookstores)
Educational institution	.edu	www.athabasca.edu (Athabasca University)
Commercial company	.com	www.ebay.com (eBay Auctions)
Not-for-profit organization	.org	www.aiesec.org (an international student organization)
Government	.gc.ca	www.cra-arc.gc.ca (Canada Revenue Agency)
Aerospace organizations	.aero	www.bas.aero (Berlin Aviation Service)
Businesses	.biz	www.secor.biz (a Canadian strategy consultancy)
Co-operatives	.coop	www.ontario.coop (a resource for co-operatives and credit unions in Ontario)
Various	.info	www.cococay.info (information about Coco Cay island in the Bahamas)
Museums	.museum	www.annefrank.house.museum (Anne Frank House museum)
Various	.name	www.yourname.name
Professionals	.pro	www.broadway.pro (Broadway theatre shows)

Using the Internet to Perform Knowledge Work Activities

A number of software applications run on the Internet, such as the World Wide Web, email, and chat rooms. Many use the client/server approach, with each server on the network providing data and information to client computers connected to the network (although BitTorrents, Skype, and others use peer-to-peer networks). The client computer must run two types of software to take advantage of the Internet: Internet conversion software and client software. The Internet conversion software enables the computer to work with Internet packets. Most operating systems, including Windows, come with this software built into the operating system.

Client software carries out the desired operation, such as sending email, downloading files from or uploading files to a server, participating in discussion groups, working on someone else's computer, or accessing the World Wide Web. For example, to send email, you would use an email client to generate the message, which then goes to the Internet conversion software that translates it into a form that can be sent over the Internet. The most widely used Internet operations are as follows:

- email (electronic mail)
- FTP (file transfer protocol)
- newsgroups
- telnet
- Internet relay chat
- World Wide Web

Email According to a Pew poll, email over the Internet is the most popular application (although email is quickly being overtaken by social media sites; see Chapter 8). Over half of the people interviewed claimed it as their number one online activity. Email has fundamentally changed the amount of personal and business communication that occurs. So what exactly is email? Email is an asynchronous electronic method of exchanging information over a network. *Asynchronous* means that the sender and receiver are not communicating at the same time. Instead, one person sends a message, and the other person reads and replies to it at another time.

A special use of email is for listservs. A *listserv* is server software that can broadcast an email message from one member of a group to all other members. Group members simply subscribe to a listserv, and any messages sent to the listserv are automatically broadcast to the group members. Depending on how the listserv is set up, a member may be able to send messages to the listserv or may only be able to receive messages. Your instructor may have set up a listserv to which you subscribe. That way, he or she can communicate information to the entire class with one email rather than sending it to a large group of email addresses.

Email also has a number of commercial applications. Many companies use it as a powerful marketing tool. Incoming email can provide them with queries about their products, information about problems with products, or suggestions for better ways to serve their customers. Companies can combine emails with other contacts to create mailing lists for either email or postal mail (often referred to as *snail mail*) as a means of communicating with customers. On the other hand, customers expect companies to respond to email queries, complaints, or comments. Failure by a company to respond to these messages can result in very unhappy customers. Companies are finding it necessary to develop systems of responding to incoming email in addition to sending an automated response that acknowledges receiving the customer's email message.

Companies are also discovering that outbound email can generate revenue in ways never before considered. This includes sending special offers to customers who have purchased items online or who have sent a question via email. For example, airlines regularly send notices of special fares that users can only purchase online. This has resulted in a significant increase in ticket sales, with almost no additional cost to the airlines.

FTP Companies and individuals frequently need to make software, data, or document files available to a wide audience over the Internet. For example, a software company may want to distribute to current users an upgrade of a software package that it markets. Or it may make a utility software package or data files freely available. Distributing files to a large audience is done by placing them on a **file transfer protocol (FTP)** server and having the users download them over the Internet. (Another protocol that is becoming increasingly popular is BitTorrent, *www.bittorrent.com*.)

Using an FTP site to download files is straightforward. You start FTP client software or a Web browser, enter the address of the FTP server that you want to use, and enter your user ID and password. At this point, you will see a list of directories or folders on the FTP server from which you can select files to download,

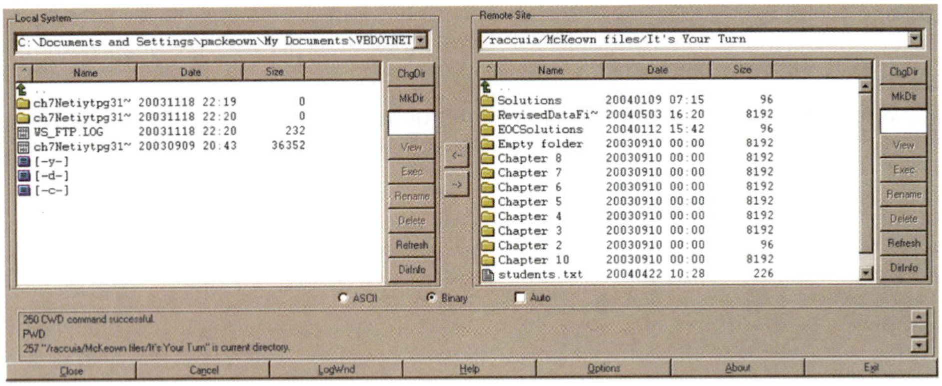

FIGURE C.14 Software for accessing an FTP server.

as Figure C.14 shows. Downloading or uploading files with this client is a simple process of highlighting the file and clicking the upload or download arrow. Other systems allow you to drag-and-drop files between client and server windows.

Newsgroups The **newsgroups** Internet application is a vast number of discussion groups on a wide range of topics. A newsgroup consists of messages written on a series of news servers, each of which transfers messages to each other. This results in replicating all postings to one newsgroup on all the other news servers through the use of the *network news transfer protocol (NNTP)*. You typically use an email client to access the newsgroups.

A tree structure of discussion topics organizes the groups. The first few letters of each newsgroup name indicates the major subject category. For example, *rec* refers to recreation and hobbies, *sci* references topics in science, *alt* refers to alternative topics (anything that's not mainstream), and so on. Each major heading has many subgroups, separated from the major heading by a period (e.g., soc.culture.australia).

Newsgroup users can post questions or comments to existing newsgroups, respond to previous posts, and create new newsgroups. Messages on newsgroups are *threaded* so that answers to or comments about a newsgroup message appear beneath it in a list of messages, regardless of the data posted. This allows readers to easily follow a discussion.

Newcomers to newsgroups should become familiar with a newsgroup before posting to it by reading the newsgroup's *frequently asked questions (FAQ)* list. FAQ lists provide answers to the most frequently asked questions about a topic.

Many companies have begun to monitor newsgroups devoted to their products as a good source of customer feedback. Because bad news travels fast on the Internet, companies must quickly detect, and respond to, any emerging problems (see Chapter 8 for more on viral social interactions and brandstorms). In our example, WildOutfitters would probably want to monitor newsgroups dedicated to outdoor products to find new ideas for marketing its products, as well as to watch for negative or erroneous postings about them. They might also want to start a newsgroup to allow customers to ask questions and exchange information on hiking equipment with other customers.

Somewhat related to newsgroups are blogs. The word "**blog**" is derived from "Web log," a user-generated website written as a journal. Blogs can cover a variety of topics, including personal reflection, commentary on current affairs, movies, food, or games. Similar to newsgroups, blogs can contain opinions on products that companies should be aware of. In fact, several companies are creating blogs to discuss and promote their own products.

Telnet One of the original purposes of the Internet was to allow researchers at one university to use a computer at another university. To make it possible to use a computer at a remote location, the telnet protocol was made a part of the Internet from the beginning. With the *telnet protocol*, you actually log on to a computer at a remote location and run the application there, with your computer acting as a terminal.

The use of telnet has diminished greatly over the last few years as organizations have found ways to replace direct access to their computers with Web access, and because organizations have security concerns about telneting. Telneting does not provide any encryption or authentication capabilities and has been largely abandoned for a system called *Secure Shell (SSH)*. This system provides all the functionality of telnet, with the addition of strong encryption to prevent sensitive data such as passwords from being intercepted, and public key authentication to ensure that the remote computer is actually what it claims to be. Furthermore, telnet is no longer a standard component of the Windows operating system since the introduction of Windows Vista in 2007.

However, telneting continues to be useful in locations where a slow Internet connection makes a typical email client or even Web-based email difficult to use. With telnet, or now more commonly SSH, a system administrator can log on to a remote system and perform any kind of maintenance or support required. This eliminates the need to be located at the same site as the system.

Internet Relay Chat **Internet relay chat (IRC)** is a *synchronous* way to use the Internet to communicate. That is, IRC allows users to communicate back and forth at the same time, similar to a telephone conversation. Chat rooms and instant messaging are two widespread uses of IRC. With *chat rooms*, many individuals can send and receive messages simultaneously regarding a subject of interest to all of them; it is a group conversation. **Instant messaging (IM)** provides a private link between two individuals over which they communicate. Although instant messaging requires a server to create the initial link between the two users, once created, the link becomes automatic, does not require the server any more, and becomes a peer-to-peer network.

Note that chat rooms allow online discussions involving multiple persons, each adding their own comments. It is a very popular way of interacting online, and provides a way of meeting other people with similar interests. Meetings in a chat room have led to a number of relationships, and even marriages. However, no one in the chat room has to provide evidence as to who they actually are. As a result, anyone using chat rooms should protect their own identity and be aware that others are doing the same. In same cases, individuals may be using chat rooms to lure unsuspecting people into dangerous situations.

THE WORLD WIDE WEB

Of the six Internet operations listed earlier, the most recent is the World Wide Web (WWW), more commonly known as simply the Web. The Web is a body of software and a set of protocols and conventions based on hypertext and multimedia that make the Internet easy to use and browse. *Hypertext* links relate information for which there is no hierarchy or menu system. *Multimedia* interactively combines text, graphics, animation, images, audio, and video displayed by and under the control of a computer.

Tim Berners-Lee, a computer scientist, developed the Web in 1989, at the European Laboratory for Particle Physics (CERN) in Geneva, Switzerland. He saw a need for physicists to be able to communicate with colleagues about their work while it was in progress, rather than waiting until a project was finished. To make this *real-time* communication possible, he wanted to create an interconnected web of documents that would allow a reader to jump between documents at will using hypertext links.

Although used only since the early 1990s on most computers, hypertext actually predates the use of personal computers. U.S. President Franklin D. Roosevelt's science advisor, Vannevar Bush, originally proposed the idea in a 1945 *Atlantic* magazine article entitled "As We May Think." Twenty years later, computer visionary Ted Nelson coined the term *hypertext*. However, hypertext remained a largely hidden concept until Apple Computers released its Macintosh HyperCard software in 1987.

As you can see, the Internet, and especially the World Wide Web, provide valuable tools and resources to business professionals. So how do you access the Web? The client computer uses software called a *Web browser* (or simply, a *browser*) that initiates activity by sending a request to a Web server for certain information.

Using Browsers to Access the Web

After using a browser to send a request to a Web server for information, the Web server responds by retrieving the information from its disk and then transmitting it to the client. Upon receiving the data, the browser formats the information for display. Web browsers use a graphical user interface (GUI) like that available on Microsoft Windows or the Apple Macintosh. With a GUI-based Web browser, you can perform various operations simply by pointing at menu selections or icons representing operations and clicking the mouse button; that is, point-and-click operations. For example, you can use a browser to navigate the Web by pointing at a hypertext link in the current document and clicking it. This operation causes the retrieval of the linked document, image file, or audio file from a distant computer and its display (or playing) on the local computer. You can also enter an address to retrieve a desired document or file.

When displaying information, the browser processes formatting instructions included in the text file retrieved from the server. For example, assume that the creator of a document stored on a Web server decides that a certain phrase should appear in italics when displayed. Instead of saving the file with an italics font, the server stores the text with tags of the form *and* that indicate the beginning and end of the text that will appear in italics when displayed.

The tags in World Wide Web documents are part of a special publishing language called **hypertext markup language (HTML)**. As such, the documents on the Web all have an .html (or .htm) extension. Documents on the Web are referred to as *web pages*, and their location is a *website*. Because HTML is standard for all computers, any Web browser can request an HTML document from any Web server. For instance, a browser running on a PC using Windows 7 can access files created on a Macintosh, which are stored on a Linux-based server.

Web servers can also store multimedia files, which include digitized text, images, animation, video, and audio. The browser retrieves these files and displays them using appropriate software. The transfer of multimedia files from the Web server to the client browser is one of the key operations that sets the Web apart from the other Internet applications. Because multimedia enables us to view photographs, graphics, and videos and listen to music, it is a major reason for the phenomenal growth in the Web's popularity.

Figure C.15 shows a fairly simple web page. The underlined words indicate a hypertext link is beneath them. Also shown in this figure is the HTML source language, or source code, necessary to create the web page. Angle brackets (< >) enclose code tags, such as *title* to indicate the title of the page, *center* to centre the text, and *b* to make the text appear in boldface. Today you can create web pages with word-processing-like software such as Microsoft Front Page and Netscape Composer, without knowing the details of HTML.

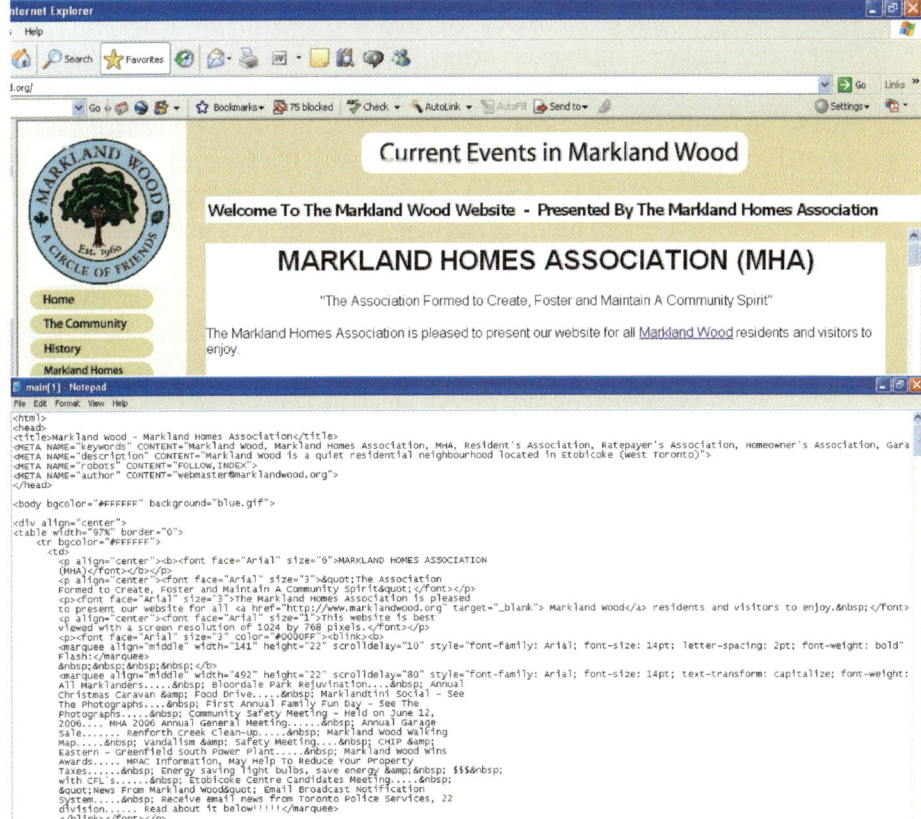

FIGURE C.15 HTML code (bottom of figure) determines a web page's appearance (top).

Browser Operations A Web browser retrieves web pages from Web servers and displays them on a client computer. In addition to being electronic rather than physical, web pages differ from pages in a book or magazine in other ways. For example, although the amount of information on a physical page is restricted to the size of the paper page, a web page can extend beyond the area shown on a screen and include audio and video.

Many individuals, companies, and organizations have created websites that contain information about themselves and their activities. They continue to add more web pages every day. A specific address identifies each web page. In Web terminology, the address of a web page is referred to as its **uniform resource locator (URL)**. A URL is a standard means of consistently locating web pages or other resources, regardless of where the Internet stores them. For example, the URL of the first page for the WildOutfitters website might be

http://www.wildoutfitters.com/welcome.htm

FIGURE C.16 The three parts of a URL.

Like every URL, this one has three parts: (1) the protocol, (2) the Internet address of the server that contains the desired resource, and (3) the path of the resource (sometimes hidden). Figure C.16 shows the three parts of the WildOutfitters welcome page address.

For Web resources, the protocol (also called the *service resource*) defines the type of resource being retrieved. The letters *http,* which, as we discussed earlier, stand for *hypertext transfer protocol*, identify a web page resource. Some of the other allowable protocols include file, telnet, FTP, mailto, and news. Table C.7 lists these protocols (service resources) and their purposes.

The second part of the URL names the Web server, in this case, *www.wildoutfitters.com*. The third part of the URL is the *path* of the Web resource, which includes the name of the web page file plus its location in any directories or folders. In our example, the path of the web page document is simply the file name, *welcome.htm*. In many cases, the path name will be much longer because it includes the folder(s) that stores the web page.

For example, the URL of the website for the Information Technology Management course offered at Ryerson University is

http://www.ryerson.ca/itm/Coursepdf/ITM700.pdf

Table C.7	Internet Protocols
Protocol	Purpose
http	Retrieve web pages
File	Retrieve files from local hard disk
telnet	Log on to a remote computer connected to the Internet
FTP	Download or upload files from an Internet FTP server
mailto	Send outgoing email
News	Display newsgroup

In this URL, Coursepdf is a subfolder in the folder called "itm". Note also that this URL ends with a .pdf, indicating that this is a document. The complete path is interpreted as itm/Coursepdf/ITM700.pdf.

Many websites make use of index.html or default.html files to save people from having to type in URLs. This also helps you to guess the URL of an organization's web page. For example, you would guess correctly if you tried *http://www.dell.com* to access Dell Inc.'s web page. In fact, most browsers now have built-in search engines that will search for the *home* website if you simply enter the name. For example, entering *Dell* will result in finding and displaying matching websites, including the one shown above.

After entering a valid address for a resource, the next step is automatic: The browser software attempts to connect to the Web server at that address, find the page referenced in the address, and return it to the user's browser. If this operation is successful, then the Web browser displays the page on the screen; otherwise, it displays an error message.

The process of moving from one website or page to another one is known as *surfing* the Web. Web surfing can quickly become a time-consuming process as you follow links looking for information or a product to purchase. You can short-circuit this process to some extent by using one of the numerous Web search engines, into which you enter a query word or term and find pages or sites that match it. However, a problem with this approach is the large number of web pages that can be returned, many of which have nothing to do with the query you entered.

As you move from website to website, you may not be aware that something called a *cookie* is saved on your PC, A **cookie** is not an application or virus, but simply a data file that will be accessed by the related website the next time you visit it. This data file tells the website any preferences you have registered with them. Obviously there are privacy concerns associated with cookies, but they do make some websites very convenient to use since you do not have to re-register your information and preferences every time you visit. Every browser has the ability to reject cookies to prevent websites from installing them. However, if this function is enabled, many websites, especially those with shopping carts, will not work.

Wireless Connectivity to the Web and Internet

In the 1990s, a number of mobile telephone companies collaborated to create a special protocol, called *wireless application protocol (WAP)*, so their telephones could connect to the Internet. These companies—Ericsson, Nokia, Matsushita (Panasonic), Motorola, and Psion—also created a company named Symbian (*www.symbian.org*) to develop and market an operating system named Symbian OS for their wireless devices. Symbian OS supports browsers and other software using WAP. Further, Symbian OS provides contact information, messaging, browsing, and wireless telephone calls.

WAP was transferred to some models of PDAs running the Palm operating system and GSM mobile phones, enabling them to take advantage of special WAP-based websites. WAP-based websites *cannot* normally be viewed with the most popular browsers, Firefox and Internet Explorer. Instead, they have been specially configured for WAP devices connected to a WAP server. A WAP server or WAP gateway supports the use of WML (wireless mark-up language), which allows content to be viewed on a mobile device, much like how HTML allows content to be viewed on a PC. This content viewed on a mobile device, however, is often stripped down to the bare minimum and may result in viewing pages in text only.

There are still mobile devices in use today that take advantage of WML and WAP and websites that provide a WAP version of their site for easy viewing on a mobile device. Newer smartphones, like the Apple iPhone, however, use embedded mini-browsers to access the Internet just as a browser on a PC would. This allows all of the content—text and graphics—to be displayed. Smartphone technology (speed and graphics capability) and the 3G (and soon 4G) telecommunications infrastructure have laid the foundation for this new generation of mobile browsing. Of course, even more important than browsing the Web is being able to access mobile applications. There are thousands of applications available for every type of smartphone, ranging from games to personal productivity tools. Check out *www.apple.com/iphone/apps-for-iphone* for the latest iPhone applications, and *http://appworld.blackberry.com/webstore* for the latest BlackBerry applications.

Another popular use of connecting mobile telephones to a WAN is **short message service (SMS)**, which sends text messages of up to 160 characters to mobile telephones. SMS can send messages to a mobile telephone when it is not active and hold the message until it becomes active. The widest use of SMS is in systems that use the **global system for mobile communication (GSM) protocol**. It is also possible to send messages to GSM mobile telephone phones using a website. Between the use of SMS and GSM, over 1.5 trillion messages were sent in 2009, amounting to almost 5 billion messages per day.[4] A variant of SMS that allows images and audio to be sent via mobile devices is called *multimedia messaging service (MMS)*. Most mobile telephones now have the ability to take photos and send them via the mobile network. Even more popular is the ability to download ring tones for mobile telephones to personalize telephone rings.

Beyond personal applications, the business applications for wireless Internet, SMS, and MMS are numerous:

- Using SMS to notify a salesperson about a request for information, along with a number to call
- Immediately sending a photo of a car accident to expedite an insurance claim
- Providing a service person with the name and location of their next service call that includes a link to an Internet site with a map to the location
- Using the company intranet via mobile phone to search for inventory while making a sale with a client

Quick Test

1. True or False. A gateway is another term used to describe a bridge.

2. True or False. A domain name is always included as a part of the server address.

---

[4]. CTIA, "CTIA—The Wireless Association® Announces Semi-Annual Wireless Industry Survey Results," http://www.ctia.org/media/press/body.cfm/prid/1936.

3. The tags in World Wide Web documents are part of a special publishing language called _____.

Answers: 1. False; 2. True; 3. HTML.

ROI STUDENT RETURN ON INVESTMENT SUMMARY

1. **What is client/server architecture, and how does it work?**

The most common architecture for computer networks is client/server architecture, in which each computer on the network is running either server software or client software, or both types of software simultaneously. Server software provides data or resources to other computers in the network. Client software requests services from the servers. Clients and servers can work in series, with the most common form being the three-tiered client/server architecture that uses a client, an application server, and a database server. It is possible for computers on a network to be both servers and clients; this is known as a peer-to-peer network.

2. **How does the network layer model describe a wide area network?**

The network layer model is used to understand the way networks operate. The layers define the standards with which each network must comply. The simplified model presented in the text consists of three layers: the application software layer, networking software layer, and data component layer. The application software layer specifies the software on each computer on the network that the user uses to send and receive messages and data between computers, as well as the software necessary to encrypt the message or data streams. The networking software layer describes how the message from the application software layer is formatted according to whatever protocol will actually be used to send it over the network. For WANs, the Internet protocols (TCP/IP) and EDI protocols are important protocols in the network layer model. The data component layer describes the hardware and media (twisted pair, coaxial cable, and so on) over which a message is sent. Radio and infrared transmissions are now being used for wireless networks. Packets are transmitted over the Internet via a packet switching methodology that uses routers or switches. Two other key considerations are the signal type (analog or digital) and the data rate (the rate at which bits are transmitted through the network).

3. **How are local area networks configured?**

The parts of a local area network include the server, client computers, cabling and hubs, the network operating system, and network interface cards (NICs). The cabling and hubs tie the server and client computers together. The network operating system directs the operations of the LAN and resides on both the server and the clients. Finally, the network interface card handles the electronic interface between the servers or clients and the rest of the network. The Ethernet protocol is used in the vast majority of LANs. Wireless LANs (WLANs), in which the usual LAN cabling is replaced with wireless transmissions between computers, are becoming increasingly popular.

4. **How does the Internet work?**

The Internet is a network of networks that have agreed to use the TCP/IP protocols for addressing computers and sending packets over the network. There is no governing authority or central computer.

The six primary operations on the Internet are email, FTP, newsgroups, telnet, and Internet relay chat (IRC). Email uses the simple mail transfer protocol (SMTP) to send asynchronous messages over the Internet to individuals and groups. A listserv is a method of easily sending email messages to a group. FTP uses the file transfer protocol to transfer files between computers over the Internet. Telnet allows users to log on to a distant computer and to use software on that computer, although its use is quickly falling out of favour. Newsgroups enable users to engage in discussions on a global network of news servers. Finally, IRC enables users to communicate synchronously in chat rooms or through instant messaging.

5. **What makes the World Wide Web valuable to business professionals?**

The World Wide Web (WWW), often referred to as the Web, is a body of software and a set of protocols and conventions based on hypertext and multimedia that make the Internet easy to use and browse. It is a client/server network by which the client browser software requests web pages created in hypertext markup language (HTML) from a Web server. Multimedia files are retrieved separately from text pages. Hypertext allows the user to jump within pages or from page to page. The address of the website is called a uniform resource locator (URL) and consists of a protocol, a Web server address, and the path of a web page.

KNOWLEDGE SPEAK

blog 415
Bluetooth 409
clients 398
cookie 419
data rate 406
Ethernet protocol 408
file transfer protocol (FTP) 413
global system for mobile communication (GSM) protocol 420
hypertext markup language (HTML) 417
instant messaging (IM) 415
Internet relay chat (IRC) 415
local area networks (LANs) 408
network architecture 398
network interface card (NIC) 411

network layer model 402
newsgroups 414
packet switching 403
packets 403
peer-to-peer network 401
personal area network (PAN) 409
servers 398
short message service (SMS) 420
signal type 405
three-tiered client/server architecture 399
transmission control protocol/Internet protocol (TCP/IP) 403
uniform resource locator (URL) 418
wireless LANs (WLANs) 408

TECH GUIDE D

THE DETAILS OF SQL, LOGICAL MODELLING, AND XML

WHAT WE WILL COVER

- Using SQL to Query Relational Databases
- Using Logical Modelling to Create a Relational Database
- Querying Multitable Databases
- Using XML for Data Transfer

STUDENT RETURN ON INVESTMENT

Through your investment of time in reading and thinking about this Tech Guide, your return—or created value—is gaining knowledge. Use the following questions as a study guide.

1. How is SQL used to query a single-table database?
2. How is logical modelling used to create effective relational database systems?
3. How is SQL used to query multiple-table databases?
4. How is XML used to transfer data between software applications?

In Chapter 6, we discussed how relational database systems are used as a way of organizing and accessing data. In this Tech Guide, we provide you with more information on relational database systems and also discuss XML as a way of transferring data between software applications and for working with Web services.

USING SQL TO QUERY RELATIONAL DATABASES

The primary function of a database is to allow business professionals to obtain information from it in a usable form. You will recall from Chapter 6 that a *relational database* is a database structured with tables that are related to one another so data can be stored and retrieved efficiently. These relations allow a user to run *queries* (questions) on the database to retrieve specific data. To query a relational database, it is common practice to use **Structured Query Language (SQL)**, which is a computer language for manipulating data in a relational database. SQL queries also enable database users to add new records, or change or delete records in a database (instead of using commands from Microsoft Access or another software package). To demonstrate how to use SQL effectively, let's begin with a simple relational database example.

Relational Database Example

Recall the relational database that we used in Chapter 6 (WildOutfitters), shown here in Figure D.1. The database tables, Product and Vendor, are related through the **primary key**, a field that holds a unique value for each record. The VendorID is the primary key for the Vendor table. The Product table includes VendorID as a **foreign key**, to relate the two tables.

What types of queries would business professionals, such as marketing analysts, use for this database? They might use a query to display all WildOutfitters products that sell for more than $100. Once a query has been used to find matching rows, the marketing analyst could then update a row by making changes to the contents of one or more rows (e.g., modify prices), or to delete a row if it is no longer needed (e.g., discontinued products). It is also possible to add new rows to a table as WildOutfitters adds new products to its inventory.

Querying a Single-Table Database

A table is known more formally as an **entity**. All tables must be given an **identifier**, or a name, as must all fields in the database. In both cases, it is best to use descriptive

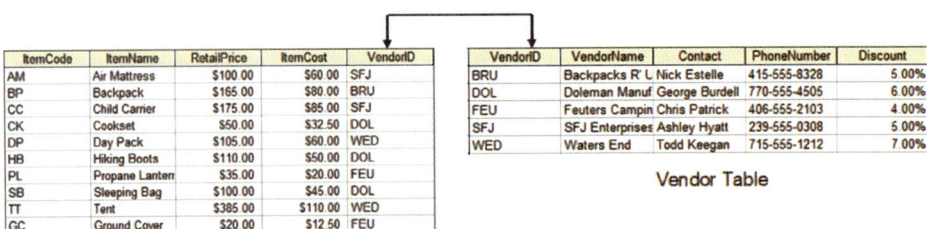

FIGURE D.1 Related WildOutfitters database tables.

names. Figure D.2 shows the Product entity with the fields shown in Figure D.1. Note that the table name is in all capitals to distinguish it from the field names. Note also that an asterisk denotes the primary key for this table, ItemCode.

How would SQL be used to query this database table? Let's begin by looking at the general form of an SQL query to search for matching records:

> **SELECT** *fields* **FROM** *tables* **WHERE** *fields match query condition*

Here, the SELECT keyword designates which fields to display as a result of the query, the FROM keyword designates which tables to search, and the WHERE keyword specifies the search criteria, or **query condition**, to use in finding records. Note that we have used upper-case for keywords to make them stand out, but otherwise case is not important when using SQL.

To display the ItemCost for all records in the PRODUCT table that have an ItemCode of BP, the SQL query is

> **SELECT ItemCost FROM Product WHERE ItemCode = 'BP'**

Enclose the BP ItemCode in single quotation marks to designate it as a character or text constant (you can also use double quotation marks). Numeric constants (such as the retail price or item cost) are not enclosed in such quotation marks. For this query, and assuming the entire product table is shown in Figure D.1, the result will show $80.

In addition to the SELECT keyword, you can use a number of other keywords to CREATE a table, to INSERT new records in a table, to DELETE records from a table, and to UPDATE one or more records in a table. You can also search for records that are *like* a specific condition, as well as calculate sums, averages, and so on for all records that match some criteria.

The next sections show how to use several SQL commands, which you should become familiar with to increase your productivity as a business professional.

PRODUCT
ItemCode*
ItemName
RetailPrice
ItemCost
VendorID

FIGURE D.2 Single database table (in all capitals) with five fields.

Using SQL to Display Specific Information

Let's begin by using SQL to display the entire table; that is, all fields for all of the records. In this case, the form of the SQL command is quite simple:

> **SELECT * FROM** *TableName*

Here, the asterisk is a placeholder for all fields in the table. Figure D.3 shows the result of this SQL command for the Product table.

Displaying Selected Fields for All Records Instead of displaying all fields for all records, you may only want to display a subset of the fields. The standard form of this query is

> **SELECT** *FieldName1, FieldName2, . . .* **FROM** *TableName*

Note that you can include one or more field names in the list. For example, if you want to display just the item names and retail prices for all products sold by WildOutfitters, the SQL command would be

> **SELECT ItemName, RetailPrice FROM Product**

ItemCode	ItemName	RetailPrice	ItemCost	VendorID
AM	Air Mattress	$100.00	$60.00	SFJ
BP	Backpack	$165.00	$80.00	BRU
CC	Child Carrier	$175.00	$85.00	SFJ
CK	Cookset	$50.00	$32.50	DOL
DP	Day Pack	$105.00	$60.00	WED
HB	Hiking Boots	$110.00	$50.00	DOL
PL	Propane Lantern	$35.00	$20.00	FEU
SB	Sleeping Bag	$100.00	$45.00	DOL
TT	Tent	$385.00	$110.00	WED
GC	Ground Cover	$20.00	$12.50	FEU

Product Table

FIGURE D.3 WildOutfitters Product Table.

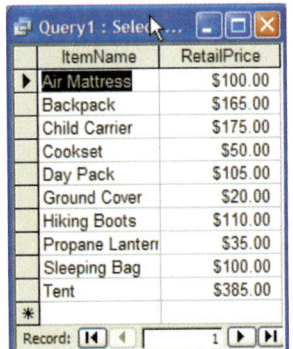

FIGURE D.4 Result of query to display specific field names.

Figure D.4 shows the resulting output, which displays all the products along with their retail prices.

If you want to display these records in some order other than in increasing order of the primary key, you can add the *Order By* clause to the SQL statement. The standard form of this query is

SELECT *FieldName1, FieldName2, . . .* FROM *TableName*

ORDER BY *FieldName*

In this case, the results of the query will be ordered according to the last field name mentioned. For example, to show the same list of items as before but now in increasing order of retail price, the SQL statement is

SELECT ItemName, RetailPrice FROM Product

ORDER By RetailPrice

Displaying Selected Fields for Matching Records In many cases, you may only want to display selected fields for records that match some condition. To do this, you need to use the WHERE keyword followed by some query condition involving one of six comparison operators: equals (=), greater than (>), less than (<), greater than or equal to (> =), less than or equal to (< =), or not equal to (< >), plus a field name and a value. The general form is

SELECT *FieldName1, FieldName2, . . .* FROM *TableName*

WHERE *Query Condition*

For example, assume that the marketing department at WildOutfitters wants to know the names and wholesale costs of products with an item cost greater than $50. To display the item name and item cost, the SQL statement is

SELECT ItemName, ItemCost FROM Product

WHERE ItemCost > 50

Here, using the WHERE keyword restricts which rows to display; that is, only those that have an ItemCost value greater than $50. In this case, this query would display the item name and item cost for the five products with an item cost over $50: Air Mattress, Backpack, Child Carrier, Day Pack, and Tent.

It is also possible to combine conditions in a query by using the AND or OR operators, known as *compound operators*. The AND operator requires both conditions to be true, while the OR operator only requires that one or both of the conditions be true. For example, consider this query:

SELECT ItemName, ItemCost FROM product WHERE

ItemCost > 15 AND VendorID = "FEU"

The results of this query show the name, cost, and vendor ID for any product with a cost greater than $15 from the vendor whose ID is FEU.

Using the LIKE Operator

Whenever you use the equals sign in a SELECT query, you are looking for an exact match. But what happens, for example, if you don't know the exact product name? Or if you're looking for information about a group of products? In that case, you should use the LIKE operator. The LIKE operator uses the **wildcard** character as a replacement for unknown or non-existing characters in an attempt to find matches to a group of characters (commonly referred to as a **character string**). The wildcard character is usually either the asterisk (*) in Microsoft Access or the percent sign (%) in other database mangement systems. The general form of this type of query is

SELECT *FieldName1, Fieldname2, . . .* **FROM** *TableName*

WHERE *FieldName* **LIKE '***value*****'**

For example, to find the item names and retail prices of all types of backpacks offered by WildOutfitters, the query in Access is

SELECT ItemName, RetailPrice FROM Product

WHERE ItemName LIKE '*Pack*'

In this query, the wildcard character represents anything on either side of the word "Pack." The query results in this case will display records for the Backpack and the Day Pack.

Inserting or Deleting Records

As discussed earlier, you can use Microsoft Access or another relational database management package to add records to or delete records from a database table. It is also possible to carry out both of these operations using SQL. To insert a record into a table, you would use an SQL statement of the form

INSERT INTO *TableName* **Values (***value1, value2, . . .***)**

Note that, in this format, you must enter the values in the exact order as the fields in the record, separated by commas. If there are null or missing values, you must still enter the corresponding comma.

For example, to insert a new record for a heater with an item code of HH, a retail price of $75, and an item cost of $45 into the Product table of the WildOutfitters database, the SQL statement is

INSERT INTO Product Values('HH', 'Heater', 75, 45)

As above, note that we use single quotation marks to set off the two character strings in this query.

To delete an existing record from a database table, you would use an SQL statement in the form

DELETE FROM *TableName* **WHERE** *FieldName* = *value*

This will delete all records that match the criteria. For example, assume that WildOutfitters no longer carries the Ground Cover product and needs to remove it from the database. To do this, the SQL command is

DELETE FROM Product WHERE ItemCode = 'GC'

Changing Values with SQL

To change values in a row of a database, you can use the UPDATE and SET keywords in the form

UPDATE *TableName* **SET** *FieldName1* = *value*

WHERE *FieldName2* = *value*

For example, assume the ItemCost for the tent has increased by 10 percent. To account for this increase in the database table, the SQL statement is

UPDATE Product SET ItemCost = ItemCost*1.1 WHERE

ItemCode = 'TT'

Executing this SQL statement will result in the ItemCost for the tent to increase from $110 to $121.

Using Aggregate Functions in SQL

Our final SQL operation is to use it to calculate certain values in the table using five different **aggregate functions**: COUNT, AVG, SUM, MIN, and MAX. As their names indicate, the purposes of these functions are to count the number of matching records, find their average value, sum the values, or find the minimum or maximum matching value, respectively. In each case, you must use a dummy field name for the result of the calculation. The form for the AVG function is

SELECT AVG(*fieldname*) **AS** *DummyName* **FROM** *TableName*

WHERE *Query condition*

In this SQL statement, the AVG function finds the average of the values of the field name in parentheses, subject to the query condition. It then stores that value in the dummy name variable, which is displayed after running the query.

For example, to find the average retail price for all items in the Product table, the query is

SELECT AVG(RetailPrice) AS AvgPrice FROM Product

Running this query on the PRODUCT table shown in Figure D.4 results in displaying the average retail price of $124.50.

The SUM, MAX, and MIN functions have the same form as the AVG function. The COUNT function, however, uses a different form, as the following shows:

SELECT COUNT(*) AS *DummyName* FROM *TableName*

WHERE *Query condition*

For example, to count the number of items in the table with a retail price of more than $75, the SQL statement is

SELECT COUNT(*) AS Over75Count FROM Product

WHERE RetailPrice > 75

The results of this query display the number of items with a retail price of more than $75.

So far in our discussion of relational databases we have been querying a single table using SQL. However, the real power of a relational database comes from the use of multiple tables. In the next section we discuss how creating a database with multiple tables usually increases the productivity of knowledge work activities.

Quick Test

For the Product table shown in Figure D.3, write queries to carry out the following operations.

1. Display the item name and retail price for all items with a retail price greater than $100.

2. Insert a new record for a product with ItemCode of 'CC,' an item name of 'Camp Chair,' an item cost of $95, and a retail price of $175.

3. Calculate the average item cost of all items in inventory.

Answers: 1. SELECT ItemName, RetailPrice FROM Product WHERE RetailPrice > 100;
2. INSERT INTO Product VALUES('CC', 'Camp Chair', 95, 175);
3. SELECT AVG(ItemCost) as AvgCost FROM Product

USING LOGICAL MODELLING TO CREATE A RELATIONAL DATABASE

Most relational databases include many tables, not just one. Why? To help you understand the reasons for this, consider the expanded version of the PRODUCT table, shown in Figure D.5. Note that the table now includes information about the vendor that provides each product to WildOutfitters. Included in the vendor information are the vendor name, the contact name and telephone number, and the discount given by the vendor if WildOutfitters pays its bill within 30 days of delivery.

ItemCode	ItemName	RetailPrice	ItemCost	VendorID	VendorName	Contact	PhoneNumber	Discount
BP	Backpack	$165.00	$80.00	BRU	Backpacks R'U	Nick Estelle	415-555-8328	5.00%
CK	Cookset	$50.00	$32.50	DOL	Doleman Manuf	George Burdell	770-555-4505	6.00%
HB	Hiking Boots	$110.00	$50.00	DOL	Doleman Manuf	George Burdell	770-555-4505	6.00%
SB	Sleeping Bag	$100.00	$45.00	DOL	Doleman Manuf	George Burdell	770-555-4505	6.00%
PL	Propane Lantern	$35.00	$20.00	FEU	Feuters Campin	Chris Patrick	406-555-2103	4.00%
GC	Ground Cover	$20.00	$12.50	FEU	Feuters Campin	Chris Patrick	406-555-2103	4.00%
AM	Air Mattress	$100.00	$60.00	SFJ	SFJ Enterprises	Ashley Hyatt	239-555-0308	5.00%
CC	Child Carrier	$175.00	$85.00	SFJ	SFJ Enterprises	Ashley Hyatt	239-555-0308	5.00%
DP	Day Pack	$105.00	$60.00	WED	Waters End	Todd Keegan	715-555-1212	7.00%
TT	Tent	$385.00	$110.00	WED	Waters End	Todd Keegan	715-555-1212	7.00%

FIGURE D.5 Using a single table to store data often results in redundancy.

In looking at Figure D.5, you can now probably see a big reason for not using a single table: *redundancy*. Note that the Product table now lists each vendor's name, contact, phone number, and discount rate multiple times. This redundancy can not only result in the database table taking up storage space (especially for a realistic-sized database table involving millions of records), but also causes problems, typically referred to as **anomalies**, when trying to insert new records, delete existing records, or update records. Therefore, to solve the problems associated with storing all the data in one table, relational databases are used.

As discussed in Chapter 6, reducing data redundancy is one advantage of using a relational database. Other advantages include improving data access and sharing by using database standards; maintaining the integrity of the data by having security and controls to prevent errors, duplication, and unauthorized entry; and allowing configurable views of the data to match the user needs.

Logical modelling is often used to create the appropriate relational tables. *Logical modelling* provides tools to help analyze and understand what data are important, and the relationships between the data.

Entity-Relationship Diagramming

The first step in logical modelling is to create an *entity-relationship diagram (ERD)*. The ERD is uncluttered by attributes so businesses can focus on the "big picture"; that is, the entities and the relationships. Businesses then use the ERD to build a *relational data model*, which adds the attributes and helps to organize them prior to creating the database.

For example, let's use the information from Figure D.5 (the Product-Vendor information), picking out the entities and attributes, to create the ERD. You first need to think about what entities you need to consider. In this case, you can easily identify two entities: PRODUCT and VENDOR. Now, using standard symbols, you can draw the entities and the relationships between the entities. Figure D.6 shows the standard symbols for an ERD. Note that 1:1 means one-to-one (a **one-to-one relationship**), and 1:M means one-to-many. The diamond indicates a relationship between two entities.

Figure D.7 shows the ERD for this example. In reading from left to right, you can see the ERD indicates that *one* vendor sells *many* products, while each product is sold by only one vendor. Note that the 1:M is next to the Product entity, as it includes *many* products.

FIGURE D.6 Standard ERD symbols, where a diamond indicates a relationship.

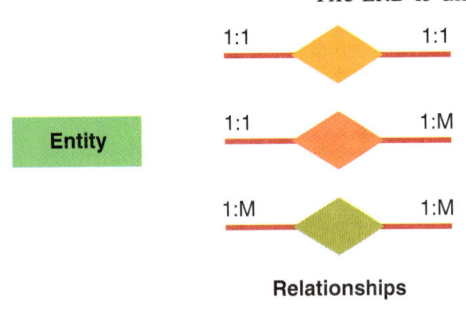

FIGURE D.7 A one-to-many relationship.

Using Logical Modelling to Create a Relational Database | 431

Let's now think of another situation involving the Product table, one involving customers instead of vendors. If you think about it, a customer can purchase many products, and many customers can purchase the same product. As a result, the 1:M is next to both the Product and Customer entities. The ERD, shown in Figure D.8, includes what is known as a **many-to-many relationship** between the Customer and Product entities.

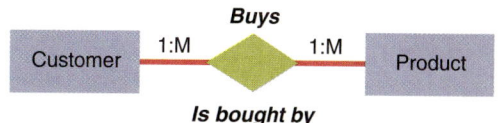

FIGURE D.8 A many-to-many relationship with no primary key–foreign key relationship.

What happens when you have this type of relationship between entities? You have a problem, because many-to-many relationships violate logical modelling rules for creating a relational database. Specifically, it is not possible to create a primary key–foreign key relationship with a many-to-many relationship. As a result, you need to draw a new **relational entity** to lie between the original two entities. As Figure D.9 shows, the relational entity is connected to each original entity by a one-to-many relationship, thereby transforming the original many-to-many relationship into two one-to-many relationships.

The Relational Data Model

After creating the ERD, the next step of logical modelling is to create the relational data model. Recall that this step fills in the details of the relationship between the entities. That is, a relational data model adds the attributes, as well as identifies primary and foreign keys. To see how to do this, let's convert the 1:M ERD (Figure D.7) into a data model.

As Figure D.10 shows, the symbols change when you convert the ERD to a data model. The relationship symbol changes from a "labelled diamond" to a "line with crow's foot." The "crow's foot" is placed on the "many" side of the relationship. The data model also adds more detail to the entities, including a listing of the attributes (fields) for the entities and indicators for the primary and foreign keys. A simple rule of thumb for determining foreign keys is that the primary key from the "one" side of the relationship is used as a foreign key on the "many" side of the relationship.

This . . .

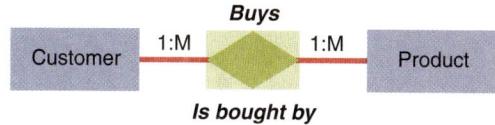

Many-to-many relationship (before transformation).

. . . Becomes this

Two one-to-many relationships with relational entity (after transformation)

FIGURE D.9 Converting a many-to-many (M:M) relationship into two one-to-many (1:M) relationships.

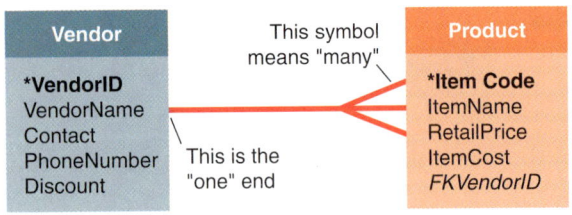

FIGURE D.10 Data model for a one-to-many (1:M) relationship.

```
CUSTOMER
*CustomerID
ShipAddress
ShipCity
ShipProvince
ShipPostal
EmailAddress
```

FIGURE D.11 CUSTOMER entity, where CustomerID is the primary key.

```
PURCHASE
*PurchaseID
FKCustomerID
FKItemCode
PurchaseDate
Number
```

FIGURE D.12 PURCHASE entity used to transform the M:M relationship into two 1:M relationships.

What about the data model for the ERD for the M:M customer-product situation discussed above? You can use the same PRODUCT table, but now you need a CUSTOMER table that includes a customer's ID number, shipping address, city, province, postal code, and email address. Figure D.11 shows the resulting entity, where the CustomerID field is the primary key.

Next, you need a PURCHASE table to convert the M:M relationship into two 1:M relationships. This entity will include the primary keys from both the CUSTOMER and PRODUCT tables (as foreign keys), as well as some unique identifier as its own primary key. The two foreign keys enable WildOutfitters to determine information on the buyer (customer) as well as information on the product purchased. Finally, you will also include the number of items purchased and the date of the purchase in this table. Figure D.12 shows the resulting entity.

Now, using the CUSTOMER, PRODUCT, and PURCHASE tables, you can create the data model that represents the purchase of a product by a customer. Note that the customer may purchase multiple products, and multiple customers can purchase the same product, by simply having one record in the PURCHASE table for each purchase. Figure D.13 shows the resulting data model, which matches the transformed M:M ERD shown in Figure D.8.

The VendorID foreign key is included in the PRODUCT table, since it is also related to the VENDOR table. You can now combine both of these entity-relationships into one complete data model, as shown in Figure D.14. As this shows, by using logical modelling, organizations can effectively expand their databases along with their businesses.

A final consideration in creating a data model is that of **referential integrity**, which enforces consistency between linked tables. To understand referential integrity, you should think of the values stored in a foreign key as a reference to a record in another table. If, for some reason, that record does not exist, then there are problems. For example, if you try to add a record to the PRODUCT table that tries to reference a VendorID for a vendor that does not exist in the VENDOR table, then a message will warn you about it. Conversely, if you try to remove a vendor record from the VENDOR table and that vendor has products listed in the PRODUCT table, a warning message will also appear. This feature helps to maintain the overall integrity of databases.

After creating a relational database with two or more tables, you can use SQL to query it, in a manner similar to querying a single-table database.

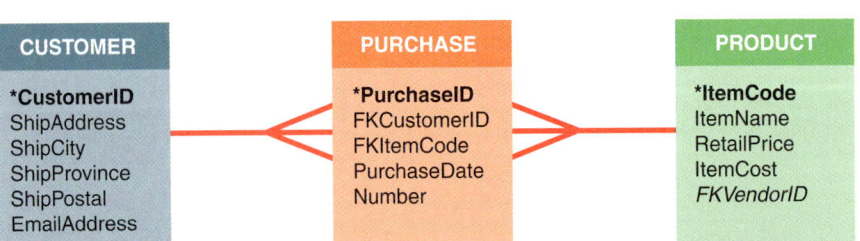

FIGURE D.13 Conversion of an M:M relationship into two 1:M relationships.

Querying Multitable Databases | 433

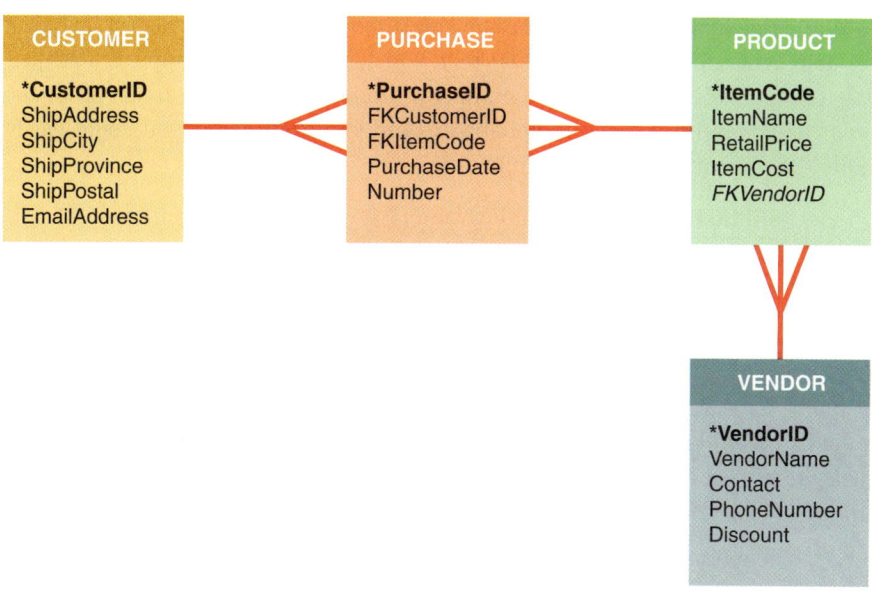

FIGURE D.14 Complete WildOutfitters data model.

QUERYING MULTITABLE DATABASES

In this section, we look at the most common operation on a two-table database: the Join operation. We then discuss how to use views to save queried results.

The Join Operation

The **Join operation** creates a single table from two (or more) tables, after which you can use it to perform calculations and carry out grouping of products. For our example, the SQL instruction to do this is as follows:

SELECT * FROM Product, Vendor WHERE

Product.VendorID = Vendor.VendorID

In looking at this query, note that because the field name for the foreign key in PRODUCT (VendorID) is the same as the primary key field name in VENDOR, we distinguish between them by combining the table name and the field name using a period; that is, Product.VendorID and Vendor.VendorID. Figure D.15 shows the result of this query.

ItemCode	ItemName	RetailPrice	ItemCost	Product.VendorID	Vendor.VendorID	VendorName	Contact	PhoneNumber	Discount
BP	Backpack	$165.00	$80.00	BRU	BRU	Backpacks R' Us	Nick Estelle	415-555-8328	5.00%
HH	Heater	$75.00	$45.00	BRU	BRU	Backpacks R' Us	Nick Estelle	415-555-8328	5.00%
CK	Cookset	$50.00	$32.50	DOL	DOL	Doleman Manufac	George Burdell	770-555-4505	6.00%
HB	Hiking Boots	$110.00	$50.00	DOL	DOL	Doleman Manufac	George Burdell	770-555-4505	6.00%
SB	Sleeping Bag	$100.00	$45.00	DOL	DOL	Doleman Manufac	George Burdell	770-555-4505	6.00%
PL	Propane Lantern	$35.00	$20.00	FEU	FEU	Feuters Camping	Chris Patrick	406-555-2103	4.00%
AM	Air Mattress	$100.00	$60.00	SFJ	SFJ	SFJ Enterprises	Ashley Hyatt	239-555-0308	5.00%
CC	Child Carrier	$175.00	$85.00	SFJ	SFJ	SFJ Enterprises	Ashley Hyatt	239-555-0308	5.00%
DP	Day Pack	$105.00	$60.00	WED	WED	Waters End	Todd Keegan	715-555-1212	7.00%
TT	Tent	$385.00	$121.00	WED	WED	Waters End	Todd Keegan	715-555-1212	7.00%

FIGURE D.15 Results of a Join query.

While this looks very much like the single table we decided earlier to avoid, it does help avoid update anomalies. Further, you can use the same approach as querying a single table to quickly do a number of things. For example, to list products, vendor name, and item cost in alphabetical order of item name, you could easily modify the previous query to the following:

SELECT ItemName, VendorName, ItemCost FROM Product,

Vendor WHERE Product.VendorID = Vendor.VendorID

ORDER BY ItemName

It is also possible to carry out calculations and display them as the result of a join query. For example, each vendor offers a different discount to WildOutfitters for paying its bill within 30 days of receiving the merchandise. The net item cost then equals the item cost times (1 − discount). You can modify the previous SQL query to output the item name, vendor name, item cost, discount, and the net cost as follows:

SELECT ItemName, VendorName, ItemCost, Discount,

ItemCost*(1-Discount) as NetCost FROM Product,

Vendor WHERE Product.VendorID = Vendor.VendorID

ORDER BY ItemName

The results of this query will list the products in order of vendor, as well as create a new field, NetCost, that will indicate the discounted cost.

Creating Views

With most relational database management systems, it is possible to save the queries you have created. Another name for a saved query is a **view**. However, note that these views are not actual tables, even though they might appear that way on the screen.

There are two main reasons for creating a view. First, it enables you to simplify query writing in the future. If you plan to reuse some aspect of a query, you can save it as a view and then use it by itself or as part of another query. For example, say you had saved a previous query as *TotalSold* and now only wanted to see the item names and revenue from this query. A new and simpler query to do this would be as follows:

SELECT ItemName, Revenue FROM TotalSold

A second reason for using a view is for security. You can create a view only showing fields that you want others to see. That way, they cannot look at fields in the database, such as customer information, that may include confidential information.

Quick Test

Indicate whether the following statements are True or False.
1. Logical modelling helps to create anomalies in relational databases.

2. Referential integrity enforces consistency between linked tables.

3. The most common operation on a two-table database is the Intersection operation, which creates a single table from two (or more) tables.

4. You must include table names when creating a multitable query.

Answers: 1. False; 2. True; 3. False; 4. True

USING XML FOR DATA TRANSFER

Until now, we have limited our discussion to creating and using relational databases within an organization. However, most companies today require the ability to share data and resources over the Web. Although companies have been using a system known as *electronic data interchange (EDI)* for many years, EDI is expensive and is useful only to very large companies. With the rapid growth of the Internet, organizations have turned to XML as a way of carrying out the same processes. An XML file can be processed purely as data by a program, it can be stored with similar data on another computer, or, like an HTML file, it can be displayed.

XML vs. HTML

A good way to understand XML is to compare it with HTML, the markup language that is the basis for the Web. First, recall that HTML is a *formatting language* that is meant to display numbers and text in a predefined way on a Web browser. As such, it does not have the structure to impart meaning to items like part numbers or prices. Because it is not a good idea to have computers infer meanings from entries on web pages, HTML is not appropriate for transmitting large amounts of purchasing and shipping information over the Internet. HTML also has predetermined tags, which reduces its flexibility, and the only way you can retrieve information from it is to search for specific text.

XML solves these problems because it is a language that emphasizes the structure and meaning of data. This means that product information such as name, identifier, and price are easily transmitted using XML. XML is also flexible in that users can define their own tags. For example, a company could use XML to define tags that their trading partners can understand. This enables searches of the data using the meaning of the data instead of just using a text search. For example, the tag < PARTID > would indicate that the field that followed was a part number and it would be easy to find all part numbers by searching for this tag. An XML file can be processed purely as data by a program, it can be stored with similar data on another computer, or, like an HTML file, it can be displayed. For example, depending on how the application in the receiving computer wanted to handle the part number field, it could be stored or displayed, or some other operation could be performed on it, depending on the content of the field. Table D.1 compares XML with HTML.

Setting Up an XML Document

The first step to creating an XML file is to decide which tags to use to describe the data that are being transferred over the Internet. As with HTML, the tags are enclosed in angle brackets (< >). Each beginning tag *must* have an ending tag. For example, if using a < PARTID > tag to describe the part ID, then there *must*

Table D.1   Comparison of HTML and XML

Feature	XML	HTML
Type of text	Structured with meaning defined	Formatted with meaning inferred
Definition of structure	User-defined	Predetermined
Retrieval	Context-sensitive	Limited
Searchability	Searchable by text or meaning	Searchable only by text or format
Hypertext linkage	Extensive	Limited

be a matching </PARTID> tag. These tags must come immediately before and after the data item to ensure that there is no ambiguity or inconsistency about the description.

While current browsers are usually capable of determining the matching tags for each data item in an XML file, it is a better practice to provide a formal definition of all the data elements in the XML file. This can be done in one of two ways: the **document type definition** method or the **XML schema** method. Both can be incorporated into the XML file or created as separate files with DTD or XSD extensions, respectively. These files are then referred to by the XML file to define the XML tags it uses to describe the data.

Using a DTD or XSD file, a program called a *parser* in a Web browser can work with the tags that the document contains. For example, Figure D.16 shows an XML schema (XSD) file for a list of WildOutfitters' vendors. Note that the first line of this XSD file with the "<?xml . . . >" tag defines it as also being an XML file. The tags that begin with *xsd:* make up the formal definition of the data elements to be used in the matching XML file. Note also that the schema defines the names of tag elements in the XML file and their data type. For instance, the schema defines an element called CompanyName, which will contain text (string) information.

```xml
<?xml version="1.0" encoding="UTF-8"?>
<xsd:schema xmlns:xsd="http://www.w3.org/2001/XMLSchema">
<!--Customer List-->
<xsd:element name="Customers">
 <xsd:complexType>
  <xsd:sequence>
   <xsd:element maxOccurs="unbounded" minOccurs="1" name="Company" type="companies"/>
  </xsd:sequence>
 </xsd:complexType>
</xsd:element>
<xsd:complexType name="companies">
 <xsd:sequence>
  <xsd:element name="CompanyName" type="xsd:string"/>
  <xsd:element name="Address" type="xsd:string"/>
  <xsd:element name="City" type="xsd:string"/>
  <xsd:element name="State" type="xsd:string"/>
  <xsd:element name="Zip" type="xsd:string"/>
 </xsd:sequence>
</xsd:complexType>
</xsd:schema>
```

FIGURE D.16 XML schema (XSD) file.

```xml
<?xml version="1.0" encoding="utf-8"?>
<?xml-stylesheet type="text/xsl" href="companynew.xsl" media="screen"?>
<NewDataSet xmlns:xsi="http://www.w3.org/2001/XMLSchema-instance" xsi:noNamespaceSchemaLocation="companynew.xsd">
    <Company>
        <CompanyName>ABC Metals</CompanyName>
        <Address>550 Montgomery Street</Address>
        <City>Minneapolis</City>
        <State>MN</State>
        <Zip>55402</Zip>
    </Company>
    <Company>
        <CompanyName>Backpacks R Us</CompanyName>
        <Address>122 Hilltop Avenue</Address>
        <City>Missoula</City>
        <State>MT</State>
        <Zip>59801</Zip>
    </Company>
    <Company>
        <CompanyName>Doleman Hiking Supplies</CompanyName>
        <Address>2532 Epson Blvd</Address>
        <City>Ocala</City>
        <State>FL</State>
        <Zip>34470</Zip>
    </Company>
    <Company>
```

FIGURE D.17 Portion of the XML file that uses the schema from Figure D.16.

Figure D.17 shows a portion of the XML file that uses this schema. Note that the file line defines it as an XML file, and the third line references the schema (XSD) file shown in Figure D.16 (companynew.xsd).

The second line refers to a stylesheet (XSL) file (which we will discuss shortly). You can see these elements used to describe actual data starting with the fourth line, which has a < company > tag. It is fairly easy to see that the first company is named ABC Metals, located at 550 Montgomery Street in Minneapolis, Minnesota, 55402. Note that a tag < /company > terminates the data for the first company.

To display an XML file in a more readable form on a Web browser, you need to use an XML **stylesheet (XSL) file**. This file uses a combination of HTML and XML tags. In our example, the XML file references it in the second line. Figure D.18 shows the actual companynew.xsl stylesheet file. Note that it is also an XML file, and the *xsl:* tags reference the stylesheet elements along with the HTML tags.

```xml
<?xml version="1.0" encoding="UTF-8"?>
<xsl:stylesheet version="1.0"
xmlns:xsl="http://www.w3.org/1999/XSL/Transform">
    <xsl:output encoding="UTF-8" indent="yes" method="html" version="1.0" />
    <xsl:template match="/">
        <html>
            <head>
                <title> Complete List of Vendors </title>
            </head>
            <body>
                <h1> Complete List of Vendors </h1>
                <xsl:apply-templates select="NewDataSet" />
            </body>
        </html>
    </xsl:template>
    <xsl:template match="NewDataSet">
        <table border = '1'>
            <xsl:for-each select="Company">
                <tr>
                    <td><xsl:value-of select="CompanyName" /></td>
                    <td><xsl:value-of select="Address" /></td>
                    <td><xsl:value-of select="City" /></td>
                    <td><xsl:value-of select="State" /></td>
                    <td><xsl:value-of select="Zip" /></td>
                </tr>
            </xsl:for-each>
        </table>
    </xsl:template>
</xsl:stylesheet>
```

FIGURE D.18 This stylesheet (XSL) file uses a combination of HTML and XML tags.

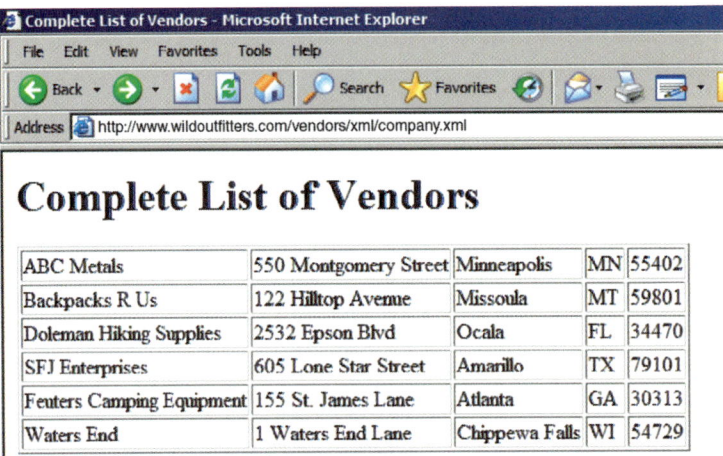

FIGURE D.19 How a browser displays the XML data from Figure D.18.

So what does the final result of these files look like on a Web browser? Figure D.19 shows the results.

Quick Test

Fill in the blanks for the following statements.

1. All XML files must include both beginning and _____ tags.

2. Unlike HTML, XML files provide _____ to the data.

3. A(n) _____ file is used to display an XML file in easily readable form.

Answers: 1. ending; 2. meaning; 3. stylesheet

RO↑ STUDENT RETURN ON INVESTMENT SUMMARY

1. How is SQL used to query a single-table database?

The primary function of a database is to enable users to obtain information from it in a usable form. Users obtain information from a database by constructing and running queries or questions to the database. For a relational database, the queries are written in Structured Query Language (SQL), which is a computer language for manipulating data in a relational database. The general form of SQL query to search for matching records is:

> **SELECT** *fields* **FROM** *tables* **WHERE** *fields match query condition*

In the SQL statement, the SELECT keyword designates which fields to display as a result of the query, the FROM keyword designates which tables to search, and the WHERE keyword specifies the search criteria or query condition to use in finding records. In addition to finding data, you can use SQL to insert, delete, and update records in the database tables, as well as to carry out calculations on records.

2. How is logical modelling used to create effective relational database systems?

Logical modelling provides tools to help businesses analyze and understand what data are important and the relationships between the data by creating a picture of this world of data and relationships. An accurate logical model provides a business with a solid foundation upon which to build its database(s).

In logical modelling, the ERD focuses on the entities and the relationships. The Data Model adds the attributes and helps to organize them prior to creating the database. Primary and foreign keys are identified as well. The Data Model is built after the ERD by adjusting some symbols and adding more detail.

3. How is SQL used to query multiple-table databases?
The most common operation on a two-table database is the Join operation, which creates a single table from two (or more) tables. The general form of a two-table join is

$$\text{SELECT*FROM } Table1, Table2 \text{ WHERE } Table1.PrimaryKey = Table2.ForeignKey$$

The Join operation is not restricted to just two tables; it is possible to carry out a three, four, or even more table join as long as all of the tables are related.

4. How is XML used to transfer data between software applications?
XML uses tags to mark up content and/or data so that software applications can recognize it. Using XML, companies can define their own tags, which their trading partners can then understand. An XML file can be processed purely as data by a program, it can be stored with similar data on another computer or, like an HTML file, it can be displayed. The first step to creating an XML file is to decide what tags will be used to describe the data that are being transferred over the Internet. While it can be left to the browser to determine the matching tags, the best way to do this is to use Document Type Definition or an XML schema, either in the XML file or as a separate file that is referenced by the XML file. To display an XML file, a stylesheet (XSL) file can be used that converts it into HTML.

KNOWLEDGE SPEAK

aggregate functions   428
anomalies   430
character string   427
document type definition   436
entity   424
forcign key   424
identifier   424
Join operation   433
many-to-many relationship   431
one-to-one relationship   430

primary key   424
query condition   425
referential integrity   432
relational entity   431
Structured Query Language (SQL)   424
stylesheet (XSL) file   437
view   434
wildcard   427
XML schema   436

TECH GUIDE

THE TECHNOLOGY OF TEAMS

WHAT WE WILL COVER

- Why Do Organizations Use Teams?
- How People Work in Teams
- How Teams Develop
- Hallmarks of Highly Effective Teams
- Bringing It All Together

STUDENT RETURN ON INVESTMENT

Through your investment of time in reading and thinking about this Tech Guide, your return—or created value—is gaining knowledge. Use the following questions as a study guide.

1. Why do organizations use teams to solve business challenges?
2. How do skills and roles work together to help people work better in teams?
3. What stages do teams need to naturally progress through in order to become high performing?
4. What are the critical success factors that characterize effective teams?
5. What tools do well-functioning teams apply to ensure their success?

A special thanks to Carol-Ann Hamilton for co-authoring this Tech Guide.

Chapter 3 examined organizations as open systems. In this approach, organizations transform inputs into outputs (i.e., use business processes to create value) and achieve their goals given market opportunities, resource limitations, and the constraints of their competitive environment.

Think about how complex the modern business environment has become. New technologies and new knowledge emerge at a rapid pace, and new demands occur from stakeholders such as customers, shareholders, employees, and the government. Nothing stands still for very long in today's fast-paced world.

To draw on expertise from colleagues in various areas, organizations often use teams. Therefore, to be a better business professional, you need to know some fundamentals about the "technology" of teams: how people work in teams, how teams develop, how teams succeed, and how teams collaborate. Let's consider the important question of the value created by using teams in an organizational context.

WHY DO ORGANIZATIONS USE TEAMS?
The Business Case for Using Teams

As Ashby's Law of Requisite Variety[1] implies, a complex and varied external environment demands a correspondingly varied and complex internal organizational environment. Ashby's Law means that in order to survive, businesses need to be as complex as their environment dictates. How does an organization meet this challenge and continue to succeed?

One way organizations meet this challenge is by hiring talented business professionals who work primarily as individuals (see Figure E.1). These people possess the required expertise and skills to ensure the organization succeeds

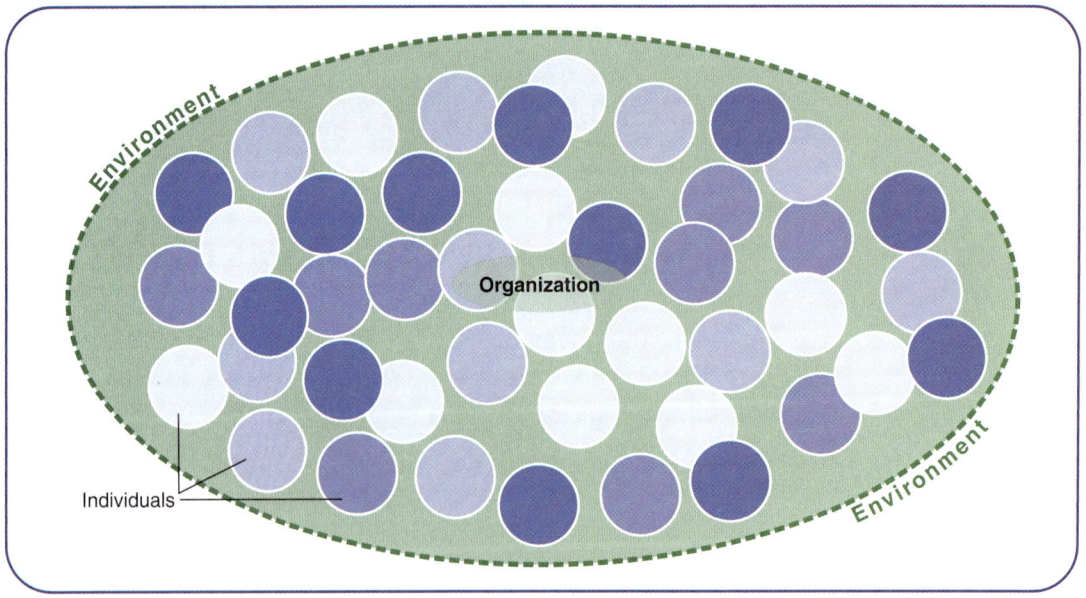

FIGURE E.1 An organization as a collection of individuals.
SOURCE: Adapted from Gareth Morgan's *Images of Organizations*, 2nd ed., Sage Publications, 1997, pp. 112–113.

---

1. For more information, see W. Ross Ashby, *An Introduction to Cybernetics*, London: Chapman and Hall, 1956. Internet (1999): http://pcp.vub.ac.be/books/IntroCyb.pdf.

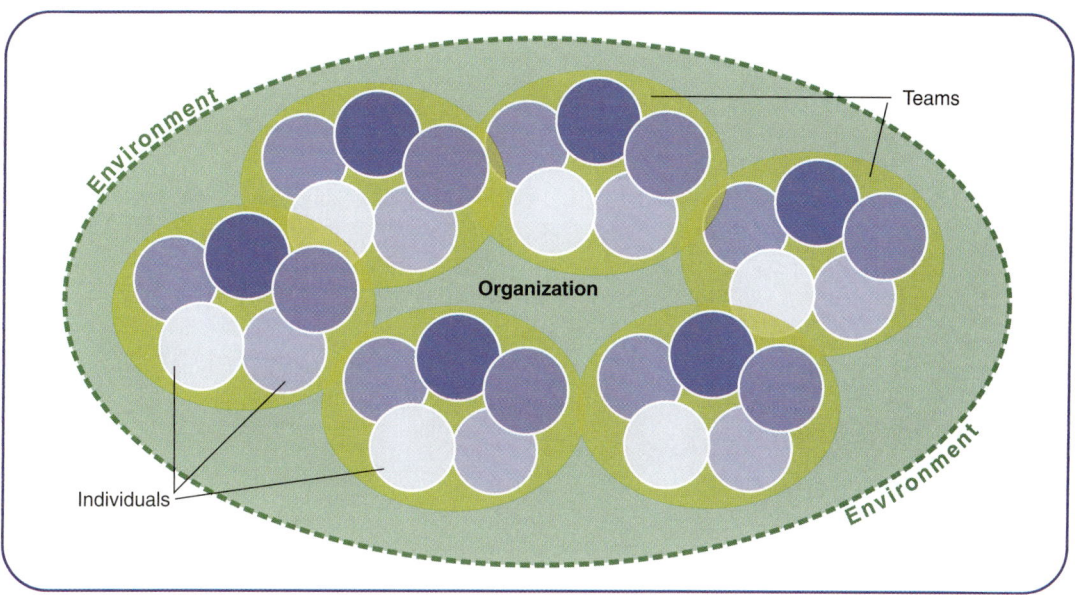

FIGURE E.2 An organization as a collection of teams.
SOURCE: Adapted from Morgan, pp. 112–113.

despite the complex environment it operates in. However, talented experts are a precious resource and may not always be available to work on every challenge that an organization faces at any point in time.

Few, if any, employees are experts in all areas of organizational knowledge, nor is this a feasible objective because of the cost and time involved. For example, if an IS development expert is managing a financial systems development project, will this expert know how the system should account for the sale of tangible assets? This is likely outside the IS expert's usual area of expertise.

To solve this problem, organizations tap into the collective power of teams. As Figure E.2 shows, team members possess a more diverse and complementary set of knowledge, expertise, and skills than any single individual. This creates powerful synergies among team members and generally produces better results. In the case of the financial systems development project, the IS expert may be on a team with an accounting expert who will provide subject matter expertise to the team.

Consequently, most modern organizations succeed through a blend of individual and team effort (see Figure E.3). As we will cover next, there are times when strong, high-potential employees working on individual goals and responsibilities are the best way for the organization to achieve its mandate. Generally speaking, though, if the organization has thoughtfully hired top talent, then a team of the right people working in an aligned fashion in the "right" direction will be greater than the sum of its parts.

Teams vs. Work Groups

When you hear the word "team," what do you think of? Perhaps you think of your favourite sports team, or maybe you work part-time and belong to a team at work, or you may think of a sales team. Although there are many different definitions of **teams**, we'll use a slightly modified version from Jon R. Katzenbach's and

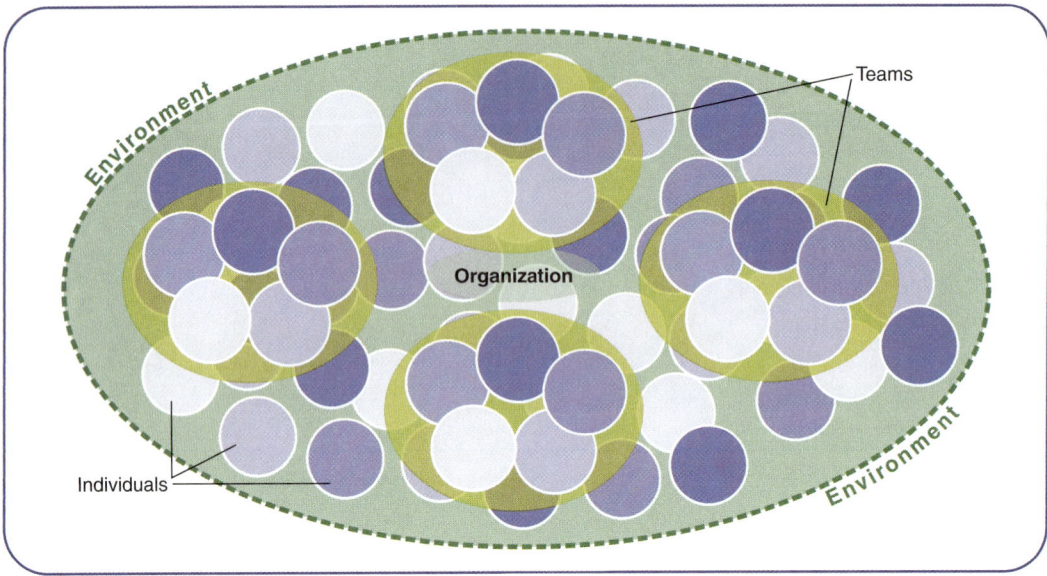

FIGURE E.3 An organization as a collection of teams and individuals.
SOURCE: Adapted from Morgan, pp. 112–113.

Douglas K. Smith's best-selling book, *The Wisdom of Teams:* "a [relatively] small number of *people with complementary skills* who *are committed to a common purpose, performance goals and approach* for which *they hold themselves mutually accountable.*"[2]

Throughout this guide, we will return often to the italicized concepts above. For the time being, think back to the teams in which you have been involved in the past and determine if they meet this definition. Some may; some may not.

A team is not just any group working together. No matter how much a leader might want to call a group of employees within a reporting relationship a team, this does not necessarily make them so. As Katzenbach and Smith point out, the entire workforce of any large and complex organization is *never* a team, despite how often that label is offered up. Table E.1 illustrates how to tell the difference between **work groups** and teams.

Notice how a work group's performance is linked directly to what its members do individually. The best work groups come together to share information, viewpoints, and learning, to make decisions that help each person accomplish their own responsibilities, and to reinforce individual performance standards. The focus is always on singular goals and accountabilities. Work group members only take responsibility for their personal results. They do not focus on continuous performance improvements requiring the combined work of two or more members. They operate independently, or at best, as a collection of individuals.

On the other hand, a team's performance includes both individual results and what we call "collective work products." A collective work product is what two or more members must work on together (e.g., interviews, surveys, experiments). A collective work product reflects the joint contribution of team members

---

2. Jon R. Katzenbach and Douglas K. Smith, *The Wisdom of Teams*, McKinsey & Company, Inc., 1993, p. 45.

Table E.1 Not All Groups Are Teams: How to Tell the Difference

Work Group	Team
Includes strong, clearly focused leader	Includes shared leadership roles
Promotes individual accountability	Promotes individual and mutual accountability
Has the same purpose as the broader organizational mission	Has a purpose that the team itself delivers
Focuses on individual work products	Focuses on collective work products
Runs efficient meetings	Encourages open-ended discussion and active problem-solving meetings
Measures its effectiveness indirectly by its influence on others (e.g., financial performance of the business)	Measures performance directly by assessing collective work products
Discusses, decides, and delegates	Discusses, decides, and does real work together

SOURCE: Adapted from Jon R. Katzenbach and Douglas K. Smith, "The Discipline of Teams," *Harvard Business Review*, March–April 1993.

and requires that they collaborate and merge their efforts into a joint output. This suggests that team members operate interdependently rather than independently, which is another important distinction between a team and a work group.

Types of Teams

Assuming the team is producing a collective work product through mutual accountability, shared contribution, group decision making, and best practice performance standards, there are many potential types of teams to which an employee can contribute, including:

- **Independent:** The team is composed of individuals who perform basically the same actions. The work of one team member has little to no direct effect on the performance of the other team members.
- **Natural Work Group:** The team reports to the same manager, works in the same department, or works together in the same area to contribute to group goals.
- **Project:** The team comes together temporarily for a specific project or assignment and when completed, disbands.
- **Functional:** The team is composed of members from the same function or department, such as customer service.
- **Cross-Functional:** The team is composed of members from varying disciplines, such as sales, parts, and manufacturing, responsible for supporting a unit or position, such as a field service engineer.
- **Virtual:** The team works in various facilities or locations, coming together "virtually" through technology (e.g., conference calling, video conferencing, VoIP).

Rather than getting caught up in specific terminology, it is important to note the variety of teams to which a business professional can belong. Team membership can enhance careers and bring other professional and personal benefits. Being part of a team can give you insight into the subject matter expertise of other functions, opportunities to develop additional skills and knowledge, along with personal growth and fulfillment as you learn to apply your skills and talents for the greater good.

HOW PEOPLE WORK IN TEAMS

Now that you know why organizations deploy teams and how they are structured, you can look inside teams and see how individuals relate to get the job done. You must consider both their skills and assigned or adopted roles that allow them to succeed.

Skills

A skill is an ability to accomplish a task. This ability is usually accompanied by a level of proficiency that enables an individual to successfully accomplish skill-related tasks (i.e., efficiently and effectively). Efficiency refers to producing an outcome with minimal waste or effort. Effectiveness is more about having a definite or desired effect. Both efficiency and effectiveness are needed to successfully apply a set of skills.

What skills can members contribute to teams? In general, team skills fall into three areas:

- **Technical skills** include expertise or functional knowledge, such as a chartered accountant's accounting knowledge or an experienced programmer's IS knowledge.
- **Problem-solving skills** include investigating and analyzing, as well as decision making and implementing. Teams must be able to identify problems and opportunities, evaluate their options, and then make appropriate decisions about how to move forward.
- **Interpersonal skills** are required for effective relationships between team members and include the ability to compromise and build consensus. Listening and supporting are two other essential interpersonal skills.

In organizational life, people are often hired (and promoted) primarily for their technical, or functional, skills and knowledge. These areas of expertise are referred to as "hard" skills, as they can be readily seen in actions performed on the job. Interpersonal skills are frequently referred to as "soft" skills, as they are perhaps less visible.

When it comes to teamwork, however, soft skills are more often the make or break point for an individual working on a team. While technical and problem-solving skills can be learned, it is more difficult to instill the attitudes that underpin positive interactions or interpersonal relationships. In this sense, organizations are wiser to hire (or compose) teams based on a superior interpersonal fit between the individuals and their responsibilities, rather than always focusing on the hard skills required to do a job. Simply stated, it's easier to repair gaps in an employee's hard job-related skills than in their interpersonal abilities.

In the end, of course, it is best when a team is composed of members who have **complementary skills** from both areas. It is a matter of balance, which is a key contributor to solid team performance. For example, an effective software application design team might include software engineers (technical skills), a certified project manager (problem-solving, decision-making, and interpersonal skills), and sales and customer service representatives (interpersonal skills).

However, complementary skills of team members will not necessarily produce desired results if the members fail to understand their team roles.

Team Roles

According to Dr. Meredith Belbin, a role is a "tendency to behave, contribute and interrelate with others in a particular way."[3] She has identified nine team roles, highlighted in Table E.2, that people tend to assume in today's organizations. **Belbin's Team Roles** are categorized by action-oriented roles, people-oriented roles, and cerebral roles.

Table E.2 Belbin's Team Roles

Category	Team-Role Type	Contributions	Allowable Weaknesses
Action-oriented roles	Shaper	Challenging, dynamic, thrives on pressure; has the drive and courage to overcome obstacles.	Prone to provocation. Offends people's feelings.
	Implementer	Disciplined, reliable, conservative, efficient; turns ideas into practical actions.	Somewhat inflexible. Slow to respond to new possibilities.
	Completer-Finisher	Painstaking, conscientious, anxious; searches out errors and omissions and delivers on time.	Inclined to worry unduly. Reluctant to delegate.
People-oriented roles	Coordinator	Mature, confident, a good chairperson; clarifies goals, promotes decision making, delegates well.	Often seen as manipulative. Off-loads personal work.
	Teamworker	Co-operative, mild, perceptive, diplomatic; listens, builds, averts friction.	Indecisive in crunch situations.
	Resource Investigator	Extroverted, enthusiastic, communicative; explores opportunities and develops contacts.	Overoptimistic. Loses interest once initial enthusiasm has passed.
Cerebral roles	Plant	Creative, imaginative, unorthodox; solves difficult problems.	Ignores incidentals. Too preoccupied to communicate effectively.
	Monitor-Evaluator	Sober, strategic, discerning; sees all options and judges accurately.	Lacks drive and the ability to inspire others.
	Specialist	Single-minded, self-starting, dedicated; provides knowledge and skills in rare supply.	Contributes only on a narrow front. Dwells on technicalities.

---
3. http://www.belbin.com

While it may be tempting to wonder if a particular role is better than another, this is just not appropriate. Although a Shaper could at first be perceived as more valuable than a Monitor-Evaluator, what do you suppose would happen if your team were only composed of Shapers and other action-oriented players?

Again, the key is balance. A team's strength lies in its diversity. Heavy weighting within a given team on only one or two roles will create a serious imbalance. Without the unorthodox Plant, confident Coordinator, strategic Monitor-Evaluator, disciplined Implementer, conscientious Completer-Finisher, enthusiastic Resource Investigator, challenging Shaper, co-operative Teamworker, or single-minded Specialist, the team is out of kilter.

Another widely accepted view of team roles divides roles into task (doing) and process (relating).[4] Some examples of each type include:

Task (Doing)

- Elaborator: builds on suggestions from others
- Clarifier: gives relevant examples, restates the problem, and probes for meaning and understanding

Process (Relating)

- Tension Reliever: uses humour or suggests breaks
- Compromiser: is willing to yield a point of view
- Harmonizer: mediates/reconciles
- Encourager: uses praise and support
- Gatekeeper: keeps communication open and encourages others

The most successful teams enjoy a well-blended mix of all the potential role profiles. Members value the variety of skill and expertise brought to bear by their teammates, and are in turn appreciated for their uniqueness. Contributory aspects of each role are highlighted; allowable weaknesses are minimized. If, by chance, the team lacks representation in a given role(s), members willingly step outside their comfort zones to adopt these missing strengths. They know that all qualities embodied by these team roles must be somehow factored into the way of working with one another.

On the other hand, high-performing teams avoid or certainly minimize the behaviours associated with the dysfunctional roles listed below:

- Aggressor: deflates others' status or disagrees aggressively
- Negator: criticizes or attacks others
- Blocker: holds onto attitudes, mentions unrelated experiences, or returns to already resolved topics
- Withdrawer: refuses to participate
- Recognition-Seeker: boasts or talks excessively
- Topic Jumper: changes the subject, sometimes frequently or randomly
- Joker: diffuses the energy by telling ill-timed or off-topic jokes

---

4. Adapted from D. Hunter, A. Bailey, and B. Taylor, *The Zen of Groups*, Tucson, AZ: Fisher Books, 1995, pp. 21–22.

You will learn later in this guide how to effectively manage or eliminate these negative behaviours using practical tools such as a code of conduct, an important part of the technology of teams (described in the section Bringing It All Together).

The What and How of Teams

Working in concert, skills and roles are key ingredients to team success. Expressed a different way, skills are *what* each person brings to the table, while roles are *how* every member executes their involvement. The *what* together with the *how* ensures effective, balanced performance.[5]

To illustrate, have you ever been part of a team where the intended outcome was accomplished, but the process left everyone dissatisfied? How did that feel? Something about *how* the result was reached left regret or anger. It could be that the team's leader treated people disrespectfully, or maybe the members did not get along. The process for accomplishing the goal may have been defective. Regardless of the cause, the experience is a negative one.

In turn, have you ever felt great about a team you were on, even though the end result was not attained? How did that leave you remembering the experience? Even though the *how* (as in team interactions and process) was satisfying, the *what* left something to be desired. At the end of the day, feeling good cannot fulfill a corporate mandate of successful outcomes, and this must be taken into account. However, leaving employees' self-esteem intact in those instances where failure is a part of the normal outcomes (as it will be from time to time) is an important behaviour.

Only when both of these occur simultaneously do we have complete organizational performance, where the required outcomes are achieved and the team feels good about the way this was done. In an organizational context, this means true performance results from each team member pulling their weight in accordance with the organization's stated vision, mission, and values and the charter or goals for the specific team they are on.

Quick Test

1. A team is a small number of people with _____ skills who are committed to _____ or which they hold themselves _____.

2. Team skills generally fall into which of these three broadly categorized areas?
   a. functional, analytical, and relationship
   b. technical, problem-solving, and interpersonal
   c. technical, decision-making, and relationship
   d. functional, implementing, and interpersonal

3. A skill is _____ the team member contributes, while a role is _____ the member contributes.

Answers: 1. complementary; a common purpose, performance goals, and approach; mutually accountable; 2. b; 3. what, how.

---

5. Carol-Ann Hamilton and James Norrie, *The A to Z Guide to Soul-Inspiring Leadership*, Epic Press, 2003.

HOW TEAMS DEVELOP

If complementary skills and roles are necessary for team success, how do team members first come together, then uncover what they each know how to do, and learn how to work effectively with each other? A good place to start is to consider what happens when people first form a team. According to Henry Ford, founder of the Ford Motor Co., "Coming together is a beginning, staying together is progress, and working together is success."

Successful teams don't just happen; they develop purposefully. Building a high-performing team takes time and effort. Each team develops differently and in its own time depending on a number of related variables including team composition, size, type, and mandate.

Something else of note is that in spite of the specific nature of any particular team, all teams are said to generally move through four or five core stages of development. Let's look at a couple of the more common models that represent team development. Perhaps the most widely accepted model of team development is **Tuckman's Stage Model**. You may have seen or heard variations of this model, which is often summarized by its five parts: forming, storming, norming, performing, and adjourning.

Wherever possible, every team should aim to reach the performing stage, the ideal state where a team is fully developed, deployed, and productive. However, it is important to recognize that moving through the stages is not a linear, step-by-step process. Often teams move back and forth fluidly between the stages for any number of valid reasons. It is also implied that eventually the team completes its work and is likely disbanded, although in some instances this may occur only in a long-term context.

As an example of a triggering event that can cause movement within the stages, if a member leaves or is added, this change in team composition and hence its dynamics may take everyone, even temporarily, from a norming or high-performing state back to the earlier forming and storming stage. Since teams are also surrounded by a broader organization, any external factors such as unexpected demands, market threats, or new information from regulators can cause shifts in performance. The mark of a high-functioning team is how quickly individuals and the total team can return to a high-performing state and recover from the occurrence of either an internal or external event.

Table E.3 lists each stage and its associated team member behaviours. Then we further describe what happens at each stage of development.

Forming

For many, the **forming** stage is an exciting one. Launching a team can feel like the beginning of a new adventure. Although team members may be eager to start, they are probably feeling somewhat unsure at the same time. The sooner the team can come to know one another's skills and expectations and begin to define their tasks and roles, the sooner members will experience the possibility of becoming a productive unit. Some testing of one another's commitment and attitude is normal at this point. However, it is important that the team not be allowed to linger unduly in this tentative state.

Table E.3	Tuckman's Stage Model of Team Development
Tuckman's Stages	**Associated Behaviours**
Forming	• Politeness; tentative interactions • Attempt to define goals • Leadership and member roles emerge • Feelings of insecurity, anxiety, excitement
Storming	• Conflict emerges regarding roles, priorities, leadership • Ideas criticized • Competition between members • Feelings of resentment, hostility, and withdrawal
Norming	• Agreement on rules • Compromising, collaborating, co-operating • Sharing of information • More accepting of differences—cohesion—"we" feeling
Performing	• Group members work toward achieving their goals • Trust, flexibility, and interdependence • Decision making, problem solving
Adjourning	• Termination of duties and reduction of dependence • Completion of tasks and disengagement • Increased emotions (e.g., celebration, sorrow over parting)

SOURCES: B. W. Tuckman, "Developmental Sequence in Small Groups," *Psychological Bulletin* (1965), *63*(6), pp. 384–399; also B. W. Tuckman and Mary Ann C. Jensen, "Stages of Small-group Development Revisited," *Group and Organization Studies*, Vol. 2 (1977), pp. 419–427. Associated behaviours column adapted from M. Lankau, unpublished presentation, Department of Management, University of Georgia, 2000.

Storming

Once team members get underway, they will likely find they are not collaborating at all, they just thought they were! If anything, the **storming** stage can bring a real sense of spinning their wheels, or even going backward. Little progress is being made as certain members compete for control. Many would like to avoid this stage altogether. They wish they could just move directly from forming to norming, where work proceeds effectively according to team norms. Skipping the storming stage is not possible, nor desirable. In fact, if natural conflict is not allowed to emerge at this early stage, it will either go underground (where it silently disrupts team functioning throughout its life cycle) or come back later in a more entrenched form (when the impact of unresolved issues is far more damaging to the final result). While uncomfortable for many, it is advisable to allow the storm clouds to gather and then to dissipate using the problem-solving and interpersonal skills described earlier.

Norming

By the time the team reaches the **norming** stage, members have gotten to know one another and find they are now able to work effectively together. While some difficulties may yet present themselves, the team is generally making real progress toward its goal. Members are using one another's ideas, giving and receiving both positive feedback and feedback for improvement in the process. Individual differences are valued and harnessed. This stage marks the establishment of team ground rules and norms (standards for the work to be done as well as how it will be produced). Agreed-upon norms, such as respecting one another's needs and capabilities, are not only set, but adhered to.

Performing

At the **performing** stage, the team is making progress toward its goal with efficiency and effectiveness. Members are legitimately excited about their accomplishments, as they use everyone's strengths to analyze and overcome obstacles. This stage has the quality of "full steam ahead" toward the destination. Feeling confident and competent, members take pride in their work, knowing they will reach their goal. If anything, a high-performing team looks for ways to continuously improve how members work together.

Adjourning

It is almost as though the **adjourning** stage marks a **transition**, defined by William Bridges as "the psychological process all people need to go through to come to terms with a new situation."[6] In this case, a new situation is the happy completion of the team's mandate, as well as the need to disband this particular team configuration. As such, adjourning encompasses the three phases of **Bridges' Transitions Model**, namely endings, neutral zone, and new beginnings, as depicted in Figure E.4.

Bridges writes that the failure to account for the ending and loss that change produces is the single largest issue encountered by organizations in transition. So, too, would it be a sad ending if after all their hard work, the team members were not allowed to properly complete the process with one another. Endings are underpinned by the very same emotions. Members must go through a grieving process to

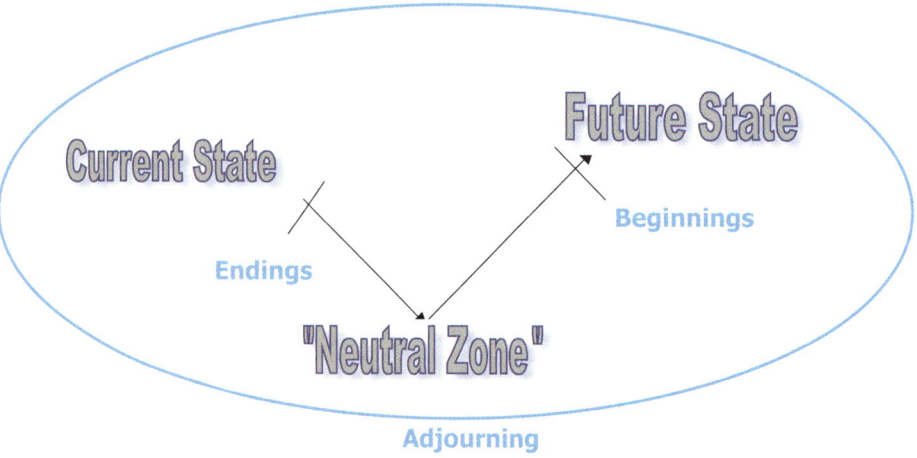

FIGURE E.4 William Bridges' Transitions Model.
SOURCE: Adapted from William Bridges, *Managing Transitions*, Perseus, 1991.

---

6. William Bridges, *Managing Transitions*, Cambridge, MA: Perseus, 1991, p. 3.

let go of those they have come to know well, and move into the ambiguous neutral zone (between assignments) to ready themselves for the new beginning of the next team launch. The process of adjourning must be properly marked, offering room for both the sadness of closure and the rightful celebration of a job well done.

Although Tuckman's Stage Model is very popular and widely accepted in business, not everyone agrees with it. For example, some researchers in the field of leadership suggest that not all teams must go through each stage to become high performing.[7] Others question how it's possible to reach a truly high-performing level of development and sustain it for any period of time.

To both, we respond that the only way out is through. This essentially means the stages of development are a process through which all teams must journey, and they cannot simply get to work. Experiencing and resolving the natural dynamics of each stage is what builds the team's cohesion, leading to eventual success. Rushing toward the end goal all the time might actually burn a team out before it can get there, and defeat the point of trying to create high-performing teams in the first place.

Speed is another matter. While each stage is necessary, a team need not spend undue time in any one stage. Especially when a team uses techniques to expedite their progress and agrees on their purpose early on, it is possible to quickly and effectively achieve high-performing status.

Quick Test

1. Match each stage of development with its appropriate descriptor:

    i. forming
    ii. storming
    iii. norming
    iv. performing
    v. adjourning

    a. full steam ahead
    b. transitions
    c. spinning wheels
    d. getting to know team members
    e. making progress

2. True or False. Every team needs to go through the same five stages of development.

3. One of the most widely accepted models of team development is Tuckman's _____ of Team Development.

Answers: 1. i-d, ii-c, iii-e, iv-a, v-b; 2. True; 3. Stage Model

HALLMARKS OF HIGHLY EFFECTIVE TEAMS

By now you should have discovered that successful team development is not a given; it requires deliberate effort. Teams consist of individuals, each with their strengths and weaknesses, and each with their own goals (which may or may not be aligned with the team's goals). For instance, some team members seek membership in high visibility project teams simply to get promoted; they participate

---

[7]. J. Beck, and N. Yeager, "Moving beyond Team Myths," *Training and Development*, 50(3), March 1996.

and perform only to the extent that this will help them gain their next high profile assignment. Do you recognize this behaviour? What impact do you think it might have on a team? To achieve a highly effective team, therefore, Katzenbach and Smith suggest that members accept mutual accountability; that is, the promises team members make to each other to be responsible for achieving the team's goals.[8] Ideally,

> *highly effective teams are comprised of groups of committed individuals who trust each other, have a clear sense of their purpose about their work, are effective communicators within and outside the team, make sure everyone in the team is involved in decisions affecting the group, follow a process that helps them plan, make decisions, and ensure the quality of their work.*[9]

Another important concept about teams is listening to each other for insights. The blending of multiple perspectives often offers teams a chance to make better decisions that incorporate a diversity of perspectives on a problem. You can use the following equation to represent this element of team effectiveness:[10]

$$\text{Organizational agility} = \text{quality of insight} + \text{speed of execution}$$

Essentially, if a team does not spend time developing its insights into the problem, the value of any solution, even one implemented quickly, is diminished and will be suboptimal in the end. Put another way, without the right directions, going fast just gets you to the wrong place faster! This creates an important distinction between simply going fast (speed) versus going fast appropriately and confidently, knowing the direction is the right one for your organization and its customers or clients (agility).

Several factors contributing to team development are listed in Table E.4.

All six of these critical success factors must be present in order for a team to advance to higher levels of development. Especially if a team intends or needs to move quickly through the five stages of team development, awareness and application of these factors can help them move more rapidly.

How these critical success factors influence performance varies depending on what stage the team is at. Since it is not unusual for a team to be strongest in one or two factors, being aware of how each factor contributes to success helps members decide what actions to take to improve their overall performance. Let's take a closer look at each factor.

Commitment

When people are wholly committed to the team, they are willing to give it their all. Commitment is the essence of a team. Without it, groups remain a conglomeration of individuals. With it, they become a powerful unit of collective performance.

Commitment lies at the heart of "owning" one's particular contributions. Commitment is what allows team members to treat their mates with honour and

---

8. Jon R. Katzenbach and Douglas K. Smith, *The Wisdom of Teams*, McKinsey & Company, Inc., 1993, pp. 60–61.

9. R. S. Wellins, W. C. Byham, and J. M. Wilson, *Empowered Teams: Creating Self-directed Work Groups that Improve Quality, Productivity, and Participation*, San Francisco: Josey-Bass, 1991, p. 188.

10. Carol-Ann Hamilton and James Norrie, *The A to Z Guide to Soul-Inspiring Leadership*, Epic Press, 2003, p. 129.

Table E.4	Critical Success Factors in Team Development
• **Commitment** Team members see themselves as belonging to a team rather than as individuals who operate autonomously. They are committed to group goals above and beyond their personal goals.	
• **Purpose** The team understands how it fits into the overall business or the organization. Team members know their roles, feel a sense of ownership, and can see how they make a difference.	
• **Communication** Communication refers to the style and extent of interaction both among members and between members and those outside the team. It also refers to the way that members handle conflict, decision making, and day-to-day interactions.	
• **Involvement** Everyone has a role in the team. Despite differences, team members feel a sense of partnership with each other. Contributions are respected and solicited, and a real consensus is established before committing the team to action.	
• **Process** Once a team has a clear purpose (why it's together and where it's going), it must have a process or means to get there. The process should include problem-solving tools, planning techniques, regular meetings, meeting agendas and minutes, and accepted ways of dealing with problems.	
• **Trust** Team members have faith in each other to honour their commitments, maintain confidences, support each other, and generally behave in a consistent and predictably acceptable fashion.	

SOURCE: Adapted from R. S. Wellins, W. C. Byham, and J. M. Wilson, *Empowered Teams: Creating Self-directed Work Groups that Improve Quality, Productivity, and Participation*, San Francisco: Jossey-Bass, 1991, p. 188.

trust, enacting their responsibilities almost like a legal contract that cannot and must not be violated.

We are referring to personal leadership here. Personal leadership has nothing to do with your job description. Have you ever known someone who holds a leadership title, but never gains followers? Others inspire everyone around them every day. What creates this difference? The answer is their personal integrity, attitude, beliefs, and values. The extent of personal leadership is squarely within a person's direct control. Personal character is what commitment is all about.

Purpose

A team's **purpose** is its reason for being. Without a clearly understood and agreed-upon purpose, team members don't know what they're supposed to do. With one in place, they can set and base short-, medium-, and longer-term goals in accordance with their larger purpose.

The best teams invest time and effort into exploring, shaping, and agreeing upon a purpose that belongs to them both collectively and individually. This development of a common purpose activity continues through the life of the team. In contrast, failed teams rarely develop a common purpose. Whether this is due to insufficient focus on performance, lack of effort, or poor leadership, they do not coalesce around a challenging aspiration.

The best teams also translate their common purpose into specific performance goals, like reducing the reject rate from suppliers by 50 percent. Indeed, if a team fails to establish specific performance goals, or if those goals do not relate directly to their purpose, team members become confused, pull apart, or revert to mediocre performance. By contrast, when the team's purpose and goals operate in harmony and are combined with commitment, they become powerful engines of performance.

Purpose gives the team direction in the sense that members can align their decisions or resources with it. Purpose allows them to concentrate on what is most important. It also offers the team a sense of identity that encourages everyone to rally around the common purpose, thereby putting the team's needs ahead of their own.

Communication

The importance of **communication** in business has been stated so often that it is almost overdone. Nonetheless, when it comes to teamwork, we can safely say you can never over-communicate. In fact, the three C's of teamwork could refer to communicate, communicate, communicate, because communication is central to team effectiveness.

When communication is authentic, people exchange not only ideas, but also feelings. Both are shared within an atmosphere of mutual trust and respect. Good communicators are therefore honest and sincere. They respect others' opinions and beliefs.

When team members communicate effectively, they resolve conflicts readily or even prevent them altogether. Constant communication also promotes continuous improvement and makes all members of the team feel their viewpoint is important.

Involvement

Involvement is another factor central to the team's effective functioning. A body of thought suggests that the employee directly performing a particular job knows it best. The premise is, they are on the frontline each day, and thus become deeply familiar with the issues, challenges, and inner workings of their function. By encouraging each person's involvement, the smart team benefits from the diverse skills and talents each member brings to the table. Involvement is what harnesses the value of these differences. Every person looks at problem solving and other challenges in his or her unique way. By encouraging these varying contributions, a highly involved team becomes greater than the sum of its individual parts.

Process

Process refers to how teams get things done (i.e., using well-defined procedures). Examples of processes include how a team identifies problems, analyzes data, makes decisions, develops solutions, or reaches agreement. Solid processes help teams reach their goals more effectively and efficiently. They further allow the team to plan and organize its work, which is especially helpful when under tight deadlines. Solid processes allow a team to uncover hidden agendas, because the team has agreed to give everyone a voice in how they arrive at decisions and solutions. A code of conduct (see the section Bringing It All Together) is an excellent example of a process mechanism.

Trust

Which comes first: trust or trust? This paradoxical question basically means, is trust given or earned? Do you know anyone who believes trust should first be granted and only taken back if it is broken in some way? Do you know anyone who believes that trust should only be accorded once earned or deserved? Either way, this subject of **trust** is a complex one because it tests the very belief systems of every team member.

Not surprisingly, many people enter new team situations somewhat cautiously because they are not sure whether those gathered can be entirely trusted. Compounding this reality is the degree to which team players have previously been on the receiving end of mistrustful behaviours. People cannot be *made* to trust one another.

Trust grows through shared purpose, process, involvement, and communication. That is why trust and commitment are so intertwined. Both climb as team members learn they can rely on one another. Promises are made and kept. Teammates are there for you when you need them. As trust builds, teams feel more comfortable to take risks and try new ideas. That is why anything a team can do to build trust sooner rather than later will stand them in good stead down the road.

Among the many benefits a team will realize by developing all six critical success factors are reduced conflict, higher productivity, better quality, and greater job satisfaction for members. To summarize this discussion of the hallmarks of highly effective teams:

- High-performance teams find ways to become highly skilled in all six critical success factors.
- A team should (regularly) evaluate its strengths or weaknesses in each factor.
- Effectiveness in one factor is closely related to effectiveness in the others.
- By focusing on all the success factors, a team can move more rapidly through the stages of team development.
- Teams work best when they combine the critical success factors with good interpersonal skills.
- As a team works on one factor, it should see improvement in the others.

BRINGING IT ALL TOGETHER
Codes of Conduct

As just discussed, effective teams develop a strong commitment to a common approach, or how they will work together to accomplish their shared purpose. Just some of the many decisions that need to be made include who will do particular jobs, how the schedule of work will be set and followed, what skills need to be developed, and how the team will make decisions.

All members of a successful team must equally share workloads and contribute in specific ways to their end product. While the team's leader may at first be viewed as owning responsibility for the team's performance, this is not completely true. Yes, the leader must provide direction and be accountable for the final result. However, as Katzenbach and Smith articulate, no group ever becomes a team until it can hold itself accountable. It is the subtle yet critical difference between "the boss holds me accountable" and "we hold ourselves accountable." Without the attitude conveyed within the second phrase, there can be no team.

Only by going through the sometimes arduous exercise of openly and honestly exploring how this diverse collection of individuals will work effectively with each other is the groundwork laid for ultimate performance. In effect, the **code of conduct** that results from this commitment-building process becomes like a social contract that obliges team players to follow it. Because everyone has presumably been given a fair voice during these discussions, by committing to this contract each person is really saying they are prepared to uphold their end of the bargain.

In this way, the code of conduct serves as a touchstone to which the team can regularly refer during its development to ensure it is on track. Indeed, it is highly advisable to review and stress the importance of these ground rules at each meeting, particularly early on in the team's development.

Some typical dos and don'ts that characterize a team code of conduct in business include:

DO

- Establish and follow clearly laid-out performance standards
- Define clear roles and goals
- Create and follow an agenda during meetings
- Give people the opportunity to openly and honestly express their concerns
- Include all team members in discussions and decisions
- Acknowledge the legitimacy of everyone's feelings
- Take advantage of everyone's individual strengths
- Keep a positive attitude
- Work out conflicts in a healthy manner
- Make decisions through consensus
- Focus on one issue at a time
- Be open to giving and receiving positive feedback and feedback for improvement
- Summarize and paraphrase discussions to ensure everyone is on the same page
- List ideas and decisions visibly so the whole team can see them
- Agree on who will do what by when
- Pay attention to opportunities for continuous improvement
- Incorporate learned lessons into the team's go-forward procedures

DON'T

- Participate in negative gossip or politics
- Assume things about others' motives
- Interrupt one another
- Criticize others' ideas
- Be closed-minded to alternative ideas and suggestions
- Jump too early to a particular conclusion
- Come unprepared to meetings
- Let people go off on tangents

- Withhold important or relevant information from the team
- Fail to alert the team if you are at risk of missing a deadline (that way, contingency plans can be instituted as soon as possible)

By now, you must have realized that becoming a highly productive team is a challenge, but not impossible. By using a process tool like the code of conduct to ensure that everyone participates openly and honestly as well as brings their full set of skills, knowledge, and talent to the table, virtually any team can become highly productive.

Collaborative Technologies

It would not be prudent for us to leave this guide without addressing the fundamentals of technology used to support teams. These are often collectively referred to as collaboration tools. They range in cost, features, and complexity.

Of course, good team members will ensure that they take advantage of the normal technology made available to them on the job. That is not what we are referring to here. Rather, we are addressing technology that is specifically designed and developed to help teams function better while doing their job.

Examples of this might include calendar systems (such as Outlook or Groupwise), email, or perhaps specially designed parts of a corporate intranet aimed at supporting collaboration. A corporate directory system could be used to help team members get to know about each other before their first meeting or connect with an expert in a certain field. For instance, at IBM, an online internal database can help any team member locate an expert in any specialized area and quickly reach out to get the most up-to-date information. Other examples include communication tools such as a BlackBerry, Web conferencing, MSN Messenger, or even something as simple as making sure that offices are equipped with speaker phones for multi-person conference calls.

Two very popular team collaboration technologies today are ProjectSpaces and Windows SharePoint. These Web-based tools allow teams, both internal and external to an organization, to share documents, use discussion boards, chat, and access integrated task lists and calendars. These tools are very powerful in that they offer the same capabilities to all team members and are highly effective in facilitating communication. Team members can no longer claim that they didn't know that a task was assigned to them, or they didn't know where to find a document, or they weren't advised of an important meeting. These tools support not only business processes and workflow, but also work accountability and responsibilities.

The range of technologies available to support teams in your organization is only as large or as small as your imagination, time, and budget permit. Like anything else in business, technology can either be a help or a hindrance, depending on how it is designed and deployed. However, what is certain is that technology is a factor in team performance, so having a technology strategy that addresses the needs of your organization's teams is essential.

CONCLUSION

Current thinking further emphasizes that rather than always focusing on weaknesses, it is more effective to build on strengths. For each of us, our innate strengths flow naturally and effortlessly. So why not harness these strengths as opposed to the often-laborious effort involved in overcoming areas that need development? We hope this discussion will help you become a player who brings your best self to teams now and in the future.

At the end of this Tech Guide is the Nut Island Case Study, a classic from the *Harvard Business Review*, which brings together all the concepts illustrated throughout this guide on the technology of teams. It will help you apply these concepts in a real organization setting.

Quick Test

1. The three C's of teamwork could refer to _____.

2. By encouraging each person's _____, the smart team benefits from everyone's diverse skills and talents.

3. A code of conduct is:
   a. a legally binding contract created among team members.
   b. an ethical statement of philosophy about teamwork.
   c. a set of rules everyone in the organization follows.
   d. a social contract created among the team that helps members stay on track process-wise and interpersonally.

Answers: 1. communicate, communicate, communicate; 2. involvement; 3. d.

ROI STUDENT RETURN ON INVESTMENT SUMMARY

1. Why do organizations use teams to solve business challenges?

Given the increasing complexity of today's organizational environment (i.e., new technologies, new knowledge, new demands), it only makes good business sense to use teams to address a number of these issues. While corporations increasingly seek out talented knowledge-enabled professionals to help them solve problems despite a complex environment, these expert individuals may not always be available to work on every challenge. As well, no one can be specialized in all fields of knowledge. That's why organizations tap into the collective power of teams. Team members possess a more diverse and complementary set of knowledge, expertise, and skills than any single individual. A well-functioning team is truly greater than the sum of its parts.

2. How do skills and roles work together to help people work better in teams?

A skill is an ability to accomplish a task efficiently and effectively. Typical examples of skills members might contribute to teams include technical or functional, problem-solving, and interpersonal. However, even team members' complementary skills will not necessarily produce desired results if members fail to understand their team roles. Roles generally can be categorized as task/action-based or process/people-oriented. Successful teamwork demands a mix of all types of roles; no one role is better than another. Skills are, therefore, what each person brings to the table, while roles are how every member executes their involvement. The *what* together with the *how* ensure balanced, complete performance.

3. What stages do teams need to naturally progress through in order to become high performing?

Successful teams don't just happen; they develop. Building a high-performing team takes time and effort. Each team develops differently and in its own time depending on a number of variables, not the least of which are member composition, team type, and mandate. Despite their specific nature, teams are generally said to go through the following stages: forming, storming, norming, performing, and adjourning (Tuckman's Stage Model of Team Development). Moving through the stages is not a linear, step-by-step process. Internal and external events will result in a team reverting back to an earlier stage of development, even temporarily. While some would like to advocate for skipping steps, resolving each stage's natural dynamics builds the means for success.

4. What are the critical success factors that characterize effective teams?

The six critical success factors include: commitment, purpose, communication, involvement, process, and trust. They must all be present for a team to advance to higher levels of development. Especially if a team intends or needs to move quickly through the five stages of development, awareness and application of these factors can help them move more rapidly. How these critical success factors influence performance varies depending on what stage the team is at. Since it is not unusual for a team to be strongest in one or two factors, being aware of how each contributes to success helps members decide what actions to take to improve their overall performance. All six factors are intertwined. These factors combined reduce conflict, as well as increase productivity and quality.

5. What tools do well-functioning teams apply to ensure their success?

The core tool examined in this Tech Guide is the code of conduct. Although it can often be a time-consuming and labour-intensive exercise to openly and honestly explore how a diverse collection of individuals will work effectively with each other, the resulting code lays the groundwork for ultimate performance. Through this commitment-building exercise, team players become obliged to follow the code of conduct because they have each been given a fair voice during the discussions. The code thus serves as a touchstone to which the team can regularly refer during its development to ensure it is on track. It is highly advisable to review and stress the importance of these ground rules at each meeting, especially early on.

KNOWLEDGE SPEAK

adjourning   452
Belbin's Team Roles   447
Bridges' Transitions Model   452
code of conduct   458
commitment   454
communication   456
complementary skills   446
cross-functional team   445
forming   450
functional team   445
independent team   445
interpersonal skills   446
involvement   456
natural work group   445

norming   451
performing   452
problem-solving skills   446
process   456
project team   445
purpose   455
storming   451
team   443
technical skills   446
transitions   452
trust   457
Tuckman's Stage Model   450
virtual team   445
work group   444

KNOWLEDGE INTEGRATING CASE: NUT ISLAND EFFECT CASE STUDY

Nut Island is a small peninsula in Quincy, Massachusetts, a city of 85,000 located about 15 kilometres south of Boston. The rickety Nut Island sewage treatment plant was decommissioned in 1997, and its core team was disbanded after 30 years of efforts that left Boston Harbour no cleaner than it was when the team came together in the late 1960s.

The Nut Island effect is a destructive organizational dynamic that pits a homogeneous, deeply committed team against its disengaged senior managers. Their conflict can be mapped as a negative feedback spiral that passes through five predictable stages:

1. Management, its attention riveted on high visibility problems, assigns a vital, behind-the-scenes task to a team and gives that team a great deal of autonomy. Team members self-select for a strong work ethic and an aversion to the spotlight. They become adept at organizing and managing themselves. The unit develops a proud and distinct identity.
2. Senior management takes the team's self-sufficiency for granted and ignores team members when they ask for help or try to warn of impending trouble. When trouble strikes, the team feels betrayed by management and reacts with resentment.
3. An us-against-the-world mentality takes hold in the team, as isolation heightens its sense of itself as a band of heroic outcasts. Driven by the desire to stay off management's radar screen, the team grows skilful at disguising its problems. Team members never acknowledge problems to outsiders or ask them for help. Management is all too willing to take the team's silence as a sign that all is well.
4. Management fails in its responsibility to expose the team to external perspectives and practices. As a result, the team begins to make up its own rules. The team tells itself that the rules enable it to fulfill its mission. In fact, these rules mask grave deficiencies in the team's performance.
5. Both management and the team form distorted pictures of reality that are very difficult to correct. Team members refuse to listen when well-meaning outsiders offer help or attempt to point out problems and deficiencies. Management, for its part, tells itself that no news is good news and continues to ignore team members and their task. Management and the team continue to shun each other until some external event breaks the stalemate.

SOURCE: Paul F. Levy, "The Nut Island Effect: When Good Teams Go Wrong," *Harvard Business Review*, March 2001.

Case Questions

Before you read ahead as to how to stop the Nut Island Effect before it starts, answer the following:
1. What critical failures do you diagnose, based on the concepts in this Tech Guide?
2. Using what you have learned, what remedies would you prescribe to senior management?
3. How can you use this Nut Island Effect information when you participate in teams in the future?

The case study goes on to talk about a fine line. The humane values and sense of commitment that distinguished the Nut Island team are precisely the kinds of values to encourage. The trick is to separate them from the isolation and lack of external focus that breeds counterproductive practices and, ultimately, failure.

As such, here are some suggested ways for a team or organization to avoid the Nut Island Effect:

- The first step is to install performance measures and reward structures tied to both internal operations and company-wide goals.

- Second, senior management must establish a hands-on presence by visiting the team. These occasions will be a chance to detect early warnings of problems and will give the team a sense they matter and are listened to.

- Third, team members must be integrated with people from other parts of the organization. This exposes team members to ideas and practices being used elsewhere, as well as encourages them to think in terms of the big picture.

- Finally, it would be helpful to periodically rotate new members into the team environment. This should not be done so frequently as to be disruptive, but often enough to discourage the institutionalization of bad habits.

PHOTO CREDITS

Logon page 1 gettyimages®.

Chapter 1 Page 5 iStockphoto/Nyul.
page 9 shutterstock.
page 15 shutterstock.
page 18 Associated Press.

Chapter 2 Page 35 iStockphoto/blackred.
Page 40: Copyright @Studio city/eStock Photo.
Page 41 (left): Courtesy of Hewlett-Packard Company.
Page 41 (right): Photodisc/Getty Images.
Page 42 (top and bottom): Courtesy of Hewlett-Packard Company.
Page 51 (top): SimonInns.
page 51 (bottom) gettyimages®.

Chapter 3 Page 85 iStockphoto/christie & cole studio inc.
page 89 Associated Press.
Page 96: Photodisc/Getty Images.
page 100 shutterstock.

Chapter 4 Page 119 iStockphoto/See Hear Media, Inc.
Page 125: Thinkstock/Media Bakery.
page 134 gettyimages®.
page 138 shutterstock.
page 147 gettyimages®.

Chapter 5 Page 165 iStockphoto/Ingvald Kaldhussæter.
page 169 gettyimages®.
page 183 iStockphoto.
page 186 iStockphoto.

Chapter 6 Page 203 iStockphoto/Andrey Prokhorov.
Page 207: Courtesy of SanDisk Inc.
page 209 corbis.

Chapter 7 Page 235 iStockphoto/David Newton.
page 243 shutterstock.

Chapter 8 Page 275 iStockphoto/Digital Planet Design.
page 280 shutterstock.
page 283 ©See-ming Lee.
page 292 MediaBakery.
page 294 shutterstock.

Chapter 9 Page 305 iStockphoto/Stephen Morris.
page 308 gettyimages®.
page 311 Associated Press.
page 313 Associated Press.
page 321 shutterstock.

Tech Guide A Page 340 ©David Ticoll.

Tech Guide B Page 360: Corbis Digital Stock.
Page 365 (top to bottom): Courtesy of Hewlett-Packard Company, Photodisc/Getty Images, Courtesy of Hewlett-Packard Company, Courtesy of Logitech, Photodisc/Media Bakery.
Page 366 (top to bottom): Courtesy of Hewlett-Packard Company, Courtesy of Logitech, Photodisc/Media Bakery, Courtesy of Hewlett-Packard.
Page 367 (top to bottom): iStockphoto, ImageSource/Media Bakery, shutterstock.
page 368 shutterstock.
Page 372 (top): Courtesy of Wacom Technology Corporation.
Page 372 (Table B.5): All photos courtesy of Hewlett-Packard Company, except thermal printer courtesy of Epson America Inc. System Device Group.

INDEX

A
Academic advisor, 106
Accenture, 345
Access point (AP), 48
Accessing, internet, 50–52
Accountant, 16
ACID, 125
  organizations, 125
  properties, 126
Action grid, example, 108
Action-oriented roles, 447
ActiveX controls, 62
Activity duration estimating, 261
Activity sequencing, 261
Address bus, 362–364
Adjourning, 450–453
Adobe Flash, 277
Advertising, 293
Advertising models, 171
AdWords, Google, 175
Affiliate, 280
Aggregate functions, 428
Agile development, 251
AI. *See* Artificial intelligence (AI)
AJAX engine, 68
Alexa.com, 300
Algorithm, 391
Alien, 333
Alpert, Jesse, 13
ALU. *See* Arithmetic Logic Unit (ALU)
Amazon.ca, 184
Amazon.com, 59
Analog sensor, 369
Analog signal, 42, 405, 407
Analog *vs.* digital data transmission, 406
Analysis paralysis process, 102
AND operator, 427
Anomalies, 430
AP. *See* Access point (AP)
API. *See* Application program interface (API)
Applet model, 171
Application program interface (API), 278, 378
Application protocol interfaces, 52, 278
Application server, 49
Application service provider (ASP), 141
  advantages, 142
Application software
  commercially developed application software, 385
    database software, 388–389
    internet-related software, 389–391
    specialized software, 391
    spreadsheets, 386–388
    web browser, 389–391
    word processing software, 385–386
  customized software, 391
  database software, 393
  desktop publishing software, 385–386
  open-source software, 393–394
  presentation software, 389
  running, 381
  specialized software, 391
Application software layer, 403
Arithmetic logic unit (ALU), 360
Artificial intelligence (AI), 100
As We May Think, 416
ASCII code, 359
Ashby's law, 442
ASP. *See* Application service provider (ASP)
Association for computing machinery (ACM), 317
Association of Information Technology Professionals (AITP), 317
ATMs. *See* Automated teller machines (ATMs)
Audio content software, 255
Audio input, 368
Auditing and Assurance Standards Oversight Council (AASOC), 147
Authentication, 71
Authorization controls, 154
Automated bank machine (ABM), 6
Automated POS-TPS process, 126
Automated teller machines (ATMs), 97–98, 126
Automating, 96
Avanzino, Stephen, 236

B
Ball, Derek, 36
Bandwidth, 362, 407
Bar code inventory systems, 97
Bar code reader, 367
Bar code scanners, 96, 134
Baseband, 407
Basel II Accord, 315
Basic input/output system (BIOS), 362, 379
B2B e-commerce
  extranet-enabled
    vs. EDI, 193
  supply chain efficiency, 190–193
B2B e-commerce exchange transactions, 188
B2B transactions
  types, 188
  BC Bid®, 193
B2C e-commerce
  advantages/disadvantages of, 184
  limitations of, 185

B2C websites, 172
Beaman, Tom, 86
Belbin, Meredith, 447
Belbin's team roles, 447
Bell, 345
Benioff, Marc, 140
Berners-Lee, Tim, 56
Best solution, 129
B2G. *See* Business-to-government (B2G)
BI system. *See* Business intelligence (BI) system
Bill 198, 315
Bill of lading (BOL), 190
Binary, 357
Binary data, 357–358
Binary mathematics, 357, 359
Biometric scanners, 367, 369
BIOS. *See* Basic input/output system (BIOS)
Bit, 357
BlackBerrys, 6, 7, 174
blogger.com, 279
Blogs, 299, 302, 415
Bluetooth, 409–410
Bluetooth chip, 410
Boeing, 190, 199
BPM. *See* Business process management (BPM)
BPO. *See* Business process outsourcing (BPO)
Brandstorm, 287
Bridges' transitions model, 452
Brin, Sergey, 106
Broadband, 407
Brochureware, 60
BS7799, 151
Buffer, 363, 373
Build-and-fix model, 248
Burns, Sherrill, 204
Bus, 361, 362
Bush, Vannevar, 416
Business benefits
  of acting ethically, 310
Business continuity plan, 150
Business environment, 248, 344, 442
  stakeholders and boundaries, 88
Business ethics, 309
Business fundamental, 87
  automating, 96–98
  business process, 93
  competitive advantage, 95–96
  feedback, 95
  organizational boundary, 89
  stakeholders, 89
  value chain, 133–139
Business information system, 204

Business intelligence (BI) system, 223, 301
  corporate information strategy, 223
  pyramid, 224
  stages of, 224
  using IT, 224–226
Business models, 172
  website, 172
Business organizations, 87–96
Business partner goals, 2
Business process, 12, 87–96
  customer service, 95
  feedback, role, 95
  performance of
    automating, informating, and transforming, 238
Business process management (BPM), 124
Business process outsourcing (BPO), 145
Business process reengineering (BPR), 95
  goals, 95
Business professional, 102, 104, 109
Business rule, 125
Business strategy, 87, 181
Business-to-business (B2B), 168
Business-to-consumer (B2C), 168
Business-to-government (B2G), 168
Business value, creation, 1, 85, 96
  informating, 98
  IT automation, use, 96–97
  transforming, 98
Businesses
  as open system, 88–90
  values creation organization, 90
Byte, 215, 359

C

C, computer languages, 392
Cable modems, 405
Cache memory, 360
Calgary, 24
Canada, top social sites in, 278
Canada Post, 64
Canada's Charter of Rights and Freedoms, 307
Canadavacationrentals.ca, 179
Canadian broadband usage, 407
Canadian context of socialized medicine, 308
Canadian Idol project, 334
Canadian Idol success, 321–322
Canadian Idol TV series, 332
Canadian Privacy Commission, 323
Canadian privacy laws, 284
Canadian Public Accountability Board (CPAB), 147
Canadian Securities Administrators (CSA), 147
Canadian Tire, 345
Capability maturity model integration (CMMI), 152

Capacitive touch screen, 371
Carcinogen, 308
Career, in ICT, 338–339, 348
Career centre, 114
Career journey, 351–352
Career management, 338
CASE. *See* Computer-aided software engineering (CASE)
Case studies
  business administration, 32–33
  buy a car, 115–116
  Dell inc., 231–232
  Google inc., 271–272
  intellectual property rights, 327–328
  Nut Island, 461–462
  selecting a computer, 82
  Walmart, 160–161
  WEB 2.0 applications at, 300–302
CASE tools, 109. *See* Computer-aided software engineering (CASE) tools
CBC radio, 76
CD-read/write (CD-RW), 374
CD-recordable (CD-R), 374
Central processing unit (CPU), 39, 40, 360
CEOs, 120
Cerebral roles, 447, 557
Champy, James, 93
Character encoding, 358
Character string, 427
Chief executive officer (CEO), 21
Chief information officer (CIO), 110, 111, 283, 314–315
Chip-based storage, 375
Cisco systems, 352
Claudio, Cecilia, 150
Client/server architecture, 398
Client/server network, 54, 398, 400
Client-side scripting, 62–63
Client software, 412
Clients, 398
Clock speed, 362
Cloud computing, 52
CMMI. *See* Capability maturity model integration (CMMI)
Co-operative websites, 179
Coaxial cable, glass fibre comparison, 404
COBIT, 151
Codd, E. F., 216
Code generation, 254
Codes of conduct, 317, 458
Collaboration, 73
Collaborative forecasting and replenishment (CFAR), 161
Collaborative management tools, 128
Collaborative software categories, 128
Command interpreter, 377
Commitment, 454
Common ethical dilemmas, involving IT, 318
Common internet security threats, 70

Communication, 212, 456
Communication security establishment (CSE), 152
Communications conference, 333
Company-centric business model, 188, 189
Competitive advantage, 95–96
  resource-based model, 99
  ways, 99
Competitive intelligence, 320–321
Complementary skills, 446
Compliance, 147
Complicit consent, 322
Compound operators, 427
Compression technologies, 283
Computer aided design/computer aided manufacturing (CAD/CAM) software, 135
Computer-aided software engineering (CASE) tool, 109, 255
Computer-enabled marketing, 288–289
Computer hierarchy, 39–40
Computer languages
  uses, 392
Computer network technologies, 47–48
  business use of, 173, 174
Computer programs
  algorithm, 391
Computer Society of the IEEE (IEEE-CS), 317
Conduct, 309
Conduct information interviews, 345
Conferencing tools, 128
Connectivity, 10, 11, 23, 48, 410
Consumer information, 185
Consumer-to-consumer (C2C), 168
Consumer-to-government (C2G), 168
Control advantage, 151
Control totals, 154–155
Control unit (CU), 360
Controls
  corrective controls, 153
  define, 152
  detective controls, 153
  effective controls, 153
  internal control, 153
  preventive controls, 154
Convergence technologies, 76
Cookie, 419
Copyright, 318–319
Core skill, 344
Corporate and IT governance, 325
Corporate governance, 313
  laws and regulations, 315–316
Corporate social responsibility (CSR), 111, 310
Corporations
  ethics and conduct, 309
Corruption, 311
COSO, 151
Cost management, 258
COTS software, 385

Council of Supply Chain Management Professionals (CSCMP), 130
CPU. *See* Central processing unit (CPU)
Crackberry, 53
Craigslist, 173
Credit card information, 185
Criteria, 107
  scoring alternatives, 108
CRM. *See* Customer relationship management (CRM)
Cross-functional team, 445
CSE. *See* Communication security establishment (CSE)
CTV's requirements, for Canadian Idol, 332–333
Customer behaviour, 19
Customer relationship management (CRM) systems, 22, 137, 140, 142, 182
  administration and finance systems, 137
  human resources service, 138
  procurement, 139
  software, 45
  technology development, 138
  up-selling, 137
Customized software, developing
  Apache Web server software, 394
  computer programs, 391
  languages, 392
  Linux operating system, 394
  opens-source software, 393
  programming languages, 391

D

Data, 205
Data analysis, 224
Data bus, 360
Data component layer, 404
Data flow diagram, 219
Data hierarchy, 215
Data-information-knowledge continuum, 205–207
Data integrity, 216
Data mart, 220
Data mining, 221
Data modelling, 218
Data rate, 406
  and bandwidth, 406
Data redundancy, 430
Data transmission, 404
Data warehouse technology, 220–222
  businesses access, 222
    multidimensional data, organizing, 221
    reasons, 221
  database, comparison of, 220
Database administrators (DBA), 214, 215
Database management system (DBMS), 214
  software, 106

Databases, 31, 81, 160
  data flow diagram (DFD), 219–220
  data hierarchy, 215–216
  data modelling, 218
  data storage, 214
  entity-relationship diagram (ERD), 218
  logical data model, 218
  relational data model, 216–218
Davda, Arti, 6
DBA. *See* Database administrators (DBA)
DBMS. *See* Database management system (DBMS)
Decentralized matrix organizational structures, 91
  advantages/disadvantages, 92
Decentralized structure, 91
Decision makers, 109
Decision making process, 99–104
  decisions classification, 100–101
  elements, 101
  information use, 101–102
  rational decision, 99
  semi-structured decision, 101
  structured decision, 100
  unstructured decision, 101
Decision support systems (DSS), 21, 22, 129
  communications-driven, 129
  data-driven, 129
  document-driven, 129
  financial models, 129
  knowledge-driven, 129
  model-driven, 129
  optimization models, 129
  simulation modelling, 129
  statistical models, 129
Dell, 167
Dell computer, 42
Dell DataSafe product, 42
Denial of service (DoS), 148
Digital data, 357
Digital products, 169
  downloading, 169
  ordering, 170
  purchasing, 169
Digital subscriber line (DSL), 406
Direct-access storage, 373
Direct marketing, 288
Disaster recovery planning, 150
Dissonance, 307
Dital signal processors (DSPs), 40
DMS. *See* Document management systems (DMS)
Document management systems (DMS), 127
  knowledge management systems, 128
Document type definition, 436
Domain names, top-level, 412
DoomJuice, 70

DoS. *See* Denial of service (DoS)
Dots per inch (dpi), 373
Drive-by hackers, 72
DVD player, 1
DVD-RW, 374
Dynamic link library (dll) files, 382
Dynamic RAM (DRAM), 363
Dynes, Sam, 333

E

E-commerce, 168
  advantage, 173–178, 187
  benefits, 184–188
  business models, 171–172
  and business strategy, 181–182
  co-operative website, 179
  competitive difference, 179–181
  credit card security codes, 186
  definition, 167–172
  limitations of, 184–188
  niche markets, 180
  between organizations
    B2B transactions, 188–190
    business models, 188–190
  and products, 169–170
  transaction, types of, 168
  vs. e-business, 167
E-commerce business model, 171, 172
E-commerce software, 153
E-commerce strategy, 181
E-commerce system, 155
E-commerce technologies, 13
  on business, impact, 174
  e-tailer, 63
  first-generation, 60
  fourth-generation, 68–69
  HTML, 60, 61
  HTTP, 61, 64
  Internet2, 53
  order and payment systems, 65–68
  second-generation, 60–64
  third-generation, 64–68
  web services, 68–69
  XML, 68
E-info, 288
e-marketer.com, 294
E-marketing, 288
E-procurement, 189, 193
E-tailer, 63
eBay, 173
Eclipse, 254
Economy, Canadian, 25
Effective controls, 153
Effectiveness, 102
Efficiency, 102
EIM systems, 75
Electromagnetic digitizer, 371
Electronic commerce, 59–60. *See* E-commerce
Electronic data files, 288

Electronic data interchange (EDI), 189, 192, 403
   extranet-enabled B2B e-commerce, 193
Electronic directory, 21
Electronic product purchasing, 170
Electronic sensors, 183
Electronic spreadsheet software, 45
Electronics Magazine, 8
Email server, 49
Embedded processors, 40
Encryption/decryption, 187
Encryption systems
   primary forms of, 187
Enterprise resource planning (ERP) system, 21, 22, 131, 232
   benefit, 132
   disadvantage, 132
   sales module, 132
Enterprise risk management (ERM)
   definition, 146
   risk acceptance, 150
   risk avoidance, 151
   risk deferral, 150
   risk framework application, 148
   risk reduction methods, 149, 150
Enterprise software, 140
Enterprise systems, 119, 133, 136, 139
   inbound logistics, 133
   value chain support, 133
Entertainment, 292
Entity, 424
Entity-relationship diagram (ERD), 218
eProcurement Scotl@nd, 193
Equity, 321
ERD. *See* Entity-relationship diagram (ERD)
Ergonomics, 41, 365, 369
Ethernet protocol, 408
Ethical breaches
   regulatory approach, imposed on public companies, 312
   remedying, 311–313
   Sarbanes-Oxley act of 2002, 312
Ethical dilemmas, in IT, 308, 325
Ethical misconduct, in business, 310–311
Ethics, 307
   personal implications of, 321–323
Etsy, 175
Evolutionary model, 250
Exchange
   horizontal exchanges, 190
   vertical exchanges, 190
Exchange model, 189
Executive information systems (EIS), 127
Expert systems, 100
Explicit knowledge, 207
eXtensible markup language (XML), 68
   for data transfer, 435
      document type definition method, 436
      portion of, 437
      stylesheet, 437
      tags, 435
      vs. HTML, 435, 436
      XML schema (XSD) file, 436
External conduit, 323
Extranet, 189, 192, 193

F

Facebook, 278, 281, 296
   privacy options, 323
Fair dealing, 328
FAQ. *See* Frequently asked questions (FAQ)
Farmers Insurance Group, 149
Feasibility study, 238
Feature creep, 262
FedEx, 64
Feedback, 95
Fibre-optic cable, 404
Field, 215
File allocation table (FAT), 383
File/disk management, 382
File transfer protocol (FTP), 413
Files, 73, 215
Finance systems, administration, 137–138
Financial analysis, 17
Financial feasibility metrics, 239
Financial IS, 123
Financial models, 129
Financially feasible, 238
FIS. *See* Functional information systems (FIS)
Flash, 176
Flash memory, 375
Flatbed scanners, 367
Flickr, 279, 292
Floating point unit (FPU), 360
Folders, 383
Folksonomy, 286
Ford, Henry, 450
Foreign key, 217, 424
Form controls, 61
Forming, 450
Foundation skills, 344
FPU. *See* Floating point unit (FPU)
Freedom of Information and Privacy Protection Act (FIPPA), 284
FremantleMedia, 332
Frequently asked questions (FAQ), 414
Friedman, Thomas, 24
Friendster, 182
Frito-Lay, 136
FTP. *See* File transfer protocol (FTP)
Functional information systems (FIS), 123–124
Functional matrix organizational structures, 91
   advantages/disadvantages, 92
Functional team, 445

G

GAN. *See* Global area network (GAN)
Gantt chart, 261
Garbage in, garbage out, 103
Gasoline, 1
Gates, Bill, 8, 9
Gateway, 408
GDP, 26
Geist, Michael, 328
General Motors, 160
GeoEye, 77
Geographic information systems (GIS), 129
Geographically dispersed team (GDT), 76
Gigahertz (GHz), 39
Global area network (GAN), 48
Global perspective, 225
   global sourcing, 340
Global sourcing, 340
Global system for mobile communication (GSM) protocol, 420
Globalization, 24, 240
Gmail, 71, 73, 407
Google, 58, 73, 77, 289
Google AdWords, 175
Google Earth, 77
Google Maps, 77
Google Toolbar, 62
Governance
   personal implications of, 321–323
GPA, 109
Graphical user interface (GUI), 369, 377
Graphics software, 45
Green IT, 321
Groove, 73, 212
Groupware, 73–74, 128
GSM mobile phones, 419

H

Hacker, 72–73
Haitian Earthquake Registry, 78
Hajaj, Nissan, 13
Hammer, Michael, 93
Handheld device, 376
Hard disk, 373–375, 379, 383
Hardware, 38
   central processing unit (CPU), 39
   communications, 42, 43
   embedded processors, 40
   input, 41
   input devices, 365–366, 368
   memory, 40
   microprocessor, 39
   modern monitors, 42
   output, 41
   overview of
      CPU, 360–362
      devices, 356–357
      electronics of, 357–360
      processing, 360–362

performance measurement, 369
processing, 38
speed, 369
storage, 42
Health care plan, 308
Henderson, Graham, 328
Hi5, 278
hidemyass.com, 284
High capacity diskettes, 374
High level system requirements, 238
Hiring practices, 321
H1N1 infection
statistics, 228
Horizontal exchanges, 190
Host computer, 411
HR management and policy, 122
HTTP request, 54, 55, 61, 64
HTTP response, 54, 55, 64
Hub, 48, 409
Human resource information systems (HRIS), 138
Hypercompetitive, 8
Hyperlink, 390
Hypertext, 55, 416
Hypertext markup language (HTML), 56, 60, 417
Hypertext transfer protocol (HTTP), 403

I
IAB. *See* Internet architecture board (IAB)
IADD model, 105
analyze stage, 106–107
decide stage, 107–108
do stage, 108–109
investigate stage, 105–106
IBM Lotus Instant Messaging & Web Conferencing, 75
ICommerce, 12, 13
ICT careers, 338, 349
ICT GDP, 26
ICT market, 27
ICT professionals
need for, 339–341
well-rounded person, 343
ICTC career clusters
and work streams, 350–351
ID code, 154
IDE. *See* Integrated development environments (IDE)
Idea phase, 245
Identifier, 424
Identity theft, 320
IETF. *See* Internet engineering task force (IETF)
IGOE model, 94–95
IM. *See* Instant messaging (IM)
Imaging technology, 127
Implementer, 448
Implicit consent, 322
In-house development, 241

vs. outsourcing, advantages and disadvantages of, 241
In-sourcing, 149
Inadequate design, 262
Inbound logistics, 121, 133
Inception phase, 238, 246, 249
Independent team, 445
Indirect sources of information, 289
Infomediaries, 171
Informating system
benefits, 98
enterprise resource planning, 131
Information, 12, 205
Information and Communications Technology Council (ICTC), 350
Information and communications technology (ICT) sector, 25, 26, 338
Information clutter
online advertising, 175–176
partnering and traffic trading, 176–178
search engine optimization, 176
web usage and statistics, 178
Information density, 175
Information economy, 13
Information evaluation criteria, 103
Information interview, 345
Information overload, 13
Information security management systems (ISMS), 151
Information system (IS), 1, 9, 204
in business, 22–23
business activities, 122
business value of, 22–23
common types of, 28
components, 10–11
decision support systems, 129
document management systems, 127
functional information systems, 123–124
input-process-output (IPO) model, 10
knowledge management systems, 128
management information, 127
supply chain management, 130
transaction processing systems, 125–126
vs IT, 11
workflow management systems, 124–125
Information technology (IT), 2, 8
for an organization, 19–20
business environment, 20–22
business organizations, 20–22
applications, 96–98, 143
automation, 96
in business, 3
compliance, support, 147
components of, 37
as fundamental for career, 16–19
governance, 144, 314
hardware, 356

importance, 110
key events in computing history, 28
knowledge, 14
manager, 321
outsourcing, 145
for personal productivity and entertainment, 14–16
professionalism, 317
professionals, 87
roles, 111, 146
for society, 24–28
software, 356
uses, 145
Information technology infrastructure library (ITIL), 152
Initial program load (IPL), 379
Innovation, 27
Input devices, 41, 365–369
Input/output (I/O) tasks, 380
Insourcing, 25
Instance, 216, 263
Instant messaging (IM), 25, 74–75, 415
Institute on Governance (IOG), 152
Instruction set, 361
Integrated development environments (IDE), 139, 254
Integrative skill, 344
Integrity commissioner, 322
Intel, 7, 342, 357, 359, 361
Intellectual property, 319
Intellectual property rights, 327–328
Internal bus, 362
Internal conduit, 322
Internal control, 153
Internal memory, 362–363
Internal rate of return (IRR), 238
Internet, 7, 12–13, 90, 114, 159, 293
accessing, 50–52, 174
cloud computing, 52
crime, 70
internetworking, 410
ISP, computer connection, 410
next-generation, 52
security, 70–73
Sophos, 70
uses of, 174
work activities, using, 412
email, 413
file transfer protocol (FTP), 413–414
internet relay chat (IRC), 415
newsgroups internet application, 414–415
telnet protocol, 415
Internet2, 53
Internet Architecture Board (IAB), 50
Internet business models, 171
Internet cafes, 174
Internet Engineering Task Force (IETF), 50
Internet explorer, 55, 62, 382, 419

Internet operations, 412
  email, 412
Internet protocol suite, 50
Internet Protocol Version 6 (IPv6), 52–53
Internet-related businesses, 171
Internet-related software, 389
Internet-related technologies, 24
Internet relay chat (IRC), 415
Internet search engines, 56–58
Internet security, 70–73
Internet service provider (ISP), 50, 407
Internet standards, 50
Internet technology, 192
  operating costs, reduction, 167
Internet TV, 292
Internet users, 174
Internet wisely, 171
Interorganizational system (IOS), 191
Interpersonal skills, 446
Interview etiquette, 346–347
Intranets, 74
Inventory management system (IMS), 136, 159
Involvement, 456
IP address, 403, 404, 409, 411
iPhone, 369
iPods, 25
IPv4, 53
IPv6, 53
Iron triangle, 256
IS. *See* Information system (IS)
IS development teams, 242–244
IS development tools, 253
  authoring software categories, 255
  case tools, 255
  code generation, 254
  integrated development environments (IDEs), 254
  modelling tools, 253–254
IS project management
  portfolio management, 263–264
  program, 263–264
  project management software, 264–266
  project management tasks, overview of, 257–260
  project time management, 260–261
  risk management, 261–263
  triple constraint/iron triangle, 256, 257
IS project team, 243–244
IS security, 94
ISO 17799, 151
IT. *See* Information technology
"IT Doesn't Matter," 144
IT-enabled businesses, 122

J
Java, 392
Java applet, 62
Java language, 392
Javascript, 68, 277

Jobloft.com, 69
Join operation, 433
Just-in-time (JIT) inventory concept, 136

K
Katzenbach, Jon R., 443, 444, 454, 457
Keller, Helen, 8, 9
Kernel, 377
Keyboard, 364, 369, 376, 380
Killin, Ken, 306
Knowledge, 205
  analysis, 209–210
  communication, 212
  discovery, 207–209
  lifelong creation, 207
  summary of, 213
  synthesis, 211–212
  transformation, 210–211
  work activities, 213
Knowledge-creation process, 207
Knowledge management (KM)
  benefits, 128
Knowledge work, 8
  activities, 207–214
  analysis, 209
  communication, 212
  discovery, 208
  overview, 213
  synthesis, 211
  transformation, 210

L
LAN. *See* Local area network (LAN)
Lands' End, 75, 169
Laser scanner, 367, 369
LCD monitors, technology, 370
Legal codes, 307
Lennie, John, 276
Lifelong knowledge creation, 207
Light pen, 366
LIKE operator, using, 427
  wildcard character, 427
LinkedIn, 278
Links, 55
Liquid crystal display (LCD), 395
Listserv, 413
Live communications, 333
Local area network (LAN), 47, 402, 408
  bridge, 408
  share information, 408
  software licences, 408
Logical data model, 224
Login IDs, 154
Logistics management systems (LMS)
  marketing and sales, 136
  operations, 135
  outbound logistics, 136

M
M-commerce, 182–184
Machine instructions, 359

Magnetic disks, 373–374
Magnetic ink character recognition (MICR), 368
Magnetic strip reader, 368
Mail box, 402
Mailto, 418
Main memory, 363
Mainframe, 39, 377
Making decisions, 22
Malcolm, Ryan, 332
Malware, 70
MAN, 48
Management information systems (MIS), 22
  demand reports, 127
  exception reports, 127
  periodic reports, 127
Manheim Auctions, 181
Many-to-many relationship, 431
Many-to-one model, 189
Marketing, 16
Marketing and sales, 121, 136
Marketing campaigns, 289
Marketing IS, 123
Mashup, 69
Mass customization, 176
Mass media, 291
MasterCard SecureCode, 185
Matrix organizational structures, 91
McCain, Michael, 324
Mead, Carver, 8
Mechanical mouse, 365, 369
Media convergence, 331
Media transparency, 290
Medication Order Entry and Administration Record System (MOE/MAR), 237
Meetings, 415
Megahertz (MHz), 39
Memory capacity, 363
Memory chips, 357
Memory management, 383
Mercedes Benz, 176
Merchant account, 66
Merge data, 31
Merge document, 31
Meta tags, 56
Metasearch engine, 58
Methodology, 247. *See also* IS methodlogy
Metrics, 109
MICR. *See* Magnetic ink character recognition
Microcell (Fido), 333
Micromarkets, 290
Microprocessor, 39
Microprocessor chips, 357
Microsoft, 345
Microsoft access, 424
Microsoft Office Live Communications Server, 75

Microsoft Visual Studio, 254
Microsoft.Net, 64
Microwaves, 405
Middleware, 45
MIDI devices. *See* Musical instrument digital interface (MIDI) devices
Mintzberg, Henry, 181
Mobile commerce, 183. *See* M-commerce
Mobile phones, 25, 174
MOE/MAR. *See* Medication Order Entry and Administration Record System (MOE/MAR)
Moen, 185
Moore's law, 7, 8
Moral code, 307
Motherboards, 360
MP3 player, 41, 76
MP3 technology, 76
MSN messenger, 75
MTS, 333
Multi-taskers, 292
Multimedia, 277
Multitasking, 380, 381
Musical instrument digital interface (MIDI) devices, 368
MyDoom, 70
MySpace, 278, 407
MySQL database software, 393

N
National network, 333–334
Natural work group, 445
Net present value (NPV), 238
NetMeeting, 213
Netscape, 24
Network, 344
Network architecture, 398
  client/server architecture
    centralized computing, 399
    four basic computing architectures, 399
    three-tiered architecture, 399
    types of software, 398
    client/server systems, work efficiency, 400–401
      client/server computing, advantage/disadvantage of, 400–401
  peer-to-peer networks, 401–402
Network Connection Layer, 402, 403
Network interface card (NIC), 42, 48, 410–411
Network layer model, 402
  application software layer, 402–403
  bandwidth, 362
  data component layer, 402, 404–407
  network connection layer, 403–404
  signal type, 405
  version of, 402
Network news transfer protocol (NNTP), 414
Network servers, 49, 127, 392

Network technology, 37, 47
  client/server architecture, 398–400
  local area network, 408
  network architecture, 398–402 (*See also* Network architecture)
  network layer model, 402–407 (*See also* Network layer model)
  peer-to-peer network, 401, 415
  wireless LANs, 408–409
Network TV, 291
Networks, 46–47
  categories, 47
  hardware, 48–49
  software, 49
Newsgroups, 414
Next-Generation Internet, 52, 53
Niche market, 180
Nielsen Online survey, 279
NNTP. *See* Network news transfer protocol (NNTP)
Nokia, 409, 419
Non-IT professionals, 14
Norming, 451
NorthernTel, 333
Nut Island effect, 461

O
Oberholzer, Felix, 328
OCR, 368
Offshoring, 25
Oktoberfest, 296
OLAP, 129, 224
Ombudsperson, 322
OMR, 368
On-campus recruiting, 345
One-to-one marketing model, 188
One-to-one relationship, 430
Online advertising, 291
Online banking, 97, 110, 138
Online community, 277
Online money earning, 171
Online security, 201
Online social advertising, 293
Online social strategy, 286
Online teens and young adults, 279
Open-source software, 46, 166, 393
Open systems model, 88
  aspect, 89
Operating system (OS) software, 376
  application software, 381
  boot process, 379
  comparison of, 376–377
  computer, starting, 378–379
  controlling access, 380
  CPU, efficient use of, 380–381
  hard disk, storage, 379
  layers of, 378
  managing hardware, 380
  overview of, 376
  parts, 377
  processing order, 382

  serves, overview of, 376
  software, 44
  works, 377–378
Operational decisions, 225
Optical mouse, 365, 369
Optimization models, 129
Oracle, 64, 132, 215
Organizational boundary, 88, 89
Organizational database, IT, 227
Organizational stakeholders, 89
Organizational value chain, 121
Organizations
  ban social networking sites, 283
  business environment, 21
  buying/leasing/building, 240–241
  core processes, advantage, 122
  development teams, 242
  in-house development, 241
  needs, 241
  outsource, 241
  strategy, 183
  teams, collection of, 443
  using teams, 442–443
Orkut, 278
Outbound logistics, 121
Output devices, 370
  display device performance, 371
  display devices, 370
  for print, 372
  printer performance, 373
  touch screens, 371–372
Outsourcing process, 25, 144, 241
Overly optimistic schedule, 262

P
Packet, 403
Packet switching, 403
Page, Larry, 106
PageRank, 271
PAN, 47, 409–410
Parallel processing, 381
Parser, 436
Partnerships, 178, 333, 334, 350
Password, 71–72
Patent violations, 319
Payback period, 238, 270
Payment gateway, 65
PayPa, 25, 27, 65, 172, 186
PC, 38, 43, 47, 379, 405, 417
PCMag.com, 175
PDA, 36, 40, 47, 359
Peer-to-peer networks, 401
  client/server networks, comparing, 401
Pen input, 366
People-oriented roles, 447
Pepsi, 136
Performance feedback, 95
Performing, 452
Periodic reports, 127, 312
Peripheral RAM, 363
Persistent data, 62

Personal area network (PAN) technology, 409–410
  enables wireless devices, 409
Personal computer (PC), 38–39, 356
Personal information management (PIM), 45
Personal Information Protection and Electronic Documents Act (PIPEDA), 284, 315, 316
Personal values, 307
Personalization, 177
PERT chart. See Program evaluation review technique (PERT) chart
Phishing, 70, 185, 320
Physical order, 169
Physical products, 169, 185
  ordering, 170
Pickett, K. H. S., 153
Piracy, 318–319
Plain old telephone system (POTS) network, 48
Plotters, 42
PM software, 264. See Project management (PM) software
PMBOK, 263
PO. See Purchase order (PO)
PodcastAlley.com, 76
Podcasting, 76, 207
Point of sale (POS) system, 136
Pop Idol, in U.K., 332
Portal, 22, 172, 192, 193, 199
Porter, Michael, 87, 121
Porter's five forces model, 87
Porter's model, 184
Porter's value chain model, 144, 145
Portfolio management, 264
POS system, 126, 136
Powell, Keith, 120
Power-on self-test (POST), 379
PPM. See Project portfolio management (PPM)
Pre-development questions, 237–238
Presentation, 31
Presentation graphics software, 45
Presentation software, 198, 213, 389
Primary key, 424
Printer buffer, 363
Printers, 42
Privacy Act, 316
Privacy Codes, 320
Privacy Commissioner, 284, 327
Problem solving, 104
Problem-solving skills, 446
Process, 456
Procurement management, 258
Procurement process, 189
Productivity, 102
Productivity software, 44, 49
Productivity zone, 12
Professional Codes, of Conduct and Practice, 317

Professional network, 344
Program, 263, 391
Program evaluation review technique (PERT) chart, 265
Program management, 263
Programming languages, 45, 264, 391–392
Project feasibility, 238–240
Project management, 256
Project Management Institute (PMI), 317
Project management integration, 259
Project management (PM) software, 264
Project portfolio management (PPM), 258
Project team, 25, 103, 243, 254, 266, 445
Project time management, 259, 260
ProjectSpaces, 459
Proprietary software, 193, 393
Prototyping, 251, 268
Provincial Privacy Legislation, 316
Public IM, 75
Public key encryption, 187
  process of, 187
Purchase order (PO), 190
Purpose, 455

Q

Quality control system, 135
Quality management, 133, 135, 139, 254, 258
Query, 58, 106, 392, 424. See also Structured Query Language (SQL)
Query condition, 425
Querying multitable databases
  creating views, 434
  join operation, 433–434

R

Radio frequency identification (RFID)
  tags, 134
  type, 134
Radio transmissions, 405
Random access memory (RAM), 40, 363
  performance, 363–364
Rational decision, 99, 101
RBC's Code of Conduct, 318
RDBMS. See Relational database management systems (RDBMS)
Read only memory (ROM), 40
Reduced instruction set computer (RISC), 361
Referential integrity, 432
Refresh rate, 371, 395
Registers, 361, 394
Relational data model, 216–218, 431–432
Relational database management package
  inserting/deleting records, 427
  logical modelling, 429
    anomalies, 430
    entity-relationship diagram, 430–431

  redundancy, 430
  relational data model, 431–433
Relational database management systems (RDBMS), 216, 218
Relational entity, 431
religionnewsblog.com, 279
Rental websites, 180
Repeater, 48
Research In Motion (RIM), 6
Reservations system, 135
Resistive touch screen, 371
Resolution, 42, 236, 371, 373
Resource investigator, 447, 448
Résumés
  career basics for, 341–342
  define, 342
  education, foundation of, 342–343
  experience, 343
  skills needed, 344
Retail innovations
  history of, 167
Retail Link, 161
Return on investment (ROI), 238, 239, 246, 270, 294
Revenue model, 171
Reverse auction, 189
Reverse engineering, 319–320
RFID. See Radio frequency identification (RFID)
Risk acceptance, 149, 150, 263
Risk appetite, 146
Risk assessment, 146, 224, 262, 265
  and management, 146
Risk avoidance, 149, 151, 263
Risk deferral, 149, 151, 263
Risk management, 146–149, 262. See also Enterprise risk management (ERM)
Risk-reduction methods, 149–151
  risk transfer, 149
Risk response, 149
Risk transfer, 149, 150, 263
Rogers AT&T, 333
Roll-back strategy, 151
Royal Bank, 318
RSS feeds, 75

S

SaaS. See Software as a service (SaaS)
Sabia, Michael, 324
Salesforce.com, 140
SAP, 132, 159, 352
Sarbanes-Oxley Act of 2002, 147
SAS® Dashboard, 223
SaskTel, 333
SAS's website, 223
Satellite transmission, 405
Scanning devices, 367
Schadenfreude, 287
Schedule control tool, 261
Schedule development, 261

Scope management, 258
Scripting language, 62
SDLC. *See* System development life cycle (SDLC)
Search criteria, 425
Search engines, 13, 56–58
Secondary storage, 363, 373, 376
Secure electronic transaction (SET), 67
Secure socket layer (SSL), 67
Security breaches, 320
Segregation of duties, 153
SELECT query, 427
Semantic web, 277
Semi-structured decision, 101
Sequence diagram, 252, 253
Server-side programming, 63, 140
Server software, 64, 399, 413
Servers, 398
Service level agreements (SLA), 149
Service marketing, 291
Service-oriented architecture (SOA), 69
ServiceOntario, 237
Short message service (SMS), 420
Signal type, 405
Silagadze, Michael, 166
Silver bullet syndrome, 255, 262
Simple mail transfer protocol (SMTP), 403
Skype, 75, 412
Smart card reader, 368
SMEs. *See* Subject matter experts (SMEs)
Smith, Douglas K., 444
Smokers' rights, 308
Smoking, 308
Social business models, 294–295
Social computing, 283
Social habit, 308
Social innovation, 284
Social media
   harnessing, power of, 290–291
   tools, 288
Social media technologies, 293
Social media websites, 284
Social networking, 279
   banning, sites of, 284
   sites, 71
Social patterns, 292
Social technologies
   business utility, 282
   define, 278–279
   design and usability, 281–282
   privacy and security, 284
   technology implications, 282–283
   utility, 279–281
Social website, 289, 297
Software, 43
   application, 44–45
   for e-commerce, 45
   middleware, 45
   open source, 45–46
   productivity, 44
   utility, 44

Software application suite, 385
Software as a service (SaaS), 52, 140
   software as outsourced service, 141
   vs. application service provider (ASP), 141
Sophos, 70
Spam, 320
Specific internal control processes categories, 153
Speechbobble.com, 296
Spiders, 57, 176
Spot buying, 188
Spreadsheet, 31, 74, 81, 114, 116, 159, 213, 230, 239, 270, 386, 388, 391
   financial status, 159
   physical condition, 159
SQL. *See* Structured Query Language (SQL)
SSL certificate, 67
Stakeholder, 88–89
Stakeholder analysis, 242
Stakeholders, importance of, 242–243
Standard, methodology, 247–248
   IS methodology, 247–248, 250–252
   IS modelling
      UML diagrams, 252–253
   waterfall model, 248–250
Standard ASCII (American Standard Code for Information Interchange), 358
Static content, 60
Static RAM (SRAM), 363
Storage, 22, 38, 42, 49, 126, 283, 370, 375, 395, 399
Storage hardware
   chip-based storage, 375
   magnetic disks, 373–374
   optical disks, 374–375
   storage performance, 375
Storming, 451
Strategic decisions, 225
Strategic sourcing, 188
Structured decision, 100
Structured Query Language (SQL), 106, 424
   aggregate functions, using, 428–429
   changing values, 428
   command, 425, 429
   to insert, delete, and update record, 438
   for programming, 395
   to query relational databases, 424–429
   questions for database through, 106
   for relational database model, 218
   server, 301
   statement, 426, 428
   uses, 228, 424
Strumpf, Koleman, 328
Stylesheet (XSL) file, 437
Subject matter experts (SMEs), 244

Sun ONE Instant Messaging, 75
Supercomputer, 39
Supervisory review, 155
Supply chain management (SCM), 120, 123, 130, 131, 200
   inventory management, 131
   logistics management, 131
   materials management, 131
   order management, 131
Supply chain system, 25, 190
Surface wave technology, 371
Survey Monkey, 75
Switching devices
   on network, 404
System design, 331
System development life cycle (SDLC), 244
   stages and importance of, 244–246
System software, 43
System unit, 360

T
T-carrier circuits, 406
Tacit knowledge, 207
Tactical decisions, 225
Tactile response, 365
Tagging, 286
TCP/IP protocol, 411
Teams, 443
   activity, 30–31
   collaboration, 141, 459
   collection of, 443
   hallmarks of, 453–457
      commitment, 454–455
      communication, 456
      critical success factors, 455
      goals, 457
      involvement, 456
      process, 456
      purpose, 455–456
      trust, 457
   organizations, 442–444
   roles, 447–449
   skills, 446–447
   types of, 445–446
   vs. work groups, 443–445
   work in, 446
Teams development
   adjourning stage, 452–453
   codes of conduct, 457–459
   collaborative technologies, 459
   forming stage, 450
   norming stage, 451–452
   performing stage, 452
   storming stage, 451
   Tuckman's stage model, 450, 451
Teamsave's application, 183
Tech Guide, 2, 3, 49, 356
Technical skills, 244, 446
Telephone, 405
Telexed, 333

TELUS, 333
The International Telecommunications Union (ITU.int), 27
The Royal Bank of Canada (RBC), 318
"The steroids" – technology, 25
The World Is Flat, 24
Three-tiered client/server architecture, 399
Ticoll, David, 349
Toner, 372
Top-level domain, 411
Touch screen, 365, 371
Touch screen monitor, 371
Touchpad, 41, 365, 369
TPS. *See* Transaction processing systems (TPS)
Trackball, 369
Tracking, 369
Trading partners, 192
Traditional procurement method, 191
Transaction process
    characteristics, 125
Transaction processing systems (TPS), 22, 23, 125–126
    software applications, 126
Transactions, 168
Transformation, 210
Transforming, 98
Transistor, 357
Transitions, 452
Transmission capacity, 406
Transmission control protocol/Internet protocol (TCP/IP), 403
    packets/datagrams, 403
Transmission speed, 406
Transportation management systems (TMS), 136
    type, 136
Triple constraint, 256
Trust, 457
Tuckman's stage model, 450, 451
turnitin.com, 319
Twisted pair wire, 404
Twitter, 12, 71, 77, 278

U

UCCnet, 152, 161
UHN. *See* University health network (UHN)
UML. *See* Unified Modelling Language (UML)
Unicode, 358
Unified Modelling Language (UML), 252
Uniform resource locator (URL), 54, 418
Universal Product Code (UPC), 367
Universal serial bus (USB), 375
University health network (UHN), 236
URL. *See* Uniform resource locator (URL)
U.S. online video advertising, 292

USB flash drives, 374, 375
USB flash memory, 42, 375
USB port, 374, 375
User-generated content (UGC), 277
    and brand risk, 286–287
    creating content, 285–286
    finding content, 286
User-generated mashup, 287
Utility computing services
    advantages, 140

V

Validation, 281
Value-added networks (VANs), 192
Value chain, 121–122
    primary activities, 122
    service activities, 121
    support activities, 122
Values, hierarchy of, 308
VB.NET, 392
    part of, 393
Verification controls, 154
Very large-scale integration (VLSI), 8
Video RAM (VRAM), 363
Viral social interactions, 286
Virtual meetings, 75–76
Virtual memory, 384
Virtual team, 445
Viruses, 70
Visa card
    security code, 185
Voice over Internet protocol (VoIP), 25, 51, 404
VRBO.com, 179

W

Walmart, 175, 185
WAN, short message service (SMS), 420
Warchalking, 72
Waterfall model, 248
W3C. *See* World Wide Web Consortium (W3C)
Web, changing social trends on, 277
Web 1.1/1.2/3.0, 276, 277
Web 2.0 technologies, 276, 277, 289, 297
    social and business impacts of, 291–294
    social business models, 294–295
Web-based tool, 58
Web crawlers, 56
Web hosting, costs, 283
Web integration, 169
Web server, 49
Web service, 68–69
WebCam, 368
Websites
    24/7/365 basis, business, 180
    type, purpose, 172

WHERE keyword, 426
Whistle-blowing, 322
Wi-Fi. *See* Wireless fidelity
Wide area network (WAN), 47
Wikipedia, 24
Wikipedia.com, 311
Wikis, 301
Wildcard, 427
WildOutfitters, 411
WildOutfitters database tables, 424
WildOutfitters product table, 426
WileyPLUS, 76
William Bridges' transitions model, 452
Windows hierarchical-based file structure, 384
Windows Vista, 44, 364
Windows XP, 364, 379, 382
Wireless access point (AP), 411
wireless application protocol (WAP)
    wireless connectivity, 419–420
Wireless fidelity (Wi-Fi), 409
Wireless LANs (WLANs), 408–409
    internet connection, 409
Wireless mark-up language (WML), 420
Wireless networking hardware, 409
Wireless networks
    mobile devices, use of, 182
Wireless transmissions, 408
Wisdom, 206
Word processing, 31, 81, 159, 299–300
Work groups, 444
Workflow management system (WMS), 124–125
Workflow software, 25
World Wide Web (WWW), 8, 12, 54, 167
    basic components, 54–56
    cookie, 419
    hypertext links, 416
    internet protocols, 418
    multimedia, 416
    surfing, 419
    URLs, 419
World Wide Web Consortium (W3C), 50
WorldWideWebSize.com, 13
Worms, 70, 71

X

XML. *See* eXtensible markup language (XML)
XML data, browser, 438
XML schema (XSD) file, 436
XML stylesheet (XSL) file, 437
XSD file. *See* XML schema (XSD) file

Y

Yahoo! Messenger, 75
YouTube, 279, 292
YouTube videos, 24